THE BARBOUR
COLLECTION
OF CONNECTICUT TOWN
VITAL RECORDS

THE BARBOUR COLLECTION OF CONNECTICUT TOWN VITAL RECORDS

WINDSOR 1637–1850

Compiled by

Lorraine Cook White

General Editor
Lorraine Cook White

INTRODUCTION

As early as 1640 the Connecticut Court of Election ordered all magistrates to keep a record of the marriages they performed. In 1644 the registration of births and marriages became the official responsibility of town clerks and registrars, with deaths added to their duties in 1650. From 1660 until the close of the Revolutionary War these vital records of birth, marriage, and death were generally well kept, but then for a period of about two generations until the mid-nineteenth century, the faithful recording of vital records declined in some towns.

General Lucius Barnes Barbour was the Connecticut Examiner of Public Records from 1911 to 1934 and in that capacity directed a project in which the vital records kept by the towns up to about 1850 were copied and abstracted. Barbour previously had directed the publication of the Bolton and Vernon vital records for the Connecticut Historical Society. For this new project he hired several individuals who were experienced in copying old records and familiar with the old script.

Barbour presented the completed transcriptions of town vital records to the Connecticut State Library where the information was typed onto printed forms. The form sheets were then cut, producing twelve small slips from each sheet. The slips for most towns were then alphabetized and the information was then typed a second time on large sheets of rag paper, which were subsequently bound into separate volumes for each town. The slips for all towns were then interfiled, forming a statewide alphabetized slip index for most surviving town vital records.

The dates of coverage vary from town to town, and of course the records of some towns are more complete than others. There are many cases in which an entry may appear two or three times, apparently because that entry was entered by one or more persons. Altogether the entire Barbour Collection--one of the great genealogical manuscript collections and one of the last to be published--covers 137 towns and comprises 14,333 typed pages.

ACKNOWLEDGMENTS

It is with great relief and yet some sadness that with this, 55th volume, we conclude Lucius Barbour's Connecticut town vital records.

The purpose of publishing this project was to make the collection more accessible to people, who do not live close to a large library or an LDS Family History center where this collection is available on microfilm.

A very special thank you to the Genealogical Publishing Company for agreeing to publish this collection; to Dr. Michael Tepper for assisting, guiding and advising this project; to Joseph Garonzik for helping when new challenges arose, and to Eileen Perkins for assisting in proofing and in many other situations. Thank you to Donna Potter Philips for suggesting that this project be published.

This project would have taken another twelve years to complete without the assistance of Christina Bailey, Nancy Schott, Wilma Moore, Dorothy Wear, Marcia Carbaugh, Debra Wilmes, Marie Crossley, Carole Magnuson, Jan Tilton, Jerri Burket, Lita Karlstrand and the members of the Greater Omaha Genealogical Society, who keyed in the information, and Cherie Mierzejewski who oversaw the project volumes and did the final correlation and proofreading.

This whole project would have been impossible if it hadn't been for my sister-in-law, Betty White, who so patiently proofread each and every page.

It is my most sincere hope this project will assist many in finding their roots.

Lorraine Cook White

ABBREVIATIONS

ae.----age
b.-----born
Col.D ---- Colonial Deeds
d.-----died or day or daughter
J.P.---Justice of Peace
m.-----married or month
MG ----- Matthew Grant Record
N. S.--- New Style
O. S.----Old Style
res.---resident
s.-----son
TR1 ----- Town Records
w.-----wife
wid.---widow
y.-----year

THE BARBOUR
COLLECTION
OF CONNECTICUT TOWN
VITAL RECORDS

WINDSOR VITAL RECORDS
1637 - 1850

	Vol.	Page

BBE, ABBY, ABEY, Caroline E., m. Richard M. **BROWN,** b. of
   Windsor, June 7, 1842, by Rev. Francis L. Robbins — 2 — 466
John, of Warehouse Point, m. Delia **MORON,** of Suffield,
   Apr. 11, 1847, by Ezra S. Cook — 2 — 464
John, m. Mary **EVANS,** Nov. 21, 1852, by Rev. James Smyth — 2 — 460
Lemuel, of Enfield, m. Sarah M. **WARDWELL,** of
   Springfield, Nov. 13, 1838, by Rev. R. Avery — 2 — 464
Louisa Harriet, m. Daniel **BACON,** Nov. 25, 1838, by Giles
   Ellsworth, J. P. — 2 — 475

BBOTT, Abiel, m. Abigail **GRANT,** b. of Windsor, Jan. 9,
   1717/18 — 2 — 123
Abiel, s. Abiel, b. June 14, 1724 — 2 — 3
Abigail, d. Abiel, b. Nov. 25, 1718 — 2 — 2
Abigail, w. Abiel, d. Aug. 22, 1724 — 2 — 214
Abigail, Mrs., m. William **WOLCOTT,** Jr., Feb. 26, 1746/7 — 2 — 209
Ann, d. Abiel, b. Aug. 3, 1721 — 2 — 3

BEL, Elisabeth, m. Henery **CURTIC,** May 13, 1645 — MG

[ABORN], EBORN, Abigal, of Tolland, m. Nathaniel **NEWEL,** of
   Windsor, Nov. 13, 1754 — 2 — 180

DAMS, ADAMES, ADDAMS, ADMES, Abigail, d. John, b. July
   8, 1681 — Col.D — 51
Abigail, d. John, b. July 8, 1681 — 1 — 1
Ambroes, of Bloomfield, m. Mrs. Lydia **PINEY,** of Hartford,
   Feb. 4, 1851, by Rev. Ralph H. Bowls, of Tariffville — 2 — 463
Danell, m. Mary **PINNE*,** d. Samuell, Sept. 20, 1677
   *(Mary **PHELPS,** dau. of Sarah (**GRISWOLD**)
   PHELPS. Corrected by Mrs. M. L. Holman) — TR1 — 1
Daniel, m. Mary **PINEY,** d. Samuel, Sept. 20, 1677 — 1 — 53
Danell, m. Mary **PINNE,** d. Samuel, Dec.* 20, 1677   *(Note
   by LBB: "Sept.") — Col.1 — 46
Edward, m. Elizabeth **BUCKLAND,** May 25, [16]60 — MG
Edward, m. Elizabeth **BUCKLAND,** May 25, 1660 — 1 — 53
Edward, had 1 child, b. in Windsor. Dated Aug. 17, 1677 — MG
Edward, d. Aug. 15, 1683 — Col.D — 56
Edward, d. Aug. 15, 1683 — 1 — 40
Edward, contributed 0-0-7 to the poor in other colonies — MG
Gillit, s. Samuel, b. Feb. 19, 1694/5 — 1 — 2
John, m. Abigall **PINNE,** Dec. 6, 1677 — Col.1 — 46
John, m. Abigal **PINNE,** Dec. 6, 1677 — TR1 — 1
John, m. Abigaile **PINNE,** Dec. 6, 1677 — Col.2 — 158
John, m. Abigail **PINEY,** Dec. 6, 1677 — 1 — 53

	Vol.	Page
DAMS, ADAMES, ADDAMS, ADMES, (cont.)		
John, s. John, b. Mar. 15, 1682/3	Col.D	51
John, s. John, b. Mar. 15, 1682/3	1	1
Mary, d. [Edward & Elizabeth], b. Aug. 28, 1671	MG	
Mary, d. Edward, b. Aug. 28, 1671	1	1
Samuel, m. Deborah GILLET, Apr. 23, 1694	1	53
Thankfull, of Simsbury, m. Robert WESTLAND, of Windsor, May 17, 1721	2	208
William, m. Olive WESTLAND, b. of Windsor, June 16, 1823, by James Loomis, J. P.	2	125
William, m. Olive HOLCOMB, b. of Windsor, Feb. 11, 1852, by Rev. H. A. Weed	2	463
ADKINS, Jane, of Hartford, m. Joseph ELMOR, of Windsor, Apr. 4, 1700	2	146
ALCOTT, [see under OLCOTT]		
ALDERMAN, John D., of Hamilton, N. Y., m. Julia Ann WESTLAND, of Windsor, Nov. 26, 1841, by [ ]	2	464
John N., m. Jerusha P. FILLEY, b. of Windsor, Mar. 14, 1833, by Rev. Ansel Nash	2	126
Mary Ann, m. William D. WESTLAND, Nov. 9, 1834, by Henry A. Rowland	2	512
Sarah, m. Gideon CASE, Deb. 5, 1750	2	137
ALEXANDER, ALEXAND, ALLEXANDER ALLIXANDER,		
Daniell, [s. George & Susan], b. Jan. 12, 1650	MG	
Daniel, s. George, b. Jan. 12, 1650	1	1
George, m. Susan [ ], Mar. 18, 1[6]	MG	
George, his child d. [ ], [16]46	MG	
George, had 5 children b. in Windsor, Dated Aug. 17, 1677	MG	
Giles, m. Abigail SKINNER, Nov. 11, 1823, by Rev. Henry A. Rowland	2	125
Henry, m. Ellen BOICE, b. of Windsor, Apr. 8, 1849, by T. A. Leet	2	463
John, s. [George & Susan], b. July 25, 1645	MG	
John, s. George, b. July 25, 1645	1	1
Mary, d. [George & Susan], b. Oct. 20, 1648	MG	
Mary, d. George, b. Oct. 20, 1648	1	1
Mindwell, of Northampton, m. Daniel PORTER, of Windsor, Feb. 19, 1706/7	2	186
Nathanaell, s. [George & Susan], b. Dec. 29, 1652	MG	
Nathaniel, s. George, b. Dec. 29, 1652	Col.2	151
Nathanael, s. John, b. Apr. beginning, 1676	1	1
Nathaniel, s. George, b. Dec. 29, [ ]	1	1
Saraa, [d. George & Susan], b. Dec. 8, 1654	MG	
Sarah, d. George, b. Dec. 8, 1654	Col.2	158
ALFOOT, [see under ALVORD]		
ALFORD, ALFORT, ALLFORT, ALFOOT, [see also ALVORD], Abigail, d. Alexander, b. Oct. 6, 1647	1	1
Abigail, d. Benedict, b. Aug. 3, 1718	2	2

	Vol.	Page
ALFORD, ALFORT, ALLFORT, ALFOOT, (cont.)		
Abigail, m. Jacob PHELPS, b. of Windsor, Dec. 30, 1745	2	188
Abigail, d. Benadict, Jr. & Jerusha, b. Oct. 23, 1746	2	285
Abigail, d. Benadict, Jr. & Jerusha, d. Jan. 16, 1746/7	2	215
Abigail, d. Benedict, Jr. & Jerusha, b. Dec. 3, 1747	2	284
Abigail, d. Apr. 30, 1773, in the 91st year of her age	2	216
Alexander, m. Mary VORE, Oct. 29, 1646	1	53
Alexander, s. Benedict, b. Mar. 31, 1721	2	3
Alexander, s. Benedict, Jr. & Jerusha, b. June 25, 1752	2	285
Anna, d. Benadict, Jr. & Jerusha, b. Apr. 7, 1759	2	287
Azubah, d. Benedick & Abagail, b. Feb. 19, 1727/8	2	4
Azubah, had d. Dorothy, b. July 28, 1750	2	284
Azubah, d. June 2, 1786	2	216
Benedict, s. Benedict, b. July 11, 1647	1	1
Benedickt, Sergt., d. Apr. 23, 1683	1	40
Benedict, s. Jeremiah, b. Apr. 27, 1688	1	1
Benedict, m. Abigael WILSON, b. of Windsor, Jan. 12, 1714/15	2	123
Benedict, s. Benedict, b. Aug. 29, 1716	2	2
Benedict, Jr., of Windsor, m. Jerusha ASHLEY, of Hartford, Aug. 9, 1744	2	124
Benedict, s. Benedict, Jr. & Jerusha, b. Feb. 27, 1757	2	287
Benedict, Jr., m. Rebeckah OWEN, b. of Windsor, Dec. 28, 1761	2	125
Benadict, d. Feb. 15, 1764	2	216
Benedictus, m. Jane NUTON, Nov. 26, 1640	1	53
Benjamin, s. Alexander, b. Feb. 11, 1657	1	1
Charity, d. Jonathan & Charity, b. June 20, 1750	2	284
Cordelia, of Windsor, m. George ANDREWS, of Waterbury, May 26, 1839, by Rev. Daniel Hemenway	2	127
Deidemia, d. Benadict, Jr. & Jerusha, b. Jan. 13, 1744/5	2	284
Dorcas, d. Joseph & Mary, b. June 10, 1742	2	284
Dorothy, d. Azubah, b. July 28, 1750	2	284
Elisha S., m. Emily SILL, b. of Windsor, Sept. 30, 1850, by Rev. James Rankin	2	463
Eliza Ann, m. Cyrus ATTLETON, b. of Springfield, Feb. 6, 1825, by Rev. Phineas Cook	2	126
Elizabeth, d. Benedict, bp. Sept. 21, 1651	1	1
Elizabeth, d. Alexander, b. Nov. 12, 1655	1	1
Elizabeth, d. Jeremiah, b. Nov. 22, 1703	1	2
Elizabeth, d. Jeremiah, d. Jan. 10, 1703/4	1	40
Elizabeth, d. May 18, 1727	2	214
Elizabeth, d. Jeremiah & Sarah, b. Aug. 2, 1727	2	3
Elizabeth, m. Jesse HOSFORD, b. of Windsor, Oct. 1, 1747	2	163
Elizabeth, m. Jesse HOSFORD, b. of Windsor, Oct. 1, 1747	2	178
Elizabeth, m. Daniel G. REMINGTON, of Hartford, Jan. 25, 1843, by Rev. S. W. Scofield	2	507
George, s. Benedict & Rebeckah, b. Mar. 30, 1761	2	288

	Vol.	Page
ALFORD, ALFORT, ALLFORT, ALFOOT, (cont.)		
Jane, m. Ambros **FOWLER,** May 6, 1646	1	56
Jane, d. Jeremiah, b. Jan. 14, 1698/9	1	2
Jane, wid., d. May 19, 1715	2	214
Jane, d. Jeremiah, b. June 1, 1715	2	2
Jane, m. John **BARBOR,** b. of Windsor, July 24, 1717	2	129
Jeremiah, s. Benedict, b. Dec. 24, 1655	1	1
Jeremiah, s. Jeremiah, b. May 8, 1692	1	2
Jerimiah, m. Sarah **ENNO,** d. John, July 4, 1711	2	123
Jeremiah, s. Jeremiah, b. June 1, 1714	2	2
Jeremiah, s. Jerimiah, d. July 9, 1714	2	213
Jeremiah, s. Jeremiah, b. May 11, 1725	2	3
Jeremiah, Jr., m. Ann **GILE,** b. of Windsor, July 15, 1746	2	124
Jeremiah, s. Jeremiah, Jr. & Ann, b. Feb. 16, 1746/7	2	284
Jeremiah, s. Jeremiah, Jr. & Ann, d. Jan. 4, 1751/2	2	214
Jerusha, d. Benedict, b. Apr. 3, 1723	2	3
Jerusha, d. Benedict, Jr. & Jerusha, b. Aug. 21, 175[ ]	2	284
Jerusha, d. Benadict & Abigal, d. Feb. 15, 1757	2	215
Jerusha, w. Benadict, Jr., d. Jan. 18, 1761	2	216
Joanna, d. Jeremiah, b. Mar. 1, 1701/2	1	2
Joanna, m. Benjamin **LOOMIS,** Jr., b. of Windsor, Dec. 9, 1725	2	171
Job, s. Job & Margerit, b. July 3, 1736	2	283
John, s. Alexander, b. Aug. 12, 1649	1	1
John, s. Job & Margerit, b. Sept. 4, 1738	2	283
Jonathan, s. Benedict, b. June 1, 1645	1	1
Jonathan, s. Jeremiah, b. Mar. 4, 1695/6	1	2
Jonathan, s. Jeremiah, d. July 14, 1700	1	40
Jonathan, s. Jeremiah, b. Sept. 16, 1720	2	2
Jonathan, m. Charity **THRALL,** b. of Windsor, Dec. 17, 1744	2	123
Jonathan, s. Jonathan & Charity, b. Dec. 21, 1745	2	284
Joseph, s. Jonathan & Charity, b. July 6, 1748	2	284
Josiah, s. Benedictus, b. July 6, 1649	1	1
Lucrece, d. Benadict, Jr. & Jerusha, b. Mar. 27, 1755	2	285
Mary, d. Alexander, b. July 6, 1651	1	1
Nathaniel R., m. Keziah **BARBER,** Apr. 14, 1829, by Henry A. Rowland	2	126
Newton, s. Jeremiah, b. Mar. 24, 1689/90	1	1
Rebeckah, s. [sic?] Benedict, Jr. & Rebeckah, b. Oct. 24, 1762	2	288
Rocittee, d. Benadict & Rebeckah, b. Nov. 18, 1765	2	288
Sarah, d. Alexander, b. June 24, 1660	1	1
Sarah, d. Jerimiah, b. June 16, 1712	2	1
Sarah, d. Jerimiah, d. June 9, 1715	2	214
Sarah, d. Jeremiah, b. Feb. 14, 1717/18	2	2
Thomas, s. Alexander, b. Oct. 27, 1653	1	1
William, m. Maria **BARBER,** July 9, 1835, by Henry A. Rowland	2	464

	Vol.	Page
ALLEN, [see also ALLIN & ALLYN], Abigael, d. Alexander, b.		
b. Feb. 4, 1716/17	2	2
Dorcas S., of Suffield, m. Samuel RAHM, of Harrisburg,		
Pa., Dec. 19, [probably 1830], by Henry A. Rowland	2	505
Eliza, m. Hiram BENNETT, Mar. 8, 1841, by Rev. S. D.		
Jewett	2	476
Elizabeth, d. Samuel, Jr. & Elizabeth, b. Apr. 8, 1763	2	288
George W., of Windsor, m. Jane DOYLE, of Suffield, Apr.		
12, 1848, by S. H. Allen	2	463
Gilbert, of Enfield, m. Caroline OWEN, of Windsor, Nov. 20,		
1823, by Rev. Francis L. Robbins, of Enfield	2	126
Huldah, d. Zachariah & Huldah, b. Nov. 16, 1767	2	289
Levi W., of So. Hadley, Mass., m. Salome H. BEMENT, of		
Windsor, Sept. 4, 1839, by Rev. S. E. Jewett	2	464
Lorenzo D., of Springfield, m. Cynthia STARKS, of Windsor,		
Jan. 1, 1827, by Rev. Henry A. Rowland	2	126
Mary E. of Windsor, m. Henry P. SWEETSER, of Hartford,		
May 21, 1842, by Rev. S. D. Jewett	2	516
Noah, s. Joseph & Mary, b. May 15, 1730	2	283
Noah, s. Noah & Anna, b. Feb. 14, 1757	2	287
Samuel, s. Samuel, Jr. & Elizabeth, b. June 16, 1764	2	288
Samuel H., Rev. of Windsor Locks, m. Julia A. PIERSON,		
of Windsor, Feb. 16, 1847, by T. A. Leete	2	462
Timothy, s. Noah & Anna, b. Nov. 25, 1759	2	287
William A., of Bloomfield, m. Harriet BARNES, of Windsor,		
Dec. 24, 1838, by D. Osborn	2	464
William A., m. Ruth Ann PHELPS, b. of Windsor, Dec. 29,		
1849, by Thomas A. Leete	2	463
Zachariah, of Windsor, m. Huldah PARSONS, of Enfield,		
Oct. 31, 1765	2	125
ALLIN, [see also ALLEN & ALLYN], Alexander, m. Hannah		
ELSWORTH, b. of Windsor, Apr. 28, 1743	2	124
Alexander, of Windsor, m. Elisabeth ALLYN, of Hartford,		
Dec. 21, [ ]	2	123
Algenion Sidney, m. Sarah E. RICHARDSON, Sept. 4,		
1835, by Henry A. Rowland	2	127
Charissa, d. Samuel Wolcott & Johannah, b. Dec. 21, 1756;		
d. Feb. 21, 1756 [7?]	2	185
David, s. Joseph & Mary, b. Nov. 22, 1734	2	283
David, m. Mary BANERAFF*, b. of Windsor, Feb. 27, 1753		
*("BANCROFT?)	2	124
David, s. David & Meriam, b. Aug. 13, 1755	2	286
David, of Windsor, m. Meriam PARSONS, of Summers, Nov.		
14, 1755	2	124
Dorcas, d. Joseph & Mary, b. June 10, 1742	2	284
Elizabeth, Mrs. of Windsor, m. John GARDINER, of Isle of		
Wight, Jan. 23, 1711/12	2	154
Elizabeth, d. John, of Enfield, m. Samuel ELSWORTH, of		

	Vol.	Page
ALLIN, (cont.)		
Windsor, Nov. 20, 1717	2	145
Ephestion, s. John & Hannah, b. Apr. 21, 1731	2	281
Fitz John, s. Alexander, b. Oct. 12, 1703	2	1
Hannah, d. Alexander & Hannah, b. Aug. 13, 1736	2	282
Hannah, d. Alexander & Hannah, b. Oct. 30, 1743	2	284
Hannah, d. Alexander & Hannah, b. Nov. 10, 1743	2	521
Hannah, 3rd, m. Roger **NEWBERRY**, b. of Windsor, Jan. 9, 1759	2	183
Hannah, m. James **HOOKER**, Jan. 6, 1763	2	164
Hannah, m. James **HOOKER**, Jan. 6, 1763	2	522
Hezekiah, s. Joseph & Mary, b. Oct. 8, 1738	2	283
John, s. John, of Enfield, d. June 3, 1714	2	213
John, 2nd, of Windsor, m. Ruth **BURNHAM**, of Farmington, Dec. 18, 1760	2	125
Loice, d. Joseph, Jr. & Loice, b. Sept. 2, 1751	2	284
Love, d. Samuel & Elizabeth, b. Aug. 13, 1718	2	283
Mary, d. Joseph & Mary, b. Jan. 2, 1731/2	2	283
Mary, d. Alexander & Hannah, b. July 14, 1733	2	282
Mary, see Mary **CHAPMAN**	2	223
Moses, s. David & Meriam, b. July 9, 1757	2	286
Noah, m. Anna **ROOT**, b. of Windsor, Mar. 25, 1756	2	124
Samuel, s. Joseph & Mary, b. June 8, 1736	2	283
Solomon, s. David & Meriam, b. June 20, 1759	2	286
Theophilus, s. Thomas & Sarah, b. May 23, 1759	2	287
William, s. William & Sibal, b. Feb. 25, 1753	2	285
Zachariah, s. Samuell & Elisabeth, b. Oct. 31, 1743	2	283
ALLIS, Laury, m. Benjamin **LORD**, b. of Windsor, Oct. 18, 1848, by Rev. Samuel Law	2	491
Sarah, m. Cicero I. **PHELPS**, b. of Windsor, June 28, 1840, by Rev. Ezra S. Cook	2	501
ALLISTON, William, d. May 30, 1684	Col.D	56
William, d. May 30, 1684	1	40
ALLYN, ALLYEN, ALLYN, ALLN, [see also **ALLEN & ALLIN**], Aaron, s. Mathew & Darcas, b. Apr. 5, 1753	2	285
Abel, s. Samuel, of Enfield & Elizabeth, b. Aug. 14, 1733	2	282
Abel, of Windsor, m. Elizabeth **CHAPIN**, of Enfield, Jan. 1, 1756	2	124
Abel, s. Abel & Elizabeth, b. Nov. 15, 1756	2	286
Abiah, d. Solomon & Abiah, b. Aug. 2, 1761	2	534
Abigal, d. [Thomas & Abigayl], b. Oct. 17, [16]72	MG	
Abigail, d. Thomas, b. Oct. 17, 1672; bp. Apr. 6, 1673	1	1
Abigail, d. Alexander, d. Sept. 20, 1719	2	214
Abigail, d. Alexander, b. Aug. 28, 1721	2	3
Abigail, d. Benjamin & Abigaiel, b. Oct. 30, 1734	2	282
Abigail, d. Benjamin & Abigail, b. Oct. 26, 1736	2	283
Abigail, d. Benjamin & Abigail, d. Sept. 12, 1737	2	214
Abigail, d. Theophilus & Tryphena, b. July 25, 1754	2	285

	Vol.	Page
ALLYN, ALLYEN, ALLYN, ALLN, (cont.)		
Abigail, m. James **BIDWELL**, b. of Windsor, June 12, 1822, by John Bartlett. Int. Pub.	2	467
Abigail E., m. William E. **HOWARD**, May 17, 1831, by H. A. Rowland	2	485
Alexander, m. Mary **GRANT**, Sept. 21, 1693	1	53
Alexander, s. Alexander, b. Sept. 9, 1695	1	2
Alexander, d. Aug. 19, 1708	2	213
Alexander, m. Hannah **MARSHEL**, b. of Windsor, May 17, 1716	2	123
Alexander, s. Alexander, b. Dec. 25, 1718	2	2
Alexander, s. Thomas & Sarah, b. Feb. 14, 1757	2	286
Amelia, m. Griswold C. **MORGAN**, June 1, 1831, by Henry A. Rowland	2	493
Amelia, m. Griswold C. **MORGAN**, June 1, 1831, by H. A. Rowland	2	495
Ann, d. Benjamin, b. Apr. 8, 1711	2	1
Ann, m. Nathanael **LOOMIS**, b. of Windsor, Mar. 27, 1718	2	170
Ann, d. Capt. Henry & Ann, b. Dec. 6, 1731	2	282
Ann, w. Capt. Henry, d. Jan. 23, 1731/2	2	214
Ann, d. Benjamin & Abigail, b. July 21, 1745	2	285
Ann, m. Josiah **ALLYN**, Jr., b. of Windsor, Dec. 3, 1751	2	124
Ann, d. Benjamin & Abigail, d. Sept. 10, 1753	2	215
Ann, d. Josiah & Ann, b. Sept. 10, 1756	2	286
Ann, d. Josiah & Ann, d. Oct. 28, 1756	2	215
Ann, d. Lieut. Josiah & Ann, b. Apr. 11, 1769	2	534
Anna, w. Lieut. Josiah, d. May 18, 1795	2	216
Benjamin, s. Lieut. Thomas, b. Oct. 14, 1680	1	11
Benjamin, m. Ann **WATSON**, b. of Windsor, Dec. 18, 1707	2	123
Benjamin, s. Benjamin, b. Apr. 8, 1711	2	1
Benjamin, d. Dec. 14, 1712	2	213
Benjamin, m. Abigail **LOOMIS**, b. of Windsor, Aug. 9, 1733	2	123
Benjamin, s. Benjamin & Abigail, b. Sept. 13, 1736	2	283
Benjamin, m. Cynthia **MATHER**, Oct. 16, 1823, by Rev. Henry A. Rowland	2	126
Betsy, m. William **JESTS**, of Wethersfield, July 10, 1823, by Rev. Henry A. Rowland	2	485
Candace, m. Samuel W. **MILLS**, May 8, 1823, by Rev. Henry A. Rowland	2	494
Charissa, d. Samuel Wolcott & Joanna, b. Jan. 13, 1766	2	289
Charles, s. John & Elizabeth, b. Mar. 19, 1762	2	287
Charles, s. Charles & Elizabeth, b. Aug. 27, 1787	2	535
Chloe, d. Solomon & Abiah, b. May 19, 1768	2	534
Chloe, d. Lieut. Josiah & Ann, b. Dec. 28, 1774	2	535
Chloe, d. Lieut. Josiah, m. Elisha Noyes **SILL**, Feb. 11, 1796	2	507
Darcas, d. Mathew, Jr. & Darcas, b. May 5, 1745	2	285
Dorethy, d. Pelitiah, b. Nov. 5, 1719	2	2
Dorothy, m. David **HAYDON**, b. of Windsor, Jan. 19, 1737/8	2	163

	Vol.	Page
ALLYN, ALLYEN, ALLYN, ALLN, (cont.)		
Dorothy, d. Lieut. Benjamin & Abigail, b. Feb. 12, 1749/50	2	285
Eli B., m. Jerusha **MATHER**, June 7, 1821, by Henry A. Rowland	2	125
Elijah, s. Mathew, Jr. & Dorcas, b. Feb. 25, 1744	2	285
Elijah, s. Mathew, Jr., was on June 5, 1764, found drowned; bd. June 5, 1764	2	523
Elijah, s. Jonathan & Eunice, b. June 21, 1776	2	535
Elijah, of Windsor, m. Miriam **PARKER**, of Southwick, Feb. 17, 1823, by Rev. Augustus Bolles, of Wintonbury	2	125
Eliphalet Gilman, s. Charles & Elizabeth, b. Jan. 18, 1797	2	535
Elisha, s. Thomas & Sarah, b. Apr. 14, 1761	2	288
Elizabeth, d. Pelitia, b. Nov. 22, 1712	2	1
Elizabeth, d. Samuell & Elizabeth, b. Apr. 20, 1724	2	3
Elizabeth, w. Samuel, d. Apr. 29, 1724	2	214
Elizabeth, d. Samuel, of Enfield & Elizabeth, b. Mar. 28, 1731	2	282
Elizabeth, w. Col. Mathew, d. June 24, 1734	2	216
Elizabeth, w. Col., Matthew & d. Henry **WOLCOTT**, d. June 24, 1734	2	522
Elizabeth, m. Joseph **MOORE**, b. of Windsor, May 29, 1735	2	178
Elisabeth, m. Simeon **BOOTH**, b. of Windsor, Mar. 19, 1752	2	133
Elizabeth, d. John & Elizabeth, b. Sept. 11, 1753	2	285
Elizabeth, w. Samuel, d. Sept. 19, 1757	2	215
Elizabeth, d. Thomas & Sarah, b. Sept. 1, 1770	2	534
Elizabeth, of Windsor, m. Samuel I. **NORTON**, of Hartford, Apr. 12, 1832, by Rev. Henry A. Rowland	2	183
Elisabeth, of Hartford, m. Alexander **ALLIN**, of Windsor, Dec. 21, [ ]	2	123
Emely, m. Josiah **PHELPS**, Jr., Dec. 26, 1820, by Rev. Henry A. Rowland	2	190
Esther, d. Mathew & Darcas, b. May 9, 1747	2	285
Esther, m. James **BARBER**, b. of Windsor, July 17, 1768	2	466
Eunice, d. Thomas & Elizabeth, b. June 27, 1730	2	281
Eunice, d. Benjamin & Abigail, b. July 30, 1743	2	283
Eunice, m. Epaphras **SHELDING**, b. of Windsor, Apr. 30, 1752	2	200
Eunice, d. Thomas & Sarah, b. Apr. 18, 1768	2	534
Eunice E., of Windsor, m. Ralph **WELLS**, of Farmington, Oct. 28, 1829, by John Bartlett	2	212
Eunice Mary Ann, m. Horatio **PINNEY**, b. of Windsor, Mar. 28, 1824, by Rev. Augustus Bolles, of Wintonbury	2	192
Fidelia, m. Ira **CLARK**, Oct. 18, 1840, by S. D. Jewett	2	475
George, s. Theophilus & Tryphena, b. July 18, 1756	2	287
Hannah, m. Caleb **BOTH**, Jr., b. of Windsor, Jan. 30, 1746/7	2	132
Harriet, m. Joseph **ATHERTON**, of Hartford, Dec. 29, 1833, by Henry A. Rowland	2	127
Haty, d. Solomon & Abiah, b. Aug. 3, 1764	2	534

	Vol.	Page
ALLYN, ALLYEN, ALLYN, ALLN, (cont.)		
Henry, s. Mathew, b. Dec. 16, 1699	1	2
Henry, Lieut., m. Ann LOOMIS, b. of Windsor, Feb. 22, 1727/8	2	123
Henry, s. Lieut. Henry & Ann, b. Feb. 4, 1728/9	2	281
Henry, Maj., d. June 23, 1753	2	215
Henry, d. May 8, 1804	2	523
Hester, d. Thomas, b. Jan. 29, [16]76; bp. Feb. 4, [16]76	1	1
James, s. Thomas & Sarah, b. Mar. 26, 1766	2	534
Jane, [d. Thomas & Abigayl], b. July 22, [16]70	MG	
Jane, d. Thomas, b. July 22, 1670	1	1
Jane, m. Henry WOLCOTT, Jr., b. of Windsor, Apr. 1, 1696	1	63
Jane, m. Odiah LOOMIS, b. of Windsor, Nov. 1, 1739	2	172
Jerusha, d. Pelitiah, b. Mar. 3, 1723/4	2	3
Jerusha, m. John PALMER, 3rd, b. of Windsor, Dec. 3, 1748/9	2	188
Joanna, d. Thomas & Joanna, b. Nov. 22, 1703	2	4
Joanna, wid., m. Samuel BANCRAFT, Feb. 23, 1709/10	2	128
Joanna, m. Daniel STOUGHTON, b. of Windsor, Sept. 3, 1730	2	199
Job, s. Lieut. Benjamin & Abigail, b. Sept. 15, 1747	2	285
Job, s. Benjamin & Abigail, d. Dec. 11, 1747	2	215
Job, s. Lieut. Benjamin & Abigail, b. Nov. 24, 1753	2	285
John, s. [Thomas & Abigayl], b. Aug. 17, [16]59; d. [ ]	MG	
John, s. Thomas, b. Aug. 17, 1659	1	1
John, s. Thomas, d. Oct. 4, [16]59	1	40
John, s. Thomas, d. [ ], [16]62	MG	
John, s. Thomas, b. June 24, 1665	Col.1	55
John, s. Thomas, b. June 24, 1665; bp. Feb. 4, 1665	1	1
John, of Windsor, m. Bridget BOOTH, of Enfield, May 3, 1694	1	53
John, s. Alexander, b. July 25, 1697	1	2
John, s. Benjamin, decd., b. July 4, 1713	2	2
John, m. Hannah CHAPMAN, b. of Windsor, Feb. 20, 1723/4	2	123
John, s. Josiah & Sarah, b. Nov. 28, 1729	2	281
John, s. Benjamin & Abigail, b. May 26, 1740	2	283
John, Jr., m. Elisabeth MATHER, b. of Windsor, May 2, 1751	2	124
John, s. John, Jr. & Elisabeth, b. Oct. 10, 1751	2	284
John Burnham, s. John, 2nd & Ruth, b. Mar. 1, 1762	2	287
Jonah, s. Thomas & Elizabeth, b. Mar. 5, 1733/4	2	282
Jonah, d. Nov. 3, 1799	2	216
Jonathan, s. Mathew & Dorcas, b. Dec. 21, 1742	2	285
Jonathan, s. Jonathan & Eunice, b. Feb. 20, 1772	2	535
Joseph, s. Thomas & Elizabeth, b. June 3, 1737	2	282
Joseph, Jr., m. Lois BURNHAM, b. of Windsor, Jan. 17, 1755	2	124
Joseph, s. Joseph, Jr. & Lois, b. Aug. 22, 1758	2	285

	Vol.	Page
ALLYN, ALLYEN, ALLYN, ALLN, (cont.)		
Josiah, s. Mathew, b. Mar. 9, 1692/3	1	2
Josiah, s. Josiah & Sarah, b. Nov. 3, 1727	2	281
Josiah, Jr., m. Ann **ALLYN**, b. of Windsor, Dec. 3, 1751	2	124
Josiah, d. Feb. [ ], 1753	2	215
Josiah, m. Sarah **ELSWORTH**, b. of Windsor, Feb. 9, 1761	2	123
Josiah, Lieut., d. Jan. 17, 1794	2	216
Laura, of Windsor, m. Addison **MORAN**, of Suffield, July 31, 1820, by James Loomis, J. P.	2	181
Louisa, of Hartford, m. Erastus **HOSKINS**, of Bennington, N. Y., Sept. 10, 1835, by Henry A. Rowland	2	164
Love, d. Samuel & Elizabeth, d. Sept. 7, 1757	2	215
Luke, s. Thomas & Sarah, b. Jan. 17, 1753	2	284
Luke, s. Thomas & Sarah, d. Dec. 26, 1753	2	215
Luke, s. Thomas & Sarah, b. Feb. 5, 1755	2	285
Martha, d. Thomas, Jr., b. Sept. 1, 1687	1	1
Martha, d. Thomas, Jr., d. Sept. 3, 1687	1	40
Marth[a], w. Thomas, Jr., d. Sept. 8, 1687	1	40
Mary, m. Beniamen **NEWBERY**, June 11, 1646	MG	
Mary, m. Benjamin **NUBERY**, June 11, 1646	1	59
Mary, d. Alexander, b. June 7, 1702	1	2
Mary, w. Alexander, d. Aug. 7, 1703	1	40
Mary, d. Samuel, b. Sept. 1, 1711	2	1
Mary, d. Pelitiah, b. Oct. 11, 1716	2	2
Mary, m. Simon **CHAPMAN**, b. of Windsor, Jan. 7, 1724/5	2	136
Mary, m. John **ROBERTS**, b. of Windsor, Oct. 22, 1734 (This entry crossed out)	2	95
Mary, m. John **ROBERTS**, b. of Windsor, Oct. 22, 1734	2	195
Mary, m. Noah **PINNEY**, b. of Windsor, Sept. 30, 1744	2	188
Mary, d. Samuel Wolcott & Joannah, b. Oct. 30, 1757	2	288
Mathew, s. [Thomas & Abigayl], b. Jan. 5, 1660	MG	
Mathew, s. Thomas, b. Jan. 5, 1660	1	1
Mathew, d. [Feb. 7*], [16]67 *(In pencil)	MG	
Mathew, d. Feb. 1, 1670	1	40
Mathew, d. Feb. 7, 1670	Col. 1	55
Mathew, m. Eliz[abeth] **WOOLCOT**, b. of Windsor, Jan. 5, 1686	Col.D	54
Mathew, m. Elizabeth **WOLCOTT**, b. of Windsor, Jan. 5, 1686	1	53
Mathew, s. Mathew, b. Aug. 9, 1687	1	1
Mathew, s.Josiah & Sarah, b. Apr. 3, 1732	2	282
Mathew, s. Mathew, Jr. & Dorcas, b. Dec. 20, 1740	2	285
Mathew, Jr., d. May 28, 1753	2	215
Mathew, Col., d. Feb. 17, 1758	2	216
Mathew, Col., d. Feb. 17, 1758	2	523
Mathew, s. Mathew, d. Nov. 13, 1768	2	216
Mathew, s. Josiah, d. Dec. 14, 1768	2	216
Moses, s. Mathew, Jr. & Darcas, b. July 16, 1750	2	285

	Vol.	Page
ALLYN, ALLYEN, ALLYN, ALLN, (cont.)		
Nathaniel, s. David & Mary, b. Jan. 2, 1754	2	286
Pelatiah, s. Mathew, b. May 3, 1689	1	1
Pelitiah, m. Mary **STOUGHTON**, b. of Windsor, Aug. 26, 1711	2	123
Pelatia, s. Pelatia, b. Oct. 4, 1714	2	2
Phinehas, s. Abel & Elizabeth, b. Oct. 31, 1758	2	286
Rhoda, d. Josiah & Ann, b. Sept. 18, 1757	2	286
Roxana, d. Josiah, Jr. & Ann, b. Apr. 20, 1753	2	285
Ruth, of Windsor, m. John **BUTLER**, of Springfield, Mar. 3, 1823, by Rev. Henry A. Rowland	2	468
Samuel, d. [ ]; bd. Apr. 28, 1648	1	40
Samuell, his child, d. [ ], [16]48	MG	
Samuell, d. [ ], [16]48	MG	
Samuell, [s. Thomas & Abigayl], b. Nov. 3, [16]67	MG	
Samuel, s. Thomas, b. Nov. 3, 1667	1	1
Samuell, had 6 children b. in Windsor. Dated Aug. 17, 1677	MG	
Samuell, s. Samuell, b. Oct. 27, 1703	2	1
Samuel, m. Elizabeth **HOPKINS**, b. of Windsor, July 17, 1723	2	123
Samuel, s. Samuel, d. Nov. 22, 1724	2	214
Samuel, s. Samuel, of Enfield & Elizabeth, b. June 13, 1729	2	282
Samuel, s. Benjamin & Abigail, b. Apr. 17, 1742	2	283
Samuel, s. Samuel, d. Jan. 23, 1759	2	215
Samuel, s. Samuel Wolcott & Joannah, b. Nov. 15, 1759	2	288
Samuel, m. Lucy **GILBERT**, b. of Windsor, Jan. 5, 1764	2	125
Samuel, s. Samuel & Lucy, b. Jan. 15, 1765	2	288
Samuel, m. Sarah **COOK**, b. of Windsor, [ ]	1	53
Samuel Wolcott, s. Sergt. Peletiah & Mary, b. Dec. 6, 1727	2	3
Samuel Wolcott, m. Joanna **MILLS**, b. of Windsor, Feb. 20, 1755	2	124
Sarah, [d. Thomas & Abigayl], b. July 13, 1674	MG	
Sarah, d. Thomas, b. July 13, 1674	1	1
Sarah, m. Timothy **THRALL**, Dec. 21, 1699	1	62
Sarah, d. Samuel, b. July [ ], 1707	2	3
Sarah, w. Samuel, d. Jan. 29, 1718/19	2	214
Sarah, of Windsor, m. John **WELLS**, of Dearfield, Jan. 2, 1728/9	2	208
Sarah, d. John & Elizabeth, b. Apr. [ ], 1756	2	286
Sarah, d. Thomas & Sarah, b. Oct. 19, 1763	2	288
Sarah, had s. Ebenezer **YOUNGS**, b. Oct. 19, 1777	2	122
Sarah, had illeg. s. Ebenezer **YOUNGS**, b. Oct. 19, 1777; reputed f. Ebenezer **YOUNGS**	2	535
Solomon, s. Capt. Pelatiah & Mary, b. Oct. 8, 1732	2	282
Solomon, m. Abiah **STOUGHTON**, b. of Windsor, Dec. 8, 1756	2	125
Solomon, s. Solomon & Abiah, b. Sept. 15, 1757	2	534
Susannah, w. Jonah, d. Mar. 26, 1800	2	216

	Vol.	Page
ALLYN, ALLYEN, ALLYN, ALLN, (cont.)		
T., his w. [ ], adm, ch. & communicant Jan. [ ], 1665	MG	
T., contributed 0-6-6 to the poor in other colonies	MG	
Tabethy, d. Samuel & Elizabeth, b. Apr. 13, 1736	2	282
Theodore, s. Jonah & Susannah, b. Feb. 25, 1762	2	287
Theodore, s. Jonah & Susannah, d. Apr. 10, 1762	2	216
Theophilos, s. Mathew, b. Aug. 26, 1702	1	2
Theophilos, s. Col. Mathew, d. Aug. 24, 1718	2	214
Theophelos, s. Pelitiah, b. Aug. 28, 1718	2	2
Theophilos, s. Pelatiah, d. Dec. 4, 1718	2	214
Theophilos, s. Thomas & Elizabeth, b. Nov. 23, 1726	2	3
Theophilus, m. Trypheny **WOLCOTT**, b. of Windsor, Oct. [ ], 1751	2	124
Theophilus, d. Sept. 3, 1757	2	215
Theophilus, s. Thomas & Sarah, d. Mar. 29, 1767	2	523
Thomas, his w. [ ], adm. to Ch. [16]	MG	
Thomas, adult, ch. men. 16[ ]	MG	
Thomas, m. Abigayl **WARRAM**, Oct. [ ], [16]	MG	
Thomas, m. Abigail **WAREHAM**, b. of Windsor, Oct. 21, 1658	1	53
Thomas, s. [Thomas & Abigayl], b. Mar. 11, [16]62/3	MG	
Thomas, s. Thomas, b. Mar. 11, [16]62/3	Col.1	54
Thomas, s. Thomas, b. Mar. 11, 1662/3	1	1
Thomas, [bp.] Mar. 15, [16]62	MG	
[Thomas], & Abigayl, had d. [ ], b. Jan. 29, 1676	MG	
Thomas, his child d. [ ], [16]76	MG	
Thomas, had 8 children b. in Windsor. Dated Aug. 17, 1677	MG	
Thomas, m. Martha **WOOLCOT**, b. of Windsor, Jan. 6, 1686	Col. D	54
Thomas, m. Martha **WOLCOTT**, b. of Windsor, Jan. 6, 1686	1	53
Thomas, s. Thomas, Jr., d. Apr. 18, 1688	1	40
Thomas, Capt., d. Feb. 14, 1695/6	1	40
Thomas, d. Apr. 6, 1709	2	213
Thomas, s. Thomas & Elizabeth, b. Nov. 7, 1725	2	3
Thomas, d. Dec. 11, 1738	2	214
Thomas, m. Sarah **PHELPS**, b. of Windsor, Dec. 13, 1750	2	124
Thomas, s. Thomas & Sarah, b. Dec. 20, 1751	2	284
Thomas, d. Nov. 13, 1781	2	216
Thomas, d. Nov. 13, 1781	2	522
Tryphena, d. Theophilus & Tryphena, b. Jan. 8, 1752	2	285
William, s. Alexander, b. Apr. 9, 1701	1	2
William, s. Alexander, d. May 16, 1701	1	40
William, s. John & Hannah, b. Apr. 22, 1728	2	4
William, s. Charles & Elizabeth, b. Mar. 25, 1791	2	535
Woloctt, s. Samuel Wolcott & Joanna, b. Sept. 11, 1763	2	289
Wolcott, of Randolph, Vt., d. Jan. 18, 1843	2	216
-----, old Mrs., adm. ch. Aug. 5, 1649	MG	
-----, Mrs., taxed 5-9 on Feb. 10, [16]73	MG	
-----, Mrs., d. Sept. 12, [16]75	MG	

	Vol.	Page
ALLYN, ALLYEN, ALLYN, ALLN, (cont.)		
----, Mrs., d. Sept. 12, 1675	Col.1	58
ALVORD, ALVARD, ALUARD, [see also **ALFORD**], Abigal, d.		
[Allixander & Mary], b. Oct. 6, 1647	MG	
Abigall, d. [Alexander], b. Oct. [ ], 1647	Col.2	161
Allixander, m. Mary **VORE**, Oct. 29, 1646	MG	
Allexander, had 7 children b. in Windsor. Dated Aug. 17, 1677	MG	
B., his w. [ ], adm. ch. & communicant Jan. [ ], 1647	MG	
Benidict, adm. ch. & communicant Oct. [ ], 1641	MG	
Bene[ ], his w. [ ], adm. ch. Jan. 13, [16]47	MG	
Benidict, his three children d. [ ], [16]48	MG	
Benedict, Sergt., d. Apr. 23, 1683	Col.D	56
Benidic, contributed 0-10-0 to the poor in other colonies	MG	
Benedictus, m. Jone **NUTON**, Nov. 26, 1640	MG	
Benidictus, taxed 4-0 on Feb. 10,]16]73	MG	
Benidictus, had 5 children b. in Windsor. Dated Aug. 17, 1677	MG	
Beniamen, s. [Benedictus & Jone], b. July 11, 1647	MG	
Beniamen, s. [Allixander & Mary], b. Feb. 11, 1657	MG	
Benjamin, [s. Alexander], b. Feb. 11, 1657	Col.2	161
Elisubth, pb. Sept. 21, [16]51	MG	
Elisabeth, d. [Benedictus & Jone], b. Sept. 21, 1651	MG	
Elisubth, bp. Sept. 21, [16]51	MG	
Elisabeth, d. [Allixander & Mary], b. Nov. 12, 1655	MG	
Elizabeth, [d. Alexander], b. Nov. 12, 1655	Col.2	161
Elisabeth, m. [ ] **DRAKE**, Mar. 20, 1671	MG	
Elizabeth, m. Job **DRAKE**, s. John, Mar. 20, 1671, by Capt. Newberry	Col.1	46
Elisabeth, d. Jerimiah, b. Apr. 27, 1706	2	1
Jeremy, [s. Benedictus & Jone], b. Dec. 24, [16]55	MG	
Jeremia, s. Benedictus, b. Dec. 24, 1655	Col.2	158
Jerimiah, d. June 6, 1709	2	213
Jerem[y], contributed 0-1-3 to the poor in other colonies	MG	
Jeremy, [s.] B. A., [ ]	MG	
Joane, m. Ambrous **FOWLLER**, May 6, 1646	MG	
Job, s. Jeremiah, b. Aug. 26, 1708	2	1
John, s. [Allixander & Mary], b. Aug. 12, 1649	MG	
John, [s. Alexander], b. Aug. 12, 1649	Col.2	161
Jonathan, s. [Benedictus & Jone], b. June 1, 1645	MG	
Josias, s. [Benedictus & Jone], b. July 6, 1649	MG	
Josias, bp. July 6, [16]49	MG	
Mary, d. [Allixander & Mary], b. July 6, 1651	MG	
Mary, [d. Alexander], b. July 6, 1651	Col.2	161
Newton, s. Jere, b. Mar. 24, 1689	Col.D	51
Sara, [d. Allixander & Mary], b. June 24, 1660	MG	
Thomas, s. [Allixander & Mary], b. Oct. 27, 1653	MG	

	Vol.	Page

ALVORD, ALVARD, ALUARD, (cont.)

Thomas, [s. Alexander], b. Oct. 27, 1653 — Col.2 — 161

----dicts, adm. communion Oct. 17, 1641 — MG

----, Sergt. taxed 4-0 on Feb. 10, [16]73 — MG

ANDERSON, Ashbel, s. Ashbel & Abigail, b. June 29, 1758 — 2 — 287

Catherin, of Wethersfield, m. W[illia]m H. **SEARS,** of
Glastenbury, June 27, 1842, by Rev. S. D. Jewett — 2 — 206

George, of Farmington, m. Charlotte **FLETCHER,** of
Windsor, Mar. 5, 1848, by Cephus Brainard — 2 — 462

Namy, d. Ashbel & Abigail, b. Apr. 29, 1756 — 2 — 287

ANDREWS, [see also **ANDRUS**], Edwin H., of Glastenbury, m.
Sarah I. **HAWLEY,** of Windsor, Aug. 18, 1850, by Rev.
S. H. Allen — 2 — 463

George, of Waterbury, m. Cordelia **ALFORD,** of Windsor,
May 26, 1839, by Rev. Daniel Hemenway — 2 — 127

Irene, of Hartford, m. Daniel **HOYT,** of Springfield,
Feb. 22, 1843, by S. D. Jewett — 2 — 476

James, m. Amelia **DRAKE,** Jan. 21, 1847, by T. A. Leete — 2 — 465

ANDROS, [see under **ANDRUS**]

ANDRUS, ANDROS, [see also **ANDREWS**], Elijah, m. Mary
ROBERTS, Jr., b. of Windsor, Dec. 1, 1763 — 2 — 125

Elijah, s. Elijah & Mary, b. Feb. 4, 1765 — 2 — 534

Elijah & Mary, had d. [ ], b. Mar. 2, 1766 — 2 — 534

Eliza, of Windsor, m. Samuel **KING,** of Enfield, Nov. 24,
1825, by Richard Miles, J. P. — 2 — 168

Eliza, of Windsor, m. [ ] **KING,** of Enfield, Nov. 24, 1825,
by Richard Niles, J. P. — 2 — 168

Elisabeth, m. Jacob **GIBBES,** Dec. 4, 1657 — MG

Elizabeth, of Hartford, m. Jacob **GIBBS,** of Windsor, Dec.
4, 1657 — 1 — 56

Jerusha, m. Abel **GILLET,** Jr., b. of Windsor, Jan. 7, 1768 — 2 — 158

Levi, of Suffield, m. Eleanor **SMITH,** of Granby, Sept. 3,
1839, by Rev. Cephas Brainard — 2 — 127

Mary, d. Elijah & Mary, b. Mar. 2, 1766 — 2 — 534

Rebeckah, d. Elijah & Mary, b. Dec. 24, 1767 — 2 — 534

ANIHUS*, D. Ameline, m. Horace **WALBRIDGE,** of Stafford,
July 4, 1821, by Henry A. Rowland *(In pencil) — 2 — 210

ANNIS, George, of Manchester, m. Martha Ann **ROWE,** of
Westfield, Mass., Sept. 16, 1839, by Rev. S. D. Jewett — 2 — 464

ARNOLD, Caroline A., of Granby, m. William **STEPHENS,** of
Southwick, Mass., Dec. 27, 1850, by Rev. S. H. Allen — 2 — 502

Maria, of Windsor, m. Charles A. **ROPER,** of Bristol, May
15, 1833, by Henry A. Rowland — 2 — 506

ASHLEY, Hannah, of Westfield, m. Nathaniel **EGELSTON,** of
Windsor, Sept. 13, 1694 — 1 — 56

Hannah, of Westfield, m. Hezekiah **PORTER,** of Windsor,
Oct. 30, 1734 — 2 — 188

Jerusha, of Hartford, m. Benedict **ALFORD,** Jr., of Windsor,

	Vol.	Page
ASHLEY, (cont.)		
Aug. 9, 1744	2	124
ATHERTON, Joseph, of Hartford, m. Harriet **ALLYN**, Dec. 29,		
1833, by Henry A. Rowland	2	127
ATKINSON, Andrew, m. Eliza **PRESCOTT**, b. of Boston, Mass.,		
Dec. 22, 1846, by Rev. George F. Kettel	2	465
Andrew, m. Eliza **PRESCOTT**, b. of Boston, Mass., Dec. 22,		
1846, by Rev. George F. Rettell	2	466
ATTLETON, Cyrus, m. Eliza Ann **ALFORD**, b. of Springfield,		
Feb. 6, 1825, by Rev. Phineas Cook	2	126
ATWELL, Benjamin, twin with Joseph, s. Joseph & Meriam, b.		
Oct. [ ], 1754	2	285
Joseph, m. Meriam **CASE**, b. of Windsor, Dec. 27, 1753	2	124
Joseph, twin with Benjamin, s. Joseph & Meriam, b. Oct.		
[ ], 1754	2	285
ATWOOD, ATTWOOD, Abigail, m. Mark **CALLSEY**, [ ].		
1683	Col.D	54
Abigail, m. Mark **KELCY**, Dec. 26, 1683	1	58
AUSTIN, Eunice, m. Nathanil **LYNDE**, of Brookfield, Mar. 26,		
1822, by Rev. Henry A. Rowland	2	174
Orson Wilson, see under Orson **WILLSON**	2	520
Samuel, of Hartford, m. Hannah **SMITH**, of Windsor, Nov.		
28, 1847, by Cephus Brainard	2	463
AVERY, Lydia, of Ashford, m. Medina **FITCH**, of Windsor,		
Dec. 19, 1744	2	152
BABCOCK, Stanton, m. Julia **WELCH**, b. of Windsor, Jan. 6,		
1840, by Rev. S. D. Jewett	2	466
BACON, Clarissa, m. Obediah **BROWN**, Aug. 20, 1832, by Henry		
Sill, J. P.	2	150
Daniel, m. Louisa Harriet **ABBY**, Nov. 25, 1838, by Giles		
Ellsworth, J. P.	2	475
BAILEY, Jane, m. Alexander **CLAPP**, Oct. 16, 184[sic?], by Giles		
Ellsworth, J. P.	2	508
BAINES, BAINS, Julia A., m. Oliver W. **MARSHALL**, b. of		
Windsor, Jan. 1, 1838, by Eli Deniston	2	493
Sarah C., of Windsor, m. C. N. **MOORE**, of Bloomfield,		
Dec. 25, 1850, by R. K. Reynolds	2	493
BAKER, Abiell, d. [Jefery & Jone], b. Dec. 23, 1652; d. [ ]	MG	
Abigall, d. Jeffery, b. Dec. 23, 1652	1	3
Abigael, d. Joseph, b. Nov. 11, 1712	2	9
Abigael, d. Joseph, d. July 11, 1714	2	218
Bezaleel, s. Nathaniel & Mary, b. Oct. 9, 1745	2	299
Cordelia, of Windsor, m. Moses **GOODWIN**, of Hartford,		
Oct. 9, 1845, by Rev. Cephas Brainard	2	508
Daniel, s. Joseph, b. Apr. 2, 1717	2	11
Ebenezer, s. John*, b. July 17, 1689 *(Note by LBB:		
"Joseph")	Col.D	51
Ebenezer, s. Joseph, b. July 17, 1689	1	5

	Vol.	Page

BAKER, (cont.)

	Vol.	Page
Ebenezer, s. Joseph, b. Jan. 31, 1714/15	2	10
Elizabeth, Mrs., m. Ebenezer **LEWIS**, July 25, 1838, by Cornelius B. Everest	2	490
Elizabeth S., m. Daniel E. **GRISWOLD**, b. of Windsor, Nov. 16, 1842, by Rev. S. D. Jewett	2	516
Hanah, d. Joseph, b. Dec. 19, 1686	Col.D	51
Hannah, d. Joseph, b. Dec. 19, 1686	1	5
Hannah, d. Joseph, d. Mar. 8, 1687/8	1	41
Hannah, w. Joseph, d. July 7, 1705	2	217
Hannah, d. Joseph, b. Apr. 9, 1709	2	6
Heman, s. Joseph, b. Apr. 27, 1719	2	11
Hepsiba, d. [Jefery & Jone], b. May 10, 1646	MG	
Hephzibah, d. Jeffery, b. May 10, 1646	1	3
Hepsiba, m. Caleb **PUMERY**, Mar. 8, 1664	MG	
Hepsiba, m. Caleb **PUMRY**, b. of Windsor, Mar. 8, 1664, by Mr. Allyn	Col.1	45
Jacob, s. Joseph, b. Jan. 11, 1710/11	2	7
Jacob, s. Joseph, b. Jan. 11, 1710/11	2	7
Jefery, m. Jone **ROCKWELL**, Nov. 15, 1642	MG	
Jeffery, d. July 7, 1655	Col.2	160
Jeffery, d. July 7, 1655	1	41
Jefery, d. [ ], [16]55	MG	
Jefry*, m. Hannah **BUCKLAND**, wid. Thomas, Jan. 30, [16]76 *(In pencil "Joseph?")	TR1	1
Jeffery, had 5 children b. in Windsor. Dated Aug. 17, 1677	MG	
John, s. Joseph, b. Dec. 28, 1707	2	6
Joseph, adult, ch. mem. 16[ ]	MG	
Joseph, b. June 18, 1655; m. Hanna **BUCKLAND**, wid. Thomas & d. Nathanell **COOK**, Jan. 30, [16]76	MG	
Joseph, s. [Jefery & Jone], b. June 18, 1655	MG	
Joseph, s. Jeffery, b. June 18, 1655	Col.2	158
Joseph, s. Jeffery, b. June 18, 1655	1	3
Joseph, m. Hanna **BUCKLAND**, wid. Thomas, Jan. 30, 1676	Col.1	46
Joseph, m. Hannah **BUCKLAND**, wid. Thomas, Jan. 30, [16]76	1	54
Joseph, s. Joseph & Hanna, b. Apr. 13, [16]78	MG	
Joseph, d. Dec. 11, 1691	1	41
Joseph, of Windsor, m. Hannah **POMERY**, of Northampton, July 8, 1702, at Northampton	1	54
Joseph, s. Joseph, b. Apr. 19, 1703	1	6
Joseph, m. Abigaell **BISSELL**, b. of Windsor, Dec. 26, 1706	2	128
Joseph, Jr., m. Elizabeth **MARSHALL**, Nov. 11, 1829, by Henry A. Rowland	2	498
Joseph W., m. Hannah M. **CLARK**, b. of Windsor, Apr. 12, 1849, by T. A. Leet	2	504
Lidia, d. [Joseph & Hanna], b. July 5, 1681	MG	
Lydia, d. May 8, 1698	1	41

	Vol.	Page
BAKER, (cont.)		
Mary, d. [Jefery & Jone], b. July 15, 1649	MG	
Mary, d. Jeffery, b. July 15, 1649	Col.2	151
Mary, d. Jeffery, b. July 15, 1649	1	3
Oliver, of Springfield, Mass., m. Harriet **BROWN**, wid.		
Samuel, of Windsor, Nov. 7, 1826, by Rev. John		
Bartlett, of Wintonbury. Int. Pub.	2	149
Samuell, communicant 16[ ]	MG	
Samuel, his w. [ ], adm. ch. Oct. 2, [16]	MG	
Samuell, s. [Jefery & Jone], b. Mar. 30, 1644	MG	
Samuel, s. Jeffery, b. Mar. 30, 1644	1	3
Samuell, m. Sara **COOK**, Jan. 30, 1670	MG	
Samuell*, m. Sara **COOK**, b. of Windsor, June 30, [16]70		
*("Samuell **BARKER**" in Col. Rec. Corrected by LBB)	Col.1	45
Sam[uel], his w. [ ], adm. ch. & communicant Dec. [ ],		
1670	MG	
Samuell, adm. communion, Apr. 7, 1672	MG	
Samuell, s. Joseph, b. Oct. 14, [16]84	Col.D	51
Samuel, s. Joseph, b. Oct. 17, 1684	1	5
Sam[uel], s. Joseph, d. Oct. 16, 1685	Col.D	56
Samuel, s. Joseph, d. Oct. 16, 1685	1	41
Samuell, s. Joseph, b. June 28, 1705	2	4
Samuel, Dea., d. Apr. 12, 1715	2	218
Samuell, contributed 0-2-6 to the poor in other colonies	MG	
Samuell, see Samuell **BARKER**	Col.1	45
Titus, s. Joseph, b. May 14, 1722	2	13
William A., m. Francis P. **GILLETT**, b. of Windsor, Dec. 7,		
1841, by Rev. S. D. Jewett	2	476
BALDWIN, BALDWINE, Ambrose, m. Harriet **MARSHALL**, b.		
of Windsor, Nov. 24, 1839, by S. D. Jewett	2	465
Charles G., m. Caroline L. **STAFFORD**, May [2], 1847, by		
Rev. S. H. Allen	2	503
Elijah, s. Daniel & Elizabeth, b. June 15, 1754	2	306
BANCROFT, BANCRAFT, [see also **BANERAFF**], Abel, s.		
Thomas & Mercy, b. July 25, 1740	2	296
Abigail, w. Isaac, d. June 17, 1758	2	220
Abigail, d. Isaac & Abigail, b. Aug. 23, 1744	2	298
Abner, s. Nathaniel & Ann, b. Oct. 20, 1739	2	296
Ann, m. John **GRIFFIN**, May 13, 1647	1	56 —
Ann, d. Thomas & Mercy, b. Oct. 8, 1744	2	299
Ann, had s. Isaac, b. Nov. 20, 1766	2	79
Anna, m. John **GRIFFEN**, May 13, 164[7]	MG	
Annah, d. John & Annah, b. Oct. 22, 1763	2	542
Benjamin, s. Ephraim, b. May 10, 1694	1	5
Daniel, s. Ephraim, b. July 16, 1700	1	6
Edward, s. Thomas & Marcy, b. July 15, 1737	2	294
Elisabeth, d. Samuell, b. Mar. 27, 1706	2	6
Elles, d. Ephraim, Jr. & Esther, b. Mar. 4, 1741/2	2	297

	Vol.	Page
BANCROFT, BANCRAFT, (cont.)		
Elliss, d. Ephraim, Jr., & Esther, d. July 13, 1750	2	220
Ephraim, s. [John & Hanna], b. June 15, 1656	MG	
Ephraim, s. John, b. June 15, 1656	Col.2	158
Ephraim, s. John, b. June 15, 1656	1	3
Ep[h]ra[i]m, m. Sarah STILLES, d. John, May 1, 1681	MG	
Ephraim, m. Sarah STILES, May 5, 1681	Col.D	54
Ephraim, m. Sarah STYLES, May 5, 1681	1	54
Ephraim, s. Ephraim, b. Feb. 8, 1682	Col.D	51
Ephraim, s. Ephraim, b. Feb. 8, 1682	1	5
Epheram, m. Frances PHELPS, b. of Windsor, Mar. 17, 1715	2	129
Ephraim, s. Ephraim, Jr., b. Oct. 8, 1717	2	11
Ephraim, s. Ephraim, Jr., b. Mar. 12, 1718/19	2	11
Ephraim, of Windsor, m. Esther LEASON, of Enfield, Dec. 6, 1739	2	131
Ephraim, s. Ephraim, Jr. & Easther, b. Feb. 6, 1748/9	2	303
Ephraim, s. Ephraim, Jr. & Esther, d. July 6, 1750	2	220
Ephraim, s. Ephraim, Jr. & Esther, b. Feb. 24, 1751	2	307
Ephraim, contributed 0-1-6 to the poor in other colonies	MG	
Esther, d. Thomas, Jr. & Martha, b. Nov. 21, 1729	2	292
Esther, d. Ephraim, Jr. & Esther, b. Dec. 23, 1744	2	299
[E]unice, d. Samuell, b. Dec. 29, 1700	2	6
Eunice, d. Isaac & Abigail, b. Feb. 16, 1747	2	303
Hannah, d. John, b. Apr. 6, 1659	1	3
Hannah, w. Samuell, d. Jan. 27, 1708/9	2	217
Hannah, d. Ephraim, b. July 23, 1723	2	14
Hannah, d. Nathaniell & Anne, b. July 22, 1735	2	294
Hannah, d. Isaac & Abigail, b. Mar. 29, 1755	2	537
Isaac, s. Ephraim, Jr., b. Aug. 17, 1720	2	12
Isaac, m. Abigail EGELSTONE, b. of Windsor, Dec. 17, 1741	2	130
Isaac, s. Isaac & Abigail, b. Sept. 8, 1742	2	297
Isaac, s. Ann, b. Nov. 20, 1766	2	79
Jerusha, d. Nathaniell & Ann, b. Apr. 11, 1742	2	297
Jerusha, d. Isaac & Abigail, b. Jan. 21, 1749/50	2	303
Jerusha, m. Oliver LOOMIS, b. of Windsor, Sept. 2, 1762	2	488
Joanna, d. [John & Hanna], b. Apr. 6, 1659	MG	
John, m. Hanna DUPER, Dec. 3, 1650	MG	
John, m. Hannah DUPPER, Dec. 3, 1650	1	53
John, s. [John & Hanna], b. Dec. [ ], 1651	MG	
John, s. John, b. Dec. [ ], 1651	1	3
John, d. [ ], [16]62	MG	
John, d. Aug. 6, 1662	Col.1	55
John, d. Aug. 6, [16]62	1	40
John, had 5 children b. in Windsor. Dated Aug. 17, 1677	MG	
John, s. Nathanell & Hanna, b. Jan. 2, [16]78	MG	
John, s. Nathanell, b. Jan. 24, 1678	Col.1	56

	Vol.	Page
BANCROFT, BANCRAFT, (cont.)		
Thomas, s. Ephraim, b. Dec. 14, 1703	1	6
Thomas, s. Thomas, b. Oct. 10, 1731	2	292
Thomas, s. Nathaniel & Ann, b. Sept. 26, 1746	2	300
Thomas, s. Thomas, d. Aug. 6, 1758, at Lake George	2	220
Triphena, d. Ephraim, Jr. & Esther, b. Aug. 10, 1740	2	296
BANERAFF, [see also **BANCROFT**], Mary*, m. David **ALLIN**,		
b. of Windsor, Feb. 27, 1753 *("Mary **BANCROFT?**")	2	124
BANKS, John, had 1 child b. in Windsor. Dated Aug. 17, 1677	MG	
Mary, m. Samuell **TAYLAR**, Oct. 27, 1670, by Mr. Wolcot	Col.1	46
BARBER, BARBAR, BARBOR, Aaron, s. Josiah, b. July 20,		
1697	1	6
Aaron, of Windsor, m. Mercy **DUGLES**, of Windsor, late of		
New London, Feb. 2, 1724/5	2	129
Aaron, s. Aaron & Marcy, b. Oct. 16, 1728	2	290
Abiel, s. William & Abigaiel, b. Apr. 8, 1730	2	295
Abigall, d. [Josia & Abigall], b. Mar. 12, 1678	MG	
Abigall, d. Josias, b. Mar. 12, 1678	Col.1	56
Abigail, d. Josiah, b. Mar. 12, 1678	1	4
Abigail, w. Josiah, d. Feb. 9, 1700/1	1	41
Abigael, m. Cornelius **BROWN**, Dec. 4, 1701	2	127
Abigail, d. Nathaniel, b. Dec. 11, 1720	2	12
Abigail, d. William & Abigail, b. Mar. 23, 1733/4	2	295
Abigail, d. Elijah & Abigail, b. Aug. 18, 1787	2	568
Abigail, m. Lucius **BROWN**, Apr. 20, 1833, by Hiram		
Roberts, J. P.	2	499
Abigail A., of Windsor, m. Lyman **STOCKBRIDGE**, of		
Hartford, Dec. 11, 1829, by Henry A. Rowland	2	507
Abner, s. Elijah & Abigail, b. Sept. 18, 1772	2	546
Allyn, s. James & Esther, b. May 14, 1774	2	547
Allyn, of Windsor, m. Charlotte **CASE**, of Canton, Dec. 25,		
1822, by Rev. John Bartlett. Int. Pub.	2	148
Almira T., m. Judson **CLARK**, Oct. 24, 1831, by Henry A		
Rowland	2	470
Ann, d. Jonathan, b. Dec. 2, 1728	2	290
Ann, m. Ebenezer **BLODGET**, b. of Windsor, Nov. 15, 1758	2	134
Ann G., m. Roman W. **LOOMIS**, Oct. 5, 1834, by Henry A.		
Rowland	2	489
Anna, d. Gideon & Anna, b. Mar. 27, 1751	2	307
Anne, d. Aaron & Mercy, b. Mar. 10, 1748/9	2	302
Asa, s. James & Esther, b. Apr. 12, 1776	2	548
Asahel, s. John & Jane, b. Dec. 6, 1725	2	289
Asahel, s. John, d. Nov. 6, 1726	2	219
Asahel, 2nd, s. John & Jane, b. Aug. 10, 1727	2	290
Ashbal, s. Jonathan & Rachel, b. July 22, 1738	2	295
Ashbel, m. Sarah **ORSBORN**, b. of Windsor, Aug. 1, 1765	2	134
Azubah, d. Jonathan, b. Dec. 20, 1724	2	15
Azubah, m. Jacob **WEBSTER**, b. of Windsor, Jan. 19, 1748/9	2	209

	Vol.	Page
BARBER, BARBAR, BARBOR, (cont.)		
Rowland	2	174
Fidelia, of Windsor, m. Alonzo **BRIDGES**, of Milford,		
N. Y., Sept. 22, 1824, by Rev. Henry A. Rowland	2	468
Freeman, d. Jan. 16, 1837, ae 69	2	221
Gideon, s. John, b. Aug. 26, 1723	2	14
Gideon, m. Anna **GILLET**, b. of Windsor, Nov. 9, 1744	2	131
Hanna, d. [Samuell & Ruth], b. Oct. 4, 1681	MG	
Hannah, d. Samuel, b. Oct. 4, [16]81	Col.D	51
Hannah, d. Samuel, b. Oct. 4, 1681	1	5
Hanah, d. Aaron & Mercy, b. June 17, 1739	2	296
Hannah, m. Simeon **MOORE**, b. of Windsor, Nov. 22, 1753	2	179
Harriet, m. Jonathan **ELLSWORTH**, Feb. 2, 1825, by Rev.		
Henry A. Rowland	2	148
Henry, s. James & Esther, b. July 1, 1785	2	562
Henry, s. James & Esther, b. July 1, 1785	2	568
Hephsibah, w. Samuell, d. Dec. 20, 1711	2	217
Hephsibah, d. Samuel, b. Apr. 8, 1716	2	10
Hephzibah, d. Nathaniell & Hephzibah, b. Mar. 9, 1739/40	2	296
Hulda, d. Jonah & Jerusha, b. Jan. 4, 1766	2	543
Jacob, s. Thomas & Jane, b. June 16, 1752	2	305
James, s. Aaron & Mercy, b. Mar. 22, 1742	2	301
James, m. Esther **ALLYN**, b. of Windsor, July 17, 1768	2	466
James, s. James & Esther, b. Nov. 19, 1771	2	546
James, s. James & Esther, b. June 2, 1778	Col.2	548
[Jane*], w. Thomas, d. Sept. 10, 1662 *(Supplied by LBB)	Col.1	55
Jane, d. John, b. June 16, 1720	2	13
Jane, d. Thomas & Jane, b. Oct. 12, 1749	2	305
Jane, d. Thomas & Jane, d. Nov. 14, 1749	2	525
Jane, wid., d. Dec. 21, 1770	2	221
Jerijah, s. John & Jane, b. Dec. 26, 1738	2	295
Jerijah, m. Joannah **FILLEY**, b. of Windsor, Dec. 5, 1765	2	134
Jerijah, s. Jerijah & Loannah, b. Aug. 23, 1766	2	543
Jerijah, d. Feb. 7, 1792, in the 53rd year of his age	2	221
Jerijah, m. Deborah **DEXTER**, b. of Windsor, May 26, 1796	2	467
Jerusha, d. John & Jane, b. Sept. 26, 1730	2	292
Jerusha, m. Jonah **BARBER**, b. of Windsor, July 10, 1747	2	132
Jerusha, d. Jonah & Jerusha, b. July 12, 1751	2	304
Jerusha, d. Jonah, d. Jan. [ ], 1781	2	526
Jerusha, w. Jonah, d. Feb. 6, 1781	2	256
Jerusha, m. Henry **WHITE**, of East Windsor, June 9, 1825,		
by Rev. Henry A. Rowland	2	211
Joanna, d. [John & Bathsheba], b. Apr. 8, [16]6[7]	MG	
Joanna, d. John, b. Apr. 8, [16]67	Col.1	56
Joanna, d. John, b. Apr. 3, [16]67	1	4
Joel, s. John & Jane, b. Oct. 22, 1736	2	294
John, s. [Thomas & Jane], bp. July 24, 1642	MG	
John, s. Thomas, bp. July 24, 1642	Col.2	151

	Vol.	Page
BARBER, BARBAR, BARBOR, (cont.)		
John, s. Thomas, bp. July 24, 1642	1	2
John, m. Bathsheba COGENS, Sept. [ ], [16]	MG	
John, of Windsor, m. Bathsheba COGGINS, of Springfield,		
Sept. 2, 1663	Col. 1	45
John, s. [John & Bathsheba], b. July 14, 1669	MG	
John, had 2 children, b. in Windsor, Dated Aug. 17, 1677	MG	
John, m. Jane ALFOOT, b. of Windsor, July 24, 1717	2	129
John, s. John, b. June 19, 1718	2	11
John, d. Mar. 29, 1767	2	221
John, s. Jerijah & Loannah, b. May 19, 1770	2	545
Jonah, s. Joseph, b. Jan. 9, 1723/4	2	14
Jonah, m. Jerusha BARBER, b. of Windsor, July 10, 1747	2	132
Jonah, s. Benjamin & Ruth, b. Sept. 20, 1783	2	569
Jonathan, s. Josiah, b. June 4, 1694	1	5
Jonathan, m. Rachel GAYLORD, b. of Windsor, Aug. 4,		
1720	2	129
Jonathan, s. Jonathan & Rachel, b. Dec. 23, 1731	2	292
Jonathan, Jr., m. Elizabeth ORSBORN, b. of Windsor, Apr.		
17, 1760	2	133
Joseph, m. Mary LOOMIS, b. of Windsor, May 6, 1708	2	128
Joseph, s. Joseph, b. Dec.* 28, 1708/9 *(In pencil "Jan.")	2	6
Joseph, Jr., m. Elizabeth COOK, b. of Windsor, June 18,		
1728	2	129
Joseph, s. Joseph, Jr. & Elizabeth, b. May 6, 1729	2	290
Josia, s. [Thomas & Jane], b. Feb. 15, 1653	MG	
Josiah, s. Thomas, b. Feb. 15, 1653	1	2
Josia, m. Abigall LOOMYS, d. Nathanell, Nov. 22, 1677,		
by Capt. [ ] Newbery	MG	
Josia, m. Abigall LOOMYS, d. Nathanell, Nov. 22, [16]77,		
by Capt. Newbery	Col. 1	46
Josiah, m. Abigail LOOMIS, d. Nathanael, Nov. 22, 1677, by		
Capt. Nubery	1	54
Josiah, s. Josia[h], b. [ ], 1685	Col.D	51
Josiah, s. Josiah, b. [ ], 1685	1	5
Josiah, m. Sarah DRAKE, b. of Windsor, Nov. 5, 1701	1	54
Josiah, s. Nathaniel, b. Mar. 6, 1714/15	2	11
Josiah, Lieut., d. Dec. 14, 1729	2	219
Josiah, of Windsor, m. Sarah FORBS, of Hartford, June 28,		
1745	2	131
Josiah, s. Josiah & Sarah, b. Oct. 9, 1747	2	304
Josiah, Jr., of Windsor, m. Naomi WILLIAMS, of Hartford,		
Mar. 26, 1767	2	134
Josias, s. [Tho[mas], b. Feb. 15, 1653	Col.2	158
Josias, [bp.] Feb. 15, [16]53	MG	
Josias, m. Abigayl LOOMYS, d. Nathanell, Nov. 22, 1677,		
by Capt. Newbery	TR1	1
Josias, contributed 0-2-6 to the poor in other colonies	MG	

	Vol.	Page
BARBER, BARBAR, BARBOR, (cont.)		
Kezia, d. Jonathan, b. Jan. 25, 1722/3	2	13
Kezia, m. Nathaniel R. **ALFORD**, Apr. 14, 1829, by Henry		
A. Rowland	2	126
Loannah, d. Jerijah & Loannah, b. Mar. 9, 1768	2	545
Loanna, wid. Jerijah, d. July 9, 1793, in the 49th y.		
of her age	2	221
Louisa, m. Simeon **LOOMIS**, Dec. 26, 1832, by Henry A.		
Rowland	2	489
Lucina, d. Jerizah & Loanna, b. Nov. 17, 1775	2	570
Luce, d. Jonathan & Rachel, b. Dec. 26, 1726	2	289
Lucie, d. Joseph & Elizabeth, b. July 11, 1734	2	293
Lucy, m. Ebenezer **ROCKWELL**, Jr., b. of Windsor, Aug.		
16, 1749	2	195
Lucy, m. William **BRITTIAN**, b. of Windsor, Oct. 13, 1755	2	133
Luther, s. William & Abigail, b. Oct.* 1, 1736 *("Nov."		
crossed out)	2	295
Lydia, m. Aaron **EATON**, b. of Windsor, Oct. 21, 1762	2	147
Marcy, d. [Thomas & Mary], b. Jan. 11, [16]	MG	
Marcy, d. Thomas, bp. Oct. 12, 1651	1	2
Marcy, d. Thomas, b. Jan. 11, 1666	Col.1	56
Marcy, m. [ ] **[GILLE[T]**, July 8, 1669	MG	
Marcy, m. John **GILLET**, b. of Windsor, July 8, 1669	Col.1	45
Maria, m. William **ALFORD**, July 9, 1835, by Henry A.		
Rowland	2	464
Martha, d. Samuel, b. May 1, 1714	2	10
Martin, m. Catharine **MOORE**, Dec. 28, 1832, by Henry		
A. Rowland	2	498
Mary, d. [Thomas & Jane], bp. Oct. 12, 1651	MG	
Mary, d. Thomas, bp. Oct. 12, 1651	Col.2	151
Mary, d. Thomas, b. Jan. 11, [16]66	1	4
Mary, m. Peter **BROWN**, July 22, 1696	1	54
Mary, d. Samuel, Jr., b. Sept. 25, 1704	2	8
Mary, d. Nathaniel, b. Aug. 26, 1713	2	9
Mary, d. Joseph, b. Mar. 24, 1714/15	2	10
Mary, m. Enoch **DRAKE**, b. of Windsor, May 1, 1735	2	142
Mary, d. Thomas & Jane, b. Aug. 14, 1754	2	306
Mary [COGGINS), w. Samuel, d. May 19, [16]76	MG	
Mary **(COGINS)***, w. Samuell, d. May 19, 1676 *(Name		
supplied by LBB)	Col.1	58
Mindwell, d. Dec. 3, 1712	2	217
Mindwell, d. Joseph, b. Oct. 8, 1716	2	11
Moses, s. Aaron & Marcy, b. Nov. 2, 1733	2	293
Naomi, d. John, b. Jan. 27, 1721/2	2	13
Naomi, d. Daniel & Naomi, b. July 20, 1743	2	197
Nath[an], d. Josi[ah], b. Apr. 6, 1691	Col.D	51
Nathaniel, s. Josiah, b. Apr. 6, 1691	1	5
Nathaniel, m. Mary **FILLEY**, b. of Windsor, July 2, 1711	2	128

	Vol.	Page
BARBER, BARBAR, BARBOR, (cont.)		
Samuel, of Windsor, m. Martha **PONDER**, of Westfield, June 18, 1713	2	129
Samuel, s. Samuel, b. Aug. 28, 1717	2	12
Samuel, s. Samuell, d. Feb. 1, 1722/3	2	219
Sary, d. [Thomas & Jane], bp. July 19, [16]46	MG	
Sarah, d. Thomas, bp. July 19, 1646	Col.2	151
Sarah, d. Thomas, bp. July 19, 1646	1	2
Sara, m. Timothy **HALL**, Nov. 26, 1663	MG	
Sara, m. Timothy **HALLE**, Nov. 26, 1663, by Mr. Alyen	Col.1	45
Sary, d. [Thomas & Mary], b. July 2, 1669	MG	
Sarah, d. Samuel, b. Aug. 28, 1698	1	6
Sarah, m. Steven **PALMER**, b. of Windsor, Oct. 17, 1717	2	187
Sarah, wid. Lieut. Josiah, d. Dec. 13, 1730	2	219
Sarah, d. Joseph & Sarah, b. Feb. 6, 1749/50	2	304
Shadrach, s. Jonathan & Rachel, b. Jan. 28, 1733/4	2	293
Shuball, s. Gideon & Anna, b. Sept. 8, 1747	2	301
Sophrona, m. Martin **PALMER**, Jr., May 20, 1835, by Rev. Nathaniel Kellogg	2	500
Submit, d. Ruth, b. Feb. 28, 1772	2	546
Tabatha, d. Jonah & Jerusha, b. May 6, 1757	2	542
Tarzah, d. Noah & Sibel, b. July 9, 1762	2	541
Thomas, adult, ch. mem. 16[ ]	MG	
Thomas, m. Mary **PHELPS**, Dec. [ ], [16]	MG	
Thomas, m. Jane [ ], Oct. 7, 1640	MG	
Thomas, m. Jone* [ ], Oct. 7, 1640 *(In pencil "Joan?")	1	53
Thomas, s. [Thomas & Jane], b. July 14, 1644	MG	
Thomas, s. Thomas, b. July 14, 1644	Col.2	151
Thomas, s. Thomas, b. July 14, 1644	1	2
Thomas, s. Thomas, b. July 14, 1644	1	4
Thomas, his w*. [ ], d. Sept. 10, 1662 *(Note by LBB: "Jane")	Col.1	55
Thomas, d. Sept. 11, 1662	Col.1	55
Thomas, his w. [ ], d. [ ], [16]62	MG	
Thomas, d. [ ], [16]62	MG	
Thomas, m. Marsey **PHELPS**, Dec. 17, 1663, by Mr. Clark	Col.1	45
Thomas, s. [Samuell & Mary], b. Oct. 7, 1671	MG	
Thomas, s. Samuel, bd. Oct. 31, 1673	Col.1	58
Thomas, s. Samuel, bd. Oct. 31, [16]73	1	41
Thomas, s. Samuel, bd. Oct. 31, [16]73	1	47
Thomas, Jr., had 4 children b. in Windsor. Dated Aug. 17, 1677	MG	
Thomas, Sr., had 6 children b. in Windsor. Dated Aug. 17, 1677	MG	
Thomas, s. Samuel, b. May 5, 1720	2	12
Thomas, s. Nathaniel, b. Oct. 1, 1725	2	15
Thomas, m. Jane **ISHAM**, b. of Windsor, Jan. 10, 1748/9	2	132
Thomas, s. Thomas & Jane, b. Nov. 13, 1750	2	305

	Vol.	Page
BARBER, BARBAR, BARBOR, (cont.)		
Thomas, contributed 0-1-0 to the poor in other colonies	MG	
Tryphena, d. Gideon & Anna, b. Dec. [ ], 1753	2	307
William, m. Esther **BROWN**, b. of Windsor, Nov. 5, 1700	1	54
William, s. William, decd., b. Dec. 31, 1701	2	10
William, s. Samuel, d. July 17, 1704	1	41
William, m. Abigail **BROWN**, b. of Windsor, Mar. 10, 1725/6	2	130
William, s. William & Abigail, b. Sept. 19, 1727	2	295
BARKER, Chancey, s. Ruben & Sarah, b. Jan. 6, 1794	2	570
Horace, m. Cynthia **BOWER**, Sept. 3, 1822, by Rev. Henry A. Rowland, of Windsor	2	467
Oliver, s. Ruben & Sarah, b. Dec. 2, 1802	2	571
Perren, s. Ruben & Sarah, b. Feb. 16, 1796	2	570
Ruben, s. Ruben & Sarah, b. Oct. 26, 1789	2	570
Samuell*, m. Sara **COOK**, b. of Windsor, June 30, [16]70 *(Note by LBB: "Samuell **BAKER**")	Col. 1	45
Samuel, adm. ch. & communicant Apr. [ ], 1672	MG	
Samuell, taxed 1-0 on Feb. 10, [16]73	MG	
Sarah, d. Ruben & Sarah, b. July 15, 1792	2	570
Susan, of Enfield, m. Sterling **DAY**, of Windsor, Aug. 11, 1824, by Richard Niles, J. P.	2	144
BARNARD, Abigaell, d. Joseph, b. July 24, 1706	2	4
Anne, d. Joseph, b. Feb. 28, 1712/13	2	10
Chloe, m. Benoni **CASE**, Jr., b. of Windsor, May 1, 1798	2	469
David, s. Joseph, b. Nov. 3, 1714	2	10
David, s. Sergt. Joseph, d. May 27, 1718	2	218
Debra, m. Beniamen **BARTLET**, Ju[ ], [16]	MG	
Debra, m. Beniamen **BARTLET**, b. of Windsor, Feb. 16, 1664, by Mr. Wolcot	Col. 1	45
Deborah, m. Benjamin **BARTLETT**, b. of Windsor, June 8, 1665, by Master Allyn	1	54
Ebenezer, s. Joseph, b. Sept. 6, 1710	2	8
Eliezer, s. Joseph, Jr. & Lydia, b. Oct. 30, 1783	2	548
Elijah, s. Joseph & Elizabeth, b. Aug. 31, 1757	2	568
Elizabeth Holcomb, d. Joseph, Jr. & Lyda, b. July 30, 1776	2	548
Frances, s. Sergt. Joseph, b. Sept. 9, 1719	2	12
James, s. John & Rebeckah, b. June 17, 1751	2	305
Jehabon, s. Joseph & Elizabeth, b. Feb. 15, 1751/2	2	568
John, m. Rebeckah **HOLCOMB**, b. of Windsor, Nov. 26, 1750	2	132
Joseph, m. Abigaell **GRISWOLD**, b. of Windsor, Oct. 4, 1705	2	127
Joseph, s. Joseph, b. Mar. 16, 1708/9	2	6
Joseph, Lieut., d. July 12, 1736	2	524
Joseph, m. Elizabeth **HOLCOMB**, b. of Windsor, Feb. 9, 1743/4	2	466
Joseph, s. Joseph & Elizabeth, b. Dec. 11, 1744	2	568

	Vol.	Page
BARNARD, (cont.)		
Joseph Stantliff, s. Joseph, Jr. & Lydia, b. Nov. 10, 1780	2	548
Juliann, m. Henry **BURR**, b. of Windsor, Oct. 22, 1824, by		
Richard Niles, J. P.	2	149
Lorinda, d. Joseph, Jr. & Lydia, b. Nov. 10, 1780	2	548
Mary, w. Robert, d. June 5, 1727	2	219
Mary, d. Robert & Mary, b. June 5, 1727	2	289
Robert, m. Ruth **LOOMIS**, b. of Windsor, Nov. 1, 1728	2	129
Sarah, d. Joseph, b. Sept. 23, 1707	2	6
Sarah, m. Hezekiah **GRISWOLD**, b. of Windsor, Dec. 14, 1738	2	157
Sarah, m. Josiah **GAYLORD**, b. of Windsor, Feb. 14, 1744	2	478
BARNES, BARNS, Abigail, m. William **BARNS**, Dec. 14, 1829, by Rev. Asa Bushnell, Jr.	2	498
Amanda, of Windsor, m. Chauncey B. **CURTIS**, of Charlton, O., Oct. 15, 1851, by Thomas R. Haskell, J. P.	2	497
Elizabeth, m. Lucius **CROCKER**, b. of Lee, Mass., June 17, 1833, by Rev. Henry Robinson	2	470
Harriet, of Windsor, m. William A. **ALLEN**, of Bloomfield, Dec. 24, 1838, by D. Osborn	2	464
Mariah L., m. Marcus **HOLCOMB**, b. of Windsor, Mar. 18, 1849, by Rev. Cephus Brainard	2	487
Oliver H., m. Anna F. **MOORE**, b. of Simsbury, July 9, 1828, by Rev. John Bartlett	2	149
Ruth Marinda, of Barkhemsted, m. Henry **VADITIN**, of East Granby, Feb. 14, 1836, by Walter Thrall, J. P.	2	511
Wealthy Ann, m. Moses **WILSON**, b. of Windsor, Feb. 5, 1824, by Joseph H. Russell, J. P.	2	211
William, m. Abigail **BARNS**, Dec. 14, 1829, by Rev. Asa Bushnell, Jr.	2	498
BARNET, Isable, m. David **BROWN**, b. of Windsor, Mar. 15, 1732/3	2	130
BARRETT, BARRET, Anne, of Hartford, m. Nathan **HIGLEY**, of Windsor, Sept. 13, 1764	2	164
Francis C., of Windsor, m. Newton **TOURTELOT**, of Thompson, June 10, 1850, by Cornelius B. Everest	2	512
Hannah, m. Ephraim **PERSON**, b. of Windsor, Apr. 23, 1754	2	189
Sarah A., m. Charles W. **HATHEWAY**, b. of Poquonock, May 26, 1852, by Thomas H. Rouse	2	521
BARTHOLOMEW, Ruth, of Windsor, m. Chester **STRONG**, of Hartford, Apr. 18, 1842, by Ezra S. Cook	2	511
BARTLETT, BARTLET, BARTLED, Abia, formerly w. of Esaia, m. John **SLATER**, July 15, 1669	Col. 1	45
Abiah, formerly w. Elisha, m. John **SLAUGHTER**, July 15, 1669	1	61
Abiia, s. [Beniamen & Debra], b. July 26, [16]73	MG	
Ann, d. Jonathan & Hannah, b. Mar. 10, 1750/1	2	303
Barnard, of Windsor, m. Elizabeth **DANKS**, of Northampton,		

	Vol.	Page
BARTLETT, BARTLET, BARTLED, (cont.)		
Jan. 14, 1702	1	54
Beniamen, s. [John], bp. Mar. 26, [16]43; d. [ ]	MG	
Beniamen, m. Debra BARNARD, Ju[ ], [16]	MG	
Beniamen, m. Debra BARNARD, b. of Windsor, Feb. 16,		
1664, by Mr. Wolcot	Col.1	45
Benjamin, m. Deborah BARNARD, b. of Windsor, June 8,		
1665, by Master Allyn	1	54
Beniamen, s. [Beniamen & Debra], b. June 21, 1668; d. [ ]	MG	
Beniamen, s. Beniamen, d. May 2, 1675	Col.1	58
Benjamin, s. Benjamin, d. Mar. 2, [16]75, near 8 years old	1	40
Beniamen, had [6] children b. in Windsor. Dated Aug. 17,		
1677	MG	
Beniamen, s. [Beniamen & Debra], b. Dec. 15, [16]77	MG	
Benjamin, s. Benjamin, b. Dec. 15, 1677	1	6
Benjamin, d. Oct. 25, 1698	1	41
Beniamen, contributed 0-1-0 to the poor in other colonies	MG	
Debora, d. [Beniamen & Debra], b. Apr. 3, 1666	MG	
Debora, m. Jeremy GILLET, Oct. 15, 1685	Col.D	54
Deborah, m. Jeremiah GILLET, Oct. 15, 1685	1	57
Elinor, had illeg. d. Meriam, b. June 25, 1750; reputed f.		
James HARPER	2	304
Elisabeth, m. Benjamin STOUGHTON, b. of Windsor, Dec.		
26, 1744	2	199
Ephraim, s. John, b. Oct. 19, 1644	1	4
Ephraim, d. [ ], [16]48	MG	
Epharem, s. Bengamn, b. Jan. 17, 1673	MG	
Esaya, s. John, b. June 13, 1641 (Isaiah)	MG	
Ezaya, m. Abia GILLET, Dec. 3, 1663	MG	
Esayah, m. Abia GILLIET, Dec. 3, 1663, by Mr. Clarke	Col.1	45
Esaih, d. July 13, 1665	Col.1	55
Esaya, s. [Beniamen & Debra], b. Dec. 9, [16]70	MG	
Esay, had 1 child b. in Windsor. Dated Aug. 17, 1677	MG	
Eunice, d. Jonathan & Hannah, b. May 18, 1749	2	302
Hannah, d. Jonathan & Hannah, b. Nov. 8, 1746	2	301
Hepsiba, d. [John], b. July 14, [16]46	MG	
Hepsiba, m. Samuell DEBLE, Jan. 21, [1]6[ ]	MG	
Hepseba, m. Samuell DEBLE, b. of Windsor, Jan. 21, 1668,		
by Mr. Wolcott	Col.1	45
Hephzibah, m. Samuel DIBLE, b. of Windsor, Jan. 21, 1668,		
by Mr. Wolcott	1	55
Isaac, s. Jehojadah, b. May 22, 1696	1	6
Isaiah, see under Esaya		
James, s. Iehoj., b. Dec. 7, [16]81	Col.D	51
James, s. Jehojada, b. Dec. 7, 1681	1	5
James, s. Jehojadah, d. Mar. 8, 1694/5	1	41
Jehoiade, s. [John], bp. Dec. 23, [16]49	MG	
Jehoggada, m. Sara HILLAR, b. of Windsor, July 10, 1673,		

	Vol.	Page
BARTLETT, BARTLET, BARTLED, (cont.)		
by Capt. Newbery	Col.1	46
Johojadah, s. Benjamin, b. Nov. 1, [16]75	1	4
Jehoiade, b. Nov. 2, 1675	MG	
Jehoidah, d. June 14, 1718	2	218
John, s. [Ezaya & Abia], b. Sept. 12, 1664	MG	
John, s. Esaya, b. Sept. 12, 1664	Col.1	54
John, s. Josiah, b. Sept. 12, 1664	1	4
John, d. [ ], [16]70	MG	
John, d. May 14, [16]70	Col.1	55
John, d. [ ]; bd. May 14, [16]70	1	40
John, had 5 children b. in Windsor. Dated Aug. 17, 1677	MG	
John, s. Benjamin, b. June 28, 1679	1	6
Jonathan, m. wid. Hannah **BISSEL,** b. of Windsor, Jan. 26,		
1743/4	2	131
Joseph, s. Jehoj[ad], b. Nov. 11, 1684	Col.D	51
Joseph, s. Gershom & Margaret, b. Jan. 23, 1748/9	2	303
Joseph, s. Jehojada, b. Nov. 11, [ ]	1	5
Josiah, see under Esayah		
Lucey, d. Gershom & Margeret, b. Nov. 18, 1750	2	303
Lydia, of Bolton, m. Jerijah **BISSELL,** of Windsor, Mar. 27,		
1755	2	132
Martha, wid., m. James **RISING,** Aug. 13, 1673	Col.1	46
Mehitable, d. John, b. Feb. 27, 1650	1	4
Mehetabell, d. [John], bp. May 11, [16]51	MG	
Meriam, d. Elinor **BARTLET,** b. June 25, 1750; reputed f.		
James **HARPER**	2	304
Samuel, s. Jehojadah, b. Apr. 11, 1688	1	5
Samuel, s. John, b. Jan. 31, 1715/16	2	10
Samuel, s. Jonathan & Hannah, b. Jan. 15, 1744/5	2	298
Samuel, m. Anne **CRANE,** b. of East Windsor, Sept. 14,		
1767	2	466
Sarah, d. Jehojad, b. May 30, 1677	Col.D	51
Sarah, d. Jehojada, b. May 30, 1677	1	5
Theophy, m. Samuell **GRANT,** b. of Windsor, Jan. 1,		
1718/19	2	155
-----efay, d. [ ], [16]65	MG	
-----, wid., d. Feb. 21, 1719/20	2	218
BASCOMB, BASCOM, Abigayl, d. Thomas, b. June 7, 1640	MG	
Abigail, d. Thomas, bp. June 7, 1640	1	2
Hannah, m. John **BROWTON,** Nov. 15, 1650	1	53
Hepsiba, d. [Thomas], b. Apr. 14, 1644	MG	
Hephzibah, d. Thomas, bp. Apr. 14, 1644	1	2
Thomas, s. [Thomas], b. Feb. 20, 1641	MG	
Thomas, s. Thomas, bp. Feb. 20, 1641	1	2
Thomas, has child d. [ ], [16]47	MG	
Thomas, had 3 children b. in Windsor. Dated Aug. 17, 1677	MG	
BATER, Samuel, taxed 5-0 on Feb. 10, [16]73	MG	

	Vol.	Page
BAXTER, Francis, of Enfield, m. Sarah **ELSWORTH**, of Windsor, May 7, 1767	2	134
Horace, of New York, m. Charlotte P. **CASE**, of Windsor, Aug. 19, 1849, by Rev. Cephus Brainard	2	504
Levi, s. Frances & Sarah, b. Aug. 14, 1764	2	542
BEACKAS, Elizabeth, of Middletown, m. David **BISSELL**, Jr., of Windsor, Feb. 25, 1761	2	133
BEAMON, BEAMAN, BEAMOND, BEMAN, BEMENT, Abigail, m. Azariah **GRANT**, July 6, 1749	2	157
Charles S., m. Julia O. **HOUSE**, b. of Windsor, July 23, 1839, by Rev. Cephas Brainard	2	465
George, of Granby, m. Caroline S. **HAMILTON**, of Suffield, Nov. 25, 1838, by Rev. Jared R. Avery	2	465
Hannah, d. Samuel, b. Apr. 2, 1698	1	6
Margaret, d. Samuell, d. Aug. 12, 1715	2	218
Salome H., of Windsor, m. Levi W. **ALLEN**, of So. Hadley, Mass., Sept. 4, 1839, by Rev. S. D. Jewett	2	464
Samuel, m. Margerit **CHAPMAN**, May 10, 1693	1	54
Samuel, s. Samuel, b. June 6, 1704	1	6
BECKWITH, Charles W., of Greenport, N. Y., m. Sophia S. **FOOTE**, of Lee, Mass., Nov. 2, 1847, by C. B. Everest	2	503
Horace, m. Nancy **MARSHALL**, Oct. 7, 1822, by Rev. Elisha Cushman, of Hartford	2	467
BECRAFFT, Damaras, of Wethersfield, m. Israel **OSBORN**, of Windsor, Apr. 18, 1751	2	185
BEDORTHA, Quartus, m. Ruth **LOOMIS**, b. of Windsor, Feb. 28, 1832, by Hiram Roberts, J. P.	2	150
[**BEEBE**], **BEBEE**, Mary G., m. Orson **CASE**, b. of Hartford, May 1, 1822, by Rev. Augustus Bolles, of Wintonbury	2	138
BELCHER, Samuel, m. Mable **STOUGHTON**, b. of Windsor, Aug. 17, 1732	2	130
BELDEN, Sarah A., m. Oliver S. **GILLETT**, Nov. 11, 1832, by Henry A. Rowland	2	506
BELKNAP, David, s. Samuel & Mary, b. Aug. 5, 1742	2	297
Ebenezer, s. Job & Phebe, b. Nov. 30, 1760	2	541
Eleanor, d. Job & Phebe, b. Feb. 9, 1757	2	541
Frances, s. Job & Phebe, b. June 22, 1755	2	541
Patience, d. Job & Phebe, b. Feb. 28, 1759	2	541
Samuel, m. Mary **NEWTON**, b. of Windsor, June 19, 1754	2	133
BEMENT, [see under **BEAMON**]		
BEMIS, Henry T., of Bloomfield, m. Aurelia H. **CASE**, of Windsor, May 21, 1846, by C. B. Everist	2	499
BENNETT, Caroline, d. James & Elizabeth, b. Dec. 12, 1815	2	517
Charles, s. James & Elizabeth, b. Sept. 9, 1817	2	517
Elizabeth, w. James, b. Aug. 15, 1785	2	517
Ellen, of Windsor, m. Elisha H. **GARDNER**, of Hartford, Feb. 19, 1849, by T. A. Leete	2	497
Frances, d. James & Elizabeth, b. Apr. 9, 1811	2	517

	Vol.	Page
BENNETT, (cont.)		
Hellen, d. James & Elizabeth, b. June 22, 1823	2	517
Hiram, m. Eliza **ALLEN**, Mar. 8, 1841, by Rev. S. D. Jewett	2	476
James, b. July 23, 1785	2	517
Jane, d. James & Elizabeth, b. July 21, 1814	2	517
BENTON, Anna, d. Thomas & Anna, b. Dec. 5, 1786	2	568
Elihu Stanley, s. Thomas & Ann, b. Dec. 8, 1762	2	541
Eliza, m. George **HOWARD**, June 18, 1844, by Rev. Shubael Bartlett	2	508
Theodore, s. Thomas & Anne, b. Apr. 12, 1769	2	545
Thomas, m. Ann **HANEY**, b. of Windsor, July 3, 1761	2	133
Thomas, s. Thomas & Ann, b. Nov. 20, 1766	2	543
William, s. Thomas & Anne, b. Feb. 2, 1772	2	545
BEST, Robert, m. Mary Ann **SIMMONS**, Apr. 1, 1849, by Cornelius B. Everest	2	503
BESUM, John, d. [Mar. 30*], [16]75 *(In pencil)	MG	
John, d. Mar. 30, 1675	Col.1	58
BIDWELL, BIDELL, BIDLE, BIDDLE, BEDWELL,		
BEDDELL, Aaron, of Manchester, m. Harriet E. **HOLCOMB**, of Windsor, Jan. 1, 1850, by Rev. Cephus Brainard	2	504
Abigail, d. Jonathan & Hannah, b. May 26, 1743	2	299
Anna, m. James **ENNO**, Aug. 18, 1648	MG	
Anna, m. James **ENNO**, Aug. 18, 1648	1	56
Anne, d. Jonathan & Hannah, b. Nov. 25, 1753	2	546
Candas, d. Jonathan, Jr. & Abigail, b. Nov. 21, 1774	2	570
Cordelia, of Windsor, m. Simeon **WHITON**, of Ashford, Apr. 18, 1832, by Ansel Nash	2	513
Elizabeth, of Hartford, m. Mooses **LOOMIS**, of Windsor, Dec. 17, 1729	2	171
Goodman, d. [ ], [16]46	MG	
Hannah, d. Richard, b. Oct. 22, 1644	1	4
Hannah, d. Jonathan & Hannah, b. Oct. 11, 1741	2	299
James, m. Abigail **ALLYN**, b. of Windsor, June 12, 1822, by John Bartlett. Int. Pub.	2	467
James, Jr., m. Electa **GRISWOLD**, b. of Windsor, Nov. 16, 1826, by Rev. Augustus Bolles	2	469
Jonathan, m. Hannah **HUBBARD**, b. of Windsor, Aug. 7, 1740	2	132
Jonathan, s. Jonathan & Hannah, b. Feb. [ ], 1744/5	2	300
Jonathan, s. Jonathan, Jr. & Abigail, b. Mar. 27, 1777	2	570
Loviey, m. Giddings **DEMING**, Aug. 5, 1823, by Rev. John Bartlett, of Wintonbury. Int. Pub.	2	144
Mabel, d. Jonathan & Hannah, b. June 26, 1749	2	546
Nabbe, d. Jonathan, Jr. & Abigail, b. Feb. 7, 1772	2	547
Rachel, d. Jonathan & Hannah, b. Aug. 30, 1751	2	546
Richard, bd. Dec. 25, 1647	1	41
Richard, d. [ ], [16]47	MG	
Richard, had 1 child b. in Windsor. Dated Aug. 17, 1677	MG	

	Vol.	Page
BIDWELL, BIDELL, BIDLE, BIDDLE, BEDWELL,		
BEDDELL, (cont.)		
Ruth, of Hartford, m. Henry **LOOMIS**, of Windsor, Apr.		
13, 1727	2	171
Theodoshe, d. Jonathan & Hannah, b. Jan. 20, 1759	2	546
BILLINGS, W[illia]m Warner, of East Windsor, m. Caroline		
Amanda **WESTLAND**, of Windsor, July 18, 1847, by		
Samuel A. Seaman	2	503
BIRGE, BIRDGE, BIRG, BURG, Abigail, wid., m. Joseph		
LOOMIS, Sr., b. of Windsor, Feb. 11, 17[0]2/3	1	59
Abigaell, d. John, b. June 13, 1706	2	4
Abigael, d. John, d. Dec. 18, 1712	2	217
Acsa, d. Pelatiah & Mary, b. Mar. 23, 1778	2	568
Alexander, s. Pelatiah & Mary, b. Aug. [ ], 1786	2	569
Ann, d. Jeremiah & Mary, b. Oct. 28, 1726	2	291
Asa, s. Pelatiah & Mary, b. Jan. 29, 1782	2	568
Cornelious, s. Daniel, b. July 30, 1694	1	6
Cornelius, m. Sarah **LOOMIS**, b. of Windsor, Feb. 8, 1721/2	2	129
Daniel, s. [Richard & Elizabeth], b. Nov. 24, 1644	MG	
Daniel, s. Richard, b. Nov. 24, 1644	Col.2	151
Daniel, s. Richard, b. Nov. 24, 1644	1	2
Daniel, s. Richard, b. Nov. 24, 1644	1	4
Daniel, m. Debra **HOLCOMB**, Nov. 5, 1668	MG	
Danell, m. Debroa **HOLCOM**, b. of Windsor, Nov. 5, [16]68,		
at Hartford, by John Allyn	Col.1	45
Daniel, m. Deborah **HOLCOMB**, b. of Windsor, Nov. 5,		
1668, at Hartford, by John Allyn	1	54
Daniell, had 3 children b. in Windsor. Dated Aug. 17, 1677	MG	
Danell, s. [Daniel & Debra], b. Sept. 16, 1680	MG	
Daniell, s. Daniell, b. Sept. 16, 1680	Col.1	57
Daniel, s. Daniel, d. Jan. 12, 1681	Col.D	56
Daniel, s. Daniell, b. Dec. 3, 1682	Col.D	51
Daniel, s. Daniel, b. Dec. 3, [16]82	1	4
Daniel, d. Jan. 26, 1697/8	1	41
Daniel, s. Pelatiah & Mary, b. July 14, 1768	2	545
Daniel, s. Daniel, d. Jan. 12, [ ]	1	41
David, s. Jeremiah & Mary, b. May 16, 1725	2	291
David, s. Pelatiah & Mary, b. Sept. 30, 1770	2	545
Debra, d. [Daniel & Debra], b. Nov. 26, 1671	MG	
Deborah, w. Daniel, d. May 26, 1686	1	41
Debora*, w. Dan, d. May 26, 1686 *(Note by LBB:		
"Deborah (**HOLCOMB**) BIRGE")	Col.D	56
Delia, of Windsor, m. Joseph **WEEKS**, of Hartford, Dec. 14,		
1836, by William H. Shailer	2	513
Eli, s. Pelatiah & Mary, b. Oct. 18, 1772	2	547
Elizabeth, d. Richard, b. July 28, 1646	1	2
Elizabeth, d. Richard & Elizabeth], b. July 28, [16]46;		
d. [ ]	MG	

	Vol.	Page
BIRGE, BIRDGE, BIRG, BURG, (cont.)		
Elizabeth, wid., m. Thomas **HOSKINS**, b. of Windsor, Apr. 20, 1653	Col.2	159
Elisabeth, d. [Daniel & Debra], b. Aug. 25, 1670; d. [ ]	MG	
Ellisabeth, d. [Daniel & Debra], b. Feb. 3, 1674	MG	
Elisabeth, wid., m. Thomas **HOSKINS**, Apr. 20, [ ]	MG	
Elizabeth **(GAYLORD)**, see Elizabeth **HOSKINS**	MG	
Esther*, m. Ebenezer **MOORE**, b. of Windsor, Jan. 10, 1733/4 *("Esther **LOOMIS**" crossed out)	2	178
Hanna, d. John, b. June 17, 1682	Col.D	51
Hannah, d. John, b. June 17, [16]82	1	4
Hanah*, w. John, d. July 24, 1690 *(Note by LBB: "Hannah **(WATSON) BIRGE**")	Col.D	57
Hannah, w. John, d. July 24, 1690	1	41
Hannah, m. Benjamin **PHELPS**, b. of Windsor, Apr. 12, 1705	2	185
Hannah, d. Jeremiah & Mary, b. Mar. 18, 1730	2	291
Hannah, m. Mathew **GRANT**, Feb. 2, 1749	2	157
Horris, s. Pelatiah & Mary, b. Aug. 30, 1784	2	568
Jeremy, s. [Richard & Elizabeth], b. May 6, 1648; d. [ ]	MG	
Jeremiah, s. Richard, b. May 6, 1648	1	2
Jeremiah, s. Richard, b. Jan. 14, 1649	Col.2	151
Jerem, d. Oct. 22, [16]68	Col.1	55
Jeremy, d. [ ], [16]68	MG	
Jeremy, s. Joseph, b. Sept. 22, 1686	Col.D	51
Jeremiah, s. John, b. Sept. 22, 1686	1	4
Jeremiah, m. Mary **GRISWOLD**, b. of Windsor, Jan. 1, 1718/19	2	130
Jeremiah, s. Jeremiah & Mary, b. Dec. 23, 1719	2	290
John, d. [ ], [16]43	MG	
John, s. [Richard & Elizabeth], b. Jan. 14, 1649	MG	
John, s. Richard, b. Jan. 14, 1649	1	2
John, bp. Jan. 14, [16]49	MG	
John, m. Hannah **WATSON**, Mar. 28, 1678	MG	
John, m. Hanna **WATSON**, Mar. 28, 1678	TR1	1
John, m. Hanna **WATSON**, Mar. 18, 1678	Col.1	46
John, m. Hannah **WATSON**, Mar. 28, 1678	1	54
John, s. [John & Hanna], b. Feb. 4, 1679	MG	
John, s. John, b. Feb. 4, [16]79	Col.1	57
John, s. Daniel, b. Sept. 19, 1689	1	6
John, d. Dec. 2, 1697	1	41
John, of Windsor, m. Abigail **MARSHEL**, of Northampton, Nov. 10, 1702	1	54
John, s. John, b. Nov. 5, 1703	2	4
John, s. Jeremiah & Mary, b. Apr. 25, 1723	2	291
John, d. [ ], in "Elenton" prior to 1740	MG	
Joseph, s. [Richard & Elizabeth], b. Nov. 2, 1651	MG	
Joseph, bp. Nov. 2, [16]51	MG	
Joseph, s. Richard, bp. Nov. 2, 1651	Col.2	151

	Vol.	Page
BIRGE, BIRDGE, BIRG, BURG, (cont.)		
Joseph, s. Richard, bp. Nov. 2, 1651	1	2
Joseph, d. July 18, 1705	2	217
Joseph, contributed 0-3-0 to the poor in other colonies	MG	
Lucie, d. Jeremiah & Mary, b. Sept. 23, 1736	2	294
Mary, d. [Daniel & Debra], b. Dec. 25, 1677	MG	
Mary, d. John, b. Sept. 9, 1688	1	5
Mary*, w. Joseph, d. Apr. 11, 1690 *(Note by LBB:		
"Mary (BISSELL) OWEN BIRGE")	Col.D	57
Mary, w. Joseph, d. Apr. 11, 1690	1	41
Mary, m. Sergt. Israel **STOUGHTON**, b. of Windsor, May 7,		
1713	2	198
Mary, d. Jeremiah & Mary, b. Aug. 23, 1721	2	291
Mindwell, d. Jeremiah & Mary, b. Mar. 24, 1732/3	2	293
Orin, s. Eli & Charlotte, b. Oct. 30, 1805	2	572
Pelletiah, s. Jeremiah & Mary, b. Sept. 8, 1728	2	291
Rhode, d. Pelatiah & Mary, b. Sept. 8, 1774	2	547
Richard, m. Elizabeth **GAYLAR**, Oct. 5, 1641	MG	
Richard, m. Elizabeth **GAYLORD**, Oct. 5, 1641	1	53
Richard, a child d. [ ], [16]43	MG	
Richard, d. [ ], [16]51	MG	
Richard, d. [ ]; bd. Sept. 29, 1651	Col.2	160
Richard, had 5 children b. in Windsor. Dated Aug. 17, 1677	MG	
Samuell, s. John, b. June 7, 1709	2	6
Sarah, d. Cornelius, b. Mar. 5, 1722/3	2	14
Seth, s. Pelatiah & Mary, b. June 17, 1776	2	547
Seth, s. Pelatiah & Mary, b. Feb. 26, 1780	2	568
William, s. Richard, b. July 28, 1646	Col.2	151
BIRT, Mary, m. William **PORTER**, Jan. 24, 1805	2	500
BISSELL, BISSEL, BISSALL, BISSILL, Aaron, m. Dorothy		
STOUGHTON, b. of Windsor, Dec. 5, 1757	2	133
Aaron, s. Aaron & Dorothy, b. July 27, 1761	2	542
Abell, s. Ephraim, b. July 27, 1709	2	6
Abigayl, d. [Thomas & Abigayl], b. Nov. 23, 1658	MG	
Abigail, d. Thomas, b. Nov. 23, 1658	1	3
Abigayl, d. [Samuel & Abigayl], b. July 6, 1661	MG	
Abigal, d. [Nathanell & Mindwell], b. Sept. 14, [16]73;		
d. [ ]	MG	
Abigail, d. Nathaniel, b. Sept. 14, 1673	1	4
Abigal, d. Nathanell, d. Dec. 7, 1673	Col.1	58
Abigail, d. Nathanael, bd. Dec. 8, [16]73	1	41
Abigal, d. [Nathanell & Mindwell], b. Mar. 9, [1676];		
bp. [Mar.] 22, 1676	MG	
Abigail, d. Nathaniel, b. Mar. 9, [16]76	1	4
Abigal, d. Thomas, ae 20, m. Nathanell **GAYLAR**, ae 22,		
Oct. 17, [16]78	MG	
Abigayell, d. Thomas, Sr., m. Nathanell **GAYLAR**, Oct. 17,		
1678	Col.1	46

	Vol.	Page
BISSELL, BISSEL, BISSALL, BISSILL, (cont.)		
Abigail, d. Thomas, m. Nathanael **GAYLORD**, Oct. 17, 1678	1	57
Abigall, d. Samuell, m. James **ENNO**, s. James, Dec. 26, 1678	MG	
Abigall, d. Samuell, m. James **ENNO**, s. James, Dec. 26, 1678, by Capt. Newbery	Col.1	46
Abigall, d. Samuell, m. James **ENNO**, s. James, Dec. 2[ ], 1678, by Capt. Newbery	TR1	1
Abigail, d. Samuel, m. James **ENNO**, s. James, Dec. 26, 1678, by Capt. Newbery	1	56
Abigall, d. [Samuell & Abigall], b. Aug. 3, 1681	MG	
Abigall, d. [Thomas & Esther], b. Oct. 20, 1681	MG	
Abigall, d. Tho[ma]s, Jr., b. Oct. 26, 1681	Col.D	51
Abigail, m. Samuel **TUDOR**, Oct. 20, 1685	1	62
Abigail, w. Samuel, d. Aug. 17, 1688	1	41
Abigail, m. George **SANDERS**, Dec. 17, 1691	1	61
Abigail, m. Jacob **STRONG**, Nov. 10, 1698	1	61
Abigail, m. Joseph **PHELPS**, b. of Windsor, Nov. 26, 1702	1	60
Abigaell, m. Joseph **BAKER**, b. of Windsor, Dec. 26, 1706	2	128
Abigael, d. Isaac, b. Jan. 16, 1710/11	2	7
Abigail, d. Jabez & Darcas, b. May 19, 1756	2	538
Allice, d. Ebenezer, Jr. & Hannah, b. Oct. 8, 1742	2	300
Ami, d. Nathaniel, b. July 20, 1716	2	11
[Ann*], d. Nathaniel, bd. [Oct. 31*], [16]73 *(In pencil)	MG	
Ann, d. John, bd. Oct. 31, 1673	Col.1	58
Ann, d. John, bd. Oct. 31, [16]73	1	41
Ann, d. John, bd. Oct. 31, [16]73	1	47
Ann, d. [John, Jr. & Jzrell], b. Apr. 28, 1675	MG	
Ann, d. John, b. Apr. 28, 1675	1	3
Ann, d. Daniel, b. Jan. 6, 1709/10	2	8
Ann, d. Thomas & Martha, b. May 22, 1732	2	292
Ann, d. Josiah & Ruth, b. Mar. 11, 1747/8	2	302
Ann, d. Jerijah & Lydia, b. Jan. 20, 1764	2	542
Anne, of Windsor, m. Daniel **WHITE**, of Hartford, July 6, 1704	2	207
Archippus, s. David & Sarah, b. Jan. 23, 1730/1	2	291
Asahell, s. Thomas, Jr., b. Nov. 29, 1716	2	10
Asahel, s. Jerijah & Lydia, b. Feb. 20, 1762	2	540
Aurelia, d. Capt. Josiah & Ruth, b. Aug. 26, 1760	2	539
Aurelia, d. Capt. Josiah & Ruth, b. Aug. 26, 1761	2	539
Benaga[h], s. [Samuel & Abigayl], b. June 30, 1671	MG	
Benajah, s. Samuel, b. June 30, 1671	1	3
Beniamen, s. [Thomas & Abigayl], b. Sept. 9, [16]69	MG	
Benjamin, s. Thomas, b. Sept. 9, 1669	1	3
Benjamin, d. May 5, 1698	1	41
Benjamin, s. John, b. Mar. 22, 1701	1	6
Benjamin, s. Ephraim, b. Feb. 23, 1711/12	2	8
Benjamin, s. Isaac, b. July 2, 1717	2	12

	Vol.	Page
BISSELL, BISSEL, BISSALL, BISSILL, (cont.)		
Benjamin, s. Josiah, b. Oct. 1, 1720	2	12
Bennoni, s. Joseph, b. Dec. 7, 1689	1	5
Bettye, d. Jerijah & Lyda, b. Mar. 21, 1756	2	536
Charles, s. Ebenezer, Jr. & Hannah, b. July 25, 1741	2	300
Chloe, d. Aaron & Dorathy, b. Aug. 30, 1758	2	542
Dan, s. Thomas, Jr., b. Dec. 3, 1721	2	13
Danell, s. [John, Jr. & Jzrell], b. Sept. 29, 1663	MG	
Daniel, s. John, b. Sept. 29, 1663	1	3
Daniel, of Windsor, m. Margerit **DEWEY**, of Westfield, Oct. 27, 1692	1	54
Daniel, of Windsor, m. Margarett **DEWEY**, of Westfield, Nov. 27, 1692	2	128
Daniel, s. Daniel, b. Oct. 31, 1694	2	7
Daniel, s. John, b. Jan. 4, 1697/8	1	6
Daniel, Jr., of Windsor, m. Jerusha **FITCH**, of Canterbery, Mar. 18, 1717/18	2	129
Daniel, s. Daniel, Jr., b. Feb. 2, 1724/5	2	14
Daniel, s. David & Sarah, b. May 3, 1741	2	297
Daniel, Jr., m. Elizabeth **NEWBERRY**, Jr., b. of Windsor, Feb. 16, 1746/7	2	132
Daniel, Jr., m. Elizabeth **LOOMIS**, b. of Windsor, Apr. 9, 1752	2	133
Daniel, s. Daniel, Jr. & Elizbeth, b. Dec. 30, 1754	2	536
Dauid, s. Nath[an], b. Nov. 18, 1681	Col.D	51
David, s. Nathaniel, b. Nov. 18, [16]82	1	4
David, m. Ruth **NORNER***, Feb. 24, 1703/4 *(Name in Pencil)	2	127
David, s. David, b. Apr. 3, 1708	2	6
David, m. Sarah **GRANT**, b. of Windsor, Sept. 30, 1730	2	130
David, s. David & Sarah, b. Apr. 28, 1732	2	292
David, s. David & Sarah, b. Apr. 28, 1732* *(Entry crossed out)	2	341
David, Lieut., d. Oct. 20, 1733	2	219
David, Lieut., d. Oct. 20, 1733	2	523
David, Jr., of Windsor, m. Elizabeth **BEACKAS**, of Middletown, Feb. 25, 1761	2	133
David, s. David & Elizabeth, b. June 6, 1764	2	543
Debora, d. [Samuel & Abigayl], b. Oct. 29, 1679	MG	
Deborah, d. Samuel, b. Oct. 29, 1679	1	4
Dorety, d. [John, Jr. & Jzrell], b. Aug. 10, 1665	MG	
Dorithy, d. John, b. Aug. 10, 1665	1	3
Dorethy, m. Nath[an] **WATSON**, b. of Windsor, Jan. 21, 1685	Col.D	54
Dorithy, d. John, b. Aug. 1, 1665	Col.1	55
Dorithy, m. Nathanael **WATSON**, b. of Windsor, Jan. 21, 1685	1	63
Dorathy, d. Nath[aniel], b. Dec. 27, 1686	Col.D	51

	Vol.	Page
BISSELL, BISSEL, BISSALL, BISSILL, (cont.)		
Dorithy, d. Nathaniel, b. Dec. 27, 1686	1	5
Dorithy,*, w. Nath[an], d. June 28, 1691 *(Note by LBB:		
"Dorothy (**FITCH**) BISSELL")	Col.D	57
Dorithy, w. Nathanael, d. June 28, 1691	1	41
Ebenezer, s. Tho[ma]s, Sr., b. Aug. 1, 1685	Col.D	51
Ebenezer, s. Thomas, Sr., b. Aug. 18, 1685	1	5
Ebenezer, s. Tho[mas], Sr., d. Aug. 22, 1685	Col.D	56
Ebenezer, s. Thomas, Sr., d. Aug. 22, 1685	1	41
Ebenezer, Jr., m. Hannah **DRAKE**, b. of Windsor, Jan. 23, 1741	2	132
Ebenezer, s. Ebenezer & Hannah, b. Jan. 6, 1758; d. Jan. 31, 1758	2	539
Ebenezer Fitch, m. Esther **HAYDON**, b. of Windsor, June 24, 1756	2	133
Edwin, of Wallingford, m. Welthan **BROWN**, of Windsor, Sept. 22, 1828, by Rev. John Bartlett	2	150
Eli, s. Ebenezer & Hannah, b. Jan. 12, 1749	2	539
Elias, s. Daniel & Elizabeth, b. June 10, 1759	2	538
Elihu, s. Daniel, Jr. & Elizabeth, b. Jan. 13, 1757	2	537
Elijah, s. Josiah & Ruth, b. June 16, 1750	2	304
Elijah, s. Elijah & Keziah, b. Mar. 24, 1779	2	571
Elisha, s. Nathaniel, b. Jan. 12, 1721/2	2	13
Elisha, s. Ens. Nathaniell, d. June 10, 1742	2	524
Elisha, s. David & Sarah, b. Oct. 1, 1743	2	297
Elizabeth, d. [Thomas & Abigayl], b. June 9, 1666	MG	
Elizabeth, d. Thomas, b. June 9, 1666	Col.1	55
Elizabeth, d. Thomas, b. June 9, 1666	1	3
Elizabeth, d. [Samuel & Abigayl], b. Jan. 4, 1677	MG	
Elizabeth, d. Samuell, bp. Jan. 6, [16]77	MG	
Elizabeth, d. Samuel, b. [ ], 1677	1	3
Elisabeth, d. [Nathanell & Mindwell], b. Mar. 15, 1679	MG	
Elizabeth, m. John **STOUGHTON**, Aug. 11, [ ]	1	61
Elizabeth, m. John **STOTON**, Aug. 24, 1682	Col.D	54
Elisabeth, d. Isaack, b. Feb. 4, 1706/7	2	5
Elizabeth, w. Samuel, d. Apr. 12, 1715	2	218
Elisabeth, d. Daniell, Jr. & Elisabeth, b. Feb. 7, 1747/8	2	302
Elizabeth, w. Daniell, Jr., d. June 9, 1749	2	257
Elizabeth, w. Daniel, Jr., d. June 9, 1749	2	525
Ellinor, d. Jonathan & Elizabeth, b. July 27, 1758	2	538
Ephraim, s. [Thomas & Abigayl], b. Apr. 11, 1676; d. 11 das. after	MG	
Ephraim, s. Thomas, b. Apr. 11, 1676	1	3
Ephraim, s. Thomas, d. Apr. 22, [16]76	MG	
Ephraim, s. Thomas, d. Apr. 22, 1676	Col.1	58
Ephraim, s. Thomas, d. Apr. 22, 1676	1	40
Ephraim, s. [Thomas & Abigayl], b. Sept. 4, 1680	MG	
Ephra[im], 2nd s. Thomas, Sr., b. Sept. 4, 1680	Col.1	57

	Vol.	Page
BISSELL, BISSEL, BISSALL, BISSILL, (cont.)		
Ephraim, s. Thomas, b. Sept. [ ], 1680	1	3
Ephraim, m. Joanna **TAYLOR**, b. of Windsor, Dec. 24, 1702	1	54
Ephraim, s. Ephraim, b. Sept. 27, 1703	2	5
Ester, d. [Thomas & Abigayl], b. Apr. 2, 1677; d. May 9, 1678	MG	
Ester, d. Thomas, b. Apr. 2, 1677	1	3
Ester, d. Thomas, d. May 9, [16]7[8]	MG	
Ester, d. Thomas, d. May 9, 1678	Col.1	58
Esth[e]r, d. [Thomas & Esther], b. Sept. 10, 1679; bp. Oct. 19*, [16]79 *(Also written "Oct. 5")	MG	
Esther, m. Jonathan **DRAKE**, Apr. 14, 1708	2	141
Esther, d. Ens. Nathaniell & Sarah, b. Apr. 15, 1729	2	290
Esther, d. Thomas, Jr. & Martha, b. Nov. 21, 1729	2	291
Esther, d. Ens. Nathaniel, d. July 31, 1747	2	524
Esther, d. Ebenezer Fitch & Esther, b. July 13, 1757	2	537
Esther, d. William & Jemima, b. Aug. 13, 1759	2	538
Esther, m. Ruben **MILLER**, b. of Windsor, Feb. 12, 1766	2	180
[E]vnice, d. Tho[mas], b. Mar. 30, 1686	Col.D	51
[E]unice, d. Thomas, Jr., b. Mar. 30, 1686	1	5
[E]unice, m. John **STOUGHTON**, Jr., b. of Windsor, May 28, 1706	2	197
Eunice, d. Thomas, Jr., b. May 1, 1724	2	14
Eunice, m. Barzilla **GREEN**, b. of Windsor, Nov. 30, 1750	2	158
Ezekiel, s. Daniel, b. Sept. 6, 1705	2	8
Ezekiel, s. Daniel, Jr. & Elizabeth, b. Apr. 22, 1764	2	569
Fitch, s. Ebenezer Fitch & Esther, b. Jan. 4, 1760	2	540
George, s. Isaac, b. Mar. 10, 1720/1	2	12
Hanna, d. [Nathanell & Mindwell], b. Jan. 12, [16]70	MG	
Hannah, d. Nathaniel, b. Jan. 12, 1670	1	4
Hanah, d. Samuell, b. Sept. 18, 1682	Col.D	51
Hannah, d. Samuel, b. Sept. 18, [16]82	1	4
Hannah, m. Nathanaell **PHELPS**, Mar. 20, 1700	2	185
Hannah, d. Jonathan, b. Dec. 14, 1711	2	8
Hannah, wid., m. Jonathan **BARTLET**, b. of Windsor, Jan. 26, 1743/4	2	131
Hannah, d. Ebenezer & Hannah, b. Jan. 17, 1761	2	539
Hanah, m. Tahan **GRANT**, [ ]	Col.D	55
Hannah, m. Tahan **GRANT**, [ ]	1	57
Harvey, of East Windsor, m. Sarah **LAMBERTON**, of Windsor, Nov. 8, 1822, by Rev. Henry A. Rowland	2	468
Hester, d. Thomas, Jr., b. Sept. 10, 1679	Col.1	56
Hester, w. Thomas, Jr., d. Mar. 4, 1726/7	2	219
Hezecia, s. [John, Jr. & Jzrell], b. Apr. 30, 1673	MG	
Hezekiah, s. John, Jr., b. Apr. 30, [16]73	1	3
Hezekiah, d. Oct. [ ], 1709, near Albany	2	217
Hezekiah, s. David, b. Jan. 30, 1710/11	2	7
Hezekiah, s. John & Hannah, b. May 9, 1736	2	296

	Vol.	Page

BISSELL, BISSEL, BISSALL, BISSILL, (cont.)

	Vol.	Page
Hezekiah, Rev. of Windsor, m. Mrs. Mary WOODBRIDGE, of Groten, Nov. 20, 1740	2	131
Hezekiah, s. Rev. Hezekiah & Mary, b. Jan. 15, 1741/2; d. July 12, following	2	298
Hezekiah, s. Hezekiah & Mary, b. Apr. 24, 1743	2	298
Hulda, d. Ebenezer & Hannah, b. June 5, 1754	2	539
Irene, d. Moses & Anna, b. July 14, 1755	2	536
Isack, s. Tho[mas], Sr., b. Sept. 22, 1682	Col.D	51
Isaac, s. Thomas, Sr., b. Sept. 22, [16]82	1	4
Isaack, m. Elisabeth OSBORN, May 2, 1706	2	127
Isaac, s. Isaac, b. Mar. 13, 1708/9	2	7
Isaac, s. Samuel & Mary, b. Jan. 25, 1749	2	538
Jabez, s. Daniel, Jr., b. Feb. 16, 1718/19	2	13
Jacob, s. [Samuel & Abigayl], b. Mar. 28, 1664	MG	
Jacob, s. Samuell, b. Mar. 28, [16]64	Col.1	54
Jacob, s. Samuel, b. Mar. 28, 1664	1	3
Jemima, d. William & Jemima, b. Oct. 25, 1767	2	545
Jeremia, s. [John, Jr. & Jzrell], b. June 22, 1677	MG	
Jeremiah, s. John, b. June 22, [16]77	1	3
Jerimiah, of Windsor, m. Mehitabel WHITE, of Hatfield, Dec. 18, 1705	2	128
Jerijah, s. Thomas, b. Apr. 20, 1698	1	6
Iiriiah*, s. Thomas, Jr., b. Mar. 11, 1712/13 *("Jerijah")	2	9
Jerijah, s. Thomas, Jr., d. May 28, 1713	2	217
Jerisiah, s. Thomas, Jr., b. Apr. 29, 1714	2	9
Jerijah, s. Jerijah & Lydia, b. Dec. 20, 1751	2	304
Jerijah, of Windsor, m. Lydia BARTLET, of Bolton, Mar. 27, 1755	2	132
Jerusha, d. Daniel, Jr., b. Apr. 11, 1721	2	13
Jerusha, m. Ens. Timothy LOOMIS, b. of Windsor, Nov. 3, 1763	2	173
Job, s. Thomas, Jr., b. Feb. 13, 1718/19	2	11
Joel, s. Isaac, b. Jan. 1, 1714/15	2	10
John, his w. [ ], d. [16]41	MG	
John, his w. [ ], d. May 2, 1641	1	40
John, Jr., m. Jzrell MASON, June 17, 1658	MG	
John, of Windsor, m. Isrell MASON, of Saybrook, June 17, 1658	1	54
John, s. [Samuel & Abigayl], b. Apr. 5, 1659	MG	
John, [s. Samuell, b. Apr. 5, [16]59; bp. Nov. 27, [16]59	MG	
John, s. Samuel, b. Apr. 5, 1659	1	3
John, bp. Nov. 27, [16]59	MG	
John, s. [Thomas & Abigayl], b. Jan. 26, 1660	MG	
John, [s.] Thomas, [bp.] Jan. 27, [16]60	MG	
John, s. [John, Jr. & Jzrell], b. May 4, 1661	MG	
John, s. John, b. May 4, 1661	Col.1	54
John, s. John, b. May 4, 1661	1	3

	Vol.	Page
BISSELL, BISSEL, BISSALL, BISSILL, (cont.)		
John, [s. John, bp.] May 12, [16]61	MG	
John, Sr., his w. [ ], d. Mar. 29, 1665	Col.1	55
John, his w. [ ], d. Mar. 29, 1665	1	40
John, his w. [ ], d. [ ], [16]65	MG	
John, Jr., had 8 children b. in Windsor. Dated Aug. 17, 1677	MG	
John, Sr., had 1 child b. in Windsor. Dated Aug. 17, 1677	MG	
John, Sr., d. Oct. 3, [16]77	MG	
John, Sr., d. Oct. 3, 1677	Col.1	58
John, of Windsor, m. Sarah LO[O]MIS, of Hatfield, Nov. 12, 1689	Col.D	55
John, of Windsor, m. Sarah LOOMIS, of Hartford, Nov. 12, 1689	1	54
John, s. John, b. Sept. 12, 1693	1	5
John, s. John, b. Sept. 10, 1698	1	6
John, s. Jeremiah, b. Sept. 1, 1709	2	7
John, m. Hannah DENSLOW, Feb. 22, 1710/11	2	128
John, s. John & Hannah, b. Feb. 18, 1717/18	2	11
John, m. Hannah WATSON, b. of Windsor, Dec. 2, 1733	2	130
John, s. John & Hannah, b. Dec. 21, 1734	2	293
John, d. July 15, 1736	2	524
John, Sr., contributed 0-2-0 to the poor in other colonies	MG	
John, Jr., contributed 0-2-0 to the poor in other colonies	MG	
John, [ ]	MG	
Jonah, s. Thomas, Jr. & Martha, b. May 3, 1727	2	289
Jonathan, s. Nathanell, b. Mar. 30, 1664	Col.1	54
Jonathan, s. [Nathanell & Mindwell], b. July 3, [16]68; d. [ ]	MG	
Jonathan, s. Nathaniel, b. July 3, 1668	1	4
[Jonathan*], s. Nathanel, d. [Sept. 22*], 1672 *(In pencil)	MG	
Jonathan, s. Nathanell, d. Sept. 22, 1672	Col.1	58
Jonathan, s. Nathanael, bd. Sept. 23, 1762	1	40
Jonathan, s. [Nathaniell & Mindwell], b. Feb. 14, [16]74	MG	
Jonathan, s. Nathanel, b. Feb. 14, [16]74	1	4
Jonathan, m. Bridgett Fitch, b. of Windsor, Mar. 17, 1708/9	2	128
Jonathan, s. Jonathan, b. May 31, 1710	2	7
Jonathan, of Windsor, m. Elizabeth HOLLIDAY, of Suffield, Nov. 29, 1744	2	131
Joseph, s. [Thomas & Abigayl], b. Apr. 18, 1663	MG	
Joseph, s. Thomas, b. Apr. 18, [16]63	Col.1	54
Joseph, s. Thomas, b. Apr. 18, [16]63	1	3
Joseph, [s.] Thomas, [bp] Apr. 19, [16]63	MG	
Joseph, m. Sarah STRONG, July 7, 1687	1	54
Joseph, s. Joseph, b. Mar. 21, 1687/8	1	5
Joseph, d. Aug. 23, 1689	Col.D	57

	Vol.	Page
BISSELL, BISSEL, BISSALL, BISSILL, (cont.)		
Joseph, d. Aug. 23, 1689	1	41
Joseph, s. Joseph, decd., d. July 29, 1713	2	218
Joseph, s. Jonathan, b. July 23, 1714	2	9
Joseph, s. Jonathan, d. Mar. 2, 1721/2	2	218
Joseph, s. Lieut. Isaac, Jr., b. Sept. 7, 1724	2	14
Josias, s. [John, Jr. & Jzrell], b. Oct. 10, 1670	MG	
Josiah, s. John, b. Oct. 10, 1670	1	3
Josiah, s. Thomas, d. Nov. 4, 1712	2	217
Josiah, m. wid. Merriam **HAYDON**, b. of Windsor, Dec. 10, 1713	2	128
Josiah, s. Josiah, b. Nov. 17, 1714	2	10
Josiah, m. Ruth **BISSEL**, b. of Windsor, Aug. 9, 1743	2	131
Josiah, s. Josiah & Ruth, b. June 8, 1744	2	298
Josiah, s. Josiah & Ruth, d. Aug. 11, 1750	2	220
Josiah, s. Josiah & Ruth, b. Nov. 27, 1757	2	537
Joyse, m. Samuell **PINNE**, Nov. 17, 1665	MG	
Joyce, m. Samuell **PINNE**, b. of Windsor, Nov. 17, 1665, by Mr. Allyn	Col.1	45
Joyce, m. Samuel **PINNEY**, b. of Windsor, Nov. 17, 1665, by Mr. Allyn	1	60
Justus, s. Jonathan & Elizabeth, b. Jan. 23, 1744/5	2	299
Lucinda, d. Daniel, Jr. & Elizabeth, b. Mar. 10, 1753	2	536
Luce, d. Lieut. John & Hannah, b. Aug. 6, 1722	2	13
Lucy, d. David & Sarah, b. Apr. 24, 1739	2	296
Luke, s. [Thomas & Abigayl], b. Sept. 22, 1682	MG	
Lydia, d. Jerijah & Lydia, b. Sept. 13, 1753	2	306
Mabel, d. Jeremiah, b. Jan. 16, 1707/8	2	7
Margaret, d. Daniel, b. Mar. 19, 1698/9	2	8
Margarett, w. Daniell, d. Nov. 27, 1712	2	217
Margaret, d. Daniel, Jr., b. May 24, 1723	2	14
Margret, m. Nathaniel **LOOMIS**, 3rd, b. of Windsor, Dec. 12, 1745	2	173
Margaret, d. Ebenezer, Jr. & Hannah, b. Oct. 21, 1746	2	301
Margret, d. Nathaniel & Azubah, b. Feb. 13, 1753	2	306
Martha, d. Thomas, Jr., b. Feb. 21, 1710/11	2	8
Martha, d. Jerijah & Lydia, b. Mar. 6, 1766	2	543
Mary, m. Jacob **DRAKE**, Apr. 12, 1649; "and never had a child"	MG	
Mary, m. Jacob **DRAKE**, Apr. 12, 1649	1	55
Mary, d. [John, Jr. & Jzrell], b. Feb. 22, 1658[9]	MG	
Mary, d. John, Jr., b. Feb. Feb. 22, 1658	1	3
Mary, d. [Samuel & Abigayl], b. Sept. 15, 1666	MG	
Mary, d. Samuell, b. Sept. 15, 1666	Col.1	55
Mary, d. Samuell, b. Sept. 15, 1666	Col.1	56
Mary, d. Samuell, b. Sept. 15, 1666	1	3
Mary, d. Samuel, b. Sept. 15, 1666	1	4
Mary, m. Daniel **OWEN**, Jan. 24, 1681	Col.D	54

	Vol.	Page
BISSELL, BISSEL, BISSALL, BISSILL, (cont.)		
Nathaniel, Sr., d. Mar. 12, 1713/14	2	218
Nathaniel, m. Sarah **GAYLORD**, b. of Windsor, July 8, 1714	2	128
Nathaniel, s. Nathaniel, b. Apr. 16, 1719	2	12
Nathaniel, s. Lieut. David, d. June 16, 1734	2	523
Nath[anie]ll, Jr., m. Azubah **ELSWORTH**, b. of Windsor, Apr. 15, 1746	2	132
Nathaniel, d. Mar. 6, 1752	2	525
Nathanell, his d. [ ], m. [ ]	MG	
Nathanell, contributed 1-0-0 to the poor in other colonies	MG	
Newberry, d. Daniell, Jr. & Elizabeth, b. June 9, 1749	2	302
Noadiah, s. Sergt. David, b. Nov. 3, 1720	2	12
Noadiah, s. David & Sarah, b. Aug. 17, 1736	2	296
Noadiah, s. David, Jr. & Elizabeth, b. Dec. 4, 1761	2	539
Noah, s. Sergt. David, b. June 27, 1715	2	12
Noah, of Windsor, m. Silence **BURT**, of Springfield, Dec. 2, 1741	2	130
Noah, s. Noah & Silence, b. Mar. 2, 1746/7	2	302
Noah, s. Noah & Silence, b. Oct. 29, 1749	2	220
Noah, s. Noah & Silence, b. Nov. 7, 1753	2	535
Oliver, s. Samuel & Mary, b. Oct. 13, 1753	2	539
Perez, s. Daniel, Jr. & Elizabeth, b. June 18, 1767	2	569
Rachel, d. Jeremiah, b. Nov. 16, 1706	2	7
Rhode, d. Ebenezer Fitch & Esther, b. Dec. 19, 1761	2	540
Rockey, d. Noah & Silence, b. Dec. 9, 1755	2	539
Roger, s. Isaac, b. Mar. 24, 1718/19	2	12
Rozzel, s. William W. & Jemima, b. May 3, 1755	2	535
Roswell, s. William & Jemima, d. Oct. 10, 1758	2	220
Rozzel, s. William & Jemima, b. Jan.* 25, 1762 *("Dec." written also)	2	541
Ruth, d. David, b. Nov. 20, 1713	2	9
Ruth, wid. Lieut. David, d. Mar. 1, 1733/4	2	523
Ruth, m. Josiah **BISSEL**, b. of Windsor, Aug. 9, 1743	2	131
Ruth, d. Josiah & Ruth, b. Mar. 5, 1745/6	2	301
Ruth, d. Josiah & Ruth, d. Aug. 15, 1750	2	220
Ruth, d. Josiah & Ruth, b. Oct*. 21, 1752 *("Nov." crossed out)	2	305
Sabra, d. Hezekiah & Sabra, b. May 25, 1763	2	543
Samuel, m. Abigayl **HOLCOM**, June 11, 1658	MG	
Samuel, m. Abigail **HOLCOMB**, b. of Windsor, June 11, 1658	1	53
Samuell, bp. Nov. 27, [16]59	MG	
Samuell, s. [Samuel & Abigayl], b. Jan. 11, 1668	MG	
Samuel, s. Samuel, b. Jan. 11, 1668	1	3
Samuel, had 6 children b. in Windsor. Dated Aug. 17, 1677	MG	
Samuell, ae 20 on Apr. 5, 1680; s. John, m. Abigall **FILLY**, ae 22 on Aug. 21, 1680, d. William, Aug. 26, 1680	MG	
Samuel, Jr., d. Mar. 4, 1697/8	1	41

	Vol.	Page
BISSELL, BISSEL, BISSALL, BISSILL, (cont.)		
Samuell, contributed 0-4-0 to the poor in other colonies	MG	
Samuell, mem. Jury 16[ ]	MG	
Samuel, ch. mem. 16[ ]	MG	
Samuel, d. Dec. 3, 1700	1	41
Samuel, s. Samuell & Mary, b. July 10, 1756	2	539
Samuel, d. Sept. 18, 1759	2	525
Sara, d. [Thomas & Abigayl], b. Jan. 8, [16]71	MG	
Sarah, d. Thomas, b. Jan. 8, [16]71	1	3
Sarah, d. John, b. Nov. 12, 1690	1	5
Sarah, d. Jeremiah, b. July 4, 1711	2	8
Sarah, d. Isaac, b. Feb. 13, 1712/13	2	9
Sarah, d. John, b. Oct. 15, 1714	2	9
Sarah, d. David & Sarah, b. Aug. 1, 1734	2	293
Sarah, m. Elishama CRANE, of Windsor, Dec. 31, 1741	2	136
Sarah, w. Ens. Nathaniell, d.Sept. 13, 1748	2	524
Sarah, d. Nathaniell, Jr. & Azubah, b. Jan. 28, 1748/9	2	304
Sarah, wid., m. Jerijah PHELPS, b. of Windsor, Feb. 10, 1763	2	190
Silee, d. Noah & Silence, b. Jan. 7, 1744/5	2	299
Silence, w. Noah, d. July 22, 1761	2	221
Silence, w. Noah, d. July 22, 1761	2	525
Stephen, s. Ephraim, b. May 8, 1706	2	5
Stephen, s. Ephraim, d. Nov. 4, 1712	2	217
Sibbel, d. Noah & Silence, b. Jan. 9, 1742/3	2	297
Sibbel, d. Noah & Silence, d. Oct. 18, 1749	2	220
Sibel, d. Noah & Silence, b. Jan. 31, 1751/2	2	535
Sibel, d. Daniel, Jr. & Elizabeth, b. June 11, 1761	2	540
Tabitha, d. Timothy & Hannah, b. Sept. 24, 1743	2	300
Thomas, adult, ch. mem. 16[ ]	MG	
Thomas, m. Abigall MOORE, b. of Windsor, Oct. 11, 1655	Col.2	159
Thomas, m. Abigayl MOORE, Oct. 11, 1655	MG	
Thomas, s. [Thomas & Abigayl], b. Oct. 2, 1656	MG	
Thomas, s. Thomas, b. Oct. 2, 1656	Col.2	158
Thomas, s. Thomas, b. Oct. 2, 1656	1	3
Thomas, b. Oct. 2, [16]56; bp. Feb. 7, [16]57	MG	
Thomas, publicly tendered himself to attain baptism for his children", Jan. 31, [16]57	MG	
Thomas, his w. [ ], bp. Feb. 28, [16]57	MG	
Thomas, had 9 children b. in Windsor. Dated Aug. 17, 1677	MG	
Thomas, s. Thomas, Sr., m. Est[h]e[r] STRONG, d. John, Elder of Northampton, Oct. 15, 1678	MG	
Thomas, Jr., s. Thomas, Sr., m. Hester STRONG, d. John, Elder, Oct. 15, 1678, at Northampton	Col.1	46
Thomas, s. Thomas, Sr., m. Hester STRONG, d. John, Elder, Oct. 15, 1678, at Northampton	TR1	1
Thomas, s. Thomas, Sr., m. Hester STRONG, d. John, Elder, Oct. 15, 1678, at Northampton	1	54

	Vol.	Page
BISSELL, BISSEL, BISSALL, BISSILL, (cont.)		
Tho[mas], s. Tho[mas], Jr., b. Dec. 8, [16]83	Col.D	51
Thomas, s. Thomas, Jr., b. Dec. 8, 1683	1	5
Tho[mas], Qt. Mast., d. July 31, 1689	Col.D	56
Thomas, d. July 31, 1689	1	41
Thomas, Jr., m. Martha **LOOMIS**, b. of Windsor, Feb. 16, 1709/10	2	128
Thomas, s. Jerijah & Lydia, b. Dec. 2, 1757	2	537
Thomas, contributed 1-0-0 to the poor in other colonies	MG	
Timothy, s. Jonathan, b. Jan. 9, 1716/17	2	10
Timothy, s. Timothy & Hannah, b. Apr. 1, 1746	2	300
Tryphena, d. Jonathan & Elizabeth, b. May 16, 1753	2	305
William, s. Ens. Nathanael, b. Sept. 15, 1725	2	289
William, s. Jabez & Dorcas. b. July 26, 1752	2	305
William, m. Jamima **SKINNER**, b. of Windsor, June 4, 1754	2	133
William, s. William & Jemima, b. Feb. 11, 1765	2	542
W[illia]m, s. William & Jemima, b. Feb. 11, 1765	2	545
------, m. Dan[i]el **GRISWOLD**, Feb. [ ]	TR1	1
----n, Sr., adm. communion, May 3, 1640	MG	
BLACK, Cyntha, of Hartford, m. Samuel A. **PERKINS**, of Windsor, Sept. 25, 1851, by Rev. Horatio N. Weed	2	461
BLACKMAN, Sarah H., of Springfield, m. Nathaniel **HOWARD**, of Windsor, Sept. 24, 1835	2	482
BLANCHARD, BLANCHAR, BLANCHER, Alidiea, d. Thomas & Ailva, b. Oct. 31, 1796	2	571
Charlotte, of Windsor, m. Dickson **GRISWOLD**, of Turin, N. Y., Nov. 16, 1826, by Richard Niles, J. P.	2	480
Cordelia, m. Samuel **CLARK**, Nov. 29, 1832, by Henry A. Rowland	2	470
Demmon, s. Thomas & Silva, b. May 21, 1794	2	569
Diana, d. Thomas & Silva, b. Feb. 15, 1799	2	571
Elisha, s. Chester & Ruba, b. May 8, 1799	2	571
Elizabeth, of Hartford, m. James **EGELSTON**, of Windsor, Nov. 31, 1732	2	146
Emma, d. Chester & Ruba, b. Dec. 21, 1795* *("Sept. 18, 179[ ]" crossed out)	2	526
George G., m. Abigail P. **GRISWOLD**, b. of Windsor, Oct. 16, 1845, by Rev. Cephas Brainard	2	508
Manin, s. Thomas & Silva, b. Nov. 4, 1807	2	571
Mannin, m. Naomi **MATHER**, Sept. 10, 1832, by Henry A. Rowland	2	469
Ransil, s. Thomas & Silva, b. Feb. 21, 1804	2	571
Sally Loiza, d. Thomas & Silva, b. June 13, 1816	2	571
Silva, d. Thomas & Silva, b. Mar. 18, 1818	2	572
Simeon, s. Thomas & Silva, b. Feb. 28, 1801	2	571
Simeon, m. Eunice **SQUIRES**, Oct. 29, 1823, by Rev. Henry A. Rowland	2	149
Thomas, m. Silva **BROWN**, b. of Windsor, Dec. 2, 1793	2	467

	Vol.	Page
BLANCHARD, BLANCHAR, BLANCHER, (cont.)		
Thomas Albirt, s. Thomas & Silva, b. Apr. 6, 1811	2	571
BELVIN, William, of Hartford, m. Aurelia **CLARKE,** Dec. 31, 1828, by John B. Ballard	2	150
BLISH, David, m. Candice **COOK,** June 20, 1836, by James Loomis, J. P.	2	499
BLISS, BLISSE, Ann, w. Pelatiah, d. Sept. 26, 1736	2	524
Anna, m. John **WATSON,** b. of Windsor, July 1, 1767	2	210
Betty, d. Rev. John & Betty, b. Nov. 30, 1766	2	543
Charlotte, m. Samuel O. **LOOMIS,** June 2, 1847, by T. A. Leete	2	175
Charlotte, m. Samuel O. **LOOMIS,** June 2, 1847, by T. A. Leete	2	491
Ebenezer, m. Ann **GAYLORD,** b. of Windsor, May 17, 1744	2	132
Ebenezer, s. Ebenezer & Ann, b. Jan. 17, 1746/7	2	300
Elizabeth, of Norwich, m. Daniel **WHITE,** of Windsor, Apr. 25, 1710	2	207
John, s. Ebenezer & Ann, b. Apr. 23, 1745	2	299
John, Rev. of Windsor, m. Mrs. Betty **WHITE,** of Bolton, Jan. 15, 1766	2	134
Jonathan, s. Jonathan, b. Feb. 4, 1711/12	2	8
Mary, of Springfield, m. Nathanell **HOLCOM,** Feb. 27, 1670	Col.1	46
Pelatiah, m. Elizabeth **STOUGHTON,** b. of Windsor, Feb. 9, 1743/4	2	131
Sarah, d. Jonathan, b. Oct. 24, 1706	2	6
Sarah, m. Thomas **MUGLESTON,** b. of Windsor, Dec. 13, 1733	2	177
BLODGET, BLOCHET, Abigail, d. Josiah & Abigail, b. Sept. 8, 1759	2	540
Ann, d. Ebenezer & Ann, b. Mar. 2, 1760	2	542
Ebenezer, m. Ann **BARBER,** b. of Windsor, Nov. 15, 1758	2	134
Elijah, of Windsor, m. Hannah **CORNING,** of Hollenston, Aug. 15, 1746	2	132
Hannah, d. Elijah & Hannah, b. Aug. 3, 1748	2	302
Josiah, m. Abigail **ROOD,** b. of Windsor, Jan. 15, 1746/7	2	132
Josiah, s. Josiah & Abigail, b. Aug. 25, 1747	2	301
Josiah, s. Josiah & Abigail, b. Aug. 29, 1752	2	540
Phenihas, s. Josiah & Abigail, b. Feb. 19, 1756	2	540
Rebeckah, d. Elijah & Hannah, b. Jan. 18, 1761	2	540
Rosel, s. Josiah & Abigail, b. Oct. 8, 1749	2	540
Susannah, d. Elijah & Hannah, b. Mar. 3, 1751	2	306
BOARDWINE, Abigail, m. Thomas **CROSBY,** Aug. 24, 1826, by Rev. Henry A. Rowland	2	139
BODGE, Joseph, m. Marsha **HOLCOMB,** b. of Windsor, July 2, 1837, by Eli Deniston	2	490
BODINE, Nathaniel, of New Jersey, m. Ellen **KENNY,** of Suffield, Apr. 21, 1850, by Rev. Samuel Warren Law	2	504
BODWELL, Jonathan, of Farmington, m. Roxy **CADWELL,** of		

	Vol.	Page
BODWELL, (cont.)		
Windsor, Oct. 14, 1828, by John Bartlett	2	469
BOLES, BOOLES, Elizabeth Putnam, d. Samuel & Ruth, b. July 31, 1750	2	542
Mary, d. Samuel & Ruth, b. Aug. 12, 1747	2	542
Ruth, d. Samuel & Ruth, b. Apr. 3, 1752	2	542
Ruth, of East Windsor, m. Benjamin **BARBER**, of Windsor, Dec. 3, 1778	2	467
BOOME, Robert, of New York, m. Elizabeth **ULRICH**, of Suffield, Apr. 21, 1850, by Rev. Samuel Warren Law	2	504
BOOTH, BOTH, Aaron, s. Caleb & Abigail, b. Sept. 8, 1735	2	295
Aaron, m. Edatha **SKINNER**, b. of Windsor, Apr. 13, 1765	2	133
Aaron, s. Aaron & Edatha, b. Mar. 10, 1757	2	537
Abigail, d. Caleb & Abigail, b. May 6, 1731	2	292
Anna, d. Ephraim & Elizabeth, b. July 26, 1760	2	543
Ashbel, s. Simeon & Elizabeth, b. July 3, 1758	2	538
Ashbel, d. Mar. 29, 1762	2	525
Beulah, d. Caleb, Jr. & Hannah, b. June 6, 1753	2	306
Bridget, of Enfield, m. John **ALLYN**, of Windsor, May 3, 1694	1	53
Caleb, Jr., m. Hannah **ALLYN**, b. of Windsor, Jan. 30, 1746/7	2	132
Caleb, s. Caleb, Jr. & Hannah, b. Apr. 22, 1751	2	306
Chloe, d. Aaron & Editha, b. July 26, 1763	2	568
David Skinner, s. Aaron & Editha, b. Apr. 30, 1765	2	568
Edatha, d. Aaron & Edatha, b. June 27, 1758	2	537
Elizabeth, d. Simeon & Elizabeth, b. Sept. 13, 1752	2	538
Ephraim, s. Caleb & Abigail, b. Jan. 11, 1740/1	2	297
Ephraim, m. Elizabeth **GAYLORD**, Mar. 27, 1765	2	134
Erastus, s. Aaron & Editha, b. Apr. 23, 1761	2	568
Esther, d. Caleb & Mary, b. Dec. 27, 1727	2	290
Esther, m. Jacob **ELMOR**, b. of Windsor, Oct. 31, 1754	2	147
Hannah, d. Caleb & Hannah, b. May 17, 1748	2	302
Irane, d. Caleb & Abigail, b. Feb. 27, 1733/4	2	293
Jemima, d. Simeon & Elizabeth, b. Apr. 22, 1756	2	538
Joshua, s. Joshua & Ruth, b. Mar. 20, 1732/3	2	293
Josiah, s. Caleb, Jr. & Hannah, b. Sept. 24, 1757	2	537
Levy, s. Caleb & Abigail, b. Jan. 25, 1738	2	296
Levi, m. Abigail **ORSBORN**, b. of Windsor, June 13, 1765	2	134
Love, twin with Peter, d. Caleb, Jr. & Hannah, b. Mar. 5, 1760	2	539
Mary, m. Calkin **MUNCIL**, b. of Windsor, May 19, 1743	2	178
Mary, d. Caleb, Jr. & Hannah, b. May 30, 1766	2	543
Merriam, d. Caleb & Abigail, b. Nov. 27, 1732	2	292
Peter, twin with Love, s. Caleb, Jr. & Hannah, b. Mar. 5, 1760	2	539
Samuel, s. Simeon & Elizabeth, b. June 14, 1761	2	540
Simeon, s. Caleb & Abigail, b. May 5, 1730	2	291

	Vol.	Page
BOOTH, BOTH, (cont.)		
Simeon, m. Elisabeth **ALLYN,** b. of Windsor, Mar. 19, 1752	2	133
Simeon, s. Simeon & Elizabeth, b. July 20, 1754	2	538
Simeon, Jr., d. Mar. 25, 1762	2	525
Sibel, m. Noah **BARBER,** b. of Windsor, Oct. 28, 1761	2	133
Tryphena, d. Caleb, Jr. & Hannah, b. May 3, 1755	2	536
William, s. Joshua & Ruth, b. Oct. 20, 1730	2	293
William, d. Aug. 1, 1753	2	220
------, had 4 children d. [ ], in "Elenton" prior to 1740	MG	
BOREMAN, Nathan[ie]ll, of Wethersfield, m. Elisabeth **STRONG,**		
of Windsor, Apr. 30, 1707	2	128
BORNE, John A., of Springfield, Mass., m. Esther C.		
GRISWOLD, of Windsor, June 22, 1852, by Rev. Pliny		
F. Sanborne	2	504
BORROUGHS, Aaron, s. Simon & Lyda, b. July 16, 1755	2	536
Daniel, s. John, Jr. & Sarah, b. May 28, 1755	2	536
BOSTON, David, m. Mary **TOWNSEND,** colored, Jan. 8, 1833,		
by Henry A. Rowland	2	498
BOWDOIN, Charles C., m. Sarah Ann **FISH,** b. of Windsor, June		
8, 1834, by Rev. Noah Porter	2	499
BOWE, Benjamin, of Springfield, m. Sarah **WARDWELL,** of		
Windsor, Aug. 22, 1847, by Cornelius B. Everest	2	503
BOWER, Anson G., m. Clarissa A. **ELLSWORTH,** b. of		
Windsor, Dec. 31, 1839, by Rev. S. D. Jewett	2	465
Anson Griswold, s. John & Ruby, b. Jan. 7, 1811	2	572
Buckland Palmer, s. Sidney & Sarah, b. Apr. 18, 1838	2	572
Cynthia, d. John & Ruby, b. Feb. 22, 1803	2	572
Cynthia, m. Horace **BARKER,** Sept. 3, 1822, by Rev. Henry		
A. Rowland	2	467
Fanny, d. John & Ruby, b. Jan. 20, 1799	2	571
Horace, s. John & Ruby, b. July 18, 1805	2	572
Horace, m. Nancy Ann **WELCH,** Nov. 18, 1835, by H. A.		
Rowland	2	499
Horace Welch, s. Horace & Nancy Ann, b. Jan. 14, 1843	2	572
John Sidney, s. Sidney & Sarah, b. Sept. 25, 1833	2	572
Nancy Ann, d. Horace & Nancy Ann, b. Apr. 5, 1838	2	572
Selene, m. Alpheus **ROCKWELL,** b. of Windsor, Dec. 19,		
1821, by Rev. Oliver Wilson, of North Haven	2	196
Sidney, s. John & Ruby, b. Nov. 25, 1800	2	571
[BOYCE], BOICE, Chester G., of Sandisfield, Mass., m. Abigail		
GRAHAM, of Windsor, Aug. 27, 1834, by Rev. Henry		
Stanwood	2	506
Ellen, m. Henry **ALEXANDER,** b. of Windsor, Apr. 8, 1849,		
by T. A. Leet	2	463
BOYNTON, BOYANTON, Irena, m. Elisha **PENDAL,** b. of		
Windsor, Apr. 15, 1762	2	189
John, s. John & Tabitha, b. June 4, 1754	2	306
BRADFORD, Cynthia M., of Haddam, m. John B. **HOLCOMB,**		

	Vol.	Page
BRADFORD, (cont.)		
of Windsor, Dec. 4, 1842, by Rev. D. L. Marks	2	517
BRAND, David, s. David & Loisa, b. Nov. 22, 1780	2	548
Dudley, s. David & Loisa, b. July 27, 1783	2	548
Polley, d. David & Loisa, b. Apr. 28, 1780	2	548
BRANKER, BRAUKER, Abigayl, Mrs., m. as 2nd w. John		
WARHAM, Oct. 9, 16[ ]	MG	
Abigail, wid., m. John WARHAM, b. of Windsor, Oct. 9,		
1662	Col.1	45
Abigail, m. John WARHAM, b. of Windsor, Oct. 9, 1662	1	63
John, d. May 27, 1662	Col.1	55
-----, Mr., d. [ ], [16]62	MG	
BRAUKER, [see under **BRANKER**]		
BRENNIN, Mary, m. Edmund CARIEER, b. of Hartford, Oct. 23,		
1842, by S. D. Jewett	2	511
BREWER, Stephen, m. Austria EVANS, b. of Berlin, Sept. 11,		
1825, by Rev. Augustus Bolles, of Wintonbury	2	149
BRIDGE, BRIDGES, Alonzo, of Milford, N. Y., m. Fidelia		
BARBER, of Windsor, Sept. 22, 1824, by Rev. Henry		
A. Rowland	2	468
Jeremiah, d. Oct. 22, [16]68, from a tree falling upon him;		
on Oct. 23, 1668, John GAYLORD, and John		
BRIDGE, brought him home; ae 20 years and half	1	40
BRITTEN, BRITTAIN, Gilbert, s. William & Lucy, b. Feb. 27,		
1764	2	542
Lucy, d. William & Lucy, b. Feb. 26, 1760	2	538
William, m. Lucy BARBER, b. of Windsor, Oct. 13, 1755	2	133
William, s. William & Lucy, b. Nov. 11, 1756	2	536
BROOKS, BROOKE, BROOKES, Elizabeth, d. [John &		
Susanna], b. June 27, [16]64	MG	
Elisabeth, d. John, b. June 27, 1664	Col.1	54
Elizabeth, d. John, b. June 27, 1664	1	4
Joanna, d. [John & Susanna], b. Feb. 2, [16] 68	MG	
Joanna, d. John, b. Feb. 2, 1668	1	4
John, m. Susanna HANMORE, May 25, 1652	MG	
John, m. Susannah HANMORE, b. of Windsor, May 25,		
1652	Col.2	159
John, m. Susannah HANMORE, May 25, 1652	1	53
John, s. [John & Susanna], b. Mar. 16, 1660; d. [ ]	MG	
John, s. John, b. Mar. 16, 1660	1	4
John, had 8 children b. in Windsor. Dated Aug. 17, 1677	MG	
[John], his w. Susanna, d. Nov. 7, [16]76	MG	
John, his w. [ ]*, d. Nov. 7, [16]76 *(Note by LBB:		
"Susanna (HANMER) BROOKS")	Col.1	58
John, his w. [ ], d. Nov. 7, 1676	1	40
John, his w. [ ], d. Nov. 7, [16]81	MG	
John, contributed 0-1-0 to the poor in other colonies	MG	
Lidia, d. [John & Susanna], b. Aug. 7, 1673	MG	

	Vol.	Page
BROOKS, BROOKE, BROOKES, (cont.)		
Lydia, d. John, b. Aug. 7, 1673	1	4
Marcy, d. [John & Susanna], b. Nov. 25, [16]70	MG	
Mary, d. [John & Susanna], b. Mar. 21, [16]65	MG	
Mary, d. John, b. Mar. 21, 1665	1	4
Mary, d. John, b. Mar. 21, [16]65/6	Col. 1	55
Mary, d. John, b. Nov. 25, 1670	1	4
Mary, m. Samuel **OSBAND**, s. James, Nov. 14, 1688	1	63
Mary, m. Nathanael **COOK**, Jr., Feb. 19, 1717/18	2	135
Samuell, s. [John & Susanna], b. Sept. 6, [16]62	MG	
Samuell, s. John, b. Sept. 6, [16]62	Col. 1	54
Samuel, s. John, b. Sept. 6, 1662	1	4
Susanna, d. [John & Susanna], b. Sept. 22, 1675	MG	
Susannah, d. John, b. Sept. 22, [16]75	1	4
[Susanna], w. of [John], d. Nov. 7, [16]76	MG	
-----, Mrs., m. Timothy **SULLIVAN**, Sept. 19, 1852, by Rev. James Smyth	2	460
BROWN, BROWNE, Aaron, s. Cornelius, b. May 31, 1725	2	14
Abigayl, d. [Peter & Mary], b. Aug. 8, 1662	MG	
Abigaile, d. Peter, b. Aug. 8, [16]62	Col. 1	54
Abigail, d. Peter, b. Aug. 8, 1662	1	39
Abigayl, [bp.] Aug. 10, [16]62	MG	
Abigail, of Windsor, m. Samuel **FOWLER**, of Westfield, Nov. [ ], 1683	1	56
Abigall, of Windsor, m. Samuel **FOWLER**, of Westfeild, Nov. [ ], 1685	Col. D	54
Abigaell, d. Cornelius, b. Sept. 6, 1702	2	4
Abigail, m. William **BARBOR**, b. of Windsor, Mar. 10, 1725/6	2	130
Abigail, m. Erastus **MANLEY**, Jan. 15, 1835, by Henry A. Rowland	2	182
Almira, m. Seymour **KINGSBURY**, Feb. 4, 1835, by Hiram Roberts, J. P.	2	168
Alpheus, s. Ephraim & Thankfull, b. May 9, 1749	2	302
Anabell, twin with Rachell, d. Cornelius, b. Nov. 21, 1704	2	4
Ann, d. John, b. Sept. 1, 1696	1	6
Ann, d. John, d. Sept. 22, 1696	1	41
Ann, d. John, b. Aug. 13, 1702	2	5
Ann, d. Jonathan & Naomi, b. Oct. 4, 1748	2	302
Ann, d. Zadock & Ann, b. Jan. 7, 1776	2	547
Anne, m. [ ] **SMITH**, b. of Windsor, Oct. 12, 1824, by Rev. John Bartlett, of Wintonbury. Int. Pub.	2	203
Azubah, d. John & Mary, b. Mar. 22, 1739/40	2	296
Azubah, d. John & Marah, d. Aug. 9, 1751	2	525
Benjamin, s. Peter, b. Aug. 11, 1711	2	8
Benjamin, s. Jonathan, b. July 14, 1721	2	14
Benjamin, m. Hannah **GRANT**, b. of Windsor, Oct. 19, 1743	2	131
Benjamin, s. Benjamin & Hannah, b. Dec. 20, 1748	2	305

	Vol.	Page

BROWN, BROWNE, (cont.)

	Vol.	Page
Benjamin E., of Suffield, m. Sarah **SMITH**, of Granby, Nov. 25, 1838, by Rev. Jared R. Avery	2	465
Bradley, s. Stephen & Eunice, b. Dec. 13, 1779 (Date conflicts with birth of Stephen)	2	547
Charles, of New Haven, m. Sophia **MOFFET**, of Windsor, June 10, 1829, by Henry A. Rowland	2	150
Chauncey, s. Peter & Margret, b. Oct. 12, 1779	2	569
Cloe, d. David & Isabel, b. Apr. 5, 1744	2	302
Cornelus, s. [Peter & Mary], b. July 30, 1672	MG	
Cornelious, s. Peter, b. July 30, 1672	1	39
Cornelius, m. Abigael **BARBER**, Dec. 4, 1701	2	127
Cornelius, s. Cornelius, b. May 31, 1707	2	5
Cornelius, Dea., d. June 26, 1747	2	220
Daniell, s. John, b. Jan. 29, 1708/9	2	6
David, s. Jonathan, b. Mar. 8, 1709/10	2	7
David, m. Isabel **BARNET**, b. of Windsor, Mar. 15, 1732/3	2	130
David, s. David & Isable, b. Feb. 20, 1733/4	2	293
David, s. David & Isabel, b. Mar. 22, 1746/7	2	303
Debora, d. [Peter & Mary], b. Feb. 12, [1678]	MG	
Deborah, m. John **HOSFORD**, Apr. 9, 1696	1	58
Deborah, d. Jonathan & Noami, b. Aug. 23, 1755	2	536
Deborah, d. Jonathan & Naomi, d. June 15, 1758	2	228
Dinah, d. Peter, b. Jan. 4, 1701/2	2	5
Ebenezer, twin with Mindwell, s. Peter, b. Aug. 26, 1719	2	12
Ebenezer, s. Ephraim & Thankful, b. May 15, 1751	2	303
Eli, s. Zadock & Ann, b. Aug. 4, 1781	2	548
Elias, s. Ephraim, Jr. & Marcy, b. Mar. 16, 1758	2	537
Elijah, s. David & Isabel, b. Mar. 24, 1753	2	306
Elizabeth, d. John, b. Feb. 11, 1692	1	5
Elizabeth, d. John, d. Aug. 12, 1715	2	218
Elizabeth, of Colchester, m. Samuel **HORSFORD**, of Windsor, Apr. 17, 1717	2	161
Elizabeth, d. Cornelius, b. Oct. 1, 1717	2	11
Elizabeth, w. John, d. Dec. 11, 1723	2	219
Emily, m. Nathan **BROWN**, b. of Windsor, Feb. 24, 1821, by Rev. John Bartlett. Int. Pub.	2	468
Ephraim, s. Jonathan, b. Aug. 25, 1712	2	9
Ephraim, s. Ephraim & Thankfull, b. Oct. 16, 1733	2	300
Ephraim, of Windsor, m. Thankfull **BURR***, of Farmington, Dec. 10, 1737 *(Name in pencil)	2	130
Ephraim, Jr., m. Mary **WESTLAND**, b. of Windsor, Apr. 13, 1757	2	133
Erastus Fitch, s. Elias & Prudance, b. Mar. 20, 1779	2	570
Esther, m. William **BARBOR**, b. of Windsor, Nov. 5, 1700	1	54
Esther, d. John, b. Mar. 13, 1712/13	2	9
Esther, d. John & Mary, b. Sept. 5, 1733	2	294
Easther, d. John & Marah, d. Aug. 7, 1751	2	525

	Vol.	Page
BROWN, BROWNE, (cont.)		
[E]unice, d. Jonathan, b. May 16, 1715	2	10
Eunice, m. Daniel ROWEL, b. of Windsor, June 23, 1736	2	194
Eunice, d. Stephen & Eunice, b. Jan. 29, 1781	2	547
Ezra, s. John & Mary, b. July 25, 1735	2	294
George, s. Ephraim & Thankfull, b. May 22, 1742	2	300
Hanna, d. [Peter & Mary], b. Sept. 29, 1660	MG	
Hannah, d. Peter, b. Sept. 29, 1660	1	39
Hanna, [bp.] Sept. 30, [16]60	MG	
Hannah, d. John, b. Aug. 24, 1697	1	6
Hannah, d. John & Mary, b. July 1, 1737	2	294
Hannah, d. John & Mary, b. Aug. 11, 1737	2	524
Hannah, d. John & Mary, b. Aug. 17, 1743	2	298
Hannah, d. Benjamin & Hannah, b. Mar. 2, 1744/5	2	299
Hannah, d. John & Marah, d. Aug. 6, 1751	2	524
Harriet, wid. of Samuel, of Windsor, m. Oliver BAKER, of Springfield, Mass., Nov. 7, 1826, by Rev. John Bartlett, of Wintonbury. Int. Pub.	2	149
Harriet Prudance, d. Elias & Prudance, b. Jan. 30, 1796	2	570
Hepsiba, d. [Peter & Mary], b. Nov. 19, 1664	MG	
Hephzibah, d. Peter, b. Nov. 19, 1664	1	39
Hepsiba, d. Peter, b. Nov. 19, 1664	Col.1	54
Hepsiba, [bp.] Nov. 20, [16]64	MG	
Hepsiba, d. Cornelius, b. June 19, 1712	2	9
Hester, d. [Peter & Mary], b. May 22, 1673	MG	
Hester, d. Peter, b.[ ], 1673; bp. 29th day	1	39
Huldah, d. Cornelius, b. Nov. 17, 1709	2	7
Huldah, m. David GRISWOLD, b. of Windsor, Dec. 23, 1731	2	156
Isaack, s. John, b. Mar. 17, 1706/7	2	5
Isaac, m. Martha BROWN, b. of Windsor, Mar. 5, 1729/30	2	130
Jesabel, m. Anthony HOSKINS, July 16, 1656	MG	
Izabell, d. [Peter & Mary], b. June 9, 1676	MG	
Isabel, d. David & Isabel, b. Nov. 3, 1735* *("Aug. 21, 1737" crossed out)	2	295
Isabel, 2nd, d. David & Isabel, b. Aug. *21, 1737 *("Mar. 9 crossed out)	2	296
Isabel, twin with Mary, d. David & Isabel, b. Nov. 14, 1750	2	304
Isable, d. Peter, b. June 9, [ ]	1	39
James, s. Stephen & Eunice, b. Dec. 2, 1776	2	547
James, of Manchester, m. Caroline HOLCOMB, of Windsor, Oct. 11, 1842, by Rev. David L. Marks	2	466
Jerusha, d. Benjamin & Hannah, b. Nov. 17, 1746	2	304
Jesse, s. Stephen & Eunice, b. May 17, 1791	2	569
Joab, m. Abigail WILSON, b. of Windsor, Nov. 30, 1801	2	467
John, s. [Peter & Mary], b. Jan. 8, 1668	MG	
John, s. Peter, b. Jan. 8, 1668	1	39
John, m. Elizabeth LOOMIS, Feb. 4, 1691/2	1	54

	Vol.	Page
BROWN, BROWNE, (cont.)		
John, s. John, b. Mar. 11, 1699/1700	1	6
John, Jr., m. Mary **EGELSTON,** b. of Windsor, Mar. 24, 1725/6	2	129
John, s. John, Jr. & Mary, b. Nov. 4, 1728	2	290
John, d. Feb. 4, 1728/9	2	219
Jonathan, s. [Peter & Mary], b. Mar. 30, 1670	MG	
Jonathan, s. Peter, b. [ ], 1670	1	39
Jonathan, m. Mindwell **LOOMIS,** Oct. 1, 1696	1	54
Jonathan, s. Jonathan, b. June 20, 1707	2	5
Jonathan, s. Jonathan, b. May 10, 1718	2	14
Jonathan, Jr., m. Naomi **ELSWORTH,** b. of Windsor, Jan. 11, 1743/4	2	131
Jonathan, s. Jonathan, Jr. & Naomi, b. Dec. 20, 1744	2	299
Jonathan, s. Jonathan & Mehitable, b. Sept. 11, 1767	2	543
Joseph, s. John & Mary, b. Aug. 17, 1744	2	298
Joseph, s. Benjamin & Hannah, b. May 25, 1753	2	306
Joseph Fitch, s. Elias & Prudance, b. July 31, 1792; d. Nov. 12, 1792	2	570
Julia Mariah, d. Elias & Prudence, b. Dec. 7, 1798	2	570
Justus, s. Jonathan & Naomi, b. Sept. 9, 1760	2	543
Lucius, m. Abigail **BARBER,** Apr. 20, 1833, by Hiram Roberts, J. P.	2	499
Luce, d. Samuel & Mary, b. Oct. 1, 1739	2	297
Luce, d. Samuel & Mary, b. Oct. 1, 1739	2	322
Lucy, d. Jonathan & Naomi, b. Oct. 4, 1750	2	303
Lucy, d. Jonthan & Naomi, d. June 16, 1758	2	228
Lucy, d. Peter & Margret, b. July 24, 1787	2	569
Lucy, m. Woodard **BROWN,** May 3, 1821, by Henry A. Rowland	2	467
Liddia, m. Thomas **PARSONS,** June 28, 1641	MG	
Lydia, m. Thomas **PARSONS,** June 28, 1641	1	60
Mabel, d. Cornelius, d. Dec. 8, 1704	2	217
Marah, w. Samuel, d. Jan. 19, 1755	2	220
Margare, d. John, b. Mar. 8, 1710/11	2	8
Margere, d. John & Mary, b. June 3, 1731	2	291
Margery*, m. David **FILLEY,** b. of Windsor, Sept. 22, 1749 *("BROWN" in pencil)	2	152
Martha, d. Jonathan, b. Sept. 7, 1704	2	5
Martha, m. Isaac **BROWN,** b. of Windsor, Mar. 5, 1729/30	2	130
Martha, d. Isaac & Martha, b. May 2, 1742	2	300
Martha, d. Stephen & Eunice, b. Dec. 22, 1784	2	569
Martin, s. Jonathan & Naomi, b. Dec. 10, 1757	2	538
Martin, s. Jonathan & Naomi, d. June 15, 1758	2	228
Mary, m. John **MOSES,** May 18, 1653	MG	
Mary, m. John **MOSES,** b. of Windsor, May 18, 1653	Col.2	159
Mary, d. [Peter & Mary], b. May 2, 1659	MG	
Mary, [bp.] July 24, [16]59	MG	

	Vol.	Page
BROWN, BROWNE, (cont.)		
Mary, d. John, b. Sept. 11, 1694	1	5
Mary, d. Peter, b. Aug. 28, 1708	2	7
Mary, w. Peter, d. Aug. 27, 1719	2	218
Mary, d. John, Jr. & Mary, b. Aug. 30, 1727	2	289
Mary, d. Samuel & Mary, b. July 3, 1731	2	292
Mary, d. Samuel & Mary, b. Apr. 23, 1737	2	295
Mary, twin with Isabel, d. David & Isabel, b. Nov. 14, 1750	2	304
Mary, m. David **BARBER**, b. of Windsor, Feb. 12, 1754	2	132
Mary, w. Samuel, d. Jan. 19, 1755	2	525
Mary, w. John, d. Aug. 25, 1789	2	221
Mary, of Windsor, m. John C. **SMITH**, of Wallingford, Oct.		
25, 1824, by Rev. John Bartlett. Int. Pub.	2	203
Mary, m. Amos **WESTLAND**, Jr., [ ]	2	210
Michael, s. Ephraim & Thankfull, b. Oct. 31, 1744	2	300
Mindwell, d. Jonathan, b. Jan. 8, 1698/9	1	6
Mindwell, twin with Ebenezer, d. Peter, b. Aug. 27, 1719	2	12
Mindwell, d. Isaac & Martha, b. Sept. 20, 1744	2	300
Mindwell, d. Peter, d. Feb. 25, 1758, at Springfield	2	525
Miriam, twin with Moses, d. David & Isabel, b. Sept. 1, 1748	2	303
Miriam, Mrs., m. Capt. Amos **GILBERT**, Sr., of Wintonbury,		
Apr. 29, 1824, by Rev. John Bartlett, of Wintonbury.		
Int. Pub.	2	160
Moses, twin with Miriam, s. David & Isabel, b. Sept. 1, 1748	2	303
Naomi, d. Jonathan & Naomi, b. Sept. 6, 1746	2	300
Nathan, s. Zadock & Ann, b. Oct. 6, 1790	2	569
Nathan, m. Emily **BROWN**, b. of Windsor, Feb. 24, 1821, by		
Rev. John Bartlett. Int. Pub.	2	468
Noah, s. David & Isabel, b. Mar. 9, 1738/9	2	296
Obediah, m. Clarissa **BACON**, Aug. 20, 1832, by Henry Sill,		
J. P.	2	150
Peggy, d. Peter & Margret, b. Jan. 5, 1778	2	569
Peggy, d. Peter & Margret, d. Dec. 1, 1788	2	221
Peter, m. Mary **GILLET**, July 15, 1658	MG	
Peter, m. Mary **GILLET**, b. of Windsor, July 15, 1658	1	54
Peter, his w. [ ], bp. July 17, [16]59	MG	
Peter, s. Peter, b. Mar. 2, 1666	1	39
Peter*, adm. ch. & communicant June 22, 1662 *(Written		
"Peter **BRUN**")	MG	
Peter, adm. ch. June 22, 1662	MG	
Peter, s. [Peter & Mary], b. Mar. 2, 1666	MG	
Peter, taxed 2-0 on Feb. 10, [16]73	MG	
Peter, had 10 children b. in Windsor. Dated Aug. 17, 1677	MG	
Peter, Sr., d. Mar. 9, 1691/2	1	41
Peter, m. Mary **BARBOR**, July 22, 1696	1	54
Peter, s. Peter, b. Jan. 28, 1699/00	2	5
Peter, communicant 16[ ]	MG	
Peter, d. Feb. 4, 1721/2	2	219

	Vol.	Page
BROWN, BROWNE, (cont.)		
Peter, of Windsor, m. Rachel **SCOTT**, of Hartford, Aug. 14, 1722	2	129
Peter, s. Peter, b. Aug. 5, 1723	2	14
Peter, d. Mar. 16, 1739/40	2	524
Peter, m. Margret **FILLEY**, b. of Windsor, Feb. 27, 1777	2	467
Peter, contributed 0-9-7 to the poor in other colonies	MG	
Peter, [ ]	MG	
Rachell, twin with Anabell, d. Cornelius, b. Nov. 21, 1704	2	4
Rachel, m. Benjamin **PHELPS**, b. of Windsor, June 24, 1731	2	187
Rebeckah, d. Stephen & Eunice, b. Dec. 6, 1786	2	569
Rebecca, m. Frederick **HUBBARD**, b. of Windsor, Sept. 12, 1820, by James Goodwin, J. P.	2	165
Richard M., m. Caroline E. **ABBE**, b. of Windsor, June 7, 1842, by Rev. Francis L. Robbins	2	466
Ruth, d. Jonathan, b. Jan. 11, 1701/2	2	4
Ruth, d. Zadock & Ann, b. Oct. 27, 1783	2	569
Samuel, s. Samuel & Mary, b. May 2, 17[ ]4	2	295
Samuell, s. Peter, b. Aug. 28, 1705	2	5
Samuel, of Lebanon, m. Joannah **LOOMIS**, of Windsor, Nov. 8, 1721	2	129
Samuel, m. Mary **PHELPS**, b. of Windsor, June 15, 1730	2	130
Samuel, had negro Cato, d. Jan. 5, 1755	2	525
Samuel, d. June 18, 1785	2	221
Samuel, of Windsor, m. Hariet **MARSHALL**, of Symsbury, Jan. 5, 1821, by Augustus Bolles	2	148
Sara, d. [Peter & Mary], b. Aug. 20, 1681	MG	
Sarah, d. John, b. Jan. 22, 1704/5	2	5
Sarah, d. John & Mary, b. Mar. 28, 1746	2	301
Sarah, d. Benjamin & Hannah, b. July 4, 1751	2	305
Sarah, d. John & Marah, d. Aug. 14, 1751	2	525
Sarah, d. Stephen & Eunice, b. June 27, 1782	2	569
Silas, s. Ephraim & Marcy, b. Mar. 31, 1761	2	542
Silas H., m. Roxey L. **REYNOLDS**, Oct. 7, 1829, by Rev. Asa Bushnell, Jr.	2	498
Silas Henry, s. Silas & Eunice, b. Aug. 30, 1810	2	572
Silva, m. Thomas **BLANCHARD**, b. of Windsor, Dec. 2, 1793	2	467
Stephen, m. Eunice **LOOMIS**, b. of Windsor, Nov. 26, 1775	2	466
Stephen, s. Stephen & Eunice, b. Apr. 30, 1779 (Date conflicts with birth of Bradley	2	547
Stephen, of Suffield, m. Ann Peris **FISH**, of Windsor, Nov. 26, 1829, by Henry A. Rowland	2	498
Sumner, of Springfield, Mass., m. Jane **HOLCOMB**, of Windsor, Dec. 14, 1834, by Rev. Luke Wood	2	150
Suse, d. Ephraim & Marcy, b. Sept. 9, 1769	2	545
Thankfull, d. Ephraim & Thankfull, b. Apr. 3, 1747	2	301
Thankfull, w. Ephraim, d. Jan. 9, 1774	2	525

	Vol.	Page
BROWN, BROWNE, (cont.)		
Timothy, s. David & Isabel, b. Oct. 27, 1741	2	302
Titus, s. Cornelius, b. Nov. 11, 1714	2	9
Tryphena, d. Jonathan & Naomi, b. Aug. 25, 1753	2	306
Tryphena, d. Jonathan & Naomi, d. May 27, 1758	2	228
Uriah, s. Daniel & Mary, b. Dec. 17, 1752	2	546
Welthan, of Windsor, m. Edwin BISSELL, of Wallingford, Sept. 22, 1828, by Rev. John Bartlett	2	150
William, s. Joab & Abigail, b. Mar. 8, 1803	2	571
William, of Windsor, m. Thirza M. GRISWOLD, of Simsbury, Jan. 16, 1823, by Rev. John Bartlett. Int. Pub.	2	468
Woodard, m. Lucy BROWN, May 3, 1821, by Henry A. Rowland	2	467
Zadock, s. Daniel & Mary, b. June 6, 1750	2	546
Zadock, m. Ann EGELSTON, b. of Windsor, Dec. 3, 1775	2	466
BROWNLY, Elizabeth, d. Robert & Presilla, b. July [ ], 1757	2	538
BROWTON, John, m. Hannah BASCOM, Nov. 15, 1650	1	53
BRUNSON, [see also **BRUSAN**], Abigayl, m. Jonathan WINCHELL, May 16, [16][ ]	MG	
Abigall, m. Jonathan WINCHELL, May [ ], 1666, at Farming Town, by Mr. H[a]wkins	Col. 1	45
Samuel, of Hartford, m. Melinda HUNT, of Windsor, Nov. 20, 1837, by Eli Deniston	2	490
BRUSAN, [see also **BRUNSON**], Abigail, m. Jonathan WINCHEL, May [ ], 1666, in Farmington, by Mr. Hukins	1	63
BUCKLAND, BUKLAND, Abigayl, d. [Timothy & Abigall], b. Nov. 11, [16]67	MG	
Abigail,d. Timothy, b. Nov. 11, 1667	1	2
Abigail, [bp.] Nov. 17, [16]67	MG	
Abigael, m. Timothy HOSFORD, Jan. 24, 1706/7	2	161
Abigael, wid. Timothy, d. Dec. 20, 1727	2	219
Abigail, w. Thomas, d. Apr. 1, 1746	2	524
Elizabeth, d. [Thomas], b. Feb. 21, [16]40	MG	
Elizabeth, m. Edward ADAMS, May 25, [16]60	MG	
Elizabeth, m. Edward ADDAMS, May 25, 1660	1	53
Elisabeth, d. [Timothy & Abigall], b. July 2, 1676	MG	
Elizabeth, d. Timothy, b. Feb. 26, 1678	1	4
Elizabeth, d. Timothy, b. Feb. 26, 1678	Col. 1	56
Elizabeth, w. Nicholos, d. Feb. 20, 1697/8	1	41
Elizabeth, d. Nicholos, b. July 19, 1692	1	5
Elisabeth, m. Fearnot BURLEY, Feb. 8, 174-5 (sic)* *(Probably "1704/5")	2	127
Ester, d. Timothy, b. Feb. 12, 1682	1	5
Hanna, d. [Thomas], b. Sept. 18, [16]54; d. [ ]	MG	
Hannah, d. Tho[mas], b. Sept. 18, 1654	Col. 2	158
Hanna, [bp.] Sept. 18, [16]54	MG	

	Vol.	Page

BUCKLAND, BUKLAND, (cont.)

Hanna, wid. Thomas & d. Nathanell **COOK**, b. Sept. 21, [16]55; m. Joseph **BAKER**, Jan. 30, [16]76	MG	
Hanna, d. Nicolas, b. Sept. 1, [1674]; d. Sept. 15, 1674	Col.1	58
Hanna, d. [ ] & Martha, b. Sept. 1, 1674; d. [ ]	MG	
Hanna, d. Nicolas, d. Sept. 15, 1674	Col.1	58
Hanna, wid. Thomas, m. Joseph **BAKER**, Jan. 30, 1676	Col.1	46
Hannah, wid. Thomas, m. Jefry* **BAKER**, Jan. 30, [16]76 *(In pencil "Joseph?")	TR1	1
Hannah, wid. Thomas, m. Joseph **BAKER**, Jan. 30, [16]76	1	54
Hannah, d. Timothy, b. June 28, 1676	1	4
[Hannah], d. Nicolas, d. [Sept. 15], [16]76	MG	
Hanna, d. wid. [ ], d. Dec. 23, 1676	Col.1	58
Hanna, d. Thomas, Sr., m. Josua **WELLES**, Aug. 11, 1681, by Capt. Newbery	MG	
Hanna, m. Josua **WELLES**, [ ] 11, 1681, by Capt. Newbery	TR1	1
Hannah, m. Joshua **WILLS**, Aug. 11, 1681, by Capt. Nubery	1	63
Hana, her child, d. Dec. 23, [16]81	MG	
Hanna, d. [Timothy & Abigall], b. June 28, [16]; bp. [ ]	MG	
Hannah, m. Nathan **GILLET**, Jr., Mar. 30, 1704	2	153
Hannah, w. Nicolas, d. Mar. 27, 1719	2	218
Hannah, m. Dr. Samuel **MATHER**, b. of Windsor, May 15, 1723	2	177
Hester, d. Tim[othy], b. Feb. 12, 1682	Col.D	51
Jarvis, m. Julia **FISH**, Sept. 18, 1827, by Rev. Henry A. Rowland	2	469
John, s. Thomas, b. Jan. 26, 1660	1	3
John, s. [ ] & Martha, b. Mar. 13, 1672; d. [ ]	MG	
John, s. Nicholas, b. Mar. 13, [16]72; d. Apr. 2, [16]73	1	41
[John*], s. Nicolas, d. [Apr. 2*], [16]72 *(In pencil)	MG	
John, s. Nicolas, d. Apr. 2, 1673	Col.1	58
John, s. Nicolas, d. Dec. 7, [16]75	MG	
John, s. Nicholos, d. Dec. 7, [16]75	1	40
John, s. Nico, d. Dec. 7, 1675	Col.1	58
John, s. [ ] & Martha, b. Dec. 7, [16]75; d. Dec. 20, 1675	MG	
John, s. Nicho[las], b. Dec. 10, 1686	Col.D	51
John, s. Nicholas, b. Dec. 10, 1686	1	5
John, s. Nicholos, d. Dec. [ ], 1686	1	41
Martha, d. Nicolas, b. Mar. 1, 1677	Col.1	56
Martha, d. Nicholos, b. Mar. 1, [16]77	1	4
Martha, d. [ ] & Martha, b. Mar. 1, [16]78/9	MG	
Martha*, w. Nicho[las], d. Oct. 28, 1684 *(Note by LBB: "Martha **(WAKEFIELD) BUCKLAND**")	Col.D	56
Martha, w. Nicholas, d. Oct. 28, 1684	1	41
Martha, m. Samuel **STRONG**, b. of Windsor, Nov. 9, 1699	1	61
Mary, d. [Thomas], b. Oct. 2, 1644; d. [ ]	MG	
Mary, d. Thomas, b. Oct. 26, 1644	1	4

	Vol.	Page
BUCKLAND, BUKLAND, (cont.)		
Mary, d. [ ], [16]57	MG	
Mary, d. Dec. 13, 1657	Col.2	160
Mary, d. Dec. [ ], 1657	1	41
Mary, d. [Timothy & Abigall], b. Nov. 7, 1670	MG	
Mary, d. Timothy, b. Nov. 7, [16]70	1	2
Mary, [bp.] Nov. 17, [16]70]	MG	
Mary, d. Feb. 6, 1738/9	2	524
Mindwell, m. Daniel **PHELPS,** b. of Windsor, Nov. 9, 1728	2	187
Nicolas, s. [Thomas], b. Feb. 21, 1646	MG	
Nicolas, of Windsor, m. Martha **WACKFELD,** of New Hauen, Apr. 14, [16]68, by Mr. Mathew Allyn	Col.1	45
Nicholas, of Windsor, m. Martha **WAKEFIELD,** of New Haven, Oct. 21, 1668, at New Haven, by Mr. Johnes	1	54
Nicolas, bp. Mar. 16, [16]72	MG	
Nicolas, had 3 children b. in Windsor. Dated Aug. 17, 1677	MG	
Nicolas, had d. [ ], b. Feb. 26, 1678; had d. [ ], b. July 18, [16]81; One d. July 24, [1681], Other d. Aug. 2, [1681]	MG	
Nicho[las], m. Eliz[abeth] **DRAKE,** Mar. 3, 1685/6	Col.D	54
Nicholas, m. Elizabeth **DRAKE,** Mar. 3, 1685/6	1	54
Nicholas, s. Nicholos, b. Jan. 8, 1687	1	5
Nicholos, s. Nicholos, d. May 9, 1688	1	41
Nicholas, m. Hannah **STRONG,** June 16, 1698	1	54
Nicolas, contributed 0-2-6 to the poor in other colonies	MG	
Sara, d. [Thomas], b. Mar. 24, 1648	MG	
Sara, bp. Apr. 1, [16]49	MG	
Sara, bp. Apr. 1, [16]49* *(Written over "Mar. 24, 1648")	MG	
Sara, d. [Timothy & Abigall], b. Apr. 10, 1673	MG	
Sarah, d. Timothy, b. Apr. 10, 1673	1	6
Sarah, d. Timothy, d. Sept. 25, 1682	Col.D	56
Sarah, d. Timothy, d. Sept. 25, 1682	1	41
Sarah, m. Joseph **GAYLORD,** Oct. 21, 1714	2	154
Sara, m. John **PHELPS,** [ ]	MG	
Tempranc[e], d. [Thomas], b. Nov. 27, [16]42	MG	
Temprannc, m. John **PONDER*,** June 26, 1668, at Hartford, by John Allyn *(Probably lived in Westfield, Mass., in 1666)	Col.1	45
Temperance, m. John **PONDER,** June 26, 1668, at Hartford, by John Allyn	1	60
Thomas, s. [Thomas], b. Feb. 2, 1650; d. [ ]	MG	
Thomas, bp. Feb. 9*, [16]50 *(Written over "2")	MG	
Thomas, s. Thomas, [b.] Feb. 25, 1650	1	4
Thomas, d. May 28, 1662	Col.1	55
Thomas, d. May 28, [16]62	1	40
Thomas, d.[ ], [16]62	MG	
Thomas, [s.] Timothy, [bp.] Jan. 21, [16]65	MG	

	Vol.	Page
BUCKLAND, BUKLAND, (cont.)		
Thomas, s. [Timothy & Abigall], b. June 23, [16]65	MG	
Thomas, s. Timothy, b. June 23, 1665	Col.1	54
Thomas, s. Timothy, b. June 23, 1665	1	2
Thomas, m. Hanna **COOK,** d. Nathanell, Oct. 21, 1675	Col.1	46
Thomas, d. May 28, [16]76	MG	
Thomas, bd. May 28, 1676	Col.1	58
Thomas, bd., May 28, [16]76, ae 25 years last Feb. 2	1	40
Thomas, Sr., had 2 children b. in Windsor. Dated Aug. 17, 1677	MG	
Thomas, Jr., had 1 child b. in Windsor. Dated Aug. 17, 1677	MG	
Thomas, m. Abigail **HANNUM,** Jan. 25, 1693	1	54
Thomas, d. Jan. 30, 1741/2	2	524
Timothy, s. [Thomas], b. Mar. 10, 1638	MG	
Timothy, m. Abigall **VORE,** Mar. 27, [16]62	MG	
Timothy, m. Abigail **VOAR,** b. of Windsor, Mar. 27, [16]62	1	54
Timothy, s. [Timothy & Abigall], b. Apr. 20, 1664; d. [ ]	MG	
Timothy, s. Timothy, b. Apr. [ ], 1664	1	2
Timothy, s. Timothy, d. [ ], [16]64	MG	
Timothy, adm. ch. Jan. 16, 1665	MG	
Timothy, adm. ch. & communicant Jan. [ ], 1665	MG	
Timothy, his w. [ ], adm. ch. & communicant Jan. [ ], 1665	MG	
Timothy, taxed 7-0 on Feb. 10, [16]73	MG	
Timothy, had 6 children b. in Windsor. Dated Aug. 17, 1677	MG	
Timothy, d. May 31, 1689	Col.D	56
Timothy, d. May 31, 1689	1	41
Timothy, his w. [ ], adm. to Ch. Jan. [ ], 16[ ]	MG	
Timot[h]y, communicant 16[ ]	MG	
------, m. Martha **WACKFEELD,** Oct. 21, [16]68	MG	
------, wid. taxed 3-0 on Feb. 10, [16]73	MG	
------ & Martha, had twins b. July 19, [16]81; d. [ ]	MG	
------, old wid., d. July 26, 1681	MG	
------, wid., d. [ ]]; bd. July 26, 1681	1	40
BUEL, BUELL, Abigall, d. William, b. Feb. 12, 1655	MG	
Abygaille, d. William, b. Feb. 12, 1655	Col.2	157
Goode, d. Dec. 3, [1639]	MG	
Hanna, d. [William], b. Jan. 8, 1646	MG	
Hannah, d. William, b. Jan. 8, 1646	1	3
Hanna, m. Timothy **PALMER,** Sept. 17, 1663	MG	
Hanna, m. Timothy **PALMER,** Sept. 17, 1663	Col.1	45
Hannah, m. Timothy **PALMER,** Sept. 17, 1663	1	60
Hannah, of Killinsworth, m. Joseph **PORTER,** of Windsor, Dec. 5, 1699	1	60
Hepsiba, d. [William], b. Dec. 11, 1649	MG	
Hephzibah, d. William, b. Dec. 11, 1649	1	3
John, m. Mary **LOOMIS,** Nov. 20, 1695	1	54

	Vol.	Page
BUEL, BUELL, (cont.)		
John, s. John, b. Feb. 1, 1698/9	1	6
Mary, d. [William], b. Sept. 3, 1642	MG	
Mary, d. William, b. Sept. 3, 1642	1	3
Mary, m. Simon MILLES, Feb. 23, 1656	MG	
Mary, m. Simon MILLS, Feb. 23, 1659	1	59
Mary, d. John, b. Dec. 11, 1696	1	6
Peter, s. [William], b. Aug. 19, 1644	MG	
Pete, s. William, [ ], Aug. 19, 1644	1	2
Peter, s. William, b. Aug. 19, 1644	1	3
Peter, m. Martha COGGINS, b. of Windsor, Mar. 31, 1670	Col.1	45
Samuell, s. [William], b. Sept. 2, 1641	MG	
Samuel, s. William, b. Sept. 2, 1641	1	3
Samuell, m. Debro GRISWOLD, Nov. 13, 1662	MG	
Samuel, m. Debora GRISWOLD, b. of Windsor, Nov. 13, 1662	Col.1	45
Samuel, m. Deborah GRISWOLD, b. of Windsor, Nov. 13, [16]62	1	54
Samuell, s. [Samuell & Debro], b. July 20, 1663	MG	
Samuell, s. Samuell, b. July 20, [16]63	Col.1	54
Samuel, s. Samuel, b. July 20, 1663	1	2
Samuell, had 1 child b. in Windsor. Dated Aug. 17, 1677	MG	
Sarah, d. [William], b. Mar. 21, 1653	MG	
Sarah, d. William, b. Mar. 21, 1653	Col.2	157
Sarah, d. William, b. Nov.*, 21, 1653 *(Note by LBB; "Mar. 21")	Col.2	181
Sarah, d. William, b. Mar. 21, 1653	1	2
Sarah, m. William GOING, b. of Windsor, Sept. 11, 1700	1	57
Sara, contributed silver, 0-1-0 to the poor in other colonies	MG	
William, m. [ ], Nov. 16, 1640	MG	
William, had 7 children b. in Windsor. Dated Aug. 17, 1677	MG	
William, d. [ ] 23, 1681	1	40
William, contributed 0-1-3 to the poor in other colonies	MG	
------, wid., d. Sept. 2, 1684	Col.D	56
------, wid., d. Sept. 2, 1684	1	41
BULKLEY, Harriet,of Windsor, m. Augustus A. **GRISWOLD,** of Simsbury, Jan. 3, 1822, by Rev. John Bartlett. Int. Pub.	2	160
BURAH, John, Ens., his six children d. [ ], in "Elenton" prior to 1740	MG	
John, Ens., his child d. [ ], in "Elenton" prior to 1740	MG	
BURG, [see under **BIRGE**]		
BURKE, James, of New York, m. Hellen J. **HALSEY,** of Windsor, Oct. 12, 1836, by Rev. Charles Walker	2	465
BURLEY, [see under **BURLISON**]		
[BURLISON], BURLISS, BURLEI, BURLEY, Daniel, s. Fearnot, b. Dec. 30, 1707	2	5

	Vol.	Page

[BURLISON], BURLISS, BURLEI, BURLEY, (cont.)

Daniell, s. Fearnot, d. Feb. 28, 1707/8 — 2 — 217

Ebenezer, s. Fearnot, b. May 8, 1711 — 2 — 8

Elizabeth, d. Fearnot, b. July 2, 1709 — 2 — 6

Esther, d. Fearnot, b. Feb. 15, 1705/6 — 2 — 4

Fearnot, m. Elisabeth BUCKLAND, Feb. 8, 174-5 (sic*)
  *(Written "Fearnot BURLEY") *(Probably "1704/5") — 2 — 127

Mary, m. John WILLIAMS, June 29, 1644 — MG

BURLISS, [see under BURLISON]

BURNHAM, BURNAM, Ann, m. Ammi TRUMBLE, May 9,
  1711 — 2 — 204

Anson B., m. Maria A. NORCOTT, Apr. 30, 1837, by
  Gamaiel W. Griswold, J. P. — 2 — 513

Elizabeth, w. Thomas, Jr., of Hartford, d. Apr. 18, 1720 — 2 — 218

Esther, d. Thomas & Elizabeth, d. Mar. 24, 1734/5, about the
  18th year of her age — 2 — 271

Hannah, m. Jeremiah DRAKE, Oct. 9, 1717 (sic?) — 2 — 141

Hannah, wid. [formerly w. of Timothy LOOMIS), d. Mar. 28,
  1784, in the 90th year of her age — 2 — 250

James Y., m. Harriet HOSKINS, Mar. 20, 1841, by Ezra S.
  Cook — 2 — 475

John, s. [Thomas, Jr. & Naomy], b. May 22, 1681 — MG

Lois, m. Joseph ALLYN, Jr., b. of Windsor, Jan. 17, 1755 — 2 — 124

Naomi, m. Josiah GAYLORD, b. of Windsor, May 7, 1713 — 2 — 154

Ruth, of Farmington, m. John ALLIN, 2nd, of Windsor, Dec.
  18, 1760 — 2 — 125

Samuel, m. Catherine P. JUDSON, Oct. 19, 1840, by S. D.
  Jewett — 2 — 475

Thomas, Jr., m. Naomy HULL, Jan. 4, 1676, at Killingworth — MG

Thomas, Jr., m. Naomy HULL, Jan. 4, 1676, at Killingworth,
  by Edward Griswold — Col.1 — 46

Thomas, Jr., m. Naomy HULL, Jan. 4, 1676, at Killingworth,
  by E. Grisell — TR1 — 1

Thomas, Jr., m. Naomi HULL, Jan. 4, 1676, at Killingsworth,
  by [ ] Griswold — 1 — 54

Thomas, s. [Thomas, Jr. & Naomy], b. Apr. 16, 1678 — MG

Thomas, s. Thomas, Jr., b. Apr. 16, 1678 — Col.1 — 57

Thomas, Jr., m. Elizabeth STRONG, Nov. 9, 1711 — 2 — 128

Thomas, s. Thomas, Jr., b. July 24, 1712 — 2 — 9

William, s. Thomas, m. Elizabeth LOOMAS, d. Nathanell,
  June 28, [16]71, by Mr. Wolcott — Col.1 — 46

BURR, Abigail, d. Benjamin & Mary, b. Apr. 4, 1736 — 2 — 294

Betsey, m. Amni WILSON, July 3, 1828, b. of Windsor, by
  Rev. John Bartlett — 2 — 212

Bissell, s. Nathaniel & Abigail, b. Dec. 14, 1771 — 2 — 545

Clarce, d. Stephen & Sarah, b. Jan. 29, 1773 — 2 — 546

Eunice, d. Stephen & Sarah, b. Aug. 8, 1769 — 2 — 545

Hannah, d. Benjamin & Mary, b. Jan. 20, 1733/4 — 2 — 294

	Vol.	Page
BURR, (cont.)		
Henry, m. Juliann **BARNARD,** b. of Windsor, Oct. 22, 1824,		
by Richard Niles, J. P.	2	149
Horris, s. Nathaniel & Abigail, b. Dec. 16, 1766	2	545
James, s. Nathaniel & Abigail, b. Dec. 12, 1779	2	547
Levi, s. Nathaniel & Abigail, b. Feb. 21, 1778	2	547
Lijah, s. Nathaniel & Abigail, b. Apr. 7, 1768	2	545
Nathan, s. Nathaniel & Abigail, b. Oct. 13, 1775	2	547
Nathaniel, Jr., of Farmington, m. Abigail **STRONG,** of		
Windsor, Apr. 3, 1766	2	134
Sarah, m. Stephen **BURR,** b. of Windsor, Oct. 22, 1761	2	134
Sarah, d. Stephen & Sarah, b. Mar. 10, 1764	2	542
Stephen, m. Sarah **BURR,** b. of Windsor, Oct. 22, 1761	2	134
Thankfull*, of Farmington, m. Ephraim **BROWN,** of		
Windsor, Dec. 10, 1737 *(Name in pencil)	2	130
BURREL, Elizabeth, of Stratford, m. Return **STRONG,** of		
Windsor, June 19, 1700	1	62
BURROUGHS, Abner, s. Abner & Margret, b. Sept. 12, 1754	2	536
Anna, d. David & Sarah, b. Mar. 1, 1744/5	2	299
David, of Windsor, m. Sarah **TYLER,** of Tolland, May 24,		
1744	2	131
David, s. Simon & Lydia, b. Jan. 26, 1749/50	2	303
Ebenezer, s. Semion & Lydia, b. July 1, 1753	2	306
Elizabeth, d. John, Jr. & Sarah, b. Nov. 10, 1740	2	297
Hannah, d. John & Sarah, b. Oct. 9, 1744	2	298
Joel, s. John & Sarah, b. Aug. 7, 1748	2	304
John, s. John, Jr. & Sarah, b. Feb. 16, 1745/6	2	301
John, s. Simon & Lydia, b. Apr. 30, 1748	2	302
Jonathan, s. John & Sarah, b. June 27, 1725	2	292
Jonathan, m. Judeth **WEBB,** b. of Windsor, Mar. 5, 1752	2	132
Jonathan, s. Jonathan & Judeth, b. Nov. 14, 1752	2	305
Sarah, d. John & Sarah, b. Aug. 19, 1731	2	292
Sarah, m. James **HARPER,** b. of Windsor, Nov. 20, 1752	2	164
Simon, of Windsor, m. Lydia **PO[ ]TER,** Oct. 30, 1745	2	131
Simon, s. Simon & Lydia, b. Sept. 30, 1746	2	301
Simon, s. Simon & Lydia, b. July 14, 1751	2	304
Stephen, s. Jonathan & Judeth, b. Jan. 3, 1755	2	536
Zebulon, s. Jonathan & Judeth, b. Sept. 3, 1758	2	538
BURT, [see also **BIRT**], James, of Springfield, m. Elizabeth		
COATS, of Windsor, Sept. 28, 1851, by C. B. Everest	2	504
Sarah, of Springfield, m. Daniel **GRANT,** of Windsor, Nov.		
18, 1717	2	155
Silence, of Springfield, m. Noah **BISSEL,** of Windsor, Dec.		
2, 1741	2	130
BUSH, John C., m. Jenette L. **DOWNING,** b. of Windsor, Apr. 4,		
1847, by Rev. George F. Kettell	2	499
BUSHON, Elizabeth, of Hartford, m. Thomas **ELMOR,** of		
Windsor, Feb. 14, 1752	2	146

	Vol.	Page
BUTLER, BUTTLER, Abigail, d. Samuel, b. Dec. 20, 1749	2	541
David, s. David & Mary, b. Nov. 8, 1736	2	294
Hannah, d. Samuel, b. Oct. 18, 1744	2	540
Henry, of Hartford, m. Harriet Esther **CADWELL**, Sept. 16, 1835, by Rev. T. H. Gallendet	2	499
Jerusha, d. Samuel, b. Sept. 21, 1746	2	540
Jerusha, d. Samuel, d. Mar. 24, 1747	2	221
Jerusha, d. Samuel, b. Oct. 26, 1747	2	541
John, of Springfield, m. Ruth **ALLYN**, of Windsor, Mar. 3, 1823, by Rev. Henry A. Rowland	2	468
Josiah, of Windsor, m. Margret **MANLY**, of Symsbury, Nov. 13, 1754	2	133
Josiah, s. Josiah & Margret, b. Sept. 2, 1755	2	541
Mabell, m. Michael **TAINTOR**, Aug. 26, 1697	1	62
Mary, d. Samuel & Hannah, b. Dec. 22, 1741	2	540
Nancy E., of Windsor, m. Alvin **WALDO**, of Bennington, N. Y., Oct. 16, 1825, by Rev. Augustus Bolles, of Wintonbury	2	211
Nancy E., of Windsor, m. Alvin **WALDO**, of Bennington, N. Y., Oct. 16, 1825, by Rev. Augustus Bolles, of Wintonbury	2	512
Samuel, s. Samuel & Hannah, b. Mar. 6, 1743	2	540
Sarah, m. Jonathan **FILLEY**, Jr., b. of Windsor, Feb. 6, 1755	2	152
Thankfull, d. Samuel, b. Jan. 24, 1759	2	541
Zachariah, s. Samuel, b. Mar. 29, 1752; d. Sept. 24, 1753	2	541
Zachariah, s. Sam[ue]ll, b. Sept. 4, 1754; d. Apr. 1, 1759	2	541
BUTT, Susanna, of Canterbury, m. Jonathan **SAFFORD**, of Windsor, Nov. 1, 1759	2	200
BUTTOLPH, BUTOLF, Abigail, of Stonington, m. Corp. Nathannael **FITCH**, of Windsor, Nov. 23, 1718	2	151
Roger, s. David & Mary, b. Oct. 4, 1734	2	293
CADWELL, CADWEL, Achsah, of Windsor, m. Bezaliel **DAVIS**, of Simsbury, Sept. 29, 1830, by J. C. Bullard	2	472
Chloe, of Windsor, m. Harvey **FILLY**, of Penn., Oct. 3, 1831, by Rev. Norman Atwood	2	477
Fidelia, m. Joab H. **HUBBARD**, b. of Windsor, May 18, 1831, by Rev. Augustus Bolles	2	485
Harriet Esther, m. Henry **BUTLER**, of Hartford, Sept. 16, 1835, by Rev. T. H. Gallendet	2	499
Huldah, of Windsor, m. Norman W. **MOSES**, of Simsbury, Nov. 23, 1831, by Rev. Ansel Nash	2	495
Jonathan, s. Mooses & Penelope, b. Mar. [ ], 1734/5	2	308
Jumin(?), of Windsor, m. Julia **ENO**, of Simsbury, June 1, 1831	2	470
Lois, d. Mooses & Penelope, b. Jan. [ ], 1729/30	2	308
Lois, d. Moses & Penelope, d. Dec. 28, 1734	2	223
Lois, d. Mooses & Penelope, b. Nov. 1, 1736	2	308
Mahala, m. Nathaniel **WHITING**, of West Hartford, Mar. 31,		

	Vol.	Page
CADWELL, CADWEL, (cont.)		
1831, by John Bartlett	2	213
Mary Ann, m. George G. **DENISON,** b. of Springfield, Oct.		
28, 1841, by Rev. S. D. Jewell	2	473
Molissa, m. William **WATSON,** of Torrington, Jan. 30, 1828,		
by Rev. John Bartlett	2	212
Penelope, d. Mooses & Penelope, b. Apr. 25, 1733	2	308
Roxy, of Windsor, m. Jonathan **BODWELL,** of Farmington,		
Oct. 14, 1828, by John Bartlatt	2	469
Russel W., m. Mary L. **SHEPHERD,** b. of Windsor, Nov. 28,		
1832, by Rev. Ansel North	2	470
Theodore C., m. Julia Ann **CORNISH,** Sept. 2, 1835, by John		
Bartlett	2	471
CALKINS, Ferdinand W., of Hamilton, N. Y., m. Julia **MOORE,**		
of Windsor, Oct. 20, 1836, by Charles Walker	2	471
CALSEY, [see under **KELSEY**]		
CALVERT, William, of Manchester, m. Hannah M. **WHEELER,**		
of Windsor, Nov. 9, 1842, by Moses Stoddard	2	516
CAMMEL, Mary L., m. Lyman **GRISWOLD,** b. of Windsor, Apr.		
2, 1848, by Cephus Brainard	2	462
CAMP, Bede, of Windsor, m. Jona A. **WATSON,** of Charleston,		
S. C., Jan. 1, 1836, by Eli Deniston	2	513
Charles, m. Amanda **LOOMIS,** b. of Windsor, Jan. 26, 1837,		
by Rev. Eli Deniston	2	490
James, m. Huldah **MAFFET,** Apr. 28, 1831, by H. A.		
Rowland	2	470
CAMPBELL, CAMPBEL, CAMPEBLE, CAMPBLE, Elizabeth,		
d. James & Jane, b. Mar. 26, 1751	2	549
James, s. James & Jane, b. Jan. 11, 1749	2	549
John, s. James & Jane, b. Nov. 2, 1753	2	549
Joseph, s. James & Jane, b. May 4, 1756	2	549
Mary, d. James & Jane, b. Feb. 13, 1743	2	549
Mathew, s. James & Jane, b. Jan. 7, 1747	2	549
Rosannah, d. James & Jane, b. June 14, 1755	2	549
William, s. James & Jane, b. Jan. 31, 1745	2	549
CANADA, Sarah, of Hartford, m. John **SKINNER,** of Windsor,		
Nov. 21, 1762	2	201
CAPIN, Henry, m. Melisa **LOOMIS,** Jan. 25, 1827, by Rev. Henry		
A. Rowland	2	139
Samuel T., of Hartford, m. Annis **WILSON,** of Windsor,		
Mar. 13, 1834, by Rev. Ansel North	2	471
CAREY, CARY, Anna, d. Samuel & Deliverance, b. May 5, 1765	2	319
Anna, d. Samuel & Deliverance, b. May 15, 1765	2	551
Austin, Rev., of Sunderland, Mass., m. Catherine **PHELPS,**		
of Windsor, May 3, 1842, by Rev. S. D. Jewett	2	516
Christopher, s. Samuel & Deliverance, b. Feb. 25, 1763	2	319
Christopher, s. Samuel & Deliverance, b. Feb. 25, 1763	2	551
Samuel, m. Deliverance **GRANT,** b. of Windsor, Dec. 7,		

	Vol.	Page
CAREY, CARY, (cont.)		
1762	2	137
CARRIER, CARIEER, Edmund, m. Mary **BRENNIN,** b. of		
Hartford, Oct. 23, 1842, by S. D. Jewett	2	511
Elizabeth, m. Nathanael **PINNEY,** s. Sergt. Nathanael, Jan.		
12, 1716/17	2	187
CARROLL, Ellen, m. James **MACKEY,** Oct. 14, 1852, by Rev.		
James Smyth	2	460
CARTER, CARTIRE, Abigal, d. Sept. 23, [1640]	MG	
Caleb, d. [ ], [16]47	MG	
Cathrine, m. Arther **WILLIAMS,** Nov. 30, 1647	1	62
Elias, s. Joshua, bp. Aug. 13, 1643	1	7
Elias, d. May 10, 1653	Col.2	160
Elias, d. May [ ], 1653	1	42
Elias, d. [ ], [16]59	MG	
Elisha, d. May 10, 1653	Col.2	160
Elisha, d. May [ ], 1653	1	42
Elisha, d. [ ], [16]59	MG	
Henery, his child d. [ ], [16]46	MG	
Jonathan, d. [ ]; bd. July 5, 1647	1	42
Joshua, s. Joshua, bp. Mar. [ ], 1638	1	7
Joshua, d. [ ] , [16]47	MG	
Josua, had 3 children b. in Windsor. Dated Aug. 17, 1677	MG	
William, had two children d. [ ], in "Elenton" prior to		
1740	MG	
CASE, CASS, CASSE, Agnes, d. Benoni & Ame, b. Jan. 19, 1776	2	554
Ame, d. Benoni & Ame, b. July 3, 1783	2	554
Aurelia H., of Windsor, m. Henry T. **BEMIS,** of Bloomfield,		
May 21, 1846, by C. B. Everist	2	499
Benoni, s. Benoni & Ame, b. Mar. 28, 1778	2	554
Benoni, Jr., m. Chloe **BARNARD,** b. of Windsor, May 1,		
1798	2	469
Charlotte, of Canton, m. Allyn **BARBER,** of Windsor, Dec.		
25, 1822, by Rev. John Bartlett. Int. Pub.	2	148
Charlotte P., of Windsor, m. Horace **BAXTER,** of New York,		
Aug. 19, 1849, by Rev. Cephus Brainard	2	504
Chloe, d. Benoni & Ame, b. July 28, 1786	2	554
Delsena, d. Benoni & Ame, b. May 19, 1797	2	555
Elizabeth, m. Joseph **LEWEIS,** Apr. 30, 1674, by Capt.		
Newbery	Col.1	46
Elizabeth, wid., d. July 23, 1728, ae 90	2	223
Frederick, s. Benoni, Jr. & Chloe, b. Mar. 4, 1803	2	555
Fredus, s. Benoni & Ame, b. June 19, 1799	2	555
Fredus, m. Ruth **PHELPS,** b. of Windsor, Feb. 14, 1828, by		
Rev. Arnold Scholefield	2	140
Gideon, m. Sarah **ALDERMAN,** Dec. 5, 1750	2	137
Harlow, s. Benoni & Ame, b. Sept. 20, 1790	2	555
James*, s. John, b. June 5, 1665 *(Note by LBB:		

	Vol.	Page
CASE, CASS, CASSE, (cont.)		
"William")	Col.1	55
Jane C., of Windsor, m. Robert L. MOFFAT, of Hartford,		
May 6, 1852, by Rev. H. N. Weed	2	494
John, s. [John], b. Nov. 5, 1662	MG	
John, s. John, b. Nov. 5, 1662	Col.1	54
John, s. John, b. Nov. 5, 1662	1	7
John, had 6 children b. in Windsor. Dated Aug. 17, 1677	MG	
Julia, d. Benoni, Jr. & Chloe, b. Jan. 27, 1807	2	556
Mary, d. [John], b. June 22, 1660	MG	
Mary, d. John, b. June 22 1660	1	7
Mary, d. Benoni, Jr. & Chloe, b. Mar. 31, 1805	2	555
Meriam, m. Joseph ATWELL, b. of Windsor, Dec. 27, 1753	2	124
Nathaniel, d. June 6, 1753	2	224
Orson, m. Mary G. BEBEE, b. of Hartfoard, May 1, 1822, by		
Rev. Augustus Bolles, of Wintonbury	2	138
Otis, s. Benoni, Jr. & Chloe, b. Nov. 14, 1798	2	555
Permela, d. Benoni & Ame, b. Feb. 8, 1788	2	555
Richard, s. [John], b. Aug. 27, [16]69	MG	
Ruth, of Simsbury, m. Hezekiah PARSONS, of Windsor,		
May 14, 1822, by Rev. John Bartlett. Int. Pub.	2	500
Ruth, m. Jehu P. ELLSWORTH, b. of Windsor, May 29,		
1837, by Eli Deniston	2	474
Samuell, s. [John], b. June 1, 1667	MG	
Sara, [d. John], b. Apr. 14, 1676	MG	
Sarah Jane, m. Lorin M. HIGGINS, b. of Windsor, Nov. 4,		
1847, by Rev. S. H. Allen	2	520
Seliana, m. Harlow MOORE, May 4, 1825, by Rev. Henry		
A. Rowland	2	181
Warren, s. Benoni, Jr. & Chloe, b. July 12, 1801	2	555
William, s. [John], b. June 5, 1665	MG	
William, s. John, b. June 5, 1665	1	7
William, m. Chloe STOUGHTON, Dec. 2, 1824, by Rev.		
John Bartlett. Int. Pub.	2	138
Zardus, s. Benoni & Ame, b. Oct. 18, 1794	2	555
Zopher, s. Benoni & Ame, b. June 26, 1792	2	555
CHACKWELL, Edward, d. Oct. 17, 1648	1	42
CHADWICK, James E., of Buffalo, N. Y., m. Martha I. CLARK,		
of Windsor, June 17, 1851, by Cornelius B. Everest	2	497
CHAFEN, Dauid, had 3 children d. [ ], in "Elenton" prior to		
1740	MG	
CHAFFEE, CHAFFE, Abigail, m. Jasper MORGAN, b. of		
Windsor, Mar. 10, 1823, by Rev. Henry A. Rowland	2	181
Esther, d. Dr. Hezakiah & Lydia, b. Apr. 24, 1765	2	552
Hepzibah, d. Hezakiah & Lydia, b. Aug. 12, 1758	2	551
Hezekiah, s. Dr. Hezakiah & Lydia, b. Mar. 21, 1762	2	551
John, s. Dr. Hezakiah & Lydia, b. Feb. 22, 1767	2	552
Mary, d. Hezakiah & Lydia, b. July 24, 1760	2	521

	Vol.	Page

CHAFFEE, CHAFFE, (cont.)

Mary, d. Hezakiah & Lydia, b. July 25, 1760	2	551
Mary, m. James **HOOKER,** Nov. 7, 1784	2	164
Mary, m. James **HOOKER,** Nov. 7, 1784	2	522
CHAKWELL, Edward, d. [ ], [16]48	MG	
CHAMPLAIN, Sally, m. John **FENNER,** b. of R. I., Oct. 8, 1827, by Rev. John Bartlett	2	477
CHANDLER, Isaac, m. Anne **LOOMIS,** b. of Windsor, Oct. 3, 1771	2	137
Isaac, s. Isaac & Ann, b. Apr. 19, 1773	2	553
Lusinda A., m. Gad **SHELDON,** Apr. 5, 1831, by Henry A. Rowland	2	508
Roger, s. Isaac, b. May 6, 1797	2	555
CHAPIN, Elizabeth, of Enfield, m. Abel **ALLYN,** of Windsor, Jan. 1, 1756	2	124
Mary E., m. Alexander **DOWNING,** May 9, 1847, by Rev. Theodore A. Leete	2	473
CHAPMAN, Ann, w. Taylor, d. Jan. 21, 1794	2	225
Asahel, of Glastonbury, m. Eunice A. **HAUSE,** of Windsor, Aug. 6, 1827, by Rev. John Bartlett	2	140
Betsy, d. Henry, b. Apr. 12, 1702	2	16
Birge, of Hartford, m. Frances C. **SOPER,** of Windsor, Nov. 27, 1851, by Cornelius B. Everest	2	497
Caroline, of Glastenbury, m. Elisha **LEFFINGWELL,** of Hartford, Feb. 22, 1821, by Rev. Coles Carpenter	2	488
Delia, d. Frederick & Lucy, b. Mar. 18, 1805	2	19
Delia, m. Samuel **WILSON,** Nov. 29, 1827, by Rev. Henry A. Rowland	2	212
Edmund, s. Taylor & Ann, b. Apr. 6, 1762	2	319
Edmund, s. Taylor & Ann, b. Apr. 6, 1762	2	551
Edward, d. Dec. 19, [16]75, in war	MG	
Edward, d. Dec. 19, 1675	Col.1	58
Edward, d. Dec. 19, 1675	1	26
Edward, d. Dec. 19, 1675	1	47
Edward, had 8 children b. in Windsor. Dated Aug. 17, 1677	MG	
Edward, s. Henry, b. Apr. 8, 1695	2	16
Edward, d. May 21, 1724	2	223
Edward, m. Hannah **FOSTER,** Apr. 4, 1754	2	157
Edward, m. Elisabeth **FOX,** [ ], in England	MG	
Edwin, s. Frederick & Lucy, b. Oct. 13, 1801	2	19
Edwin, m. Abigail **DRAKE,** Apr. 29, 1824, by Rev. Henry A. Rowland	2	138
Elisabeth, d. [Edward & Elisabeth], b. Jan. 15, 1667	MG	
Elizabeth, d. Elizabeth, b. Jan. 15, 1667; bp. [ ] 27, [16]77	MG	
Elizabeth, adm. ch. & commnicant Apr. [ ], 167[ ]	MG	
Elizabeth, adm. communion, Apr. 22, 167[ ]	MG	
Elizabeth, wid. Edward, m. Samuell **CROSS,** July 12, [16]77	Col.1	46
Elizabeth, wid. Edward, m. Samuell **CROSS,** July 12, 1677	TR1	1

	Vol.	Page
CHAPMAN, (cont.)		
1729	2	223
Mary, d. Henry & Mary, b. May 5, 1748	2	310
Mary, m. Daniel **ELA***, b. of Windsor, May 20, 1779 *(In		
pencil)	2	147
Reuben, s. Samuel, b. Dec. 9, 1713	2	17
Reuben, s. Samuel, d. Jan. 3, 1718/19	2	222
Samuel, s. Simeon, b. Mar. 2, 1695/6	2	16
Samuel, m. Hannah **STRONG**, b. of Windsor, Aug. 8, 1717	2	135
Samuel, s. Samuel, of Stanford, b. Oct. 15, 1723	2	18
Sara, d. [Edward & Elisabeth], b. May 24, 1675	MG	
Sara, d. Elizabeth, b. May 24, 1675; bp. [ ] 27, [16]77	MG	
Sarah, d. Henry, b. Nov. 10, 1706	2	16
Sarah, d. Samuel, b. May 23, 1720	2	17
Sarah, m. Samuel **DENSLOW**, b. of Windsor, Oct. 1, 1730	2	141
Sarah, w. Simon, d. May 21, 1735	2	223
Sarah, w. Simon, d. May 21, 1735	2	224
Simeon, s. Simeon, b. Nov. 14, 1700, at Stanford	2	16
Simon, s. [Edward & Elisabeth], b. Apr. 30, 1669	MG	
Simon, s. Elizabeth, b. Apr. 30, 1669; bp. [ ] 27, [16]77	MG	
Simon, m. Mary **ALLYN**, b. of Windsor, Jan. 7, 1724/5	2	136
Simon, s. Simon, Jr. & Mary, b. Dec. 27, 1726	2	18
Simon, s. Simon, Jr. & Mary, d. Jan. 3, 1726/7	2	223
Simon, m. Silence **WINCHEL**, b. of Windsor, Dec. 25, 1730	2	136
Simon, of Windsor, m. Mrs. Elizabeth **LATHROP**, of		
Tolland, Dec. 2, 1736	2	136
Symon, d. [ ], in "Elenton" prior to 1740	MG	
Taylor, m. Ann **ELSWORTH**, b. of Windsor, Nov. 1, 1759	2	137
Taylor, s. Taylor & Ann, b. Apr. 25, 1764	2	551
Taylor, had d. [ ], b. Nov. 5, 1765; d. Nov. 30, 1765	2	551
------, wid., m. Samuell **CROSS**, July 12, 1677	MG	
------, contributed 0-10-6 to the poor in other colonies	MG	
CHASE, Charles A., of Warehouse Point, m. Nancy H.		
POMEROY, of New London, Apr. 11, 1841, by Ezra S.		
Cook	2	475
[CHAUNCEY], **CHANCY**, Abiah, s. Charles, b. Jan. 22, 1699	1	8
Abigall, d. [Isack], b. Oct. 14, 1677	Col. 1	56
Abigayl, d. [Nathanell & Abigayl], b. Oct. 14, 16[ ];		
bp. same day	MG	
Cathrien, [d.] Nathaniel, b. Jan. 12, [16]75	1	7
Charles, s. [Isack], b. Sept. 3, 1679	Col. 1	56
Charles, s. [Nathanell & Abigayl], b. Sept. 3, [16]79;		
bp. [Sept.] 7, [1679]; d. Oct. 31, [16]79	MG	
Charles, of Fairfield, m. Sarah **WOLCOTT**, of Windsor, Mar.		
16, 1698/9	1	55
Ichabod Wolcott, s. Charles, b. Jan. 4, 1703/4	1	8
Isack, s. Nathanell & Abigayl, b. Sept. [5], [16]74;		
bp. Sept. 6, [16]74	MG	

	Vol.	Page
[CHAUNCEY], CHANCY, (cont.)		
Kettarn, d. [Isack], b. Jan. 12, 1675	Col.1	56
Kathren, d. Nathanell & Abigayl, b. Jan. 12, 1675;		
bp. [Jan.] 16, [1675]	MG	
Nathaniel, adm. ch. & communicant Jan. [ ],1667	MG	
Nathanell, adm. ch. Jan. 12, 1667	MG	
Nathanell, of Windsor, m. Abigayl **STRONG**, d. Elder John,		
at Northampton, Nov. 12, 1673	MG	
Nathanell, m. Abigail **STRONG**, d. of Elder **STRONG**, Nov.		
12, 1673, at Northampton	Col.1	46
Nathanell, s. Isack, b. Sept. 6, 1674	Col.1	56
Robert, s. Charles, b. Nov. 29, 1701	1	8
Sarah, w. Charles, d. Jan. 5, 1703/4	1	42
-----, resumed practice of publicly catechizing		
candidates for church membership June 21, [16]64	MG	
-----, Mr., taxed 2-0 on Feb. 10, [16]73	MG	
-----, Mr., had 2 children b. in Windsor. Dated Aug. 17,		
1677	MG	
-----, communicant 16[ ]	MG	
-----, [ ], [16]	MG	
-----, Mr., contributed 1-0-0 to the poor in other colonies	MG	
CHESTER, Mary, Mrs., m. John **WOOLCOTT**, Feb. 14, 1676	Col.D	54
Sara, of Wethersfield, m. Simon **WOLCOT**, of Windsor,		
Dec. 5, 1689	Col.D	54
Sarah, of Weathersfield, m. Simon **WOLCOTT**, of Windsor,		
Dec. 5, 1689	1	63
CHURCH, Samuel, m. Sophronia **CLARK**, b. of Windsor, Apr.		
28, 1824, by Rev. Augusuts Bolles	2	138
Sarah, m. Arba **GRANNIS**, b. of Windsor, July 24, 1839, by		
Rev. Cephas Brainard	2	481
CIBBE, [see under **KIBBE**]		
CIESAR*, Emeline, m. Asahel **WILLIAM**, Oct. 1, 1829, by		
Henry A. Rowland *(In pencil)	2	212
CLAPP, CLAP, Alexander, m. Huldah **GRISWOLD**, b. of		
Windsor, Mar. 22, 1837, by Rev. Eli Deniston	2	490
Alexander, m. Jane **BAILEY**, Oct. 16, 184[sic?], by Giles		
Ellswoth, J. P.	2	508
Charles, m. Jennett **ENO**, b. of Windsor, Feb. 8, 1842, by		
Ezra S. Cook	2	515
Preserve, s. Capt. Roger, of Dorchester, m. Sarah **NUBERY**,		
d. Capt. Benjamin, of Windsor, June 4, 1668, by Mr.		
Talcutt	1	55
Preserve, see Presance **CLAY**	Col.1	45
Spencer, Jr., of Easthampton, Mass., m. Drusilla M.		
THRALL, of Windsor, Jan. 26, 1848, by T. A. Leete	2	496
William, m. Emerette **GRISWOLD**, b. of Windsor, July 7,		
1839, by Rev. Cephas Brainard	2	475
Zebulah, of Norwich, Mass., m. Adeline **HEMPSTED**, of		

	Vol.	Page
CLAPP, CLAP, (cont.)		
Windsor, Oct. 3, 1822, by Rev. Henry A. Rowland	2	469
CLARK, CLARKE, Abigail, d. Benoni & Abigail, b. Apr. 16,		
1763	2	551
Ann, d. John, b. Jan. 12, 1706/7	2	16
Ann, d. John, d. Aug. 16, 1713	2	222
Ann, d. Solomon, b. Apr. 24, 1722	2	18
Ann, d. Solomon & Ann, b. Apr. 24, 1722	2	18
Augusta F., m. David **PINNEY**, b. of Windsor, Apr. 31,		
1848, by Rev. Cephas Brainard	2	501
Aurelia, m. William **BLEVIN**, of Hartford, Dec. 31, 1828, by		
John B. Ballard	2	150
Benjamin, s. Benoni & Abigail, b. Apr. 4, 1761	2	551
Benoni, s. John, b. Oct. 21, 1708	2	16
Benoni, m. Abigail **LATTEMORE**, b. of Windsor, Apr. 12,		
1759	2	137
Betsey, Mrs. of Windsor, m. Josiah **STANNARD**, of Haddam,		
Apr. 21, 1839, by Rev. Daniel Heminway	2	206
Bushrod, of Granby, m. Juliann **GRISWOLD**, of Windsor,		
Aug. 11, 1825, by Richard Niles, J. P.	2	139
Bushrod, of Granby, m. Juliann **GRISWOLD**, Aug. 11, 1825,		
by Richard Niles, J. P.	2	140
Cornelia, of Windsor, m. Isaac **ROBERTS**, of West		
Springfield, Apr. 3, 1834, by Henry A. Rowland	2	506
D., his w. [ ], adm. ch. [ ] 22, [16]58	MG	
Danell, adm. ch. & communicant June [ ], 1643	MG	
Daniell, m. Mary **NEWBERY**, June 13, 1644	MG	
Daniell, his child d. [ ], [16]48	MG	
Daniell, s. [Daniell & Mary], b. Apr. 4, 1654	MG	
Daniell, s. Daniell, b. Apr. 4, 1654	Col.2	157
Daniell, s. Daniell, b. Apr. 4, 1654	Col.2	181
Daniel, s. Daniel, b. Apr. 4, 1654	1	7
Dani[e]ll, [bp] Apr. 10, [16]54	MG	
Daniell, had 9 children b. in Windsor. Dated Aug. 17, 1677	MG	
Daniell, s. John, b. Dec. 31, 1704	2	16
Daniell, Capt., d. Aug. 12, 1710, in the 88th y. of his age or		
there about	2	222
Daniell, s. John & Kaziah, b. Dec. 24, 1760	2	550
David, s. Samuel, b. Apr. 7, 1696	1	7
Deborah, d. John & Kaziah, b. Apr. [ ], 1757	2	550
Deliverance, d. Josiah & Deliverance, b. [ ]	2	310
Elias, s. Benoni & Abigail, b. May 6, 1765	2	552
Elisabeth, d. [Daniell & Mary], b. Oct. 28, 1651	MG	
Elizabeth, d. Daniel, b. Oct. 28, 1651	1	7
Elisabeth, of Windsor, m. Moses **COOKE**, of Warronock,		
Nov. 25, 1669	Col.1	45
Elizabeth, of Windsor, m. Mooses **COOK**, of Worronoke,		
Nov. 25, 1669	1	55

	Vol.	Page
CLARK, CLARKE, (cont.)		
Elisabeth, d. John, b. May 16, 1701	2	16
Elisabeth, d. Ezekiel & Elisabeth, b. Oct.10, 1750	2	310
Elisabeth, see Elisabeth **COOK**	MG	
Ezekiel, s. Solomon & Ann, b. Feb. 5, 1728/9	2	19
Fanny, m. Alfred **GRIFFIN**, b. of Windsor, Nov. 27, 1823, by Richard Niles, J. P.	1	160
Frances, m. Thomas **DEWEY**, Mar. 22, 1638	MG	
Frances, m. Thomas **DEWEY**, Mar. 22, 1638	1	55
Hanna, d. [Daniell & Mary], b. Aug. 29, 1665; d. [ ]	MG	
Hannah, d. Daniel, b. Aug. 29, 1665	1	7
Hannah, m. Thomas **GILLET**, Feb. 26, 1704/5	2	153
Hannah, of Symsbury, m. Charles **THRALL**, of Windsor, Mar. 24, 1744	2	205
Hannah M., m. Joseph W. **BAKER**, b. of Windsor, Apr. 12, 1849, by T. A. Leet	2	504
Harriet, m. Levi G. **GRISWOLD**, b. of Windsor, Jan. [ ], 1826, by Richard Niles, J. P.	2	480
Henry, his [sister & wid. of [ ] **FOX**, d. Apr. 13*], [16]73 *(In pencil)	MG	
Henery, his sister wid. [ ] **FFOX**, d. Apr. 13, 1673	Col.1	58
Henry, his s. [ ] & wid. of [ ] **FOX**, d. Apr. 13, [16]73	1	43
Henry, m. Chloe **RILEY**, Jan. 1, 1821, by Rev. Henry A. Rowland	2	138
Hezakiah, s. Benoni & Abigail, b. Aug. 18, 1767	2	552
Hosea, s. Solomon & Ann, b. Mar. 10, 1730/1	2	307
Ira, m. Fidelia **ALLYN**, Oct. 18, 1840, by S. D. Jewett	2	475
Isaac S., m. Fidelia **PHELPS**, [, 1835], by Richard G. Drake, J. P.	2	471
Jason, m. Dolly B. **WATROUS**, b. of Windsor, Aug. 1, 1821, by Augustus Bolles	2	469
Jemimah, d. John & Keziah, b. Feb. [ ], 1759	2	550
Joel B., m. Jane **GRISWOLD**, b. of Windsor, June 12, 1836, by Rev. James Shugley, of No. Granby	2	472
John, s. [Daniell & Mary], b. Apr. 10, 1656	MG	
John, s. Daniell, b. Apr. 10, 1656	Col.2	158
John, s. Daniel, b. Apr. 10, 1656	1	7
John, [bp.] Apr. 15, [16]56	MG	
John, s. John, d. Mar. 6, 1708/9	2	222
John, d. Sept. [ ], 1715	2	222
John, s. Solomon, b. July 1, 1720	2	17
John, s. John & Kaziah, b. Oct. 26, 1755	2	550
John S., m. Eunice A. **LOOMIS**, Mar. 5, 1833, by H. A. Rowland	2	470
Joseph, s. Joseph, bp. Sept. 30, 1638	1	7
Joseph, his w. [ ], d. Apr. 3, 1639	MG	
Joseph, bd. Apr. 19, 1641	1	42
Joseph, d. [ ], [16]41	MG	

	Vol.	Page
CLARK, CLARKE, (cont.)		
Joseph, d. May 2, [16]59	1	42
Joseph, d. [ ], [16]59	MG	
Joseph, had 2 children b. in Windsor. Dated Aug. 17, 1677	MG	
Joseph, s. Samuel, b. July 13, 1697	1	7
Joseph, s. Samuel, d. July 7, 1718	2	222
Joseph Adams, of Simsbury, m. Catherine **TURNBULL**, of Windsor, June 18, 1843, by Rev. S. D. Jewett	2	517
Josiah, s. Daniel, b. Jan. 21, 1648	1	7
Josiah, s. Josiah, b. Jan. 1683	Col.D	51
Josiah, s. Josiah, b. Jan. 13, 1682	1	7
Josiah, s. Solomon & Ann, b. Jan. 25, 1726/7	2	18
Josias, s. [Daniell & Mary], b. Jan. 21, 1648	MG	
Josias, [bp.] Jan. 28, [16]48	MG	
Judson, m. Almira T. **BARBER**, Oct. 24, 1831, by Henry A. Rowland	2	470
Keziah, d. John & Keziah, b. Apr. 14, 1751	2	311
Lydia, of Symsbury, m. Elijah **OWEN**, of Windsor, Mar. 8, 1762	2	185
Martha, d. John, b. Mar. 19, 1697	2	16
Martha, m. James **EGELSTON**, b. of Windsor, Aug. 28, 1718	2	145
Martha, d. Solomon & Ann, b. Nov. 5, 1733	2	307
Martha, d. John & Keziah, b. Oct. 9, 1753	2	311
Martha, m. Eli **HOSKINS**, b. of Windsor, Aug. 13, 1772	2	164
Martha I., of Windsor, m. James E. **CHADWICK**, of Buffalo, N. Y., June 17, 1851, by Cornelius B. Everest	2	497
Mary, d. Joseph, bp. Sept. 30, 1638	1	7
Mary, d. Daniel, b. Apr. 24, 1645	1	6
Mary, m. John **STRONG**, Jr., Nov. 26, 1656	MG	
Mary, m. John **STRONG**, Nov. 26, 1656	Col.2	159
Mary, m. John **STRONG**, b. of Windsor, Nov. 26, 1656	1	61
Mary, d. [Daniell & Mary], b. Sept. 22, 1658	MG	
Mary, d. Daniel, b. Sept. 22, 1658	1	7
Mary, bp. Sept. 26, [16]5[ ]	MG	
Mary, m. John **GAYLOR**, Dec. 13, 1683	Col.D	54
Mary, m. John **GAYLORD**, Dec. 13, 1683	1	57
Mary, w. Capt. Daniel, d. Aug. 29, 1688	1	42
Mary, w. Capt. Daniel, d. Aug. 29, 1688	1	44
Mary, of Windsor, m. Samuel **COOLEY**, of Springfield, Oct. 24, 1711	2	135
Mary Morton, m. Charles **KUCHEL**, b. of Hartford, Jan. 16, 1849, by Rev. Charles R. Fisher	2	169
Meheteble, w. Samuel, d. Aug. 15, 1723	2	223
Monimia, of Windsor, m. Joel **ROCKWELL**, of Granville, Mass., July 7, 1823, by Rev. Augustus Bolles, of Wintonbury	2	196
Morgan, m. Julia **FOX**, of Windsor, Jan. 27, 1830, by		

	Vol.	Page
CLARK, CLARKE, (cont.)		
Henry A. Rowland	2	140
Nathanell, s. [Daniell & Mary], b. Sept. 8, 1666	MG	
Nathanell, s. Daniell. Sept. 8, 1666	Col.1	55
Nathanael, s. Daniel, b. Sept. 8, 1666	1	7
Nathanael, [bp.] Sept. 9, [16]66	MG	
Nathanael, s. Samuel, b. Oct. 11, 1699	1	8
Oliver, s. Ezekiel & Elizabeth, b. Feb. 6, 1747/8	2	310
Oliver, s. Moses & Ursuler, b. Apr. 2, 1781	2	554
Russell T., of Hartford, m. Sarah N. **MATHER,** of Windsor, Oct. 3, 1838, by Rev. Cephas Brainard	2	475
Samuell, s. [Daniell & Mary], b. July 6, 1661	MG	
Samuel, s. Daniel, b. July 6, 1661	1	7
Samuell, [bp.] July 7, [16]61	MG	
Samuel, s. Samuel, b. Nov. 10, 1688	1	7
Samuel, m. Cordelia **BLANCHARD,** Nov. 29, 1832, by Henry A. Rowland	2	470
Sary, d. [Daniell & Mary], b. Aug. 7, 1663	MG	
Sarah, d. Daniel, b. Aug. 7, [16]63; bp. the 9th day	1	7
Sara, [bp.] Aug. 9, [16]63	MG	
Sarah, d. John, b. Oct. 28, 1702	2	16
Sarah, wid. of Farmington, m. Job **ELSWORTH,** of Windsor, Oct. 25, 1711	2	145
Solomon, s. John, b. May 20, 1699	2	16
Sollomon, m. Ann **EGELSTON,** b. of Windsor, Feb. 24, 1719/20	2	135
Solomon, s. Solomon & Ann, b. Sept. 25, 1725	2	18
Sophronia, m. Samuel **CHURCH,** b. of Windsor, Apr. 28, 1824, by Rev. Augustus Bolles	2	138
Sumner, m. Prudence B. **MURPHY,** Mar. 15, 1841, by Ezra S. Cook	2	475
Susan, m. George W. **MUNN,** Jan. 14, 1821, by James Loomis, J. P.	2	492
Silvia, m. Eleazer **GAYLORD,** b. of Windsor, Aug. 24, 1780	2	159
Theodocia, d. Solomon & Ann, b. Aug. 8, 1723	2	18
William, m. Ruth W. **MOORE,** Jan. 9, 1828, by Rev. Henry A. Rowland	2	469
------, Mr., his sister d. Sept. 5, [1640]	MG	
------, adm. communion June 18, 1643	MG	
------, Capt., his w. [ ], adm. ch. & communicant Apr. [ ], 1658	MG	
------, Capt., taxed 4-0 on Feb. 10, [16]73	MG	
------, Capt., contributed 0-5-0 to the poor in other colonies	MG	
CLARKHAN, ------, Mrs., m. John **MURPHY,** Oct. 15, 1852, by Rev. James Smyth	2	460
CLARKSON, Peter, m. Mary Jane **TAB,** Sept. 5, 1852, by Rev. James Smyth	2	460

	Vol.	Page
CLAY, Presance*, s. Capt. Roger, of Dorchester, m. Sara NEWBERY, d. Capt. Beniamen, of Windsor, June 4, 1668, by Mr. Talcott *(Note by LBB: "Preserve CLAPP")	Col.1	45
CLEAVELAND, Cyrus, of Dalton, Mass., m. Elizabeth GRISWOLD, of Windsor, Dec. 14, 1826, by Rev. Tobias Spirer	2	139
COATS, Elizabeth, of Windsor, m. James BURT, of Springfield, Sept. 28, 1851, by C. B. Everest	2	504
COGGINS, COGGENS, Bathsheba, m. John BARBER, Sept. [ ], [16]	MG	
Bathsheba, of Springfield, m. John BARBER, of Windsor, Sept. 2, 1663	Col.1	45
Martha, m. Peter BUELL, b. of Windsor, Mar. 31, 1670	Col.1	45
Mary, m. Samuell BARBER, [ ], [16]	MG	
Mary, m. Samuell BARBER, Dec. 1, 1670, by Capt. Newbery	Col.1	46
Mary, see Mary BARBER	MG	
COGSWELL, Sarah, d. Joseph & Elizabeth, b. Mar. 31, 1754	2	311
Sarah, w. Joseph, d. Apr. 15, 1754	2	224
COLGROVE, COLGRAVE, Allyn Mather, s. Joseph & Hannah, b. Dec. 27, 1790	2	556
Almena, d. Joseph & Hannah, b. Feb. 16, 1793	2	556
Hannah, d. Joseph & Hannah, b. Aug. 12, 1788	2	555
COLLINS, Abigail, of Hartford, m. Salmon McKEE, of Glastenbury, July 7, 1822, by Rev. Augustus Bolles	2	494
Anson A., m. Sally Maria NEWBERRY, b. of Windsor, Mar. 14, 1827, by Rev. Augustus Bolles	2	139
Elizabeth, of Hartford, m. Joab GRISWOLD, of Windsor, Oct. 6, 1763	2	158
Mary, of Wallingford, m. Salvanus GRISWOLD, of Windsor, Apr. 1, 1762	2	158
Mary, of Wallinsford, m. Salvanus GRISWOLD, of Windsor, Apr. 1, 1762	2	353
Nathan, m. Anna COOLEY, ae about 30, Feb. 6, 1710/11; Samuel WARNER & Ebenezer WARINER made affidavit before John Hollihock, J. P., that Int. Pub. of said Nathan COLLENS & Anna COOLEY, also her mother did not wish the marriage	2	135
COLT, Esther, m. Stephen LOOMIS, b. of Windsor, Jan. 1, 1690	1	58
Jabez, s. J[ ], b. Apr. 1, 1703	1	8
Joseph, m. Ruth LOOMIS, Oct. 29, 1691	1	55
Joseph, d. Jan. 11, 1719	2	222
COLTON, Abigaell, of Springfield, m. Francis GRISWOLD, of Windsor, Dec. 7, 1703	2	154
Jonathan, of East Windsor, m. Mary PHELPS, of Windsor, Mar. 31, 1831, by Stephen Crosby	2	140
COOK, COOKE, A[a]ron, s. [Capt. Aaron], bp. Feb. 21, 1640	MG	
Aaron, s. Aaron, bp. Feb. 21, 1640	Col.2	151

	Vol.	Page
COOK, COOKE, (cont.)		
Aaron, s. Aaron, bp. Feb. 21, 1640	1	6
Aaron, had 7 children b. in Windsor. Dated Aug. 17, 1677	MG	
Aaron, s. Nathaniel, b. Apr. 22, 1715	2	17
Aaron, s. Joseph & Jochebah, b. Oct. 1, 1745	2	309
Abel, s. Theophilus, Jr. & Hannah, b. Apr. 12, 1755	2	311
Abigall, d. [Nathanell & Lidia], b. Mar. 1, 1659	MG	
Abigail, d. Nathanael, b. Mar. 1, [16]59/60	1	7
Abigayl, bp. Mar. 7, [16]59	MG	
Abigael, d. Nathaniell, b. Jan. 12, 1705/6	2	15
Abigail, w. Eliakim, d. Apr. 4, 1760	2	224
Abigail, d. Benjamin & Abigail, b. Apr. 27, 1760	2	549
Abijah, s. Theophilus, Jr. & Hannah, b. Sept. 26, 1773	2	553
Abner, s. Richard & Martha, b. May 6, 1737	2	308
Abner, m. Ann HOSKINS, b. of Windsor, Feb. 18, 1762	2	137
Abner, s. Abner & Ann, b. Nov. 13, 1765	2	551
Abner, s. Abner & Margret, b. Dec. 21, 1796	2	554
Agnis, d. Joel & Sarah, b. Aug. 29, 1767	2	553
Alexander, s. Theophilus, Jr. & Hannah, b. Aug. 19, 1766	2	552
Allen, m. Mary GRISWOLD, Sept. 1, 1831, by Henry A. Rowland	2	470
Allis, w. Thomas, d. June 13, 1705	2	222
Almira, m. Norman COOK, b. of Windsor, May 22, 1827, by Luther Fitch, J. P.	2	140
Almira G., m. Francis W. MADISON, of New York, Nov. 19, 1840, by S. D. Jewett	2	515
Ama, d. Josiah, Jr. & Hannah, b. Apr. 11, 1772	2	553
Amanda, of Windsor, m. Asa PRIOR, of East Windsor, Dec. 22, 1839, by Rev. W. C. Hoyt	2	501
Ann, d. William, b. Oct. 30, 1719	2	17
Ann, m. Charles PHELPS, Jr., b. of Windsor, Apr. 13, 1776	2	190
Annmariah, d. William & Keziah, b. Mar. 30, 1793	2	555
Anna, d. Elisha & Anna, b. Dec. 7, 1768	2	552
Anna, d. Elisha, d. Sept. 10, 1787	2	225
Anne, d. Joel & Sarah, b. Apr. 4, 1757	2	553
Asa, s. Noah & Lydia, b. July 10, 1766; d. Aug. 25, following	2	552
Ashbill, s. Theophilus & Hannah, b. Apr. 22, 1753	2	311
Benjamin, s. Nathaniel, b. Mar. 26, 1711	2	15
Benjamin, m. Abigail SKINNER, b. of Windsor, Nov. 30, 1758	2	137
Benjamin, s. Benjamin & Abigail, b. Sept. 3, 1765	2	551
Bettsena, d. Abner, Jr. & Margret, b. Aug. 28, 1788	2	554
Candice, m. David BLISH, June 20, 1836, by James Loomis, J. P.	2	499
Chloe, d. Noah & Lydia, b. Jan. 30, 1772	2	553
Chloe, m. Henry WRIGHT, b. of Windsor, Aug. 12, 1840, by Rev. Ezras Cook	2	515
Clera, d. Elisha & Anna, b. Sept. 24, 1783	2	554

	Vol.	Page
COOK, COOKE, (cont.)		
Daniell, s. Nathaniell, b. Jan. 9, 1693/4	2	15
Daniel, s. Abner & Ann, b. Apr. 10, 1763	2	550
David, twin with Jonathan, s. Theophilus & Mindwell, b. Jan. 26, 1733/4	2	307
David, d. July 1, 1796, in the 62nd year of his age	2	225
Delia, of Windsor, m. Samuel **VOLLENTINE**, of Eastbury, Sept. 18, 1828, by Henry A. Rowland	2	498
Dorithy, d. Nathaniell & Mary, b. July 20, 1721	2	308
Dudley, s. Richard & Martha, b. Feb. 14, 1732/3	2	19
Dudley, s. Richard & Martha, d. Dec. 28, 1754	2	224
Ebenezer, s. Nathaniell, b. June [ ], 1692	2	15
Ebenezer, s. Richard & Martha, b. Apr. 17, 1728	2	18
Edee, d. William, b. Dec. 30, 1717	2	17
Elikim, s. Benjamin & Abigail, b. June 18, 1762	2	550
Eliacem, Jr., contributed 0-2-6 to the poor in other colonies	MG	
Elijah*, s. Theophilus & Mindwel, b. Nov. 19, 1738 *("Phinehas" crossed out)	2	309
Elijah, s. Theophilus, Jr. & Hannah, b. Mar. 26, 1764	2	550
Elisha, s. John & Hannah, b. Feb. 14, 1721/2	2	19
Elisha, s. Dea. John & Hannah, b. Dec. 24, 1745	2	310
Elisha, m. Anna **RAYMOND**, b. of Windsor, Jan. 16, 1767	2	137
Elisha, s. Elisha & Anna, b. Aug. 13, 1769	2	552
Elisha, s. Abner & Ann, b. June 9, 1776; d. July 9, following	2	552
Elisha, s. Dea. John, d. May 24, 1785, in the 40th year of his age	2	224
Elisabeth, d. [Capt. Aaron], b. Aug. 7, 1653	MG	
Elizabeth, d. Aaron, b. Aug. 7, 1653	Col.2	151
Elizabeth, d. Aaron, b. Aug. 7, 1653	1	6
Elisabeth, wid. & d. Daniell **CLARK**, m. Job **DRAKE**, s. Job, Sept. 13, 1677	MG	
Elizabeth, wid., m. Job **DRAKE**, s. Job, Sept. 13, [16]77	Col.1	46
Elizabeth, wid., m. Job **DRAK[E]**, s. Job, Sr., Sept. 13, 1677	TR1	1
Elizabeth, wid., m. Job **DRAKE**, s. Job, Sr., Sept. 13, 1677	1	55
Elizbeth, m. Benjamin **GRISWOLD**, Jan. 4, 1693	1	57
Elizabeth, d. Nathaniell, b. Oct. 3, 1707	2	15
Elizabeth, m. Joseph **BARBOR**, Jr., b. of Windsor, June 18, 1728	2	129
Elizabeth, d. William & Kaziah, b. Feb. 24, 1791	2	555
Elizabeth, m. David **PEASE**, 2nd, Mar. 14, 1841, by Ezra S. Cook	2	501
Elkenah, s. Nathanael & Marah, b. May 31, 1738	2	309
Esther M., of Windsor, m. Reuben **SCOTT**, of Poultney, Vt., June 11, 1835, by John Bartlett	2	509
Fanny, m. Uriah **SMITH**, b. of Windsor, July 13, 1823, by James Loomis, J. P.	2	202
Francis, s. John, b. July 17, 1715	2	17
Frances, s. John (s. John), d. Nov. 17, 1722, ae about		

COOK, COOKE, (cont.)

	Vol.	Page
7 y. 4 m.	2	223
Francis, s. Dea. John & Hannah, b. Sept. 16, 1737	2	309
Francis, s. Dea. John & Hannah, d. Oct. 22, 1737	2	224
Frances Ellen, d. Thomas & Laware, b. Aug. 31, 1841	2	556
George, s. Josiah, Jr. & Hannah, b. Dec. 30, 1769	2	553
Hanna, d. [Nathanell & Lidia], b. Sept. 21, 1655	MG	
Hannah, d. Nathaniell, b. Sept. 21, 1655	Col.2	158
Hanna, d. Nathan[i]ell, b. Sept. 21, [16]55; m. Thomas BUCKLAND, [ ]; m. Joseph BAKER, Jan. 30, [16]76	MG	
Hanna, bp. Oct. 28, [16]55	MG	
Hanna, d. Nathanell, m. Thomas BUCKLAND, Oct. 21, 1675	Col.1	46
Hannah, m. Charles PHELPS, b. of Windsor, [17]	2	137
Hannah, d. Nathaniell & Mary, b. Jan. 13, 1718/19	2	307
Hannah, d. Richard & Martha, b. June 29, 1726	2	18
Hannah, d. Dea. John & Hannah, b. Aug. 7, 1742	2	309
Hannah, d. Theophilus, Jr. & Hannah, b. Feb. 12, 1762	2	550
Hannah, m. Josiah COOK, Jr., b. of Windsor, Apr. 14, 1762	2	137
Hannah, d. Nathanael, b. Sept. 21, [ ]	1	6
Harriet S., m. Lemuel A. WELCH, Jan. 12, 1848, by Rev. Samuel A. Stedman	2	519
Horace F., m. Faney M. DANIELS, b. of Windsor, Nov. 25, 1849, by Rev. Sameul W. Law	2	497
Horace M., m. Almira G. FISH, Nov. 16, 1834, by Richard G. Drake, J. P.	2	471
Isaac, s. Theophilus, Jr. & Hannah, b. July 5, 1757	2	311
Jemimah, d. Nathaniell, b. Sept. 23, 1709	2	15
Jemima, m. Mathew ROCKWELL, b. of Windsor, Jan. 19, 1743/4	2	195
Joanna, d. [Capt. A[a]ron], b. or bp. Aug. 5, 1638	MG	
Joanna, d. Aaron, bp. Aug. 5, 1638	Col.2	151
Joanna, d. Aaron, bp. Aug. 15, 1638	1	6
Joanna, m. Simon WOOLCOT, Mar. 19, 1656	Col.2	159
Joanna, m. Simon WOLCOTT, b. of Windsor, Mar. 19, 1656/7	1	63
Joanna, d. Josiah, b. May 24, 1719	2	17
Joanna, m. Samuel MARSHEL, Jr., b. of Windsor, Nov. 17, 1743	2	178
Joanna, see Simon WOOLCOT	Col.2	160
Job, s. Dea. John & Hannah (2nd w.), b. Apr. 19, 1740	2	309
Joel, s. Richard & Martha, b. Mar. 17, 1734/5	2	307
Joel, s. Joel & Sarah, b. May 19, 1763	2	553
John, s. [Nathanell & Lidia], b. Aug. 3, 1662	MG	
John, s. Nathanell, b. Aug. 3, [16]62	Col.1	54
John, s. Nathanael, b. Aug. 3, 1662	1	7
John, bp. Aug. 10, [16]62	MG	
John, of Windsor, m. Sarah FISKE, of Wenham, Sept. 14,		

	Vol.	Page
COOK, COOKE, (cont.)		
1688	1	55
John, s. John, b. Nov. 3, 1692	1	7
John, Sr., d. Feb. 27, 1711/12	2	222
John, s. John, decd., m. Hannah **DRAKE**, d. Symon, decd., July 15, 1714	2	135
John, s. John (s. John), b. June 14, 1719	2	17
John, Dea., m. Hannah **LOOMIS**, b. of Windsor, Jan. 1, 1735/6	2	136
John, Dea., d. May 25, 1751	2	224
Jonathan, twin with David, s. Theophilus & Mindwell, b. Jan. 26, 1733/4	2	307
Joseph, s. Nathaniel, b. Apr. 1, 1713	2	17
Joseph, m. Jochebah **MILLINGTON**, b. of Winsor, Nov. 26, 1744	2	136
Josia, s. [Nathanaell & Lidia], b. Dec. 22, 1664	MG	
Josia, s. Nathanell, b. Dec. 22, 1664	Col.1	55
Josiah, s. Nathanel, b. Dec. 22, 1664	1	7
Josia, [bp.] Dec. 25, [16]64	MG	
Josiah, s. Josiah, b. Aug. 4, 1690	1	8
Josiah, of Windsor, m. Sarah **PONDER**, of Westfield, Jan. 14, 1702/3	1	55
Josiah, m. Joanna **KELCY**, b. of Windsor, June 5, 1718	2	135
Josiah, s. Theophilus & Mindwel, b. Feb. 11, 1740/1	2	309
Josiah, Jr., m. Hannah **COOK**, b. of Windsor, Apr. 14, 1762	2	137
Josiah, s. Josiah, Jr. & Hannah, b. Oct. 13, 1766	2	552
Josiah, d. Dec. 4, 1773	2	224
Justin, m. Fanny **MOORE**, Jan. 18, 1835, by Henry A. Rowland	2	471
Keziah, d. Josiah, Jr. & Hannah, b. July 18, 1762	2	550
Lewis, of Hartford, m. Lucia **LATHAM**, of Windsor, Nov. 6, 1836, by Rev. Eli Deniston	2	513
Louisa, of Windsor, m. Daniel W. **FROST**, of Hartford, Jan. 14, 1847, by Rev. George F. Kettell	2	478
Lucie, d. Richard & Martha, b. July 20, 1730	2	18
Lucy, d. Richard, d. Apr. 21, 1747	2	224
Lidia, d. [Nathanell & Lidia], b. Jan. 9, 1652	MG	
Lydia, d. Nathanael, b. Jan. 9, 1652	Col.2	152
Lydia, d. Nathanael, b. Jan. 9, 1652	1	6
Lidia, bp. Jan. 17, [16]52	MG	
Lidia, d. May 23, [16]76, ae 24	MG	
Lidia, d. Nathanell, d. May 23, [16]76, in her 24th y.	Col.1	58
Lidia, d. Nathanaell, d. May 23, [16]76, in her 24th y.	1	42
Lydia, d. Nathaniell, b. Mar. 13, 1696/7	2	15
Lydia, wid., d. June 14, 1698	1	42
Lydia, d. Nathaniell & Mary, b. Feb. [ ], 1724	2	308
Lydia, d. Joseph & Jochebah, b. Feb. 1, 1746/7	2	310
Lyda, d. Noah & Lyda, b. Jan. 26, 1759	2	549

	Vol.	Page
COOK, COOKE, (cont.)		
Lydia, m. Enoch **DRAKE**, b. of Windsor, [17]	2	141
Marah, d. Nathanael & Mary, b. Nov. 26, 1736	2	308
Margerit, d. Theophilous, b. July 20, 1722	2	17
Margaret, d. Noah & Lydia, b. Apr. 25, 1764	2	550
Martha, d. Tho[mas], d. Nov. 8, [16]83	Col.D	56
Martha, d. Thomas, d. Nov. 8, [16]83	1	42
Mary, d. Thomas, d. Mar. 10, 1688/9	1	42
Mary, d. Nathaniell, b. Jan. 16, 1700/1	2	15
Mindwell, d. Theophilous, b. Dec. 14, 1724	2	18
Mindwell, d. May 7, 1801, in the 78th y. of his age	2	225
Mirriam, d. [Capt. Aaron], bp. Mar. 12, 1642	MG	
Miriam, d. Aaron, bp. Mar. 12, 1642	Col.2	151
Meriam, d. Aaron, bp. Mar. 12, 1642	1	6
Mooses, s. Aaron, b. Nov. 13, 1645	1	6
Moses, s. [Capt. Aaron], bp. Nov. 16, 1645	MG	
Mooses, s. Aaron, bp. Nov. 16, 1645	1	6
Moses, s. Aaron, bp. Nov. 16, 1645	Col.2	151
Moses, of Warroncok, m. Elisabeth **CLARKE**, of Windsor, Nov. 25, 1669	Col.1	45
Mooses, of Worronocke, m. Elizabeth **CLARK**, of Windsor, Nov. 25, 1669	1	55
Mooses, s. Mooses, b. Apr. 17, [16]75; bp. [ ] 21, [ ]	1	7
Moses, d. May 5, 1714	2	223
Moses, d. May 15, 1714	2	222
N., his w. [ ], adm. ch. & communicant Aug. [ ], 1652	MG	
Nama, d. Abner & Ann, b. July 16, 1767	2	552
Nancy, m. Crayton **FOWLER**, b. of Hartford, July 24, 1843, by Rev. S. D. Jewett	2	478
Nat[han], his w. [ ], adm. ch. Aug. 29, [16]52	MG	
Nathanell, m. Lidia **VORE**, June 29, 1649	MG	
Nathanael, m. Lydia **VOAR**, June 29, 1649	1	55
Nathanell, s. [Nathanell & Lidia], b. May 13, 1658	MG	
Nathanael, s. Nathanael, b. May 13, 1658	1	7
Nathanell, bp. May 16, [16]58	MG	
Nathaniel, adm. ch. & communicant June 22, 1662	MG	
Nathanel, adm. ch. June 22, 1662	MG	
Nathanell, had 7 children b. in Windsor. Dated Aug. 17, 1677	MG	
Nathanael, d. May 19, 1688	1	42
Nathaniel, s. Nathaniell, b. Apr. 6, 1689	2	15
Nathanell, communicant 16[ ]	MG	
Nathanell, contributed 0-1-0 to the poor in other colonies	MG	
Nathanel, Jr. & his sister contributed 0-1-3 to the poor in other colonies	MG	
Nathanael, Jr., m. Mary **BROOKS**, Feb. 19, 1717/18	2	135
Nathanael, d. Feb. 28, 1724/5	2	223
Nathaniell, s. Nathaniell & Mary, b. Mar. 2, 1726	2	308

	Vol.	Page
COOK, COOKE, (cont.)		
Noah, s. [Capt. Aaron], b. June 14, 1657	MG	
Noah, s. Aaron, b. June 14, 1657	Col.2	161
Noah, s. Aaron, b. June 14, 1657	1	6
Noah, s. Theophilous & Mindwell, b. May 7, 1736	2	307
Noah, m. Lydia **WESTLAND**, b. of Windsor, Feb. 21, 1758	2	137
Noah, s. Noah & Lyda, b. Sept. 5, 1761	2	550
Norman, m. Almira **COOK**, b. of Windsor, May 22, 1827, by Luther Fitch, J. P.	2	140
Olive, d. Elisha & Ann, b. May 1, 1774	2	553
Olive, d. Elisha, d. Sept. 1, 1775	2	224
Olive, d. Elisha & Ann, b. June 12, 1776	2	553
Phena, d. Elisha & Ann, b. Aug. 12, 1771	2	553
Phena, d. Elisha, d. Sept. 17, 1788	2	225
Pinney, s. Joel & Sarah, b. Jan. 19, 1765	2	553
Reuben, s. Richard, b. Feb. 5, 1722/3	2	17
Ruben, s. Abner & Margret, b. Mar. 23, 1795	2	554
Richard, s. Nathaniell, b. Aug. 30, 1703	2	15
Richard, m. Martha **EVINS**, b. of Windsor, Apr. 11, 1722	2	136
Rodney, m. Lorania **MOORE**, b. of Windsor, Mar. 8, 1825, by Richard Niles, J. P.	2	139
Roger, s. Theophilus, Jr. & Hannah, b. Dec. 4, 1768	2	552
Roswell, s. Abner, Jr. & Margret, b. May 29, 1791	2	554
Ruth, d. Josiah, b. Apr. 22, 1692	1	8
Ruth, w. Josiah, d. Sept. 29, 1697	1	42
Ruth, d. Josiah, Jr., b. Apr. 4, 1723	2	17
Ruth*, m. Noah **MARSHEL**, b. of Windsor, Jan. 19, 1748/9 *("Joanna" crossed out)	2	179
Ruth, d. Noah & Lydia, b. June 23, 1767	2	552
Samuell, d. [ ], [16]49	MG	
Samuell, s. [Capt. Aaron], b. Nov. 21, 1650	MG	
Samuel, s. Aaron, b. Nov. 21, 1650	1	7
Samuel, s. Aaron, bp. Nov. 22, 1650	Col.2	151
Samuel, s. Aaron, b.*, Nov. 22, 1650 *(bp.)	1	6
Samuel, s. Theophilous & Mindwell, b. July 6, 1726	2	18
Samuel, m. Dorothy **GILLET**, b. of Windsor, Nov. 25, 1747	2	137
Samuell, s. Samuel & Dorothy, b. Apr. 29, 1748	2	310
Samuel, s. Samuel & Jane, b. July 15, 1748	2	310
Sara, m. Richard **SAXTON**, Apr. 16, [164[ ]	MG	
Sarah, m. Richard **SAXTON**, Apr. 16, 1647	1	61
Sara, d. [Nathanell & Lidia], b. June 28, 1650	MG	
Sarah, [d.] Nathaniel, b. June 28, 1650; bp. Oct. 17, [16]52	MG	
Sarah, d. Nathanael, b. June 28, 1650	Col.2	151
Sara, m. Samuell **BAKER**, Jan. 30, 1670	MG	
Sara, m. Samuell **BARKER***, b. of Windsor, June 30, [16]70 *(Note by LBB: "BAKER")	Col.1	45
Sarah, d. Nathaniell, b. Feb. 10, 1690/1	2	15
Sarah, d. John, m. Josiah **GRANT**, Mar. 30, 1710	2	154

	Vol.	Page
COOK, COOKE, (cont.)		
Sarah, d. Nathaniell, b. Josiah **GRANT**, Aug. 4, 1714	2	154
Sarah, d. John (s. John), b. June 22, 1717	2	17
Sarah, d. Nathaniell & Mary, b. Oct. 31, 1731	2	308
Sarah, m. Asahel **SPENCER**, b. of Windsor, Dec. 25, 1736	2	199
Sarah, d. Dea. John & Hannah, b. Mar. 15, 1748/9	2	310
Sarah, d. Joseph & Jochebah, b. Nov. 23, 1750	2	310
Sarah, d. Joseph & Jochebah, d. Sept. 7, 1753	2	224
Sarah, d. Joseph & Jochrbah, b. May 12, 1754	2	311
Sarah, d. Joel & Sarah, b. July 26, 1755	2	553
Sarah, d. Josiah, Jr. & Hannah, b. Apr. 11, 1764	2	550
Sarah, d. Nathan, b. June 24, [ ]	1	6
Sarah, m. Samuel **ALLYN**, b. of Windsor, [ ]	1	53
Seliner, m. Joel A. **LOOMIS**, b. of Windsor, Jan. 24, 1847,		
by George F. Kettell	2	491
Shuball, s. Theophilus, Jr. & Hannah, b. Apr. 20, 1751	2	310
Simeon, s. Nathaniell & Mary, b. Oct. 18, 1729	2	308
Sula, d. Elisha & Anna, b. May 7, 1779	2	554
Theophilous, m. Mindwell **HOLCOMB**, b. of Windsor, Sept.		
26, 1721	2	136
Theophilous, s. Theophilous & Mindwell, b. June 3, 1729	2	18
Theophilus, Jr., m. Hannah **GRAYHAM**, b. of Windsor, Oct.		
19, 1746	2	137
Theophilus, s. Theophilus, Jr. & Hannah, b. Jan. 5, 1749/50	2	310
Thomas, d. Nov. 18, 1697	1	42
Thomas, had negro Peter, d. Aug. 6, 1715	2	222
Thomas, had negro William, d. Sept. 30, 1722	2	222
Thomas, d. Nov. 29, 1724	2	223
Timothy, s. Theophilus, Jr. & Hannah, b. Jan. 30, 1746/7	2	310
William, s. Josiah, b. Nov. 4, 1695	1	8
William, m. Edei **DRAKE**, b. of Windsor, Feb. 28, 1716/17	2	135
William, s. Theophilus, Jr. & Hannah, b. Dec. 11, 1759	2	549
William, of Windsor, m. Keziah **MATSON**, of Hartford, May		
13, 1790	2	137
COOLEY, Abigail, of Springfield, m. Henry **WOLCOT**, Jr., of		
Windsor, Dec. 28, 1716	2	208
Anna, ae about 30, m. Nathan **COLLENS**, Feb. 6, 1710/11.		
Affidavit made before John Hollihock, J. P., by Samuel		
WARNER & Ebenezer **WARINER**, of Springfield, that		
Int. had been Pub. and that her mother did not wish the		
marriage	2	135
Deborah, of Springfield, m. Joshua **LOOMIS**, Oct. 26, 1715	2	170
Mary, of Springfield, m. Joseph **LOOMIS**, Jr., of Windsor,		
June 28, 1710	2	170
Mary, m. Timothy **WOODWORTH**, Sept. 28, 1829, by Asa		
Bushnell, Jr.	2	212
Samuel, of Springfield, m. Mary **CLARK**, of Windsor, Oct.		
24, 1711	2	135

	Vol.	Page

COOLIDGE, Sally, m. John **SMITH**, June 11, 1826, by Rev.
    David Miller   2   507

[COOMBES], COMBS, Amanda, m. John **CROSLEY**, Nov. 13,
    1836, by Rev. Eli Deninston   2   489

COOPER, Joseph M., of Springfield, Mass., m. Susan Ann
    ENDERTON, of Suffield, July 4, 1825, by Rev. Henry
    A. Rowland   2   138

COPLEY, COPLY, COOPLEY, Elizabeth, m. Nathanell
    PHELPS, Sept. 17, 1650   MG

    Elizabeth, wid., m. Nathanael **PHELPS**, Sept. 17, 1650   1   60

    Nathanael, m. Mary **GAYLORD**, b. of Windsor, Apr. 30,
    1730   2   136

    Nathaniel, s. Nathaniel & Mary, b. Apr. 9, 1733   2   19

    Nathaniel, m. Esther **GRISWOLD**, b. of Windsor, Sept. 19,
    1749   2   136

    Noah, s. Nathaniell & Esther, b. June 25, 1746   2   309

CORCORAN, Bridget, m. Patrick **GAYNOR**, Sept. 12, 1852, by
    Rev. James Smyth   2   460

CORNING, Elizabeth, d. Josiah & Hannah, b. Apr. 10, 1808   2   556

    Hannah, of Hollenston, m. Elijah **BLOCHET**, of Windsor,
    Aug. 15, 1746   2   132

    Josiah, m. Ursula **WELLS**, Oct. 15, 1834, by Henry A.
    Rowland   2   471

    Levi Crosby, s. Josiah & Hannah, b. June 2, 1810   2   556

    Mary, of Enfield, m. Bigget **EGELSTONE**, of Windsor, Nov.
    7, 1745   2   146

CORNISH, Damiris, of Windsor, m. William **TULLER**, of
    Symsbury, Apr. 12, 1711   2   204

    Elizabeth, d. James, b. Sept. 25, 1695   1   7

    Elizabeth, of Westfield, m. Phillip **MINOR**, of Windsor, May
    31, 1704   1   59

    Gabriel, of Westfeild, m. Eliz[abeth] **WOOLCOT**, d. George,
    Dec. 15, 1686   Col.D   54

    Gabriell, of Westfield, m. Elizabeth **WOLCOTT**, d. George,
    Dec. 15, 1686   1   55

    Gabrel, contributed 0-1-3 to the poor in other colonies   MG

    James, of Westfield, m. Elizabeth **THRALL**, of Windsor,
    Nov. 10, 1693   1   55

    James, contributed 0-5-0 to the poor in other colonies   MG

    Joseph, s. James, b. Oct. 18, 1697   1   7

    Julia Ann, m. Theodore C. **CADWELL**, Sept. 2, 1835, by
    John Bartlett   2   471

    Phebe, m. Shubael **GRISWOLD**, b. of Windsor, Nov.* 3,
    1725 *("Dec." crossed out)   2   156

    Sarah, m. John **PHELPS**, Jr., b. of Windsor, Oct. 24, 1728   2   187

    ------, taxed 4-0 on Feb. 10, [16]73   MG

COSSITT, Moses, m. Chloe **HUMPHREY**, Apr. 15, 1835, by
    Rev. Ansel Nash   2   471

	Vol.	Page
COSTO, Michael, m. Honora LALLY, Sept. 7, 1852, by Rev.		
James Smyth	2	460
COTTON, COTTEN, Dorithy, d. Sebrow, b. Nov. 11, 1656	1	7
Seboun, had 1 child b. in Windsor. Dated Aug. 17, 1677	MG	
COY, David, s. David & Abigail, b. May 19, 1759	2	549
Eunice, d. Uriah & Hannah, b. Dec. 11, 1758	2	550
Hannah, d. Uriah & Hannah, b. Sept. 4, 1761	2	550
Josiah, s. Samuel, b. Jan. 31, 1764	2	554
Mabel, d. Samuel, b. Feb. 5, 1757	2	553
Temphena, d. Samuel, b. Jan. 3, 1766	2	554
CRAA——, —— had 1 child d. [ ], in "Elenton" prior		
to 1740	MG	
CRANE, Anne, m. Samuel BARTLET, b. of East Windsor, Sept.		
14, 1767	2	466
Elishama, m. Sarah BISSELL, b. of Windsor, Dec. 31, 1741	2	136
Hezekiah, m. Rachel ROCKWELL, Apr. 2, 1747	2	136
Hezekiah, s. Hezekiah & Rachel, b. Aug. 7, 1747	2	310
Rhoda, m. Job THOMSON, b. of Windsor, July 12, 1750	2	205
CRANTON, Francis, of Gilford, m. Samuel DIBLE, Sr., of		
Windsor, Mar. 25, 1703	1	55
CRESEY, Welthe Ann, d. Benjamin & Welthe, b. Nov. 18, 1788	2	554
CROCKER, Elihu, d. Nov. 4, 1768	2	224
Lucius, m. Elizabeth BARNES, b. of Lee, Mass., June 17,		
1833, by Rev. Henry Robinson	2	470
[CROFOOT], [see under CROWFOOT]		
CROSBY, Harriet, m. Luke GRAHAM, May 20, 1841, by Rev. S.		
D. Jewett	2	481
Thomas, m. Abigail BOARDWINE, Aug. 24, 1826, by Rev.		
Henry A. Rowland	2	139
CROSLEY, John, m. Amanda COMBS, Nov. 13, 1836, by Rev.		
Eli Deninston	2	489
CROSS, Ann, of Windsor, m. Jeremiah M. SPENCER, of		
Hartford, Dec. 3, 1826, by Rev. Joseph Hough	2	507
Hanna, d. [Samuell], b. Jan. 11, [16]78	MG	
Hanna, d. Samuell, b. June 11, 1678	Col.1	56
[Hanna], [d. Samuell], d. July 7, 1680	MG	
Hannah, d. John, b. Apr. 10, 1694	1	7
Hannah, d. John, d. Dec. [ ], 1696	1	42
John, m. Mary GRANT, Nov. 3, 1686	Col.D	54
John, m. Mary GRANT, Nov. 3, 1686	1	55
John, d. July 23, 1721	2	222
Mary, wid., d. June 24, 1726	2	223
Mary, d. Peter & Sarah, b. June 3, 1759	2	549
Peter, s. Peter & Sarah, b. Dec. 17, 1756	2	549
Samuell, m. wid. Chapman, July 12, 1677	MG	
Samuell, m. Elizabeth CHAPMAN, wid. Edward, July 12,		
[16]77	Col.1	46
Samuell, m. Elizabeth CHAPMAN, wid. Edward, July 12,		

	Vol.	Page
DANIELS, (cont.)		
1830, by John Bartlett	2	144
DANKS*, Elizabeth, of Northampton, m. Barnard **BARTLET**, of		
Windsor, Jan. 14, 1702 *("**DUNKS**?")	1	54
Mary, m. Joshua **WILLIS**, Jr., May 19, 1709	2	207
DARE, DEARE, Sara, m. Thomas **PARSON**, Dec. 24, 1668	MG	
Sara, m. Thomas **PARSONS**, Dec. 24, [16]6[8]?, by Mr.		
Wolcott	Col.1	45
Sarah, m. Thomas **PARSONS**, Dec. 6, 1668, by Mr. Wolcott	1	60
DART, Simeon, d. Dec. 4, 1763	2	228
DAVIS, DAVICE, Bezaliel, of Simsbury, m. Achsah **CADWELL**,		
of Windsor, Sept. 29, 1830, by J. P. Bullard	2	472
Deborah, d. Nathaniell & Mary, b. Oct. 12, 1740	2	314
Isaac, Jr., of Windsor, m. Rachel **SHELDEN**, of Suffield,		
May 15, 1745	2	142
Isaac P., of Northampton, m. Nancy **STRATTON**, Nov. 19,		
1840, by S. D. Lewett	2	145
Nathanel, of Windsor, m. Mary **GLEASON**, of Enfield, Oct.		
4, 1739	2	142
Rachel, d. Isaac & Deborah, b. Feb. 15, 1722	2	23
Rebeckah, of Harwinton, m. John **THRALL**, of Windsor, Oct.		
18, 1748	2	205
DAWSON, Catharine, m. Henry **SHEFFINGTON**, Nov. 21, 1852,		
by Rev. James Smyth	2	460
DAY, Ezra, of Ottawa, Ill., m. Nancy **PARMELE**, of Windsor,		
May 18, 1848, by Rev. Cephus Brainard	2	474
Grove, m. Lois **ELLSWOTH**, b. of Windsor, Dec. 11, 1822,		
by Rev. Oliver Willson, of North Haven	2	472
Isaac, m. Sarah **MAY**, Apr. 17, 1823, b. of Windsor, by		
Richard Niles, J. P.	2	472
Jonathan, d. Sept. 9, 1721	2	226
Justus, s. Nathan & Deborah, b. Apr. 10, 1735	2	312
Mary A., m. Calvin W. **HOSKINS**, Sept. 5, 1847, by		
Samuel A. Seaman	2	484
Nancy, of Windsor, m. Henry W. **ENDERS**, of Suffield, Jan.		
5, 1875, by R. K. Reynolds	2	519
Nathan, m. Deborah **PORTER**, b. of Windsor, Dec. 15, 1729	2	142
Oliver, s. Nathan & Deborah, b. Jan. 3, 1732/3	2	312
Sterling, of Windsor, m. Susan **BARKER**, of Enfield, Aug.		
11, 1824, by Richard Niles, J. P.	2	144
William W., of Windsor, m. Emeline E. **RUSSELL**, of		
Springfield, Mar. 12, 1848, by Cephus Brainard	2	474
DAYTON, Henry W., of Glastenbury, m. Amanda **SOUTHARD**,		
of Ware, Mass., Apr. 5, 1847, by Rev. T. A. Leete	2	473
DEARE, [see under **DARE**]		
DEMING, DEMEN, DEMMING, Abigail, of Hartford, m.		
Humphrey **PINNEY**, of Windsor, July 22, 1717	2	187
Giddings, m. Loviey **BIDWELL**, Aug. 5, 1823, by Rev. John		

	Vol.	Page
DEMING, DEMEN, DEMMING, (cont.)		
Bartlett. Int. Pub.	2	144
Levi L., m. Laura R. **ROBERTS**, Oct. 12, 1840, by Rev. Ezra		
S. Cook	2	473
-----, had 2 children d. [ ], in "Elenton" prior		
to 1740	MG	
DENISON, George G., m. Mary Ann **CADWELL**, b. of		
Springfield, Oct. 28, 1841, by Rev. S. D. Jewell	2	473
DENSLOW, DENSLO, Abigayl, d. [Henery], b. Feb. 6, 1655	MG	
Abigaile, d. Henery, b. Feb. 6, 1655	Col.1	54
Abigail, d. Henry, b. Feb. 6, 1655	1	9
Abigall, d. [John & Mary], b. Nov. 7, 1677; bp. July 14,		
[16]78	MG	
Abigall, d. John, d. Apr. 5, 1690	Col.D	57
Abigail, d. John, d. Apr. 5, 1690	1	43
Abraham, s. [John & Mary], b. Mar. 8, 1669	MG	
Albert, m. Eliza **FISH**, Sept. 18, 1827, by Rev. Henry A.		
Rowland	2	144
Albert, m. Eliza **FISH**, Sept. 18, 1827, by [ ]* *(Entry		
crossed out)	2	153
Anne, d. Joseph & Anne, b. Nov. 15, 1735	2	312
Anne, wid. of Windsor, m. Joseph **WINCHEL**, of Suffield,		
Apr. 11, 1751	2	209
Benajah, s. Joseph & Anne, b. June 6, 1743	2	314
Benajah, s. Joseph & Ann, d. Sept. 10, 1746	2	227
Beniamen, s. [John & Mary], b. Mar. 30, 1668	MG	
Benjamin, d. Nov. 23, 1688	1	42
Benjamin, s. Samuel, b. Mar. 29, 1701	1	10
Benjamin, s. Samuel, Jr. & Sarah, b. July 30, 1743	2	314
Benjamin, s. John, b. Mar. 30, [ ]	1	9
Benoni, m. Sarah **GRISWOLD**, Nov. 17, 1748	2	142
Debora, d. [Henery], b. Dec. 21, 1657; m. [ ]	MG	
Debora, d. Henery, b. Dec. 21, 1657	Col.1	54
Deborah, d. Henry, b. Dec. 21, 1657	1	9
Debro, m. John **HOSKINES**, Jan. 21, 1677	MG	
Debra, m. John **HOSKINS**, Jan. 29, 1677	Col.1	46
Debora, m. John **HOSKINS**, Jan. 29*, 1677 *(In pencil		
"21"?)	TR1	1
Deborah, m. John **HOSKINS**, Jan. 29, 1677	1	58
Elihu, s. Samuell, Jr. & Hannah, b. Aug. 13, 1757	2	318
Elijah, s. Samuel & Sarah, b. May 9, 1738	2	313
Eliza, m. Ephraim **HARRIS**, Jan. 27, 1831, by Henry A.		
Rowland	2	485
Elisabeth, d. [Henery], b. Feb. 11, 1665	MG	
Elisabeth, d. Henery, b. Feb. 11, 1665	Col.1	55
Elizabeth, d. Samuel, b. Mar. 9, 1692/3	1	9
George, s. [John & Mary], b. Apr. 8, 1672	MG	
George, d. Jan. 17, 1737/8	2	227

	Vol.	Page
DENSLOW, DENSLO, (cont.)		
H., his w.[ ], adm. ch. & communicant Apr. [ ], 1665	MG	
Hannah, d. Henry, b. Sept. 3, 1646	1	9
Hannah, [d. Henery], b. Mar. 1, 1661	MG	
Hanna, d. Henery, b. Mar. 1, 1661	Col.1	54
Hannah, d. Henry, b. Mar. 1, 1661	1	9
Hanna, d. Hanna, b. Nov. 14, 1690	Col.D	51
Hanna, had d. Hanna, b. Nov. 14, 1690	Col.D	51
Hannah, d. Samuel, b. Nov. 14, 1690	1	9
Hannah, m. John **BISSELL,** Feb. 22, 1710/11	2	128
Hannah, d. Samuel & Sarah, b. Apr. 24, 1746	2	315
Hannah, m. Moses **WING,** b. of Windsor, Dec. 13, 1781	2	512
Henry, his w. had [ ], bp. Jan. 31, [16]55	MG	
Henry, his w. [ ], adm. to ch. Apr. 2, [16]55	MG	
Henery, had 8 children b. in Windsor. Dated Aug. 17, 1677	MG	
Henry, his w. [ ], adm. ch. Apr. [ ], [16]	MG	
Huldah, d. Martin & Lois, b. Apr. 3, 1771	2	556
Huldah, m. Moses **WING,** b. of Windsor, Apr. 8, 1793	2	512
Isack, s. [John & Mary], b. Apr. 12, 1674	MG	
Isaac, s. John, b. Apr. 12, 1674	1	9
Joel, s. Benoni & Sarah, b. Apr. 28, 1758	2	319
John, m. Mary **EGGLESTON,** b. of Windsor, Jan. 7, 1653	Col.2	159
John, m. Mary **EGELSTON,** June 7, 1655	MG	
John, s. [John & Mary], b. Aug. 13, 1656	MG	
John, s. John, b. Aug. 13, 1656	Col.1	54
John, s. John, b. Aug. 13, 1656	1	9
John, had 9 children b. in Windsor. Dated Aug. 17, 1677	MG	
John, Sr., d. Sept. 14, 1689	Col.D	57
John, Sr., d. Sept. 14, 1689	1	42
John, m. Elizabeth **STYLES,** b. of Windsor, Mar. [ ], 1720/1	2	141
John, d. Oct. 25, 1732	2	226
John, contributed with flax 0-0-9 to the poor in other		
colonies	MG	
Joseph, s. [John & Mary], b. Aug. 12, 1665	MG	
Joseph, s. John, b. Aug. 12, 1665	Col.1	54
Joseph, s. Samuel, b. Mar. 24, 1703/4	1	10
Joseph, m. Ann **HOLCOMB,** b. of Windsor, Oct. 10, 1733	2	142
Joseph, s. Joseph & Anne, b. Sept. 25, 1734	2	312
Joseph, s. Joseph & Anne, d. Oct. 1, 1734	2	226
Joseph, s. Joseph & Anna, b. Dec. 9, 1740	2	314
Joseph, d. Oct. 2, 1749	2	227
Joseph Gaylord, s. Benoni & Sarah, b. June 6, 1769	2	557
Louisa Ann, m. Edward G. **HAYDEN,** Nov. 10, 1836, by		
Rev. Henry Robinson	2	489
Marcy, d. Henery, b. Apr. 10, 1651	Col.1	54
Martin, s. Joseph & Anne, b. Apr. 25, 1745	2	315
Martin, of Windsor, m. Lois **WIARD,** of Farmington, Apr.		
11, 1770	2	143

	Vol.	Page
DENSLOW, DENSLO, (cont.)		
Martin, s. Martin & Lois, b. Feb. 19, 1773	2	557
Mary, d. [Henery], b. Apr. 10, 1651	MG	
Mary, d. [John & Mary], b. Mar. 10, 1658	MG	
Mary, d. John, b. Mar. 10, [16]58	Col.1	54
Mary, d. John, b. Mar. 10, 1658	1	9
Mary, m. Thomas **ROWLY**, May 5, [16]69	MG	
Mary, m. Thomas **ROWLY**, May 5, 1669, by Mr. Wolcott	Col.1	45
Mary, m. Thomas **ROWEL**, May 5, 1669, by Mr. Wolcott	1	61
Mary*, w. John, d. Aug. 29, 1684 *(Note by LBB:		
"Mary (EGGLESTON) DENSLOW")	Col.D	56
Mary, w. John, d. Aug. 29, 1684	1	43
Mary, d. Samuel, Jr. & Mary, b. May 23, 1729	2	23
Mary, w. Samuel, Jr., d. May 25, 1729	2	226
Mary Caroline, of Windsor, m. Myron Safford **WEBB**, of		
Bennington, Vt., Oct. 12, 1800, by Dwight Ives, of		
Suffield	2	510
Nicolas, d. [Mar. 8*], [16]65, ae 90 *(In pencil)	MG	
Nicolas, d. Mar. 8, [16]66	Col.1	55
Olive, m. Walter **PEASE**, Jr., Sept. 4, 1822, by Rev. Henry		
A. Rowland	2	500
Oliver, s. Benoni & Sarah, b. May 15, 1756	2	318
Oliver, s. Joseph Gaylord & Olive, b. June 16, 1794	2	557
Patience, d. Samuel, d. Dec. 7, 1697	1	43
Patience, w. Samuel, d. Oct. 1, 1736	2	226
Patience, d. Samuel & Sarah, b. Sept. 5, 1740	2	314
Patience, m. John **ROSS**, b. of Windsor, Mar. [ ], 1763	2	196
Phebe, d. Enoni & Sarah, b. Sept. 22, 1763	2	557
Rebeca, [d. John & Mary], b. May 29, 1663	MG	
Rebeca, d. John, b. May 29, [16]63	Col.1	54
Rebekah, m. Samuel **OSBAND**, Feb. 7, [ ]	1	63
Rebeckah, m. Samuel **OSBORN**, [ ]	Col.D	54
Ruben, s. Samuel & Sarah, b. Aug. 4, 1735	2	312
Rosabella, d. Joseph & Ann, b. May 27, 1738	2	316
Rosarilla, d. Joseph & Anna, d. Oct. 4, 1740	2	227
Rosabella, d. Joseph & Ann, b. May 9, 1748	2	316
Rosabilla, d. Joseph & Ann, d. Oct. 21, 1749	2	227
Ruth, d. [Henery], b. Sept. 19, 1653	MG	
Ruth, d. Henery, b. Sept. 19, 1653	Col.1	54
Ruth, d. Henry, b. Sept. 19, 1653	1	9
Samuell, s. [Henery], b. Dec. 19, 1659	MG	
Samuell, s. Henry, b. Dec. 19, 1659	Col.1	54
Samuel, s. Henry, b. Dec. 19, 1659	1	9
Samuel, m. Patience **GIBBS**, Dec. 2, 1686	Col.D	54
Samuel, s. Samuel, b. July 14, 1697	1	10
Samuel, m. Mary **GRANT**, b. of Windsor, Mar. 7, 1727/8	2	141
Samuel, m. Sarah **CHAPMAN**, b. of Windsor, Oct. 1, 1730	2	141
Samuel, s. Samuel & Sarah, b. Apr. 24, 1733	2	312

	Vol.	Page
DENSLOW, DENSLO, (cont.)		
Samuel, d. Oct. 1, 1743	2	227
Samuel, Jr., m. Hannah **LEVIT**, b. of Windsor, May 24, 1756	2	143
Samuel, s. Samuel, Jr. & Hannah, b. Sept. 15, 1759	2	319
Sarah, d. Samuel, b. Feb. 13, 1694	1	9
Sarah, d. Samuell & Sarah, b. July 5, 1721	2	24
Sarah, d. Benoni & Sarah, b. Sept. 11, 1749	2	316
Sarah, d. Samuel & Sarah, d. July 23, 1756	2	228
Sarah, d. Benoni & Sarah, b. Apr. 30, 1761	2	319
Sarah, d. Benoni & Sarah, d. June 13, 1761	2	228
Sarah, d. Joseph Gaylord & Ollive, b. May 20, 1791	2	557
Submitte, d. Benoni & Sarah, b. May 15, 1765	2	557
Susan, m. George **MURPHY**, Nov. 23, 1820, by Rev. Henry A. Rowland	2	181
Susana, d. [Henery], b. Sept. 3, 1646	MG	
Susanna, d. Henery, b. Sept. 3, 1646	Col.1	54
Susanna, d. Henery, m. John **HODG[E]**, Aug. 1, 1666	MG	
Susanna, d. Henery, m. John **HODGE**, Aug. 1, 1666	Col.1	45
Susannah, d. Henry, m. John **HODG[E]**, Aug. 12, 1666	1	57
Susanna, m. John **HODGE**, Aug. 1, 16[ ]	MG	
Susanna, d. Aug. 26, 1683	Col.D	56
Susanna, d. Aug. 26, 1683	1	43
Thomas, s. [John & Mary], b. Apr. 22, 1661	MG	
Thomas, s. John, b. Apr. 22, [16]61	Col.1	54
Thomas, s. John, b. Apr. 22, 1661	1	9
Tryphena, d. Benoni & Sarah, b. Nov. 19, 1751	2	317
Zuhma, d. Benoni & Sarah, b. Mar. 13, 1754	2	318
-----, wid., d. [ ], [16]69, ae 84	MG	
-----, wid., d. Aug. 14, [16]69	Col.1	55
DEWEY, Anna, d. [Thomas & Frances], bp. Oct. 15, 1643	MG	
Ann, d. Thomas, bp. Oct. 15, 1643	1	8
David, s. Israel, b. Jan. 11, 1675	1	9
Frances, wid. Thomas, m. as 2nd w. George **PHELPS**, Nov. [ ], 164[ ]	MG	
Frances, m. George **PHELPS**, Nov. 30, 1648	1	60
Hannah, of Westfield, m. Benjamin **NUBERY**, of Windsor, Mar. 3, 1691/2	1	59
Isrell, s. [Thomas & Frances], b. Sept. 25, 1645	MG	
Isrell, s. [Thomas & Frances], b. Sept. 25, 1645; d. [ ]	MG	
Israel, s. Thomas, b. Sept. 25, 1645	1	8
Isrell, d. Oct. 23, 1678	MG	
Isrell, d. Oct. 23, [16]78	Col.1	58
Isrel, contributed 0-4-0 to the poor in other colonies	MG	
Isrel, his w. [ ] contributed 0-4-0 to the poor in other colonies	MG	
Jededia, s. [Thomas & Frances], b. Dec. 15, 1647	MG	
Jedidiah, s. Thomas, b. Dec. 15, 1647	1	8
John, d. June 23, [1640]	MG	

	Vol.	Page
DEWEY, (cont.)		
Joseph, s. Isrell, bp. Jan. 27, [16]77	MG	
Josia, s. [Thomas & Frances], bp. Oct. 10, 1641	MG	
Josiah, s. Thomas, bp. Oct. 10, 1641	1	8
Margerit, of Westfield, m. Daniel **BISSELL**, of Windsor, Oct. 27, 1692	1	54
Margarett, of Westfield, m. Daniel **BISSELL**, of Windsor, Nov. 27, 1692	2	128
Thomas, m. Frances **CLARK**, Mar. 22, 1638	MG	
Thomas, m. Frances **CLARK**, Mar. 22, 1638	1	55
Thomas, s. [Thomas & Frances], b. Feb. 16, 1639	MG	
Thomas, s. Thomas, bp. Feb. 16, 1639	1	8
Thomas, d. Apr. 27, 1648	MG	
Thomas, bd. Apr. 27, 1648	1	42
Thomas, d. [ ], [16]48	MG	
Thomas, had 5 children b. in Windsor. Dated Aug. 17, 1677	MG	
DEXTER, DEXTOR, Abigail Church, d. David & Mary, b. Apr. 25, 1802	2	558
Charles H., m. Lydia **PIERSON**, of Windsor, Sept. 19, 1838, by William Thompson	2	473
Charles Haskell, s. Seth & Sylvia, b. Sept. 19, 1810	2	558
David, s. Seth & Deborah, b. May 17, 1770	2	556
David, of Windsor, m. Mary **PITKIN**, of East Hartford, Dec. 22, 1796	2	472
David, s. David & Mary, b. Apr. 15, 1799	2	558
Deborah, d. Seth & Deborah, b. June 25, 1774	2	556
Deborah, m. Jerijah **BARBER**, b. of Windsor, May 26, 1796	2	467
Edward, s. David & Mary, b. Feb. 18, 1807	2	558
Harriet C., of Windsor, m. Edwin A. **DUGLAS**, of Stephentown, N. Y., Feb. 6, 1834, by Henry A. Rowland	2	473
Harriet Clark, d. Seth & Sylvia, b. Apr. 5, 1809	2	558
Horace, s. David & Mary, b. Dec. 29, 1803	2	558
James Pitkin, s. David & Mary, b. Sept. 8, 1797	2	558
Joanna, d. Seth & Deborah, b. Mar. 23, 1772	2	556
Lucretia, d. David & Mary, b. June 15, 1805	2	558
Mary, d. David & Mary, b. Oct. 17, 1800	2	558
Seth, d. Aug. 1, 1797, in the 53rd y. of his age	2	229
Seth, m. Sylvia **GAYLORD**, May 5, 1808	2	143
William, s. David & Mary, b. Sept. 13, 1809	2	558
DIBBLE, DEBLE, DIBLE, DEBL, DEBELL, Abigayl, d. [Samuell & "his former w."], b. Jan. 19, [16]66	MG	
Abigail, m. George **HAY**, Aug. 29, 1683	Col.D	54
Abigail, m. George **HAYES**, Aug. 29, 1683	1	58
Abigail, d. Wakefield, b. Oct. 1, 1703	1	10
Abigail, d. Abraham & Hannah, b. Mar. 30, 1728/9	2	23
Abraham, s. Abraham, d. Mar. 15, [16]76	MG	
Abraham, s. Abraham, d. Mar. 15, 1676	Col.1	58
Abraham, s. Abraham, d. [ ]; bd. May 15, 1676; ae 6 y.		

	Vol.	Page
DIBBLE, DEBLE, DIBLE, DEBL, DEBELL, (cont.)		
Feb. last	1	42
Abraham, s. Thomas, b. May 12, 1684	1	10
Abraham, s. Thomas, b. May 15, 1684	1	9
Abraham, m. Hannah **HORSFORD**, Aug. 18, 1709	2	141
Abraham, s. Abraham, b. May 4, 1711	2	20
Abram, s. Tho[mas], b. May 15, 1684	Col.D	51
Abram, contributed 0-1-3 to the poor in other colonies	MG	
Ann, d. Abraham, b. Dec. 16, 1714	2	21
Daniel, s. Abraham, b. Nov. 5, 1721/2	2	22
Daniel, s. Thomas & Hannah, b. Oct. 20, 1744	2	315
Ebenezer, s. [Thomas], bp. Sept. 26, [16]41; d. [ ]	MG	
Ebenezer, s. Thomas, bp. Sept. 21, 1641	Col.2	152
Ebenezer, s. Thomas, bp. Sept. 26, 1641	1	8
Ebenezer, m. Mary **WAKEFIELD**, Oct. 27, [16]63	MG	
Ebenezer, of Windsor, m. Mary **WAKEFELD**, of New		
Hauen, Oct. 27, 1663, by Mr. Jones, at New Hauen	Col.1	45
Ebenezer, bp. Dec. 11, [16]64	MG	
Ebenezer, d. [ ], [16]70	MG	
Ebenezer, s. Ebenezer, bp. Aug. 17, [16]71	MG	
Ebenezer, s. [Ebenezer & Mary], b. Aug. 18, 1671	MG	
Ebenezer, d. Dec. 19, [16]75, in war	MG	
Ebenezer, d. Dec. 19, 1675	Col.1	58
Ebenezer, d. Dec. 19, 1675	1	26
Ebenezer, d. Dec. 19, 1675	1	47
Ebenezer, had 5 children, b. in Windsor. Dated Aug. 17, 1677	MG	
Ebenezer, m. Mary **LOOMIS**, July 16, 1696	1	55
Elisabeth, d. [Osrell & Elisabeth], b. Mar. 27, 1673	MG	
Elizabeth, d. Isreal, b. Mar. 27, 1673	1	9
Elizabeth, w. Thomas, Sr., d. Sept. 15, 1689	1	43
Elizabeth*, w. Thomas, Sr., d. Sept. 25, 1689 *(Note by		
LBB: "Elizabeth (**HINSDALE**) **DEBLE**")	Col.D	57
Ezra, s. Wakefield, b. June 12, 1695	1	10
Ezra, s. Wakefield, d. June 20, 1695	1	43
Ezra, s. Wakeffield, b. Oct. 7, 1697	1	10
George, s. [Osrell & Elisabeth], b. Jan. 25, [16]75	MG	
George, s. Thomas, b. Apr. 13, 1687	1	9
George, s. Thomas, b. Apr. [ ], 1687	1	10
Hannah, d. Abraham, b. Dec. 2, 1712	2	21
Hannah, d. Abraham, d. Jan. 13, 1721/2	2	226
Hannah, d. Abraham, b. May 6, 1724	2	23
Hepsiba, d. [Thomas], bp. Dec. 25, [16]42	MG	
Hephziba, d. Thomas, bp. Dec. 25, 1642	Col.2	152
Hephzibah, d. Thomas, bp. Dec. 25, 1642	1	8
Hepsiba, m. Samuell **GIBBES**, Apr. 15, 1664	MG	
Hepsiba, m. Samuell **GIBBES**, Apr. 15, 1664, by Mr. Clark	Col.1	45
Hepsiba, d. [Samuell & Hepsiba], b. Dec. 19, 1669	MG	
Hephzibah, w. Samuel, d. Dec. 7, 1701	1	43

	Vol.	Page
DIBBLE, DEBLE, DIBLE, DEBL, DEBELL, (cont.)		
Isrell, s. [Thomas], b. Aug. 29, 1637	MG	
Israel, s. Thomas, b. Aug. 29, 1637	Col.2	152
Israel, s. Thomas, b. Aug. 29, 1637	1	8
Osrell, m. Elisabeth HULL, Nov. 28, 1661	MG	
Isreal, m. Elizabeth HULL, b. of Windsor, Nov. 28, 1661	1	55
Isrel, bp. Sept. 18, [16]70	MG	
Isrell, his w. [ ], bp. Oct. 6, [16]7[2]	MG	
Isrell, had 4 children b. in Windsor. Dated Aug. 17, 1677	MG	
Isrell, his s. [ ], d. Dec. 1, 1679	Col.1	58
Israel, d. Dec. 11, 1697	1	43
Joana, d.[ ], [16]51	MG	
Joanna, d. Samuel, b. Oct. 4, [16]72	1	9
Joanna, d. [Samuell & Hepsiba], b. Oct. 24, 1672	MG	
Johamiah, d. Thomas, b. Feb. 1, 1650	1	9
John, s. [Ebenezer & Mary], b. Feb. 9, 1673	MG	
John, s. Ebenezer b. Feb. 9, 1673	1	8
John, s. [Osrell & Elisabeth], b. Aug. 18, [16]78; bp. Oct. 6, [1678]	MG	
Joseph, s. Wakefield, b. May 26, 1696	1	10
Josias, s. [Osrell & Elisabeth], b. May 15, 1667	MG	
Josiah, s. Israel, b. May 15, [16]67	1	9
Martha, d. [Ebenezer & Mary], b. Mar. 10, 1669; d. [ ]	MG	
Martha, d. Ebenezer, b. Mar. 10, [16]69/70	1	8
Martha, d. Ebenezer, d. June 13, [16]70	Col.1	55
Martha, d. Abraham, b. Dec. 25, 1719	2	21
Mary, d. [Ebenezer & Mary], b. Dec. 24, 1664	MG	
Mary, d. Ebenezer, b. Dec. 24, 1664	Col.1	54
Mary, d. Ebenezer, b. Dec. 24, 1664	1	8
Mary, d. Ebenezer, b. Dec. 24, 1664	1	9
Mary, d. Ebenezer, b. Dec. 24, [16]64; bp. [Dec.] 25, [16]64	MG	
Mary, formerly w. Ebenzer, m. James HILLAR, June 28, 1677, by Capt. Newbery	Col.1	46
Mary, wid. Ebenezer, m. James HILLER, June 28, 1677, by Capt. Newbery	TR1	1
Mary, formerly w. Ebenezer, m. James HELLIOR, June 28, 1677, by Capt. Nubery	1	58
Mary, d. [Thomas, Jr. & Mary], b. Aug. 9, 1680	MG	
Mary, d. Ebenezer, m. John ENNO, s. James, May 10, 1681, by Capt. [ ] Newbery	MG	
Mary, d. Ebenezer, ae 17, m. John ENNO, s. James, ae 27, May 10, [16]81	Col.1	46
Mary, d. Thomas, Jr., d. Apr. 9, 1685	1	43
Mary, d. Tho[mas], d. Apr. 9, 1685	Col.D	56
Mary, d. Thomas, b. July 22, 1689	1	10
Mary, d. Ebenezer, b. Jan. 13, 1698/9	1	10
Mary, d. Wakefield, b. Mar. 5, 1698/9	1	10
Mary, m. Benjamin EGESTONE, b. of Windsor, Dec. 2,		

	Vol.	Page
DIBBLE, DEBLE, DIBLE, DEBL, DEBELL, (cont.)		
1708	2	145
Mary, d. Abraham, b. Sept. 24, 1716	2	21
Mary, m. Henry **CHAPMAN**, b. of Windsor, May 24, 1744	2	136
Mindwell, d. [Samuell & Hepsiba], b. Feb. 17, 1680	MG	
Miriam, d. [Thomas], bp. Dec. 7, [16]45	MG	
Miriam, bp. Dec. 7, [16]45	MG	
Miriam, d. Thomas, bp. Dec. 7, 1645	Col.2	152
Merriam, d. Thomas, bp. Dec. 7, 1645	1	8
Meriam, m. Jonathan **GILLET**, Jr., Dec. 14, [16]76	MG	
Meriam, d. Thomas, Sr., m. Jonathan **GILLET**, Sr., Dec. 14, 1676, by Capt. Newbery	Col.1	46
Meriam, m. Jonathan **GILLET**. Jr., Dec. 14, [16]76, by Capt. Unbery	TR1	1
Merriam, m. Jonathan **GILLIT**, Jr., Dec. 14, 1676, by Capt. Nubery	1	57
Mindwell, d. Samuell, b. Feb. 17, [16]80	Col.1	57
Patience, d. Samuel, b. Oct. 25, 1687	1	9
Rachel, d. Ebenezer, b. Jan. 23, 1699/1700	1	10
Samuel, bd. May 31, [1640]	MG	
Samuell, s. [Thomas], b. Feb. 19, [16]43; bp. Mar. 24, [16]43	MG	
Samuel, s. Thomas, bp. Mar. 24, 1643	Col.2	152
Samuel, s. Thomas, bp. Mar. 24, 1643	1	8
Samuell, m. Hepsiba **BARTLET**, Jan. 21, [1]6[ ]	MG	
Samuell, m. Hepseba **BARTLET**, b. of Windsor, Jan. 21, 1668, by Mr. Wolcott	Col.1	45
Samuel, m. Hephzibah **BARTLET**, b. of Windsor, Jan. 21, 1668, by Mr. Wolcott	1	55
Samuell, bp. Oct. 2, 1670	MG	
Samuell, s. [Samuell & Hepsiba], b. Apr. 13, 1675; d. Feb. 8, [ ]75	MG	
Samuell, 2nd, [s. Samuell & Hepsiba], b. May 4, 1677	MG	
Samuel, had 5 children, b. in Windsor. Dated Aug. 17, 1677	MG	
Samuell, s. Samuell, bp. May 13, [16]79	MG	
Samuel, Sr., of Windsor, m. Francis **CRANTON**, of Gilford, Mar. 25, 1703	1	55
Samuell, Sr., d. June 5, 1709	2	225
Sarah, d. Wakefield, b. Feb. 9, 1701/2	1	10
Thankfull, d. Samuell, b. June 19, 1685	Col.D	51
Thankful, d. Samuel, b. June 19, 1685	1	9
Thomas, s. [Thomas], b. Sept. 3, 1647	MG	
Thomas, s. Thomas, b. Sept. 3, 1647	Col.2	152
Thomas, s. Thomas, b. Sept. 3, 1647	1	8
Thomas, bp. Sept. 3, [16]47	MG	
Thomas, s. [Osrell & Elisabeth], b. Sept. 16, 1670	MG	
Thomas, Jr., m. Mary **TUKER**, of England, Oct. 10, [16]72	Col.1	46
Thomas, taxed 3-6 on Feb. 10, [16]73	MG	
Thomas, Jr., m. Mary **TUCKER**, Oct. 10, 1676	MG	

	Vol.	Page

DIBBLE, DEBLE, DIBLE, DEBL, DEBELL, (cont.)

	Vol.	Page
Thomas, Jr., m. Mary **TUCKER**, Oct. 10, 1676* *(In pencil "1672?")	TR1	1
Thomas, Jr., m. Mary **TUCKER**, Oct. 10, 1676	1	55
Thomas, had 6 children b. in Windsor. Dated Aug. 17, 1677	MG	
Thomas, s. [Thomas, Jr. & Mary], b. Aug. 21, 1677	MG	
Thomas, s. Thomas, bp. Aug. 26, [16]77	MG	
Thomas, Sr., communicant from Dorchester; living in Windsor, Dec. 22, 1677	MG	
Thomas, Jr. & Mary, had s. [ ], st. b. July 30, [16]79	MG	
[Thomas], his w.[ ], d. May 14, 1681	MG	
Thomas, Sr., his w. [ ], d. May 14, 1681	MG	
Thomas, Sr., his w. [ ], d. May 14, 1681	Col.1	58
Thomas, Sr., his w. [ ],, d. May 14, [16]81	1	42
Tho[mas], Sr., of Windsor, m. Eliz[abeth] **HENSDELL**, of Hadley, June 25, 1683	Col.D	54
Thomas, Sr., of Windsor, m. Elizabeth **HENSDELL**, of Hadly, June 25, 1683	1	55
Thomas, communicant 16[ ]	MG	
Thomas, adult, ch. mem. 16[ ]	MG	
Tho[ma]s, his w. [ ], ch. mem. 16[ ], from Dorchester	MG	
Thomas, Sr., d. Oct. 17, 1700	1	43
Thomas, s. Abraham, b. July 10, 1718	2	21
Thomas, of Windsor, m. Hannah **WOOLWORTH**, of Suffield, Dec. 22, 1743	2	142
Thomas, Sr., contributed 0-1-3 to the poor in other colonies	MG	
Wakefield, s. [Ebenezer & Mary], b. Sept. 15, 1667	MG	
Wakefield, s. Ebenez[e]r, [b.] Sept. 15, [16]67; bp. May 17, [16]68	MG	
Wakefield, s. Ebenezer, b. Sept. 15, 1667	1	8
Wakefield, m. Sarah **LOOMIS**, Dec. 27, 1692	1	55
Wakefield, m. Jane **FYLER**, Sept. 20, 1694	1	55
------, wid. Ebenezer, m. James **HILLAR**, June 28, [16]77	MG	
------, sister communicant from Dorchester; living in Windsor, Dec. 22, 1677	MG	
------, Sr., ch. mem. 16[ ], from Dorchester	MG	
DICKINSON, Azariah, of Rhoadtown, m. Eunice **STOUGHTON**, of Windsor, Sept. 16, 1747	2	143
Jonathan, of Rhoadtown, m. Dorathy **STOUGHTON**, of Windsor, Sept. 26, 1745	2	143
Nehemiah, of Rhodtown, m. Amy **STOUGHTON**, of Windsor, Nov. 14, 1749	2	143
DIGGONS, Joseph, s. Jerimiah, Jr., b. Apr. 2, 1710	2	20
Thomas, m. Mary **LOOMIS**, b. of Windsor, Dec. 31, 1719	2	141
Thomas, d. Mar. 11, 1719/20	2	226
DILL, Dorothy, m. Obadiah **FULLER**, b. of Windsor, July 16, 1772	2	152
DIXON, Henry, of New Canan, N. Y., m. Thankful **PETTIS**, of		

	Vol.	Page
DIXON, (cont.)		
Bolton, Conn., Oct. 24, 1830, by John Bartlett	2	473
William, m. Clarisa **MATHER**, b. of Windsor, Dec. 9, 1836, by Rev. Eli Deniston	2	145
DOD[D], Elizabeth, of Hartford, m. Nathanael **PORTER**, of Windsor, Oct. 3, 1838 [1738?]	2	188
DOLMAN, Elizabeth, see Elizabeth **FYLER**	Col.D	56
Elizabeth, of England, m. John **FFILAR**, of Windsor, Oct. 17, 1670, by Mr. Wolcot	Col.1	46
Elisabeth, m. John **FFYLAR**, Oct. 1[7?], 1672	MG	
DORCHESTER, DOCHESTER, Abigail, m. Jonathan **MASON**, b. of Windsor, Aug. 29, 1754	2	179
Alexander, see under John **DORCHESTER**		
John, s. Anthony, b. Nov. 5, 1644	1	9
John*, of Springfield, m. Sara **GAYLAR**, d. Samuell, of Windsor, Nov. 29, 1671, by Capt. Newbery *(Note by LBB: "Alexander")	Col.1	46
John, m. Mary **SLADE**, Dec. 13, 1744	2	142
Mary, d. John & Mary, b. Dec. 4, 1745	2	315
DOUGLASS, DOULASS, DUGLAS, DUGLES, Edwin A., of Stephentown, N. Y., m. Harriet C. **DEXTER**, of Windsor, Feb. 6, 1834, by Henry A. Rowland	2	473
Hannah, of New London, m. Thomas **KELCY**, of Windsor, Dec. 11, 1723	2	167
Hannah, d. Robert & Martha, b. Mar. 18, 1726/7	2	23
James, s. Robert & Martha, b. Oct. 2, 1721, at Sea	2	23
John, s. Robert & Martha, b. June 24, 1730	2	23
Martha, d. Robert & Martha, b. Dec. 24, 1722	2	23
Mercy, of Windsor, late of New London, m. Aaron **BARBER**, of Windsor, Feb. 2, 1724/5	2	129
DOUGTRUS, -----, of Westfield, Mass., m. Fanny **GRISWOLD**, of Simsbury, d. Elijah, Aug. 15, 1822, by John Bartlett. Int. Pub.	2	472
DOWLING, Cathrine, m. John **DUN[N]**, [ ] [1852], by Rev. James Smyth	2	460
DOWNING, Alexander, m. Mary E. **CHAPIN**, May 9, 1847, by Rev. Theodore A. Leete	2	473
Jenette L., m. John C. **BUSH**, b. of Windsor, Apr. 4, 1847, by Rev. George F. Kettell	2	499
DOWNS, Burrett, of New Haven, m. Laury F. **HOLCOMB**, of Windsor, Oct. 16, 1849, by Rev. Cephus Brainard	2	474
DOYLE, Jane, of Suffield, m. George W. **ALLEN**, of Windsor, Apr. 12, 1848, by S. H. Allen	2	463
DRAKE, DRAK, Aaron, s. Jacob, b. Nov. 25, 1710	2	20
Aaron, d. May 20, 1734	2	226
Aaron, d. May 20, 1734 (Crossed out)	2	312
Aaron, s. Jacob & Kathraien, b. Aug. 30, 1735	2	226
Aaron, s. Jacob & Catherin, b. Aug. 30, 1735	2	317

	Vol.	Page
DRAKE, DRAK, (cont.)		
Aaron, s. Josiah & Hannah, b. Apr. 13, 1751	2	317
Aaron,m. Chlotilde **GILLETT**, b. of Windsor, July 21, 1757	2	143
Abell, s. Josiah, b. Mar. 24, 1710/11	2	20
Abigayl, d. [Job & Mary], b. Sept. 28, 1648	MG	
Abigail, d. Jobe, b. Sept. 28, 1648	Col.2	152
Abigail, d. Job, b. Sept. 28, 1648	1	8
Abigail, d. Lemuel & Abigail, b. Apr. 22, 1752	2	317
Abigail, m. Abijah **MOORE,** b. of Windsor, Aug. 20, 1772	2	180
Abigail, m. Edwin **CHAPMAN,** Apr. 29, 1824, by Rev. Henry A. Rowland	2	138
Abigail, m. William **HOWARD,** Nov. 15, 1829, by Henry A. Rowland	2	484
Abner, s. Thomas & Eunice, b. Sept. 23, 1758	2	318
Adonis, d. Jacob, Jr. & Rhoda, b. May 12, 1765	2	319
Almira, m. Alonzo **SMITH,** Nov. 26, 1835, by H. A. Rowland	2	509
Amasa, s. Thomas & Eunice, b. Dec. 8, 1750	2	317
Amelia, m. James **ANDREWS,** Jan. 21, 1847, by T. A. Leete	2	465
Amee, d. Jeremiah, b. Sept. 22, 1724	2	23
Amy, d. Samuel & Amy, b. Oct. 24, 1749	2	316
Amy, d. Samuel & Amy, b. Apr. 18, 1750	2	228
Amy, d. Samuel & Amy, b. July 7, 1755	2	319
Ann, d. Joseph, b. Jan. 30, 1701	2	20
Ann, w. Joseph, d. Aug. 28, 1716	2	225
Ann, d. Jeremiah, b. Sept. 2, 1722	2	22
Ann, d. Jeremiah, b. Sept. 2, 1722 (This entry crossed out)	2	108
Ann, m. Ebanezer **STYLES,** b. of Windsor, Nov. 2, 1725	2	198
Asahel, s. Jacob, b. June 24, 1722	2	22
Asahel, of Windsor, m. Damaras **KELSEY,** of Hartford, Feb. 7, 1744/5	2	142
Asahel, s. Asahel & Damaras, b. Oct. 10, 1745	2	317
Augustine, s. Job & Martha, b. Nov. 7, 1742	2	314
Aurel, d. Ebenezer, Jr. & Martha, b. Nov. 1, 1764	2	551
Benjamin, s. Job, d. Jan. 17, 1697/8	1	43
Benjamin, s. Joseph, b. Apr. 14, 1699	2	20
Benjamin, s. Jonathan, b. Feb. 1, 1709/10	2	20
Benjamin, s. Jonathan, d. Oct. 28, 1730	2	226
Cathrain, d. Jacob & Catharain, b. July 5, 1729	2	23
Chloe, d. Aaron & Chlotilde, b. May 17, 1758	2	318
Creley, d. Job, 2nd & Hannah, b. June 12, 17[ ]	2	557
Cyrene, of Windsor, m. Chester **SEDGWICK,** of Hartford, Nov. 27, 1822, by Rev. John Bartlett. Int. Pub.	2	202
Damaras, d. Asahel & Damaras, b. Dec. 26, 1752	2	317
David, m. Elizabeth **STRONGE,** b. of Windsor, Mar. 12, 1747	2	142
David, Jr., m. Eunice **EGELSTON,** Dec. 12, 1820, by Rev. Henry A. Rowland	2	143

	Vol.	Page
DRAKE, DRAK, (cont.)		
Deborah, m. Asahel **OWEN,** b. of Windsor, June [ ], 1752	2	185
Delia, m. Daniel **PHELPS,** b. of Windsor, Apr. 4, 1832, by		
Rev. Henry A. Rowland	2	193
Darcos, d. Enoch, b. Sept. 11, 1723	2	22
Dudley, s. Enoch & Dorcas, b. Aug. 30, 1725	2	313
Ebenezer, s. Enoch & Dorcas, b. Nov. 28, 1729	2	313
Ebenezer, s. Nathanael & Elizabeth, b. June 12, 1739	2	313
Ebenezer, Jr., m. Martha **STEADMAN,** b. of Windsor, Feb.		
18, 1762	2	143
Edee, d. Simon, b. Nov. 14, 1697	1	10
Edei, m. William **COOKE,** b. of Windsor, Feb. 28, 1716/17	2	135
Edee, d. Phinehas & Edee, b. July 6, 1737	2	313
Edmund, of Windsor, m. Eliza Jane **KNOX,** of Hartford, Mar.		
18, 1849, by Rev. Cephus Brainard	2	474
Edward, m. Almira **GAYLORD,** Jan. 18, 1827, by Rev.		
Henry A. Rowland	2	144
Eliner, d. Thomas & Eunice, b. Oct. 27, 1756	2	318
Eleanor, m. Samuel W. **ELLSWORTH,** b. of Windsor, Nov.		
27, 1834, by H. A. Rowland	2	148
Elihu, s. Augustine & Mary, b. Sept. 24, 1763	2	319
Elihu, d. Jan. 17, 1839	2	229
Elijah, s. Enoch, Jr. & Mary, b. June 20, 1744	2	315
Elijah, s. Phinehas, b. Aug. 4, 1748	2	316
Elijah, s. Phenihas, d. Oct. 3, 1769	2	229
Elisabeth, m. William **GAYLOR,** b. of Windsor, Feb. 9, 1653	Col.2	159
Elizabeth, m. William **GAILER,** b. of Windsor, Feb. 9, 1653	Col.2	159
Elisabeth, d. [Job & Mary], b. Nov. 14, 1654	MG	
Elizabeth, d. Jobe, b. Nov. 14, 1654	Col.2	158
Elisabeth, d. Job, b. Nov. 14, 1654	1	8
Elisabeth, wid. of Windsor, m. John **ELDERKIN,** of New		
London, Mar. 1, 1660	Col.1	45
Elisabeth, d. [John & Hanna], b. July 22, 1664	MG	
Elizabeth, d. John, b. July 22, 1664	1	9
Elisabeth, [bp.] July 24, [16]64	MG	
Elisabeth, d. [ ] & Elisabeth, b. Nov. 2, 1675	MG	
Eliz[abeth], wid., d. Oct. 7, 1681	Col.D	56
Elizabeth, wid., d. Oct. 7, 1681	1	43
Eliz[abeth], m. Nicho[las] **BUCKLAND,** Mar. 3, 1685/6	Col.D	54
Elizabeth, m. Nicholas **BUCKLAND,** Nov. 3, 1685/6	1	54
Elizabeth, m. Joseph **ROCKWELL,** Jan. 23, 1694	1	61
Elizabeth, m. Enoch **DRAKE,** b. of Windsor, [,17]	2	141
Elizabeth, d. Enoch, b. Feb. 3, 1707/8	2	19
Elizabeth, w. Enoch, d. Apr. 2, 1717	2	225
Elizabeth, d. Jeremiah, b. May 4, 1721	2	22
Elizabeth, wid. Lieut. Job, d. Dec. 22, 1729	2	226
Elisabeth, m. John **GILLET,** b. of Windsor, Sept. 30, 1731	2	156
Elizabeth, d. Nathanael & Elizabeth, b. Sept. 8, 1732	2	311

	Vol.	Page
DRAKE, DRAK, (cont.)		
Elizabeth, d. Enoch, Jr. & Mary, b. Nov. 14, 1739	2	313
Elizabeth, d. Job & Jemima, b. Nov. 12, 1797	2	557
Elizabeth, d. Enoch, b. [ ]	2	22
Enock, s. [John & Hanna], b. Dec. 8, 1655	MG	
Enoch, s. John, b. Dec. 8, 1655	Col.2	181
Enoch, s. John, Jr., b. Dec. 8, 1655	1	9
Enock, [bp.] Dec. 10, [16]55	MG	
Enoch, ae 25, [on Dec.] 8, [1680], m. Sarah **PORTER,** who was ae 25 on June 5, 1680, Nov. 11, 1680	MG	
Enock, s. John, m. Sara **PORTER,** d. John, Sr., Nov. 11, 1680	Col.1	47
Enoch, s. Enoch, b. May 5, 1683	Col.D	51
Enoch, s. Enoch, b. May 5, 1683	1	9
Enoch, d. Aug. 21, 1698	1	43
Enoch, m. Lydia **COOK,** b. of Windsor, [,17]	2	141
Enoch, m. Elizabeth **DRAKE,** b. of Windsor, [,17]	2	141
Enoch, m. Elizabeth **BARBER,** Apr. 20, 1704	1	55
Enoch, s. Enoch, b. Jan. 12, 1705/6	2	19
Enoch, m. Dorcas **EGELSTON,** b. of Windsor, May 6, 1719	2	141
Enoch, m. Mary **BARBER,** b. of Windsor, May 1, 1735	2	142
Enoch, s. Enoch, Jr. & Mary, b. Aug. 24, 1741	2	314
Enoch, s. Enoch, b. [ ]	2	22
Esther, d. Jonathan, b. May 4, 1712	2	21
Ester, m. Dr. Joseph **SKINER,** b. of Windsor, Aug. 21, 1718	2	198
Esther, d. Jonathan, d. June 20, 1730	2	226
Esther, m. Hezekiah **HILLS,** b. of Windsor, Apr. 10, 1823, by Rev. Henry A. Rowland	2	165
[E]unice, d. Jonathan, b. Feb. 4, 1715/16	2	21
Eunice, d. Phinehas & Deborah, b. Apr. 5, 1740 (Crossed out)	2	309
Eunice, d. Phinehas & Deborah, b. Apr. 5, 1740	2	313
Eunice, d. Enoch, Jr. & Mary, b. June 22, 1749	2	317
Eunice, m. Isaac **HAYDON,** b. of Windsor, Jan. 25, 1753	2	163
Eunice, d. Enoch, b. [ ]	2	20
Eunice, d. Enosh, b. [ ]	2	22
Frances, s. Simon, b. Oct. 16, 1701	1	10
Frances, s. Symon, decd., d. June 5, 1715	2	225
Francis, s. Phinehas & Deborah, b. Apr. 12, 1733	2	311
Frances, s. Phinehas, d. Sept. 3, 1762	2	228
Frederick, m. Eliza D. **PHELPS,** b. of Windsor, Mar. 6, 1843, by Rev. S. D. Jewett	2	473
Frederick Augustin, s. Job & Jemima, b. June 11, 1810	2	558
Gideon, s. Jeremiah & Hannah, b. Aug. 31, 1729	2	23
Hana, [d.] John, b. Aug. 8, [16]53; bp. Apr. 15, [16]55	MG	
Hanna, d. [John & Hanna], b. Aug. 8, 1653	MG	
Hannah, d. John, b. Aug. 8, 1653	Col.2	152
Hannah, d. John, b. Aug. 8, 1653	1	9
Hanna, m. John **HIGLY,** Nov. 9, [16]71	MG	

	Vol.	Page
DRAKE, DRAK, (cont.)		
Hanna, d. John, m. John **HEGLEE**, Nov. 9, [16]71	Col.1	46
Hanna, taxed 2-0 on Feb. 10, [16]73	MG	
Hanna, taxed 2-0 on Feb. 10, [16]73	MG	
Hanah, w. John, Sr., d. Feb. 16, 1686	Col.D	56
Hannah, w. John, d. Feb. 16, 1686	1	42
Hannah, d. Simon, b. Sept. 29, 1694	1	10
Hannah, d. Ennoch, b. Oct. 6, 1695	1	.10
Hannah, d. Jacob, b. Jan. 3, 1706/7	2	19
Hannah, wid., m. Sergt. Daniel **LOOMIS**, b. of Windsor, July 9, 1713	2	170
Hannah, d. Symon, decd., m. John **COOKE**, s. John, decd., July 15, 1714	2	135
Hannah, d. Enoch, b. Mar. 29, 1717	22	21
Hannah, d. Jeremiah, b. Apr. 20, 1718	2	21
Hannah, of Windsor, m. Remembrance **SHELDING**, of Hartford, Feb. 19, 1718/19	2	198
Hannah, w. Jacob, d. July 6, 1722	2	226
Hannah, m. Ebenezer **BISSELL**, Jr., b. of Windsor, Jan. 23, 1741	2	132
Hannah, m. Daniel **MARSHEL**, b. of Windsor, Nov. 10, 1742	2	178
Hannah, d. Phinehas & Deborah, b. June 14, 1744	2	315
Hannah, d. Jacob, Jr. & Catharine, b. Nov. 13, 1746	2	316
Hannah, d. Job, 2nd & Hannah, b. July 4, 1753	2	317
Hanah, d. Enoch, b. [ ]	2	22
Hepsiba, d. [Job & Mary], b. July 14, 1659	MG	
Hephzibah, d. Job, b. July 14, 1659	1	8
Hephzibah, d. Jacob, Jr. & Catharine, b. May 20, 1744	2	315
Hepzibah, d. Job, 2nd & Hannah, b. Feb. 14, 1784	2	557
Hester, d. [Job & Mary], b. Oct. 10, 1662	MG	
Hester, d. Job, b. Oct. 10, [16]62	Col.1	54
Hester, d. Job, b. Oct. 10, [16]62	1	8
Hester, d. Job, m. Thomas **GRISWOLD**, s. George, Aug. 11, 1681, by Capt. Nubery	1	57
Hester, ae 19 on Oct. 10, 1681, d. Job, m. Thomas **GRISWOLD**, ae 23 on Dec. 29, 1681, s. George, Aug. 11, 1681, by Capt. Newbery	MG	
Hester, d. Job, m. Thomas **GRISWOLD**, s. George, [ ], by Capt. Nubery	TR1	1
Hezekiah, s. Enoch, b. Jan. 17, 1721/2	2	22
Isaac, s. Enoch & Dorcas, b. July 13, 1733	2	313
Jacob, m. Mary **BISSELL**, Apr. 12, 1649; "and never had a child"	MG	
Jacob, m. Mary **BISSELL**, Apr. 12, 1649	1	55
Jacob, adm. ch. Apr. 11, 1658	MG	
Jacob, adm. ch. & communicant Apr. [ ], 1658	MG	
Jac[ob], his w. [ ], adm. ch. & communicant June [ ],		

	Vol.	Page
DRAKE, DRAK, (cont.)		
1666	MG	
Jacob, s. Job (s. Job, Sr.), b. Jan. 29, [16]83	Col.D	51
Jacob, s. Job (s. Job, Sr.), b. Jan. 29, 1683	1	9
Jacob, Sergt., d. Aug. 6, 1689	Col.D	57
Jacob, his f. [ ], d. Aug. 18, [ ]; his mother d.		
Oct. 7, 1681, ae 100 yrs; she was a widow 22 y.	MG	
Jacob, his w. [ ], adm. to Ch. June 3, [16]	MG	
Jacob, contributed 0-8-0 to the poor in other colonies	MG	
Jacob, s. Job, m. Hannah **LOOMIS**, d. Thomas, June 28,		
1704	1	55
Jacob, s. Jacob, b. May 27, 1705	2	19
Jacob, m. Kathrien **PORTER**, b. of Windsor, Jan. 10, 1727/8	2	142
Jacob, s. Jacob & Kathrine, b. Mar. 23, 1732/3	2	311
Jacob, d. Jan. 20, 1762	2	228
Jacob, s. Jacob, Jr. & Rhoda, b. Jan. 20, 1768	2	319
Jacob, d. Sept. 11, 1775	2	229
Jeremiah, m. Hannah **BURNHAM**, Oct. 9, 1717 (sic?)	2	141
Jeremy, s. Job (s. John, Sr.), b. Sept. 11, [16]84	Col.D	51
Jerusha, d. Enoch, b. June 14, 1720	2	22
Job, m. Mary **WOLCOT**, June 25, 1646	MG	
Job, m. Mary **WOLCOTT**, June 25, 1646	1	55
Job, b. Jan. 15, [16]51; bp. Apr. 15, [16]55	MG	
Job, s. [John & Hanna], b. June 15, 1651	MG	
Jobe, s. John, b. June 15, 1651	Col.2	152
Job, s. John (the younger), b. June 15, 1651	1	9
Job, s. John, Jr., b. June 15, 1651	1	9
Jobe, s. [Job & Mary], b. Mar. 28, 1652	MG	
Jobe, s. Jobe, bp. Mar. 28, 1652	Col.2	152
Job, s. Job. bp. Mar. 28, 1652	1	8
Jo[b], his w. [ ], adm. ch. & communicant Apr. [ ], 1655	MG	
Job, s. John, m. Elizabeth **ALUARD**, Mar. 20, 1671, by Capt.		
Newbery	Col.1	46
Job, s. John, had 2 children b. in Windsor. Dated Aug. 17,		
1677	MG	
Job, had 7 children b. in Windsor. Dated Aug. 17, 1677	MG	
Job, s. Job, m. Elisabeth **COOK**, wid. & d. of Daniell		
CLARK, Sept. 13, 1677	MG	
Job, s. Job, m. Elizabeth **COOKE**, wid. Sept. 13, [16]77	Col.1	46
Job, s. Job, Sr., m. wid. Elizabeth **COOK**, Sept. 13, 1677	TR1	1
Job, s. Job, Sr., m. Elizabeth **COOK**, wid., Sept. 13, 1677	1	55
Job, s. [Job & Elisabeth], b. Jan*. 26, 1678 *(Also written		
"Oct.")	MG	
Job, s. Job, Jr., b. Oct. [ ], 1678	Col.1	56
Job, Sergt., d. Aug. 6, 1689	1	42
Jobe, Sr., d. Sept. 16, 1689	Col.D	57
Job, Sr., d. Sept. 16, 1689	1	42
Job, adult, s. John, ch. mem. 16[ ]	MG	

	Vol.	Page
DRAKE, DRAK, (cont.)		
Job, brother of John, Jr., contributed 0-1-3 to the poor		
in other colonies	MG	
Job, Sr., contributed 0-5-6 to the poor in other colonies	MG	
Job, Jr., contributed 0-3-0 to the poor in other colonies	MG	
Job, Lieut., d. Dec. 19, 1711	2	225
Job, s. Lieut. Job, d. Oct. 15, 1712	2	225
Job, s. Jacob, b. Nov. 6, 1714	2	21
Job, s. Jeremiah & Hannah, b. Feb. 1, 1725/6	2	23
Job, m. Martha **MOORE,** b. of Windsor, Nov. 16, 1730	2	141
Job, Dea., d. Apr. 19, 1733	2	226
Job, 2nd, m. Hannah **GOODRICH,** b. of Windsor, Apr. 27,		
1749	2	142
Job, s. Job, 2nd & Hannah, b. Oct. 15, 1750	2	316
Job, s. Augustine & Mary, b. Aug. 23, 1767	2	319
Job, 3rd, m. Hepzibah **WALTERS,** b. of Windsor, Feb. 7,		
1774	2	143
Job, m. Jemima **GILLIT,** b. of Windsor, Oct. 4, 1796	2	143
Joel, s. Josiah* & Hannah, b. Jan. 20, 1738/9 *("Samuel"		
crossed out)	2	313
John, m. Hannah **MOORE,** Nov. 30, 1648	1	55
John, s. [John & Hanna], b. Sept. 14, 1649	MG	
John, s. John, b. Sept. 14, 1649	Col.2	152
John, s. John, Jr., b. Sept. 14, 1649	1	8
John, b. Feb. 14, [16]49; bp. Apr. 15, [16]55	MG	
John, his w. [ ], adm. ch. [ ] 8, [16]55	MG	
John, Sr., d. Aug. 17, 1659; bd. Aug. 18, [1659]	1	42
John, Sr., d. [ ], [16]62	MG	
John, s. Job, d. [ ], [16]64	MG	
John, s. John, m. Mary **WATSON,** b. of Windsor, Mar. 20,		
[16]71, by Capt. Newbery	Col.1	46
John, had 11 children b. in Windsor. Dated Aug. 17, 1677	MG	
John, m. Hanna **MOORE,** Nov. [ ], [16]	MG	
John, Sr., adult, ch. mem. 16[ ]	MG	
John, Jr., adult, ch. mem. 16[ ]	MG	
John, Jr., contributed 0-3-0 to the poor in other colonies	MG	
John, s. Joseph, b. May 6, 1703	2	20
John, s. Jacob* & Cathrien, b. Oct. 27, 1739 *("John"		
crossed out)	2	313
John, s. Jacob, Jr. & Catharine, d. Oct. 28, 1741	2	227
John, s. Job, 2nd & Hannah, b. Oct. 20, 1751	2	317
Jonah, s. Josiah & Hannah, b. Aug. 6, 1747	2	316
Jonathan, s. [ ] & Elisabeth, b. Jan. 4, 1672	MG	
Jonathan, s. Job (s. of John), b. Jan. 4, [16]72	1	9
Jonathan, m. Esther **BISSEL,** Apr. 14, 1708	2	141
Jonathan, s. Jeremiah, b. Sept. 28, 1719	2	22
Joseph, s. [John & Mary], b. Apr. 16, 1657	MG	
Joseph, s. Job, b. Apr. 16, 1657	Col.2	161

	Vol.	Page
DRAKE, DRAK, (cont.)		
Joseph, s. Job, b. Apr. 16, 1657	1	8
Joseph, d. May 22, 1664	Col.1	55
Joseph, s. [John & Hanna], b. June 26, [16]74; bp. June 28, [1674]	MG	
Joseph, s. John, Jr., bp. June 28, [16]7[ ]	MG	
Joseph, s. Joseph, b. Apr. 24, 1697	2	20
Joseph, Jr., of Windsor, m. Sarah EASSON, of Hartford, Mar. 31, 1721	2	141
Joseph, s. Enoch, Jr. & Mary, b. Aug. 22, 1752	2	317
Joseph, d. Jan. 14, 1754	2	228
Josia, s. Jobe (s. John), d. Jan. 23, [16]81	Col.D	56
Josiah, s. Job (s. of John), d. Jan. 28, 1681	1	43
Josiah, s. Nathaniell, b. Apr. 18, 1711	2	20
Josiah, m. Hannah WILLSON, b. of Windsor, May 7, 1735	2	142
Josiah, s. Josiah & Hannah, b. July 28, 1737	2	313
Lemiwell, s. Joseph, Jr., b. Sept. 12, 1723	2	22
Lemuel, d. Jan. 17, 1837, ae 82	2	229
Levi, s. Josiah & Hannah, b. Aug. 6, 1743	2	314
Levy, illeg. s. Lydia DRAKE, b. May 4, 1745; reputed f. John SOOPER	2	316
Lois, d. Enoch, b. June 15, 1710	2	20
Lois, m. Mathew HOLCOMB, b. of Windsor, Jan. 20, 1729/30	2	162
Loes, d. Enoch, b. [ ]	2	22
Louisa, m. William B. REED, of Granby, Sept. 20, [1830?], by Henry A. Rowland	2	505
Lidia, d. [John & Hanna], b. Jan. 21, 1661	MG	
Lydia, d. John, b. Jan. 26, 1661	1	9
Lidia, [d. John], [bp.] Feb. 2, [16]61	MG	
Lidea, d. John, m. Joseph LOOMAS,s. Joseph, Apr. 10, 1681	MG	
Lidea, d. John, Sr., m. Joseph LOOMYS, s. Joseph, Sr., Apr. 10, 1681	Col.1	46
Lydia, w. Enoch, d. May 18, 1718	2	225
Lydia, d. Enoch & Dorcas, b. Nov. 15, 1727	2	313
Lydia, had illeg. s. Levy, b. May 4, 1745; reputed f. John SOOPER	2	316
Lyda, m. Benjamin LOOMIS, Jr., b. of Windsor, Apr. 27, 1760	2	488
Lidia, sister of John, Jr. & Job, contributed 0-0-6 to the poor in other colonies	MG	
Malory, d. Job, 2nd & Hannah, b. Aug. 14, 1778	2	557
Marcus, s. Jeremiah & Hannah, b. Jan. 13, 1727/8	2	23
Martha, d. Job & Martha, b. Oct. 31, 1731	2	311
Martha, d. Job & Martha, d. July 25, 1765	2	228
Martha, d. Augustine & Mary, b. Sept. 20, 1765	2	319
Mary, d. [Job & Mary], b. Dec. 12, 1649	MG	
Mary, d. Jobe, b. Dec. 12, 1649	Col.2	152

	Vol.	Page
DRAKE, DRAK, (cont.)		
Mary, d. Job, b. Dec. 12, 1649	1	8
Mary, m. John **GAYLAR,** Nov. 17, 1653	MG	
Mary, m. John **GAYLER,** b. of Windsor, Nov. 17, 1653	Col.2	159
Mary, m. John **GAYLER,** b. of Windsor, Nov. 17, 1655	Col.2	159
Mary, d. [John & Hanna], b. Jan. 29, 1666	MG	
Mary, d. John, b. Jan. 29, 1666	Col.1	55
Mary, d. John, b. Jan. 29, 1666	1	9
Mary, [d. John], [bp.] Feb. 3, [16]66	MG	
Mary, d. [Job & Elisabeth], b. Apr. 29, 1680	MG	
Mary, d. Job, Jr., b. Apr. 29, 1680	Col.1	57
Mary, m. Tho[mas] **MARSHALL,** b. of Windsor, Mar. 3, 1685/6	Col.D	54
Mary, m. Thomas **MARSHEL,** b. of Windsor, Mar. 3, 1685/6	1	59
Mary, m. Thomas **MARSHALL,** Mar. 2, 1686	2	175
Mary,*, Mrs., d. Sept. 11, 1689 *(Note by LBB: "Mary (**WATSON?**) **DRAKE**")	Col.D	57
Mary, wid., d. Sept. 11, 1689	1	42
Mary, w. Job, Sr., d. Sept. 16, 1689	Col.D	57
Mary, w. Job, Sr., d. Sept. 16, 1689	1	42
Mary, m. John **PORTER,** Sept. 23, 1697	1	60
Mary, d. Enoch & Mary, b. Dec. 31, 1736	2	312
Mary, d. Augustine & Mary, b. Sept. 3, 1761	2	319
Mary, see Mary **GAYLOR**	Col.D	56
Mary Seward, d. Frederick A. & Mary A., b. Feb. 20, 1840	2	558
Matilda, d. Job, 3rd, b. May 15, 1774	2	556
Mindwell, d. [John & Hanna], b. Nov. 10, 1671	MG	
Moses, s. Joseph, b. July 20, 1716	2	21
Moses, d. Josiah & Hannah, b. Apr. 2, 1749		316
Nancy, d. Ebenezer, Jr. & Martha, b. [ ] 15, 1767	2	556
Nathaniel, m. Rebeckah **BARBOR,** Jan. 23, 1706/7		140
Nathaniel, s. Nathaniell, b. June 4, 1708	2	19
Nathanael, m. Elizabeth **WARNER,** b. of Windsor, Feb. 4, 1730/1	2	141
Nathanael, s. Nathanael & Elizabeth, b. Mar*. 4, 1736/7 *("Jan." crossed out)	2	313
Nathaniel, Jr., Dea. & Elizabeth, had d. [ ], b. Sept. 7, 1747; d. within 24 hours after birth	2 2	316
Nathaniel, Dea., d. May 23, 1769	2	229
Noah, s. Enoch, b. June 13, 1714	2	21
Noah, m. Hannah **SKINNER,** b. of Windsor, Oct. 1, 1741	2	142
Noah, s. Noah & Hannah, b. May 30, 1743	2	298
Noah, s. Noah & Hannah, b. May 30, 1743	2	315
Noah, s. Noah & Hannah, d. June 13, 1743	2	227
Noah, s. Noah & Hannah, b. May 5, 1744	2	298
Noah, s. Noah & Hannah, b. May 5, 1744	2	315
Noah, s. Noah & Hannah, d. July 21, 1744	2	227
Noah, s. Noah & Hannah, b. Sept. 3, 1745	2	315

	Vol.	Page
DRAKE, DRAK, (cont.)		
Noah, s. Noah & Hannah, d. Nov. 4, 1745	2	227
Noah, s. Enoch, b. [ ]	2	22
Patty, d. Job, 2nd & Hannah, b. Oct. 23, 1780	2	557
Phineas, s. Symon, b. Sept. 21, 1706	2	19
Phinehas, m. Deborah MOORE, b. of Windsor, Feb. 29, 1727/8	2	141
Phinehas, s. Phinehas & Deborah, b. Feb. 20, 1728/9	2	23
Prudence, d. Phinehas & Deborah, b. Apr. 5, 1735	2	312
Prudence, m. Joseph FITCH, Jr., b. of Windsor, July 9, 1760	2	152
Rebeccah, d. Job. b. Jan. 16, 1689	Col.D	51
Rebekah, d. Job (s. John), b. Jan. 16, 1689	1	9
Rebeckah, d. Nathaniel, b. Dec. 30, 1715	2	21
Rebeckah, m. John FILLEY, Jan. 18, 1736/7	2	151
Rebeckah, d. Samuel & Amy, b. Jan. 24, 1745/6	2	315
Rebeckah, Jr., m. Thomas EGELSTON, Jr., b. of Windsor, Feb. 13, 1766	2	147
Rebeckah, w. Dea. Nathaniell, d. May 22, 1768	2	229
Rebeckah, see Rebeckah FILLEY	2	227
Reuben, s. Josiah & Hannah, b. May 19, 1741	2	314
Rhoda, d. Asahel & Damaras, b. Aug. 15, 1747	2	317
Rhoda, m. Samuel SOPER, of Sandersfield, Mass., Nov. 30, 1828, by Rev. Henry A. Rowland	2	507
Richard, s. Job & Jemima, b. Sept. 13, 1801	2	557
Roger, s. Phinehas & Deborah, b. Mar. 25, 1742	2	317
Ruth, d. [John & Hanna], b. Dec. 1, 1657	MG	
Ruth, d. John, b. Dec. 1, 1657	Col.2	161
Ruth, d. John, b. Dec. 1, 1657	1	9
Ruth, d. John, [bp.] Dec. 6, [16]57	MG	
Ruth, d. John, m. as 2nd w. Samuell BARBER, Jan. 25, 1676	MG	
Ruth, d. John, m. Samuell BARBER, Jan. 25, [16]76	Col.1	46
Ruth, d. John, m. Samuell BARBER, Jan. 30*, [16]76 *(In pencil "25?")	TR1	1
Ruth, d. John, m. Samuel BARBOR, June 25, [16]76	1	54
Ruth, [d.] John, [bp.] Dec. [ ], [16]	MG	
Sabra, d. Job, 2nd & Hannah, b. Mar. 27, 1786	2	557
Samuel, s. Enoch, b. July 27, 1688	1	9
Samuel, s. Nathaniel, b. Sept. 6, 1713	2	21
Samuel, s. Samuel & Amy, b. Apr. 14, 1744	2	315
Sara, d. [Enoch & Sara], b. [ ] 31, 1681	MG	
Sarah, d. Job, Jr., b. May 10, 1686	Col.D	51
Sarah, d. Job, Jr., b. May 10, 1686	1	9
Sarah, m. Josiah BARBOR, b. of Windsor, Nov, 5, 1701	1	54
Sarah, m. Roger WOLCOTT, b. of Windsor, Dec. 3, 1702	1	63
Sarah, m. Benoni TRUMBLE, Aug. 31, 1709	2	203
Sarah, m. Joel ROCKWELL, b. of Windsor, Dec. 3, 1741	2	195
Sarah, d. Jacob, Jr. & Cathraine, b. Dec. 12, 1741	2	314
Sarah Eason, d. Joseph, Jr., b. Jan. 15, 1722	2	22

	Vol.	Page
DRAKE, DRAK, (cont.)		
Shubal, s. Dea. Nathaniell, Jr. & Elizabeth, b. Jan.		
27, 1744/5	2	315
Silas, s. Dea. Nathaniel, Jr. & Elizabeth, b. Jan. 8, 1741/2	2	314
Simon, s. [John & Hanna], b. Oct. 28, 1659	MG	
Simon, s. Simon, b. Oct. 28, 1659	1	9
Simon, [s.] John, [bp.] Oct. 30, [16]59	MG	
Simon, m. Hannah **MILLS**, Dec. 15, 1687	1	55
Simon, s. Simon, b. Aug. 27, 1690	Col.D	51
Simon, s. Simon, b. Aug. 27, 1690	1	9
Simon, s. Simon, d. Sept. 19, 1690	1	43
Symon, d. Dec. 21, 1711	2	225
Thomas, s. Joseph, b. May 18, 1708	2	20
Thomas, m. Eunice **SKINNER**, b. of Windsor, Jan. 25, 1750	2	143
Thomas, s. Thomas & Eunice, b. Nov. 1, 1753	2	317
Waitstill, d. Nathaniell & Elizabeth, b. Nov. 2, 1734	2	312
William, s. Joseph, b. Dec. 30, 1705	2	20
-----, wid. adm. ch. & Communicant Feb. [ ], 1639	MG	
-----, old. wid. adm. ch. Feb. 23, 1639	MG	
-----, m. Elisabeth **ALUARD**, Mar. 20, 1671	MG	
-----, wid. Oct. 7, [16]81, ae in her 100th year	1	42
-----, had 4 children d. [ ], in "Elenton" prior		
to 1740	MG	
DRISCOLL, Fflurance, m. Mary **WEBSTER**, b. of Windsor, Apr.		
24, 1674, by Capt. Newbery	Col.1	46
DROWN, Abigail, m. Jeremiah **HUBBARD**, Feb. 12, 1832, by		
Rev. Edwin E. Griswold	2	485
DUFFY, Patrick, m. Catharine **MACKELL**, Sept. 3, 1852, by Rev.		
James Smyth	2	460
----, Mrs., m. Patrick **TROY**, May [ ] , 1852, by Rev. James		
Smyth	2	460
DUNBAR, Heman, of Windsor, m. Mary **EVANS**, of Hartford,		
Sept. 11, 1825, by Rev. Augustus Bolles, of Wintonbury	2	144
DUNLAP, Chloe, of Windsor, m. Eri **RISLEY**, of East Hartford,		
Sept. 20, 1826, by Rev. Joseph Hough	2	197
John W., of So. Hadley, Mass., m. Rhoda B. **PHELPS**, of		
Windsor, Jan. 16, 1844, by S. D. Jewett	2	473
DUN[N], John, m. Cathrine **DOWLING**, [ ], [1852], by Rev.		
James Smyth	2	460
DUPER, Hanna, m. John **BANCROFT**, Dec. 30, 1650	MG	
Hannah, m. John **BANCRAFT**, Dec. 3, 1650	1	53
EARL, Mary C., m. A. R. **WILLIAMS**, b. of Buffalo, N. Y., May		
17, 1847, by T. A. Leete	2	519
EASTON, EASSON, Deidamia, of Granby, m. Abel **GRISWOLD**,		
of Windsor, June 19, 1799	2	159
Prudence, of Hartford, m. Benjamin **SKINNER**, of Windsor,		
Nov. 9, 1747	2	200
Sarah, of Hartford, m. Joseph **DRAKE**, Jr., of Windsor,		

	Vol.	Page
EASTON, EASSON, (cont.)		
Mar. 31, 1721	2	141
EATON, Aaron, m. Lydia **BARBER,** b. of Windsor, Oct. 21, 1762	2	147
Daniel, s. Daniel & Rebeckah, b. Feb. 23, 1762	2	328
John, s. Daniel & Hannah, b. June 6, 1739	2	323
Keziah, wid. of Springfield, m. Justavous **ELSWORTH,** of Windsor	2	147
Nathaniel, s. Daniel & Hannah, b. Apr. 26, 1736	2	323
EBORN, [see under **ABORN**]		
EDWARDS, Abigael, d. Timothy, b. Dec. 25, 1707	2	25
Ann, d. Timothy, b. Apr. 28, 1699	1	12
Ann, m. John **ELSWORTH,** b. of Windsor, Nov. 8, 1734	2	146
Anne, d. Timothy, b. Apr. 28, 1699	2	25
Elizabeth, d. Timothy, b. Apr. 14, 1697	1	12
Elizabeth, d. Timothy, b. Apr. 14, 1697	2	25
Esther, d. Timothy, b. Aug. 6, 1695	1	12
Esther, d. Timothy, b. Aug. 6, 1695	2	25
Eunice, d. Timothy, b. Aug. 20, 1705	2	25
Hannah, d. Timothy, b. Feb. 8, 1712/13	2	27
Jerusha, d. Timothy, b. May 30, 1710	2	27
Jonathan, s. Timothy, b. Oct. 5, 1703	2	25
Luce, d. Timothy, b. May 25, 1715	2	28
Martha, d. Rev. Timothy, b. Jan. 5, 1717/18	2	320
Mary, d. Timothy, b. Feb. 11, 1700/1	2	25
Mary, d. Timothy, b. Feb. 11, 1701	1	12
EGGLESTON, EGELSTON, EGLESTONE, EGESTONE,		
EGLESTON, EAGGELSTON, EGGLLSTON, EGLSTON,		
Abiah, d. Benjamin, Jr. & Mary, b. Apr. 29, 1728	2	31
Abigayl, [d. Begat], b. June 12, 1648	MG	
Abigail, d. Bagget, bp. June 18, 1648	1	10
Abigail, m. John **OSBO[R]N,** Jr., Oct. 14, 1669	MG	
Abigail, m. John **OSBAND,** Oct. 4, 1669	1	59
Abigall, m. John **OSBON,** Jr., Oct. 14, [16]69	Col.1	45
Abigall, d. [James], b. Sept. 1, 1671	MG	
Abigail, d. James, b. Sept. 1, 1671	1	11
Abigael, d. John, b. Dec. 14, 1683	2	26
Abigal, d. Benj[amin], b. Apr. 11, 1685	Col.D	51
Abigail, d. Benjamin, b. Apr. 11, 1685	1	11
Abigaell, m. Samuell **OSBORN,** Jr., May [ ], 1704	2	184
Abigael, d. Benjamin, Jr., b. June 21, 1710	2	25
Abigail, d. James & Elizabeth, b. Jan. 6, 1733/4	2	321
Abigail, m. Isaac **BANCRAFT,** b. of Windsor, Dec. 17, 1741	2	130
Abigail, see Abigall **OSBORN**	Col.D	56
Ann, d. John, b. Jan. 18, 1697/8	2	26
Ann, m. Sollomon **CLARK,** b. of Windsor, Feb. 24, 1719/20	2	135
Ann, m. Zadock **BROWN,** b. of Windsor, Dec. 3, 1775	2	466
Begat, d. Sept. 1, [16]74, ae almost 100 yrs.	MG	
Bagget, d. Sept. 1, [16]74	1	43

	Vol.	Page
EGGLESTON, EGELSTON, EGLESTONE, EGESTONE, EGLESTON, EAGGELSTON, EGGLLSTON, EGLSTON,(cont.)		
Begut, d. Sept. 1, 1674	Col.1	58
Begat, d. Sept. 1, [16]76	MG	
Begat, had 7 children b. in Windsor. Dated Aug. 17, 1677	MG	
Biget, s. Benjamin, Jr., b. Mar. 17, 1724/5	2	30
Bigget, of Windsor, m. Mary CORNING, of Enfield, Nov. 7, 1745	2	146
Beniamen, [s. Begat], b. Dec. 18, 1653	MG	
Benjamin, s. Bagget, b. Dec. 18, 1653	1	10
Beniamen, m. Hanna SHADOCK, wid., Mar. 6, 1678, by Capt. Newbery	MG	
Beniamen, m. Hanna SHADOCK, wid. & d. John OSBON, Mar. 6, 1678, by Capt. Newbery	Col.1	46
Beniamen, m. Hanna [ ], wid. Shadock, & d. John OSBORN, Mar. 6, 1678, by Capt. Newbery	TR1	1
Benjamin, m. wid. Hannah SHADRAKE, d. of John OSBAND, Mar. 6, 1678, by Capt. Nubery	1	56
Benjamin, s. Benjamin, b. May [ ], 1687	1	11
Benjamin, m. Mary DIBLE, b. of Windsor, Dec. 2, 1708	2	145
Benjamin, s. Benjamin, Jr., b. Sept. 28, 1713	2	27
Benjamin, d. Oct. 30, 1732	2	231
Benjamin, s. Benjamin, d. Aug. 9, 1733	2	231
Benjamin, s. Edward & Easther, b. Mar. 16, 1742/3	2	297
Benjamin, s. Edward & Esther, b. Mar. 16, 1742/3	2	324
Benjamin, s. Bigett & Mary, b. Jan. 2, 1747/8	2	325
Bigget, see under Begat		
Clarissa, of Windsor, m. John HOLT, of Norwich, Dec. 28, 1820, by Rev. John Bartlett. Int. Pub.	2	165
Constant, see under Sconstant		
Damaris, d. John, b. July 14, 1700	2	26
Daniell, s. Isaak, b. June 12, 1705	2	24
Daniel, s. Daniel & Elizabeth, b. Oct. 29, 1737	2	322
David, s. John & Constant, b. May 3, 1736	2	357
Debroa, d. [James], b. May 1, 1674	MG	
Deborah, d. James, b. May 1, 1674	1	11
Deborah, d. Thomas, b. May 10, 1700	1	12
Deborah, m. Aaron LOOMIS, b. of Windsor, Feb. 5, 1718/19	2	170
Deliverance, d. John, b. Apr. 7, 1695	2	26
Deliverance, d. John, d. July 12, 1715	2	230
Deliverance, d. John, Jr. & Constant, b. Feb. 5, 1729/30	2	320
Dorcas, d. John, b. Sept. 7, 1692	2	26
Dorcas, m. Enoch DRAKE, b. of Windsor, May 6, 1719	2	141
Dorathy, d. Benj[amin], b. Feb. 28, 1689	Col.D	51
Dorithy, d. Benjamin, b. Feb. 28, 1689/90	1	11
Dorithee, m. Samuell WEST, Feb. 24, 1708/9	2	207
Edward, s. John, b. Jan. 31, 1707/8	2	27

	Vol.	Page
EGGLESTON, EGELSTON, EGLESTONE, EGESTONE,		
EGLESTON, EAGGELSTON, EGGLLSTON,		
EGLSTON,(cont.)		
Edward, s. Edward & Esther, b. Apr. 14, 1736	2	322
Edward & Esther, had s. [ ], b. May 11, 1747;		
d. [ ], ae 6 d.	2	325
Elijah, s. Jedadiah & Sarah, b. July 2, 1747	2	325
Elijah, s. Thomas & Rebeckah, b. Dec. 10, 1771	2	330
Elisha, s. James, b. Sept. 25, 1720	2	30
Elizabeth, m. Abel **HOSKINS**, Mar. 22, 1759	2	164
Ephraim, s. Thomas, b. Mar. 3, 1708/9	2	25
Ephraim, s. Joseph & Naome, b. Mar. 8, 1762	2	327
Ester, d. James, b. Dec. 1, 1663	Col.1	54
Ester, d. James, b. Dec. 1, 1663	1	11
Ester, d. John, b. Mar. 14, 1682/3	1	11
Easter, m. John **WILLIAMS**, Sr., b. of Windsor, June 10,		
1686	1	63
Ester, d. Benjamin, b. July 10, 1697	1	12
Esther, m. Josiah **FILLEY**, b. of Windsor, Dec. 9, 1703	1	56
Esther, m. Josiah **FILLY**, Dec. 29, 1703	2	151
Esther, d. Thomas, b. Oct. 19, 1710	2	26
Esther, see Esther **WILLIAMS**	2	277
Eunice, m. David **DRAKE**, Jr., Dec. 12, 1820, by Rev. Henry		
A. Rowland	2	143
Francis, s. Thomas & Rebeckah, b. Mar. 20, 1774	2	330
Freman, s. Jonathan & Mindwell, b. Nov. 19, 1766	1	329
Grace, d. Thomas, b. Nov. 11, 1687		11
Grace, d. Thomas, of Windsor, m. Nathan **WAPLES**, of	2	
Hartford, Aug. 3, 1714	2	208
Grace, d. Jedediah & Sarah, b. Jan. 12, 1730/1	2	320
Grace, d. Gedediah & Sarah, d. May 30, 1734	2	231
Grace, wid., d. Mar. 27, 1739	2	231
Grace, d. Jedadiah & Sarah, b. June 17, 1744	MG	324
Hanna, d. [James], b. Dec. 19, 1676	1	
Hannah, d. Thomas, b. Feb. 7, 1691/2	2	11
Hannah, w. Benjamin, d. Aug. 17, 1715	2	230
Hannah, m. Isaac **LOOMIS**, b. of Windsor, Apr. 26, 1716	2	170
Hannah, d. Benjamin, b. Apr. 9, 1722	MG	30
Hester, d. [James], b. Dec. 1, 166[ ]		
Hester, formerly w. James, m. James **ENNO**, Sr., Apr. 29,	MG	
1680		
Hester, formerly w. James, m. James **ENNO**, Sr., Apr. 29,	Col.1	
1680, by Capt. Newbery		46
Hester, wid. James, m. James **ENNO**, Sr., Apr. 29, 1680,	TR1	
by Capt. Newbery		1
Hester, formerly w. James, m. James **ENNO**, Sr., Apr. 29,	1	
1680, by Capt. Nubery	Col.D	56
Hester, d. John, b. Mar. 14, 1682/3	MG	51

	Vol.	Page
EGGLESTON, EGELSTON, EGLESTONE, EGESTONE,		
EGLESTON, EAGGELSTON, EGGLLSTON,		
EGLSTON,(cont.)		
Isack, s. [James], b. Feb. 27, 1668	MG	
Isaac, s. James, b. Feb. 27, 1668	1	11
Isaac, m. Mary STYLES, Mar. 21, 1694/5	1	56
Isaak, m. Mary STILES, b. of Windsor, Mar. 21, 1694/5	2	145
Isaac, s. Isaac, b. Dec. 30, 1695	1	11
Isaak, s. Isaak, b. Dec. 30, 1695	2	24
Isaac, Jr., s. Isaac, d. Feb. 10, 1716/17	2	230
Isabell, d. Thomas, b. Jan. 25, 1697	1	12
Isabel, m. Abraham LOOMIS, b. of Windsor, Feb. 5, 1718/19	2	170
Isabel, d. Jedediah & Sarah, b. Apr. 11, 1732	2	321
James, s. James, b. Jan. 1, 1656; d. [ ]	MG	
James, s. James, b. Jan. 1, 1656	Col.2	161
James, s. James, st. b. Jan. 1, 1656	1	11
James, had 8 children, b. in Windsor. Dated Aug. 17, 1677	MG	
James, d. evening before Dec. 2, [16]79; bd. that day	MG	
James, d. Dec. 2, 1679	Col.1	58
James, s. John, b. June 18, 1684	Col.D	51
James, s. John, b. June 18, 1689	1	11
James, m. Martha CLARK, b. of Windsor, Aug. 28, 1718	2	145
Jemes, s. James, b. Sept. 4, 1719	2	29
James, s. James, d. Nov. 5, 1719	2	230
James, s. James, b. Sept. 15, 1724	2	30
James, of Windsor, m. Elizabeth BLANCHER, of Hartford, Nov. 31, 1732	2	146
James, contributed 0-1-6 to the poor in other colonies	MG	
Jedidiah, s. Thomas, b. June 14, 1696	1	11
Jedidiah, m. Sarah MOORE, b. of Windsor, Apr. 6, 1726	2	146
Jedediah, s. Jedediah & Sarah, b. July 7, 1736	2	322
Jedediah, s. Thomas, Jr. & Rebeckah, b. Apr. 11, 1764	2	330
Jedediah, d. July 15, 1766	2	232
Jehiel, s. Biget & Mary, b. Feb. 17, 1745/6	2	324
John, d. [ ], [16]46	MG	
John, s. [James], b. Mar. 27, 1659	MG	
John, s. James, b. Mar. 27, 1659	1	11
John, m. Hester MILLS, June 1, 1682	Col.D	54
John, m. Esther MILLS, June 1, 1682	1	56
John, s. Isaac, b. Sept. 10, 1700	1	12
John, s. Isaak, b. Sept. 10, 1700	2	24
John, s. Isaac, d. Jan. 12, 1701/2	1	43
John, s. Isaak, d. Jan. 12, 1701/2	2	229
John, s. John, b. Mar. 13, 1702/3	1	12
John, s. John, b. Mar. [ ], 1702/3	2	28
John, Jr., m. Constant HOSKINS, b. of Windsor, June 3, 1725	2	146

	Vol.	Page
EGGLESTON, EGELSTON, EGLESTONE, EGESTONE,		
EGLESTON, EAGGELSTON, EGGLLSTON,		
EGLSTON,(cont.)		
John, Corp., d. Mar. 10, 1730/1	2	231
Jonathan, s. John & Constant, b. May 14, 1738	2	357
Jonathan, m. Mindwell **HOSKINS**, b. of Windsor, June 24,		
1762	2	147
Joseph, [s. Begat], bp. Mar. 30, 1651	MG	
Joseph, s. Bagget, bp. Mar. 30, 1651	1	10
Joseph, s. Benjamin, b. Mar. 3, 1694/5	1	11
Joseph, s. Thomas, b. Apr. 4, 1706	2	24
Joseph, s. Benjamin, d. July 27, 1715	2	230
Joseph, s. Benjamin, Jr., b. Apr. 9, 1716	2	28
Joseph, s. Edward & Esther, b. Aug. 13, 1744	2	324
Joseph, of Windsor, m. wid. Naomi **PHELPS**, of Symsbury,		
Dec. 21, 1757	2	147
Joseph, twin with Mary, s. Joseph & Naomi, b. May 15, 1760	2	327
Lydia, d. Jedediah & Sarah, b. Jan. 12, 1728/9	2	31
Marcy, [d. Begat], b. May 29, 1641	MG	
Marcy, d. Bagget, b. [ ], 1641	1	10
Marcy, d. [ ], [16]57	MG	
Marcy, d. [Beniamen & Hanna], b. Oct. 20, 1680	MG	
Martha, d. John, b. Nov. 20, 1705	2	26
Martha, w. James, d. May 25, 1728	2	231
Mary, m. John **DENSLOW**, b. of Windsor, Jan. 7, 1653	Col.2	159
Mary, m. John **DENSLOW**, June 7, 1655	MG	
Mary, d. Dec. 8, 1657	Col.2	160
Marey, d. Dec. 8, [16]57	1	43
Mary, d. Beniamen, b. Oct. 2, 1680	Col.1	57
Mary, d. Thomas, b. Jan. 11, 1689	1	11
Mary, d. Thom[as], b. Jan. 11, 1690	Col.D	51
Mary, d. Isaac, b. July 20, 1697	1	12
Mary, d. Isaak, b. July 20, 1697	2	24
Mary, d. Thomas, b. May 13, 1702	1	12
Mary, d. Benjamin, Jr., b. Feb. 1, 1718/19	2	28
Mary, m. John **BROWN**, Jr., b. of Windsor, Mar. 24, 1725/6	2	129
Mary, d. Daniel & Elizabeth, b. Jan. 20, 1735/6	2	322
Mary, twin with Joseph, d. Joseph & Naomi, b. May 15, 1760	2	327
Mary, d. Benjamin, d. June 28, 1761	2	232
Mary, see Mary **DENSLOW**	Col.D	56
Mina, d. Jonathan & Mindwell, b. Oct. 1, 1764	2	329
Mindwell, d. Thomas, b. Nov. 29, 1703	1	12
Mindwell, m. Ebenezer **PHELPS**, b. of Windsor, Dec. 7,		
1727	2	187
Nathanell, s. [James], b. Aug. 15, 1666	MG	
Nathanell, s. James, b. Aug. 15, 1666	Col.1	55
Nathanael, s. James, b. Aug. 15, 1666	1	11
Nathaniel, of Windsor, m. Hannah **ASHLEY**, of Westfield,		

	Vol.	Page
EGGLESTON, EGELSTON, EGLESTONE, EGESTONE,		
EGLESTON, EAGGELSTON, EGGLLSTON,		
EGLSTON,(cont.)		
Sept. 13, 1694	1	56
Nathanael, s. Isaac, b. Jan. 8, 1702/3	1	12
Nathanaell, s. Isaack, b. Jan. 8, 1702/3	2	24
Polly, of Windsor, m. Solomon **CURTICE**, of Ohio, July 15,		
1831, by Rev. Norman Atwood	2	470
Rebeckah, d. Bagget, b. Sept. 8, 1644	1	10
Rebeca, [d. Begat], b. Dec. 8, 1644	MG	
Rebekah, d. Benjamin, d. Oct. 11, 1718	2	230
Sabra, d. Jonathan & Mindwell, b. Sept. 19, 1762	2	329
Sara, [d. Begat], b. Mar. 28, 1643	MG	
Sarah, d. Bagget, b. Mar. 28, 1643	1	10
Sara, m. John **PETTEBON**, Feb. 16, 1664	MG	
Sara, m. John **PETTEBON**, b. of Windsor, Feb. 16, 1664,		
by Mr. Wollcot	Col.1	45
Sarah, m. John **PETTIBONE**, b. of Windsor, Feb. 16, 1664,		
by Mr. Wolcott	1	60
Sarah, d. Benjamin, b. Apr. 20, 1683	1	11
Sarah, d. Benjamin, b. Apr. 20, 1683	1	12
Sarah, d. Benj[amin], b. Apr. 20, 1683	Col.D	51
Sarah, d. John, b. Jan. 4, 1686/7	2	26
Sarah, m. Daniel **PRIOR**, Feb. 8, 1692	1	60
Sarah, of Middletown, m. Daniel **PRIOR**, of Windsor, Feb.		
9, 1692/3	1	60
Sarah, m. Jonathan **STILES**, Jan. 12, 1708/9	2	197
Sarah, d. Jedediah & Sarah, b. Mar. 16, 1726/7	2	30
Sarah, d. Benjamin, Jr. & Mary, b. Nov. 25, 1730	2	321
Sarah, d. Benjamin & Mary, d. Oct. 30, 1741	2	231
Sarah, d. Biget & Mary, b. July 10, 1750	2	326
Sarah, m. Remembrance **SHELDING**, Jr., b. of Windsor, Jan.		
31, 1751	2	200
Sarah, d. Thomas & Rebeckah, b. Dec. 22, 1766	2	329
Sconstant, m. Charles **LOOMIS**, b. of Windsor, July 3, 1750	2	487
Thomas, s. Begat, b. Aug. 26, 1638	MG	
Thomas, s. Bagget, b. Aug. 26, 1638	1	10
Thomas, bp. Nov. 22, [16]46	MG	
Thomas, s. [James], b. July 27, 1661	MG	
Thomas, s. James, b. July 27, 1661	1	11
Thomas, s. Thomas, b. Jan. 16, 1693	1	11
Thomas, Sr., d. May [ ], 1697	1	43
Thomas, d. Apr. 6, 1732	2	231
Thomas, s. Jedadiah & Sarah, b. Sept. 26, 1740	2	323
Thomas, Jr., m. Rebeckah **DRAKE**, Jr., b. of Windsor, Feb.		
13, 1766	2	147
Thomas, contributed 0-2-6 to the poor in other colonies	MG	
Timothy, s. Edward & Esther, b. Apr. 7, 1747	2	324

	Vol.	Page
EGGLESTON, EGELSTON, EGLESTONE, EGESTONE,		
EGLESTON, EAGGELSTON, EGGLLSTON,		
EGLSTON,(cont.)		
----, wid., d. July 25, 1689	Col.D	56
----, wid. d. July 25, 1689	1	43
----, wid. contributed cloth 0-4-0 to the poor in other		
colonies	MG	
ELA*, Daniel, m. Mary **CHAPMAN**, b. of Windsor, May 20, 1779		
*(In pencil)	2	147
Daniel, s. Daniel & Mary, b. Jan. 6, 1783	2	331
Mary, d. Daniel & Mary, b. Dec. 26, 1784	2	331
ELDERKIN, James, d. Apr. 26, 1698	1	43
John, of New London, m. wid. Elizabeth **GAYLORD**, of		
Windsor, Mar. 1, 1660	1	56
John, of New London, m. Elisabeth **DRAKE**, wid., of		
Windsor, Mar. 1, 1660	Col.1	45
ELGAR, ELGER, Abner, s. Thomas & Rachel, b. Sept. 8, 1734	2	326
Ann, d. Thomas, b. Oct. [ ], 1715	2	28
Ann, of Windsor, m. Samuel **MILLINGTON**, late of		
Coventry, now of Windsor, Apr. 23, 1733	2	178
David, s. Thomas, b. Aug. 5, 1718	2	28
Elizabeth, d. Thomas & Rachel, b. May 8, 1731	2	321
Ezra, s. Thomas & Rachel, b. Sept. 16, 1728	2	320
Hannah, d. Thomas & Rachel, b. May 10, 1738	2	323
Hannah, d. Thomas & Rachel, d. Nov. 3, 1753	2	232
Jerusha, d. Thomas & Rachel, b. Feb. 1, 1723/4	2	320
Rachel, d. Thomas, b. Dec. 26, 1720	2	30
Thomas, m. Rachel **KELCY**, Dec. 22, 1714	2	145
Thomas, his s. [ ], d. Oct. 15, 1727	2	230
ELLIOT, ELIOT, Anne, d. John, b. Feb. 12, 1709/10	2	25
Elizabeth, w. John, d. Nov. 24, 1702	1	43
Elizabeth, d. John, b. May 14, 1712	2	27
Hannah, d. John, b. Nov. 9, 1719	2	30
John, m. Mrs. Elizabeth **MACKMAN**, Oct. 31, 1699	1	56
John, m. Mary **WOLCOT**, b. of Windsor, Dec. 19, 1706	2	145
John, s. John, of Enfield* & Mary, b. Jan. 21, 1716/17		
*(Crossed out)	2	322
John, d. Mar. 25, 1719	2	230
Mary, d. John, b. Mar. 28, 1708	2	25
Thomas D., m. Elizabeth **ROCKWELL**, b. of Windsor, Nov.		
30, 1843, by Rev. S. D. Jewett	2	508
ELLIS, ELLICE, John, m. Silence **ROCKWELL**, b. of Windsor,		
Oct. 13, 1826, by Rev. David Miller	2	196
Rachel, m. Ichabod Cromwell **GRINES**, b. of Windsor, Jan.		
14, 1747/8	2	157
Sarah Ann, m. Luther **PORTER**, b. of Windsor, Feb. 12,		
1850, by Rev. Cephas Brainard	2	194

	Vol.	Page
ELLSWORTH, ELSWORTH, ELSEWORTH, ELESWORT, ELESWORTH, ELSWORT, Abbey W., of Windsor, m. David A. HALL, of Washington City, Dec. 25, 1838, by Rev. Daniel Hemenway	2	483
Abigail, d. Josiah, b. [ ], 1694	1	11
Abigael, d. Thomas, b. Sept. 14, 1712	2	27
Abigail, d. Nathaniell & Abigail, b. Aug. 7, 1731	2	322
Abigaiel*, m. John LOOMIS, b. of Windsor, Apr. 5, 1733 *("BISSEL" crossed out)	2	171
Abigail, d. Nathaniell & Abigail, d. Aug. 8, 1739	2	231
Abigail, w. Nathaniel, d. Jan. 20, 1745/6	2	232
Abigail, d. Nathaniel & Catharine, b. Aug. 3, 1752	2	326
Alexander, s. Jonathan & Abigail, b. June 9, 1747	2	327
Ame, d. Benjamin & Deborah, b. Apr. 17, 1730	2	320
Ame, m. John THOMSON, May 24, 1753	2	204
Ann, d. Ens. Jonathan, b. Aug. 12, 1719	2	29
Ann, d. Giles & Hannah, b. Feb. 25, 1729/30	2	320
Ann, d. John & Ann, b. Jan. 23, 1741	2	323
Ann, twin with Oliver, d. William & Mary, b. Aug. 25, 1745	2	324
Ann, m. Taylor CHAPMAN, b. of Windsor, Nov. 1, 1759	2	137
Anna, d. John, b. Apr. 27, 1705	2	26
Anna M., m. Alexander JOHNS, b. of Windsor, Mar. 30, 1834, by Rev. Ansel Nash	2	168
Anne, m. Ebenezer GRANT, b. of Windsor, Nov. 10, 1737	2	156
Asahel, s. Nathanael & Abigail, b. July 17, 1734	2	322
Asael, s. Nathaniell & Abigael, d. May 2, 1753	2	259
Azubah, d. Benjamin, b. Apr. 16, 1722	2	30
Azubah, m. Nath[anie]ll BISSELL, Jr., b. of Windsor, Apr. 15, 1746	2	132
Beniamen, s. [Josia], b. Jan. 19, 1676	MG	
Beniamen, [s. Josias], b. Jan. 19, 1676	Col.1	56
Benjamin, s. Josiah, b. Jan. 19, 1676	1	11
Benjamen, b. Jan. 19, [16]76; bp. Aug. 19, [16]77	MG	
Benja[min], s. Sergt. Josi., d. Apr. 14, 1690	Col.D	57
Benjamin, s. Sergt. Josiah, d. Apr. 14, 1690	1	43
Benjamin, s. Job, b. Oct. 1, 1696	1	12
Benjamin, m. Deborah HOSFORD, b. of Windsor, Oct. 25, 1721	2	146
Benjamin, s. Job & Mary, b. Feb. 9, 1763	2	328
Caroline, d. William & Mary, b. Mar. 24, 1742	2	325
Charles, s. Samuel, b. Dec. 13, 1721	2	30
Charles, s. Charles & Elizabeth, b. Feb. 25, 1763	2	330
Clarissa A., m. Anson G. BOWER, b. of Windsor, Dec. 31, 1839, by Rev. S. D. Jewett	2	465
Daniel, s. John, b. Mar. 20, 1699/1700	1	12
David, s. Jonathan, b. Aug. 8, 1709	2	320
David, s. David & Jemimah, b. Mar. 27, 1742	2	324
Deborah, d. Thomas, b. Sept. 24, 1714	2	28

	Vol.	Page

**ELLSWORTH, ELSWORTH, ELSEWORTH, ELESWORT,
ELESWORTH, ELSWORT, (cont.)**

Deborah, d. Thomas & Sarah, b. Nov. 2, 175[sic?]	2	325
Delia W., m. Henry G. TAINTOR, of Hampton, [ ] 25,		
[ ], by Rev. S. D. Jewett	2	510
Dinah, d. Thomas & Sarah, b. Dec. 5, 1745	2	325
Elijah, s. Samuel, b. Feb. 11, 1723/4	2	30
Eliphelet, s. Samuel & Elizabeth, b. July 23, 1740	2	326
Elisabet[h], bp. Mar. 7, [16]5[ ]	MG	
Elizabeth, d. [Josia & Elizabeth], b. Nov. 11, 1657	MG	
Elizabeth, d. Josiah, b. Nov. 11, 1657	Col.2	161
Elizabeth, d. Josiah, b. Nov. 11, 1657	1	10
Elizabeth, ae 23 on Nov. 11, 1680, m. Nathaniel LOOMYS,		
s. Nathanell, who was ae 24 on Mar. 20, [1681], Dec.		
23, 1680	MG	
Elizabeth, m. Nathaniell LOOMYES, Dec. 23, 1680	TR1	1
Elizabeth, d. Josias, m. Nathaniell LOOMYS, s. Nathanell		
Dec. 23, 1680, by Capt. Newbery	Col.1	46
Elizabeth, m. Nathanel LOOMIS, s. Nathanael, Dec. 23, 1680	1	58
Eliz[abeth], d. Josi[ah], Jr., b. Jan. 22, 1683	Col.D	51
Elizabeth, d. Josiah, Jr., b. Jan. 22, 1683	1	11
Elisabeth, d. Job, b. Apr. 5, 1706	2	24
Elisabeth, d. Thomas, b. Nov. 18, 1706	2	24
Elizabeth, wid., d. Sept. 18, 1712	2	229
Elisabeth, m. Hugh TOMSON, b. of Windsor, Jan. 11, 1727/8	2	204
Elizabeth, m. David SKINNER, b. of Windsor, Nov. 20, 1728	2	200
Esther, d. John, b. Mar. 9, 1701/2	2	26
Esther, d. Thomas, Jr. & Sarah, b. Mar. 29, 1734	2	321
Eunice, d. Sergt. Thomas & Deborah, b. Mar. 29, 1717	2	321
Frances Maria, m. Henry A. HALSEY, Jan. 11, 1836, by		
Charles Walker	2	484a
Fraderick, s. John & Ann, b. Oct. 26, 1738	2	323
Frederick, m. Elizabeth HALSEY, b. of Windsor, Apr. 27,		
1846, by Rev. T. A. Leete	2	519
Gilburt, s. Giles, Jr. & Keziah, b. June 17, 1762	2	328
Giles, s. Jonathan, b. Aug. 6, 1703	2	24
Giles, m. Hannah STOUGHTON, b. of Windsor, Feb. 6,		
1728/9	2	146
Giles, s. Giles & Hannah, b. Sept. 6, 1732	2	321
Giles, Jr., m. Keziah MOORE, b. of Windsor, Feb. [ ], 1756	2	158
Giles, s. Giles, Jr. & Kezia, b. Sept. 7, 1758	2	327
Giles, d. Mar. 21, 1768	2	232
Grove, s. Jonathan, Jr. & Jerusha, b. Feb. 23, 1765	2	329
Gustavous, s. Thomas & Sarah, b. June 21, 1743	2	325
Hamutal, d. Benjamin & Deborah, b. Jan. 11, 1725/6	2	30
Hannah, d. Job, b, Feb. 10, 1700/1	1	12
Hannah, d. Thomas, b. Nov. 25, 1704	2	24
Hannah, d. Ens. Jonathan, b. Sept. 10, 1713	2	29

	Vol.	Page
ELLSWORTH, ELSWORTH, ELSEWORTH, ELESWORT,		
ELESWORTH, ELSWORT, (cont.)		
Hannah, d. Giles & Hannah, b. May 18, 1740	2	323
Hannah, m. Alexander **ALLIN**, b. of Windsor, Apr. 28, 1743	2	124
Hannah, w. Giles, d. Dec. 29, 1756	2	232
Hannah, d. Jonathan, Jr. & Jerusha, b. July 1, 1767	2	329
Jehu P., m. Ruth **CASE**, b. of Windsor, May 29, 1837, by		
Eli Deniston	2	474
Jehu P., m. Mary **WELLS**, b. of Windsor, Nov. 28, 1843, by		
Rev. S. W. Scofield	2	501
Jemima, d. William & Mary, b. Sept. 4, 1742	2	323
Jemima, m. Oliver **MATHER**, b. of Windsor, Mar. 21, 1778	2	180
Jerusha, d. Giles & Hannah, b. Nov. 9, 1743	2	323
Jerusha, Mrs., of Windsor, m. Rev. Nath[anie]ll		
HUNTINGTON, b. of Windsor, Nov. 28, 1850 [1750?]	2	163
Job, s. Josia, b. Apr. 13, 167[4]	MG	
Job, s. Josias, b. Apr. 13, 1674	Col.1	56
Job, s. Josiah, b. Apr. 13, 1674	1	11
Job, m. Mary **TROUMBLE**, Dec. 19, 1695	1	56
Job, s. Job, b. June 5, 1698	1	12
Job, of Windsor, m. Sarah **CLARK**, of Farmington, wid.		
Oct. 25, 1711	2	145
Job, Jr., s. Capt. Job. d. June 29, 1724, at Newport, R. I.	2	230
Job, s. Benjamin & Deborah, b. Apr. 15, 1737	2	322
Job, m. Mary **TRUMBEL**, b. of Windsor, May 4, 1762	2	147
Job, s. Job & Mary, b. Aug. 26, 1765	2	328
Joel, s. Nathaniel & Cathrine, b. Feb. 9, 1749/50	2	326
John*, s. Josias, b. Nov. 5, 1655 *(Note by LBB: "Should		
be Josias")	Col.2	181
John, s. [Josia & Elizabeth], b. Oct. 7, 1671	MG	
John, [bp.] Oct. 15, [16]71	MG	
John, s. Josiah, b. Oct. 7, 1671; bp. the 15th day	1	11
John, of Windsor, m. Esther **WHITE**, of Hatfield, Dec. 9,		
1696	1	56
John, s. John, b. Nov. 7, 1697	1	12
John, Lieut., d. Oct. 26, 1720	2	230
John, m. Ann **EDWARDS**, b. of Windsor, Nov. 8, 1734	2	146
John, s. Capt. John & Anne, b. Aug. 24, 1735	2	322
John, s. John & Ann, b. Aug. 24, 1735	2	323
John, s. Thomas & Sarah, b. Dec. 31, 1737	2	325
Jonathan, [s. Josia & Elizabeth], b. June 28, 1669;		
[bp.] July 4, [16]69	MG	
Jonathan, s. Josiah, b. June 28, 1669; bp. July 4,		
[probably 1669]	1	11
Jonathan, m. Sarah **GRANT**, Oct. 26, 1693	1	56
Jonathan, s. Jonathan, b. Mar. 11, 1695/6	1	11
Jonathan, s. Ens. Jonathan, d. Sept. 22, 1712	2	230
Jonathan, s. Jonathan, d. Sept. 22, 1712	2	230

	Vol.	Page
ELLSWORTH, ELSWORTH, ELSEWORTH, ELESWORT,		
ELESWORTH, ELSWORT, (cont.)		
Jonathan, s. Ens. Jonathan, b. Aug. 22, 1716	2	29
Jonathan, s. Jonathan, Jr. & Abigail, b. May 28, 1743	2	327
Jonathan, m. Harriet **BARBER,** Feb. 2, 1825, by Rev. Henry		
A. Rowland	2	148
Joseph, s. Josiah, b. Mar. 23, 1700/1	1	12
Josiah, s. Josiah, b. Nov. 5, 1655	1	10
Josiah, Sr., d. Aug. 20, 1689	Col.D	57
Josiah, Sr., d. Aug. 20, 1689	1	43
Josiah, s. Josi[ah], b. Mar. 3, 1690/1	Col.D	51
Josiah, s. Josiah, b. Mar. 3, 1690/1	1	11
Josiah, s. Samuel & Elizabeth, b. Sept. 18, 1726	2	30
Josia, m. Elizabeth **HOLCOMB,** Nov. 16, 1654	MG	
Josias, m. Elisabeth **HOLCOM,** b. of Windsor, Nov. 16, 1654	Col.2	159
Josias, s. [Josia & Elizabeth], b. Nov. 5, 1655	MG	
Josia, bp. Mar. 7, [16]57	MG	
Josias, had 9 children b. in Windsor. Dated Aug. 17, 1677	MG	
Josias*, s. Josias, ae 24, m. Martha **GAYLAR,** d. Samuell in		
her 20th y. Oct. 30, [16]79 *(Also written "John")	MG	
Josias, his w., adm. ch. Sept. [ ], [16]	MG	
Josias, adult, ch. mem. 16[ ]	MG	
Josias, contributed 0-3-0 to the poor in other colonies	MG	
Julia, d. Allyn & Hanna, d. Sept. 5, 1839, ae 27	2	233
Justavous, of Windsor, m. wid. Keziah **EATON,** of		
Springfield, Apr. 14, 1766	2	147
Kezia, d. Giles, Jr. & Kezia, b. Aug. 13, 1756	2	327
Kezia, w. Giles, Jr., d. June 27, 1762	2	530
Keziah, d. Justavous & Keziah, b. Sept. 5, 1766	2	328
Levy, s. Thomas & Sarah, b. Mar. 22, 1747/8	2	325
Levy, s. Thomas & Sarah, d. Nov. 9, 1750	2	228
Levy, s. Thomas & Sarah, d. Nov. 9, 1750	2	232
Lois, m. Grove **DAY,** b. of Windsor, Dec. 11, 1822, by		
Rev. Oliver Willson, of North Haven	2	472
Lucy, m. William **HOWARD,** b. of [ ], [ ], 1803, by		
Henry A. Rowland (Crossed out)	2	164
Lucy, m. William **HOWARD,** b. of Windsor, Apr. 8, 1805	2	482
Lucy, see Lucy **HOWARD**	2	244
Mabel, d. Benjamin & Deborah, b. June 15, 1732	2	321
Margarett, d. Job. b. Apr. 3, 1709	2	25
Margaret, d. Job, d. Jan. 9, 1709/10	2	229
Margaret, d. Benjamin, b. Mar. 6, 1723/4	2	30
[Martha?*], [d. Josia & Elizabeth], b. Dec. 7, 1662		
*(Supplied in pencil by LBB)	MG	
Martha, d. Josias, b. Dec. 7, 1662	Col.1	54
Martha, d. Josiah, b. Dec. 7, 1662	1	10
Martha, [bp.] Dec. 13, [16]62	MG	
Martha, d. [Josias* & Martha], b. Oct. 1, 1680 *(Also		

	Vol.	Page
ELLSWORTH, ELSWORTH, ELSEWORTH, ELESWORT,		
ELESWORTH, ELSWORT, (cont.)		
written "John")	MG	
Martha, d. Josias, Jr., b. Oct. 5, 1680	Col. 1	57
Martha, m. Samuel **STYLES**, b. of Windsor, Dec. [ ], 1701	1	62
Martha, d. John, b. Feb. 27, 1708/9	2	26
Martha, m. Nathanael **STOUGHTON**, b. of Windsor, Sept. 11, 1729	2	198
[Mary?*], [d. Josia & Elizabeth], b. May 7, 1660 *(Supplied in pencil by LBB)	MG	
Mary, d. Josiah, b. May 7, 1660	1	10
Mary, ae 20 on May 7, 1680, m. Danell **LOOMIS**, s. John, who was ae 23 on June 16, 1680, Dec. 23, 1680	MG	
Mary, [bp.] May 9, [16]60	MG	
Mary, m. Danell **LOOMAS**, s. John, Dec. 23, 1680, by Capt. Newbery	Col. 1	46
Mary, m. Daniel **LOOMIS**, s. John, Dec. 23, 1680	1	58
Mary, d. Josiah, Jr., b. Oct. 12, 1687	1	11
Mary, d. Job, b. Aug. 29, 1703	1	12
Mary, d. Jonathan, b. Mar. 1, 1706/7	2	25
Mary, d. Job, d. Feb. 28, 1707/8	2	229
Mary, w. Job, d. Sept. 15, 1710	2	229
Mary, d. Thomas, b. Jan. 7, 1710/11	2	26
Mary, d. Benjamin & Deborah, b. Feb. 20, 1727/8	2	320
Mary, d. William & Mary, b. June 27, 1738	2	323
Mary, of Windsor, m. Allen **HAWLEY**, of Granby, Dec. 15, 1829, by Henry A. Rowland	2	484
Mary Ann, m. Nathaniel L. **HAYDON**, Jr., b. of Windsor, Oct. 2, 1838, by Bennet Tyler	2	483
Moses, s. Nathaniel & Catharine, b. May 11, 1748	2	325
Naomi, d. Sergt. Thomas & Deborah, b. Feb. 23, 1719	2	321
Naomi, m. Jonathan **BROWN**, Jr., b. of Windsor, Jan. 11, 1743/4	2	131
Nathanel, s. Thomas, b. Sept. 3, 1699	1	12
Nathanael, m. Abigail **STRONG**, b. of Windsor, Jan. 1, 1729/30	2	146
Nathanael, d. (sic) Nathanael & Abigail, b. Sept. 9, 1730	2	321
Nathanael, s. Nathanaell & Abigail, d. Sept. 16, 1730	2	231
Nathanael, s. Nathanaell & Abigail, b. Apr. 30, 1738	2	322
Nathaniel, s. Nathaniel & Abigail, d. May 28, 1742	2	232
Oliver, twin with Ann, s. William & Mary, b. Aug. 25, 1745; d. Nov. 10, following, ae 11 wks.	2	324
Oliver, s. William & Mary, b. Mar. 24, 1746/7	2	324
Phebe L., m. Daniel B. **PHELPS**, b. of Windsor, Mar. 21, 1848, by Cephus Brainard	2	501
Ruben, s. Giles & Hannah, b. Feb. 19, 1736/7	2	322
Roger, s. Giles, Jr. & Keziah, b. July 28, 1760	2	328
Roger, s. Roger & Lucy, d. Oct. 1, 1837	2	233

	Vol.	Page

ELLSWORTH, ELSWORTH, ELSEWORTH, ELESWORT, ELESWORTH, ELSWORT, (cont.)

	Vol.	Page
Samuel, s. Josiah, b. July 18, 1697	1	12
Samuel, of Windsor, m. Elizabeth **ALLIN**, d. John, of Enfield, Nov. 20, 1717	2	145
Samuel, s. Samuel, b. Oct. 1, 1718	2	29
Samuel W., m. Eleanor **DRAKE**, b. of Windsor, Nov. 27, 1834, by H. A. Rowland	2	148
Sarah, d. Thomas, b. Dec. 9, 1696	1	12
Sarah, d. Jonathan, b. Jan. 8, 1698/9	2	24
Sarah, d. Jonathan, Jr. & Abigail, b. Sept. 16, 1739	2	327
Sarah, d. Thomas & Sarah, b. Nov. 11, 1740	2	325
Sarah, m. Josiah **ALLYN**, b. of Windsor, Feb. 9, 1761	2	123
Sarah, of Windsor, m. Francis **BAXTER**, of Enfield, May 7, 1767	2	134
Sarah G., of Windsor, m. Lucius W. **THAYRE**, of Westfield, Mass., Sept. 5, 1848, by C. B. Everest	2	511
Solomon, s. John & Ann, b. Apr. 30, 1737	2	323
Sibbel, d. Benjamin & Deborah, b. Mar. 7, 1734/5	2	321
Thomas, [s. Josia & Elizabeth], b. Sept. 2, 1665	MG	
Thomas, s. Josiah, b. Sept. 2, 1665	Col.1	55
Thomas, s. Josiah, b. Sept. 2, 1665	1	11
Thomas, bp. Sept. 9, [16]66	MG	
Thomas, s. Thomas, b. Mar. 10, 1708/9	2	26
Thomas, m. Sarah **LOOMIS**, b. of Windsor, Mar. 26, 1733	2	130
Thomas, Jr., m. Sarah **LOOMIS**, b. of Windsor, Mar. 26, 1733	2	146
Thomas, s. Thomas & Sarah, b. Jan. 21, 1735/6	2	325
Thomas, Sergt., d. Sept. 26, 1750	2	228
Thomas, Sergt., d. Sept. 26, 1750	2	232
William, s. Thomas, b. Apr. 15, 1702	1	12
William, of Windsor, m. Mary **OLIVE**, of Boston, June 16, 1737	2	146
William, s. William & Mary, b. Mar. 24, 1740	2	323
William H., m. Emily M. **MILLER**, b. of Windsor, Apr. 5, 1842, by Ezra J. Cook	2	148
-----, his w. [ ], adm. ch. & communicant Sept. [ ], 1666	MG	
-----, Lieut., d. [ ], in "Elenton" prior to 1740	MG	
-----, Capt., had 5 children d. [ ], in "Elenton" prior to 1740	MG	
-----, Capt., his child d. [ ], in "Elenton" prior to 1740	MG	
ELMOR, ELMER, ELMAR, Aaron, s. Joseph, b. Oct. 8, 1703	2	27
Aaron, s. Joseph, d. May 7, 1719	2	231
Abiel, s. Daniel & Elizabeth, b. May 9, 1752; d. Aug. 29, 1752	2	327
Abigail, d. Samuel, b. Apr. 28, 1710	2	27
Alexander, twin with Daniel, s. Daniel & Elizabeth, b. Aug.		

	Vol.	Page

ELMOR, ELMER, ELMAR, (cont.)

30, 1739	2	326
Ann, m. Thomas ELMOR, b. of Windsor, May 2, 1728	2	146
Anna, d. Thomas & Anna, b. Feb. 28, 1730	2	321
Anna, w. Thomas, d. Mar. 9, 1730/1	2	231
Aurelia, of Windsor, m. Elisha SHEPPARD, Jr., of Hartford, May 20, 1824, by Rev. Augustus Bolles	2	202
Cloe, d. Daniel & Elizabeth, b. May 17, 1737	2	326
Cloe, d. Jacob & Esther, b. Jan. 5, 1757	2	327
Cloe, d. Jacob & Esther, d. Oct. 26, 1757	2	232
Chloe, m. Archelaus FLINT, b. of Windsor, Apr. 6, 1764	2	152
Daniell, s. Samuel, b. Mar. 1, 1707/8	2	25
Daniel, twin with Alexander, s. Daniel & Elizabeth, b. Aug. 30, 1739	2	326
Elizabeth, d. Joseph, b. Feb. [ ], 1710/11	2	27
Elizabeth, d. Rev. Daniell & Margaret, b. Mar. 21, 1724/5	2	31
Elizabeth, d. Daniel & Elizabeth, b. Apr. 23, 1746; d. Sept. 1, 1752	2	326
Eunice, d. Joseph & Jane, b. Sept. 30, 1720	2	320
France, d. Thomas & Elizabeth, b. Jan. 16, 1754	2	326
Hannah, m. Thomas ROWEL, b. of Windsor, Dec. 7, 1743	2	195
Hezakiah, s. Daniel & Elizabeth, b. Mar. 5, 1744; d. Sept. 9, 1752	2	326
Jacob, s. Joseph, b. Feb. 27, 1714/15	2	28
Jacob, m. Esther BOOTH, b. of Windsor, Oct. 31, 1754	2	147
Jane, d. Joseph, b. Nov. 19, 1711	2	28
Jerusha, d. Daniel & Elizabeth, b. Aug. 31, 1735	2	326
Joel, s. Jacob & Esther, b. July 24, 1758	2	327
John, Sr., d. Dec. 24, 1711	2	231
Joseph, of Windsor, m. Jane ADKINS, of Hartford, Apr. 4, 1700	2	146
Joseph, s. Joseph, b. Mar. 28, 1701	2	27
Joseph, s. Joseph, d. Sept. 10, 1717	2	231
Joseph, s. Joseph & Jane, b. Sept. 6, 1718	2	320
Margret, d. Jacob & Esther, b. Aug. 17, 1755	2	327
Margret, d. Jacob & Esther, d. Oct. 23, 1757	2	232
Martha, m. Thomas FOSTER, b. of Windsor, Dec. 24, 1761	2	152
Nodiah, s. Jacob & Esther, b. Feb. 14, 1768	2	329
Phinehas, s. Joseph, b. Sept. 6, 1716	2	28
Samuel, s. Joseph, b. Dec. 12, 1705	2	27
Solomon, s. Joseph, b. Mar. 5, 1708/9	2	27
Solomon, s. Jacob & Esther, b. Feb. 10, 1761	2	328
Thomas, m. Ann ELMOR, b. of Windsor, May 2, 1728	2	146
Thomas, of Windsor, m. Elizabeth BUSHON, of Hartford, Feb. 14, 1752	2	146
Timothy, s. Daniel & Elizabeth, b. Sept. 23, 1741	2	326
ELY, Eunice, of Springfield, m. Roger NEWBERRY, of Windsor, July 29, 1762	2	183

	Vol.	Page
ENDERS, Henry W., of Suffield, m. Nancy **DAY**, of Windsor,		
Jan. 5, 1875, by R. K. Reynolds	2	519
ENDERTON, Susan Ann, of Suffield, m. Joseph M. **COOPER**, of		
Springfield, July 4, 1825, by Rev. Henry A. Rowland	2	138
ENDICOT, [see under **INDICOT**]		
ENGLISH, Thomas, m. Bridget **McDERMOT**, Oct. 13, 1852, by		
Rev. James Smyth	2	460
ENO, ENNO, ENNOE, ENOE, ENOS, Abygel, d. James, b. Mar.		
1, 1684	Col.D	51
Abigail, d. James, b. Mar. 1, 1686/7	1	11
Abigaell, m. Samuell **PHELPS**, b. of Windsor, Apr. 3, 1707	2	185
Allen, of Simsbury, m. Fanny **LEWIS**, of Windsor, May 21,		
1823, by Richard Niles, J. P.	2	148
Ann, d. James, b. Apr. 10, [16]82	1	11
Ann, m. Joseph **PHELPS**, grandson of Capt. Timothy, [17]	2	187
Ann, d. John, m. John **LOOMIS**, s. Daniell, Apr. 24, 1712	2	170
[Anna], w. John, d. Oct. 7, [16]79; bd. the 8th day	MG	
Anne, d. Erasmus & Anne, b. Sept. 27, 1784	2	330
Ashbel, s. Capt. Samuel & Eunice, b. Aug. 2, 1744	2	318
Ashbel, s. Capt. Samuel & Eunice, b. Aug. 2, 1744	2	329
Benjamin, s. James, b. Mar. 1, 1715/16	2	28
Benjamin, s. James, d. Nov. 9, 1716	2	230
Benjamin, s. Sergt. James, b. Oct. 5, 1719	2	29
Benjamin, s. Benjamin & Jerusha, b. Dec. 2, 1741	2	324
Benjamin, m. wid. Jerusha **PINNEY**, Jan. [ ], 1741/2	2	146
Carolina, d. Mary **ENOS**, b. Feb. 7, 1774	2	330
Daniel, s. Capt. Samuel & Eunice, b. Apr. 12, 1742	2	318
Daniel, s. Capt. Samuel & Eunice, b. Apr. 12, 1742	2	329
Daniel, s. Samuel & Marcy, b. Jan. 12, 1780	2	330
Daniel, m. Esther **PHELPS**, b. of Windsor, Jan. 23, 1783	2	147
David, s. James, b. Aug. 12, 1702	1	12
Eliphelet, s. Samuel & Eunice, b. Mar. 29, 1740	2	318
Eliphalet, s. Samuel & Eunice, b. Mar. 29, 1740	2	328
Elizabeth, d. Capt. Roger & Jerusha, b. May 20, 1774	2	330
Emily Augusta, m. George Milo **GRISWOLD**, b. of Windsor,		
Oct. 13, 1847, by C. B. Everest	2	481
Ester, d. Daniel & Ester, b. July 19, 1785	2	331
Esther, w. Daniel, d. July 10, 1787, at Colebrook	2	232
Eunice, d. Samuel & Eunice, b. Mar. 14, 1737; d. 23rd day of		
same month	2	318
Eunice, d. Samuel & Eunice, b. Mar. 14, 1737; d. same		
month, 23rd day	2	328
Eunice, d. Capt. Samuell & Eunice, b. Oct. 5, 1746	2	318
Eunice, d. Capt. Samuel & Eunice, b. Oct. 5, 1746	2	329
Eunice, wid. Samuel, d. May 7, 1792	2	232
Eunice, w. Samuel, d. May 7, 1792, ae 83	2	233
Hannah, d. James, Jr., b. Sept. 1, 1710	2	26
Hannah, m. Job **LOOMIS**, b. of Windsor, [ ], 1736	2	172

	Vol.	Page
ENO, ENNO, ENNOE, ENOE, ENOS, (cont.)		
Hezekiah, s. Daniel & Esther, b. July 1, 1783	2	331
James, m. Anna **BEDWELL,** Aug. 18, 1648	MG	
James, m. Anna **BIDELL,** Aug. 18, 1648	1	56
James, his two children, d. [ ], [16]48	MG	
James, s. [James & Anna], b. Oct. 30, 1651	MG	
James, s. James, bp. Nov. 2, 1651	1	10
James, his w. [ ], d. [ ], [16]57	MG	
James, m. Elizabeth **HOLCOMB,** wid., Aug. 5, 1658	1	56
James, had 3 children b. in Windsor. Dated Aug. 17, 1677	MG	
James, s. James, m. Abigall **BISSELL,** d. Samuel, Dec. 26, 1678	MG	
James, s. James, m. Abigall **BISSELL,** d. Samuell, Dec. 26, 1678, by Capt. Newbery	Col.1	46
James, s. James, m. Abigail **BISSELL,** d. Samuel, Dec. 26, 1678, by Capt. Nubery	1	56
James, s. James, m. Abigall **BISSELL,** d. Samuell, Dec. 2[ ], 1678, by Capt. Newbery	TR1	1
James, s. [James & Abigall], b. Sept. 23, 1679	MG	
James, s. James, Jr., b. Sept. 23, 1679	Col.1	56
James, Sr., his 1st w. [ ], d. Oct. 7, 1679; m. 2nd w. Hester **EGELSTON,** formerly w. James, Apr. 29, 1680	MG	
James, his w. [ ], d. Oct. 7, 1679	Col.1	58
James, Sr., m. Hester **EGELSTON,** formerly w. James, Apr. 29, 1680, by Capt. Newbery	Col.1	46
James, Sr., m. Hester **EGELSTON,** wid. James, Apr. 29, 1680, by Capt. Newbery	TR1	1
James, Sr., m. Hester **EGELSTON,** formerly w. James, Apr. 29, 1680, by Capt. Nubery	1	56
	Col.D	51
James, his d. [ ], b. Apr. 10, 1682	Col.D	56
James, Sr., d. June 11, 1682	1	43
James, Sr., d. June 11, 1682	1	56
James, Jr., m. Mary **GRANT,** Apr. 15, 1703	1	12
James, s. James, b. Dec. 30, 1703	2	28
James, s. James, Jr., b. Dec. 30, 1703	2	145
James, Jr., m. Hannah **PHELPS,** wid., July 15, 1708	2	230
James, Sr., d. July 16, 1714	2	324
James, s. Benjamin & Jerusha, b. June 17, 1743		
Jennett, m. Charles **CLAPP,** b. of Windsor, Feb. 8, 1842, by Ezra S. Cook	2	515
	2	328
Jerusha, d. Capt. Roger & Jerusha, b. Feb. 6, 1764	2	324
Joab, s. Benjamin & Jerusha, b. Mar. 6, 1744/5	MG	
John, s. [James & Anna], b. Dec. 2, 1654	Col.2	158
John, s. James, b. Dec. 2, 1654	1	10
John, s. James, b. Dec. 2, 1654		
John, s. James, m. Mary **DEBLE,** d. Ebenezer, May 10, 1681,	MG	

	Vol.	Page
ENO, ENNO, ENNOE, ENOE, ENOS, (cont.)		
John, s. James, ae 27, m. Mary **DEBLE**, d. Ebenezer, ae 17, May 10, [16]81	Col.1	46
John, s. James, b. Jan. 5, 1693	1	11
John, m. [Mary] [　], [　]	TR1	1
Joseph, s. Sergt. James, b. Jan. 20, 1721/2	2	30
Julia, of Simsbury, m. Jumin **CADWELL**, of Windsor, June 1, 1831	2	470
Marcy, d. Samuel & Marcy, b. Mar. 4, 1783	2	330
Martha, d. John, b. Apr. 6, 1685	Col.D	51
Martha, m. John **WINCHEL**, Jan. 3, 1705/6	2	207
Mary, d. Jno, b. Oct. 12, 1682	Col.D	51
Mary, d. James, b. May 5, 1691	1	11
Mary, d. Sept. 15, 1697	1	43
Mary, m. Daniel **GILLIT**, b. of Windsor, Jan. 28, 1702/3	1	57
Mary, w. James, Jr., d. Mar. 6, 1704/5	2	229
Mary, had d. Carolina, b. Feb. 7, 1774	2	330
Moses, s. Capt. Samuel & Eunice, b. Aug. 13, 1752	2	318
Moses, s. Capt. Samuel & Eunice, b. Aug. 13, 1752	2	329
Paoli, s. Capt. Roger & Jersha, b. Feb. 19, 1770	2	330
Roger, Capt., m. Jerusha **HAYDON**, b. of Windsor, Mar. 10, 1763	2	147
Roger, s. Capt. Roger & Jerusha, b. Feb. 14, 1768	2	330
Samuel, s. James, b. July 7, 1696	1	12
Samuel, m. Eunice **MARSHALL**, b. of Windsor, Dec. 24, 1735	2	147
Samuel, s. Samuel & Eunice, b. Mar. 19, 1738	2	318
Samuel, s. Samuel & Eunice, b. Mar. 19, 1738	2	328
Samuel, Jr., m. wid. Marcy **MANLEY**, b. of Windsor, May 7, 1777	2	147
Samuel, s. Samuel, Jr. & Marcy, b. Feb. 4, 1778; d. Feb. 27, 1781	2	330
Samuel, d. Aug. 17, 1778	2	232
Samuel, d. Aug. 17, 1778, ae 82	2	233
Samuel, s. Samuel & Marcy, d. Feb. 27, 1781	2	233
Samuel, s. Samuel & Marcy, b. Nov. 4, 1785	2	330
Sara, d. [James & Anna], b. June 15, 1649	MG	
Sarah, d. James, bp. June 17, 1649	1	10
Sarah, m. Benaga **HOLCOMB**, Apr. 11, 1667	MG	
Sarah, m. Beniaga **HOLCOMB**, Apr. 11, 1667, by Mr. Allyen	Col.1	45
Sarah, m. Benajah **HOLCOMB**, b. of Windsor, Apr. 11, 1667	1	57
Sarah, d. John, m. Jerimiah **ALFORD**, July 4, 1711	2	123
Sarah, d. Sergt. James, b. Nov. 7, 1717	2	28
Susannah, d. James, b. May 16, 1699	1	12
Sibbel, d. Capt. Roger & Jerusha, b. Feb. 6, 1766	2	328
William, s. James, b. Dec. 15, [16]84	Col.D	51
William, s. James, b. Dec. 15, 1684	1	11

	Vol.	Page
ENSIGN, ENSIGNE, Elizabeth, d. David & Elizabeth, b. Oct.		
17, 1761	2	327
Sara, m. John **ROCKWELL,** May 6, 1651	MG	
EPEEN, Daniell, his child d. [ ], in "Elenton" prior to 1740	MG	
ETON, Daniel, d. [ ], in "Elenton" prior to 1740	MG	
Daniell, his three children d. [ ], in "Elenton" prior		
to 1740	MG	
EVANS, EVINS, EUENES, EVENS, Austria, m. Stephen		
BREWER, b. of Berlin, Sept. 11, 1825, by Rev.		
Augusuts Bolles, of Wintonbury	2	149
Bennoni, d. May 7, 1698	1	43
Ebenezer, s. Samuel, b. July [ ], 1714	2	29
John, s. Samuel, b. Sept. 26, 1716	2	29
Joseph, s. Samuel, b. July 19, 1706	2	29
Martha, d. Samuel, b. [ ], 1699	2	29
Martha, m. Richard **COOK,** b. of Windsor, Apr. 11, 1722	2	136
Mary, m. Joel **GRISWOLD,** b. of Windsor, May 11, 1758	2	158
Mary, of Hartford, m. Heman **DUNBAR,** of Windsor, Sept.		
11, 1825, by Rev. Augustus Bolles, of Wintonbury	2	144
Mary, m. John **ABEY,** Nov. 21, 1852, by Rev. James Smyth	2	460
Nicolas, m. Mary **PARSON,** b. of Windsor, Nov. 17, 1670,		
by Capt. Newbery	Col.1	46
Nicolas, s. Samuel, b. July [ ], 1710	2	29
Phebe, d. Abigael, b. Jan. 16, 1713/14	2	27
Samuel, s. Samuel, b. Dec. 10, 1703	2	29
Sarah, of Hartford, m. Elijah **HOLCOMB,** of Windsor, Nov.		
23, 1758	2	163
Thankfull, d. Samuel, b. Mar. 31, 1712	2	29
Thankfull, m. John **HOSKINS,** b. of Windsor, June 15, 1735	2	162
Thomas, s. Samuel, b. Jan. [ ], 1708	2	29
FAIRBANKS, Ephraim, twin with Willard Blackmer, s.		
Lyman & Sarah, b. Dec. 11, 1835	2	35
Willard Blackmer, twin with Ephraim, s. Lyman & Sarah, b.		
Dec. 11, 1835	2	35
FARNSWORTH, FARNESWORTH, FFARNWORTH, Joseph,		
s. Samuel, b. June 19, 1694	2	31
Joseph, s. Samuel, b. June 20, 1694	1	13
Mary, d. [Samuell & Mary], b. May 17, 1678; d. [May]		
26, [1678]	MG	
Mary, d. Samuel, b. May 17, 1678; d. May 26, 1678	1	13
Mary, w. Samuel, d. Aug. 28, 1684	1	44
Mary*, w. Sam[uel], d. Aug. 28, 1684 *(Note by LBB:		
"Mary **(STOUGHTON) FARNSWORTH**")	Col.D	56
Mary, m. John **MOOR,** Sr., Dec. 17, 1701	2	175
Samuell, of Dorchester, m. Mary **STOTON,** d. Thomas, of		
Windsor, June 3, [16]77	MG	
Samuel, of Dorchester, Mass., m. Mary **STOTON,** d. Thomas,		
of Windsor, June 3, 1677, by Capt. Newbery	Col.1	46

	Vol.	Page

FARNSWORTH, FARNESWORTH, FFARNWORTH, (cont.)

Samuell, of Dorchester, Mass., m. Mary **STOUGHTON,** d.		
Thomas, of Windsor, June 3, 1677, in Hartford Cty., by		
Capt. Newbery	TR1	1
Samuel, of Dorchester, Mass., m. Mary **STOUGHTON,** d.		
Thomas, of Windsor, June 3, 1677, by Capt. Nubery	1	56
Samuel, m. Mary **MOOSES,** Nov. [ ], 1685	1	56
Samuel, d. Nov. 17, 1697	1	44

FENCHON, FENSHON, Mathias, had 3 children b. in Windsor.

Dated Aug. 17, 1677	MG	
Mathias, [ ]	MG	
Nicolas, s. Isabell [ ], June 12, 1645; "in 1680 they has		
been m. 35 yrs and had no child"	MG	
Nicolas, contributed 0-2-6 to the poor	MG	
Sara, d. [ ], [16]46	MG	
Thomas, d. May 16, [16]39	MG	

FENNER, John, m. Sally **CHAMPLAIN,** b. of R. I., Oct. 8, 1827,

by Rev. John Bartlett	2	477

FENTON, Alvah, m. Elizabeth B. **PORTER,** Sept. 8, 1830, by

Rev. Asa Bushnell, Jr.	2	153
Frederick, of Vernon, m. Caroline E. **GRISWOLD,** of		
Windsor, Feb. 28, 1848, by Cephus Brainard	2	478

FIELD, Edithea, m. Augustus **FITCH,** Jan. 22, 1760

FIELD, Edithea, m. Augustus FITCH, Jan. 22, 1760	2	152
John, s. Benjamin & Sarah, b. June 9, 1761	2	336
Sarah, d. Benjamin & Sarah, b. Oct. 4, 1759	2	336

FILER, [see under **FYLER**]

FILLEY, FILLY, FFILLY, FFILE, FFILLYF, FILLE, FELLY, FILLIE, FILLIS, FFILLEY, FYLLEY, FILLER, Abiah, d.

William & Abiah, b. Mar. 11, 1743	2	332
Abigal, [d. William & Margret], b. Aug. 21, 1658	MG	
Abigail, d. William, b. Aug. 21, 1658	1	13
Abigayl, [d. William], [bp.] Aug. 22, [16]58	MG	
Abigayl, [d. William], bp. Aug. 28, [16]58	MG	
Abigayl, d. [Samuell & Anna], b. Jan. 20, 1668; d. [ ]	MG	
Abigail, d. Samuel, b. Jan. 20, 1668	1	13
Abigayl, d. Samuell, b. Jan. 30, 1679	MG	
Abigall, ae 22 on Aug. 21, 1680, d. of William, m.		
Samuell **BISSELL,** ae 20 on Apr. 5, 1680, s. John, Aug.		
26, 1680	MG	
Abigal, d. Samuell, bp. [16]	MG	
Abigael, d. John, m. Isaack* **PINNEY,** Jan. 26, 1709/10		
*("Josia" crossed out)	2	186
Abigaell, m. Job **LOOMIS,** Apr. 27, 1710	2	170
Abigail, d. Josiah & Esther, b. July 4, 1719	2	34
Abigail, d. Joseph & Ann, b. May 17, 1746	2	333
Abigail, d. Joseph & Anne, d. May 19, 1747	2	234
Abigail, d. Joseph, [ ] (Crossed out)	2	333
Abraham, s. William & Abiah, b. Apr. 28, 1739	2	331

FILLEY, FILLY, FFILLY, FFILE, FFILLYF, FILLE, FELLY,
FILLIE, FILLIS, FFILLEY, FYLLEY, FILLER, (cont.)

	Vol.	Page
Amelia, d. Oliver & Tabitha, b. Sept. 20, 1792	2	560
Amos, s. John, b. July 29, 1713	2	33
Amos, d. Sept. 7, 1734, in the 83rd y. of his age	2	235
Ann, d. Samuel, b. Aug. 16, 1664	1	13
Ann, m. John FILLEY, b. of Windsor, Apr. 27, 1764	2	152
Ann, d. John & Ann, b. Feb. 19, 1765	2	337
Anna, d. Samuell & Anna, b. Aug. 16, 1664	MG	
Anna, d. Samuell, b. Aug. 16, 1664	Col.1	54
Anna, [d.] Sam[uel], [bp.] Sept. 25, [16]64	MG	
Anna, m. Samuel GRANT, Dec. 6, 1683	MG	
Anna, m. Samuell GRANT, Dec. 6, 1683	2	154
Annah, d. Jonathan, b. Sept. 23, 1708	2	32
Anna, w. Samuel, d. Nov. 18, 1711	2	233
Anna, m. Daniel GILLET, b. of Windsor, Jan. 6, 1726	2	155
Anne, d. Joseph & Anne, b. Feb. 24, 1740/1	2	331
Asher, s. William & Abiah, b. [ ]	2	334
Daniel, s. John, b. Jan. 29, 1718/19	2	33
Daniel, s. Joseph & Ann, b. Nov. 8, 1757	2	334
David, s. John, b. Nov. 20, 1715	2	33
David, m. Margery BROWN*, b. of Windsor, Sept. 22, 1749 *(In pencil)	2	152
David, s. John & Ann, b. Apr. 30, 1773	2	559
David, s. David & Lydia, b. Nov. 4, 1777	2	559
David H., m. Nancy LOOMIS, b. of Windsor, Mar. 5, 1828, by Rev, John Bartlett	2	153
Debroa, d. [William & Margret], b. Mar. 21, 1661	MG	
Deborah, d. William, b. Mar. 21, 1661	1	13
Debro, [d. William, [bp.] Mar. 24, [16]61	MG	
Deborah, of Windsor, m. John SACKET, of Westfeild, Dec. 1, 1686	Col.D	54
Deborah, of Windsor, m. John SACKIT, of Westfield, Dec. 1, 1686	1	61
Deborah, d. Jonathan, b. Feb. 22, 1701/2	2	31
Deborah, d. Jonathan, d. Mar. 29, 1702	2	233
Deborah, d. Jonathan, b. Mar. 24, 1705/6	2	31
Deborah, m. John PALMER, Jr., b. of Windsor, Sept. 12, 1723	2	187
Deborah, d. Nathaniel & Hannah, b. Oct. 15, 1743	2	332
Deliverance, d. Josiah, b. Nov. 17, 1716	2	33
Dorcas, d. Josiah, b. May 14, 1714	2	33
Edee, d. Amos & Edee, b. Aug. 7, 1737; d. 4 wks. after	2	34
Edee, d. Amos, d. Sept. 4, 1738, ae 4 wks.	2	234
Elijah, s. David & Lydia, b. Nov. 19, 1778	2	559
Elisabeth, d. [William & Margret], b. Mar. 4, 1650	MG	
Elizabeth, d. William, b. Mar. 4, 1650	1	13
Elizabeth, d. William, b. Mar. 4, 1650	1	13

	Vol.	Page
FILLEY, FILLY, FFILLY, FFILE, FFILLYF, FILLE, FELLY,		
FILLIE, FILLIS, FFILLEY, FYLLEY, FILLER, (cont.)		
Elisabeth, d. William, bp. Aug. 3, [1651]	MG	
Elizabeth, m. Dauid WINCHELL, Nov. 17, 1669	MG	
Elizabeth, m. Daued WINCHELL, Nov. 17, 1669	Col.1	45
Elizabeth, m. David WINCHEL, Nov. 17, 1669	1	63
Elizabeth, wid. m. John HOSKINS, May 27, 1708	2	161
Elizabeth, d. Jonathan, b. Mar. 8, 1716/17	2	33
Elizabeth, d. Nathanael & Hannah, b. July 25, 1738	2	331
Elnathan, s. Nathaniel & Hannah, b. Mar. 22, 1753	2	334
Emily, of Windsor, m. Hector MILLER, of Avon, Aug. 30,		
1830, by John Bartlett	2	492
Erasmus, s. Josiah & Esther, b. Dec. 1, 1721	2	34
Esther, d. Josiah, b. May 26, 1712	2	32
Eunice M., m. Lucius NEWBERRY, b. of Windsor, Sept. 15,		
1834, by Rev. A. C. Washburn	2	183
Gad, s. William & Abiah, b. Jan. 28, 1747/8	2	333
Gilbert, m. Lucy WELLS, b. of Windsor, Dec. 29, 1821, by		
Rev. Augusuts Bolles, of Wintonbury	2	476
Hannah, bp. July 3, [16]53	MG	
Hanah, m. Samuel GRANT, Dec. 6, 1683	Col.D	54
Hannah, m. Samuel GRANT, Dec. 6, 1683	1	57
Hannah, d. Nathaniell & Hannah, b. Mar. 8, 1740/1	2	331
Hannah, 3rd, m. Nathaniel MATHER, Jr., b. of Windsor,		
Nov. 11, 1762	2	180
Hannah, see Hanna GRANT	Col.D	56
Harvey, s. Oliver & Tabitha, b. June 30, 1794	2	560
Harvey, of Penn., m. Chloe CADWELL, of Windsor, Oct. 3,		
1831, by Rev. Norman Atwood	2	477
Horrace, s. John & Ann, b. Nov. 16, 1779	2	559
Horace H., m. Irene K. FRANCIS, b. of Windsor, Oct. 19,		
1842, by S. D. Jewett	2	477
Isaac, s. William & Abia, b. Feb. 25, 1736/7	2	34
Jane, d. Joseph & Ann, b. June 29, 1751	2	334
Jay H., m. Julia A. NEWBURY, b. of Wintonbury, Sept. 25,		
1833, by Stephen Berrunnigton	2	519
Jerusha, d. Samuell & Jerusha, b. June 3, 1740	2	331
Gerusha, d. Oliver & Tabitha, b. July 19, 1788	2	560
Jerusha P., m. John N. ALDERMAN, b. of Windsor, Mar. 14,		
1833, by Rev. Ansel Nash	2	126
Jesse, s. John & Ann, b. Apr. 27, 1775; d. May 2, 1775	2	559
Joannah, m. Jerijah BARBER, b. of Windsor, Dec. 5, 1765	2	134
John, s. [William & Margret], b. Dec. 15, 1645	MG	
John, b. Dec. 15, [16]45; bp. Aug. 3, [16]51	MG	
John, s. William, b. Dec. 15, 1645	1	13
John, s. William, bp. Aug. 3, [1651]	MG	
John, s. [Samuell & Anna], b. Feb. 10, 1677; bp. Feb. 17,		
1677	MG	

	Vol.	Page
FILLEY, FILLY, FFILLY, FFILE, FFILLYF, FILLE, FELLY, FILLIE, FILLIS, FFILLEY, FYLLEY, FILLER, (cont.)		
John, s. [Samuell], b. Feb. 10, 1677	Col.1	56
John, s. Samuel, b. Feb. 10, 1677	1	13
John, s. Samuell, bp. Feb. 17, 1677	MG	
John, m. Mary WILSON, b. of Windsor, Oct. 9, 1707	2	151
John, s. John, b. Sept. 19, 1708; d. [ ]	2	32
John, s. John, d. Sept. 28, 1709	2	233
John, 2nd, s. John, b. Nov. 4, 1709	2	32
John, d. Dec. 9, 1736	2	234
John, m. Rebeckah DRAKE, Jan. 18, 1736/7	2	151
John, s. John & Rebeckah, b. Apr. 18, 1737	2	34
John, s. John, d. June 26, 1737	2	234
John, m. Ann FILLEY, b. of Windsor, Apr. 27, 1764	2	152
John, s. John & Ann, b. May 28, 1769	2	339
John, contributed 0-2-6 to the poor in other colonies	MG	
Jonah, s. Jonathan & Mary, b. Aug. 9, 1740	2	331
Jonathan, s. [Samuell & Anna], b. Nov. 30, 1672	MG	
Jonnathan, s. Samuell, b. Nov. 30, 1672	Col.1	56
Jonathan, s. Samuel, b. Nov. 30, [16]72; bp. Dec. 1, [16]72	1	13
Jonathan*, m. Deborah LOOMIS, Sept. 5, 1700 *(In pencil)	2	150
Jonathan, s. Jonathan, b. Oct. 28, 1703	2	31
Jonathan, m. Mary WILSON, b. of Windsor, Jan. 2, 1728/9	2	151
Jonathan, s. Jonathan & Mary, b. Mar. 15, 1732/3	2	34
Jonathan, d. May 17, 1740	2	234
Jonathan, Jr., m. Sarah BUTLER, b. of Windsor, Feb. 6, 1755	2	152
Joseph, s. John, b. Nov. 1, 1711	2	32
Joseph, m. Anne MORTON, b. of Windsor, May 8, 1740	2	151
Joseph, s. Joseph & Anne, b. May 18, 1744	2	332
Joseph, twin with Mary, s. William & Mary, b. July 9, 1752	2	334
Joseph, d. July 18, 1775	2	235
Josia, s. [Samuell & Anna], b. Jan. 21, 1675	MG	
Josiah, s. Samuel, b. Jan. 21, 1675	1	13
Josiah, m. Esther EGELSTON, b. of Windsor, Dec. 9, 1703	1	56
Josiah, m. Esther EGLSTONE, Dec. 29, 1703	2	151
Josiah, s. Josiah, b. Nov. 24, 1704	2	31
Josiah, s. Josiah & Mary, b. Nov. 25, 1737	2	34
Josias, s. Samuell, b. June 21, 1675	Col.1	56
Keziah, d. Jonathan & Mary, b. Sept. 17, 1748	2	333
Keziah, d. Amos & Edee, b. Dec. 6, 1758	2	335
Lauranna, d. Nathaniel & Hannah, b. Dec. 17, 1745	2	332
Loanna, d. Amos & Edee, b. Oct. 19, 1744	2	333
Luke, s. Joseph & Ann, b. Mar. 1, 1747/8	2	334
Margaret, d. Jonathan, b. Oct. 7, 1710	2	32
Margarett, d. Jonathan, d. Feb. 27, 1711/12	2	233
Margaret, d. Jonathan & Mary, b. Aug. [ ], 1743	2	332
Margret, d. Nathaniell & Hannah, b. June 13, 1748	2	333
Margret, m. Thomas HOSKINS, b. of Windsor, Apr. 15,		

	Vol.	Page
FILLEY, FILLY, FFILLY, FFILE, FFILLYF, FILLE, FELLY, FILLIE, FILLIS, FFILLEY, FYLLEY, FILLER, (cont.)		
[Samuel*], s. Samuel, d. [Nov. 10*], [16]67 *(In pencil)	MG	
Samuel, s. Samuell, d. Nov. 10, [16]67	Col. 1	55
Samuell, s. [Samuell & Anna], b. Apr. 2, 1670; d. [ ]	MG	
Samuel, s. Samuel, b. Apr. 2, 1670	1	13
Samuell, s. Samuell, [bp.], Apr. 3, [16]70	MG	
Samuell, adm. communion Dec. 18, [16]70	MG	
Samuel, adm. ch. & communicant Dec. [ ], 1670	MG	
Samuell, taxed 4-0 on Feb. 10, [16]73	MG	
Samuell, s. [Samuell & Anna], b. Mar. 7, 1673; d. [ ]	MG	
Samuell, s. Samuell, b. Mar. 7, 1673	Col. 1	56
Samuel, s. Samuel, b. Mar. 7, 1673	1	13
Samuel, had 7 children, b. in Windsor. Dated Aug. 17, 1677	MG	
Samuell, s. Samuell, d. Oct. 7, 1679	Col. 1	58
Sam[ue]l, his w. [ ], adm. ch. & communicant Dec. [ ], 1670	MG	
Samuel, his w. [ ], adm. ch. & communicant Dec. [ ], 167[ ]	MG	
Samuell, s. Samuell, b. Dec. 8, 1681	Col. D	51
Samuel, s. Samuel, b. Dec. 8, 1681	1	13
Samuel, his w. [ ], adm. ch. Dec. 8, [16]	MG	
Samuell, communicant 16[ ]	MG	
Samuell, s. Josiah, b. Oct. 22, 1706	2	31
Samuel, d. Jan. 4, 1711/12	2	233
Samuel, contributed 0-5-0 to the poor in other colonies	MG	
Sarah, d. Joseph & Ann, b. Sept. 18, 1742	2	331
Susannah, m. Ruben **LOOMIS**, Jr., b. of Windsor, Aug. 17, 1769	2	173
Susanna, d. John & Ann, b. June 29, 1784	2	560
Thomas, m. Charlotte M. **BARBER**, Nov. 12, 1833, by Henry A. Rowland	2	477
Timothy, s. Joseph & Ann, b. Oct. 21, 1753	2	334
W., his w. [ ], adm. ch. & communicant July [ ], 1651	MG	
William, m. Margret [ ], Sept. 2, 164[ ]	MG	
William, his w. [ ], adm. ch. July 17, [16]51	MG	
William, s. William, [bp.] Nov. 12, [16]64	MG	
William, s. [William & Margret], b. Mar. 7, 1664/5	MG	
William, s. William, b. Mar. 7, [16]64/5	Col. 1	55
William, s. William, b. Mar. 7, 1664/5	1	13
William, taxed 2-0 on Feb. 10, [16]73	MG	
William, taxed 4-0 on Feb. 10, [16]73	MG	
William, adm. communion, Mar. 8, 1673	MG	
William, adm. ch. & commiunicant Mar. [ ], 1673	MG	
William, had 7 children b. in Windsor. Dated Aug. 17, 1677	MG	
William, communicant 16[ ]	MG	
William, s. Josiah, b. Apr. 2, 1709	2	32
William, m. Abia **MILLINGTON**, b. of Windsor, June 15,		

	Vol.	Page

FILLEY, FILLY, FFILLY, FFILE, FFILLYF, FILLE, FELLY, FILLIE, FILLIS, FFILLEY, FYLLEY, FILLER, (cont.)

1730	2	151
William, m. Abiah MILLINTON, b. of Windsor, June 16, 1730	2	151
William, s. William & Abia, b. Mar. 5, 1734/5	2	34
William, contributed 0-0-7 to the poor in other colonies	MG	
----, Lieut., his w. [ ], ch. mem. 16[ ], from Dorchester	MG	
FISH, Almira G., m. Horace M. COOK, Nov. 16, 1834, by Richard G. Drake, J. P.	2	471
Ann Peris, of Windsor, m. Stephen BROWN, of Suffield, Nov. 26, 1829, by Henry A. Rowland	2	498
Eliza, m. Albert DENSLOW, Sept. 18, 1827, by Rev. Henry A. Rowland	2	144
Eliza, m. Albert DENSLOW, Sept. 18, 1827, by [ ]*, *(Entry crossed out)	2	153
Elizabeth, m. Lewis REED, b. of Windsor, Sept. 28, 1830, by Henry Sill, J. P.	2	505
Julia, m. Jarvis BUCKLAND, Sept. 18, 1827, by Rev. Henry A. Rowland	2	469
Mary Ann, m. Fredus WATERS, of Chester, Sept. 19, 1838, by William Thompson	2	514
Mary Jane, of Windsor, m. Greenleaf KEENY, of Manchester, Apr. 22, 1840, by Rev. S. D. Jewett	2	485
Sarah Ann, m. Charles C. BOWDOIN, b. of Windsor, June 8, 1834, by Rev. Noah Porter	2	499
FISHER, Thomas, m. Elisabeth GRANT, Nov. 20, 1707	2	151
FISKE, Sarah, of Wenham, m. John COOK, of Windsor, Sept. 14, 1688	1	55
FITCH, FFITCH, Abigail, w. Corp. Nathanael, d. Apr. 4, 1719	2	234
Alice, d. Ebenezer, b. June 30, 1713	2	32
Ales, d. Joseph & Prudence, b. July 30, 1762	2	336
Ann, Mrs., d. Jan. 20, 1686	Col.D	56
Ann, Mrs., d. Jan. 20, 1686	1	44
Ann, m. Benjamin LOOMIS, b. of Windsor, Jan. 6, 1703	1	59
Augustus, m. Edithea FIELD, Jan. 22, 1760	2	152
Bridgett, m. Jonathan BISSELL, b. of Windsor, Mar. 17, 1708/9	2	128
Charles H., m. Mary E. PALMER, b. of Windsor, Sept. 15, 1847, by F. A. Leete	2	478
Daniel, s. Jeremiah & Abigal, b. Jan. 17, 1760	2	335
Dorathy, m. Nathaniel BISSELL, July 4, 1683	Col.D	54
Dorethy, m. Nathan[ie]ll BISSELL, July 4, 1683	1	54
Dorothy, see Dorithy BISSELL	Col.D	57
Ebenezer, d. Nov. 20, 1724	2	234
Ebenezer, s. Ebenezer, b. Mar. 10, 1724/5	2	34
Eleazer, s. Ebenezer, b. May 28, 1720	2	34
Elijah, s. Ebenezer, b. Feb. 23, 1717/18	2	33

	Vol.	Page
FITCH, FFITCH, (cont.)		
Elijah, m. Mary **LOOMIS,** b. of Windsor, Oct. 28, 1742	2	152
Fanny, of Windsor, m. Samuel **GREEN,** of Palmer, Mass.,		
Dec. 2, 1827, by Rev. Augustus Bolles	2	480
George, s. Joseph & Prudance, b. Apr. 22, 1774	2	339
Hannah, d. James & Phebe, b. Apr. 7, 1757	2	335
James, s. Ebenezer, b. July 24, 1715	2	33
James, s. James & Phebe, b. May 2, 1762	2	336
Jerusha, of Canterbery, m. Daniel **BISSEL,** Jr., of Windsor,		
Mar. 18, 1717/18	2	129
John, of Hartford, m. Ann **HELLER,** wid. of Windsor,		
Dec. 9, 1656	Col.2	159
John, his w. [ ], d. [Aug. 11*] [16]73 *(In pencil)	MG	
John, his w. [ ], d. Aug. 11, [16]73	Col.1	58
John, his w. [ ], d. Aug. 11, [16]73	1	43
John, d. May 10, [16]76	MG	
John, bd. May 10, 1676	Col.1	58
John, bd. May 10, 1676	1	43
John Field, s. Augustus & Edithea, b. Feb. 7, 1766	2	337
Jonathan, s. Medinah & Lydia, b. Feb. 15, 1745/6	2	333
Joseph, s. Joseph, d. Feb. 18, 1697/8	1	44
Joseph, Jr., m. Prudence **DRAKE,** b. of Windsor, July 9, 1760	2	152
Joseph, s. Joseph, Jr. & Prudence, b. Aug. 1, 1765	2	337
Justis, s. Joseph & Prudance, b. May 20, 1769	2	339
Justus, of Windsor, m. Hannah **INDICOT,** of Hartford, July		
13, 1825, by Rev. Augusuts Bolles, of Wintonbury	2	153
Leuther, s. Joseph, Jr. & Prudence, b. May 20, 1767	2	339
Mary, d. Elijah & Mary, b. Apr. 25, 1744	2	332
Mary, w. Elijah, d. May 5, 1744	2	234
Mary, m. Ebenezer **READ,** b. of Windsor, Dec. 6, 1759	2	195
Medina, s. Ebenezer, b. Nov. 20, 1722	2	33
Medina, of Windsor, m. Lydia **AVERY,** of Ashford, Dec. 19,		
1744	2	152
Nathannael, Corp. of Windsor, m. Abigail **BUTOLF,** of		
Stonington, Nov. 23, 1718	2	151
Olef, d. Joseph, Jr. & Prudence, b. Dec. 12, 1763	2	337
Prudence, d. Joseph & Prudence, b. Mar. 15, 1761	2	336
Roxana, d. Jeremiah & Abigail, b. June 13, 1763	2	336
Russell, s. James & Phebe, b. Sept. 29, 1760	2	336
Sary, m. John **STOUGHTON,** Jan. 23, 1689	Col.D	55
Sarah, m. John **STOUGHTON,** Jan. 23, 1689	1	61
Sarah, m. Timothy **KING,** b. of Windsor, Apr. 19, 1753	2	167
Sarah, d. James & Phebe, b. Feb. 3, 1755	2	335
Thaddeus, s. Jeremiah & Abigail, b. July 27, 1761	2	335
Thankfull, d. Jeremiah & Abigail, b. Jan. 16, 1765	2	337
FLETCHER, Charlotte, of Windsor, m. George **ANDERSON,** of		
Farmington, Mar. 5, 1848, by Cephus Brainard	2	462
FLINT, Archelaus, m. Chloe **ELMOR,** b. of Windsor, Apr. 6, 1764	2	152

	Vol.	Page
FLINT, (cont.)		
Elizabeth, d. Achelaus & Chloe, b. Oct. 19, 176?	2	338
Talcott, d. Archelaus & Chloe, b. June 17, 1764	2	337
FOOTE, FOOT, Russell, m. Solome **PARSONS**, May 29, 1825,		
by Benjamin F. Lambord, of Warehouse Point	2	153
Sophia S., of Lee, Mass., m. Charles W. **BECKWITH**, of		
Greenport, N. Y., Nov. 2, 1847, by C. B. Everest	2	503
FORBS, Sarah, of Hartford, m. Josiah **BARBER**, of Windsor, June		
28, 1745	2	131
FORD, FOORD, Ann, m. Thomas **NEWBURY**, Mar. 12, [16]76	MG	
Ann, m. Thomas **NEWBERY**, Mar. 12, 1676	Col.1	46
Ann, m. Thomas **NEWBERY**, Mar. 12, 1676	TR1	1
Ann, m. Thomas **NUBERY**, Mar. 12, 1676/7	1	59
Thomas, his w. [ ], d. [16]43	MG	
Thomas, his w. [ ], bd. Apr. 18, 1643	1	44
Thomas, his w. [ ], adm. ch. [ ] 30, [16]60	MG	
----f, ch. mem. 16[ ], from Dorchester	MG	
FORWARD, FOWARD, Abel, s. Samuel, b. Nov. 4, 1710	2	32
Ann, d. June 22, 1685	Col.D	56
Ann, d. June 22, 1685	1	44
Deborah, d. Samuel, b. Apr. 6, 1713	2	32
John, s. Samuell, b. Apr. 29, 1717	2	33
Joseph, s. Samuell, b. Nov. 10, 1707	2	31
Rachell, d. Samuel, b. Apr. 30, 1715	2	33
Samuell, had child b. July 23, 1671; had child b. Nov. 10,		
1674	MG	
Samuell, adm. communion Oct. 8, [16]71	MG	
Samuel, adm. ch. & communicant Oct. [ ], 1671	MG	
Samuel, had 2 children b. in Windsor. Dated Aug. 17, 1677	MG	
Samuel, d. Sept. 16, 1684	Col.D	56
Samuel, d. Oct. 16, 1684	1	44
Samuell, communicant 16[ ]	MG	
Samuel, s. Samuel, b. Aug. 20, 1703	1	13
Samuel, s. Samuell, b. Aug. 20, 1703	2	31
Samuel, contributed 0-1-3 to the poor in other colonies	MG	
-----, Mr., taxed 2-0 on Feb. 10, [16]73	MG	
FOSTER, Abel, s. Abraham & Elizabeth, b. Oct. 11, 1728	2	332
Abel, m. Hannah [ ], b. of Windsor, Dec. 18, 1755	2	335
Abel, m. Hannah [ ], b. of Windsor, Dec. 18, 1757	2	152
Abraham, m. Elisabeth **MOORE**, b. of Windsor, Nov. 30,		
1727	2	151
Abraham, s. Abel & Hannah, b. Feb. 16, 1765	2	338
Ann, had illeg. d. Ann, b. Oct. 2, 1721	2	33
Ann, illeg. d. Ann **FOSTER**, b. of Oct. 2, 1721	2	33
Ann, d. Oct. 18, 1721	2	234
Chanse, s. Abel & Hannah, b. Jan. 15, 1759	2	335
Elisabeth, d. Abraham & Elisabeth, b. Jan. 20, 1745/6	2	333
Hacoliah, d. Abraham & Elisabeth, b. July 4, 1740	2	333

	Vol.	Page
FOSTER, (cont.)		
Hannah, d. Abraham & Elizabeth, b. Oct. 4, 1730	2	332
Hannah, m. Edward **CHAPMAN,** Apr. 4, 1754	2	157
Hannah, m. Jonathan B. **GILLETT,** b. of Windsor, July 1,		
1835, by Rev. Ansel Nash	2	481
Hittey, d. Abel & Hannah, b. June 17, 1761	2	336
John, s. Abraham & Elisabeth, b. Sept. 19, 1742	2	333
Mar*, s. Abel & Hannah, b. Oct. 22, 1766 *(In pencil)	2	338
Mary, d. Thomas & Martha, b. Feb. 13, 1763	2	336
Mary Chapman, d. Abel & Hannah, b. June 12, 1763	2	336
Pellatiah, s. Abraham & Elizabeth, b. Nov. 30, 1732	2	34
Pelatiah, s. Abraham & Elisabeth, b. Nov. 30, 1732	2	332
Phenihas, s. Thomas & Pheba, b. May 13, 1763	2	337
Prudance, d. Thomas & Pheba, b. Sept. 14, 1764	2	338
Sibil, d. Abraham & Elisabeth, b. May 19, 1735	2	332
Sibbel, m. Thomas **SEXTON,** b. of Windsor, Nov. 26, 1759	2	200
Thomas, s. Abraham & Elisabeth, b. July 25, 1737	2	333
Thomas, m. Martha **ELMOR,** b. of Windsor, Dec. 24, 1761	2	152
Thomas, m. Pheba **POMROY,** b. of Windsor, Jan. 12, 1762	2	152
Wareham, s. Abel & Hannah, b. Oct. 8, 1757	2	335
FOUKS, Henry, bd. Sept. 12, 1640	1	43
FOWLER, FOWLLER, FOULER, FFOWLER, Abigayl, d.		
[Ambrous & Joane], b. Mar. 1, 1646	MG	
Abigail, d. Ambros, b. [ ], 1646	1	13
Ambrous, m. Joane **ALUARD,** May 6, 1646	MG	
Ambros, m. Jane **ALFORD,** May 6, 1646	1	56
Ambrous, s. [Ambrous & Joane], b. May 8, 1658	MG	
Ambros, s. Ambros, b. May 8, 1658	1	13
Ambros, had 7 children b. in Windsor. Dated Aug. 17, 1677	MG	
Crayton, m. Nancy **COOK,** b. of Hartford, July 24, 1843,		
by Rev. S. D. Jewett	2	478
Elisabeth, d. [Ambrous & Joane], b. Dec. 2, 1656	MG	
Elizabeth, d. Ambros, b. Dec. 2, 1656	1	13
George W., m. Susan Maria **MACROBIES,** b. of Windsor,		
Aug. 15, 1852, by Rev. Joseph D. Hull	2	461
Hanna, d. [Ambrous & Joane], b. Dec. 20, 1654	MG	
Hana, d. Ambous, b. Dec. 20, [16]55	Col.2	181
John, s. [Ambrous & Joane], b. Nov. 19, 1648	MG	
John, s. Ambros, b. Nov. [ ], 1648	1	13
Mary, d. [Ambrous & Joane], b. May 15, 1650	MG	
Samuell, s. [Ambrous & Joane], b. Nov. 18, 1652	MG	
Samuel, s. Ambros, b. Nov. 18, 1652	1	13
Samuel, of Westfield, m. Abigail **BROWN,** of Windsor, Nov.		
[ ], 1683	1	56
Samuel, of Westfield, m. Abigall **BROWN,** of Windsor, Nov.		
[ ], 1685	Col.D	54
FOX, FFOXE, FFOX, Charly, of New Hartford, m. Salinas A.		
HOLCOMB, of Windsor, Oct. 4, 1841, by Ezra S. Cook	2	477

	Vol.	Page
FOX, FFOXE, FFOX, (cont.)		
Elisabeth, m. Edward **CHAPMAN**, [ ], in England	MG	
Hanna, m. Thomas **LOOMYS**, Nov. 1, 1653	MG	
Hannah, m. Thomas **LOOMAS**, b. of Windsor, Nov. 1, 1653	Col.2	159
Hanna, m. Thomas **LOOMES**, b. of Windsor, Nov. 1, [ ]	Col.2	159
Hannah, m. Thomas **LOOMIS**, Nov. 1, 1653	1	59
Julia, m. Morgan **CLARK**, Jan. 27, 1830, by Henry A. Rowland	2	140
Lorin, m. Louisa **HOUSE**, b. of Windsor, June 12, 1839, by Rev. Cephas Brainard	2	477
Rowland L., of East Hartford, m. Olive H. **GRISWOLD**, of Windsor, Sept. 9, 1840, by Rev. S. D. Jewett	2	477
-----, wid., adm. ch. June [ ], [16]	MG	
-----, wid. & [sister of Henry **CLARK**, d. Apr. 13*], [16]73 *(In pencil)	MG	
-----, wid. & s. of Henry **CLARK**, d. Apr. 13, [16]73	1	43
-----, wid. & sister of Henery **CLARK**, d. Apr. 13, 1673	Col.1	58
FRANCIS, FRANCES, Ann, of Windsor, m. Owen **ROCKWELL**, of Terris Vill, Apr. 25, 1827, by Rev. Henry A. Rowland	2	197
Edward, m. Mariah **HUBBARD**, b. of Windsor, Nov. 18, 1823, by Rev. John Bartlett, of Wintonbury. Int. Pub.	2	476
Harriet, d. William & Agnes, b. Jan. 1, 1795	2	560
Irene K., m. Horace H. **FILLEY**, b. of Windsor, Oct. 19, 1842, by S. D. Jewett	2	477
Louisa, d. William & Agnis, b. June 2, 1786	2	559
William, m. Agnis **LOOMIS**, b. of Windsor, Sept. 7, 1783	2	152
William, s. William & Agnis, b. Apr. 4, 1790	2	560
FRISBIE, Lemuel T., of Bloomfield, m. Caroline E. **GILLETT**, of Windsor, Apr. 5, 1848, by T. A. Leete	2	478
FROST, Daniel W., of Hartford, m. Louisa **COOK**, of Windsor, Jan. 14, 1847, by Rev. George F. Kettell	2	478
David, s. Josiah, b. Feb. 1, 1750	2	338
Ephraim, s. Josiah, b. Oct. 4, 1757	2	338
Joel, s. Josiah, b. May 16, 1763	2	338
Mary, d. Josiah, b. Apr. 15, 1752	2	338
Noah, s. Josiah, b. Apr. 8, 1755	2	338
Ruben, s. Josiah, b. Sept. 18, 1760	2	338
Sarah, d. Josiah, b. May 8, 1765	2	338
FULLER, Cyntha, d. Obadiah & Dorothy, b. Aug. 9, 1780	2	559
Dorothy, d. Obadiah & Dorothy, b. Sept. 7, 1777	2	559
Josiah, d. Obadiah & Abigal, b. July 10, 1755	2	334
Martha, d. Obadiah & Dorothy, b. Mar. 21, 1773	2	339
Obadiah, m. Dorothy **DILL**, b. of Windsor, July 16, 1772	2	152
Obadiah, s. Obadiah & Dorothy, b. Dec. 25, 1786	2	560
Pitts, s. Obadiah & Dorothy, b. Oct. 23, 1782	2	559
FURBER, John C., of Hartford, m. Mary **MILLER**, of Windsor, Apr. 8, 1834, by Rev. Ansel Nash	2	153

	Vol.	Page

FYLER, FILER, FILOR, FFYLAR, FFYLER, FFILAR,
FYLAR, FILAR, (cont.)

John, s. [Zurobabel & Experence], b. Mar. 2, [16[ ]; bp. Mar. 11, [16]	MG	
John, s. Zerubbabel, d. Aug. 10, 1715	2	234
John, d. Oct. 9, 1723	2	234
John, twin with Bethesda, s. Silas & Catharin, b. Apr. 28, 1760	2	335
John, contributed 0-2-6 to the poor in other colonies	MG	
Josanna, d. [ ], [16]50	MG	
Katharean, d. Silas & Katharean, b. Feb. 17, 1849/50* *("1749/50?")	2	334
Normond, s. Jeremiah & Jerusha, b. May 13, 1756	2	337
Paris, s. Jeremiah & Jerusha, b. Apr. 26, 1754	2	337
Rachell, d. Zerubbabell, Jr., b. Sept. 29, 1706	2	31
Rachel, d. Jeremiah & Jerusha, b. June 19, 1745	2	336
Rhoda, m. Daniel WEBSTER, b. of Windsor, Oct. 14, 1821, by Augustus Bolles	2	210
Roger, s. Jeremiah & Jerusha, b. May 3, 1743	2	332
Roger, s. Roger & Tryphena, b. July 15, 1767	2	339
Roman, s. Silas & Catharine, b. Aug. 12, 1769	2	339
Roxe, d. Roger & Tryphena, b. Feb. 2, 1764	2	338
Sabra, d. Silas & Catharine, b. Apr. 27, 1764	2	338
Samuell, d. [ ], [16]46	MG	
Samuel, of Hebron, d. Sept. 13, 1710	2	233
Samuel, s. Thomas, b. Nov. 6, 1712	2	32
Samuel, s. Thomas, d. Aug. 27, 1714	2	233
Samuel, s. Thomas, b. Dec. 19, 1716	2	33
Samuel, m. Ann STOUGHTON, b. of Windsor, Oct. 11, 1739	2	152
Silas, s. Silas & Catharein, b. Mar. 22, 1751/2	2	334
Stephen, d. [ ], [16]49	MG	
Stephen, s. Zerubbable, b. Mar. 27, 1688	1	13
Stephen, s. Silas & Catharin, b. May 21, 1756	2	335
Stephen, s. Stephen & Polle, b. Mar. 6, 1780	2	559
Silvia, d. Jeremiah & Jerusha, b. Mar. 29, 1750	2	337
Thomas, s. [Zurobabel & Experence], b. Jan. 25, 1669	MG	
Thomas, s. Zerubbable, b. Jan. 25, 1669; bp. Mar. 6, 1669	1	13
Thomas, [bp.] Mar. 6, [16]69	MG	
Thomas, s. Thomas, b. Nov. 9, 1709	2	32
Ulysses, s. Jeremiah & Jerusha, b. Jan. 11, 1752	2	337
Wa[l]ter, had 6 children b. in Windsor. Dated Aug. 17, 1677	MG	
Walter, communicant from Dorchester, living in Windsor Dec. 22, 1677	MG	
Walter, Lieut., d. Dec. 12, 1683	Col.D	56
Walter, Lieut., d. Dec. 12, 1683	1	44
Walter, contributed 0-8-0 to the poor in other colonies	MG	
Zurobabel, [s. Walter], b. Dec. 23, 1644	MG	

	Vol.	Page

GAYLORD, GAYLER, GAYLAR, GAYLOR, GAILERD,
GAILER, (cont.)

Almira, m. Edward DRAKE, Jan. 18, 1827, by Rev. Henry A. Rowland	2	144
Ann, d. [William, Jr. & Ann], b. Apr. 24, 1645	MG	
Ann, d. William, b. Apr. 24, 1645	Col.2	153
Ann, d. William, Jr., b. Apr. 24, 1645	1	14
Ann, w. William, Jr., d. July 21, 1653	Col.2	160
Ann, m. Isack PHELPS, Mar. 11, 1662	MG	
Ann, m. Isack PHELPS, b. of Windsor, Mar. 11, 1662/3, by Mr. Allyn	Col.1	45
Ann, d. John, Sr., b. Apr. 20, 1693	2	43
Ann, d. Nathaniel, Jr., b. Mar. 1, 1710/11	2	39
Ann, d. John, Jr., b. Apr. 6, 1718	2	42
Ann, d. John, Sr., d. Apr. 4, 1718	2	237
Ann, d. Nathanael, d. Sept. 14, 1725	2	238
Ann, m. Ebenezer BLISS, b. of Windsor, May 17, 1744	2	132
Ann, see Ann PHELPS	Col.D	57
Anna, d. Eliakim & Anna, b. Mar. 22, 1790	2	563
Anne, d. Eliakim & Elizabeth, b. July 27, 1756	2	352
Anne, d. Eliakim & Elizabeth, d. Feb. 20, 1758	2	529
Beniamen, s. [Walter & Mary], b. Apr. 12, 1655	MG	
Beniamin, s. Walter, b. Apr. 12, 1655	Col.2	158
Benjamin, s. Walter, b. Apr. 12, 1655	1	14
Beniamn, bp. Apr. 15, [16]55	MG	
Bennoni, illeg. s. Ruth GAYLORD, b. Sept. 9, 1723; reputed f. Benjamin DENSLOW	2	43
Betsiey, d. Elazar & Silvia, b. Oct. 1, 1781	2	561
Betsey, m. Roswell MILLER, July 2, 1828, b. of Windsor, by Rev. Henry A. Rowland	2	495
Daniel, s. Nathaniel, Jr., b. June 13, 1715	2	40
Daniel, s. Lieut. Nathaniell, d. May 6, 1734	2	238
Eliazer, s. [Walter & Sarah], b. Mar. 7, 1662	MG	
Eleezor, [bp.] Mar. 15, [16]62	MG	
Eleazer, s. Walter, b. Mar. 7, [16]62/3	Col.1	54
Eleazer, s. Walter, b. Mar. 7, 1662/3	1	14
Eliezer, m. Martha THOMPSON, Aug. 18 (?), 1686	Col.D	54
Eleazer, m. Martha THOMPSON, Aug. 18, 1686	1	57
Eleazer, s. Eleazer, b. Feb. 26, 1694/5	1	17
Eleazer, m. Silvia CLARK, b. of Windsor, Aug. 24, 1780	2	159
Eleazer, s. Eleazar & Silvia, b. Oct. 11, 1785	2	562
Eliezer, s. Walter, contributed flax 0-1-6 to the poor in other colonies	MG	
Eliakim, s. Nathaniel, Jr., b. Dec. 4, 1717	2	42
Eliakim, s. Eliakim & Elisabeth, b. June 23, 1749	2	348
Eliakim, of Windsor, m. Anna DANA, of Ashford, Nov. 5, 1788	2	159
Eliakim, of Windsor, m. Anna DANA, of Ashford, Nov. 5,		

	Vol.	Page
GAYLORD, GAYLER, GAYLAR, GAYLOR, GAILERD, GAILER, (cont.)		
1788	2	479
Eliakim, s. Eliakim & Anna, b. Oct. 31, 1796	2	563
Eliakim, Ens., d. Nov. 10, 1796	2	531
Eliakim, s. Eliakim, d. Feb. 18, 1797	2	531
Eliakim, s. Ithamer & Lydia, b. Feb. 4, 1802	2	573
Elijah, s. Josiah, b. Sept. 12, 1725	2	44
Elizabeth, m. Richard BIRG, Oct. 5, 1641	MG	
Elizabeth, m. Richard BIRDGE, Oct. 5, 1641	1	53
Elisabeth, d. [Samuell & Elisabeth], b. Oct. 4, 1647	MG	
Elizabeth, d. Samuel, b. Oct. 4, 1647	1	14
Elizabeth, wid. of Windsor, m. John ELDERKIN, of New London, Mar. 1, 1660	1	56
Elisabeth, d. [John & Mary], b. Feb. 19, 1670	MG	
Elizabeth, d. John, Jr., b. Feb. 19, 1670	1	15
Elisabeth, bp. Feb. 26, [16]	MG	
Eliz[abeth], d. Eben[ezer], b. Nov. 26, 1690	Col.D	51
Eliz[abeth], d. Eben[eze]r, b. Nov. 26, 1690	Col.D	51
Elizabeth, d. Eleazer, b. Nov. 26, 1690	1	17
Elizabeth, d. Nathanael, b. July 28, 1693	1	17
Elizabeth, m. Samuel ROCKWELL, Jan. 10, 1694	1	61
Elisabeth, d. John, Sr., b. Jan. 1, 1704/5	2	35
Elizabeth, m. Nathaniel GAYLORD, Jr., June 1, 1710	2	154
Elizabeth, d. Nath[anie]ll & Elizabeth, b. Oct. 25, 1727	2	45
Elizabeth, m. John Mack MORAN, b. of Windsor, Jan. 10, 1727/8	2	177
Elizabeth, d. Lieut. Nathaniell & Elizabeth, d. Apr. 12, 1737	2	527
Elizabeth, d. William & Elizabeth, b. Nov. 18, 1740	2	345
Elizabeth, d. William & Elizabeth, b. Nov. 18, 1740	2	346
Elisabeth, d. Eliakim & Elisabeth, b. Nov. 16, 1744	2	347
Elizabeth, wid., d. Mar. 15, 1758	2	529
Elizabeth, m. Ephraim BOOTH, Mar. 27, 1765	2	134
Elizabeth, w. Ens. Eliakim, d. Sept. 21, 1776	2	531
Elizabeth, see Elizabeth HOSKINS	MG	
Esther, d. Nath[aniel], b. Apr. 8, 1702	1	17
Esther, m. Benjamin GRISWOLD, b. of Windsor, July 6, 1726	2	156
Ezekia, d. Sept. 12, 1677	MG	
Ezekia, d. Sept. 12, [16]77	Col.1	58
F., his w. [ ], adm. ch. & communicant Apr. [ ], 1645	MG	
Fanna, d. Eliakim & Anna, b. Oct. 18, 1793	2	563
Fluvia, d. Elazer & Silvia, b. Sept. 19, 1783	2	562
Giles, s. Josiah & Naomi, b. Dec. 19, 1728	2	340
Giles, s. Josiah & Naomi, d. Feb. 12, 1736/7	2	527
Hanna, d. [William, Jr. & Ann], b. Jan. 30, 1646	MG	
Hannah, d. William, b. Jan. 30, 1646	Col.2	153
Hannah, d. William, b. Jan. 30, 1646	1	14

	Vol.	Page
GAYLORD, GAYLER, GAYLAR, GAYLOR, GAILERD,		
GAILER, (cont.)		
Hannah, d. Eleazer, b. Sept. 4, 1700	1	17
Harriet, twin with Huldia, d. Eleazar & Silvia, b. Dec.		
15, 1790	2	562
Hezeciah, s. [William, Jr. & Ann], b. Feb. 11, 1652; d.[ ]	MG	
Hezekiah, s. William, b. Feb. 11, 1652	Col.2	153
Hezekiah, s. William, b. Feb. 11, 1652	1	14
Hezecia, s. [Nathanell & Abigal], b. Aug. 23, 1679	MG	
Hezekia, s. Nathanell, b. Aug. 23, 1679	Col.1	56
Hezekiah, s. Josiah & Sarah, b. Nov. 15, 1745	2	347
Hezakiah, s. Eleazer & Silvia, b. Mar. 18, 1793	2	562
Huldia, twin with Harriet, d. Eleazar & Silvia, b. Dec. 15,		
1790	2	562
Isack, s. [Walter & Mary], b. June 21, 1657; d. [ ]	MG	
Isaack, s. Walter, b. June 21, 1657	Col.2	161
Isaac, s. Walter, b. June 21, 1657	1	14
Ithamar, s. Eliakim & Elizabeth, b. Apr. 9, 1758	2	352
Ithamer, of Windsor, m. Lydia **PETTIBONE**, of Simsbury,		
Dec. 4, 1800	2	479
James, s. Josiah, b. May 24, 1714	2	40
James, s. Josiah, d. June 22, 1714	2	236
Jerusha, d. William & Elizabeth, b. Apr. 9, 1753	2	350
Joanna, d. [Walter & Mary], b. Feb. 5, 1652	MG	
Joanaa, d. Walter, b. Feb. 5, 1652	1	14
Joanna, m. John **PORTER**, Jr., Dec. 16, 1669	MG	
Joanna, m. John **PORTER**, Jr., Dec. 16, 1669, by Capt.		
Newbery	Col.1	45
Joanna, d. Walter, m. John **PORTER**, Jr., Sept. 16, 1669, by		
Capt. Nubery	1	60
John, s. [William, Jr. & Ann], b. Jan. 27, 1648	MG	
John, s. William (the younger), b. Jan. 27, 1648	1	14
John, bp. Feb. 4, [16]48	MG	
John, s. William, b. June 27, 1648	Col.2	153
John, m. Mary **DRAK[E]**, Nov. 17, 1653	MG	
John, m. Mary **DRAKE**, b. of Windsor, Nov. 17, 1653	Col.2	159
John, m. Mary **DRAKE**, b. of Windsor, Nov. 17, 1655	Col.2	159
John, s. [John & Mary], b. June 15, 1656; d. [ ]	MG	
John, s. John, b. June 15, 1656	1	15
John, s. John, bp. June 25, [16]	MG	
John, s. John, d. Nov. 18, 1656	1	44
John, his s. [ ], d. [ ], [16]56	MG	
John, his w. [ ], bp. Feb. 28, [16]57	MG	
John, adm. ch. & communicant Apr. [ ], 1666	MG	
John, adm. ch. Apr. 3, [16]66	MG	
John, s. [John & Mary], b. June 23, 1667	MG	
John, s. John, b. June 23, 1667	1	15
John, had 4 children b. in Windsor. Dated Aug. 17, 1677	MG	

	Vol.	Page
GAYLORD, GAYLER, GAYLAR, GAYLOR, GAILERD,		
GAILER, (cont.)		
John, s. [Joseph & Sarah], b. Aug. 21, [16]77; bp. May		
12, [16]78	MG	
John, s. Joseph, b. Aug. 21, 1677	Col.1	56
John, s. Joseph, b. Aug. 21, 1677, at Hadly	1	16
John, m. Mary CLARKE, Dec. 13, 1683	Col.D	54
John, m. Mary CLARK, Dec. 13, 1683	1	57
John, s. John, Jr., b. Jan. 8, 1686	Col.D	51
John, s. John, Jr., b. June 8, 1686	1	16
John, Sergt., d. July 31, 1689	Col.D	56
John, Sergt., d. July 31, 1689	1	44
John, Sr., d. Apr. 27, 1699	1	45
John, Sr., communicant 16[ ]	MG	
John, Jr., adult, ch. mem. 16[ ]	MG	
John, m. Elizabeth MARSHEL, b. of Windsor, May 27, 1701	1	57
John, m. Hannah GRANT, b. of Windsor, Apr. 3, 1712	2	155
John, s. John, Jr., b. Jan. 7, 1713/14	2	42
John, Jr., d. June 25, 1722	2	237
John, d. Nov. 24, 1740	2	527
John, s. William & Elizabeth, b. June 26, 1743	2	346
John, m. Elizabeth STOUGHTON, Mar. 5, 1751	2	157
John, s. Alexander & Hephzibah, b. Nov. 18, 1752	2	350
John, Sr., contributed 0-2-6 to the poor in other colonies	MG	
John, Jr., contributed 0-3-0 to the poor in other colonies	MG	
John Hefecia, [s. William], [bp.] Feb. 14, [16]52	MG	
Joseph, s. [Walter & Mary], b. May 13, 1649	MG	
Joseph, s. Walter, b. May 13, 1649	1	14
Jos[ ], d. [May 16*], [16]67 *(In pencil)	MG	
Joseph, s. William, d. May 16, 1667	Col.1	55
Joseph, s. William, d. May 16, 1667	1	44
Joseph, s. Walter, m. Sarah STANDLY, July 11, 1670	MG	
Joseph, s. Walter, of Windsor, m. Sara STANDLY, of		
Farmingtown, July 14, 1670	Col.1	45
Joseph, bp. July 16, [16]71	MG	
Joseph, s. [Joseph & Sarah], b. Aug. 22, 1673	MG	
Joseph, s. Joseph, b. Aug. 22, [16]73	1	16
Joseph, had 2 children b. in Windsor. Dated Aug. 17, 1677	MG	
Joseph, twin with Thomas, s. John, b. June 20, 1690	Col.D	51
Joseph, twin with Thomas, s. Nathanael, b. June 20, 1690	1	17
Joseph, s. Joseph, bp. Aug. [ ], [16]	MG	
Joseph, m. Sarah BUCKLAND, Oct. 21, 1714	2	154
Joseph, d. Dec. 15, 1757	2	530
Josia, s. [William, Jr. & Ann], b. Feb. 13, 1654	MG	
Josiah, s. William, b. Feb. 13, 1654	Col.2	158
Josiah, s. William, b. Feb. 13, 1654	1	14
Josiah, s. Nathanael, b. Feb. 24, 1686	1	16
Josiah, m. Naomi BURNHAM, b. of Windsor, May 7, 1713	2	154

	Vol.	Page

GAYLORD, GAYLER, GAYLAR, GAYLOR, GAILERD, GAILER, (cont.)

	Vol.	Page
Josiah, s. Josiah, b. Mar. 7, 1719/20	2	43
Josiah, d. June 25, 1741	2	528
Josiah, m. Sarah BARNARD, b. of Windsor, Feb. 14, 1744	2	478
Josiah, s. Josiah & Sarah, b. Mar. 6, 1747/8	2	348
Josiah, s. Josiah & Sarah, d. Aug. 15, 1750	2	528
Josiah, twin with Thomas, s. Josiah & Sarah, b. May 13, 1756	2	353
Lucinda, d. Eliakim & Anna, b. Oct. 25, 1800	2	564
Lydia, d. John, Sr., b. June 2, 1709	2	36
Lydia, d. John, d. Oct. 2, 1718	2	237
Martha, d. [Samuell & Elisabeth], b. June [ ], 1660	MG	
Martha, [bp.] June 24, [16]60	MG	
Martha, d. Samuell, in her 20th y., m. Josias* ELESWORTH, s. Josias, ae 24, Oct. 30, [16]79		
*("John" also written)	MG	
Martha, d. Eleazer, b. May 21, 1687	1	17
Martha, m. Ebenezer WILCOKEN, Jan. 15, 1707/8	2	207
Mary, d. [Samuell & Elisabeth], b. Nov. 10, 1649	MG	
Mary, d. Samuel, b. Nov. 10, 1649	1	15
Mary, d. [Walter & Mary], b. Mar. 19, 1650	MG	
Mary, d. Walter, b. Mar. 19, 1650	1	14
Mary, d. Walter, b. Mar. 19, 1650	1	16
Mary, w. Walter, d. June 29, 1657	MG	
Mary, d. [John & Mary], b. Jan. 19, 1663	MG	
Mary, d. John, b. Jan. 19, [16]63	Col.1	54
Mary, d. John, b. Jan. 19, 1663	1	15
Mary, d. Samuell, m. Joseph GRISWOLD, June 10, [16]70, by Capt. Newbery	Col.1	46
Mary, m. Joseph GRISWOLD, July 14, 1670	MG	
Mary, w. Sergt. John, d. June 12, 1683	1	44
Mary*, w. Sergt. John, d. June 12, 1683 *(Note by LBB: "Mary (DRAKE) GAYLOR")	Col.D	56
Mary, m. Mathew LOOMYS, b. of Windsor, Jan. 6, 1686	Col.D	54
Mary, m. Mathew LOOMIS, b. of Windsor, Jan. 6, 1686	1	58
Mary, m. Nathanael OWIN, b. of Windsor, June 14, 1694	1	63
Mary, d. John, bp. Jan. 2, [16]	MG	
Mary, m. Nathanael COPLEY, b. of Windsor, Apr. 30, 1730	2	136
Mary Dana, d. Eliakim & Anna, b. Mar. 26, 1798	2	564
[Mary (STEBBINS)*], w. William, Sr., d. June 20, 1657 *(Name supplied by LBB)	Col.2	160
Naomi, d. Josiah, b. Nov. 3, 1715	2	41
Naomi, m. Nathanael HAYDON, b. of Windsor, Apr. [ ], 1737	2	163
Naomi, wid., d. Oct. 16, 1755	2	529
Nath[an], s. Nath[an], b. Nov. 23, 1681	Col.D	51
Nathanell, s. [William, Jr. & Ann], b. Sept. 3, 1656	MG	
Nathaniell, s. William, b. Sept. 3, 1656	2	158

	Vol.	Page
GAYLORD, GAYLER, GAYLAR, GAYLOR, GAILERD,		
GAILER, (cont.)		
Nathanael, s. William, b. Sept. 3, 1656	1	14
Nathanell, ae 22 m. Abigal BISSELL, d. Thomas, ae 20, Oct.		
17, [16]78	MG	
Nathanaell, m. Abigayell BISSELL, d. Thomas, Sr., Oct.		
17, 1678	Col.1	46
Nathaniell, m. [ ], [ ]sell, [Oct.] 17, 1678	TR1	1
Nathanael, m. Abigail BISSELL, d. Thomas, Oct. 17, 1678	1	57
Nathanael, s. Nathanael, b. Nov. 23, 1681	1	16
Nathaniel, Jr., m. Elizabeth GAYLORD, June 1, 1710	2	154
Nathaniel, s. Nathaniel, Jr., b. July 14, 1713	2	40
Nathanael, Lieut., d. Apr. 26, 1720	2	237
Nathanael, s. Sergt. Nathaniell, d. Jan. 29, 1728/9	2	238
Nathaniel, s. Eliakim & Elisabeth, b. Sept. 13, 1746	2	348
Nathaniell, s. Eliakim & Elisabeth, d. Sept. 16, 1749	2	528
Nathaniel, s. Eliakim & Elisabeth, b. Apr. 15, 1751	2	349
Nathaniel, Lieut., d. Dec. 28, 1762	2	530
Nathanael, s. Nath[aniel], b. Nov. 23, [ ]	1	16
Nathanel, contributed 0-2-0 to the poor in other colonies	MG	
Nehemiah, s. Josiah, b. June 15, 1722	2	43
Nehemiah, of Torrington, m. Lucy LOOMIS, of Windsor,		
Nov. 10, 1748	2	157
Rachel, m. Jonathan BARBOR, b. of Windsor, Aug. 4, 1720	2	129
Ruth, d. Nathanael, b. Apr. 10, 1699	1	17
Ruth, had illeg., s. Bennoni, b. Sept. 9, 1723; reputed f.		
Benjamin DENSLOW	2	43
Ruth, m. Nathanael GRISWOLD, b. of Windsor, Oct. 14,		
1731	2	156
Sabrah, d. Josiah, b. Dec. 11, 1717	2	41
Sabra, m. Ammi TRUMBEL, b. of Windsor, Nov. 9, 1738	2	204
Samuel, his w. [ ], adm. ch. Apr. 27, [16]45	MG	
Samuell, m. Elisabeth HULL, Dec. 4, 1646	MG	
Samuel, m. Elizabeth HULL, Dec. 4, 1646	1	56
Samuell, bp. Feb. 28, [16]57	MG	
Samuell, s. [Samuell & Elisabeth], b. July [ ], 1657	MG	
Samuel, s. Samuel, b. July [ ], 1657	1	15
Samuell, s. Samuel, [bp.] July [ ], [16]57	MG	
Samuell, taxed 1-6 on Feb. 10, [16]73	MG	
Samuell, taxed 3-6 on Feb. 10, [16]73	MG	
Samuell, adm. communion Jan. 28, 1674	MG	
Samuel, adm. ch. & communicant June [ ], 1674	MG	
Samuel, had 6 children b. in Windsor. Dated Aug. 17, 1677	MG	
Samu[e]l, his w. [ ], d. May 2, 1680	MG	
Samuell, his w. [ ], d. May 2, 1680	Col.D	58
Samuel, s. Nath[an], d. June 21, 1690	Col.D	57
Samuel, d. Aug. 19, 1690	Col.D	57
Samuel, d. Aug. 19, 1690	1	45

	Vol.	Page
GAYLORD, GAYLER, GAYLAR, GAYLOR, GAILERD,		
GAILER, (cont.)		
Samuel, s. Eleazer, b. Mar. 9, 1696/7	1	13
Samuell, communicant 16[ ]	MG	
Sara, d. [Samuell & Elisabeth], b. Jan. 18, 1651	MG	
Sara, bp. Jan. 18, [16]51	MG	
Sarah, d. Samuel, bp. Jan. 18, 1651	1	15
Sara, adm. ch. & communicant Apr. [ ], 1661	MG	
Sara, d. [Walter & Sarah], b. Apr. 13, 1665	MG	
Sarah, d. Walter, b. Apr. 13, 1665	Col.1	54
Sarah, d. Walter & Sarah, b. Apr. 13, 1665	1	14
Sara, [d.] Wa[l]ter, bp. Feb. 19, [16]70	MG	
Sara, d. [Joseph & Sarah], b. July 11, 1671	MG	
Sara, d. Samuell, of Windsor, m. John* **DORCHESTER**, of Springfield, Nov. 29, 1671, by Capt. Newbery *(Note by LBB: "Alexander")	Col.1	56
Sarah*, w. Walter, d. Aug. 17, 1683 *(Note by LBB: "Sarah (**ROCKWELL**) GAYLOR")	Col.D	56
Sarah, w. Walter, d. Aug. 17, 1683	1	45
Sarah, d. Walter, m. Timo[thy] **PHELPS**, s. Sam[ue]l, Nov. 18, 1686	Col.D	54
Sarah, d. Walter, m. Timothy **PHELPS**, s. Samuel, Nov. 18, 1686	1	60
Sarah, m. Nathaniel **BISSELL**, b. of Windsor, July 8, 1714	2	128
Sarah, d. Josiah & Sarah, b. Aug. 15, 1751	2	349
Sarah, d. Josiah & Sarah, d. Oct. 20, 1759	2	530
Sarah, w. Joseph, d. June 12, 1761	2	228
Sarah, w. Joseph, d. June 12, 1761	2	530
Silvia, d. Eleazar & Silvia, b. Sept. 8, 1787	2	562
Sylvia, m. Seth **DEXTER**, May 5, 1808	2	143
Thomas, twin with Joseph, s. John, b. June 20, 1690	Col.D	51
Thomas, twin with Joseph, s. Nathanael, b. June 20, 1690	1	17
Thomas, s. Nathanael, d. June 21, 1690	1	45
Thomas, twin with Josiah, s. Josiah & Sarah, b. May 13, 1756	2	353
Walter, m. Mary **STEBENS**, Apr. [ ], 1648	MG	
Walter, adult, adm. ch. May 5, [16]51	MG	
Walter, adm, ch. & communicant May [ ], 1651	MG	
Walter, his w. [ ], d. June 29, 1657	Col.2	160
Walter, his w. [ ], d. June 29, 1657	1	44
Walter, his w. [ ], d. [ ], [16]57	MG	
Walter, m. 2nd w. Sarah **ROCKWELL**, Mar. 22, 1658	MG	
Walter, m. Sarah **ROCKWELL**, b. of Windsor, Mar. 22, 1659/60	1	56
Walter, taxed 4-0 on Feb. 10, [16]73	MG	
Walter, taxed 4-0 on Feb. 10, [16]73	MG	
Walter, had 7 children b. in Windsor. Dated Aug. 17, 1677	MG	
Walter, d. Aug. 9, 1689	Col.D	57
Walter, d. Aug. 9, 1689	1	44

	Vol.	Page
GAYLORD, GAYLER, GAYLAR, GAYLOR, GAILERD, GAILER, (cont.)		
Walter, communicant 16[ ]	MG	
Waltel, contributed 0-2-6 to the poor in other colonies; his w. [ ], contributed in cloth 0-6-3 to the poor in other colonies	MG	
William, Jr., m. Ann **PORTER**, Feb. 24, 1641	MG	
William, m. Anna **PORTER**, Feb. 24, 1641	1	56
William, s. [William, Jr. & Ann], b. Feb. 25, 1650	MG	
William, s. William, b. Feb. 25, 1650	Col.2	153
William, s. William (the younger), b. Feb. 25, 1650	1	14
William, s. William (younger), b. Feb. 25, 1650	1	16
William, m. Elisabeth **DRAKE**, b. of Windsor, Feb. 9, 1653	Col.2	159
William, his w. [ ], d. [ ], [16]53	MG	
William, d. Dec. 14, 1656	MG	
William, the younger, d. Dec. 14, 1656	Col.2	160
William, the younger, d. Dec. 14, 1656	1	44
William, d. [ ], [16]56	MG	
William, Sr., his w. [ ]*, d. June 20, 1657 *(Note by LBB: "Mary (**STEBBINS**) GAILOR")	Col.2	160
William, Sr., his w. [ ], d. June 20, 1657; bd. June 21, 1657	1	44
William, Sr., his w. [ ], d. [ ], [16]57	MG	
William, Jr., had 7 children b. in Windsor. Dated Aug. 17, 1677	MG	
William, s. John, Jr., b. Apr. 24, 1712	2	39
William, m. Elizabeth **STOUGTON**, b. of Windsor, Feb. 18, 1739/40	2	157
William, d. Aug. 16, 1753	2	529
William, s. Eliakim & Anna, b. Nov. 26, 1791	2	563
Zeruiah, d. John & Elizabeth, b. Mar. 31, 1761	2	354
-----, Dea., d. [July 20*], [16]73, ae 88 *(In pencil)	MG	
-----, Dea., d. July 20, 1673	Col.1	58
-----, Dea., d. July 20, [ ]; bd. July 21, [ ], ae 88	1	44
-----, ch. mem. 16[ ], from Dorchester	MG	
GAYNOR, Patrick, m. Bridget **CORCORAN**, Sept. 12, 1852, by Rev. James Smyth	2	460
GEORGE, John, d. Apr. 28, 1724	2	238
GIBBS, GIBBES, Abigayl, d. [Jacob & Elisabeth], b. Jan. 7, 1661	MG	
Abigail, d. Jacob, b. Oct. 3, 1694	1	17
Abigael, d. Benjamin, b. Mar. 16, 1714/15	2	40
Abigail, d. Giles & Rachel, b. May 25, 1744	2	346
Benjamin, m. Abigaell **MARSHALL**, Sept. 16, 1708	2	154
Benjamin, s. Benjamin, b. Apr. 23, 1710	2	37
Catherine, wid., d. Oct. 24, 1660	1	44
Setran, d. [ ], [16]60 (Catharine)	MG	
Cattarn, d. [Samuell & Hepsiba], b. Apr. 29, 1675; d. [ ]	MG	
Katherine, d. Samuel, d. June 29, [16]76	MG	
Catherine, d. Samuel, d. June 29, [1676]; bd. [June] 30, 1676	1	44

	Vol.	Page
GIBBS, GIBBES, (cont.)		
Cattarn, d. Samuel, d. June 29, 1676	Col.1	58
David, s. Benjamin, b. Apr. 7, 1720	2	43
Deborah, d. Giles & Rachel, b. Jan. 30, 1765	2	354
Ebenezer, s. Jacob, Jr., b. Nov. 8, 1703	1	18
Elizabeth, d. [Samuell & Hepsiba], b. Jan. 30, 1668	MG	
Elisabeth, [bp.] Jan. 31, [16]68	MG	
Elisabeth, d. [Jacob & Elisabeth], b. Apr. 1, 1672	MG	
Elizabeth, w. Jacob, d. Jan. 13, 1695/6	1	45
Elizabeth, m. John OSBAND, Jr., Dec. 7, 1696	1	64
Elizabeth, d. Jacob, Jr., b. Aug. 26, 1697	1	17
Elizabeth, d. Samuell, 3rd & Elizabeth, b. Oct. 5, 1756	2	352
Esther, d. Jacob, b. July 9, 1709	2	36
Experence, d. Samuel, b. Dec. 2, [16]66	1	16
Experience, d. [Samuell & Hepsiba], b. Apr. 4, 1673	MG	
Experience, d. Samuel, b. Apr. 4, [16]73	1	16
Experience, of Windsor, m. John SPENSER, of Suffield, Oct. 30, 1706	2	197
Giles, d. [ ] , [16]41	MG	
Gyles, bd. May 21, 1641	1	44
Giles, s. Samuell, Jr., b. Aug. 8, 1706	2	35
Giles, s. Samuell, Jr., d. Oct. 28, 1708	2	235
Giles, s. Giles & Rachel, b. June 6, 1742	2	346
Giles, s. Giles & Rachel, b. May 25, 1760	2	353
Giles, s. Giles & Rachel, d. Oct. 20, 1760	2	530
Hannah, d. Benjamin, b. Nov. 2, 1716	2	41
Henry, s. Benjamin, b. Aug. 5, 1713	2	40
Hepsiba, d. Samuell, b. Jan. 12, 1664	Col.1	54
Hephzibah, d. Samuel, b. Jan. 12, 1664	1	18
Hepsiba, d. [Samuell & Hepsiba], b. Jan. 12, 1664[5]	MG	
Hepsiba, d. Samuel, bp. Mar. 12, [16]64	MG	
Hephzibah, w. Samuel, d. Feb. 22, 1697/8	1	45
Huldah, d. Samuel & Elizabeth, b. Sept. 5, 1751	2	352
Jacob, m. Elisabeth ANDROUS, Dec. 4, 1657	MG	
Jacob, of Windsor, m. Elizabeth ANDROS, of Hartford, Dec. 4, 1657	1	56
Jacob, s. [Jacob & Elisabeth], b. Dec. 1, 1664; d. [ ]	MG	
Jacob, s. Jacob, d. [ ], [16]64	MG	
Jacob, 2nd, s. [Jacob & Elisabeth], b. June 22, 1666	MG	
Jacob, s. Jacob, b. June 22, 1666	Col.1	55
Jacob, had 7 children, b. in Windsor. Dated Aug. 17, 1677	MG	
Jacob, m. Abigail OSBAND, May 16, 1689	1	57
Jacob & Elisabeth, had d. [ ], b. Sept. 12, 16[ ]	MG	
Jocob, mem. Jury 16[ ]	MG	
Jacob, s. Jacob, Jr., b. July 30, 1700	1	17
Jacob, Sr., d. Mar. 1, 1708/9	2	236
Jacob, 2nd, d. Jan. 16, 1711/12	2	236
Jacob, contributed 0-2-0 to the poor in other colonies	MG	

	Vol.	Page
GIBBS, GIBBES, (cont.)		
Joanna, d. [Samuell & Hepsiba], b. Mar. 26, 1671	MG	
Joanna, [bp.] Apr. 2, [16]71	MG	
Joanna, m. Mooses **LOOMIS**, Apr. 27, 1694	1	59
John, s. Jacob, b. Mar. 18, 1711/12	2	39
Jonathan, s. Samuell, b. Jan. 16, 1679	Col. 1	57
Jonathan, s. [Samuell & Hepsiba], b. Feb. 16, 1679	MG	
Josiah, s. Samuel, 3rd & Elizabeth, b. Mar. 11, 1754	2	352
Katherine, see under Catherine		
Levy, s. Giles & Rachel, b. July 20, 1756	2	351
Mary, s. [Jacob & Elisabeth], b. Apr. 21, 1659	MG	
Mary, d. Jacob, Jr., b. Apr. 26, 1706	2	35
Mary, d. Samuel, Jr. & Rebeckah, b. Aug. 17, 1735	2	342
Mary, d. Giles & Rachel, b. July 13, 1762	2	354
Mehitable, m. Samuel **HARRIS**, b. of Windsor, Sept. 23,		
1824, by Rev. Phineas Cook	2	166
Miriam, d. Samuell, b. Dec. 12, 1681	Col. D	51
Meriam, m. William **HAYDON**, s. Daniel, b. of Windsor,		
Jan. 21, 1702/3	1	58
Oliver, s. Giles & Rachel, b. Aug. 3, 1758	2	352
Patience, d. [Samuell & Hepsiba], b. Dec. 2, 1666	MG	
Patienc[e], d. Samuell, b. Dec. 2, 1666	Col. 1	56
Patience, m. Samuel **DENSLOW**, Dec. 2, 1686	Col. D	54
Patience, d. Samuel, bp. Dec. 9, [16]66	MG	
Rachel, d. Giles & Rachel, b. Apr. 14, 1746	2	347
Rachel, d. Giles & Rachel, d. Mar. 23, 1767	2	530
S., his w.[ ], adm. ch. & communicant Sept. [ ], 1666	MG	
Samuell, bp. Mar. 12, [16]64	MG	
Samuell, m. Hepsiba **DEBLE**, Apr. 15, 1664	MG	
Samuell, m. Hepsiba **DEBLE**, Apr. 15, 1664, by Mr. Clark	Col. 1	45
Samuel, taxed 1-0 on Feb. 10, [16]73	MG	
Samuell, taxed 3-0 on Feb. 10, [16]73	MG	
Samuell, s. [Samuell & Hepsiba], b. Apr. 16, 1677	MG	
Samuel, s. Samuel, bp. Apr. 22, [16]77	MG	
Samuel, had 7 children b. in Windsor. Dated Aug. 17, 1677	MG	
Samuel, his w. [ ], adm. ch. Sept. [ ], [16]	MG	
Samuell, mem. Jury 16[ ]	MG	
Samuell, adult, ch. mem. 16[ ]	MG	
Samuel, m. Mary **WINCHEL**, b. of Windsor, Mar. 4,		
17[0]2/3	1	57
Samuell, s. Samuell, Jr., b. Nov. 30, 1704	2	35
Samuel, Sr., d. Feb. 8, 1719/20	2	237
Samuel, s. Samuel, Jr. & Rebeckah, b. May 2, 1729, at		
Enfield	2	342
Samuell, his d. [ ], d. [ ], in "Elenton" prior		
to 1740	MG	
Samuell, had three children b. [ ], in "Elenton" prior		
to 1740	MG	

	Vol.	Page

GIBBS, GIBBES, (cont.)

Samuell, Jr., had 2 children d. [ ], in "Elenton" prior to 1740	MG	
Samuell, contributed 0-3-0 to the poor in other colonies	MG	
Sara, m. John SHARE, Dec. 5, 1661	MG	
Sarah, m. John SHARE, b. of Windsor, Dec. 5, 1661	1	61
Sara, d. [Jacob & Elisabeth], b. Feb. 28, 1668	MG	
Sarah, d. Giles & Rachel, b. Mar. 20, 1753	2	350
Seth, s. Giles & Rachel, b. Feb. 4, 1748/9	2	348
Titus, s. Giles & Rachel, b. Sept. 7, 1750	2	349
William, s. Benjamin, b. June 10, 1718	2	11
William, s. Benjamin, b. June 10, 1718	2	42
Zebulun, s. Benjamin, b. Aug. 10, 1711	2	39

GIDDINGS, Linus, m. Electa PARSONS, b. of Windsor, Nov. 27,

1821, by Rev. John Bartlet. Int. Pub.	2	159

GILBERT, GILBURS, Amos, Sr., Capt. of Wintonbury, m. Mrs. Miriam BROWN, Apr. 29, 1824, by Rev. John Bartlett,

of Wintonbury. Int. Pub.	2	160
Benjamin, s. Benjamin & Jane, b. Mar. 28, 1751	2	349
Lucy, m. Samuel ALLYN, b. of Windsor, Jan. 5, 1764	2	125
Nathaniell, of Coulchester, m. Mary BISSELL, of Windsor, Feb. 8, 1720/1	2	155

GILE, Ann, m. Jeremiah ALFORD, Jr., July 15, 1746 | 2 | 124

GILLETT, GILLET, GILLIET, GILLIT, GELLET, Aaron, s.

Josiah, b. Mar. 8, 1698/9	1	17
Abell, s. Thomas, b. Oct. 18, 1705	2	36
Abel, s. Abel & Abigail, b. May 16, 1744	2	347
Abel, Jr. m. Jerusha ANDRUS, b. of Windsor, Jan. 7, 1768	2	158
Abel, s. Abel, Jr. & Jerusha, b. Apr. 19, 1769	2	355
Abia, d. [Nathan], b. Aug. 22, 1641	MG	
Abia, m. Ezaya BARTLET, Dec. 3, 1663	MG	
Abia, m. Esayah BARTLET, Dec. 3, 1663, by Mr. Clarke	Col.1	45
Abbigayel, d. [Jonathan, Sr.], bp. June 28, 1646	MG	
Abigail, d. Jonathan, bp. June 28, 1646	1	14
Abigail, d. [ ], [16]48	MG	
Abigayl, d. [Cornelius], b. Sept. 20, 1663	MG	
Abigayl, d. Cornelus, b. Sept. 20, [16]63	Col.1	54
Abigail, d. Cornellious, b. Sept. 20, 1663	1	15
Abigail, d. Jeremiah, b. Feb. 21, 1687	1	16
Abigall, d. Jeremy, d. Feb. 16, 1689	Col.D	57
Abigail, d. Jeremiah, d. Feb. 16, 1689	1	45
Abigail, d. Abel & Abigail, b. Nov. 28, 1731	2	342
Abigail, d. Jonathan, 3rd & Abigail, b. Mar. 25, 1746	2	347
Abigal, d. Abel & Jerusha, b. Jan. 22, 1796	2	564
Abigail, of Torrington, m. Orson MOORE, of Windsor, Jan. 17, 1797	2	180
Agnis, d. Abel & Abigail, b. Nov. 1, 1739	2	345
Almerin, of Windsor, m. Eunice, GRISWOLD, 2nd, of Lyme		

	Vol.	Page
GILLETT, GILLET, GILLIET, GILLIT, GELLET, (cont.)		
Lyme, Dec. 29, 1790	2	159
Amos, s. Jonathan, 3rd & Abigail, b. Oct. 15, 1743	2	346
Amy, d. Daniel & Amy, b. July 30, 1770	2	355
Amy, w. Daniel, d. Oct. 27, 1785	2	531
Ann, d. Daniel, b. Mar. 12, 1710/11	2	39
Ann, d. John & Elizabeth, b. Aug. 16, 1740	2	345
Ann, m. Josiah **MOORE,** b. of Windsor, Nov. 18, 1762	2	180
Anna, d. Jonathan, Sr., b. Dec. 29, 1639	MG	
Anna, m. Samuell **FILLY,** Oct. 29, 1663	MG	
Anna, m. Samuell **FFILLY,** b. of Windsor, Oct. 29, 1663, by		
Mr. Allyn	Col.1	45
Anna, d. Daniel & Anna, b. Dec. 13, 1726	2	45
Anna, m. Gideon **BARBER,** b. of Windsor, Nov. 9, 1744	2	131
Anne, d. Nathan, Jr., b. Apr. 3, 1707	2	36
Ara*, s. Isaac & Elizabeth, b. Dec. 28, 1731 *("Ava" in		
Stile's Windsor)	2	341
Asa*, s. Isaac & Elizabeth, d. Dec. 28, 1736 *("Ava"in		
Stile's Windsor)	2	527
Asa*, s. Sergt. Isaac & Elizabeth, b. Dec. 10, 1739		
*("Ava" in Stiles" Windsor)	2	344
Ashbel, s. Abel & Abigail, b. Dec*. 26, 1754 *("Jan."		
crossed out)	2	351
Ashor, s. Abel, Jr. & Jerusha, b. May 1, 1786	2	561
Ava*, s. Isaac & Elizabeth, b. Dec. 28, 1731 *("Ara" in		
copy)	2	341
Ava*, s. Isaac & Elizabeth, d. Dec. 28, 1736 *("Asa" in		
copy)	2	527
Ava*, s. Sergt. Isaac & Elizabeth, b. Dec. 10, 1739		
*("Asa" in copy)	2	344
Azariah, s. Nathan, Jr., b. Mar. 28, 1705	2	35
Beniamen, s. [Nathan], b. Aug. 29, 1653; d. [ ]	MG	
Benjamin, s. Nathan, b. Aug. 29, 1653	Col.2	153
Benjamin, s. Nathan, b. Aug. 29, 1653	1	14
Benjamin, s. Nathan, d. July 13, 1655	Col.2	160
Bethuel, s. Abel, Jr. & Jerusha, b. Apr. 16, 1791	2	564
Caroline E., of Windsor, m. Lemuel T. **FRISBIE,** of		
Bloomfield, Apr. 5, 1848, by T. A. Leete	2	478
Chancey, s. Abel, Jr. & Jerusha, b. Nov. 8, 1788	2	564
Clotilda, d. Abel & Abigail, b. Sept. 24, 1733	2	342
Chlotilde, m. Aaron **DRAKE,** b. of Windsor, July 21, 1757	2	143
Cornelius, adm. ch. Jan. 16, 1665	MG	
Cornelius, adm. ch. & communicant, Jan. [ ], 1665	MG	
Cornelius, s. [Cornelius], b. Dec. 15, 1665	MG	
Cornelius, s. Cornelius, b. Dec. 15, 1665	Col.1	55
Cornellious, s. Cornellious, b. Dec. 15, 1665; bp. Jan.		
28, 1665	1	15
Cor[nelius], his w. [ ], adm. ch. & communicant Feb. [ ],		

	Vol.	Page
GILLETT, GILLET, GILLIET, GILLIT, GELLET, (cont.)		
1671	MG	
Cornelius, had s. [ ], b. June 10, 1671	MG	
Cornelius, taxed 2-0 on Feb. 10, [16]73	MG	
Cornelius, taxed 0-2 on Feb. 10, [16]73	MG	
Cornelius, had 8 children b. in Windsor. Dated Aug. 17, 1677	MG	
Cornelious, s. Cornellious, b. [ ], 1693	1	17
Cornelius, his w. [ ], adm. ch. F[eb] [ ], [16]	MG	
Corn[e]l[ius], communicant 16[ ]	MG	
Cornelius, Sr., d. June 26, 1711	2	236
Cornelius, d. Sept. 5, 1746	2	528
Cornelius, contributed 0-2-6 to the poor in other		
colonies	MG	
Cynthia, d. Almeron & Eunice, b. Nov. 15, 1798	2	573
Daniel, [s. Cornelius], b. June 30, 1678	MG	
Daniell, s. Cornelius, b. June 30, 1679; bp. July 27, [16]79	MG	
Daniel, s. Cornellious, b. July 1, 1679; bp. 27th day	1	15
Daniel, s. Cornellious, Jr., b. Mar. 11, 1695	1	17
Daniel, m. Mary ENNO, b. of Windsor, Jan. 28, 1702/3	1	57
Daniel, s. Daniel, b. Nov. 17, 1703	1	18
Daniel, m. Anna FILLEY, b. of Windsor, Jan. 6, 1726	2	155
Daniel, s. Daniel, Jr. & Anna, b. Jan. 26, 1728/9	2	339
Daniel, of Windsor, m. Ruth LOOMIS, of Bolton, Aug. 27,		
1735	2	156
Daniel, of Windsor, m. Ruth LOOMIS, of Bolton, Aug. 29,		
1735 (Entry crossed out)	2	343
Daniel, s. Daniel, Jr. & Anna, d. Apr. 25, 1743	2	527
Daniel, s. John & Elisabeth, b. Nov. 22, 1748	2	348
Daniel, d. Aug. 16, 1753	2	529
Daniel, m. Amy PALMER, b. of Windsor, Nov. 2, 1769	2	159
Daniel, s. Daniel & Amy, b. Nov. 25, 1781	2	356
Daniel, Capt., m. Mrs. Alelhina ROWLAND, b. of Windsor,		
Feb. 15, 1789	2	159
Daniel, d. Aug. 13, 1837	2	531
David, twin with Jonathan, s. Jonathan, b. July 5, 1711	2	40
David, s. Jonathan, d. Aug. 14, 1711	2	236
David, s. Jonathan & Mary, b. Sept. 22, 1733	2	341
Debora, d. Jere, b. Aug. 6, 1686	Col.D	51
Deborah, d. Jeremiah, b. Aug. 6, 1686	1	16
Deborah, d. Jeremiah, d. Apr. 22, 1693	1	45
Deborah, m. Samuel ADDAMS, Apr. 23, 1794	1	53
Deborah, d. Cornelius, Jr., b. Feb. 28, 1708/9	2	36
Deborah, d. Daniel & Amy, b. Oct. 2, 1777	2	356
Dina, d. Nathan, b. Oct. 18, 1696	1	17
Dorithy, d. Josiah, b. Apr. 15, 1689	1	16
Dorethy, d. Daniel, Sr. & Mary, b. May 15, 1726	2	45
Dorothy, m. Samuel COOK, b. of Windsor, Nov. 25, 1747	2	137
Ebenezer, s. [Jonathan, Jr. & Meriam], b. Oct. 28, 1679;		

	Vol.	Page
GILLETT, GILLET, GILLIET, GILLIT, GELLET, (cont.)		
d. [ ] 19, [16[7][ ]	MG	
Elias, s. [Nathan], b. July 1, 1649	MG	
Elias, s. Nathan, bp. July 1, 1649	1	14
Elias, d. Feb. 15, 1731/2	2	238
Elisabeth, d. [Nathan], b. Oct. 6, 1639	MG	
Elisabet[h], d. [Joseph], b. June 12, 1666	MG	
Elizabeth, d. Joseph, b. June 12, 1666	Col.1	55
Elizabeth, d. Joseph, b. June 12, 1666	1	39
Elizabeth, d. Josiah, b. Jan. 16, 1682	1	16
Eliz[abeth], d. Josiah, b. Jan. 16, 1683	Col.D	51
Elizabeth, d. Cornelius, Jr., b. May 31, 1707	2	36
Elizabeth, d. Elias, d. July 5, 1709	2	235
Elizabeth, of Colchester, m. Nathaniel PORTER, of Windsor,		
June 4, 1712	2	186
Elizabeth, d. Isaac, d. Sept. 18, 1722	2	237
Elizabeth, d. Isaac, & Elizabeth, b. Feb. 2, 1728/9	2	340
Elizabeth, m. Eleazer HILL, b. of Windsor, July 8, 1731	2	162
Elizabeth, d. John & Elizabeth, b. Sept. 26, 1732	2	341
Elizabeth, m. Eli PALMER, b. of Windsor, Apr. 1, 1756	1	189
Elizabeth, wid., d. Jan. 5, 1802	2	531
Elizabeth, d. Almerin & Eunice, b. [ ]	2	573
Esther, m. John LOOMIS, s. Joseph, Aug. 30, 1705	2	169
Eunice, d. Daniel, b. Feb. 21, 1716/17	2	41
Eunice, d. Abel & Abigail, b. Nov. 6, 1741	2	345
Eunice, d. Almerin & Eunice, b. Apr. 20, 1796	2	573
Francis P., m. William A. BAKER, b. of Windsor, Dec. 7,		
1841, by Rev. S. D. Jewett	2	476
George Griswold, s. Almeron & Eunice, b. June 10, 1804	2	573
Gideon, s. Nathan, Jr., b. Aug. 12, 1717	2	41
Hanna, d. Joseph, b. Jan. 30, [16]74	MG	
Hanna, [d. Cornelius], b. Jan. 30, 1674	MG	
Hannah, d. Joseph, b. June 30, [16]74	1	40
Hannah, d. Jonath[an], b. Sept. 18, 1682	Col.D	51
Hannah, d. Jonathan, b. Sept. 18, [16]82	1	16
Hanna, d. Jos., d. Aug. 11, [16]83	Col.D	56
Hannah, d. Joseph, d. Aug. 11, 1683	1	44
Hannah, w. Thomas, d. Feb. 20, 1708/9	2	235
Hannah, d. Nathan, Jr., b. Aug. 11, 1712	2	40
Hannah, d. Daniel, b. Dec. 21, 1719	2	43
Hannah, d. Nathan, 2nd, d. Dec. 28, 1721	2	237
Hannah, d. Abel & Abigail, b. Sept. 24, 1735	2	343
Hannah, m. William SHEPARD, b. of Windsor, Mar. 28,		
1754	2	200
Hester, d. [Cornelius], b. May 24, 1671	MG	
Hester, d. Cornellious, b. May 24, 1671	1	15
Isaac, s. Nathan, b. Aug. 2, 1693	1	17
Isaac, m. Elizabeth GRISWOLD, b. of Windsor, Oct. 29,		

	Vol.	Page
GILLETT, GILLET, GILLIET, GILLIT, GELLET, (cont.)		
1719	2	155
Isaac, s. Isaac, b. May 16, 1720	2	43
Isaac, of Windsor, m. Hannah **STEPHENS**, of Symsbury, Dec. 28, 1742	2	157
Ithniel, s. Nathan, Jr., b. Jan. 7, 1714/15	2	40
Jabiz, twin with John, s. John & Elizabeth, b. July 30, 1738	2	344
Jabez, s. Jacob* & Lydia, b. Jan. 13, 1761 *(In pencil)	2	353
Jacob, s. Isaac & Elizabeth, b. Jan. 27, 1726/7* *(In pencil "1728/9")	2	340
Jacob, of Windsor, m. Lydia **PHELPS**, of Symsbury, Dec. 13, 1744	2	157
Jacob, s. Jacob & Lydia, b. Oct. 13, 1745	2	347
Jacob, s. Jacob & Lydia, b. Aug. 8, 1755	2	352
James, s. Abel, Jr. & Jerusha, b. Jan. 28, 1781	2	356
Jane, w. Benjamin, d. Apr. 15, 1751	2	529
Jemima, d. Daniel & Amy, b. Dec. 28, 1774	2	356
Jemima, m. Job **DRAKE**, b. of Windsor, Oct. 4, 1796	2	143
Jeremia, s. [Jonathan, Sr.], b. Feb. 12, 1647	MG	
Jeremiah, s. Jonathan, b. Feb. 12, 1647	1	14
Jfremy, bp. Feb. 20, [16]47	MG	
Ifremy, bp. Feb. 20, [16]47 (Jeremiah)	MG	
Jeremiah, m. Deborah **BARTLIT**, Oct. 15, 1685	1	57
Jeremiah, s. Jeremiah, d. Apr. 21, 1692	1	45
Jeremiah, d. Mar. 1, 1692/3	1	45
Jeremy, m. Debora **BARTLET**, Oct. 15, 1685	Col.D	54
Jerusha, d. Abel & Abigail, b. Sept. 30, 1737	2	343
Jerusha, m. John **HOSKINS**, 3rd, b. of Windsor, June 10, 1755	2	163
Jerusha, d. Abel, Jr. & Jerusha, b. Aug. 15, 1773	2	356
Joab, s. Jacob & Lydia, b. Nov. 6, 1747	2	348
Joanna, d. [Cornelius], b. Apr. 22, 1676; bp. [Apr.] 23, 1676	MG	
Joanna, d. Cornellious, b. Apr. 22, 1676; bp. 23rd day	1	15
Johanna, d. Josias [& Johana], b. Oct. 28, 1680	MG	
Johana, d. Josias, b. Oct. 28, 1680	Col.1	57
Joannah, m. Josiah **STRONG**, Jan. 5, 1698/9	1	61
Joel, s. Thomas, b. May 1, 1707	2	36
John, s. [Jonathan, Sr.], b. Oct. 5, 1644	MG	
John, s. Jonathan, b. Oct. 5, 1644	1	16
John, m. Marcy **BARBER**, b. of Windsor, July 8, 1669	Col.1	45
John, s. [Joseph], b. June 10, 1671	MG	
John, s. Joseph, b. June 10, [16]71	1	40
John, s. [ ] & Marcy, b. Aug. 6, 1673	MG	
John, s. John, b. Aug. 6, [16]73	1	17
John, had 2 children b. in Windsor. Dated Aug. 17, 1677	MG	
John, d. July 4, 1699	1	45
John, s. Daniell, b. Sept. 11, 1707	2	36
John, m. Elizabeth **DRAKE**, b. of Windsor, Sept. 30, 1731	2	156

	Vol.	Page
GILLETT, GILLET, GILLIET, GILLIT, GELLET, (cont.)		
Jonathan, s. Jonathan, b. July 26, 1708; d. [ ]	2	40
Jonathan, s. Jonathan, d. Sept. 5, 1708	2	236
Jonathan, twin with David, s. Jonathan, b. July 5, 1711	2	40
Jonathan, m. Mary **LEWIS**, b. of Windsor, Dec. 17, 1731	2	156
Jonathan, s. Jonathan, Jr. & Mary, b. Oct. 21, 1735	2	343
Jonathan, Jr., m. Abigail **HUBBARD**, b. of Windsor, Dec. 11, 1740	2	157
Jonathan, Sr., contributed 0-4-6 to the poor in other colonies	MG	
Jonathan, Jr., contributed 0-2-6 to the poor in other colonies	MG	
Jonathan B., m. Hannah **FOSTER**, b. of Windsor, July 1, 1835, by Rev. Ansel Nash	2	481
Joseph, s. [Jonathan, Sr.], bp. July 25, 1641	MG	
Joseph, s. Jonathan, bp. July 25, 1641	1	14
Joseph, s. Joseph, b. Nov. 2, 1664	MG	
Joseph, s. Joseph, b. Nov. 20, 1664	Col.1	54
Joseph, s. Joseph, b. Nov. 20, 1664	1	18
Joseph, had 7 children b. in Windsor. Dated Aug. 17, 1677	MG	
Joseph, s. Joseph, b. Feb. 16, 1692	1	17
Joseph, s. Josiah, b. Mar. 3, 1694/5	1	15
[Jos[ep]h, adult, ch. mem. 16[ ]	MG	
Josiah, s. Jonathan, bp. July 14, 1650	1	14
Josia, m. Hanna **TAINTOR**, b. of Windsor, June 30, 1676, by Capt. John Allyen	Col.1	46
Josias, s. [Jonathan, Sr.], bp. July 14, 1650	MG	
Josias, bp. July 14, [16]50	MG	
Josia, m. Johana **TAINTER**, June 30, 1676, by John Allyn	MG	
Josia, m. Johana **TAINTER**, June 30, 1676, by John Allyn	MG	
Josias, s. Josias [& Johana], b. Nov. 24, 1678	MG	
Josia, s. [Josia & Johana], b. Nov. 24, 1678; bp. Dec. 1, [16]78	MG	
Josias, s. Josias, b. Nov. 24, 1678	Col.1	56
Josias, contributed 0-2-6 to the poor in other colonies	MG	
Julia, m. William L. **PERKINS**, Nov. 8, 1826, by Rev. Henry A. Rowland	2	193
Julia Ann, d. Almeron & Eunice, b. Mar. 23, 1802	2	573
Justice Elmer, s. Abel, Jr & Mary, b. Jan. 7, 1798	2	564
Lemuel, s. Benjamin & Elizabeth, b. Nov. 7, 1754	2	350
Leonard, s. Abel, Jr. & Jerusha, b. July 23, 1793	2	564
Loie, d. Abel & Abigail, b. June 1, 1746	2	347
Lucy, d. John & Elizabeth, b. Nov. 23, 1735	2	343
Lucie, d. Joel & Mary, b. Feb. 18, 1739/40	2	345
Lucy, d. Jonah & Elizabeth, b. Jan. 17, 1751	2	350
Lydia, d. Jacob & Lydia, b. Aug. 1, 1750	2	348
Marcy, d. John, b. Jan. 31, 1682	1	16
Marcy, of Windsor, m. George **NORTON**, of Suffield, June		

	Vol.	Page
GILLETT, GILLET, GILLIET, GILLIT, GELLET, (cont.)		
14, 1683	1	59
Marcy, d. Jonah & Elizabeth, b. Feb. 23, 1746	2	350
Margeret, d. Daniel, b. Dec. 31, 1723	2	44
Margaret, m. Timothy **PHELPS**, b. of Windsor, Apr. 24, 1746	2	188
Margere, m. Elijah **GOODRICH**, b. of Windsor, Aug. 20, 1752	2	158
Mary, m. Peter **BROWN**, July 15, 1658	MG	
Mary, m. Peter **BROWN**, b. of Windsor, July 15, 1658	1	54
Mary, d. Jonathan, Jr., b. Apr. 5, 1665	Col.1	54
Mary, d. Jonathan, Jr., b. Apr. 5, 1665	1	18
Mary, d. Joseph, b. Sept. 1, 1667	1	39
Mary, d. [Joseph], b. Sept. 10, 1667	MG	
Mary, d. [Jonathan, Jr & Mary], b. Oct. 21, 1667	MG	
Mary, d. Jonathan, Jr., b. Oct. 21, 1667	1	15
Mary, d. Jonathan, Jr., bp. Oct. 27, [16]67	MG	
Marey, d. [Cornelius], b. Aug. 12, 1668	MG	
Mary, d. Cornellious, b. Aug. 12, 1668	1	15
Mary, w. Jonathan, Jr., d. Apr. 18, [16]76	MG	
Mary, wid., d. Jan. 5, 1685	Col.D	56
Mary, wid., d. Jan. 5, 1685	1	45
Mary, d. Josia, b. Mar. 8, [16]86	Col.D	51
Mary, d. Josiah, b. Mar. 8, 1686/7	1	16
Mary, m. Robert **HOSKINS**, Oct. 27, 1686	1	58
Mary, d. Daniell, b. July 9, 1705	2	35
Mary, m. Anthony **HOSKINS**, Jr., b. of Windsor, Dec. 23, 1725	2	162
Mary, alias **CROW**, b. May 24, 1726	2	44
Mary, m. Richard **SKINNER**, b. of Windsor, Sept. 5, 1727	2	198
Mary, d. Jonathan & Mary, b. Sept. 30, 1732	2	341
Mary, wid., d. Dec. 6, 1773	2	531
Mercy, d. John, b. Jan. 31, 1682	Col.D	51
Mercy, of Windsor, m. George **NORTON**, of Sowthfeild, June 14, 1683	Col.D	54
Merila, d. Abel, Jr. & Mary, b. July 1, 1799	2	564
Mindwell, d. Josiah, b. Feb. 4, 1696	1	17
Nancy, 2nd, of Windsor, m. William **WESTLAND**, of Ohio, June 13, 1822, by Rev. John Bartlett. Int. Pub.	2	512
Nathan, his child d. [ ], [16]46	MG	
Nathan, had s. [ ] & d. [ ], d. [ ], [16]53	MG	
Nathan, s. [Nathan], b. Aug. 17, 1655	MG	
Nathan, s. Nathan, b. Aug. 17, 1655	Col.2	158
Nathan, s. Nathan, b. Aug. [ ], 1655	1	14
Nathan, his w. [ ], d. [Feb. 21*], [16]67 *(In pencil)	MG	
Nathan, his w. [ ], d. Feb. 21, [16]70	Col.1	55
Nathan, his w. [ ], d. Feb. 21, 1670	1	44
Nathan, taxed 6-0 on Feb. 10, [16]73	MG	

	Vol.	Page
GILLETT, GILLET, GILLIET, GILLIT, GELLET, (cont.)		
Nathan, had 8 children b. in Windsor. Dated Aug. 17, 1677	MG	
Nathan, Sr., d. Sept. 15, 1689	Col.D	57
Nathan, m. Rebekah **OWIN**, b. of Windsor, June 30, 1692	1	57
Nathan, communicant 16[ ]	MG	
Nathan, Jr., m. Hannah **BUCKLAND**, Mar. 30, 1704	2	153
Nathan, d. Jan. 30, 1751/2	2	529
Nathan, contributed 0-2-6 to the poor in other colonies	MG	
Nathanell, s. [Joseph], b. May 4, 1673	MG	
Nathanell, s. [Cornelius], b. May 4, 1673	MG	
Nathanael, s. Joseph, b. May 4, [16]73	1	40
Nathanell, s.[ ] & Marcy, b. Oct. 3, 1680; bp. Oct. 30,		
1681, at Hartford (?)	MG	
Noadiah, m. Sarah **OWIN**, b. of Windsor, Sept. 29, 1737	2	156
Noadiah, s. Noadiah & Sarah, b. Nov. 29, 1737	2	345
Noadiah, s. Noadiah & Sarah, d. Dec. 13, 1737	2	527
Noah, s. Josiah, b. Dec. 5, 1701	1	17
Oliver, s. Daniel, d. Sept. 14, 1841	2	532
Oliver S., m. Sarah A. **BELDEN**, Nov. 11, 1832, by Henry		
A. Rowland	2	506
Oliver Sherman, s. Daniel & Alethina, b. May 15, 1796	2	573
Pamela G., of Windsor, m. James H. **SPENCER**, of		
Windham, Jan. 19, 1823, by Rev. Augustus Bolles	2	202
Priscilla, d. Cornellious, b. Jan. 22, 1659	1	15
Prissella, d. [Cornelis], b. Jan. 23, 1659; d. [ ]	MG	
Prissilla, 2nd, d. [Cornelius], b. Mar. 30, 1661	MG	
Priscilla, d. Cornellious, b. May 30, 1661	1	15
Priscilla, w. Cornelius, decd., d. Jan. 7, 1722/3	2	237
Prudence, d. John & Elizabeth, b. May 22, 1743	2	346
Rachel, d. Jonah & Elizabeth, b. Mar. 9, 1737/8	2	345
Rachel, m. Stephen **GOODRICH**, b. of Windsor, Jan. 3, 1754	2	158
Rebeca, d. [Nathan], b. June 14, 1646	MG	
Rebekah, d. Nathan, b. June 14, 1646	1	14
Rebeckah, d. Nathan, d. July 13, 1655	Col.2	160
Rebeca, d. [Nathan], b. Dec. 8, 1657	MG	
Rebeckah, d. Nathan, b. Dec. 8, 1657	Col.2	161
Rebeckah, d. Noadiah & Sarah, b. Sept. 10, 1741	2	347
Rebekah, d. Abel, Jr. & Jerusha, b. Sept. 6, 1783	2	357
Rebekah, d. Nathan, d. July 13, [ ]	1	44
Rhoda, d. Jonathan, 3rd & Abigail, b. Jan. 25, 1750/1	2	349
Roseana, d. Jonathan, Jr. & Abigail, b. Oct. 13, 1741	2	345
Ruth, d. Daniel & Ruth, b. Oct. 13, 1736	2	343
Samuell, s. [Jonathan, Sr.], bp. Jan. 22, 1642	MG	
Samuel, s. Jonathan, bp. Jan. 22, 1642	1	14
Samuell, s. [ ] & Marcy, b. Feb. 16, 1677	MG	
Samuell, [s. Jonathan, Jr. & Meriam], b. Dec. 17, [16]80	MG	
Samuell, s. Josi[ah], b. Oct. 1, 1690	Col.D	51
Samuel, s. Josiah, b. Oct. 1, 1690	1	17

	Vol.	Page
GILLETT, GILLET, GILLIET, GILLIT, GELLET, (cont.)		
Samuel, s. Cornellious, Jr., b. Mar. 19, 1702/3	1	17
Samuel, s. Abel, Jr. & Jerusha, b. May 6, 1776	2	356
Sarah, d. [Nathan], b. July 13, 1651	MG	
Sarah, d. Nathan, bp. July 13, 1651	1	14
Sarah, d. [Cornelius], b. Jan. 3, 1673	MG	
Sarah, d. Cornellious, b. Jan. 3, 1673	1	15
Sarah, m. Joseph **PHELPS**, s. Capt. Timothy, Feb. 22, 1709/10	2	186
Sarah, d. Noadiah & Sarah, b. Apr. 21, 1739	2	345
Sarah, of Hartford, m. Isaac **LOOMIS**, Jr., of Windsor, Mar. 10, 1742/3	2	172
Sarah, d. Abel & Abigail, b. May 3, 1748	2	348
Sarah, w. Noadiah, d. Mar. 16, 1748/9	2	528
Sarah, d. Abel & Abigail, d. Dec. 25, 1757	2	529
Sarah, d. Abel, Jr. & Jerusha, b. Nov. 27, 1778	2	356
Sarah M., m. Jasper **MORGAN**, Sept. 12, 1832, by Henry A. Rowland	2	495
Sarah Macanley, d. Daniel & Alethina, b. Oct. 22, 1793	2	573
Shuball, s. Daniel, Jr. & Anna, d. July 19, 1744	2	527
Simon, s. Jonah & Elizabeth, b. Oct. 16, 1745	2	350
Stephen, s. Cornelius, b. June 30, 1713	2	42
Stephen, m. Ann **LOOMIS**, b. of Windsor, Sept. 21, 1738	2	156
Stephen, s. Stephen & Ann, b. Nov. 1, 1738	2	344
Stephen, s. Jonathan, 3rd & Abigail, b. July 4, 1748	2	348
Thomas, s. John, b. Jan. 7, [16]71; bp. the 14th	1	16
Thomas, s. [ ] & Marcy, b. July 18, [1676], bp. [July] 23, 1676	MG	
Thomas, s. John, b. July 18, [16]76	1	16
Thomas, s. [Jonathan, Jr. & Meriam], b. May 31, 1678; d. July 11, [1678]	MG	
Thomas, s. Jonathan, d. June 11, [16]78	MG	
Thomas, s. Jonathan, d. June 11, 1678	Col.1	58
Thomas, m. Martha **MILLS**, b. of Windsor, Nov. 21, 1700	1	57
Thomas, m. Hannah **CLARKE**, Feb. 26, 1704/5	2	153
Thomas, s. Cornelius, Jr., b. Aug. 1, 1705	2	35
Thomas, s. Jonah & Elizabeth, b. Jan. 17, 1751	2	350
Tryphena, d. Jonah & Elizabeth, b. Aug. 15, 1740	2	350
Triphena, d. Jonah & Elizabeth, b. Aug. 13, 1746	2	345
William, s. [Jonathan, Jr. & Mary], b. Dec. 4, 1673	MG	
William, s. [Jonathan], b. Dec. 4, 1673	1	15
William Rowland, s. Daniel & Alethina, b. Jan. 18, 1801	2	573
Zabud, s. Nathan, Jr., b. Apr. 6, 1710	2	37
Zacheus, s. Isaac & Elizabeth, b. Dec. 18, 1724	2	340
Zacheus, of Windsor, m. Ruth **PHELPS**, of Symsbury, Mar. 15, 1743/4	2	157
Zemira, s. Abel & Mary, b. Nov. 15, 1801	2	573
-----, m. Marcy **BARBER**, July 8, 1669	MG	

	Vol.	Page
GILLETT, GILLET, GILLIET, GILLIT, GELLET, (cont.)		
-----, wid. communicant from Dorchester, living in Windsor, Dec. 22, 1677	MG	
-----, Sr., ch. mem. 16[ ], from Dorchester	MG	
-----, ch. mem. 16[ ], from Dorchester	MG	
GILLMAN, Damaras, of Hartford, m. Asahel **HODGE**, of Windsor, Jan. 27, 1740/1	2	163
GLAZER, Betsey, d. Eliphalet & Rachel, b. June 18, 1794	2	562
Martha, d. Eliphlet & Rachel, b. June 26, 1792	2	562
GLEASON, GLESON, Isaac, s. Isaac & Martha, b. Sept. 14, 1745	2	349
Isaac, s. Isaac & Martha, b. Sept. 13, 1747	2	352
Isaac, s. Isaac & Martha, b. Sept. 13, 1747	2	444
Martha, wid., m. John **SLADE**, b. of Windsor, Sept. 12, 1751	2	200
Mary, of Enfield, m. Nathanel **DAVIS**, of Windsor, Oct. 4, 1739	2	142
GODDARD, Ann, m. Theodore **SPERRY**, b. of East Windsor, Mar. 5, 1847, by T. A. Leete	2	482
Nicolas, contributed 0-2-6 to the poor in other colonies	MG	
GOFF, GOFFE, GOFE, Abia, m. Henery **WOLCOT**, Jr., Oct. 12, 1664	MG	
Abia, m. Henery **WOLCOT**, Oct. 12, 1664, by Mr. Wolcot	Col.1	45
Hanna, m. John **MOORE**, Sept. 21, 1664	MG	
Hanna, m. John **MOOR**, Sept. 21, 1664, by Mr. Woolcot	Col.1	45
GOING, [see also **GOREN**], William, m. Sarah **BUELL**, b. of Windsor, Sept. 11, 1700	1	57
GOODELL, Jesie, m. Mara **WOLCOTT**, b. of Windsor, Apr. 22, 1764	2	158
GOODMAN, Fanny, m. Enoch **KINGSBURY**, Nov. 1, 1830, by John Bartlett	2	168
Osmer, of Hartford, m. [ ] **WILTON**, wid. Daued, May 6, [16]79, at Hartford	MG	
Richard, of Hartford, m. Mary **TERY**, of Windsor, Dec. 8, 1659	Col.1	45
Richard, of Hartford, m. Mary **TERRY**, of Windsor, Dec. 8, 1659	1	56
GOODRICH, Daniel, s. Elijah & Margere, b. Aug. 8, 1765	2	354
Elijah, m. Margere **GILLET**, b. of Windsor, Aug. 20, 1752	2	158
Elijah, s. Elijah & Margere, b. Jan. 23, 1757	2	351
Hannah, m. Job **DRAKE**, 2nd, b. of Windsor, Apr. 27, 1749	2	142
Jacob, s. Stephen & Rachel, b. Feb. 5, 1755	2	350
Jeremiah, s. Elijah & Margere, b. Aug. 4, 1757	2	353
Jesse, s. Elijah & Margere, b. Oct. 28, 1759	2	353
John, s. Elijah & Margere, b. Dec. 26, 1755	2	351
Justus, s. Elijah & Margere, b. June 16, 1769	2	355
Margere, d. Elijah & Margere, b. July 24, 1763	2	354
Maria Chloe, of Windsor, m. Thomas **MOORE**, of Plymouth, Penn., Nov. 21, 1830, by Rev. Augustus Bolles	2	493
Rebeckah, m. Reuben **LOOMIS**, b. of Windsor, Feb. 5,		

	Vol.	Page
GRANGER, (cont.)		
at Samuell Moores	2	235
GRANNIS, Arba, m. Sarah **CHURCH**, b. of Windsor, July 24, 1839, by Rev. Cephas Brainard	2	481
GRANT, Abiel, m. Elizabeth **LOOMIS**, b. of Windsor, May 26, 1754	2	158
Abiel, d. [sic] Abiel & Mary, b. May 26, 1762	2	354
Abiel, d. May 28, 1762	2	530
Abiel, d. May 28, 1762	2	530
Abigal, d. [John & Mary], b. Jan. 27, 1679; bp. July 17, 168[ ], at Hartford, by Mr. Foster	MG	
Abigall, d. [John], b. Jan. 27, 1679	Col. 1	56
Abigael, d. Samuel, Jr., b. Dec. 18, 1695	2	38
Abigail, m. Dr. Samuel **MATHER**, Apr. 13, 1704	1	59
Abigail, m. Abiel **ABBOTT**, b. of Windsor, Jan. 9, 1717/18	2	123
Ann, d. Ebenezer & Ann, b. Nov. 18, 1739	2	344
Ann, d. Capt. Ebenezer & Ann, d. Oct. 21, 1747	2	528
Ann, d. Capt. Ebenezer & Ann, b. May 6, 1748	2	348
Ann, d. Edward Chapman & Hannah, b. Aug. 22, 1757	2	352
Anna, d. [Samuel & Anna], b. Sept. 2, 1684	MG	
Anna, w. Samuel, Jr., d. Apr. 18, 1686	2	236
Ashbel, s. David & Elizabeth, b. Aug. 20, 1737	2	344
Ashbel, m. Elizabeth **CHAPMAN**, b. of Windsor, Mar. 29, 1764	2	158
Ashbel, d. June 8, 1774	2	531
Azariah, m. Abigail **BEAMAN**, July 6, 1749	2	157
Bathsheba, d. William & Sarah, b. Oct. 20, 1728	2	342
Benjamin, s. Nathaniel, b. July 8, 1708	2	39
Benjamin, of Windsor, m. Ann **HUNT**, of Enfield, Feb. 10, 1737	2	156
Benjamin, s. Benjamin & Ann, b. Dec. 9, 1737	2	343
Benjamin, had 2 children d. [ ], in "Elenton" prior to 1740	MG	
Bethia, d. Nathaniel, b. June 17, 1700	2	39
Daniel, s. Mathew, b. Feb. 2, 1692/3	1	17
Daniel, of Windsor, m. Sarah **BURT**, of Springfield, Nov. 18, 1717	2	155
David, s. Samuel, Jr., b. Dec. 10, 1703	2	39
David, m. Elizabeth **CHAPMAN**, b. of Windsor, Dec. 21, 1727	2	155
David, s. David & Elizabeth, b. June 8, 1734	2	344
David, s. Ens. David & Elisabeth, d. June 15, 1748	2	528
David, s. Ashbel & Elizabeth, b. July 6, 1770	2	355
Deliverance, m. Samuel **CARY**, b. of Windsor, Dec. 7, 1762	2	137
Ealsna, d. Thomas, b. Oct. 21, 1696	2	37
Ebenezer, s. Samuel, Jr., b. Oct. 20, 1706	2	39
Ebenezer, s. Josiah, b. Mar. 2, 1723/4	2	44
Ebenezer, m. Anne **ELLSWORTH**, b. of Windsor, Nov. 10,		

	Vol.	Page
GRANT, (cont.)		
1737	2	156
Ebenezer, s. Ebenezer & Ann, b. Apr. 24, 1744	2	347
Ebenezer, s. Capt. Ebenezer & Ann, d. Dec. 4, 1747	2	528
Edward Chapman, s. John, b. Jan. 13, 1725/6	2	44
Elijah, s. Josiah, b. June 22, 1719	2	42
Elijah, s. Josiah, d. Aug. 13, 1724	2	238
Elijah, s. David & Elizabeth, b. May 8, 1729	2	344
Elijah, s. Ens. David & Elizabeth, d. Aug. 14, 1749	2	528
Elizabeth, d. [John], b. July 10, [16]77	Col.1	56
Elissabeth, d. [John & Mary], b. July 10, [16]77; bp. [ ]	MG	
Elizabeth, d. John, bp. July 15, [16]77	MG	
Elizabeth, m. Joshua **WILLS,** May 12, 1697	1	63
Elisabeth, m. Thomas **FISHER,** Nov. 20, 1707	2	151
Elizabeth, d. John, b. Dec. 1, 1717	2	41
Elizabeth, d. Thomas, Jr. & Elizabeth, b. June 8, 1724	2	45
Elizabeth, d. Thomas, Jr. & Elizabeth, d. Jan. 9, 1725	2	238
Elizabeth, d. Thomas & Elizabeth, b. Nov. 15, 1730	2	340
Elizabeth, m. Nathaniel **STRONG,** b. of Windsor, Apr. 20, 1755	2	200
Elizabeth, d. Ashbel & Elizabeth, b. Oct. 14, 1767	2	355
Elizabeth, d. Ashbel & Elizabeth, d. May 10, 1772	2	530
Ephraim, s. Samuel, Jr., b. Aug. 24, 1698	2	38
Esther, d. Nathaniel, b. Oct. 31, 1710	2	39
Eunice, d. Ebenezer & Anne, b. Oct. 21, 1741	2	345
Eunice, d. Capt. Ebenezer & Ann, d. Oct. 28, 1747	2	528
Eunice, d. Capt. Ebenezer & Ann, b. Mar. 27, 1752	2	349
Eunice, d. Capt. Ebenezer & Ann, d. Feb. 3, 1754	2	529
Grace, d. Samuell, Jr., b. Aug. 17, 1701	2	38
Grace, d. Jonathan & Mary, b. Sept. 27, 1756	2	351
Hanna, d. [Tahan & Hanna], b. June 8, 1668	MG	
Hanna, d. [Tahan], b. June 8, 1668	Col.1	56
Hannah, d. Tahan, b. June 8, [16]68	1	16
Hannah, d. Samuell, Jr., b. Sept. 2, 1684	Col.D	51
Hannah, d. Samuel, Jr., b. Sept. 2, 1684	1	16
Hannah, w. Samuel, Jr., d. Apr. [ ], 1685* *(Date in penciil)	1	45
Hannah, d. Samuell, Jr., b. Mar. 28, 1689	2	38
Hannah, m. Henry **CHAPMAN,** May 11, 1692	1	55
Hannah, d. Mathew, b. Mar. 9, 1694/5	1	17
Hannah, m. John **GAYLORD,** b. of Windsor, Apr. 3, 1712	2	155
Hannah, d. Sergt. Joseph, b. Oct. 1, 1716	2	41
Hannah, d. John & Mary, b. Mar. 7, 1730/1	2	340
Hannah, m. Benjamin **BROWN,** b. of Windsor, Oct. 19, 1743	2	131
Hannah, d. Tahan, b. [ ]	Col.D	51
Hanna*, w. Samuell, Jr., d. [ ] *(Note by LBB: "Hannah (**FILLEY**) GRANT")	Col.D	56
Huldah, d. Josiah, b. May 25, 1721	2	43
Increase, s. Josiah, b. Feb. 13, 1716/17	2	41

	Vol.	Page
GRANT, (cont.)		
Jehiel, s. Thomas, b. June 25, 1705	2	38
Jerusha, d. Josiah, b. Jan. 21, 1725/6	2	44
John, b. Apr. 30, 1642; m. Mary **HULL,** Aug. 2, 1666	MG	
John, [s. Mathew, Sr.], b. Apr. 30, 1642	Col.1	56
John, s. Mathew, b. Apr. 30, 1642	1	14
John, s. John, bp. [ ], [16]62	MG	
John, s. [Samuel & Mary], b. Apr. 24, 1664	MG	
John, s. Samuell, b. Apr. 24, 1664	Col.1	54
John, [s. Samuell], b. Apr. 24, 1664	Col.1	56
John, s. Samuel, b. Apr. 24, 1664	1	15
John, m. Mary **HULL,** Aug. 2, 1666, by Mr. Clark	Col.1	45
John, m. Mary **HULL,** Aug. 2, 1666, by Mr. Clark	1	57
John, s. [John & Mary], b. Oct. 20, 167[ ]	MG	
John, s. John (s. of Mathew), b. Oct. 20, 1671	Col.1	56
John, bp. Oct. 22, [16]71	MG	
John, had 3 children b. in Windsor. Dated Aug. 17, 1677	MG	
John, d. July 22, 1684	Col.D	56
John, d. July 22, 1684	1	45
John, s. John, d. May 17, 1686	Col.D	56
John, s. John, d. May 17, 1686	1	45
John, s. Peter, d. Sept. 29, 1687	1	44
John, m. Elizabeth **SKINER,** June 1, 1690	Col.D	55
John, m. Elizabeth **SKINNER,** June 5, 1690	1	57
John, s. John, b. Mar. 3, 1690/1	Col. D	51
John, s. John, b. Mar. 3, 1690/1	1	17
John, d. July 19, 1695	1	45
John, adult, ch. mem. 16[ ]	MG	
John, m. Mary **CHAPMAN,** b. of Windsor, Nov. 11, 1714	2	155
John, s. Josiah, b. May 17, 1715	2	40
John, s. John, b. Jan. 1, 1720/1	2	43
John, contributed 0-2-6 to the poor in other colonies	MG	
Jonathan, s. Nathaniel, b. Aug. 18, 1713	2	40
Jonathan, s. Nathaniel, d. Sept. 10, 1713	2	236
Jonathan, of Windsor, m. Mary **LADD,** of Tolland, July 9, 1741	2	478
Joseph, s. [Tahan & Hanna], b. May 14, 1673	MG	
Joseph, s. [Tahan], b. May 14, 1673	Col.1	56
Joseph, s. Tahan, b. May 14, [16]73; bp. May 18, [16]73	1	16
Joseph, m. Mary **WARRIN,** b. of Windsor, May 1, 1701	1	57
Joseph, s. Joseph, b. June 29, 1706	2	35
Joseph, s. Sergt. Joseph, d. Dec. 24, 1716	2	237
Josia, s. [Samuel & Mary], b. Mar. 19, 1668	MG	
Josia, s. [Samuell], b. Mar. 19, 1668	Col.1	56
Josiah, s. Samuel, b. Mar. 19, 1668	1	15
Josiah, s. Josiah, b. Nov. 24, 1678	1	16
Josiah, s. John, b. Jan. 28, 1682	1	16
Josiah, s. John, b. Jan. 28, 1683	Col.D	51

	Vol.	Page
GRANT, (cont.)		
Mathew, m. Henry* **CHAPMAN**, Oct. 29, 1690 *(Note by		
LBB: "Hannah")	Col.D	55
Mathew, m. Hannah **CHAPMAN**, Oct. [ ], 1690	1	57
Mathew, s. Mathew, b. Oct. 22, 1691	1	17
Mathew, communicant 16[ ]	MG	
Mathew, contributed silver 0-3-0 to the poor in other colonies	MG	
Mathew, s. Mathew, d. Apr. 19, 1710	2	236
Mathew, s. John, b. June 27, 1723	2	44
Mathew, s. William & Sarah, b. Feb. 8, 1730	2	342
Mathew, his w. [ ], d. Feb. 9, 1734/5	2	527
Mathew, m. Hannah **BIRGE**, Feb. 2, 1749	2	157
Nathanell, s. [Samuel & Mary], b. Apr. 14, 1672	MG	
Nathanell, s. [Samuell], b. Apr. 14, 1672	Col.1	56
Nathanael, s. Samuel, b. Apr. 14, [16]72	1	15
Nathanael, m. Bethia **WARNER**, Oct. 12, 1699	1	57
Nathaniel, s. Nathaniel, b. Oct. 18, 1705	2	39
Nathaniell, had two children d. [ ], in "Elenton"		
prior to 1740	MG	
Nathaniell, his child d. [ ], in "Elenton" prior		
to 1740	MG	
Nathaniell, Jr., had 3 children d. [ ], in "Elenton"		
prior to 1740	MG	
Nathanell, [ ]	MG	
Noah, s. Samuel, Jr., b. Dec. 16, 1693	2	38
Phebe, d. Jonathan & Mary, b. Mar. 15, 1747	2	351
Prissilla, m. Micall **HUMFERY**, Oct. 14, 1647	MG	
Priscilla, m. Michael **HUMPHRY**, Oct. 14, 1647	1	57
Prudence, d. Jonathan & Mary, b. Sept. 15, 1754	2	351
Rachell, d. Mathew, b. Apr. 17, 1704	2	35
Rachel, d. Jonathan & Mary, b. June 20, 1762	2	354
Rhoda, d. Jonathan & Mary, b. Apr. 12, 1749	2	351
Rhoda Emma, m. Asahel C. **WASHBURN**, of Royalton, Vt.,		
Sept. 24, 1828, by Rev. John Bartlett, of Wintonbury	2	212
Roswell, s. Ebenezer & Ann, b. Mar. 9, 1745/6	2	347
Russell, s. Edward Chapman & Hannah, b. Dec. 29, 1754	2	350
Ruth, d. Nathaniel, b. Feb. 26, 1702/3	2	39
S., [ ]	MG	
Samuel, b. Nov.12, 1631, in Dorchester; m. Mary **PORTER**,		
May 27, 1658	MG	
Samuell, s. Mathew, Sr., b. Nov. 12, 1631	Col.1	56
Samuell, s. Samuel & Mary, b. Apr. 20, 1659	MG	
Samuell, s. Samuell, b. Apr. 20, 1659	Col.1	56
Samuel, s. Samuel, b. Apr. 20, 1659	1	15
Samuell, bp. May 22, [16]59	MG	
Samuel, had 8 children b. in Windsor. Dated Aug. 17, 1677	MG	
Samuel, m. Anna **FILLIE**, Dec. 6, 1683	MG	
Samuel, m. Hanah **FILLEY**, Dec. 6, 1683	Col.D	54

GRANT, (cont.)

	Vol.	Page
Samuel, m. Hannah **FILLEY**, Dec. 6, 1683	1	57
Samuell, m. Anna **FILLEY**, Dec. 6, 1683	2	154
Samuel, m. Grace **MINOR**, Apr. 11, 1688	2	154
Samuel, s. Samuel, Jr., b. Sept. 19, 1691	2	38
Samuell, adult, ch. mem. 16[ ]	MG	
Samuel, Jr., d. May 8, 1710	2	236
Samuell, m. Theophy **BARTLET**, b. of Windsor, Jan. 1, 1718/19	2	155
Samuel, s. Samuel, s. Samuell, decd., b. Nov. 30, 1720	2	43
Samuell, s. Azariah & Abigail, b. Mar. 6, 1752	2	351
Samuel, s. Mathew, b. Nov. 12, [ ]	1	14
Samuel, s. Samuel, Jr., d. [ ]	Col.D	56
Samuell, contributed 0-5-0 to the poor in other colonies	MG	
Samuel Rockwel, s. Thomas, Jr. & Elizabeth, b. June 30, 1726	2	45
Sara, d. [Tahan & Hanna], b. Sept. 19, 1675; bp. same day	MG	
Sary, d. [Tahan], b. Sept. 19, 1675	Col.1	56
Sarah, d. Tahan, b. Sept. 19, [16]75	1	16
Sara, d. [Samuel & Mary], b. Jan. 19, 167[ ]; bp. Feb. 2, [16]78; d. [ ]	MG	
Sara, d. [Samuell], b. Jan. 19, 1678	Col.1	56
Sarah, d. Samuell, Jr., b. Sept. 2, 1684	2	38
Sarah, m. Jonathan **ELSWORTH**, Oct. 26, 1693	1	56
Sarah, d. Thomas, b. Jan. 8, 1699/00	2	37
Sarah, m. Thomas **SKINNER**, July 19, 1705	2	197
Sarah, d. Mathew, b. July 17, 1710	2	37
Sarah, d. Josiah, b. Mar. 11, 1711/12	2	39
Sarah, w. Josiah, d. July 30, 1713	2	236
Sarah, m. David **BISSELL**, b. of Windsor, Sept. 30, 1730	2	130
Sarah, d. William & Sarah, b. June 8, 1735	2	343
Sarah, d. Samuell, d. [ ]	Col.D	56
[Susanna*], w. M[ ], d. [Nov. 13*], [16]65 *(In pencil)	MG	
Susanna, w. Mathew, d. Nov. 13, 1666, ae 65 years wanting 20 weeks	1	44
Susanna, d. Nov. 13, 1666	Col.1	55
Susannah, d. Jonathan & Mary, b. Sept. 5, 1744	2	347
Tahan, b. Feb. 3, 1633, in Dorchester; m. Hanna **PALMER**, Jan. 22, 1662	MG	
Tahan, s. [Mathew, Sr.], b. Feb. 3, 1633	Col.1	56
Tahan, s. Mathew, b. Feb. 3, [16]33	1	14
Tahan, m. Anna **PALMER**, b. of Windsor, Jan. 22, 1662	Col.1	45
Tahan, m. Anna **PALMER**, b. of Windsor, Jan. 22, 1662	1	57
Tahan, his w. [ ], bp. Dec. 27, [16]63	MG	
Tahan, s. [Tahan & Hannah], b. Sept. 27, 1665	MG	
Tahan, s. Tahan, b. Sept. 27, 1665	Col.1	55
Tahan, s. [Tahan], b. Sept. 27, 1665	Col.1	56
Tahan, s. Tahan, b. Sept. 27, 1665	1	16

	Vol.	Page

GRANT, (cont.)

Tahan, had 6 children b. in Windsor. Dated Aug. 17, 1677	MG	
Tahan & Hannah, had s. [ ], s. b. Nov. 11, 1680	MG	
Tahan, Sr., d. May 30, 1693	1	45
Tahan, adult, ch. mem. 16[ ]	MG	
Tahan, s. Joseph, b. Feb. 25, 1702/3	1	17
Tahan, m. Hanah **BISSELL,** [ ]	Col.D	55
Tahan, m. Hannah **BISSELL,** [ ]	1	57
Tahan, contributed 0-8-0 to the poor in other colonies	MG	
Thomas, s. [Tahan & Hanna], b. Feb. 20, 1670	MG	
Thomas, s. [Tahan], b. Feb. 20, 1670	Col.1	56
Thomas, s. Tahan, b. Feb. 20, [16]70; bp. the 26th day	1	16
Thomas, m. Sarah **PINNEY,** Feb. 13, 1695/6	1	57
Thomas, s. Thomas, b. Oct. 5, 1710	2	38
Thomas, Jr., m. Elizabeth **ROCKWELL,** b. of Windsor, July 9, 1722	2	155
Triphene, d. William & Sarah, b. Jan. 16, 1737/8	2	343
William, s. Mathew, b. Jan. 23, 1700/1	1	17
William, s. Mathew, d. May 26, 1701	1	45
William, s. Mathew, b. June 7, 1706	2	36
William, s. Thomas & Elizabeth, b. Apr. 24, 1727	2	339
W[illia]m, m. [ ]	MG	
Zerviah, d. William & Sarah, b. Nov. 13, 1731	2	342
-----, ch. mem. 16[ ], from Dorchester	MG	
GRAVES, Mary, of Hartford, m. Nathanael **WINCHEL,** of Windsor, Mar. 15, 1693/4	1	63
GRAYMES, Gody, d. [ ], in [Elenton" prior to 1740	MG	
GREEN, Asahel, s. Barzilla & Eunice, b. June 19, 1763	2	354
Barzilla, m. Eunice **BISSELL,** b. of Windsor, Nov. 30, 1750	2	158
Joel, s. Barzilla & Eunice, b. Oct. 3, 1761	2	354
Julia S., m. Edwin F. **STOUGHTON,** of East Windsor, Sept. 5, 1839, by Rev. S. D. Jewett	2	514
Maria T., m. Jason A. **TAINTOR,** b. of Windsor, June 25, 1829, by Rev. Henry A. Rowland	2	206
Nancy, of Windsor, m. Elijah **ROCKWELL,** of East Windsor, Oct. 3, 1832, by Henry A. Rowland	2	505
Roxa, m. William **HUNT,** Jr., b. of Windsor, Dec. 31, 1828, by John B. Ballard	2	484
Roxana, m. Joel **THRALL,** b. of Windsor, Nov. 23, 1820, by Rev. Augustus Bolles	2	205
Samuel, of Palmer, Mass., m. Fanny **FITCH,** of Windsor, Dec. 2, 1827, by Rev. Augustus Bolles	2	480
GREENAN, Margaret, m. Farl (?) **ROARK,** June 13, 1852, by Rev. James Smyth	2	460
GREGORY, Sturgis G., of New Milford, m. Susannah A. **PHELPS,** of Windsor, [18], by Rev. Ansel Nash	2	480
GRIDLEY, Rhoda, of Windsor, m. Eleazer **HOWLET,** of Hartford, Jan. 11, 1827, by Rev. Tobias Spicer, of		

	Vol.	Page
GRIDLEY, (cont.)		
Hartford	2	166
Roswel, of Windsor, m. Flona **HUMPHREY**, of Farmington, Sept. 1, [ ], by Rev. John Bartlett, of Wintonbury. Int. Pub.	2	160
Truman, of Farmington, m. Cinthia **KING**, of West Hartford, June 27, 1820, by Rev. John Bartlett, of Wintonbury	2	479
GRIFFIN, GRIFFEN, Abigaill, d. [John & Anna], b. Nov. 12, 1660	MG	
Abigail, d. John, b. Nov. 12, [16]60	1	15
Alfred, m. Fanny **CLARK**, b. of Windsor, Nov. 27, 1823, by Richard Niles, J. P.	2	160
Epharam, s. [John & Anna], b. Mar. 1, 1668	MG	
Ephraim, s. John, b. Mar. 1, [16]68/9	1	15
Hanna, d. [John & Anna], b. July 4, 1649	MG	
Hannah, d. John, b. July 4, 1649	Col.2	158
Hana, m. Isack **POND**, May 10, 166[7?]	MG	
Hannah, m. Isaac **POND**, b. of Windsor, May 1, 1667, by Mr. Allyn	1	60
Hanna, m. Isack **POND**, May 10, [16]67, at Hartford, by Capt. John Allin	Col.1	45
John, m. Anna **BANCROFT**, May 13, 164[7]	MG	
John, m. Ann **BANCRAFT**, May 13, 1647	1	56
John, s. [John & Anna], b. Oct. 20, 1656	MG	
John, had 10 children b. in Windsor. Dated Aug. 17, 1677	MG	
John S., m. Mariette **MOFFAT**, b. of Windsor, Dec. 23, 1851, by Rev. H. A. Weed	2	498
Julia, m. Samuel **HOLCOMB**, Nov. 3, 1825, by Richard Niles, J. P.	2	166
Julia, m. Samuel **HOLCOMB**, b. of Windsor, Nov. 3, 1825, by Richard Niles, J. P.	2	167
Mary, d. [John & Anna], b. Mar. 1, 1651	MG	
Mary, d. [John], b. Mar. 4, 1651	Col.2	158
Mary, m. [ ] **WILSON**	MG	
Mary, m. Samuell **WILSON**, b. of Windsor, May 1, 1672	Col.1	46
Mary, m. Samuel **WILSON**, b. of Windsor, May 1, 1672	1	63
Mary, m. Julius **PEASE**, Mar. 23, 1826, by Rev. Jeremiah F. Bridges	2	193
Mindwell, d. [John & Anna], b. Feb. 11, 1662	MG	
Mindwell, d. John, b. Feb. 11, 1662	1	15
Nathanell, s. [John & Anna], b. May 31, 1673	MG	
Nathanael, b. May 31, [16]73	1	15
Ruth, d. [John & Anna], b. Jan. 21, 1665	MG	
Ruth, d. John, b. Jan. 21, 1665	1	15
Sarah, d. [John], b. Feb. 10, 1654	Col.2	158
Sara, d. [John & Anna], b. Dec. 25, 1654	MG	
Thomas, s. [John & Anna], b. Oct. 3, 1658	MG	
Thomas, s. John, b. Oct. 3, 1658	1	15

	Vol.	Page
GRINES, Ichabod Cromwell, m. Rachel **ELLICE**, b. of Windsor,		
Jan. 14, 1747/8	2	157
GRISWOLD, GRISWALD, Aaron, s. Francis, Jr. & Jerusha, b.		
Oct. 22, 1743	2	346
Abel, s. Joseph, b. Feb. [ ], 1713/14	2	42
Abel, s. George, Jr., & Mary, b. May 16, 1760	2	353
Abel, m. Chloe **MOORE**, b. of Windsor, Oct. 14, 1779	2	159
Abel, of Windsor, m. Deidamia **EASTON**, of Granby, June		
19, 1799	2	159
Abel Trumbull, s. Abel & Chloe, b. Jan. 3, 1789	2	563
Abiel, s. Isaac & Mindwell, b. June 14, 1755	2	351
Abiel, of Windsor, m. Huldah **PINNEY**, of Symsbury, Oct.		
25, 1775	2	159
Abiel B., m. Mary **PINNEY**, b. of Windsor, Sept. 8, 1800	2	479
Abigayl, d. [George & Mary], b. Oct. 31, 1676	MG	
Abigail, d. George, b. Oct. 31, 1676	1	15
Abigail, d. George, d. May 7, [16]82	Col.D	56
Abigail, d. Sergt. Joseph, b. Aug. 11, 1689	1	17
Abigael, d. Francis, b. Dec. 23, 1704	2	35
Abigaell, m. Joseph **BARNARD**, b. of Windsor, Oct. 4, 1705	2	127
Abigael, d. John, b. Feb. 1, 1706/7	2	35
Abigael, d. Ens. Jos., m. Josiah **PHELPS**, s. John, June 21,		
1711	2	186
Abigael, d. John, d. Feb. 9, 1712/13	2	236
Abigail, d. Sergt. John & Abigail, b. May 21, 1727	2	45
Abigail, m. Edward **GRISWOLD**, b. of Windsor, June 23,		
1728	2	156
Abigail, d. Edward & Abigail, b. May 5, 1732	2	341
Abigail, w. Edward, d. Aug. 7, 1763	2	350
Abigail P., m. George G. **BLANCHARD**, b. of Windsor, Oct.		
16, 1845, by Rev. Cephas Brainard	2	508
Abram, s. Abiel & Huldah, b. Nov. 28, 1788	2	562
Ann, d. Edward, bp. June 19, 1642	MG	
Ann, d. Edward, bp. June 19, 1642	1	14
Ann, m. Isaac **PHELPS**, b. of Windsor, Mar. 11, 1662, by		
Mr. Allyn	1	60
Ann, d. Benjamin, b. May 28, 1708	2	37
Ann, d. Daniel, Jr., b. Mar. 20, 1718	2	42
Ann, m. Josiah **PHELPS**, b. of Windsor, Sept. 14, 1733	2	187
Ann, d. Jonah & Ruth, b. Apr. 31 (sic), 1757	2	352
Anna, d. Edward, bp. June 19, 1642	Col.2	153
Anna, d. Francis, b. July 29, 1716	2	41
Anne, d. Moses, Jr. & Anna, b. Feb. 17, 1766	2	355
Anson, s. Moses, Jr. & Anne, b. Sept. 30, 1769	2	355
Arthur, s. Abel & Chloe, b. Jan. 30, 1783	2	561
Asaph, m. Anna A. **PHELPS**, b. of East Granby, Dec. 8,		
1829, by John Bartlett	2	480
Asenah, d. David & Huldah, b. Sept. 6, 1751	2	349

	Vol.	Page
GRISWOLD, GRISWALD, (cont.)		
Augustus A., of Simsbury, m. Harriet **BULKLEY**, of		
Windsor, Jan. 3, 1822, by Rev. John Bartlett. Int. Pub.	2	160
Avery, s. George, Jr. & Mary, b. May 22, 1767	2	355
Avery, s. Abel & Chloe, b. May 28, 1785	2	562
Azubah, d. Benjamin, b. Aug. 2, 1710	2	37
Azubah, m. John Wareham **STRONG**, b. of Windsor, Mar.		
27, 1734/5	2	199
Azuba, d. Ens. Nathaniell & Ruth, b. July 16, 1736	2	344
Bathsheba, d. Daniel, Jr., b. Dec. 2, 1720	2	43
Bathsheba, d. Daniel, b. Dec. 2, 1720* *(Crossed out)	2	155
Beniamen, s. [George & Mary], b. Apr. 16, 1671	MG	
Benjamin, s. George, b. Apr. 16, 1671	1	15
Benjamin, m. Elizabeth **COOK**, Jan. 4, 1693	1	57
Benjamin, s. Benjamin, b. Apr. 14, 1701	2	37
Benjamin, m. Esther **GAYLORD**, b. of Winsor, July 6, 1726	2	156
Benjamin, s. Benjamin & Esther, b. Dec. 15, 1727	2	339
Benjamin, d. Apr. 4, 1747	2	528
Benjamin, s. Silvanus & Mary, b. Feb. 19, 1765	2	563
Benjamin, Capt., d. July 26, 1772	2	531
Candice M., of Poquonock, m. Ephraim **SIZER**, of Westfield,		
Feb. 26, 1852, by Rev. T. H. Rouse	2	503
Caroline, of Windsor, m. John E. **GRISWOLD**, Nov. 5, 1832,		
by Henry A. Rowland	2	505
Caroline E., of Windsor, m. Frederick **FENTON**, of Vernon,		
Feb. 28, 1848, by Cephus Brainard	2	478
Catherine S., m. Cicero **PHELPS**, b. of Windsor, Jan. 31,		
1822, by Richard Niles, J. P.	2	500
Catherine S., m. Lester F. **GRISWOLD**, b. of Windsor,		
May 31, 1849, by Cornelius B. Everest	2	497
Charles, s. Abel & Chloe, b. Nov. 11, 1796	2	564
Chloe, d. Abel & Chloe, b. Jan. 21, 1780	2	561
Chloe, w. Abel, d. Apr. 2, 1798	2	531
Chloe, d. Abel & Chloe, d. July 24, 1798	2	531
Chloe, twin with Clarissa, d. Abel & Deidamia, b. June 27,		
1802	2	573
Christiana, d. Isaac & Christiana, b. May 23, 1784	2	561
Clarrissa, d. Isaac & Christiana, b. Apr. 3, 1775	2	561
Clarissa, twin with Chloe, d. Abel & Deidamia, b. June		
27, 1802	2	573
Cyrus, s. Isaac & Christiana, b. Feb. 15, 1786	2	561
Dan, twin with Nath[an], s. Daniel, b. Feb. 14, [16]84	Col.D	51
Dan, s. Dan, d. Mar. [ ], 1684/5	Col.D	56
Daniell, s. [George & Mary], b. Oct. 1, 1656	MG	
Daniell, s. George, b. Oct. 1, 1656	Col.2	158
Danell, s. George, m. Mindwell **BISSELL**, d. Nathanell,		
Feb. 3, 1680	Col.1	46
Daniel, s. George, m. Mindwell **BISSELL**, d. Nath[anie]ll,		

	Vol.	Page
GRISWOLD, GRISWALD, (cont.)		
Feb. 3, 1680	1	57
Daniel, twin with Nathanael, s. Daniel, b. Feb. 14, 1684	1	16
Daniel, s. Daniel, d. Mar. [ ], 1684/5	1	45
Daniell, Jr., m. Sarah **WHITE**, b. of Windsor, Sept*. 5, 1716 *("Dec." crossed out)	2	155
Daniel, s. Daniel, Jr., b. May 26, 1723	2	43
Dan[ie]l, m. [ ] **BISSELL**, Feb. [ ]	TR1	1
Daniel E., m. Elizabeth S. **BAKER**, b. of Windsor, Nov. 16, 1842, by Rev. S. D. Jewett	2	516
David, s. Daniel, b. Aug. 26, 1701	1	17
David, m. Huldah **BROWN**, b. of Windsor, Dec. 23, 1731	2	156
David, s. David & Huldah, b. May 25, 1733	2	342
David, s. David & Huldah, d. Mar. 14, 1736/7	2	527
David, s. David & Huldah, b. Feb. 15, 1748	2	349
Debroa, d. [Edward], bp. June 28, 1646	MG	
Deborah, d. Edward, bp. June 28, 1646	Col.2	153
Deborah, d. Edward, bp. June 28, 1646	1	14
Debro, m. Samuell **BUELL**, Nov. 13, 1662	MG	
Debora, m. Samuel **BUELL**, b. of Windsor, Nov. 13, 1662	Col.1	45
Deborah, m. Samuel **BUELL**, b. of Windsor, Nov. 13, [16]62	1	54
Debrow, d. [George & Mary], b. May 30, 1674	MG	
Deborah, d. George, b. May 30, 1674	1	15
Deborah, m. Thomas **MOORE**, b. of Windsor, Dec. 12, 1695	1	59
Deborah, m. Thomas **MOORE**, b. of Windsor, Dec. 12, 1695	2	175
Deborah, d. Benjamin, b. Jan. 16, 1697/8	2	37
Deborah, d. Benjamin, d. Jan. 26, 1697/8	2	236
Deborah, d. Daniel, b. Nov. 7, 1698	1	17
Deborah, d. Joseph, b. Mar. 10, 1715/16	2	42
Deborah, w. Joseph, d. June 5, 1717	2	237
Deborah, w. Joseph, d. June [ ], 1717	2	237
Deborah, d. Joseph, b. Jan. 26, 1723	2	44
Deborah, d. David & Huldah, b. Mar. 15, 1745	2	349
Deidamia, d. Abel & Deidamia, b. Apr. 6, 1800	2	564
Dickson, of Turin, N. Y., m. Charlotte **BLANCHARD**, of Windsor, Nov. 16, 1826, by Richard Niles, J. P.	2	480
Dorothy S., m. William C. **WHEELER**, May 4, 1842, by Rev. David S. Marks	2	516
Edward, s. [George & Mary], b. Mar. 19, 1660/1	MG	
Edward, had 6 children b. in Windsor. Dated Aug. 17, 1677	MG	
Edward, m. Abigail **WILLIAMS**, Nov. 3, 1681	Col.D	54
Edward, s. Daniel, b. Mar. 8, 1695/6	1	17
Edward, d. July 8, 1715	2	236
Edward, m. Abigail **GRISWOLD**, b. of Windsor, June 23, 1728	2	156
Edward, s. Edward & Abigail, b. July 13, 1729	2	340
Edward, Jr., of Windsor, m. Abigal **PHELPS**, of Symsbury, Apr. 3, 1755	2	158

	Vol.	Page
GRISWOLD, GRISWALD, (cont.)		
Edward, m. Abigail **WILLIAMS**, Nov. 3, [ ]	1	57
Edwin, of Simsbury, m. Nancy **WEBSTER**, of Windsor, Apr. 20, 1825, by Rev. John Bartlett. Int. Pub.	2	479
Electa, m. James **BIDWELL**, Jr., b. of Windsor, Nov. 16, 1826, by Rev. Augustus Bolles	2	469
Elizabeth, d. Benjamin, b. Feb. [ ], 1694	1	17
Elizabeth, d. Benjamin, b. Feb. 25, 1697/8	2	37
Elizabeth, m. Isaac **GILLET**, b. of Windsor, Oct. 29, 1719	2	155
Elizabeth, of Windsor, m. Cyrus **CLEAVELAND**, of Dalton, Mass., Dec. 14, 1826, by Rev. Tobias Spirer	2	139
Elizabeth, m. Charles **HOLLISTER**, May 1, 1828, by Rev. Henry A. Rowland	2	167
Elizabeth, of Windsor, m. William S. **LOOMIS**, of Granby, Apr. 11, 1838, by Eli Deniston	2	175
Emmillie, d. Isaac & Christian, b. Apr. 28, 1790	2	572
Emely, m. Samuel W. **STOUGHTON**, b. of Windsor, Nov. 22, 1824, by Rev. Augustus Bolles, of Wintonbury	2	203
Emerette, m. William **CLAPP**, b. of Windsor, July 7, 1839, by Rev. Cephas Brainard	2	475
Erastus, s. Silvanus & Hannah, b. Jan. 3, 1783	2	564
Esther, w. Thomas, d. Feb. 9, 1691/2	1	45
Esther, d. Benjamin & Elizabeth, b. Apr. 4, 1712	2	341
Esther, of Windsor, m. Daniel **GUNN**, of Westfield, Oct. 15, 1712	2	154
Esther, had illeg. s. William, b. Sept. 5, 1738; reputef f. Lieut. William **THRALL**	2	109
Esther, m. Nathaniel **COOPLEY**, b. of Windsor, Sept. 19, 1749	2	136
Easther, d. Silvanus & Mary, b. Dec. 22, 1763	2	563
Esther, wid. Capt. Benjamin, d. Sept. 3, 1776	2	531
Esther Bates, d. Phenihas & Vashti, b. Dec. 24, 1780	2	560
Esther C., of Windsor, m. John A. **BORNE**, of Springfield, June 22, 1852, by Rev. Pliny F. Sanborne	2	504
Eunice, 2nd, of Lyme, m. Almerin **GILLET**, of Windsor, Dec. 29, 1790	2	159
Ezekiel, s. David & Huldah, b. Feb. 21, 1736/7	2	343
Fanny, of Simsbury, d. Elijah, m. [ ] **DOUGTRUS**, of Westfield, Mass., Aug. 15, 1822, by John Bartlett. Int. Pub.	2	472
Francis, s. Joseph, b. July 11, 1683	Col.D	51
Frances, s. Joseph, b. July 11, 1683	1	16
Francis, of Windsor, m. Abigaell **COLTON**, of Springfield, Dec. 7, 1703	2	154
Frances, s. Frances & Abigail, b. Nov. 8, 1719	2	45
Francis, s. Francis, Jr. & Jerusha, b. Apr. 23, 1741	2	346
Frederick, s. Hezekiah & Sarah, b. June 6, 1748	2	348
Frederick, s. Hezekiah & Sarah, d. Apr. 1, 1751	2	528

	Vol.	Page
GRISWOLD, GRISWALD, (cont.)		
Fredus, s. Isaac & Christian, b. Feb. 14, 1792	2	572
Gaylord, s. Silvanus & Mary, b. Dec. [ ], 1767	2	563
George, m. Mary HOLCOM[B], Oct. [ ], [16]	MG	
George, m. Mary HOLCOM, b. of Windsor, Oct. 3, 1655	Col.2	159
George, s. [George & Mary], b. Dec. 3, 1665	MG	
Georg[e], s. George, b. Dec. 3, 1665	Col.1	55
George, s. George, b. Dec. 3, 1665	1	15
George, had 9 children, b. in Windsor. Dated Aug. 17, 1677	MG	
George, Sr., d. Sept. 3, 1704	2	235
George, s. Joseph, Jr., b. Feb. 26, 1709/10	2	38
George, m. Zeruiah GRISWOLD, b. of Windsor, Mar. 6, 1734/5	2	156
George, s. George & Zeruiah, b. Sept. 28, 1737	2	344
George, Capt., d. Feb. 1, 1747/8	2	528
George, Jr., m. Mary HAYDON, b. of Windsor, Aug. 16, 1759	2	158
George, s. George, Jr. & Mary, b. June 8, 1762	2	354
George, contributed 0-3-9 to the poor in other colonies	MG	
George Milo, m. Emily Augusuta ENO, b. of Windsor, Oct. 13, 1847, by C. B. Everest	2	481
Giles, m. Charlotte HATHEWAY, b. of Windsor, Dec. 25, 1823, by Richard Niles, J. P.	2	160
Hanna, m. Jonas WESTOUER, Nov. 19, 1663	Col.1	45
Hannah, d. Benjamin, b. Mar. 16, 1698/9	2	37
Hannah, d. Daniel, Jr. & Sarah, b. Feb. 8, 1725/6	2	44
Hannah, d. Silvanus & Hannah, b. July 14, 1780	2	564
Harvey, s. Silvanus & Mary, b. May 20, 1766	2	563
Henry, s. Benjamin & Sarah, b. Sept. 23, 1792	2	562
Hepzibah, d. Phenihas & Vashti, b. Oct. 11, 1778	2	560
Hester, d. Thomas, b. Jan. 1, 1689	1	17
Hezekiah, s. Thomas, b. Feb. 18, 1687	1	16
Hezekiah, s. John, b. Sept. 6, 1715	2	40
Hezekiah, m. Sarah BARNARD, b. of Windsor, Dec. 14, 1738	2	157
Hezekiah, s. Hezekiah & Sarah, b. Feb. 28, 1741/2	2	346
Hezekiah, s. Hezekiah & Sarah, d. Feb. 28, 1742/3	2	527
Homer, s. Abel & Chloe, b. June 3, 1793	2	563
Hulda, d. David & Hulda, b. Apr. 23, 1739	2	344
Hulda, m. Theophilus MOORE, b. of Windsor, May [ ], 1779	2	180
Huldah, d. Abiel & Huldah, b. Sept. 15, 1783	2	562
Huldah, m. Alexander CLAPP, b. of Windsor, Mar. 22, 1837, by Rev. Eli Deniston	2	490
Isaac, s. Sergt. John, b. Sept. 24, 1718	2	41
Isaac, m. Mindwell PHELPS, b. of Windsor, May 19, 1748	2	479
Isaac, s. Isaac & Mindwel, b. Aug. 8, 1749	2	348
Isaac, d. Oct. 21, 1755	2	529
Isaac, s. Isaac & Christiana, b. Oct. 27, 1779	2	561

	Vol.	Page
GRISWOLD, GRISWALD, (cont.)		
Isaac P., m. Cynthia M. **HILLYER,** Apr. 7, 1841, by Rev.		
S. D. Jewett	2	481
Jane, m. Joel B. **CLARK,** b. of Windsor, June 12, 1836, by		
Rev. James Shugley, of No. Granby	2	472
Jane E., m. Vernon **LINDSLEY,** Dec. 9, 1846, by Rev. S. H.		
Allen	2	491
Jane M., of Windsor, m. Philemon P. **SPERRY,** of Avon,		
Sept. 23, 1832, by Rev. Ansel Nash	2	508
Jared, s. Isaac & Christian, b. Mar. 3, 1798	2	572
Jea[ ]*, s. Abiel & Huldah, b. Dec. 24, 1781 *(In pencil)	2	357
Jerusha, d. Mathew, b. Apr. 19, 1714	2	42
Jerusha, d. Francis, Jr. & Jerusha, b. Dec. 6, 1747	2	349
Joab, s. George, Jr. & Zeruiah, b. Sept. 11, 1740	2	345
Joab, of Windsor, m. Elizabeth **COLLINS,** of Hartford,		
Oct. 6, 1763	2	158
Joab, s. Joab & Elizabeth, b. Aug. 23, 1764	2	354
Joel, m. Mary **EVENS,** b. of Windsor, May 11, 1758	2	158
Joel, s. Joel & Mary, b. Nov. 4, 1758	2	352
John, d. [ ], [16]42	MG	
John, s. [Edward], bp. Aug. 1, 1652	MG	
John, s. Edward, bp. Aug. 1, 1652	Col.2	153
John, s. Edward, bp. Aug. [ ], 1652	1	14
John, s. [George & Mary], b. Sept. 17, 1668	MG	
John, s. George, b. Sept. 17, 1668	1	15
John, m. Abigaell **GAYLORD,** Nov. 22, 1705	2	154
John, s. John, b. June 16, 1712	2	40
John, Sergt., had 4th s. [ ], b. about middle Apr. 1721;		
d. about four days after	2	43
John, Sergt., his 4th s. [ ], b. about middle Apr. 1721;		
d. about 4 days after	2	49
John, s. Abiel & Huldah, b. Oct. 10, 1776	2	356
John E., m. Caroline **GRISWOLD,** of Windsor, Nov. 5, 1832,		
by Henry A. Rowland	2	505
Jonah, s. Joseph, Jr., b. Apr. 12, 1704	2	36
Joseph, s. [Edward], bp. Mar. 12, 1647	MG	
Joseph, s. Edward, bp. Mar. 12, 1647	Col.2	153
Joseph, s. Edward, bp. Mar. 12, 1647	1	14
Joseph, m. Mary **GAYLAR,** d. Samuell, June 10, [16]70, by		
Capt. Newbery	Col.1	46
Joseph, m. Mary **GAYLARS,** July 14, 1670	MG	
Joseph, d. [Jan. 6*], [16]72, [ae 23*] *(In pencil)	MG	
Joseph, d. Jan. 6, 1672, ae 23 yrs.	Col.1	58
Joseph, bd. Jan. 6, 1672, ae 23 years	1	44
Joseph, s. [Joseph & Mary], b. Jan. 24, 1677	MG	
Joseph, had 3 children b. in Windsor. Dated Aug. 17, 1677	MG	
Joseph, s. Joseph, Jr., b. May 31, 1700	1	17
Joseph, Ens., d. Nov. 14, 1716	2	236

	Vol.	Page
GRISWOLD, GRISWALD, (cont.)		
Joseph, s. Joseph, b. Jan. 6, 1724/5	2	44
Joseph, d. Feb. 17, 1724/5	2	44
Joseph, d. Feb. 17, 1724/5	2	238
Joseph, his w. [ ], contributed 0-2-6 to the poor in other colonies	MG	
Joseph, contributed 0-2-6 to the poor in other colonies	MG	
Julia, d. Phenihas & Vashti, b. Jan. 20, 1789	2	560
Juliann, of Windsor, m. Bushrod **CLARK**, of Granby, Aug. 11, 1825, by Richard Niles, J. P.	2	139
Juliann, m. Bushrod **CLARK**, of Granby, Aug. 11,1825, by Richard Niles, J. P.	2	140
Juliette, of Windsor, m. Samuel **PHILLIPS**, of Wilmantic, Nov. 26, 1851, by Rev. H. N. Weed	2	461
Keziah, d. Francis, b. Sept. 11, 1714	2	41
Keziah, d. Francis, d. Dec. 1, 1714	2	237
Kezia, d. Edward & Abigail, b. July 5, 1737	2	344
Laura, d. Abel & Chloe, b. Feb. 27, 1787	2	563
Lester F., m. Catherine S. **GRISWOLD**, b. of Windsor, May 31, 1849, by Cornelius B. Everest	2	497
Levi, s. George, Jr. & Mary, b. Apr. 26, 1769	2	355
Levi G., m. Harriet **CLARK**, b. of Windsor, Jan. [ ], 1826, by Richard Niles, J. P.	2	480
Livea, d. Abel & Chloe, b. Mar. 3, 1791	2	563
Liois, d. Joseph, b. Aug. 19, 1721	2	44
Lucia Ann, of Windsor, m. Cadwell **STRICKLAND**, of Simsbury, July 29, 1834, by Henry A. Rowland	2	509
Lucinda, of Windsor, m. Hayden G. **PECK**, of Simsbury, Dec. 9, 1824, by Rev. Augustus Bolles, of Wintonbury	2	192
Luce, d. Matthew, b. June 10, 1716	2	42
Lydia, d. Mathew & Mary, b. Sept. 18, 1725	2	342
Lydiah, of Symsbury, m. Dr. Hezekiah **PHELPS**, of Windsor, Feb. 21, 1749/50	2	189
Lydia, d. George, Jr. & Mary, b. July 5, 1772	2	356
Lydia, m. Shirley **KELLOGG**, b. of Windsor, Feb. 19, 1832, by Rev. Ansel Nash	2	168
Lyman, m. Mary L. **CAMMEL**, b. of Windsor, Apr. 2, 1848, by Cephas Brainard	2	462
Marcus, of Windsor, m. Martha **HOLCOMB**, Feb. 15, 1827, by Rev. Henry A. Rowland	2	480
Margarett, d. Francis, b. Oct. 20, 1710	2	41
Margerit, m. Samuel **OWIN**, b. of Windsor, Nov. 19, 1730	2	184
Maria D. S., of Windsor, m. Samuel L. **SMITH**, of North Haven, Oct. 18, 1849, by E. B. Everest	2	515
Mary, d. Edward, b. Oct. 5, 1644	1	14
Mary, d. Edward, b. Oct. 5, 1644	1	15
Mary, d. [Edward], bp. Oct. 13, 1644	MG	
Mary, d. Edward, bp. Oct. 13, 1644	Col.2	153

	Vol.	Page
GRISWOLD, GRISWALD, (cont.)		
Noah, s. Mathew & Mary, b. Sept. 11, 1722	2	342
Noah, Jr., of Bloomfield, m. Ruth R. **LOOMIS**, of Windsor,		
Apr. 27, 1836, by Rev. Charles Walker	2	481
Norman, of Norwich, N. Y., m. Altemira **HAYDEN**, of		
Windsor, Oct. 16, 1822, by Rev. Henry A. Rowland	2	479
Olive H., of Windsor, m. Rowland L. **FOX**, of East Hartford,		
Sept. 9, 1840, by Rev. S. D. Jewett	2	477
Oliver, s. Phinehas & Zibiah, b. Dec. 9, 1754	2	351
Oliver, s. Phenihas & Zibah, d. Mar. 24, 1757	2	529
Oliver, s. Phenihas & Vashti, b. June 11, 1784	2	560
Origan, s. Abiel & Huldah, b. Oct. 31, 1785	2	562
Pelatiah, s. Daniel, b. Sept. 13, 1689	1	17
Phebe, d. Shubell & Phebe, b. Sept. 14, 1726	2	45
Phinehas, s. Sergt. Thomas, b. Nov. 15, 1725	2	44
Phinehas, s. Phinehas & Zibiah, b. Aug. 13, 1750	2	348
Phenihas, s. Phenihas & Vashti, b. Aug. 21, 1782	2	560
Prudence, d. Isaac & Mindwell, b. Nov. 26, 1751; d. Nov.		
27, 1752	2	351
Rachell, d. John, b. Feb. 28, 1709/10	2	36
Rebecca G., of Windsor, m. Albert G. **WICKWARE**, of		
Bristol, Jan. 20, 1834, by Rev. Stephen Martindale	2	213
Roger, s. Joseph, Jr., b. Jan. 30, 1707/8	2	36
Rosalia E., m. Orator P. **ROCKWELL**, of Bloomfield, Aug.		
15, 1852, by Rev. T. H. Rouse	2	502
Ruth, d. Nathaniell & Ruth, b. Aug. 3, 1732	2	341
Salvanus, of Windsor, m. Mary **COLLINS**, of Wallingford,		
Apr. 1, 1762	2	158
Salvanus, of Windsor, m. Mary **COLLINS**, of Wallingford,		
Apr. 1, 1762	2	353
Salvanus Collins, s. Salvanus & Mary, b. Sept. 5, 1762	2	354
Samuell, s. [Edward], bp. Nov. 18, 1649; d. [ ]	MG	
Samuel, s. Edward, [ ] Nov. 18, 1649	Col.2	153
Samuel, s. Edward, bp. Nov. 18, 1649	1	14
Samuel, s. George, b. Nov. 5, 1681	1	15
Samuell, s. George, d. June 1, 1682	Col.D	56
Samuel, s. George, d. June 1, 1682	1	44
Samuel, s. Tho[mas], b. Dec. 15, 1684	Col.D	51
Samuel, s. Thomas, b. Aug. 7, 1685	1	16
Samuel S., m. Elizabeth A. **WATROUS**, b. of Windsor, Oct.		
5, 1851, by Rev. Horatio N. Weed	2	462
Sara, m. Samuell **PHELPS**, Nov. 10, 1650	MG	
Sarah, m. Samuel **PHELPS**, Nov. 10, 1650	1	60
Sarah, d. Daniel, Jr., b. Oct. 14, 1717	2	41
Sarah, d. Shubael & Phebe, b. July 1, 1732	2	342
Sarah, d. Hezekiah & Sarah, b. June 5, 1740	2	346
Sarah, d. Hezekiah & Sarah, d. July 14, 1740	2	527
Sarah, m. Benoni **DENSLOW**, Nov. 17, 1748	2	142

	Vol.	Page
GRISWOLD, GRISWALD, (cont.)		
Sarah, w. Capt. Hezekiah, d. Sept. 13, 1777	2	531
Selina, d. Isaac & Christiana, b. Jan. 2, 1787	2	561
Seneca, s. Abiel B. & Mary, b. July 21, 1801	2	564
Shubell, s. Joseph, Jr., b. May 2, 1701	1	17
Shubael, m. Phebe **CORNISH,** b. of Windsor, Nov.* 3, 1725		
*("Dec." crossed out)	2	156
Shubael, s. Shubael & Phebe, b. Nov. 30, 1729	2	340
Shubael, d. Mar. 6, 1732/3	2	238
Susannah, d. Silvanus & Mary, b. June 20, 1769	2	563
Sebel, d. David & Huldah, b. Apr. 17, 1742	2	349
Sylvanus, see under Salvanus		
Thaddeus, of Windsor, m. Electa **WOODWARD,** of Suffield,		
Mar. 5, 1833, by Rev. Daniel Hemienway	2	480
Thirza M., of Simsbury, m. William **BROWN,** of Windsor,		
Jan. 16, 1823, by Rev. John Bartlett. Int. Pub.	2	468
Thomas, s. [George & Mary], b. Sept. 29, 165[ ]	MG	
Thomas, ae 23 on Dec. 29, 1681, s. George, m. Hester		
DRAKE, ae 19 on Oct. 10, 1681, d. Job. Aug. 11, 1681,		
by Capt. Newbery	MG	
Thomas, s. George, m. Hester **DRAKE,** d. Job, Aug. 11,		
1681, by Capt. Nubery	1	57
Tho[mas], his s. [ ], b. Dec. 10, 1682	Col.D	51
Thomas, s. Thomas, b. Dec. 10, 1682	1	18
Thomas, Sergt. of Windsor, m. Abigail **SACKET,** of		
Westfield, Sept. 5, 1725	2	155
Thomas, Ens., d. Jan. 29, 1727/8, at Westfield	2	238
Thomas, s. Ens. Thomas & Abigail, b. Jan. 5, 1728/9	2	340
Thomas, s. George, m. Hester **DRAKE,** d. Job, [ ], by		
Capt. Nubery	TR1	1
Treuman, s. Joab & Elizabeth, d. Feb. 5, 1767	2	355
Ursula, d. George, Jr. & Mary, b. Sept. 22, 1778	2	356
Vashty, d. Moses, Jr. & Anne, b. Apr. 1, 1774	2	355
Vashti, d. Phenihas & Vashti, b. Sept. 26, 1786	2	560
Welthe, d. Abel & Chloe, b. Jan. 1, 1795	2	564
White, s. Daniel, Jr. & Sarah, b. Oct. 22, 1727	2	45
William, illeg. s. Esther **GRISWOLD,** b. Sept. 5, 1738;		
reputed f. Lieut William **THRALL**	2	109
William, s. Silvanus & Hannah, b. June 3, 1778	2	563
Zacheus, s. Benjamin, b. Dec. 10, 1705	2	37
Zacheus, m. Mary **GRISWOLD,** b. of Windsor, Nov. 15,		
1728	2	156
Zacheus, s. Zacheus & Mary, b. Nov. 15, 1730	2	341
Zerviah, d. Benjamin, b. Dec. 26, 1703	2	37
Zeruiah, m. George **GRISWOLD,** b. of Windsor, Mar. 6,		
1734/5	2	156
Zeruiah, d. George & Zeruiah, b. Dec. 22, 1735	2	343
Zerviah, d. George, Jr. & Mary, b. July 1, 1774	2	356

	Vol.	Page
GRISWOLD, GRISWALD, (cont.)		
Zibeah, d. Benjamin & Esther, b. May 31, 1730	2	340
GROVER, Daniel, s. Edmond & Elizabeth, b. Sept. 3, 1755; d.		
Sept. 13, 1755	2	353
Daniel Thomas, s. Edmond & Elizabeth, b. Sept. 3, 1761	2	353
Edmond, s. Edmond & Elizabeth, d. Jan. 2, 1763	2	530
Elijah, s. Edmond & Elizabeth, b. Dec. 13, 1753	2	353
Elijah, s. Edmond & Elizabeth, d. Jan. 1, 1763	2	530
Elizabeth, d. Edmond & Elizabeth, b. Oct. 5, 1757	2	353
Hozea, s. Edmond & Elizabeth, d. Sept. 23, 1762	2	530
GUNN, Daniel, of Westfield, m. Esther **GRISWOLD,** of Windsor,		
Oct. 15, 1712	2	154
Debroa, d. [Thomas], b. Feb. 21, 1641	MG	
Deborah, d. Thomas, bp. Feb. 27, 1641	Col.2	152
Deborah, d. Thomas, b. Feb. 27, 1641	1	14
Debro, m. Timothy **TRALL,** Nov. 10, 1659	MG	
Deborah, m. Timothy **THRALL,** b. of Windsor, Nov. 10,		
1659	1	62
Elisabet[h], d. Aug. 22, [1640]	MG	
Elisabeth, d. [Thomas], b. Oct. 14, 1640; d. [ ]	MG	
Elizabeth, d. Thomas, b. Oct. 14, 1649	Col.2	152
Elizabeth, d. Thomas, b. Oct. 14, 1649	1	14
Elizabeth, d. Thomas, d. [ ], [16]55	MG	
Elisabeth, d. Thomas, d. Jan. 3, 1655	Col.2	160
John, s. [Thomas], b. July 8, 1647	MG	
John, s. Thomas, bp. July 11, 1647	Col.2	153
Mehetabell, d. [Thomas], b. July 28, 1644	MG	
Mehetabel, d. Thomas, b. July 28, 1644	Col.2	152
Mahitable, d. Thomas, b. July 28, 1644	1	16
Thomas, had 4 children b. in Windsor. Dated Aug. 17, 1677	MG	
HADLOCK, Benjamin, s. John & Hannah, b. Mar. 20, 1743/4	2	360
Hannah, m. Hezekiah **READ,** b. of Windsor, Feb. 16, 1746/7	2	195
HAGER, ------, d. [ ], [16]44	MG	
HAKES, HAKS, HAWKES, Ann, d. John, bp. Oct. 1, 1648	Col.2	154
Ann, d. John, bp. Oct. 1, 1648	1	18
Anna, d. [John], b. Oct. 1, 1648	MG	
Eliezer, s. [John], b. Dec. 20, 1655	MG	
Elizabeth, d. [John], b. Jan. 10, 1646	MG	
Elizabeth, d. John, bp. Jan. 10, 1646	Col.2	154
Elizabeth, d. John, bp. Jan. 10, 1646	1	18
Eliesor, s. John, b. Dec. 20, [16]55	Col.2	181
Jersom, s. [John], b. Apr. 12, 1659 (Gershom)	MG	
Gershom, s. John, b. Apr. 12, 1659	1	18
Isack, s. John, b. Aug. 11, 1650	Col.2	154
Isaac, s. John, b. Aug. 11, 1650	1	18
Isack, s. John, b. Aug. 11, 1650; d. [ ], [16]59	MG	
Isaac, d. June 22, 1659; drowned in the Great River	1	45
Joanna, d. John, b. Feb. 8, 1653	Col.2	181

	Vol.	Page
HAKES, HAKS, HAWKES, (cont.)		
Johanne, d. John, b. Feb. 8, 1653	Col.2	157
Johana, d. [John], b. Feb. 8, 1653; d. [ ]	MG	
John, s. John, b. Aug. 10, 1643	Col.2	154
John, s. [John], b. Aug. 13, 1643	MG	
John, s. John, bp. Aug. 13, 1643	1	18
John, had 11 children b. in Windsor. Dated Aug. 17, 1677	MG	
Mary, d. [John], b. May 23, 1652	MG	
Mary, d. John, b. May 23, 1652	Col.2	154
Mary, d. John, b. May 23, 1652	1	18
Nathanell, s. [John], b. Feb. 15, 1644	MG	
Nathanael, s. John, bp. Feb. 16, 1644	Col.2	154
Nathanael, s. John, bp. Feb. 16, 1644	1	18
Sara, d. [John], b. Sept. 29, 1657	MG	
Sarah, d. John, b. Sept. 29, 1657	Col.2	161
HALE, Frederick H., of Glastenbury, m. Julia **STILES**, of		
Windsor, Apr. 7, 1825, by Rev. Henry A. Rowland	2	166
William, of Sandisfield, Mass., m. Mrs. Emily **PARSONS**,		
of Windsor, Jan. 4, 1846, by Rev. T. A. Leete	2	519
HALL, HALLE, Abigail, of Summers, m. Samuel **HAYDON**, of		
Windsor, Nov. 17, 1737	2	162
David A., of Washington, m. Abbey W. **ELLSWORTH**, of		
Windsor, Dec. 25, 1838, by Rev. Daniel Hemenway	2	483
John, s. [Timothy & Sara], b. Aug. 24, 1670	MG	
Josias, s. [Timothy & Sara], b. Sept. 22, [16]78; bp.		
[Sept.] 29, [16]78	MG	
Lydia A., of Worcester, Mass., m. James M. **JOHNSON**,		
of Havana, N. Y., Oct. 22, 1848, by Rev. S. H. Allen	2	462
Richmond, of Suffield, m. Nancy **REYNOLDS**, of Windsor,		
Nov. 26, 1834, by Richard G. Drake, J. P.	2	243
Samuell, s. [Timothy & Sara], b. Jan. 3, 1673	MG	
Sara, d. [Timothy & Sara], b. Apr. 9, 1665	MG	
Sara, d. Timothy, b. Aug. 9, 1665	Col.1	54
Thomas, s. [Timothy & Sara], b. Aug. 26, 1672	MG	
Timothy, m. Sara **BARBER**, Nov. 26, 1663	MG	
Timothy, m. Sara **BARBER**, Nov. 26, 1663, by Mr. Alyen	Col.1	45
Timothy, s. [Timothy & Sarah], b. Dec. 12, 1667	MG	
Timothy, his w. [ ], bp. July 5, [16]68	MG	
Timothy, adm. communion, Apr. 28, [16]72	MG	
Timothy, adm. ch. & communicant, Apr. [ ], 1672	MG	
Timothy, taxed 2-0 on Feb. 10, [16]73	MG	
Timothy, contributed 0-2-6 to the poor in other colonies	MG	
Vines, d. [Timothy & Sarah], b. Nov. 28, 1675; bp. Dec. 5,		
[1675]; d. [ ]	MG	
HALLIBUTT, [see under **HURLBURT**]		
HALSEY, Charlott S., of Windsor, m. George N. **REMINGTON**,		
of Suffield, Sept. 24, 1838, by Rev. Cephas Brainard	2	474
Elizabeth, m. Frederick **ELLSWORTH**, b. of Windsor, Apr.		

	Vol.	Page
HALSEY, (cont.)		
27, 1846, by Rev. T. A. Leete	2	519
Frederick P., m. Julia R. **OSBORN**, Nov. 25, 1840, by S. D.		
Jewett	2	483
Frederick P., s. James R. & Keziah, d. Nov. 17, 1841	2	244
Hellen J., of Windsor, m. James **BURKE**, of New York,		
Oct. 12, 1836, by Rev. Charles Walker	2	465
Henry, m. Eunice **TALCOTT**, July 12, 1832, by Rev. Henry		
A. Rowland	2	485
Henry A., m. Frances Maria **ELLSWORTH**, Jan. 11, 1836,		
by Charles Walker	2	484a
Julia O., of Windsor, m. Hezekiah H. **SEARS**, of Hartford,		
June 23, 1847, by T. A. Leete	2	514
Sarah L., m. Samuel B. **HAYDEN**, b. of Windsor, Apr. 16,		
1849, by T. A. Leete	2	487
HAMILTON, Caroline S., of Suffield, m. George **BEMAN**, of		
Granby, Nov. 25, 1838, by Rev. Jared R. Avery	2	465
[HAMNER], [see under **HANMER, HANMORE & HANNUM**]		
HANEY, Ann, m. Thomas **BENTON**, b. of Windsor, July 3, 1761	2	133
HANFORD, Susan, m. Robard **OULD**, b. of Windsor, Dec. 31,		
1669	Col. 1	45
Susanna, m. Robard **OULD**, Dec. [ ]	MG	
HANMER, [see also **HANMORE & HANNUM**], Susanna, see		
John **BROOKS**	Col. 1	58
HANMORE, [see also **HANMER & HANNUM**], Susanna, m.		
John **BROOKS**, May 25, 1652	MG	
Susannah, m. John **BROOKE**, b. of Windsor, May 25, 1652	Col. 2	159
Susannah, m. John **BROOKS**, May 25, 1652	1	53
HANNUM, HANUM, [see also **HANMER & HANMORE**],		
Abigail, d. William, bp. Nov. 22, 1640	1	18
Abigail, m. Thomas **BUCKLAND**, Jan. 25, 1693	1	54
Elizabeth, d. William, b. Apr. 24, 1645	1	18
Elizabeth, d. Will[ia]m, b. Apr. 24, 1645	1	21
Joanna, d. William, b. July 24, 1642	1	18
Mary, d. William, b. Apr. 5, 1650	1	18
Susanna, d. [ ], [16]46	MG	
William, had 4 children, b. in Windsor. Dated Aug. 17, 1677	MG	
HARGER, Addison, s. Benjamin & Chloe, b. Dec. 19, 1808	2	53
Caroline, d. Benjamin & Chloe, b. Apr. 27, 1811	2	53
Esther, d. Benjamin & Chloe, b. Dec. 11, 1815	2	53
Rollin, s. Benjamin & Chloe, b. May 10, 1813	2	53
Thilissa, d. Benjamin & Chloe, b. Dec. 27, 1817	2	53
HARMON, Paul, of Suffield, m. Charity **PHELPS**, of Windsor,		
Apr. 13, 1826, by Rev. Asahel Morse	2	166
HARPER, Ann, d. James & Sarah, b. Mar. 22, 1758	2	367
Cathrien, d. Joseph & Jemima, b. Aug. 28, 1729	2	51
Hannah, d. James & Sarah, b. Feb. 15, 1765	2	368
	2	

	Vol.	Page

HARPER, (cont.)

James, m. Sarah **BURROUGHS,** b. of Windsor, Nov. 20,
 1752 — 2, 164

James, s. James & Sarah, b. May 21, 1756 — 2, 367

Jinnet, d. James & Sarah, b. Feb. 20, 1762 — 2, 367

Joseph, s. Joseph & Merriam, b. Jan. 14, 1726/7 — 2, 51

Merriam, d. Joseph, b. June 25, 1724 — 2, 50

Ruth, d. James & Sarah, b. Sept. 1, 1759 — 2, 367

Sarah, d. James & Sarah, b. Oct. 20, 1753 — 2, 367

HARRIS, Ann E., of Windsor, m. Daniel **PORTER,** of Windsor
 Locks, Dec. 15, 1850, by T. A. Leete — 2, 502

Ephraim, m. Eliza **DENSLOW,** Jan. 27, 1831, by Henry A.
 Rowland — 2, 485

Nancy, m. William **TERRY,** Dec. 24, 1821, by Rev. Henry
 A. Rowland — 2, 205

Samuel, m. Mehitable **GIBBS,** b. of Windsor, Sept. 23, 1824,
 by Rev. Phineas Cook — 2, 166

HART, HEART, Elisha, d. Aug. 15, 1683 — Col.D, 56

Elisha, d. Aug. 15, 1683 — 1, 46

Thomas, d. Sept. 2, 1688 — 1, 46

HARTLEY, Lunsford W., of Oswegotche, N. Y., m. Adeline H.
 PINNEY, of Windsor, Jan.4, 1842, by Rev. A. C.
 Washburn — 2, 515

HARVEY, Horace, m. Elizabeth **HATHEWAY,** Oct. 13, 1823, by
 Richard Niles, J. P. — 2, 166

HASKELL, Arathusa, m. Herleigh **HASKELL,** Nov. 19, 1823, by
 Rev. Henry A. Rowland — 2, 166

Carmaralzaman, s. Jabez & Elizabeth, b. Sept. 12, 1790 — 2, 566

Elizabeth Newberry, d. Jabez & Elizabeth, b. Aug. 6, 1771 — 2, 565

Ely, s. Jabez & Elizabeth, b. Oct. 17, 1778 — 2, 566

Harriss, s. Jabez & Elizabeth, b. Sept. 8, 1782 — 2, 566

Herlehigh, s. Jabez & Elizabeth, b. Oct. 30, 1780 — 2, 566

Herleigh, m. Arathusa **HASKELL,** Nov. 19, 1823, by Rev.
 Henry A. Rowland — 2, 166

Jabez, s. Jabez & Elizabeth, b. Dec. 13, 1784 — 2, 566

Lucinda, d. Jabez & Elizabeth, b. Feb. 11, 1775 — 2, 566

Roxa, d. Jabez & Elizabeth, b. Mar. 8, 1773 — 2, 565

Sidney, s. Jabez & Elizabeth, b. June 13, 1786 — 2, 566

Weltha, d. Jabez & Elizabeth, b. Dec. 13, 1775 — 2, 566

HATHEWAY, Amos, m. Mary G. **THRALL,** b. of Windsor, Jan.
 5, 1831, by Stephen Crosby — 2, 485

Charles W., m. Sarah A. **BARRETT,** b. of Poquonock, May
 26, 1852, by Thomas H. Rouse — 2, 521

Charlotte, m. Giles **GRISWOLD,** b. of Windsor, Dec. 25,
 1823, by Richard Niles, J. P. — 2, 160

Clarissa, of Pocconock, m. E. H. **TALCOTT,** of Sweden, N.
 J., May 27, 1852, by Thomas H. Rouse — 2, 461

Elizabeth, m. Horace **HARVEY,** Oct. 13, 1823, by Richard

	Vol.	Page
HATHEWAY, (cont.)		
Niles, J. P.	2	166
Emely, of Windsor, m. Harvey **HATHEWAY**, of Suffield,		
Nov. 16, 1826, by Richard Niles, J. P.	2	167
Harvey, of Suffield, m. Emely **HATHEWAY**, of Windsor,		
Nov. 16, 1826, by Richard Niles, J. P.	2	167
Lorenda, of Windsor, m. Martin **KENT**, of Suffield, O.,		
June 16, 1825, by Rev. Augusuts Bolles, of Wintonbury	2	168
HAUSE, Eunice A., of Windsor, m. Asahel **CHAPMAN**, of		
Glastenbury, Aug. 6, 1827, by Rev. John Bartlett	2	140
HAWARD, [see under **HAYWARD**]		
HAWKINS, HOWKINS, Anthony, his child d. [ ], [16]46	MG	
Anthony, his w. [ ], d. July 12, 1655	Col.2	160
Anthony, had 3 children b. in Windsor. Dated Aug. 17, 1677	MG	
John, s. [Anthony], b. Feb. 18, 1651	MG	
John, s. Anthony, b. Feb. 28, 1651	Col.2	154
Mary, d. [Anthony], b. July 16, 1644	MG	
Mary, d. Anthony, bp. July 21, 1644	Col.2	154
Ruth, d. [Anthony], b. Oct. 24, 1649	MG	
Ruthe, d. Anthony, b. Oct. 24, 1649	Col.2	154
HAWLEY, HAWLY, Abiah, m. William **WOLCOT**, b. of		
Windsor, Nov. 5, 1707	2	207
Allen, of Granby, m. Mary **ELLSWORTH**, of Windsor, Dec.		
15, 1829, by Henry A. Rowland	2	484
Elizabeth, m. Charles **WOLCOT**, Dec. 19, 1706	2	207
Elizabeth A., of Windsor, m. Ira **JENNINGS**, of Natick,		
July 3, 1848, by Rev. S. H. Allen	2	486
Julia Ann, of Windsor, m. George W. **WARREN**, of		
Hartford, Dec. 12, 1847, by S. H. Allen	2	519
Mary, of Middletown, m. John **WOLCUT**, 3rd, of Windsor,		
Jan. 9, 1734/5	2	208
Mary C., m. Horace B. **LITTLE**, Nov. 25, 1846, by Rev.		
S. H. Allen, of Windsor Locks	2	490
Mathew, d. Feb. 16, 1695/6	1	46
Sarah I., of Windsor, m. Edwin H. **ANDREWS**, of		
Glastenbury, Aug. 18, 1850, by Rev. S. H. Allen	2	463
HAY, George, m. Abigail **DIBLE**, Aug. 29, 1683	Col.D	54
HAYDEN, HAYDON, HEYDON, HAIDEN, Aaron, s. Samuell &		
Abigail, b. May 4, 1750	2	363
Abigail, d. Samuell & Abigail, b. Dec. 21, 1745	2	360
Alla, d. Isaac & Lucy, b. Mar. 5, 1781	2	567
Altemira, of Windsor, m. Norman **GRISWOLD**, of Norwich,		
N. Y., Oct. 16, 1822, by Rev. Henry A. Rowland	2	479
Ann, d. Nathaniel & Naomi, b. June* 6, 1737 *("Dec."		
crossed out)	2	357
Ann, wid., d. June 13, 1756	2	242
Anna, d. Isaac & Hannah, b. Mar. 25, 1744	2	359
Anne, d. Samuell, b. May 2, 1706	2	46

	Vol.	Page
HAYDEN, HAYDON, HEYDON, HAIDEN, (cont.)		
Anne, m. Joel **PALMER**, b. of Windsor, July 23, 1761	2	189
Anne, d. John & Anne, b. Oct. 12, 1772	2	368
Augustin, s. Samuel & Abigail, b. Aug. 24, 1740	2	358
Daniel, s. William, b. Sept. 2, 1640	1	19
Daniell, s. William, b. Sept. 21, 1640	MG	
Daniell, m. Hanna **WILCOKSON**, Mar. 17, 1664	MG	
Daniel, m. Hanna **WILLCOCKSON**, Mar. 17, [16]64/5, by		
Mr. Allyn	Col.1	45
Daniel, m. Hannah **WILCOXSON**, Mar. 17, 1664, by Mr.		
Allyn	1	57
Daniell, s. [Daniell & Hanna], b. Oct. 5, 1666	MG	
Danell, s. Danell, b. Oct. 5, 1666	Col.1	56
Daniel, s. Daniel, b. Oct. 5, 1666	1	19
Daniell, had 4 children b. in Windsor. Dated Aug. 17, 1677	MG	
Daniel, s. Daniel, Jr., b. Aug. 27, 1703	1	21
Daniel, Lieut., d. Mar. 22, 1712/13	2	239
Daniel, m. Esther **MOORE**, b. of Windsor, Dec. 31, 1735	2	162
Daniel, s. Daniel, Jr. & Easther, b. Nov. 10, 1742	2	358
Daniel, Jr., m. Elizabeth **McMORAN***, wid. John, Jr., Apr.		
13, 1748 *(In pencil)	2	163
David, s. Ebenezer, b. Jan. 21, 1715/16	2	48
David, m. Dorothy **ALLYN**, b. of Windsor, Jan. 19, 1737/8	2	163
David, s. David & Dorethy, b. Oct. 8, 1738	2	357
Dorothy, d. David & Dorothy, b. Nov. 10, 1748	2	361
Ebenezor, s. Dan[iel], b. Dec. 14, 1681	Col.D	51
Ebenezer, m. Mindwell **GRISWOLD**, Jan. 12, 1709/10	2	161
Ebenezer, s. Ebenezer, b. Dec. 9, 1710	2	47
Ebenezer, Jr., m. Mary **TRUMBLE**, b. of Windsor, June 16,		
1737	2	163
Ebenezer, s. Ebenezer & Mary, b. May 11, 1738	2	357
Ebenezer, s. Ebenezer, Jr. & Mary, d. May the last, 1746	2	241
Ebenezer, s. Ebenezer, Jr. & Mary, b. Aug. 28, 1747	2	361
Ebenezer, m. Dorithy **LOOMIS**, b. of Windsor, July 16, 1752	2	163
Ebenezer, s. Ebenezer & Mary, d. Dec. 15, 1753	2	242
Edward G., m. Louisa Ann **DENSLOW**, Nov. 10, 1836, by		
Rev. Henry Robinson	2	489
Eli, twin with Oliver, s. Ebenezer & Dorithy, b. June 29, 1753	2	362
Eli, s. Ebenezer & Dorithy, d. Sept. 2, 1753	2	242
Elijah, s. David & Dorithy, b. July 4, 1741	2	358
Elizabeth, d. William, m. Apr. 24, 1712	2	48
Elizabeth, d. Daniel, Jr. & Esther, b. June 6, 1738	2	357
Elizabeth, w. Daniell, d. Oct. 18, 1740	2	240
Elizabeth, w. Daniel, d. Feb. 18, 1776	2	243
Esther, d. Daniel & Esther, b. Nov. 28, 1736	2	52
Esther, w. Daniell, Jr., d. Nov. 2, 1747	2	241
Esther, m. Ebenezer Fitch **BISSELL**, b. of Windsor, June 24,		
1756	2	133

	Vol.	Page
HAYDEN, HAYDON, HEYDON, HAIDEN, (cont.)		
Eunice, d. Isaac & Eunice, b. Mar. 17, 1754	2	363
Ezra, s. Isaac & Hannah, b. Dec. 20, 1742	2	359
Ezra, s. Isaac & Hannah, d. Jan. 23, 1742/3	2	241
Ezra, s. Isaac & Eunice, b. Feb. 27, 1758	2	363
George P., m. Francis A. **LOOMIS**, b. of Windsor, Dec. 31, 1841, by Rev. S. D. Jewett	2	515
H. Sidney, of Charleston, S. C., m. Abba S. **LOOMIS**, of Windsor, Aug. 9, 1848, by Rev. William Payne	2	486
Hanna, d. [Daniell & Hanna], b. Nov. 9, 1668	MG	
Hannah, m. William **PHELPS**, Jan. 4, 1693	1	60
Hannah, w. Lieut. Daniel, d. Apr. 19, 1722	2	239
Hannah, d. Isaac & Hannah, b. Aug. 30, 1737	2	357
Hannah, w. Isaac, d. Aug. 27, 1750	2	241
Hannah, d. Isaac & Lucy, b. Oct. 19, 1776; d. Sept. 8, 1777	2	567
Hannah, d. Isaac & Lucy, d. Sept. 8, 1777	2	243
Hannah, d. Isaac & Lucy, b. Dec. 10, 1778	2	567
Hezekiah, s. Nathaniel & Naomi, b. Apr. 24, 1741	2	358
Isaac, s. Daniel, Jr., b. July 3, 1706	2	47
Isaac, m. Hannah **STYLES**, Nov. 19, 1736	2	162
Isaac, s. Isaac & Hannah, b. Nov. 27, 1741	2	358
Isaac, s. Isaac & Hannah, d. Jan. 23, 1741/2	2	241
Isaac, s. Isaac & Hannah, b. Mar. 12, 1748/9	2	361
Isaac, m. Eunice **DRAKE**, b. of Windsor, Jan. 25, 1753	2	163
Isaac, s. Isaac & Lucy, b. Apr. 13, 1787	2	567
Isaac Lathrop, s. Isaac, Jr. & Susan, b. Oct. 3, 1817	2	567
Jerusha, d. Daniel, Jr. & Esther, b. Nov. 23, 1739	2	357
Jerusha, m. Capt. Roger **ENOS**, b. of Windsor, Mar. 10, 1763	2	147
John, s. Ebenezer, Jr. & Mary, b. Nov. 4, 1750	2	362
John, m. Mary **PALMER**, Nov. 28, 1830, b. of Windsor, by Henry A. Rowland	2	485
Joseph, s. Samuel, b. Nov. 17, 1711	2	48
Julia A., m. Edward W. **MARSHALL**, Nov. 10, 1836, by Rev. Charles Walker	2	489
Juliet, d. Isaac & Susan, b. Sept. 15, 1814	2	567
Juletta, d. Isaac & Lucy, d. Apr. 13, 1814	2	243
Juletta, d. Isaac, Jr. & Lucy, b. Aug. 3, 1791; d. Apr. 13, 1814	2	567
Levy, s. Nathaniel & Naomi, b. May 22, 1747	2	369
Lucey, d. Isaac & Hannah, b. Mar. 5, 1739/40	2	358
Lucy, d. Isaac & Hannah, d. Mar. 10, 1747/8	2	241
Lucy, d. Isaac & Eunice, b. Dec. 30, 1755	2	363
Lucy, d. Isaac & Lucy, b. Apr. 1, 1784	2	567
Leucey, d. David & Dorithy, b. Nov. [ ]	2	361
Luke, s. Samuell & Abigail, b. June 7, 1752	2	363
Luke, s. Samuel & Abigail, d. Mar. 22, 1756	2	243
Mable, twin with Merriam, d. Isaac & Hannah, b. Nov. 6, 1746	2	360

	Vol.	Page
HAYDEN, HAYDON, HEYDON, HAIDEN, (cont.)		
Samuell, s. Samuell, b. Oct. 7, 1707	2	46
Samuel, of Windsor, m. Abigail **HALL**, of Summers, Nov. 17, 1737	2	162
Samuel, s. Samuell & Abigail, b. Oct. 22, 1738	2	357
Samuel, s. Samuel & Abigail, d. Dec. 14, 1743/4	2	241
Samuel, s. Samuell & Abigail, b. Jan. 17, 1748	2	363
Samuel, s. Daniel, b. Feb. 28, [ ]	1	20
Samuel B., m. Sarah L. **HALSEY**, b. of Windsor, Apr. 16, 1849, by T. A. Leete	2	487
Sarah, d. Samuel, b. Sept. 17, 1716	2	49
Sarah Ann, m. James H. **WELLS**, Feb. 26, 1840, by S. D. Jewett	2	514
Sarah N., of Windsor, m. John N. **POWERS**, of Charleston, S. C., Aug. 25, 1847, by T. A. Leete	2	501
Seth, s. Samuel & Abigail, b. Apr. 2, 1756	2	365
Susan Ann, d. Isaac, Jr. & Susan, b. Jan. 3, 1811	2	567
Sibil, d. Daniel, Jr. & Easther, b. Dec. 28, 1746; d. Jan. 27, 1746/7	2	360
Thomas, s. Daniel, Jr. & Esther, b. June 14, 1745	2	360
William, his w. [ ], d. [ ], [16]53	MG	
William, his w. [ ], d. July 17, 1655	Col.2	160
William, s. [Daniell & Hanna], b. Apr. 27, 1673; d. [ ]	MG	
William, s. Daniel, b. Apr. 27, 1673	1	20
William, 2nd s. [Daniell & Hanna], b. Jan. 1, 1675	MG	
William, s. Danell, b. Jan. 1, 1675	Col.1	56
William, s. Daniell, d. June 11, [16]75	MG	
William, s. Danell, d. June 11, 1675	Col.1	58
William, s. Daniel, d. June 11, 1675	1	45
William, had 3 children b. in Windsor. Dated Aug. 17, 1677	MG	
William, s. Daniel, m. Meriam **GIBBS**, b. of Windsor, Jan. 21, 1702/3	1	58
William, d. July 3, 1713	2	239
William, s. Samuel, b. Mar. 13, 1713/14	2	48
HAYES, HAYS, Abigail, d. George, b. Apr. 11, 1685	Col.D	51
Abigail, d. George, b. Aug. 31, 1684	1	20
Daniel, s. George, b. Jan. 22, [16]81	Col.D	51
Daniel, s. George, b. Apr. 26, 1686	1	20
Deliuerance, m. as 2nd w. John **ROCKWELL**, Aug. 18, 1662	MG	
George, s. George, b. Mar. 26, 1682/3	1	20
George, s. George, b. Mar. 26, 1683	Col.D	51
George, s. George, d. Apr. 3, 1683	Col.D	56
George, s. George, d. Apr. 3, 1683	1	46
George, m. Abigail **DIBLE**, Aug. 29, 1683	1	58
George, s. George, b. Mar. 9, 1694/5	1	21
Joanna, d. George, b. Oct. 2, 1692	1	20
Mary, d. George, b. Jan. 6, 1689	1	20
Sarah, w. George, d. Mar. 27, 1682/3	Col.D	56

	Vol.	Page
HAYES, HAYS, (cont.)		
Sarah, w. George, d. Mar. 27, 1682/3	1	46
Sarah, d. George, b. Jan. 22, 1687	1	20
William, s. George, b. June 13, 1697	1	21
HAYNES, Deliverance, of Dorchester, Mass., m. John		
ROCKWELL, of Windsor, Aug. 18, [16]62, at		
Dorchester, Mass.	1	61
HAYT, HAYTE, [see under **HOYT**]		
HAYWARD, HAWARD, HAYWERD, HAWOD, [see also		
HOWARD], Ephra[i]m, s. [Robard], b. Jan. 11, 1656	MG	
Ephraim, s. Robert, b. Jan. 11, 1656	Col.2	161
Epharim, bp. Jan. 11, [16]56	MG	
Ephraim, m. Abigail **NEWBERY**, Jan. 8, 1684	Col.D	54
Ephraim, contributed 0-2-6 to the poor in other colonies	MG	
Esther, d. Dec. 5, 1657	Col.2	160
Ester, d.[ ], [16]57	MG	
Hester, d. [Robard], b. June 8, 1651; d. [ ]	MG	
Lydia, d. Robbert, b. June 13, 1655	Col.2	158
Lidea, d. [Robard], b. June 13, 1655; d. [ ]	MG	
Lidia, bp. June 16, [16]55	MG	
Lidea, d. May 4, 1676	Col.1	58
Marcy, d. [ ], [16]46	MG	
Mary, d.[ ], [16]50	MG	
Rebeca, d. [Robard], b. Aug. 17, 1648	MG	
Robard, adm. ch. & communicant July [ ], 1642	MG	
Robard, had 5 children b. in Windsor. Dated Aug. 17, 1677	MG	
Rob[ert], d. Aug. [ ], 1684	Col.D	56
Rob[er]t, s. Ephraim, d. Nov. 9, 1685	Col.D	56
Rober[t], communicant 16[ ]	MG	
Robard, contributed 0-5-0 to the poor in other colonies	MG	
Sara, d. [ ], [16]47	MG	
Taphath, d. Robard, b. Jan. 1, 1646	MG	
-----, adm. commnion July 10, [16]42	MG	
HAZARD, Caroline C., of Windsor, m. Nathan **HOLCOMB**, of		
Thomsonville, Feb. 22, 1848, by Rev. S. H . Allen	2	486
HAZE, Joana, of Symsbury, m. Philander **ROWEL**, of Windsor,		
Jan. 5, 1775	2	196
HEATH, Mary, m. Horace **PALMER**, Dec. [ ], 1823, by Rev.		
James F. Bridges, of Enfield	2	500
Stephen, of East Windsor, m. Mary **HAYDEN**, of Windsor,		
Apr. 27, 1842, by Rev. S. D. Jewett	2	516
HELLER, [see under **HILLYER**]		
HELLIOR, [see under **HILLYER**]		
HELYAR, [see under **HILLYER**]		
HEMMINGWAY, Mary Ann, Mrs. of Windsor, m. Gilbert **WEST**,		
of Rockville, Sept. 21, 1857, by Levi Smith	2	520
HEMPSTED, Adeline, of Windsor, m. Zebulah **CLAP[L]**, of		
Norwich, Mass., Oct. 3, 1822, by Rev. Henry A. Rowland	2	469

HEMPSTED, (cont.)

John A., m. Sarah **STOUGHTON**, Sept. 7, 1830, by John
Bartlett 2   484

HENBERY, A[ ]th[ ], had 1 child b. in Windsor. Dated Aug.
17, 1677 .... MG

HENDERSON, Mary, d. Walter & Mary, b. May 17, 1743; d. July
12, 1743 2   364

Mary, wid., m. Caleb **PHELPS**, b. of Windsor, June 22, 1749 2   189

Walter, m. Mary **LOTHROP**, b. of Windsor, June 23, 1742 2   163

Walter, d. Jan. 6, 1746, in the 39th year of his age 2   242

William, s. Walter & Mary, b. Sept. 30, 1744 2   364

HENRY, Martin, m. Mary **ROCHE**, Oct. 18, 1852, by Rev. James
Smyth 2   460

HENSDELL, [see under **HINSDALE**]

HERMAN, Elizabeth, m. David **LOOMIS**, Nov. 24, 1715 2   170

HERNE, Mathias, d. Dec. 16, 1690 .... Col.D   57

Mathias, d. Dec. 16, 1690 1   46

HEWIT, HUIT, HUEIT, HWEIT, Ephraim, d. [ ]; bd. Sept. 5,
1644 1   45

Mary, d. Ephraim, bp. Aug. 2, 1640 1   18

Mary, m. Thomas **STRONG**, b. of Windsor, Dec. 5, 1660 ..... Col.1   45

Mary, m. Thomas **STRONG**, b. of Windsor, Dec. 5, 1660 1   61

Nathanel, d. [ ], [16]47 .... MG

Sara, d. [ ], [16]42 .... MG

Susana, d. [ ], [16]44 .... MG

-----, Mr., came from up the bay & settled in Windsor
Aug. 17, 1639 .... MG

-----, Mr., d.[ ], [16]44 .... MG

-----, Mr., d. Mar. 8, 1660; bd. the 9th day, ae 21 years 1   45

-----, Mrs., d. [ ], [16]61 .... MG

-----, Mr. had 1 child b. in Windsor. Dated Aug. 17, 1677 ..... MG

HIGGINS, Lorin M., m. Sarah Jane **CASE**, b. of Windsor, Nov. 4,
1847, by Rev. S. H. Allen 2   520

HIGLEY, HIGLEE, HIGLY, HEGLEE, HIGLE, Anna, d. Elijah
& Anna, b. Aug. 27, 1772 2   369

Elijah, s. Elijah & Anna, b. July 7, 1770 2   369

Hanna, d. [John & Hanna], b. Mar. 13, 1677; bp. [Mar.] 17,
[1677]; d. [ ] .... MG

Hanna, d. [John], b. Mar. 13, [16]77; d. [ ] Col.1   56

Hanna, contributed 0-1-3 to the poor in other colonies ..... MG

Horrece, s. Nathan & Anne, b. June 17, 1765 2   366

Isaac, m. Sarah **PORTER**, b. of Windsor, Feb. 13, 1734/5 2   162

John, m. Hanna **DRAKE**, d. John, Nov. 9, [16]71 .... Col.1   46

John, m. Hanna **DRAKE**, Nov. 9, [16]71 .... MG

John, s. [John], b. Aug. 10, 1673 .... Col.1   56

John, s. [John & Hannah], b. Aug. 16, 1673 .... MG

John, adult, ch. mem. 16[ ] .... MG

Jonathan, s. [John & Hannah], b. Feb. 16, [16]75; bp. [Feb.]

	Vol.	Page
HILL, HILLS, (cont.)		
Mary, m. John SAXTON, July 30, 1677	1	61
Sara, m. Joseph LOOMYS, Sept. 17, 1646	MG	
Sarah, m. Joseph LOOMIS, Sept. 17, 1646	1	58
Sarah, m. John PORTER, b. of Windsor, June 27, 1723	2	187
Sarah, wid., d. Sept. 30, 1737	2	240
Stephen, s. Eleazer & Elizabeth, b. Oct. 2, 1737	2	52
Tahan, s. [Luke & Mary], b. Nov. 23, 1659	MG	
Tahan, s. Luke, b. Nov. 23, 1659	1	19
William, had 1 child b. in Windsor. Dated Aug. 17, 1677	MG	
William W., m. Charlotte SCOVILL, b. of Windsor, Mar. 24,		
1852, by Theodore A. Leet	2	487
HILLYER, HELLER, HELLIOR, HELYAR, HILLAR,		
HILLIER, HILEIR, HILLARS, HILLER, Abigayl, d. [John], b.		
Aug. 21, 1654	MG	
Abgaile, d. John, b. Aug. 21, 1654	Col.2	158
Andrew, s. [John], b. Nov. 4, 1646	MG	
Andrew, contributed 0-2-6 to the poor in other colonies	MG	
Ann, wid. of Windsor, m. John FFITCH, of Hartford, Dec.		
9, 1656	Col.2	159
Ann, d. [John], b. May 8, 1677; d. July 17, [16]8[ ]	MG	
Ann, d. John, b. May 8, 1677	Col.1	56
Ann, d. John, b. May 8, 1677	1	20
Cynthia M., m. Isaac P. GRISWOLD, Apr. 7, 1841, by Rev.		
S. D. Jewett	2	481
Elin, d. Jno, b. Dec. 23, [16]82; d. same day	Col.D	51
Elisabeth, d. [James], b. May 6, [16]80	MG	
Elizabeth, d. James, b. May 6, 1680	Col.1	57
Elizabeth, d. John, b. Dec. 8, 1680	MG	
James, s. John, b. July 23, 1644	1	19
James, s. [John], b. Aug. 24, 1644	MG	
James, m. [ ] DEBELL, wid. Ebenezer, June 28, [16]77	MG	
James, m. Mary DEBLE, formerly w. Ebenezer, June 28,		
1677, by Capt. Newbery	Col.1	46
James, m. Mary DEBLE, wid. Ebenezer, June 28, 1677, by		
Capt. Newbery	TR1	1
James, m. Mary DIBLE, w. Ebenezer, June 28, 1677, by		
Capt. Nubery	1	58
James, s. [James], b. Jan. 28, 1678; d. [ ]	MG	
James, s. James, d. Apr. 27, 1679	Col.1	58
James, s. James, b. Apr. 14, 1683	Col.D	51
James, s. James, b. Apr. 14, 1683	1	20
John, s. [John], b. June 3, 1637	MG	
John, Sr., d. [ ], [16]53	MG	
John, Sr., d. July 16, 1655	MG	
John, d. July 16, 1655	Col.2	160
John, had 9 children b. in Windsor. Dated Aug. 17, 1677	MG	
John, Sr., d.[ ]; bd. July 16, [ ]	1	45

	Vol.	Page
HILLYER, HELLER, HELLIOR, HELYAR, HILLAR,		
HILLIER, HILIER, HILLARS, HILLER, (cont.)		
John, his d. [ ], d. July 25, 1680	Col.1	58
Mary, d. [John], b. Dec. 25, 1639	MG	
Mary, of Windsor, m. Joseph **CROWFOOT**, of Springfield,		
Apr. 14, 1658	1	55
Nathanell, s. [John], b. Jan. 1, 1650	MG	
Nathanael, s. John, b. Jan. 5, 1650	1	19
Sara, d. [John], b. Aug. 25, 1652	MG	
Sarah, d. John, b. Aug. 25, 1652	Col.2	157
Sarah, d. John, b. Aug. 25, 1652	1	20
Sara, m. Jehoggada **BARTLIT**, b. of Windsor, July 10, 1673,		
by Capt. Newbery	Col.1	46
Simon, s. [John], b. Dec. 25, 1648	MG	
Timothy, s. [John], b. June 3, 1642	MG	
[HINE], see under HYNE]		
HINSDALE, HENSDELL, Elizabeth, see Elizabeth **DEBLE**	Col.D	57
Eliz[abeth], of Hadley, m. Tho[mas] **DIBLE,** Sr., of Windsor,		
June 25, 1683	Col.D	54
Elizabeth, of Hadly, m. Thomas **DIBLE,** Sr., of Windsor,		
June 25, 1683	1	55
HITCHCOCK, Abigail, d. Dr. Caleb & Elinor, b. Mar. 21, 1783	2	565
Caleb, s. Dr. Caleb & Elinor, b. Sept. 6, 1767	2	368
Caleb, s. Dr. Caleb & Elinor, b. July 14, 1776	2	565
Charles, s. Dr. Caleb & Elinor, b. Aug. 14, 1771	2	369
Elinor, d. Dr. Caleb & Elinor, b. May 11, 1771	2	369
Eliza, of Windsor, m. Elazer **JONKINS**, of Winchester,		
Mar. 29, 1821, by Rev. John Bartlett. Int. Pub.	2	485
Elizabeth, d. Dr. Caleb & Elinor, b. May 28, 1764	2	368
Tamer, d. Dr. Caleb & Elinor, b. Nov. 11, 1765	2	368
HODGE, HODG, Asael, s. John, b. Oct. 10, 1697	1	20
Asahel, s. John & Mary, b. Oct. 4, 1717, at Springfield	2	50
Asahel, of Windsor, m. Damaras **GILLMAN**, of Hartford,		
Jan. 27, 1740/1	2	163
Asahel, s. Asahel & Damaris, b. Nov. 7, 1741	2	358
Beniamen, s. [John & Susanna], b. June 17, 1674	MG	
Beniamen, s. [John], b. June 17, 1674	Col.1	56
Benjamin, s. John, b. June 17, 1674	1	20
Henery, s. [John & Susanna], b. Aug. 19, 1676	MG	
Henery, s. [John], b. Aug. 19, 1676	Col.1	56
John, m. Susanna **DENESLOW**, Aug. 1, 16[ ]	MG	
John, m. Susanna **DENSLOW**, d. Henery, Aug. 1, 1666	MG	
John, m. Susanna **DENSLOW**, d. Henery, Aug. 1, 1666	Col.1	45
John, m. Susannah **DENSLOW**, d. Henry, Aug. 12, 1666	1	57
John, s. [John & Susanna], b. June 16, 1667, at Killingworth	MG	
John, 1st s. [William], b. June 16, 1667, at Kininsworth	1	20
John, had 5 children b. in Windsor. Dated Aug. 17, 1677	MG	
John*, s. William, b. Apr. 10, 1678 *("this probably should		

	Vol.	Page
HODGE, HODG, (cont.)		
read, "William, s. of John")	1	20
John, s. John, b. July 26, 1694	1	20
John, s. John, b. July 11, 1724	2	50
John, d. Sept. 9, 1751	2	241
Joseph, s. [John & Susanna], b. Dec. 14, 1672	MG	
Joseph, s. [John], b. Dec. 14, 1672	Col.1	56
Joseph, s. John, b. Dec. 14, 1672	1	20
Margeret, d. John, b. June 5, 1720	2	49
Mary, d. [John & Susanna], b. Feb. 15, 1670	MG	
Mary, d. [John], b. Feb. 15, 1670	Col.1	56
Mary, d. John, b. Feb. 24, 1718/19	2	49
Nathanael, s. John, b. June 15, 1696	1	20
Sarah, d. John, b. Feb. 24, 1721/2	2	49
Sarah, m. Eliakim **MARSHEL**, b. of Windsor, Nov. 10, 1743	2	178
Susanna, d. John, b. May 30, 1699	1	21
Thankfull, d. John & Mary, b. July 28, 1726	2	51
Thomas, s. [John & Susanna], b. Feb. 13, 1668	MG	
Thomas, s. John, b. Feb. 13, 1668	Col.1	56
William, s. [John & Susanna], b. Apr. 10, 1678	MG	
William, s. John, b. Apr. 10, 1678	Col.1	56
William, see John **HODG[E]**	1	20
HOLCOMB, HOLCOM, HOLCOMBE, HOKOM, Abigayl, d.		
Thomas, b. or bp. Jan. 6, [16]38	MG	
Abigail, d. Thomas, bp. Jan. 6, 1638	Col.2	153
Abigail, d. Thomas, bp. June 6, 1638	1	18
Abigayl, m. Samuel **BISSELL**, June 11, 1658	MG	
Abigail, m. Samuel **BISSELL**, b. of Windsor, June 11, 1658	1	53
Abigail, d. Benaj[ah], b. May 12, 1681	Col.D	51
Abigail, d. Benajah, b. May 12, 1681	1	20
Ann, d. Benajah, b. Mar. 19, 1675	1	20
Ann, m. Samuel **HAYDON**, b. of Windsor, Jan. 26, 1703/4	1	58
Ann, m. Joseph **DENSLOW**, b. of Windsor, Oct. 10, 1733	2	142
Anna, m. Titus **MEACHAM**, June 22, 1820, by Richard		
Niles, J. P. Int. Pub.	2	181
Benaga, s. [Thomas], b. June 23, 1644	MG	
Benajah, s. Thomas, b. June 23, 1644	Col.2	153
Benajah, s. Thomas, b. June 23, 1644	1	18
Benaja, m. Sarah **ENNOS**, Apr. 11, 1667	MG	
Benaiaga, m. Sarah **ENNO**, Apr. 11, 1667, by Mr. Allyen	Col.1	45
Benajah, m. Sarah **ENNO**, b. of Windsor, Apr. 11, 1667	1	57
Benaga, s. [Benaga & Sarah], b. Apr. 16, 1668	MG	
Benagah, s. Benja[min], b. Apr. 16, 1668	1	19
Benaj[ah], his d. [ ], b. Mar. 19, 1675	Col.D	51
Benaga, had 2 children, b. in Windsor. Dated Aug. 17, 1677	MG	
Benajah, of Windsor, m. Martha **WINCHEL**, of Suffield,		
May 17, 1705	2	161
Bonajah, s. Bonajah, Jr., b. July 10, 1710	2	48

	Vol.	Page
HOLCOMB, HOLCOM, HOLCOMBE, HOKOM, (cont.)		
Benajah, Jr., d. Oct. 30, 1716	2	239
Benajah, Sergt., d. Jan. 25, 1736/7	2	240
Benajah, s. Samuel & Phebe, b. July 28, 1743	2	359
Benajah, s. Samuell & Phebe, d. Nov. 1, 1751	2	241
Benjamin, s. Benajah, b. June 1, 1689	1	20.
Betsey, or Elizabeth, of Windsor, m. Chauncey **PEASE,** of Springfield, Nov. 7, 1821, by Richard Niles, J. P.	2	191
Caroline, of Windsor, m. James **BROWN,** of Manchester, Oct. 11, 1842, by Rev. David L. Marks	2	466
Catherine, m. William **HOUSE,** of Manchester, Oct. 16, 1842, by Rev. David L. Marks	2	483
Christian, d. Martin & Christian, b. Feb. 17, 1755	2	366
Christian, d. Martin & Christian, b. Feb. 17, 1755	2	367
Clarissa, m. John **WARD,** Dec. 25, 1833, by Richard Niles, J. P.	2	213
Climena, d. Mathew & Lydia, b. Apr. 13, 1747	2	361
David, s. Joseph, b. Jan. 7, 1723/4	2	50
David, s. Joseph, d. Apr. 21, 1724	2	240
David S., m. Catharine M. **LACY,** b. of Windsor, Dec. 31, 1849, by Rev. Cephas Brainard	2	487
Debroa, d. [Thomas], b. Oct. 15, 1646; d. [ ]	MB	
Deborah, d. Thomas, b. Oct. 15, 1646	1	18
Deborah, d. Thomas, b. Feb. 5, 1650	1	19
Debroa, 2nd, d. [Thomas], b. Feb. 15, 1650	MG	
Deborah, d. Thomas, b. Feb. 15, 1650	Col.2	154
Deborah, d. Thomas, b. Feb. 15, 1650	1	18
Debra, m. Daniel **BIRG,** Nov. 5, 1668	MG	
Debroa, m. Daniell **BIRG,** b. of Windsor, Nov. 5, [16]68, at Hartford, by John Allyn	Col.1	45
Deborah, m. Daniel **BIRDGE,** b. of Windsor, Nov. 5, 1668, at Hartford, by John Allyn	1	54
Debora, d. Benaj[ah], b. Oct. 26, 1690	Col.D	51
Deborah, d. Benajah, b. Oct. 26, 1690	1	20
Deborah, d. Samuell, b. July 20, 1716	2	48
Deborah, d. Samuel & Phebe, b. Apr. 2, 1741	2	358
Deborah, see Deborah **BIRGE**	Col.D	56
Edwin B., m. Sarah E. **SOPER,** b. of Windsor, Apr. 4, 1852, by Cornelius B. Everest	2	520
Eli, s. Mathew & Lois, b. Aug. 30, 1736 (Conflicts with birth of Lois **HOLCOMB**)	2	52
Eli, s. Elijah & Sarah, b. Aug. 27, 1766	2	368
Elihu, m. Miriam **PHELPS,** b. of Windsor, Mar. 22, 1832, by Henry A. Rowland	2	485
Elijah, s. Mathew & Lois, b. Mar. 5, 1731/2	2	52
Elijah, of Windsor, m. Sarah **EVENS,** of Hartford, Nov. 23, 1758	2	163
Elijah, s. Elijah & Sarah, d. Feb. 4, 1761	2	243

	Vol.	Page
HOLCOMB, HOLCOM, HOLCOMBE, HOKOM, (cont.)		
Elijah, s. Elija & Sarah, b. June 29, 1764	2	367
Elizabeth, m. Josia **ELESWORTH**, Nov. 16, 1654	MG	
Elisabeth, m. Josias **ELSEWORTH**, b. of Windsor, Nov. 16, 1654	Col.2	159
Elizabeth, wid., m. James **ENNO**, Aug. 5, 1658	1	56
Elizabeth, d. Joseph, b. May 9, 1722	2	50
Elizabeth, m. Joseph **BARNARD**, b. of Windsor, Feb. 9, 1743/4	2	466
Elizabeth, d. Martin & Christian, b. Feb. 14, 1757	2	366
Elizabeth, d. Martin & Christian, b. Feb. 14, 1757	2	367
Elizabeth, see Betsey **HOLCOMB**	2	191
Fidelia H., m. Horace B. **HOSKINS**, b. of Windsor, Dec. 13, 1841, by Rev. Daniel L. Marks	2	483
George Worthington, s. Elijah & Sarah, b. Aug. 13, 1776	2	565
Harriet E., of Windsor, m. Chester **TRACY**, of Vernon, May 23, 1849, by Cornelius B. Everest	2	511
Harriet E., of Windsor, m. Aaron **BIDWELL**, of Manchester, Jan. 1, 1850, by Rev. Cephus Brainard	2	504
Hiram, m. Maria **LATHAM**, Mar. 27, 1827, by Rev. Henry A. Rowland	2	167
James, s.[Benaga & Sarah], b. Oct. 13, 1671	MG	
James, s. Benaj[ah], d. Feb. 11, 1681	Col.D	56
James, s. Benajah, d. Feb. 11,1681	1	46
Jane, of Windsor, m. Sumner **BROWN**, of Springfield, Mass., Dec. 14, 1834, by Rev. Luke Wood	2	150
John, s. Mathew & Lydia, b. Oct. 5, 1749	2	364
John B., of Windsor, m. Cynthia M. **BRADFORD**, of Haddam, Dec. 4, 1842, by Rev. D. L. Marks	2	517
Jonathan, s. [Thomas], b. Mar. 23, 1652; d. [ ]	MG	
Jonathan, s. Thomas, b. Mar. 23, 1652	Col.2	154
Jonathan, s. Thomas, b. Mar. 23, 1652	1	18
Jonathan, s. Thomas, d. Sept. 13, 1656	Col.2	160
Jonathan, s. Thomas, d. Sept. 15, 1656	1	46
Jonathan, d. [ ], [16]56	MG	
Joseph, s. Benj[ah], b. Nov. 7, 1686	Col.D	51
Joseph, s. Benajah, b. Nov. 7, 1686	1	21
Joseph, of Windsor, m. Mary **WINCHEL**, Nov. 15, 1714	2	161
Joseph, s. Joseph, b. Aug. 5, 1715	2	48
Joseph, s. Martin & Christian, b. Jan. 20, 1759	2	366
Joseph, s. Martin & Christian, b. Jan. 20, 1759	2	367
Josua, s. [Thomas], bp. Sept. 27, 1640	MG	
Joshua, s. Thomas, bp. Sept. 27, 1640	Col.2	153
Joshua, s. Thomas, bp. Sept. 27, 1640	1	18
Josua, m. Ruth **SHARWOOD**, June 4, 1663	MG	
Josua, m. Ruth **SHARWOOD**, June 4, 1663, by Mr. Wolcot	Col.1	45
Josua, had 3 children b. in Windsor. Dated Aug. 17, 1677	MG	
Justis, s. Elijah & Sarah, b. Mar. 27, 1779	2	565

	Vol.	Page
HOLCOMB, HOLCOM, HOLCOMBE, HOKOM, (cont.)		
Laury F., of Windsor, m. Burrett **DOWNS**, of New Haven,		
Oct. 16, 1849, by Rev. Cephus Brainard	2	474
Lois, d. Mathew & Lois, b. Oct. 25, 1736 (Date conflicts		
with birth of "Eli **HOLCOMB**")	2	52
Lois, d. Elijah & Sarah, b. Sept. 4, 1768	2	368
Luther, m. Mathew & Lydia, b. Aug. 12, 1752	2	364
Lydia, d. Mathew & Lydia, b. Feb. 21, 1744	2	360
Madusa, d. Martin & Christian, b. Feb. 17, 1763	2	566
Marah, d. Corp. Samuel, b. Nov. 8, 1722	2	50
Marcus, of Windsor, m. Mariah L. **BARNES**, of Windsor,		
Mar. 18, 1849, by Rev. Cephus Brainard	2	487
Maria, m. William **MARBLE**, of East Windsor, Oct. 17,		
1826, by Richard Niles, J. P.	2	182
Marsha, m. Joseph **BODGE**, b. of Windsor, July 2, 1837, by		
Eli Deniston	2	490
Martha, d. Boorajah, Jr., b. Sept. 16, 1706	2	46
Martha, d. Samuel, b. Aug. 6, 1710	2	47
Martha, w. Benajah, d. Sept. 8, 1722	2	240
Martha, m. Marcus **GRISWOLD**, Feb. 15, 1827, by Rev.		
Henry A. Rowland	2	480
Martin, s. Joseph & Mary, b. Nov. 21, 1725	2	50
Martin, s. Martin & Christian, b. May 27, 1753	2	365
Martin, s. Martin & Christian, b. May 27, 1753	2	367
Mary, m. George **GRISWOLD**, Oct. [ ], [16]	MG	
Mary, m. George **GRISWOLD**, b. of Windsor, Oct. 3, 1655	Col.2	159
Mary, d. Nathanael, b. May 17, 1675	1	20
Mary, d. Joseph, b. Feb. 2, 1717/18	2	49
Mary, d. Martin & Christian, b. Apr. 12, 1761	2	366
Mary, d. Martin & Christian, b. Apr. 12, 1761	2	367
Mary, m. Henry **MOSHIER**, b. of Windsor, Sept. 4, 1834, by		
Henry A. Rowland	2	496
Mathew, m. Lois **DRAKE**, b. of Windsor, Jan. 20, 1729/30	2	162
Mathew, s. Mathew & Lois, b. May 30, 1730	2	51
Mindwell, m. Theophilus **COOK**, b. of Windsor, Sept. 26,		
1721	2	136
Nathan, of Thomsonville, m. Caroline C. **HAZARD**, of		
Windsor, Feb. 22, 1848, by Rev. S. H. Allen	2	486
Nathanell, s. [Thomas], b. Nov. 4, 1648	MG	
Nathanael, s. Thomas, b. Nov. 4, 1648	Col.2	153
Nathanael, s. Thomas, b. Nov. 4, 1648	1	18
Nathanell, m. Mary **BLISSE**, of Springfield, Feb. 27, 1670	Col.1	46
Nathanael, s. Nathan[ie]ll, b. June 11, 1673	1	20
Nathanel, had 2 children b. in Windsor. Dated Aug. 17, 1677	MG	
Olive, d. Elijah & Sarah, b. Dec. 16, 1770	2	368
Olive, m. William **ADAMS**, b. of Windsor, Feb. 11, 1852, by		
Rev. H. A. Weed	2	463
Oliver R., of East Granby, m. Mary M. **SILL**, Mar. 3, 1851,		

	Vol.	Page
HOLCOMB, HOLCOM, HOLCOMBE, HOKOM, (cont.)		
by Rev. James Rankin	2	476
Parnel, d. Benajah, Jr., b. July 8, 1708	2	48
Phebe, w. Samuel, d. Aug. 20, 1750	2	241
Rebekah, d. Corp. Samuel, b. Aug. [ ], 1719	2	50
Rebeckah, m. John BARNARD, b. of Windsor, Nov. 26, 1750	2	132
Rhoderec, s. Martin & Christian, b. Oct. 21, 1764	2	566
Ruth, d. [Josua & Ruth], b. May 26, 1664	MG	
Ruth, d. Josua, b. May 26, [16]64	Col.1	54
Salinas A., of Windsor, m. Charly FOX, of New Hartford, Oct. 4, 1841, by Ezra S. Cook	2	477
Samuel, s. Benaj[ah], b. Nov. 29, 1683	Col.D	51
Samuel, s. Benaja[h], b. Nov. 29, 1683	1	20
Samuel, m. Martha PHELPS, Oct. 13, 1709	2	161
Samuell, s. Samuell, b. Jan. 16, 1712	2	48
Samuel, d. Aug. 13, 1722	2	239
Samuel, s. Samuell & Phebe, b. Aug. 22, 1746	2	362
Samuell, s. Samuel & Phebe, d. Oct. 31, 1751	2	241
Samuel, m. Julia GRIFFIN, Nov. 3, 1825, by Richard Niles, J. P.	2	166
Samuel, m. Julia GRIFFIN, b. of Windsor, Nov. 3, 1825, by Richard Niles, J. P.	2	167
Sara, d. [Thomas], b. Aug. 14, 1642; d. [ ]	MG	
Sarah, d. Thomas, bp. Aug. 14, 1642	Col.2	153
Sarah, d. Thomas, bp. Aug. 14, 1642	1	18
Sara, d. [ ], [16]54	MG	
Sara, d. [Josua & Ruth], b. June 23, 1668	MG	
Sarah, d. Joshua, b. June 23, 1668	1	20
Sarah, d. Benajah, b. Feb. 1, 1673	1	20
Sarah, d. Benaj[ah], b. Feb. 12 (?), 1673	Col.D	51
Sarah, m. Isaac OWIN, Dec. 20, 1694	1	64
Sarah, d. Corp. Samuell, b. Dec. 20, 1717	2	50
Sarah, w. Sergt. Benajah, d. Apr. [ ], 1732	2	240
Sarah Cade, d. Elijah & Sarah, b. May 16, 1762	2	365
Suffiah, d. Corp. Samuel, b. Jan. 16, 1720/1	2	50
Susanna, m. Josiah PHELPS, Nov. 6, 1822, by Horace Clark, J. P.	2	191
Thomas, his child d. [ ], [16]48	MG	
Thomas, d. [ ], [16]57	MG	
Thomas, d. Sept. 7, 1657	Col.2	160
Thomas, d. Sept. 7, 1657	1	46
Thomas, s. [Josua & Ruth], b. Mar. 30, 1666	MG	
Thomas, s. Josua, b. Mar. 30, 1666	Col.1	55
Thomas, s. Joshua, b. Mar. 30, 1666	1	20
Thomas, had 8 children b. in Windsor. Dated Aug. 17, 1677	MG	
Zurviah, d. Elijah & Sarah, b. Aug. 13, 1773	2	369
HOLLIDAY, Abigael, m. Samuel MILLER, Nov. 1, 1710	2	176

	Vol.	Page
HOOKER, (cont.)		
James, m. Hannah **ALLIN**, Jan. 6, 1763	2	164
James, m. Hannah **ALLIN**, Jan. 6, 1763	2	522
James, m. Dolly **GOODWIN**, Apr. 30, 1777	2	164
James, m. Dolly **GOODWIN**, Apr. 30, 1777	2	522
James, m. Mary **CHAFFEE**, Nov. 7, 1784	2	164
James, m. Mary **CHAFFEE**, Nov. 7, 1784	2	522
James, s. James & Mary, b. July 12, 1792	2	521
James, s. James & Mary, b. July 12, 1792	2	567
James, Capt., s. Nathaniel & Eunice, d. Dec. 10, 1805	2	243
James, s. Nathaniel & Eunice, d. Dec. 10, 1805	2	522
James, m. Helen S. **REED**, Jan. 24, 1816	2	522
James, Jr., m. Helen S. **REEDE**, Jan. 24, 1841	2	165
Jarus, s. Nathaniel & Eunice, b. Aug. 15, 1742	2	521
Mary Chaffee, d. James & Mary, b. Mar. 31, 1796	2	521
Mary Chaffee, d. James & Mary, b. Mar. 31, 1796	2	567
HOPEWELL, Sarah, d. Thomas, b. July 31, 1658	1	19
Thomas, d. Aug. 17, 1683	Col.D	56
Thomas, d. Aug. 17, 1683	1	46
HOPKINS, Elizabeth, m. Samuel **ALLYN**, b. of Windsor, July 17, 1723	2	123
Mary R., m. Alfred H. **SILL**, b. of Cugahoga Falls, O., [ ], 1852, by Theodore A. Leete	2	503
-----, wid., adm. ch. Apr. 9, [16]48	MG	
HORTEN, Thomas, had 1 child b. in Windsor. Dated Aug. 17, 1677	MG	
HOSFORD, HORSFORD, Abigaell, d. Timothy, b. Feb. 28, 1707/8	2	46
Ann, m. Stephen **TAYLOR**, Nov. 1, 1642	1	62
Ann, d. Nathanael, b. Aug. 3, 1702	1	21
Ann, d. Nathanael, d. Oct. 28, 1702	1	46
Ann, d. Obadiah, b. Feb. 23, 1705/6	2	46
Anne, d. Nathaniel, b. Aug. 3, 1712	2	85
Benjamin, s. Samuel, b. Jan. 1, 1700/1	1	21
Daniel, s. Timothy, b. July 5, 1695	1	20
Deborah, m. Benjamin **ELSWORTH**, b. of Windsor, Oct. 25, 1721	2	146
Elizabeth, d. Samuel, b. Feb. 8, 1721/2	2	50
Hanah, d. Tim[othy], b. Oct. 12, 1690	Col.D	51
Hannah, d. Timothy, b. Oct. 12, 1690	1	20
Hannah, w. Timothy, d. Jan. 8, 1701/2	1	46
Hannah, m. Abraham **DIBLE**, Aug. 18, 1709	2	141
Hester, d. John, b. May 26, [16]64	Col.1	54
Hester, d. [John & Phillup], b. May 27, 1664	MG	
Hester, d. John, b. May 27, 1664	1	18
Isaac, s. Nathanael, b. Feb. 4, 1717/18	2	49
Jeremiah, s. Jess & Elizabeth, d. June 8, 1761	2	242
Jesse, s. Samuel, b. May 24, 1719	2	49

	Vol.	Page
HOSFORD, HORSFORD, (cont.)		
Jesse, m. Elizabeth **ALFORD**, b. of Windsor, Oct. 1, 1747	2	163
Jesse, m. Elizabeth **ALFORD**, b. of Windsor, Oct. 1, 1747	2	178
Jesse, s. Jesse & Elizabeth, b. Feb. 20, 1747/8	2	360
John, m. Phillup **TRALL**, Nov. 5, 1657	MG	
John, m. Phillip* **TRALL**, Nov. 5, 1657 *(Female)	Col.2	159
John, m. Phillip* **THRALL**, b. of Windsor, Nov. 5, 1657		
*(Female)	1	57
John, s. [John & Phillup], b. Oct. 16, 1660	MG	
John, s. John, b. Oct. 16, 1660	1	18
John, had 8 children b. in Windsor. Dated Aug. 17, 1677	MG	
John, d. Aug. 7, 1683	Col.D	56
John, d. Aug. 7, 1683	1	46
John, m. Deborah **BROWN**, Apr. 9, 1696	1	58
John, d. Nov. 8, 1698	1	46
John, s. Timothy, b. June 16, 1699	1	21
John, s. Timothy, d. July 18, 1701	1	46
John, s. Nathanael, b. Oct. 3, 1703	1	21
John, contributed 0-1-6 to the poor in other colonies	MG	
Martha, d. Samuell, d. Dec. 6, 1707	2	239
Martha, d. Samuell, b. Sept. 6, 1708	2	47
Mary, d. [John & Phillup], b. Apr. 12, 1674	MG	
Mary, d. John, b. Apr. 12, 1674	Col.1	56
Mary, d. John, b. Apr. 12, 1674	1	18
Mary, d. Samuel, b. Feb. 15, 1690/1	1	20
Mary, d. Samuell, b. Feb. 15, 1691	Col.D	51
Mary, m. Josiah **OWIN**, Jr., Dec. 3, 1698	1	64
Mary, d. Nathaniel, b. Aug. 8, 1710	2	47
Mary, w. Samuel, d. May 9, 1715	2	239
Nathanaell, s. [John & Phillup], b. Aug. 19, 167[ ]	MG	
Nathanael, s. John, b. Aug. 19, 1671	1	18
Nathanael, m. Mary **PHELPS**, b. of Windsor, Apr. 19, 1700	1	58
Nathaniell, s. Nathaniell, b. Oct. 31, 1708	2	47
Obadia[h], s. John, b. Sept. [ ], [16]	MG	
Obadia, s. John, b. Sept. 28, 1677	Col.1	56
Obediah, s. John, b. Sept. 28, 1677	1	18
Obediah, m. Mindwell **PHELPS**, May 4, 1705	2	161
Phillip, wid., d. May [ ], 1698	1	46
Samuell, s. [John & Phillup], b. June 2, 1669	MG	
Samuel, s. John, b. June 2, 1669	1	18
Samuel, m. Mary **PALLMOR**, Apr. 4, 1690	Col.D	55
Samuel, m. Mary **PALMER**, Apr. 4, 1690	1	58
Samuel, of Windsor, m. Elizabeth **BROWN**, of Colchester,		
Apr. 17, 1717	2	161
Samuel, s. Samuel, b. Jan. 11, 1717/18	2	49
Sara, m. Stephen **TAYLAR**, Nov. 1, 1642	MG	
Sara, d. [John & Phillup], b. Sept. 27, 1666	MG	
Sara, d. John, b. Sept. 27, 1666	Col.1	55

	Vol.	Page
HOSFORD, HORSFORD, (cont.)		
Sarah, d. John, b. Sept. 27, 1666	1	18
Sara, m. Joseph **PHELPS**, s. Tim[othy], Nov. 18, 1686	Col.D	54
Sarah, m. Joseph **PHELPS**, s. Sergt. Timothy, Nov. 18, 1686	1	60
Sarah, d. Nathanael, b. Apr. 3, 1701	1	21
Sarah, d. Nathaniell, d. Dec. 1, 1705	2	239
Sarah, d. Nathaniel, b. July 11, 1706	2	46
Timothy, s. [John & Phillup], b. Oct. 20, 1662	MG	
Timothy, s. John, b. Oct. 20, [16]62	Col.1	54
Timothy, s. John, b. Oct. 20, 1662	1	18
Timothy, m. Hannah **PALMER**, Dec. 5, 1689	Col.D	54
Timothy, m. Hannah **PALMER**, Dec. 5, 1689	1	58
Timothy, s. Timothy, b. Feb. 5, 1692/3	1	20
Timothy, s. Timothy, d. Sept. 15, 1701	1	46
Timothy, m. Abigael **BUCKLAND**, Jan. 24, 1706/7	2	161
Timothy, s. Timothy, b. Sept. 3, 1709	2	47
William, his w. [ ], d. [ ], [16]41	MG	
William, his w. [ ], bd. Aug. 26, 1641	1	45
William, s. [John & Phillup], b. Oct. 25, 1658	MG	
William, s. John, b. Oct. 25, 1658	1	18
William, d. May 29, 1688	1	46
William, s. Samuel, b. June 24, 1692	1	20
William, s. Nathaniel, b. Mar. 26, 1715	2	48
William, s. Samuel, d. Apr. 13, 1715	2	239
HOSKINS, HOSKINES, Abel, s. Zebulon & Lois, b. June 28,		
1734	2	52
Abel, m. Elizabeth **EGELSTON**, Mar. 22, 1759	2	164
Abel, s. Abel & Elizabeth, b. Jan. 12, 1766	2	367
Abiah, d. Abel & Elizabeth, d. June 21, 1772	2	368
Abiah, d. Abel & Elizabeth, d. June 30, 1775	2	243
Abigael, d. John, Jr., [s. Thomas], b. May 23, 1710	2	47
Alexander, s. Anthony, Jr., b. Mar. 3, 1705/6	2	46
Alexander, s. Alexander & Mindwell, b. Aug. 25, 1739	2	359
Alton, s. Zebulon, Jr. & Mary, b. Nov. 2, 1761	2	365
Ann, d. Anthony, Jr., b. Aug. 1, 1699	2	46
Ann, d. John, 3rd & Thankfull, b. Dec. 8, 1743	2	359
Ann, m. Abner **COOK**, b. of Windsor, Feb. 18, 1762	2	137
Anna, d. Abel & Elizabeth, b. Apr. 9, 1770	2	368
Anthony, m. Jesabel **BROWN**, July 16, 1656	MG	
Anthony, m. Izabell **BROWNE**, b. of Windsor, July 16, 1656	Col.2	159
Anthony, s. [Anthony & Jesabel], b. Mar. 19, 1663/4	MG	
Anthony, s. Anthony, b. Mar. 19, [16]63/4	Col.1	54
Anthony, s. Anthony, b. Mar. 19, 1663/4	1	19
Anthony, had 9 children b. in Windsor. Dated Aug. 17, 1677	MG	
Anthony, s. Anthony, Jr., b. Sept. 1, 1687	1	20
Anthony, s. Anthony, d. Oct. 6, 1687	1	46
Anthony, s. Anthony, Jr., b. Jan. 19, 1694/5	2	45
Anthony, Jr., m. Mary **GILLET**, b. of Windsor, Dec. 23,		

	Vol.	Page
HOSKINS, HOSKINES, (cont.)		
1725	2	162
Anthony, s. Anthony & Mary, b. Apr. 12, 1731	2	51
Asa, s. Anthony, Jr. & Mary, b. May 4, 1728	2	51
Asa, s. Abel & Elizabeth, b. May 16, 1760	2	364
Benjamin, twin with Joseph, s. Anthony, b. May 5, 1710	2	47
Benjamin, s. John & Catharine, b. Dec. 7, 1752; d. Jan. 15, 1753	2	362
Benjamin, s. John & Catharine, b. Dec. 25, 1753	2	362
Caleb, s. Thomas, b. Nov. 7, 1705	2	46
Caleb, d. Mar. 10, 1758	2	242
Calvin W., m. Mary A. DAY, Sept. 5, 1847, by Samuel A. Seaman	2	484
Catharine, d. John & Catharine, b. Sept. 16, 1750	2	362
Chloe, d. John & Thankfull, b. Mar. 5, 1739/40	2	358
Constant, d. Anthony, Jr., b. Jan. 1, 1703/4	2	46
Constant, m. John EGELSTON, Jr., b. of Windsor, June 3, 1725	2	146
Daniel, s. Thomas, Jr. & Lydia, b. Oct. 27, 1731	2	51
Daniel, s. John & Catharine, b. Sept. 6, 1744	2	362
David, s. John, 2nd & Catharine, b. May 24, 1741	2	358
David, s. John & Thankfull, b. June 22, 1747	2	361
Debro, d. John, b. June 9, 1679	Col. 1	57
Elener, w. Thomas, Jr., d. Mar. 17, 1722/3	2	240
Eli, s. John & Thankfull, b. Nov. 24, 1750	2	361
Eli, m. Martha CLARK, b. of Windsor, Aug. 13, 1772	2	164
Eli, s. Eli & Martha, b. Jan. 25, 1773	2	368
Elijah, s. Zebulon & Lois, b. July 22, 1730	2	51
Elijah, s. Thomas & Margret, b. July 20, 1760	2	366
[Elisabeth], wid. Thomas, d. Dec. 22, 1675	MG	
Elizabeth, wid. & formerly Elizabeth (GAYLORD) BIRGE, d. Dec. 22, [16]75	MG	
Elisabeth, wid., d. Dec. 22, [16]75	Col. 1	58
Elizabeth, wid., d. Dec. 22, 1675; bd. Dec. 23, 1675	1	45
Elisabeth, d. [John & Debro], b. June 9, 1679; bp. Oct. 19, 1679	MG	
Elizabeth, m. Thomas THRALL, Nov. 2, 1699	1	62
Elizabeth, w. John (s. of Anthony), d. May 9, 1719	2	239
Elizabeth, d. Thomas & Lydia, b. July 7, 1734	2	52
Elizabeth, d. Abel & Elizabeth, b. Feb. 20, 1766	2	368
Erastus, of Bennington, N. Y., m. Louisa ALLYN, of Hartford, Sept. 10, 1835, by Henry A. Rowland	2	164
Eunice, d. Alexander & Mindwell, b. Sept. 14, 1734	2	52
Eunice, d. Alexander & Mindwell, b. Jan. 14, 1746/7	2	360
Ezekiel, s. John & Catharine, b. Jan. 3, 1748/9	2	362
George, s. John, 3rd & Jerusha, b. Feb. 9, 1758	2	364
Grace, d. [Anthony & Jesabel], b. July 26, 1666	MG	
Grace, d. Anthony, b. July 26, [16]66	Col. 1	55

	Vol.	Page
HOSKINS, HOSKINES, (cont.)		
Grace, d. Anthony, b. July 26, [16]66	1	19
Hannah, d. Anthony, Jr., b. Jan. 19, 1690/1	2	45
Hannah, d. Robert & Elizabeth, of Simsbury, b. Feb.		
13, 1726/7	2	51
Hannah, d. Alexander & Mindwel, b. Feb. 7, 1748/9	2	361
Harriet, m. James Y. BURNHAM, Mar. 20, 1841, by Ezra S.		
Cook	2	475
Henry, s. Abel & Elizabeth, b. Mar. 19, 1775	2	565
Henry H., m. Fidelia SKINNER, Sept. 28, 1832, by Henry A.		
Rowland	2	486
Horace B., m. Fidelia H. HOLCOMB, b. of Windsor, Dec.		
13, 1841, by Rev. Daniel L. Marks	2	483
Jesabell, d. [Anthony & Jesabel], b. May 16, 1657	MG	
Ezabell, d. Anthony, b. May 16, 1657	Col.2	161
Isable, d. Anthony, b. May 16, 1657	1	19
Isable, w. Anthony, Sr., d. [ ]	1	46
Jane, d. [Anthony & Jesabel], b. Apr. 30, 1671	MG	
Jane, d. Anthony, b. Apr. 30, 1671	1	19
Jane, d. Anthony, b. Feb. 18, 1708/9	2	47
Jemima, d. Alexander & Mindwell, b. Apr. 1, 1736	2	359
Jemima, d. Alexander & Mindwell, d. Feb. 9, 1757, in the		
21st y. of her age	2	242
Jerusha, d. John, 3rd & Jerusha, b. Dec. 4, 1755	2	364
John, d. [ ]; [16]48	MG	
John, d. [ ], bd. May 5, 1648	Col.2	160
John, s. [Thomas & Elisabeth], b. May 29, 1654	MG	
John, s. Tho[mas], b. May 29, 1654	Col.2	158
John, s. Thomas, b. [ ], 1654	1	19
John, s. [Anthony & Jesabel], b. Oct. 14, 1659	MG	
John, s. Anthony, b. Oct. 14, [16]59	1	19
John, m. Debro DENESLOW, Jan. 21, 1677	MG	
John, m. Debra DENSLO, Jan. 29, 1677	Col.1	46
John, m. Debora DENSLO[W], Jan. 29*, 1677 *(In pencil		
"21?")	TR1	1
John, m. Deborah DENSLOW, Jan. 29, 1677	1	58
John, s. John, b. June 13, 1688	1	20
John, s. John, b. Dec. 5, 1701	1	21
John, m. wid. Elizabeth FILLEY, May 27, 1708	2	161
John, s. John, Jr. (s. Anthony), b. Oct. 22, 1713	2	48
John, Sr., d. Feb. 21, 1733/4	2	240
John, m. Thankfull EVINS, b. of Windsor, June 15, 1735	2	162
John, s. John & Thankfull, b. Mar. 18, 1735/6	2	52
John, of Windsor, m. Cathrien VIETTS, of Simsbury, Aug.		
17, 1738	2	162
John, s. John, 2nd & Catharine, b. May 5, 1740	2	358
John, 3rd, m. Jerusha GILLET, b. of Windsor, June 10, 1755	2	163
John, contributed 0-1-0 to the poor in other colonies	MG	

	Vol.	Page
HOSKINS, HOSKINES, (cont.)		
Jonah, s. Thomas & Margret, b. Sept. 23, 1761	2	366
Joseph, s. [Anthony & Jesabel], b. Feb. 28, 1674	MG	
Joseph, s. Anthony, b. Feb. 28, 1674	1	19
Joseph, twin with Benjamin, s. Anthony, b. May 4, 1710	2	47
Joseph, m. Mary **LOOMIS**, b. of Windsor, Jan. 10, 1733/4	2	162
Lois, d. Zebulon & Lois, b. May 22, 1732	2	51
Lois, w. Zebulon, d. Oct. 31, 1754, ae 50 yrs., wanting 16 days	2	242
Lyaid, d. Thomas & Lydia, b. Dec. 8, 1732	2	52
Mabell, d. Anthony, Jr., b. May 11, 1692	2	45
Mabell, m. Stephen **LOOMIS**, Dec. 7, 1715	2	170
Mabel, d. Alexander & Mindwell, b. Dec. 5, 1737	2	359
Margarett, d. John, Sr., b. May 10, 1712	2	48
Margret, d. Thomas & Margret, b. Dec. 28, 1762	2	366
Mary, d. John (s. Thomas), b. Apr. 12, 1707	2	46
Mary, d. John, Sr., d. Nov. 19, 1727	2	240
Mary, d. Joseph & Mary, b. Dec. 9, 1734	2	357
Mary, d. Joseph & Mary, b. Dec. 9, 1734 (Crossed out)	2	375
Mary, d. John & Catherine, b. Jan. 31, 1746/7	2	362
Mary, d. Daniel & Abigail, b. July 2, 1770	2	368
Mindwell, d. Alexander & Mindwell, b. Dec. 29, 1732	2	51
Mindwell, d. Alexander & Mindwell, b. Jan. 1, 1742/3	2	359
Mindwell, m. Jonathan **EGELSTON**, b. of Windsor, June 24, 1762	2	147
Moses, s. Thomas & Margret, b. Sept. 23, 1764	2	366
Name, d. John, 3rd & Thankfull, b. July 22, 1745	2	360
Nathan, s. Abel & Elizabeth, b. Mar. 13, 1764	2	365
Noah, s. Anthony, Jr., b. Aug. 29, 1688	1	20
Noah, s. Anthony, Jr. & Mary, b. Dec. 9, 1726	2	50
Peere, s. Abel & Elizabeth, b. Dec. 4, 1761	2	365
Rebekah, m. Mark **KELCIE**, b. of Windsor, Mar. 8, 1658/9	1	58
Rebeca, d. [Anthony & Jesabel], b. Dec. 3, 1668; d. [ ]	MG	
Rebekah, d. Anthony, b. Dec. 3, 1668	1	19
Rebeca, d. Anthony, d. Oct. [ ], 1673	Col.1	58
Rebecah, d. Anthony, d. Oct. [ ], 1673, ae about 5 years	1	45
[Rebecca*], d. Anthony, bd. [Oct.*], [ ], [16]73		
*(In pencil)	MG	
Robard, s. [Anthony & Jesabel], b. June 6, 1662	MG	
Robart, s. Anthony, b. June 6, 1662	Col.1	54
Robert, s. Anthony, b. June 6, 1662	1	19
Robert, m. Mary **GILLIT**, Oct. 27, 1686	1	58
Robert, s. Robert, b. July 9, 1687	1	21
Robert, s. Robert, d. July 30, 1687	1	46
Sarah, d. Anthony, b. Dec. 10, 1707	2	47
Simeon, s. John, 2nd & Catharine, b. Jan. 1, 1742/3	2	359
Susannah, d. John, b. Aug. 22, 1682	1	20
Thankfull, d. John, Jr. (s. Anthony), b. May 25, 1711	2	48

	Vol.	Page
HOSKINS, HOSKINES, (cont.)		
Thomas, m. wid. Elisabeth **BIRG**, Apr. 20, [ ]	MG	
Thomas, m. Elizabeth **BIRG**, wid., b. of Windsor, Apr. 20, 1653	Col.2	159
Thomas, d. Apr. 13, 1666	MG	
Thomas, d. Apr. 13, 1666	Col.1	55
Thomas, d. Apr. 13, 1666	1	45
Thomas, s. [Anthony & Jesabel], b. Mar. 14, 1672	MG	
Thomas, s. Anthony, b. Mar. 14, 1672	1	19
Thomas, had 1 child b. in Windsor. Dated Aug. 17, 1677	MG	
Thomas, s. John, b. May 21, 1693	1	20
Thomas, m. Elizabeth **MILLS**, Feb. 23, 1698/9	1	58
Thomas, s. Thomas, b. July 1, 1703	1	21
Thomas, s. Thomas, d. Aug. 2, 1718	2	239
Thomas, of Windsor, m. Elenor **WARNER**, of Suffield, June 28, 1719	2	162
Thomas, s. Thomas, s. John, b. Sept. 3, 1719	2	49
Thomas, m. Lydia **LOOMIS**, b. of Windsor, Dec.* 17, 1729 *("Nov." crossed out)	2	162
Thomas, d. Aug. 1, 1737	2	240
Thomas, s. John & Thankfull, b. Sept. 8, 1737	2	52
Thomas, m. Margret **FILLEY**, b. of Windsor, Apr. 15, 1760	2	164
Timothy, s. Alexander & Mindwell, b. Dec. 21, 1744	2	359
Zebulun, s. Anthony, Jr., b. May 6, 1696	2	46
Zebulon, of Windsor, m. Lois **MOORE**, of Simsbury, Aug. 1, 1727	2	162
Zebulon, s. Zebulon & Lois, b. Mar. 5, 1728	2	51
Zebulon, s. Zebulon, Jr. & Mary, b. Oct. 17, 1758	2	363
-----, wid., d. Mar. 6, 1662	Col.1	55
-----, wid., d. [ ], [16]70	MG	
HOSMER, Maria, of Granby, m. Arly **GRANDER,** of East Windsor, Jan. 30, 1825, by Rev. Phinehas Cook	2	161
HOUGH, Levi, of Glastonbury, m. Emaly **HUBBARD,** of Windsor, Oct. 18, 1830, by John Bartlett	2	484
HOUSE, Hulah P., m. Elihu **PHELPS,** b. of Windsor, Dec. 31, 1843, by Rev. S. W. Scofield	2	501
Jehiel, m. Eunice C. **WINCHEL,** b. of Windsor, Jan. 13, 1839, by Rev. Cephas Brainard	2	483
Julia O., m. Charles S. **BEMENT,** b. of Windsor, July 23, 1839, by Rev. Cephas Brainard	2	465
Louisa, m. Lorin **FOX,** b. of Windsor, June 12, 1839, by Rev. Cephas Brainard	2	477
William, of Manchester, m. Catherine **HOLCOMB,** Oct. 16, 1842, by Rev. David L. Marks	2	483
HOUT, [see also **HOYT**], Mary, m. Luke **HILL,** May 6, 1651	MG	
Mary, m. Luke **HILL,** May 6, 1651	1	57
HOW, Cyrus, m. Sally **PHELPS,** Feb. 7, 1830, by Rev. Asa Bushnell, Jr.	2	484

	Vol.	Page
HOWARD, HOWART, [see also HAYWARD], Abigail, d.		
William E. & Abigail, b. Apr. 10, 1835	2	54
Abigail, d. William E. & Abigail, d. Apr. 28, 1840	2	244
Abigail, w. William, d. Sept. 10, 1845, ae 58 y. 6 m.	2	244
Anne, d. Nathaniel & Anne, b. June 4, 1785; d. July 15, 1787	2	565
Anne, d. Nathaniel &Anne, d. July 15, 1787	2	244
Anne, wid. Nathaniel, d. July 14, 1833, ae 84	2	243
Anne Watson, d. Nathaniel, Jr. & Nancey, b. Dec. 7, 1801	2	54
Elizabeth, d. William E. & Abigail, b. Mar. 1, 1837	2	54
Ephraim, s. Ephraim, bp. Jan. 11, 1656	1	19
Ephraim, m. Abigail NUBERY, Jan. 8, 1684	1	58
George, s. Nathaniel & Anne, b. Jan. 23, 1787	2	565
George, of Windsor, m. Sarah TRUMBULL, of East		
Windsor, May 28, 1810	2	482
George, s. George & Sarah, d. Mar. 20, 1819	2	244
George, s. George & Sarah, b. Nov. 15, 1819	2	53
George, m. Eliza BENTON, June 18, 1844, by Rev. Shubael		
Bartlett	2	508
Hester, d. Robert, b. June 8, 1651	Col.2	154
Hester, d. Robert, d. Dec. 5, 1657	1	46
John, s. Nathaniel & Anne, b. May 29, 1779	2	565
John, s. Nathaniel & Anne, d. Mar. 25, 1819	2	244
Julia Trumbull, d. George & Sarah, b. Mar. 11, 1811	2	53
Lucy, w. William (d. of Roger ELLSWORTH), d. Mar. 28,		
1828	2	244
Lucy Ann, d. William & Lucy, b. Oct. 12, 1815; d. Nov. 4,		
1816	2	53
Lucy Ann, d. William E. & Abigail, b. Jan. 10, 1831	2	54
Lida, d. May 4, [16]76	MG	
Lydia, d. May 4, 1676	1	45
Mary, m. William MITCHELSON, Apr. 26, 1713	2	176
Mary, d. Nathaniel, Jr. & Nancey, b. Oct. 14, 1805	2	54
Mary, d. Nathaniel, Jr. & Nancy, d. Oct. 14, 1805	2	244
Mary Ann, d. George & Sarah, b. Nov. 5, 1814	2	53
Nath[an], s. Nathaniell & Anne, d. Feb. 16, 1809, at St. Lucia	2	244
Nathaniel, of Windsor, m. Anna WATSON, of East Windsor,		
Apr. 26, 1776. Mar. 25, 1773* *(Two date are so		
written in copy)	2	164
Nathaniel, s. Nathaniel & Anne, b. Apr. 26, 1777	2	565
Nathaniel, Jr., of Windsor, m. Nancey VIBBERT, of		
Hartford, Nov. 30, 1800	2	482
Nathaniel, s. Nathaniel, Jr. & Nancy, b. Aug. 7, 1807	2	53
Nathaniel, s. Nathanie, Jr. & Nancy, d. Jan. 17, 1809	2	244
Nathaniel, s. William & Lucy, b. July 1, 1813	2	53
Nathaniel, d. June 3, 1819	2	244
Nathaniel, of Windsor, m. Sarah H. BLACKMAN, of		
Springfield, Sept. 24, 1835	2	482
Nathaniel Watson, s. Nathaniel & Sarah, b. Aug. 24, 1836	2	54

	Vol.	Page

HOWARD, HOWART, (cont.)

Rebeckah, d. Robert, b. Aug. 17, 1648	Col.2	154
Robert, d. Aug. 23, 1684	1	46
Robert, s. Ephraim, d. Nov. 9, 1685	1	46
Sarah, d. Robert, b. Nov. 1, 1644	1	19
Sarah, w. George, d. Sept. 24, 1839, at Staten Island	2	244
Sarah Harper, d. George & Sarah, b. May 30, 1817	2	53
Taphath, d. Robert, b. Jan. 1, 1646	Col.2	154
Taphat, d. Robert, b. [ ] 1, 1646	1	19
William, s. Nathaniel & Anne, b. July 6, 1781	2	565
William, m. Lucy **ELLSWORTH**, [ ], 1803, by Henry A. Rowland (crossed out)	2	164
William, m. Lucy **ELLSWORTH**, b. of Windsor, Apr. 8, 1805	2	482
William, m. Abigail **DRAKE**, Nov. 15, 1829, by Henry A. Rowland	2	484
William E., s. William & Lucy, b. Apr. 4, 1808	2	53
William E., m. Abigail E. **ALLYN**, May 17, 1831, by H. A. Rowland	2	485

HOWLET, Eleazer, of Hartford, m. Rhoda **GRIDLEY**, of Windsor, Jan. 11, 1827, by Rev. Tobias Spicer, of Hartford | 2 | 166

HOYT, HAYT, HAYTE, HOITE, [see also **HOUT**], Benjamin, s.

Simon, b. Feb. 2, 1644	1	19
Daniell, s. [Nicolas & Susana], b. Apr. 10, 1653; d. [ ]	MG	
Daniel, s. Nicholos, b. Apr. 10, 1653	1	19
Daniel, s. Nicholos, b. Apr. 10, 1653	1	21
Daniel, s. Nickholas, b. Apr. 10, 1653	Col.2	154
Daniell, d. [ ], [16]53	MG	
Daniell, s. Nicholas, d. July 15, 1655	Col.2	160
Daniel, of Springfield, m. Irene **ANDREWS**, of Hartford, Feb. 22, 1843, by S. D. Jewett	2	476
Daniel, s. Nicholas, d. July 15, [ ]	1	45
Dauid, s. [Nicolas & Susana], b. Apr. 22, 1651	MG	
David, s. Nickholas, b. Apr. 22, 1651	Col.2	154
David, s. Nicholos, b. Apr. 22, 1651	1	18
David, s. Nicholos, b. Apr. 22, 1651	1	19
Goode, "old", d. [ ], [16]44	MG	
John, s. Walter, b. July 13, 1644	1	19
Jonathan, s. [Nicolas & Susana], b. June 7, 1649	MG	
Jonathan, s. Nickholas, b. June 7, 1649	Col.2	154
Jonathan, s. Nicholos, b. June 7, 1649	1	19
Jonathan, s. Nicholos, b. June 7, 1649	1	21
Nicholas, m. Susanna **JOYSE**, June 12, 1646	1	57
Nicolas, m. Susana **JOYCE**, July 12, 1646	MG	
Nicolas, d. [ ], [16]55	MG	
Nicolas, his w. [ ], d. [ ], [16]55	MG	
Nicolas, his w. [ ], d. July 4, 1655	Col.2	160

	Vol.	Page
HOYT, HAYT, HAYTE, HOITE, (cont.)		
Nicholas, his w. [ ], d. [ ]; bd. July 4, 1655	1	45
Nicholas, d. July 7, 1655	Col.2	160
Nicolas, had 4 children b. in Windsor. Dated Aug. 17, 1677	MG	
Samuel, s. Nicholos, b. Mar. 1, 1647	1	18
Samuell, s. [Nicolas & Susana], b. May 1, 1647	MG	
Samuel, s. Nicholos, b. May 1, 1647	1	21
Samuel, s. Nickholas, b. May 7, 1647	Col.2	154
Simon, had 2 children b. in Windsor. Dated Aug. 17, 1677	MG	
Walter, had 3 children b. in Windsor. Dated Aug. 17, 1677	MG	
-----, his child d. [ ], [16]47	MG	
HUBBARD, [see also **HULBARD**], Abigail, m. Jonathan GILLET, Jr., b. of Windsor, Dec. 11,1740	2	157
Abigail, d. Nathaniell & Mary, b. Sept. 24, 1758	2	363
Agness, d. John & Hannah, b. July 2, 1752	2	366
Anna Sophia, of Windsor, m. Edward **MEADCALF**, of East Hartford, Mar. 25, 1824, by Rev. John Bartlett. Int. Pub.	2	494
Asa, s. Nathaniel & Mary, b. Mar. 16, 1753	2	363
Deidemia, d. John & Hannah, b. Apr. 17, 1754	2	366
Emaly, of Windsor, m. Levi **HOUGH**, of Glastonbury, Oct. 18, 1830, by John Bartlett	2	484
Frederick, m. Rebecca **BROWN**, b. of Windsor, Sept. 12, 1820, by James Goodwin, J. P.	2	165
Hannah, m. Jonathan **BIDWELL**, b. of Windsor, Aug. 7, 1740	2	132
Hannah, d. John, Jr. & Hannah, b. Nov. 16, 1746	2	360
Hannah, wid., m. Jonathan **PALMER**, b. of Windsor, Jan. 19, 1764	2	189
Harriet, of Windsor, m. Edwin C. **VINING**, of Simsbury, Dec. 11, 1831, by Rev. Ansel Nash	2	511
Hector, m. Elisa **WILSON**, b. of Windsor, Mar. 4, 1822, by Rev. John Bartlett. Int. Pub.	2	165
Jeremiah, m. Abigail **DROWN**, Feb. 12, 1832, by Rev. Edwin E. Griswold	2	485
Joab, s. John, Jr. & Hannah, b. Aug. 16, 1758	2	366
Joab, 2nd, of Windsor, m. Almira **WHITING**, of Hartford, May 9, 1822, by Rev. Augustus Bolles, of Wintonbury	2	165
Joab H., m. Fidelia **CADWELL**, b. of Windsor, May 18, 1831, by Rev. Augustus Bolles	2	485
John, s. John & Hannah, b. Dec. 28, 1748	2	361
Lamitha, of Windsor, m. Edward **PHELPS**, of Simsbury, Nov. 28, 1822, by Rev. John Bartlett. Int. Pub.	2	191
Mariah, m. Edward **FRANCIS**, b. of Windsor, Nov. 18, 1823, by Rev. John Bartlett, of Wintonbury. Int. Pub.	2	476
Mary, d. Nathaniel & Mary, b. Aug. 17, 1755	2	363
Nathaniel, s. Nathaniell, b. Oct., 24, 1750	2	361

	Vol.	Page

HUBBARD, (cont.)

Nathaniel, Jr., m. Sarah **HUBBARD**, b. of Windsor, Aug. 27, 1828, by Rev. John Bartlett, of Wintonbury	2	484
Oliver, s. John, Jr. & Hannah, b. Apr. 16, 1761	2	367
Sally, of Windsor, m. Oliver C. **PHELPS**, of Simsbury, Jan. 1, 1822, by Rev. John Bartlett. Int. Pub.	2	191
Sally, of Windsor, m. James **SMITH**, of Morrisvill, N. Y., June 15, 1824, by Luther Fitch, J. P. Int. Pub.	2	202
Sarah, m. Nathaniel **HUBBARD**, Jr., b. of Windsor, Aug. 27, 1828, by Rev. John Bartlett, of Wintonbury	2	484
Timothy, s. John, Jr. & Hannah, b. Dec. 5, 1750	2	362
Trumble, m. Julia Ann **MILLS**, May 12, 1831, by Henry A. Rowland	2	485
Trumble, m. Julia Ann **MILLS**, May 12, 1831, by Henry A. Rowland	2	485
------, Lieut., his child d. [ ], in "Elenton" prior to 1740	MG	
------, Lieut., had 2 children d. [ ], in "Elenton" prior to 1740	MG	

HUDSON, William, of Hartford, m. Anna **MILLER**, of Windsor, May 15, 1832, by Rev. Ansel Nash | 2 | 485 |

HUIT, [see under **HEWITT**]

HULBARD, [see also **HUBBARD** & **HURLBURT**], John, d. Aug. 25, [1639] | MG | |

William, had 2 children b. in Windsor. Dated Aug. 17, 1677	MG	

HULL, Elisabeth, d. [Josias & Elisabeth], b. Feb. 18, 1646 | MG | |

Elizabeth, d. Josiah, b. Feb. 18, 1646	1	40
Elisabeth, m. Samuell **GAYLAR**, Dec. 4, 1646	MG	
Elizabeth, m. Samuell **GAYLORD**, Dec. 4, 1646	1	56
Elisabeth, m. Osrell **DEBLE**, Nov. 28, 1661	MG	
Elizabeth, m. Israel **DIBLE**, b. of Windsor, Nov. 28, 1661	1	55
George, s. [Josias & Elisabeth], b. Apr. 28, 1662; d. [ ]	MG	
Georg[e], s. Josias, b. Apr. 28, [16]62	Col.1	54
George, s. Josiah, b. Apr. 28, [16]62; bp. May 4, [ ]	1	40
John, s. [Josias & Elisabeth], b. Dec. 17, 1644	MG	
John, s. Josiah, b. Dec. 17, 1644	1	40
John, s. Josiah, b. Dec. 27, 1644	1	18
Joseph, s. [Josias & Elisabeth], b. Aug. 10, 1652	MG	
Joseph, s. Josiah, bp. Aug. 15, 1652	1	40
Josias, m. Elisabeth **LOOMYS**, May 20, 1641	MG	
Josias, m. Elizabeth **LOOMIS**, May 20, 1641	1	57
Josias, s. [Josias & Elisabeth], b. Sept. [ ], 1642; d. [ ]	MG	
Josias, d. Nov. 16, [16]75	MG	
Josias, had 10 children b. in Windsor. Dated Aug. 17, 1677	MG	
Martha, d. [Josias & Elisabeth], b. June 10, 1650	MG	
Martha, d. Josiah, b. June 10, 1650	1	40
Mary, d. [Josias & Elisabeth], b. Oct. 2, 1648	MG	
Mary, d. Josiah, bp. Oct. 8, 1648	1	40

	Vol.	Page
HULL, (cont.)		
Mary, m. John **GRANT**, Aug. 2, 1666	MG	
Mary, m. John **GRANT**, Aug. 2, 1666, by Mr. Clark	Col.1	45
Mary, m. John **GRANT**, Aug. 2, 1666, by Mr. Clark	1	57
Mary, m. Houmfery **PINNE**, [ ], in Dorchester	MG	
Naomy, d. [Josias & Elisabeth], b. Feb. 17, 1656	MG	
Naomy, d. Josias, b. Feb. 17, 1656	Col.2	161
Naomi, d. Josiah, b. Feb. 17, 1656	1	40
Naomy, m. Thomas **BURNAM**, Jr., Jan. 4, 1676, at Killingworth	MG	
Naomy, m. Thomas **BURNAM**, Jr., Jan. 4, 1676, at Killingworth, by Edward Griswold	Col.1	46
Naomy, m. Thomas **BURNAM**, Jr., Jan. 4, 1676, at Killingworth, by E. Griswold	TR1	1
Naomi, m. Thomas **BURNHAM**, Jr., Jan. 4, 1676, at Killingsworth, by [ ] Griswold	1	54
Rebeca, d. [Josias & Elisabeth], b. Aug. 10, 1659	MG	
Rebekah, d. Josiah, b. Aug. 10, 1659	1	40
Sarah, d. Josias, b. Apr. 9, 1654	Col.2	158
Sara, d. [Josias & Elisabeth], b. Aug. 9, 1654	MG	
Sarah, d. Josiah, b. Aug. 9, 1654	1	40
Thomas, s. [Josias & Elisabeth], b. May 29, 1665	MG	
Thomas, s. Josiah, bp. July 30, [16]65; b. 9 wks before at Homenosset	1	39
Timothy, had 6 children b. in Windsor. Dated Aug. 17, 1677	MG	
HULSE, Persilla, m. Benjamin **OSBAND**, b. of Windsor, June 11, 1720	2	184
HUMASON, Jane M., m. Daniel **SAWN**, b. of Windsor, [ ] 31, [ ], by Rev. Francis L. Robins, of Enfield	2	509
HUMPHREY, HUMPHRY, HOMFRY, HUMPHRIS, OMFERY, OUMPHERY, HUMFERY, Abigayl, d. [Micall & Prissilla], b. Mar. 23, 1665	MG	
Abigail, d. Michal, b. Mar. 23, [16]65	1	19
Abigail, d. Micall, b. Mar. 23, [16]65/6	Col.1	55
Abigail, d. Thomas & Abigail, d. Sept. 20, 1736	2	242
Abigail, d. Thomas & Abigail, b. Dec. 12, 1738	2	364
Abijah, s. Thomas & Abigail, b. Aug. 23, 1740	2	365
Anna, d. Thomas & Abigail, b. Feb. 26, 1736/7	2	364
Annis, m. Oliver **FILLEY**, May 8, 1805	2	153
Benajah, m. Olive **GOODWIN**, of Simsbury, May 4, 1831, by John Bartlett	2	485
Chloe, m. Moses **COSSITT**, Apr. 15, 1835, by Rev. Ansel Nash	2	471
Daniel, s. Thomas & Abigail, b. Nov. 13, 1754	2	365
Daniel, s. Petcey, b. Aug. 12, 1797	2	566
Flona*, of Farmington, m. Roswel **GRIDLEY**, of Windsor, Sept. 1, [ ], by Rev. John Bartlett, of Wintonbury. Int. Pub. *("Flora?")	2	160

	Vol.	Page

HUMPHREY, HUMPHRY, HOMFRY, HUMPHRIS,
OMFERY, OUMPHERY, HUMFERY, (cont.)

	Vol.	Page
Hanna, d. [Micall & Prissilla], b. Oct. 21, 1669	MG	
Hannah, d. Michal, b. Oct. 21, [16]69	1	19
John, s. [Micall & Prissilla], b. June 7, 1650	MG	
John, s. Michal, b. June 7, 1650	Col.2	154
John, s. Michal, b. June 7, 1650	1	19
Josiah, s. Thomas & Abigail, b. July 12, 1749	2	365
Lucy, d. Thomas & Abigail, b. Aug. 13, 1746	2	365
Malissa, of Farmington, m. Orson WELLS, of Simsbury, Aug. 21, 1822, by John Bartlett. Int. Pub.	2	512
Martha, d. [Micall & Prissilla], b. Oct. 5, 1663	MG	
Martha, d. Mical, b. Oct. 5, [16]63	Col.1	54
Martha, d. Michal, b. Oct. 5, 1663	1	19
Mary, d. [Micall & Prissilla], b. Oct. 24, 1653	MG	
Mary, d. Michal, b. Oct. 24, 1653	1	19
Mary, d. Thomas & Abigail, b. Dec. 13, 1743	2	365
Mary, d. Micall, m. John LEWEIC, of Windsor, June 16, 1675, at Hartford, by Capt. John Allyen	Col.1	46
Micall, m. Prissilla GRANT, Oct. 14, 1647	MG	
Michael, m. Priscilla GRANT, Oct. 14, 1647	1	57
Mical, had 7 children b. in Windsor. Dated Aug. 17, 1677	MG	
Petcey, had s. Daniel, b. Aug. 12, 1797	2	566
Samuell, s. [Micall & Prissilla], b. May 15, 1656	MG	
Samuell, s. Michael, b. May 15, 1656	Col.2	161
Samuel, s. Michal, b. May 15, 1656	1	19
Sara, d. [Micall & Prissilla], b. Mar. 6, 1658	MG	
Sara, d. Mical, b. Mar. 6, [16]58	Col.1	54
Sarah, d. Michal, b. Mar. 6, 1658	1	19
Susannah, d. Thomas & Abigail, b. [ ]	2	365

HUNT, Ann, of Enfield, m. Benjamin GRANT, of Windsor, Feb. 10, 1737

	Vol.	Page
	2	156
Elizabeth, m. James I. YOUNGS, b. of Windsor, Jan. 10, 1843, by Rev. S. W. Scofield	2	517
Harriet N., of Northampton, m. James R. MOORE, of Windsor, Dec. 1, 1850, by A. T. Leete	2	493
Martha, m. James YOUNGS, b. of Windsor, Apr. 27, 1834, by Rev. David Miller	2	213
Melinda, of Windsor, m. Samuel BRUNSON, of Hartford, Nov. 20, 1837, by Eli Deniston	2	490
William, Jr., m. Roxa GREEN, b. of Windsor, Dec. 31, 1828, by John B. Ballard	2	484

HUNTINGTON, Christopher, had 1 child b. in Windsor. Dated Aug. 17, 1677

	Vol.	Page
	MG	
Eunice, d. Rev. Nathaniell & Jerusha, b. Oct. 5, 1754	2	363
Hannah, m. Joseph ROCKWELL, Jr., Nov. 11 or 15, 1714	2	194
Jerusha, d. Rev. Nathaniell & Jerusha, b. Apr. 30, 1753	2	363
Joseph W., of Lancaster, Mass., m. Julia MILLER, of		

	Vol.	Page
JESS, (cont.)		
Dated Aug. 17, 1677	MG	
JESTS, [see also **JESS**], William, of Wethersfield, m. Betsy		
ALLYN, July 10, 1823, by Rev. Henry A. Rowland	2	485
JEWETT, [see also **SEWETT**], Jeremiah P., of Lowell, Mass., m.		
Harriet E. **LOOMIS**, of Windsor, May 27, 1841, by S.		
D. Jewett	2	486
JOHNS, Alexander, m. Anna M. **ELLSWORTH**, b. of Windsor,		
Mar. 30, 1834, by Rev. Ansel Nash	2	168
JOHNSON, **JONSON**, Chauncey R., m. Rhoda **WEBSTER**, b. of		
Avon, Jan. 9, [1830 (?)], by John Bartlett	2	486
James M., of Havana, N. Y., m. Lydia A. **HALL**, of		
Worcester, Mass., Oct. 22, 1848, by Rev. S. H. Allen	2	462
L. F., m. Susan Jane **PINNEY**, b. of Windsor, June 2, 1852,		
by Rev. Ralph N. Bowles	2	462
Richard, d. Aug. 30, 1687	1	46
----, of Harwinton, m. Sarah **WELLS**, of Farmington, Aug.		
22, 1827, by Rev. John Bartlett	2	486
JONES, [see also **JANES**], Keziah, d. David & Keziah, b. Dec.		
20, 1782	2	369
JONKINS, Elazer, of Winchester, Va., m. Eliza **HITCHCOCK**, of		
Windsor, Mar. 29, 1821, by Rev. John Bartlett. Int.		
Pub.	2	485
JOY, Levi, of Amherst, Mass., m. Melinda **HAYDEN**, Dec. 29,		
1829, by Henry A. Rowland	2	486
Philo, of Amherst, Mass., m. Mary A. **MALLORY**, of		
Windsor, Nov. 15, 1835, by Rev. Daniel Heminway	2	169
JOYCE, **JOICE**, **JOYS**, **JOYSE**, Abigail, d. William, b. Jan. 31,		
1644	1	21
Esther, d. William & Eunice, b. Oct. 22, 1758	2	369
Susanna, m. Nicholas **HOYT**, June 12, 1646	1	57
Susana, m. Nicolas **HAYT**, July 12, 1646	MG	
JUDD, **JUDG**, Mary, m. as 2nd w. Thomas **LOOMYS**, Jan. 1,		
1662	MG	
Mary, of Ffarmingtown, m. Thomas **LOMAS**, of Windsor,		
Jan. 1, [16]62, at Hartford, by Mr. Willes	Col.1	45
Mary, m. Thomas **LOOMIS**, Jan. 1, 1662, by Mr. Willis	1	58
Mary, see Mary **LOOMYS**	Col.D	56
JUDSON, Catherine P., m. Samuel **BURNHAM**, Oct. 19, 1840, by		
S. D. Jewett	2	475
JUPSON, Elizabeth, of West Springfield, m. Samuel **WIGHT**, of		
Windsor, Nov. 4, 1849, by Cephas Brainard	2	516
KEENY, [see also **KENNY**], Greenleaf, of Manchester, m. Mary		
Jane **FISH**, of Windsor, Apr. 22, 1840, by Rev. S. D.		
Jewett	2	485
Marcy, m. Remembrance **SHELDON**, b. of Windsor, Mar.		
17, 1762	2	201
Sheldon, Jr., of Winchester, m. Eliza A. **PHELPS**, of		

	Vol.	Page
KEENY, (cont.)		
Windsor, Nov. 25, 1846/7, by Rev. Cephus Brainard	2	462
KELLOGG, Margret, m. Nathan **WEBB**, b. of Windsor, Mar. 20,		
1755	2	209
Shirley, m. Lydia **GRISWOLD**, b. of Windsor, Feb. 19,		
1832, by Rev. Ansel Nash	2	168
KELSEY, KELCY, KELSIE, KELCEY, CALLSEY, KELCIE,		
CALSEY, Abigail, d. William, b. Dec. 10, 1694	1	21
Abigail, m. Ebenezer **WATSON**, b. of Windsor, Apr. 1, 1703	1	63
Abigael, w. Mark, d. Mar. 28, 1713	2	245
Almira, of Windsor, m. Harlow **WELLS**, of Farmington, Oct.		
22, 1823, by Rev. Augustus Bolles, of Wintonbury	2	211
Damaras, of Hartford, m. Asahel **DRAKE**, of Windsor, Feb.		
7, 1744/5	2	142
Elizabeth, m. Josiah **LOOMIS**, Jan. 22, 1707/8	2	170
Elizabeth, wid., d. Jan. 31, 1725/6	2	245
Easther, of Hartford, m. Seth **LOOMIS**, of Windsor, Mar. 1,		
1747/8	2	173
Hannah, d. Thomas, b. June 6, 1707	2	54
Hannah, d. Thomas & Hannah, b. Sept. 27, 1726	2	55
Jerusha, of Hartford, m. Jeremiah **FYLER**, of Windsor, June		
29, 1738	2	151
Joanna, d. William, b. Nov. 14, 1696	1	21
Joanna, m. Josiah **COOK**, b. of Windsor, June 5, 1718	2	135
John, s. Mark, d. June 18, 1685	1	46
John, s. Marke, d. June 18, 1685	Col.D	56
Mabel, d. Thomas, b. June 9, 1712	2	54
Mark, m. Rebekah **HOSKINS**, b. of Windsor, Mar. 8, 1658/9	1	58
Mark, had 1 child b. in Windsor. Dated Aug. 17, 1677	MG	
Mark, m. Abigail **ATTWOOD**, [ ], 1683	Col.D	54
Mark, m. Abigail **ATWOOD**, Dec. 26, 1683	1	58
Mary, m. Jonathan **GILLET**, Jr., Apr. 23, 1661	MG	
Mary, of Hartford, m. Jonathan **GILLIT**, Jr., of Windsor,		
Apr. 23, 1661	1	57
Rachel, m. Thomas **ELGER**, Dec. 22, 1714	2	145
Rebekah, d. Mark, b. Jan. 2, 1659	1	21
Rebeckah, m. Nathan **MESSENGER**, Apr. 5, 1678	Col.D	54
Rebekah, m. Nathan **MESSENGER**, Apr. 5, 1678	1	59
Rebeccah, w. Mark, d. Aug. 28, 1683	Col.D	56
Rebekah, w. Mark, d. Aug. 28, 1683	1	46
Rebeckah, d. Thomas, b. Jan. 10, 1709/10	2	54
Rebekah, of Windsor, m. Hezekiah **LANE**, formerly of Rye,		
N. Y., now of Windsor, Oct. 29, 1730	2	171
Ruth, d. William, b. Jan. 16, 1698	1	21
Ruth, d. William, d. May 9, 1700	1	46
Ruth, d. Thomas, b. Jan. 10, 1704/5	2	54
Ruth, d. Jan. 1, 1724/5	2	245
Ruth, d. Thomas & Hannah, b. Jan. 30, 1724/5	2	54

	Vol.	Page
KELSEY, KELCY, KELSIE, KELCEY, CALLSEY, KELCIE, CALSEY, (cont.)		
Thomas, s. Thomas, b. July 10, 1701	2	54
Thomas, d. May 9, 1715	2	245
Thomas, of Windsor, m. Hannah **DUGLES**, of New London, Dec. 11, 1723	2	167
Thomas, s. Thomas & Hannah, b. Nov. 6, 1729	2	55
William, m. Abigail **WHITTCOMB**, b. of Windsor, Mar. 23, 1694/5	1	58
William, d. Nov. 8, 1698	1	46
[KENNEDY], **KANADY**, Andrew, s. Thomas & Martha, b. Jan. 2, 1745/6	2	369
Margaret, d. Thomas & Martha, b. Nov. 15, 1740	2	369
Thomas, s. Thomas & Martha, b. Feb. 23, 1742/3	2	369
KENNY, [see also **KEENY**], Ellen, of Suffield, m. Nathaniel **BODINE**, of New Jersey, Apr. 21, 1850, by Rev. Samuel Warren Law	2	504
KENT, Martin, of Suffield, O., m. Lorenda **HATHEWAY**, of Windsor, June 16, 1825, by Rev. Augustus Bolles, of Wintonbury	2	168
Mercey, of Suffield, m. Aaron **PHELPS**, of Windsor, Aug. 13, 1742	2	188
KEONSAN, Phillip, m. Bridget **O'DONALL**, [ ], [1852], by Rev. James Smyth	2	460
KIMBALL, KIMBAL, Benjamin, twin with Joseph, s. Andrew & Benjamin, b. Aug. 1, 1761	2	370
Daniel, s. Andrew & Elizabeth, b. Apr. 4, 1755	2	370
Joseph, twin with Benjamin, s. Andrew & Benjamin, b. Aug. 1, 1761	2	370
Luke, s. Andrew & Elizabeth, b. Sept. 7, 1757	2	55
Luke, s. Andrew & Elizabeth, b. Sept. 7, 1757	2	370
KING, Abial, of Suffield, m. Melincha **LOOMIS**, of Windsor, May 12, 1841, by Rev. S. D. Jewett	2	169
Alexander, s. Zebulon & Keziah, b. Dec. 6, 1749	2	370
Augustus, s. Titus & Mindwell, b. July 18, 1764	2	371
Caroline, d. Zebulon & Keziah, b. Mar. 6, 1752	2	370
Charles, of Hartford, m. Maria C. **OLMSTED**, of Windsor, June 17, 1850, by Rev. T. A. Leete	2	169
Charlotte, m. Nelson **PASCO**, Feb. 1, 1827, by Rev. Henry A. Rowland	2	193
Cinthia, of West Hartford, m. Truman **GRIDLEY**, of Farmington, June 27, 1820, by Rev. John Bartlett, of Wintonbury	2	479
George, s. Timothy & Sarah, b. Jan. 25, 1754	2	370
Huldah, d. Titus & Mindwell, b. Aug. 6, 1766	2	371
Huldah, of East Windsor, m. Asa **MOORE**, of Windsor, Nov. 1, 1790	2	180
Jerusha, d. Zebulon & Keziah, b. Dec. 9, 1747	2	370

	Vol.	Page
LADD, (cont.)		
Zuriviah, m. Joel **NASH,** b. of Windsor, June 11, 1754	2	183
LAIHAY, Thomas P., of Manchester, m. Mary R. **PIKE,** of East		
Hartford, Mar. 14, 1848, by Samuel A. Seaman	2	491
LALLY, Honora, m. Michael **COSTO,** Sept. 7, 1852, by Rev.		
James Smyth	2	460
LAMBERSON, [see also **LAMBERTON**], Richard S., m.		
Elizabeth **PARMELE,** b. of Suffield, Sept. 20, 1852, by		
Rev. S. H. Allen	2	492
LAMBERT, Belinda, of Windsor, m. Hannebal **TAYLOR,** of		
Fowler, O., June 2, 1850, by Rev. T. A. Leet	2	206
LAMBERTON, [see also **LAMBERSON**], Malissa L., of		
Windsor, m. Austin **SIGLUR,** of Fowler, O., May 13,		
1849, by Rev. Cephus Brainard	2	514
Nathaniel, s. Obed & Elizabeth, b. Oct. 14, 1749	2	380
Obed, m. Elisabeth **TAYLOR,** b. of Windsor, Aug. 27, 1747	2	173
Obed, s. Obed & Elisabeth, b. Nov. 2, 1747	2	380
Sarah, of Windsor, m. Harvey **BISSELL,** of East Windsor,		
Nov. 8, 1822, by Rev. Henry A. Rowland	2	468
William, m. Aulia **SKINNER,** b. of Windsor, Aug. 5, 1822,		
by Joseph H. Russell, J. P.	2	488
LAMSON, Asubath, m. Josua **WELLES,** May 5, 1670, by Capt.		
Newbery	MG	
Asubath, m. Josua **WELLS,** May 5, 1670, by Capt. Newbery	Col.1	46
Azubah, see Josua **WELLS**	Col.1	58
LANE, Hezekiah, formerly of Rye, N. Y., now of Windsor, m.		
Rebeckah **KELCY,** of Windsor, Oct. 29, 1730	2	171
Samuel, m. Abigael **HUSSY,** b. of Suffield, Oct. 6, 1709.		
Witnesses: John Kent, Jr. & Benjamin King. Int. Pub.	2	169
LATHAM, Henry, m. Harriet **PORTER,** b. of Windsor Locks, Jan.		
5, 1851, by Rev. S. H. Allen	2	491
Lucia, of Windsor, m. Lewis **COOK,** of Hartford, Nov. 6,		
1836, by Rev. Eli Deniston	2	513
Maria, m. Hiram **HOLCOMB,** Mar. 27, 1827, by Rev. Henry		
A. Rowland	2	167
LATHROP, LOTHROP, LOTHRUP, Abigail, of Hartford, m.		
Capt. Thomas **STOUGHTON,** of Windsor, May 19,		
1697	1	62
Ann R., of Middletown, m. Elihu **ROBERTS,** of Windsor,		
Dec. 6, 1826, by Rev. Henry A. Rowland	2	196
Cynthia L., m. Stillman F. **WHITMAN,** b. of Windsor, Mar.		
28, 1852, by Rev. S. H. Allen	2	520
Elizabeth, Mrs. of Tolland, m. Simon **CHAPMAN,** of		
Windsor, Dec. 2, 1736	2	136
Mary, m. Walter **HENDERSON,** b. of Windsor, June 23,		
1742	2	163
Mehitable, of Norwich, m. Thomas **STOUGHTON,** Jr., of		
Windsor, Oct. 3, 1722	2	198

	Vol.	Page
LATHROP, LOTHROP, LOTHRUP, (cont.)		
William, m. Lucy I. WARD, May 15, 1849, by Rev. S. H.		
Allen	2	491
LATIMER, LATTEMORE, Abigail, m. Benoni CLARK, b. of		
Windsor, Apr. 12, 1759	2	137
Aholiab, s. Bazaleel & Elizabeth, b. Sept. 1, 1762	2	386
Christian, d. Bezaleel & Elizabeth, b. June 19, 1760	2	386
Ebenezer, s. Bezaleel & Elizabeth, d. Oct. 8, 1762	2	249
Ebenezer, Jr., m. Laura MILLS, Jan. 19, 1825, by Rev.		
Henry A. Rowland	2	489
Elihu, Jr., m. Triphena L. ROBERTS, b. of Wintonbury, Oct.		
17, 1834, by John Bartlett	2	489
Eliza, of Windsor, m. Luther PRAT[T], of Granby, Aug.		
30, 182[ ], by Rev. John Bartlett. Int. Pub.	2	190
Elizabeth, d. Bezaleel & Elizabeth, b. Dec. 1, 1755	2	385
Elizer, m. Betsey McLEAN, Nov. 15, 1830, by John Bartlett	2	174
George, s. Bezaleel & Elizabeth, b. Nov. 15, 1757	2	386
George, m. Eunice ROWLAND, Nov. 16, 1826, by Rev.		
Henry A. Rowland	2	174
Harvey, m. Almira WESTON, Apr. 11, [18], by Rev. Asa		
Bushnell, Jr.	2	175
Luceretia, m. James NEWBERRY, Jr., b. of Wintonbury,		
Oct. 1, 1834, by John Bartlett	2	184
Mahala, of Windsor, m. Roger ROWLEY, of Bennington, N.		
Y., Feb. 8, 1829, by John Bartlett	2	197
Mary Ann, m. Asahel H. NEARING, b. of Windsor, Oct.		
19, 1820, by Rev. John Bartlett. Int. Pub.	2	183
William, s. Barzilleel & Elizabeth, b. Sept. 30, 1773	2	390
LAWRENCE, Sarah, Mrs. of Groton, Mass., m. Rev. Joseph		
PERRY, of Windsor, Oct. 24, 1755	2	189
LAYTON, William, s. John, d. May 7, [16]77	MG	
William, s. John, d. May 7, 1677	Col.1	58
LEASON, Esther, of Enfield, m. Ephraim BANCROFT, of		
Windsor, Dec. 6, 1739	2	131
LEE, Abigail, d. Oliver & Abigail, b. Feb. 23, 1770	2	388
Anna Larg, d. Oliver & Abigail, b. May 30, 1777	2	388
Josiah, s. Oliver & Abigail, b. Dec. 7, 1772	2	388
Lemuel, s. Oliver & Abigail, b. July 23, 1774	2	388
Oliver, s. Oliver & Abigail, b. Apr. 15, 1778	2	388
LEET, Sarah, of Gilford, m. Eliakim MARSHALL, of Windsor,		
Aug. 23, 1704	2	175
LEFFINGWELL, Elisha, of Hartford, m. Caroline CHAPMAN, of		
Glastenbury, Feb. 22, 1821, by Rev. Coles Carpenter	2	488
LEVIT, [see also LOVETT], Hannah, m. Samuel DENSLOW, Jr.,		
b. of Windsor, May 24, 1756	2	143
LEWIS, LEWES, LUIS, LEWEIC, Ebenezer, m. Mrs. Elizabeth		
BAKER, July 25, 1838, by Cornelius B. Everest	2	490
Eliz[abeth], d. John, b. Mar. 6, 1681	Col.D	51

	Vol.	Page
LEWIS, LEWES, LUIS, LEWEIC, (cont.)		
Elizabeth, d. John, b. Mar. 6, 1681	1	23
Elizabeth, m. John **PHELPS,** Jan. 15, 1707/8	2	196
Fanny, of Windsor, m. Allen **ENO,** of Simsbury, May 21, 1823, by Richard Niles, J. P.	2	148
Hannah, m. Benjamin **BARBOR,** b. of Windsor, June 30, 1720	2	129
Jemima, of East Haddam, m. Samuel **WILSON,** of Windsor, May 9, 1723	2	208
John, s. John, b. Feb. 24, 1675	1	22
John, of Windsor, m. Mary **HUMPHREY,** d. Micall, June 16, 1675, by Capt. John Allyen, at Hartford	Col. 1	46
John, his s. [ ], d. May 10, [16]76	MG	
John, his s. [ ], d. May 10, 1676	Col. 1	58
John, had 1 child b. in Windsor. Dated Aug. 17, 1677	MG	
John, s. John, b. Feb. 1, 1693/4	1	24
John, Sr., d. Apr. 22, 1713	2	246
Joseph, m. Elizabeth **CASE,** Apr. 30, 1674, by Capt. Newbery	Col. 1	46
Marey, d. John, b. Dec. 18, [16]79	MG	
Mary, m. Jonathan **GILLET,** b. of Windsor, Dec. 17, 1731	2	156
Samuel, s. John, b. Aug. 6, 1677	MG	
Sarah, d. John, b. Mar. 6, 1683/4	Col.D	51
Sarah, d. John, b. Mar. 6, 1683/4	1	25
LINDSEY, LINSLEE, Jane C., m. Harris H. **MORAN,** Aug. 22, 1852, by Rev. H. N. Weed	2	494
John, of Toket, m. wid. Sarah **POND,** of Windsor, July 9, 1655	Col. 2	159
Vernon, m. Jane E. **GRISWOLD,** Dec. 9, 1846, by Rev. S. H. Allen, of Windsor Locks	2	491
LITTLE, [see also **LYTEL**], Horace B., m. Mary C. **HAWLEY,** Nov. 25, 1846, by Rev. S. H. Allen, of Windsor Locks	2	490
Mary, d. Thomas & Ann, b. May 14, 1728	2	373
LOOMIS, LOOMYS, LOOMAS, LOMAS, LOOMYES, Aaron, s. David, b. Sept. 5, 1696	1	24
Aaron, m. Deborah **EGELSTON,** b. of Windsor, Feb. 5, 1718/19	2	170
Aaron, s. Aaron, b. Jan. 30, 1722/3	2	61
Aaron, s. Charles & Constant, b. Mar. 21, 1768	2	387
Abba S., of Windsor, m. H. Sidney **HAYDEN,** of Charleston, S. C., Aug. 9, 1848, by Rev. William Payne	2	486
Abell, s. John, b. Aug. 3, 1716	2	58
Abel, m. Eunis **PORTER,** b. of Windsor, Nov. 3, 1741	2	172
Abiah, s. Timothy, b. Apr. 4, 1705	2	56
Abia, d. Aaron & Deborah, b. Apr. 22, 1740	2	377
Abiel, s. Ichabod, Jr. & Dorothy, b. Sept. 13, 1748	2	380
Abigayl, d. [Nathanell & Elisabeth], b. Mar. 27, 1659	MG	
Abigail, d. Nat[han], bp. Apr. 1, [16]5[9]	MG	
Abigall, d. Nathanell, m. Josiah **BARBER,** Nov. 22, 1677, by		

	Vol.	Page
LOOMIS, LOOMYS, LOOMAS, LOMAS, LOOMYES, (cont.)		
Capt. [ ] Newbery	MG	
Abigall, d. Nathanell, m. Josia BARBER, Nov. 22, [16]77,		
by Capt. Newbery	Col.1	46
Abigayl, d. Nathanell, m. Josias BARBER, Nov. 22, 1677, by		
Capt. Newbery	TR1	1
Abigail, d. Nathanael, m. Josiah BARBOR, Nov. 22, 1677, by		
Capt. Nubery	1	54
Abigail, d. Josiah, b. Aug. 10, 1691	1	23
Abigaell, d. Ebenezer, b. Oct. 31, 1706	2	56
Abigaell, d. Joseph, Sr., b. Apr. 8, 1708	2	56
Abigail, d. Job. b. Apr. 10, 1713/14	2	58
Abigail, m. James ROCKWELL, b. of Windsor, Nov. 7,		
1728	2	194
Abigail, m. Benjamin ALLYN, b. of Windsor, Aug. 9, 1733	2	123
Abigail, d. Ichabod & Hephzibah, b. Aug. 2, 1734	2	375
Abigail, d. John & Abigail, b. Mar. 28, 1735	2	378
Abigail, d. Job & Hannah, b. Jan. 19, 1738/9	2	377
Abigail, d. Odiah & Jane, b. Oct. 20, 1740	2	377
Abigail, d. Joel & Name, b. Nov. 27, 1758	2	385
Abigail, w. John, of the East Side of River, d. May 6, 1761	2	249
Abigail M., m. George G. LOOMIS, May 4, 1851, by T. A.		
Leete	2	491
Abijah, s. Ruben & Rebeckah, b. Jan. 23, 1756	2	383
Abner, s. Aaron & Deborah, b. Nov. 26, 1727	2	372
Abraham, s. Daniel, b. Dec. 13, 1696	1	25
Abraham, m. Isabel EGELSTON, b. of Windsor, Feb. 5,		
1718/19	2	170
Abraham, s. Abraham, b. Oct. 17, 1724	2	61
Agnis, m. William FRANCES, b. of Windsor, Sept. 7, 1783	2	152
Alexander, s. Jonah & Anna, b. June 8, 1744	2	378
Amanda, m. Charles CAMP, b. of Windsor, Jan. 26, 1837, by		
Rev. Eli Deniston	2	490
Amasa, s. Gershom & Mary, b. Feb. 19, 1737/8	2	376
Amasa, of Windsor, m. Hannah HURLBUT, of Hartford, July		
16, 1763	2	173
Amasa, s. Amasa & Hannah, b. Sept. 29, 1763	2	386
Amelea, d. Simeon & Keziah, b. Nov. 28, 1772	2	389
Amos, s. Stephen, b. Aug. 12, 1707	2	56
Amme, d. John, b. May 8, 1724	2	61
Ame, d. Ens. John & Ann, d. Nov. 11, 1734	2	247
Ann, d. Joseph (s. of John), b. Jan. 10, 1678	1	22
Ann, d. Timothy, b. June 15, 1698	1	24
Ann, d. Timothy, b. June 15, 1698	2	60
Ann, d. Hezekiah, b. Feb. 20, 1710/11	2	57
Ann, d. John (s. Sergt. Daniell), b. Mar. 7, 1718/19	2	61
Ann, m. Lieut. Henry ALLYN, b. of Windsor, Feb. 22,		
1727/8	2	123

	Vol.	Page
LOOMIS, LOOMYS, LOOMAS, LOMAS, LOOMYES, (cont.)		
Ann, d. David & Elizabeth, b. Sept. 23, 1733	2	375
Ann, m. Stephen **GILLET**, b. of Windsor, Sept. 21, 1738	2	156
Ann, d. Reuben & Anne, b. Jan. 14, 1743/4	2	378
Ann, w. Reuben, d. Feb. 13, 1743/4	2	247
Ann, d. Benjamin, Jr. & Lydia, b. Oct. 23, 1762	2	386
Anna, d. Joseph (s. John), b. Jan. 10, 1678; bp. [Jan.]		
12, [1678]	MG	
Anna, d. Joseph (s. John), b. Jan. 10, 1678	Col.1	56
Anna, d. Jonah & Anna, b. Oct. 5, 1734	2	376
Anna, w. Jonah, d. Nov. 23, 1748	2	248
Ana, d. Simeon & Keziah, b. Dec. 2, 1763	2	389
Anne, d. Ichabod & Hephzibah, b. Sept. 19, 1741	2	377
Anne, m. Isaac **CHANDLER**, b. of Windsor, Oct. 3, 1771	2	137
Anne, of Suffield, m. George **LOOMIS**, of Windsor, Dec. 7,		
1780	2	174
Anne, d. George & Anne, b. Oct. 20, 1781	2	389
Anne, w. George, d. Oct. 24, 1789, in the 34th y. of her age	2	250
Anson, s. Jacob, Jr. & Jerusha, b. Oct. 23, 1800	2	390
Anson, of Bethlem, Conn., m. Eunice N. **SIMMONS**, of		
Windsor, Oct. 25, 1836, by Rev. Charles Walker	2	489
Apphia, d. Uriah, Jr. & Apphia, b. Jan. 15, 1771	2	387
Asa, s. Isaac, Jr. & Sarah, b. Feb. 29, 1756	2	382
Asher, s. Serajah & Sibbell, b. Apr. 4, 1772	2	387
Azubah, d. Jonah & Anna, b. Nov. 6, 1748	2	380
Benajah, s. Daniel, b. Jan. 20, 1702	1	25
Benajah, s. Daniel, d. May 6, 1702	1	47
Benajah, s. Josiah, b. Jan. 28, 1710/11	2	57
Beniamen, s. [Samuell], b. Feb. 11, [166[7]	MG	
Benjamin, s. Samuel, b. Feb. 11, [16]67	1	22
Beniamen, s. [Thomas & Mary], b. May 20, [16]79; bp. June		
1, [16]79	MG	
Benjamin, s. Thomas, b. May 20, 1679	1	22
Beniamen, s. Thomas, b. May 20, 1690	Col.1	56
Benjamin, s. Daniel, b. Feb. 7, 1698	1	25
Benjamin, m. Ann **FITCH**, b. of Windsor, Jan. 6, 1703	1	59
Benjamin, Jr., m. Joanna **ALFORD**, b. of Windsor, Dec. 9,		
1725	2	171
Benjamin, s. Benjamin & Joanna, b. Jan. 12, 1728/9	2	373
Benjamin, s. Benjamin & Joanna, d. Feb. 8, 1728/9	2	246
Benjamin, s. Benjamin & Joanna, b. Apr. 19, 1732	2	374
Benjamin, Jr., m. Elizabeth **BARBER**, b. of Windsor, Feb. 3,		
1757	2	487
Benjamin, s. Benjamin, Jr. & Elisabeth, b. Nov. 27, 1757	2	383
Benjamin, s. Benjamin, Jr. & Elizabeth, b. Nov. 28, 1757	2	537
Benjamin, Jr., m. Lyda **DRAKE**, b. of Windsor, Apr. 27,		
1760	2	488
Benjamin, Jr., d. Jan. 2, 1763	2	249

	Vol.	Page
LOOMIS, LOOMYS, LOOMAS, LOMAS, LOOMYES, (cont.)		
Benjamin Newberry, s. Oliver & Jerusha, b. Dec. 7, 1765	2	386
Bennoni, s. Abraham & Isabel, b. Sept. 28, 1738	2	376
Benoni, s. Abraham & Isabel, d. Feb. 27, 1741/2	2	247
Betse, d. Uriah, Jr. & Apphia, b. Apr. 2, 1772	2	387
Betsey, d. Jacob, Jr. & Jerusha, b. Feb. 6, 1819	2	391
Bulah, d. Jonah & Anna, b. Aug. 9, 1746	2	380
Brigadore, s. Charles & Constant, b. Sept. 18, 1761	2	385
Caleb, s. Joseph (s. of Joseph), b. Oct. 10, 1686	1	23
Caleb, s. Joseph, d. Mar. 5, [16]86/7	Col.D	56
Caleb, s. Joseph, d. Mar. 5, 1686/7	1	47
Caleb, s. Josiah, b. Dec. 23, 1693	1	24
Caroline, d. Gideon & Joanna b. Nov. 28, 1758	2	384
Charles, s. Nathanael, b. Feb. 20, 1696	1	24
Charles, m. Sconstant **EGELSTON**, b. of Windsor, July 3, 1750	2	487
Charles, s. Steven, b. Feb. 8, 1717/18	2	59
Charlotte M., m. Horace **DANIELS**, b. of Windsor, Feb. 18, 1830, by John Bartlett	2	144
Chauncey, s. Uriah, Jr. & Apphia, b. Apr. 22, 1775	2	388
Chancey, s. Uriah, Jr. & Apphia, d. Oct. 27, 1776	2	250
Chancy, s. Uriah, Jr. & Apphia, b. Sept. 11, 1780	2	389
Chauncey, s. Jacob, Jr. & Jerusha, b. Apr. 30, 1811	2	390
Cloe, d. Joel & Name, b. Dec. 13, 1748	2	385
Christian, d. Noah, b. Apr. 13, 1719	2	59
Constant, d. Charles & Constant, b. Mar. 25, 1756	2	382
Damoros, d. Joseph, b. July 29, 1699	1	24
Damirus, d. Joseph, Sr., d. June 1, 1705	2	245
Damaris, d. John, b. Dec. 1, 1712	2	57
Damaris, m. Daniel **PHELPS**, Jr., b. of Windsor, Feb. 28, 1744/5	2	188
Dan[i]el, s. John, bp. Jan.* 21, [16]57 *("June?")	MG	
Daniell, s. [John & Elisabeth], b. June 16, 1657	MG	
Daniell, s. John, b. June 16, 1657	Col.2	161
Daniel, s. John, b. June 16, [16]57	1	22
Danell, ae 23 on June 16, 1680, s. John, m. Mary **ELESWORTH**, who was ae 20 on May 7, 1680, Dec. 23, 1680	MG	
Danell, s. John, m. Mary **ELSWORTH**, Dec. 23, 1680, by Capt. Newbery	Col.1	46
Danell, m. Mary [ ]ELS, [ ] 23, 1680	TR1	1
Daniel, s. John, m. Mary **ELSWORTH**, Dec. 23, 1680	1	56
Daniel, s. Daniel, b. Nov. 15, 1682	1	25
Daniell, Jr., m. Elizabeth **BARBAR**, Nov. 10, 1709	2	169
Daniel, s. Daniel, b. Nov. 2, 1710	2	57
Daniel, Sergt., m. wid. Hannah **DRAKE**, b. of Windsor, July 9, 1713	2	170
Daniel, s. Daniel & Sarah, b. July 25, 1739	2	377

	Vol.	Page
LOOMIS, LOOMYS, LOOMAS, LOMAS, LOOMYES, (cont.)		
Daniel, Sergt., d. June 25, 1740	2	247
Daniel, s. Ichabod & Dorithy, b. Nov. 28, 1756	2	383
Daniel, contributed 0-1-0 to the poor in other colonies	MG	
Daued, s. [John & Elisabeth], b. May 30, 1665; d. June [ ],		
[16]65	MG	
David, s. John, b. May 30, 1665	1	22
Dauid, s. John, bp. June 4, [16]65	MG	
Dauid, s. John, d. [ ], [16]65	MG	
Dauid, s. John, d. June 24, 1665	Col.1	55
Dauid, s. [Nathaniel & Elisabeth], b. Jan. 11, 1667	MG	
David, s. Nathanael, b. Jan. 11, [16]67	1	22
Dauid, [s. N[ ], [bp.] Jan. 12, [16]67	MG	
David, m. Lydia MARSH, Dec. 8, 1692	1	59
David, s. David, b. Dec. 2, 1694	1	24
David, m. Elisabeth HERMAN, Nov. 24, 1715	2	170
David, s. David, Jr., b. Mar. 13, 1718/19	2	59
David, d. Jan. 9, 1751/2	2	248
Deborah, d. John, b. Jan. [ ], 1679	1	23
Deborah, m. Jonathan FILLY*, Sept. 5, 1700 *(In Pencil)	2	150
Deborah, d. Joshua, b. Sept. 6, 1718	2	59
Deborah, d. Aaron, b. Apr. 10, 1720	2	60
Deborah, m. Nathaniel LOOMIS, Jr., b. of Windsor, Sept. 22,		
1743	2	172
Dorcas, d. Stephen & Grace, b. Apr. 9, 1752	2	383
Dorithy, d. Daniel, Jr. & Elizabeth, b. June 21, 1718	2	371
Dorothy, d. Nathaniel, b. Apr. 30, 1722	2	61
Dorethy, m. Ichabod LOOMIS, b. of Windsor, Jan. 25,		
1738/9	2	172
Dorethy, d. Ichabod & Dorethy, b. July 5, 1740	2	377
Dorithy,m. Ebenezer HAYDON, b. of Windsor, July 16, 1752	2	163
Ebenezer, s. [Nathaniel & Elisabeth], b. Mar. 22, 1674/5	MG	
Ebenezer, m. Jemimah WHITCOMB, Apr. 15, 1697	1	59
Ebenezer, s. Ebenezer, b. July 16, 1698	1	24
Ebenezer, d. Oct. 2, 1709	2	245
Ebenezer, s. Josiah, b. Nov. 9, 1712	2	58
Ebenezer, s. Ebenezer, decd., d. [ ], 1712	2	245
Ebenezer, s. David, Jr., b. Aug. 6, 1723	2	61
Ebenezer, s. Noah & Sarah, b. Apr. 28, 1724	2	372
Elinor, d. Gedion & Joanna, b. June 29, 1765	2	387
Eli, s. Aaron & Deborah, b. Feb. 18, 1733/4	2	375
Eliakim, s. David, b. July 27, 1701	1	24
Eliakim, m. Mary LOOMIS, b. of Windsor, Dec. 4, 1735	2	171
Eliakim, s. Eliakim & Mary, b. Sept. 25, 1738	2	377
Elihu, s. John & Abigail, b. Dec. 15, 1746	2	381
Ellihu, s. John, 2nd & Abigail, d. Aug. 21, 1751	2	248
Elihu, s. John, Jr. & Redexsaelano, b. Jan. 28, 1758	2	385
Elihu, s. Simeon & Keziah, b. Feb. 19, 1776	2	389

	Vol.	Page
LOOMIS, LOOMYS, LOOMAS, LOMAS, LOOMYES, (cont.)		
Enoch, s. Joseph, Sr., b. Mar. 23, 1694/5	1	24
Epaphras, s. Abraham & Isabel, b. Nov. 13, 1732	2	374
Ephipra, s. George & Reumah, b. Nov. 10, 1792	2	390
Ephraim, s. John, b. Nov. [ ], 1685	1	23
Ephraim, s. Dea. John, d. Jan. 10, 1697	1	47
Ephraim, s. Josiah, b. May 2, 1698	1	24
Ephraim, s. Aaron & Deborah, b. Apr. 1, 1731	2	374
Esther, d. John (s. Joseph), b. Sept. 13, 1708	2	56
Esther, wid., d. Nov. 6, 1714	2	246
Esther, d. Aaron & Deborah, b. June 30, 1729	2	373
Esther, d. John & Esther, d. May 11, 1730	2	246
Esther, d. Timothy & Hannah, b. Nov. 14, 1730	2	374
Esther, d. John & Abigail, b. May 14, 1738	2	379
Esther, d. Seth & Esther, b. July 7, 1748	2	381
Esther, d. Seth & Esther, d. Mar. 28, 1752	2	248
Esther, d. Timothy & Sarah, b. May 19, 1756	2	382
[E]unice, d. James, b. May 1, 1705	2	55
Eunice, d. Job, b. July 25, 1716	2	58
Eunice, d. Isaac, b. Jan. 23, 1723/4	2	61
Eunice, m. Stephen **BROWN**, b. of Windsor, Nov. 26, 1775	2	466
Eunice A., m. John S. **CLARK**, Mar. 5, 1833, by H. A. Rowland	2	470
Ezekiel, s. John, b. Oct. [ ], 1683	1	23
Ezekiel, s. Jonah & Anna, b. Aug. 20, 1742	2	378
Ezra, s. John, b. Sept. 10, 1721	2	61
Fitch, s. Nathaniell, 3rd & Margeret, b. Dec. 8, 1748; d. 24 hrs. after birth	2	380
Fitch, s. Capt. Nathaniel & Margrit, b. May 14, 1751	2	383
Francis A., m. George P. **HAYDEN**, b. of Windsor, Dec. 31, 1841, by Rev. S. D. Jewett	2	515
George, s. Joshua & Deborah, b. Feb. 6, 1725/6	2	371
George, s. Jonathan & Sarah, b. Nov. 22, 1727	2	372
George, s. Timothy & Sarah, b. Sept. 20, 1753	2	382
George, s. Joseph & Keziah, b. July 17, 1761	2	384
George, s. Amasa & Hannah, b. July 16, 1762	2	386
George, of Windsor, m. Anne **LOOMIS**, of Suffield, Dec. 7, 1780	2	174
George, s. Benjamin & Chloe, b. Sept. 24, 1783	2	390
George, s. George & Anne, b. June 25, 1787	2	389
George, of Windsor, m. Reumah **MOORE**, of East Windsor, Dec. 29, 1719	2	174
George, m. Hannah **WILSON**, b. of Windsor, Feb. 10, 1807	2	488
George G., m. Abigail M. **LOOMIS**, May 4, 1851, by T. A. Leete, V. D. M.	2	491
Gershom, s. Thomas, b. Apr. 9, 1701	1	24
Gersham, s. Thomas, b. Apr. 9, 1701	2	59
Gershom, m. Mary **GRANT**, b. of Windsor, June [ ], 1736	2	172

	Vol.	Page
LOOMIS, LOOMYS, LOOMAS, LOMAS, LOOMYES, (cont.)		
Gershom, d. Dec. 27, 1738	2	247
Gershom, m. Mary GRANT, b. of Windsor, [ ]		
(Crossed out)	2	178
Gideon, s. Stephen & Mabel, b. Nov. 17, 1725	2	371
Gideon, s. Henry & Ruth, b. Dec. 30, 1735	2	376
Gideon, m. Joanna LOOMIS, b. of Windsor, Dec. 8, 1748	2	173
Giles, s. Joel & Name, b. Apr. 19, 1750	2	385
Giles, s. Joel & Name, d. Aug. 31, 1751	2	249
Giles, s. Joel & Name, b. Nov. 6, 1756	2	385
Grace, d. Joseph (s. John), b. Mar. 17, 1684	Col.D	51
Grace, d. Joseph (s. John), b. Mar. 17, 1684/5	1	23
Grace, d. Aaron, b. Apr. 28, 1721	2	60
Grace, m. Stephen LOOMIS, Jr., b. of Windsor, June 9, 1743	2	172
Grace, d. Stephen, Jr. & Grace, b. Dec. 5, 1745	2	379
Graves, s. Sergt. Nathanael & Ann, b. Nov. 6, 1717	2	372
Gurdon, m. Meriim WARNER, Jan. 21, 1830, by Henry A. Rowland	2	174
Hannah, d. Thomas, b. Feb. 3, 1657	Col.2	161
Hannah, d. [Thomas & Hanna], b. Feb. 8, 1657	MG	
Hannah, d. Thomas, b. Feb. 8, 1658	1	22
Hana, d. [Joseph & Sara], b. Feb. 2, 1661	MG	
Hannah, d. Joseph, b. Feb. 2, 1661	1	22
Hannah, [d.] Joseph, [bp.] Feb. 8, [16]61	MG	
Hanna, w. Thomas, d. Apr. 25, 1662	MG	
Hannah, d. Joseph (s. John), b. Jan. 10, 1678	1	24
Hannah, d. Thomas, Jr., b. Oct. 9, 1685	1	23
Hana, [d.] T[homas], bp. Feb. 14, [16[ ]	MG	
Hannah, d. Stephen, b. Apr. 13, 1703	2	56
Hannah, d. Thomas, m. Jacob DRAKE, s. Job, June 28, 1704	1	55
Hannah, d. Philip, b. May 21, 1705	2	55
Hannah, d. James, b. Apr. 19, 1707	2	56
Hannah, d. David, b. Aug. 2, 1709	2	57
Hannah, d. Isaac, b. Feb. 15, 1721/2	2	61
Hannah, d. Timothy & Hannah, b. Dec. 23, 1728	2	373
Hannah, d. Henry & Ruth, b. Oct. 22, 1733	2	375
Hannah, m. Dea. John COOK, b. of Windsor, Jan. 1, 1735/6	2	136
Hannah, d. David & Elizabeth, b. Sept. 28, 1736	2	376
Hannah, d. Job & Hannah, b. July 13, 1737	2	377
Hannah, w. Thomas, d. Jan. 1, 1738/9	2	247
Hannah, d. Uriah & Hannah, b. Oct. 11, 1747	2	380
Hannah, w. Isaac, d. Nov. 6, 1752	2	248
Hannah, d. Isaac, Jr. & Sarah, b. Jan. 16, 1753	2	381
Hannah, d. Amasa & Hannah, b. July 29, 1765	2	387
Hannah, w. Uriah, d. Dec. 19, 1766	2	249
Hannah, see Hannah BURNHAM	2	250
Harriet E., of Windsor, m. Jeremiah P. JEWETT, of Lowell Mass., May 27, 1841, by S. D. Jewett	2	486

	Vol.	Page
LOOMIS, LOOMYS, LOOMAS, LOMAS, LOOMYES, (cont.)		
Henry, s. James, b. Sept. 14, 1701	1	25
Henry, of Windsor, m. Ruth **BIDWELL**, of Hartford, Apr. 13, 1727	2	171
Henry, s. Henry & Ruth, b. Feb. 12, 1727/8	2	373
Hephzibah, d. David, b. Dec. 2, 1698	1	24
Hepzibah, m. Ichabod **LOOMIS**, Dec. 20, 1716	2	170
Hephzibah, d. Ichabod, b. July 5, 1722	2	61
Hephzibah, m. Nathanael **BARBOR**, b. of Windsor, Sept. 13, 1739	2	130
Hezekia, s. [Nathaniel & Elisabeth], b. Feb. 21, 1668	MG	
Hezekiah, s. Nathanael, b. Feb. 21, [16]68	1	22
Hesekia, s. N[ ], [bp.] Feb. 28, [16]68	MG	
Hezekiah, m. Mary **LOOMIS***, Apr. 30, 1690 *("Porter" written over "LOOMIS")	2	169
Hezekiah, s. Hezekiah, b. Nov. 7, 1697	2	55
Horice, s. Serajah & Sibbel, b. Aug. 4, 1774	2	388
Huldah, d. Stephen & Grace, b. Dec. 31, 1755	2	383
Hulda, d. Gideon & Jonah, b. Sept. 14, 1757	2	383
Ichobod, s. Timothy, b. Jan. 25, 1692	1	24
Ichabod, s. Timothy, b. Jan. 25, 1692	2	60
Ichabod, m. Hepzibah **LOOMIS**, Dec. 20, 1716	2	170
Ichabod, s. Ichabod, b. Dec. 10, 1717	2	58
Ichabod, m. Dorethy **LOOMIS**, b. of Windsor, Jan. 25, 1738/9	2	172
Ichabod, s. Ichabod, Jr. & Dorothy, b. Jan. 17, 1742/3	2	378
Ichabod, d. Feb. 21, 1776	2	249
Ichabod, s. Ruben, Jr. & Laurana, b. Mar. 11, 1777	2	388
Ira, s. Serajah & Sibbel, b. Feb. 13, 1770	2	387
Isack, s. [John & Elisabeth], b. Aug. 31, 1668	MG	
Isaac, s. John, b. Aug. 31, 1668	1	22
Isaac, s. John, bp. Sept. 6, [16]68	MG	
Isack, s. [Joseph & Sara], b. Oct. 28, 1677	MG	
Isaac, d. Dec. 12, 1688	1	47
Isaac, s. Samuel, b. Dec. 23, 1693	1	24
Isaac, s. Daniel, b. Aug. 23, 1694	1	25
Isaac, s. Joseph, d. Mar. 17, 1704	1	47
Isaack, s. Joseph, Sr., b. Sept. 14, 1705	2	55
Isaac, m. Hannah **EGLSTON**, b. of Windsor, Apr. 26, 1716	2	170
Isaac, had eldest s. [ ], s. b. Dec. 3, 1717	2	58
Isaac, s. Isaac, b. July 19, 1719	2	59
Isaac, Jr., of Windsor, m. Sarah **GILLET**, of Hartford, Mar. 10, 1742/3	2	172
Isaac, s. Isaac, Jr. & Sarah, b. Aug. 11, 1750	2	381
Isabel, d. Abraham & Isabel, b. Oct. 26, 1729	2	373
Isaiah, s. Noah & Sarah, b. June 28, 1730	2	374
Israell, s. Stephen, b. Aug. 6, 1705	2	56
J., his w. [ ], adm. ch. & communicant Apr. [ ],1655	MG	

	Vol.	Page
LOOMIS, LOOMYS, LOOMAS, LOMAS, LOOMYES, (cont.)		
Job, m. Abigaell FFILLY, Apr. 27, 1710	2	170
Job, s. Job, b. Mar. 11, 1710/11	2	57
Job, m. Hannah ENNO, b. of Windsor, [ ], 1736	2	172
Job, s. Job, Jr. & Hannah, b. Mar. 22, 1743/4	2	379
Job, s. Job & Hannah, d. Aug. 29, 1744	2	247
Job, Ens., d. Jan. 6, 1765	2	249
Job, s. Simeon & Keziah, b. Mar. 29, 1771	2	389
Joel, s. David, Jr., b. June 2, 1721	2	60
Joel, s. Joshua, b. June 21, 1722	2	61
Joel, s. Joel & Name, b. Nov. 4, 1763	2	386
Joel A., m. Seliner COOK, b. of Windsor, Jan. 24, 1847, by George F. Kettell	2	491
Joel A., m. Faney E. THOMAS, b. of Windsor, Mar. 24, 1850, by Rev. Samuel W. Law	2	175
John, adm. ch. & communicant Oct. [ ], 1640	MG	
John, m. Elisabeth SCOT, Feb. 3, 1648	MG	
John, m. Elizabeth SCOTT, Feb. 3, 1648, at Hartford	1	58
John, s. [John & Elisabeth], b. Nov. 9, 1649	MG	
John, s. John, b. Nov. 9, 1649	Col.2	161
John, s. John, b. Nov. 9, 1649	1	22
John, s. [Joseph & Sara], b. Oct. 1, 1651	MG	
John, [s.] Joseph, bp. Oct. 5, [16]51	MG	
John, his w. [ ], adm. ch. [ ], [16]55	MG	
John, taxed 7-0 on Feb. 10, [16]73; taxed 4-0 on Feb. 10, [16]73	MG	
John, taxed 4-0 on Feb. 10, [16]73	MG	
John, had 13 children b. in Windsor. Dated Aug. 17, 1677	MG	
John, Dea., d. Sept. 2, 1688	1	47
John, s. Daniel, b. Oct. 11, 1688	1	25
John, s. John, b. Mar. 28, 1691/2	1	23
John, mem. Jury 16[ ]	MG	
John, s. Joseph, m. Esther GILLET, Aug. 30, 1705	2	169
John, s. John (s. Joseph), b. Feb. 12, 1706/7	2	56
John, s. Daniell, m. Ann ENNO, d. John, Apr. 24, 1712	2	170
John, s. John, b. Sept. 21, 1713	2	58
John, d. Nov. 30, 1732	2	246
John, m. Abigaiel ELSWORTH*, b. of Windsor, Apr. 5, 1733 *("BISSEL" crossed out)	2	171
John, s. John & Abigail, b. Mar. 4, 1733/4	2	375
John, Jr., m. Redexselano WOLCOTT, b. of Windsor, June 8, 1756	2	173
John, s. John, Jr. & Redexselano, b. June 22, 1759	2	385
John, s. Joseph, bp. [ ]	1	22
John, contributed 0-6-0 and in money 0-5-9 to the poor in other colonies	MG	
Jonah, s. Hezekiah, b. Apr. 11, 1705	2	55
Jonah, m. Anna SKINNER, b. of Windsor, June 19, 1734	2	172

	Vol.	Page
LOOMIS, LOOMYS, LOOMAS, LOMAS, LOOMYES, (cont.)		
Jonah, s. Jonah & Anna, b. Feb. 1, 1736/7	2	376
Jonathan, s. [Nathaniel & Elisabeth], b. Mar. 30, 1664	MG	
Jonathan, [s.] N[ ], [bp.] Apr. 3, [16]64	MG	
Jonathan, d. Oct. 23, 1707	2	245
Jonathan, m. Sarah HIGLEY, b. of Windsor, Dec. 24, 1723	2	171
Jonathan, s. Jonathan, b. Nov. 14, 1725	2	62
Jonathan, s. Jonathan & Sarah, d. Sept. 26, 1730	2	246
Jonathan, s. Jonathan & Sarah, b. June 16, 1734	2	375
Jonathan, s. Joseph & Keziah, b. Mar. 25, 1757	2	383
Jonathan, s. Nathanael, b. Mar. [ ]	1	22
Jos[ ], his w. [ ], adm. ch. & communicant Dec. [ ], 1660	MG	
Jose, his w. [ ], adm. ch. [ ] 25, [16[ ]	MG	
Joseph, adult, ch. mem. 16[ ]	MG	
Joseph, m. Sara HILL, Sept. 17, 1646	MG	
Joseph, m. Sarah HILL, Sept. 17, 1646	1	58
Joseph, s. [Joseph & Sara], b. July 15, 1649	MG	
Joseph, s. Joseph, b. July 15, 1649	1	22
Joseph, s. [John & Elisabeth], b. Nov. 7, 1651	MG	
Joseph, s. John, b. Nov. 7, 1651	Col.2	161
Joseph, s. John, b. Nov. 7, 1651	1	22
Joseph, [s.] John, [bp.] Nov. 7, [16]51	MG	
Joseph, Sr., his w. [ ], d. [ ], [16]52	MG	
Joseph, Sr., his w. [ ], d. [ ]; bd. Aug. 23, 1652	Col.2	160
Joseph, Elder, his w. [ ], bd. Aug. 23, 1652	1	47
Joseph, Sr., d. [ ], [16]58	MG	
Joseph, had 8 children b. in Windsor. Dated Aug. 17, 1677	MG	
Joseph, s. Joseph (s. John), b. Feb. 13, 1681	Col.D	51
Joseph, s. Joseph (s. of John), b. Feb. 13, 1681	1	23
Joseph, s. Joseph, m. Lidea DRAKE, d. John, Apr. 10, 1681	MG	
Joseph, s. Joseph, Sr., m. Lidea DRAKE, d. John, Sr. Apr. 10, 1681	Col.1	46
Joseph, his w. [ ], d. Apr. 22, 1681	Col.1	58
Joseph, s. Joseph, b. Nov. 28, [16]82	Col.D	51
Joseph, s. Joseph, b. Nov. 28, [16]82	1	23
Joseph, s. Joseph (s. Joseph), d. Mar. 19, [16]82/3	Col.D	56
Joseph, s. Joseph (s. Joseph), d. Mar. 19, 1682/3	1	47
Joseph, s. Joseph (s. Joseph, Sr.), b. Oct. 8, 1684	1	23
Joseph, Sr., d. June 26, 1687	1	47
Joseph, [s.] J[ ], ch. mem. 16[ ]	MG	
Joseph, Sr., m. wid. Abigail BIRGE, b. of Windsor, Feb. 11, 17[0]2/3	1	59
Joseph, Jr., of Windsor, m. Mary COOLEY, of Springfield, June 28, 1710	2	170
Joseph, s. Isaac, b. Aug. 29, 1725	2	62
Joseph, m. Keziah LOOMIS, b. of Windsor, Jan. 23, 1752	2	173
Joseph, s. Joseph & Keziah, b. Mar. 23, 1755	2	382

	Vol.	Page

LOOMIS, LOOMYS, LOOMAS, LOMAS, LOOMYES, (cont.)

	Vol.	Page
Joseph, Jr., contributed 0-1-3 to the poor in other colonies	MG	
Josephus, s. Joseph (s. Joseph), b. Oct. 8, [16]84	Col.D	51
Joshua, s. Thomas, b. Nov. 6, 1692	1	24
Joshua, m. Deborah **COOLEY**, of Springfield, Oct. 26, 1715	2	170
Joshua, s. Joshua, b. Nov. 16, 1716	2	58
Josia, s. [Nathaniel & Elisabeth], b. Feb. 17, 1660	MG	
Josiah, s. Nathanael, b. Feb. 17, [16]60	1	22
Josia, [s.] Natha[n], [bp.] Feb. 24, [16]60	MG	
Josiah, m. Mary **ROCKWELL**, Oct. 23, 1683	Col.D	54
Josiah, m. Mary **ROCKWELL**, Oct. 23, 1683	1	58
Josia, s. Josia, b. Feb. 17, [16]84	Col.D	51
Josiah, s. Daniel, b. Nov. 28, 1684	Col.D	51
Josiah, s. Daniel, b. Nov. 28, 1684	1	23
Josiah, s. Josiah, b. Jan. 23, 1687/8	1	23
Josiah, m. Elizabeth **KELCY**, Jan. 22, 1707/8	2	170
Josiah, s. Josiah, b. Mar. 11, 1708/9	2	57
Jssear*, s. Aaron & Deborah, b. May 28, 1736 *(In pencil)	2	376
Justin, s. Uriah, Jr. & Apphia, b. Mar. 2, 1785	2	389
Justus, s. Moses, Jr. & Elizabeth, b. Aug. 25, 1745	2	381
Katherine, d. Mooses, b. Dec. 19, 1702	1	25
Keziah, d. Joseph, b. Dec. 12, 1715	2	58
Keziah, d. Jonathan & Sarah, b. June 18, 1729	2	373
Keziah, m. Zebulon **KING**, Dec. 8, 1743	2	167
Keziah, m. Joseph **LOOMIS**, b. of Windsor, Jan. 23, 1752	2	173
Keziah, d. Joseph & Keziah, b. Feb. 27, 1753	2	381
Keziah, d. Simeon & Keziah, b. Jan. 24, 1778	2	389
Keziah, w. Simeon, d. Feb. 7, 1778	2	249
Laurana, d. Ruben, Jr. & Laurana, b. May 15, 1771	2	388
Lois, d. Timothy, b. Aug. 15, 1695	1	24
Lois, d. Timothy, b. Aug. 15, 1695; d. Dec. 20, 1695	2	60
Lois, d. James, b. Oct. 26, 1725	2	58
Lois, d. Ichabod, b. Nov. 26, 1724	2	62
Louisa, d. Uriah, Jr. & Apphia, b. June 6, 1779	2	389
Lovel, s. Charles & Constant, b. May 18, 1764	2	386
Lucrecia, d. Jonah & Anna, b. Dec. 18, 1738	2	376
Lucie, d. Ichabod & Hephzibah, b. Aug. 5, 1727	2	372
Lucy, d. John & Ann, b. Aug. 21, 1729	2	374
Lucy, d. John & Abigail, b. Dec. 15, 1739	2	379
Lucy, of Windsor, m. Nehemiah **GAYLORD**, of Torrington, Nov. 10, 1748	2	157
Lucy Ann, of Windsor, m. Isaac P. **WATERMAN**, of Hanover, N. H., June 30, 1840, by Ezra S. Cook	2	514
Luke, s. John & Abigail, b. Oct. 15, 1736	2	378
Lydia, d. Joseph [s. John], b. Apr. 15, 1686	1	24
Lydia, d. Joseph (s. Joseph), b. Feb. 17, 1687	1	23
Lydia, d. David, b. Oct. 21, 1693	1	24
Lydia, w. Joseph, d. May 7, 1702	1	47

	Vol.	Page
LOOMIS, LOOMYS, LOOMAS, LOMAS, LOOMYES, (cont.)		
Lydia, had d. Mary, b. Jan. 13, 1718/19	2	59
Lydia, m. Thomas HOSKINS, b. of Windsor, Dec.* 17, 1729		
*("Nov." crossed out)	2	162
Liddia, d. John & Abigail, b. Oct. 5, 1748	2	381
Maybell, d. [Thomas & Mary], b. Oct. 27, 1672	MG	
Mabel, d. James, b. May 20, 1710	2	57
Mabel, d. James, d. Aug. 20, 1710	2	245
Mabel, d. Joseph, Jr., b. Mar. 6, 1711/12	2	57
Mabel, d. Charles & Constant, b. Oct. 28, 1758	2	384
Margeret, d. Jonathan & Sarah, b. Mar. 15, 1730/1	2	374
Margrit, of Lebanon, m. Daniel ROCKWELL, of Windsor,		
Feb. 20, 1732/3	2	195
Margret, m. John WARNER, b. of Windsor, Dec. 25, 1754	2	210
Mariah, m. Rev. Peter C. OAKLEY, Sept. 12, 1827, by Rev.		
Arnold Scholefield	2	185
Martha, d. Joseph (s. Joseph), b. Oct. 3, 1690	Col.D	51
Martha, d. Joseph (s. Joseph), b. Oct. 13, 1690	1	23
Martha, m. Thomas BISSELL, b. of Windsor, Feb. 16,		
1709/10	2	128
Marten, s. Seth & Esther, b. June 6, 1754	2	382
Mary, d. [Joseph & Sara], b. Aug. 3, 1653	MG	
Mary, d. [Thomas & Hanna], b. Jan. 16, 1659	MG	
Mary, d. Thomas, b. Jan. 16, 1659	1	22
Mary, d. Thomas, bp. Jan. 17, [16]5[9]	MG	
Mary, d. John (s. John), b. Mar. 20, 1672	1	23
Mary, d. [John & Elisabeth], b. Aug. 7, 1673; d. May		
14, [16]7[ ]	MG	
Mary, d. John, b. Aug. 7, 1673	1	22
Mary, d. John, bp. Aug. 10, [16]7[ ]	MG	
[Mary], d. John, d. [May 14], [16]75	MG	
Mary, d. John, d. May 14, 1675	Col.1	58
Mary, d. John, d. May 14, 1675	1	47
Mary, d. [Nathaniel & Elisabeth], b. Jan. 5, [16]79	MG	
Mary, d. Nathanell, b. Jan. 5, 1679	Col.1	57
Mary, d. Thomas, m. Mical TAINTOR, Apr. 3, 1679	MG	
Mary, d. Thomas, m. Micall TAINTOR, Apr. 3, 1679	Col.1	46
Mary, d. Thomas, m. Mical TAINTOR, Apr. 3, 1679	TR1	1
Mary, d. Thomas, m. Michael TAINTOR, Apr. 3, 1679	1	62
Mary, w. Joseph, d. Apr. 22, 1681	MG	
Mary, d. Tho[mas], Jr., b. Sept. 2, 1683	Col.D	51
Mary, d. Thomas, b. Sept. 2, 1683	1	23
Mary*, w. Thom[as], Sr., d. Aug. 8, 1684 *(Note by LBB:		
"Mary (JUDD) LOOMYS")	Col.D	56
Mary, w. Thomas, Sr., d. Aug. 8, 1684	1	47
Mary, d. Josiah, b. Jan. 18, 1685	Col.D	51
Mary, d. Josiah, b. Jan. 18, 1685	1	23
Mary, d. Mathew, b. Oct. 31, [16]87	1	23

	Vol.	Page
LOOMIS, LOOMYS, LOOMAS, LOMAS, LOOMYES, (cont.)		
Mary, d. Daniel, b. Jan. 15, 1690	1	25
Mary, d. Hezekiah, b. Nov. 15, 1694	2	55
Mary, m. John **BUELL**, Nov. 20, 1695	1	54
Mary, m. Ebenezer **DIBLE**, July 16, 1696	1	55
Mary, m. Joseph **BARBER**, b. of Windsor, May 6, 1708	2	128
Mary, d. James, b. Jan. 3, 1708/9	2	56
Mary, d. Stephen, b. Mar. 26, 1709	2	56
Mary, d. James, d. Mar. 31, 1709	2	245
Mary, d. Daniel, Jr., b. May 10, 1714	2	59
Mary, d. Lydia, b. Jan. 13, 1718/19	2	59
Mary, m. Thomas **DIGGONS**, b. of Windsor, Dec. 31, 1719	2	141
Mary, d. Joseph, Jr., b. Jan. 12, 1720/1	2	60
Mary, d. David, Jr. & Elizabeth, b. Oct. 6, 1728	2	373
Mary, m. Joseph **HOSKINS**, b. of Windsor, Jan. 10, 1733/4	2	162
Mary, m. Eliakim **LOOMIS**, b. of Windsor, Dec. 4, 1735	2	171
Mary, m. Elijah **FITCH**, b. of Windsor, Oct. 28, 1742	2	152
Mary, d. Joel & Name, b. Sept. 15, 1752	2	385
Mary, of Windsor, m. George **TUTTLE**, of Hartford, Jan. 8, 1832, by Rev. Gurdon Robins, of East Windsor	2	206
Mary, w. Dea. John, d. [ ]	1	45
Mary, w. Dea. John, d. [ ]	1	47
Mathew, s. [Joseph & Sara], b. Nov. 4, 1664	MG	
Mathew, s. Joseph, b. Nov. 4, 1664	Col.1	55
Mathew, s. Joseph, b. Nov. 4, 1664	1	22
Mathew, s. Joseph, bp. Nov. 6, [16]64	MG	
Mathew, m. Mary **GAYLER**, b. of Windsor, Jan. 6, 1686	Col.D	54
Mathew, m. Mary **GAYLORD**, b. of Windsor, Jan. 6, 1686	1	58
Mathew, d. Apr. 12, 1688	1	47
Mathew, s. Stephen, b. Nov. 15, 1691	1	23
Mathew, s. James, b. Oct. 25, 1703	1	25
Melincha, of Windsor, m. Abial **KING**, of Suffield, May 12, 1841, by Rev. S. D. Jewett	2	169
Melisa, m. Henry **CAPIN**, Jan. 25, 1827, by Rev. Henry A. Rowland	2	139
Michael, s. Isaac, Jr. & Sarah, b. Oct. 13, 1747	2	380
Mindwell, d. [Nathaniel & Elisabeth], b. July 20, 1673	MG	
Mindwell, d. Nathaniel, b. July 20, [16]73	1	23
Mindwell, d. [Thomas & Mary], b. Aug. 6, 1676; bp. Aug. 13, 176[ ]	MG	
Mindwell, m. Jonathan **BROWN**, Oct. 1, 1696	1	54
Mindwell, d. James, b. Dec. 28, 1697	1	24
Mindwell, d. Aaron, b. Mar. 16, 1724/5	2	62
Mindwel, d. Henry & Ruth, b. Nov. 3, 1739	2	377
Mindwell, m. Titus **KING**, b. of Windsor, June 1, 1761	2	167
Minerva, m. Hervey **RISLEY**, of East Windsor, June 23, 1825, by Rev. Henry A. Rowland	2	196
Moses, s. [Nathaniel & Elisabeth], b. May 15, 1671	MG	

	Vol.	Page
LOOMIS, LOOMYS, LOOMAS, LOMAS, LOOMYES, (cont.)		
Mooses, s. Nathanael, b. May 15, [16]71	1	22
Moses, s. N[ ], [bp.] May 21, [16]71	MG	
Mooses, m. Joanna GIBBS, Apr. 27, 1694	1	59
Mooses, s. Mooses, b. June 24, 1696	1	24
Moses, m. Rebekah LOOMIS, b. of Windsor, Aug. 12, 1725	2	171
Moses, s. Aaron & Deborah, b. Sept. 12, 1726	2	371
Mooses, of Windsor, m. Elizabeth BIDWELL, of Hartford, Dec. 17, 1729	2	171
Moses, s. Moses & Elizabeth, b. Dec. 24, 1734	2	376
Moses, d. Apr. 15, 1754, in the 83rd y. of his age	2	248
Moses, m. Nancy LOOMIS, May 8, 1834, by H. A. Rowland	2	175
Name, d. Joel & Name, b. Jan. 12, 1755	2	385
Name, see also Naomi		
Nancy, m. David H. FILLEY, b. of Windsor, Mar. 5, 1828, by Rev. John Bartlett	2	153
Nancy, m. Moses LOOMIS, May 8, 1834, by H. A. Rowland	2	175
Naomi, d. Aaron & Deborah, b. May 10, 1738	2	376
Naomi, d. John & Abigail, b. Apr. 9, 1743	2	379
Naomy, d. John, 2nd & Abigail, d. Oct. 17, 1749	2	248
Naomi, d. John & Abigail, d. Oct. [ ], 1749	2	248
Naomi, see also Name		
Nath[an], m. Elizabeth MOORE, b. of Windsor, Nov. 24, 1653	Col.2	159
Nat[han], his w. [ ], adm. ch. & Communicant Sept. [ ], 1673	MG	
Nath[an], s. John, m. Ruth PORTER, Nov. 28, 1689	Col.D	55
Nathanell, m. Elisabeth MOORE, Nov. 27, [16]	MG	
Nathaniell, m. Elisabeth MO[O]RE, b. of Windsor, Nov. 24, 1653	Col.2	159
Nathanell, s. [Nathanell & Elisabeth], b. Mar. 20, 1656/7	MG	
Nathaniell, s. Nathaniell, b. Mar. 20, 1656	Col.2	161
Nathan[i]el*, his w. [ ], "publicly tendered herself to attain baptism for her children", Jan. 31, [16]57		
*(First written "Nathan[i]el BISSELL")	MG	
Nathanel, s. Nath[aniel], bp. Feb. 7, [16]57	MG	
Nathanell, adm. ch. May 3, [16]63	MG	
Nathaniel, adm. ch. & Communicant May [ ], 1663	MG	
Nathanell, s. [John & Elisabeth], b. July 8, 1663	MG	
Nathanael, s. John, b. July 8, [16]63	1	22
Nathanel, s. J[ ], bp. [ ] 12, [16]63	MG	
Nathan[ie]l, taxed 4-0 on Feb. 10, [16]73	MG	
Nathanell, s. [Joseph & Sara], b. Aug. 8, 1673	MG	
Nathanael, s. Joseph, b. Aug. 8, 1673	1	22
Nathanell, had 10 children b. in Windsor. Dated Aug. 17, 1677	MG	
Nathan[i]e[l], his w. [ ], adm. ch. Sept. 28, [16]7[ ]	MG	
Nathanell, s. Nathanell, m. Elizabeth ELESWORTH, d.		

	Vol.	Page
LOOMIS, LOOMYS, LOOMAS, LOMAS, LOOMYES, (cont.)		
Josias, Dec. 23, 1680, by Capt. Newbery	Col. 1	46
Nathaneill, m. Elizabeth **ELSWORTH**, Dec. 23, 1680	TR1	1
Nathanael, s. Nathanael, m. Elizabeth **ELSWORTH**, Dec. 23, 1680	1	58
Nathanel, s. Nathanell, ae 24 on Mar. 20, [1681], m. Elizabeth **ELSWORTH** who was ae 23 on Nov. 11, 1680, Dec. 23, 1680	MG	
Nathanael, Sr., d. [ ] 19, 1688	1	47
Nathanael, s. John, m. Ruth **PORTER**, Nov. 28, 1689	1	58
Nathanael, s. Nathanael (s. John), b. Mar. 7, 1694/5	1	24
Nathanael, s. Josiah, b. Oct. [ ], 1700	1	24
Nathaniel, s. James, b. Feb. 15, 1711/12	2	57
Nathanael, m. Ann **ALLYN**, b. of Windsor, Mar. 27, 1718	2	170
Nathaniel, s. Nathaniel & Ann, b. Apr. 11, 1719	2	59
Nathaniel, s. Nathaniel & Sarah, b. May 13, 1724	2	383
Nathanael, Lieut., d. Sept. 29, 1733	2	246
Nathaniel, 2nd, m. wid. Ruth **NEWBERRY**, b. of Windsor, Mar. 9, 1740/1	2	172
Nathaniel, Jr., m. Deborah **LOOMIS**, b. of Windsor, Sept. 22, 1743	2	172
Nathaniel, 3rd, m. Margret **BISSEL**, b. of Windsor, Dec. 12, 1745	2	173
Nathaniel, Sergt. of the East Side of the River, d. Aug. 2, 1758	2	248
Nathaniel, d. Mar. 8, 1768	2	249
Nathaniel, Capt., d. June 14, 1784, in the 65th y. of his age	2	250
Nathanel, contributed 0-5-0 to the poor in other colonies	MG	
Nehemiah, s. [Samuell], b. July 15, 1670	MG	
Nider, s. Serajah & Sibbel, b. Apr. 9, 1768	2	387
Noah, s. Hezekiah, b. Apr. 1, 1692	2	55
Noah, m. Sarah **MORTON**, b. of Windsor, May 7, 1713	2	170
Noah, s. Noah, b. Jan. 27, 1713/14	2	58
Obiah, s. Timothy, b. Aug. 4, 1705	2	60
Odiah, m. Jane **ALLYN**, b. of Windsor, Nov. 1, 1739	2	172
Odiah, s. Odiah & Jane, b. Feb. 8, 1741/2	2	378
Oliver, s. Uriah & Hannah, b. Dec. 17, 1741	2	377
Oliver, s. Uriah & Hannah, d. Jan. 21, 1741/2, ae 5 wks.	2	247
Oliver, s. Nathaniell, 4th* & Deborah, b. Dec. 18, 1743 *("John Egleston" crossed out)	2	379
Oliver, m. Jerusha **BANCRAFT**, b. of Windsor, Sept. 2, 1762	2	488
Oliver, s. Oliver & Jerusha, b. Sept. 24, 1763	2	386
Oliver, s. Uriah, Jr. & Apphia, b. Oct. 30, 1768	2	387
Oliver, of Windsor, m. Chloe **WOOD**, of East Windsor, Feb. 9, 1792	2	488
Ozias, s. Odiah & Jane, b. Oct. 25, 1743	2	378
Ozias, s. Odiah & Jane, d. Dec. 17, 1744	2	247
Ozias, s. Odiah & Jane, b. Jan. 13, 1745/6	2	379

	Vol.	Page
LOOMIS, LOOMYS, LOOMAS, LOMAS, LOOMYES, (cont.)		
Phebe, m. Jacob MONSELL, b. of Windsor, Feb. 15, 1718	2	176
Phinehas, s. Eliakim & Mary, b. Mar. 15, 1744/5	2	380
Polly, d. George & Anne, b. Dec. 12, 1784	2	389
Prudence, m. Curtis TUTTLE, of Otis, Mass., Sept. 17, 1833, by Henry A. Rowland	2	206
Rachel, d. Joseph, [s. of Joseph, s. of Joseph], b. Jan. 12, 1692/3	1	23
Rachel, d. Benjamin & Joanna, b. Aug. 5, 1735	2	376
Rachel, d. Jonah & Anna, b. Sept. 17, 1740	2	377
Rebeck[a], d. [Nathaniel & Elisabeth], b. Dec. 10, 16[ ]	MG	
Rebeckah, d. Nath[an], b. Dec. 10, 1682	Col.D	51
Rebekah, d. Nathaniel, b. Dec. 10, [16]82	1	23
Rebekah, d. John, b. Dec. [ ], 1687	1	23
Rebekah, d. Timothy, b. May 24, 1700	2	60
Rebekah, d. Timothy, b. May 29, 1700	1	24
Rebeckah, of Lebanon*, m. Josiah ROCKWELL, of Windsor, Dec. 10, 1713 *("Hebron" crossed out)	2	194
Rebekah, d. Moses & Rebekah, b. June 4, 1726	2	371
Rebekah, w. Moses, d. June 10, 1726	2	246
Rebekah, m. Moses LOOMIS, b. of Windsor, Aug. 12, 1725	2	171
Rebeckah, d. Reuben & Rebeckah, b. Mar. 4, 1747/8	2	381
Rebeckah, Mrs., d. Apr. 21, 1750	2	248
Rebeckah, d. Odiah & Jane, b. Oct. 25, 1750	2	381
Rebecca, d. Jacob, Jr. & Jerusha, b. Jan. 20, 1805	2	390
Rebecca, m. Ammi MILLS, b. of Windsor, Nov. 16, 1826, by Rev. John Bartlett, of Winstonbury	2	492
Redexselano, d. John, Jr. & Redexselano, b. Nov. 29, 1761	2	385
Remembrance, s. Abraham & Isabel, b. Sept. 30, 1743	2	378
Remembrance, s. Abraham & Isabel, d. Jan. 18, 1744/5	2	247
Reuben, s. Ichibod, b. Mar. 4, 1719	2	59
Reuben, m. Ann MOORE, b. of Windsor, Dec. 2, 1742	2	172
Reuben, m. Rebeckah GOODRICH, b. of Windsor, Feb. 5, 1745/6	2	173
Reuben, s. Reuben & Rebeckah, b. Nov. 11, 1746	2	380
Ruben, Jr., m. Susannah FILLEY, b. of Windsor, Aug. 17, 1769	2	173
Ruben, Jr. & Luranna, had child b. May 13, 1770; d. May 14, 1770	2	387
Ruben, s. Ruben, Jr. & Laurana, b. Apr. 16, 1773	2	388
Ruben, Jr., d. Sept. 12, 1776	2	249
Rhoda, d. Isaac, 3rd & Sarah, b. July 11, 1746	2	379
Rhoda, m. Orson WILLSON*, b. of Windsor, Apr. 11, 1849, by Rev. Samuel Law *("Orson Wilson AUSTIN" crossed out in the original)	2	520
Richard, s. David, b. Jan. 1, 1706/7	2	56
Richard, s. David, Jr. & Elizabeth, b. Oct. 11, 1725	2	371
Richard, s. David, Jr. & Elizabeth, d. Dec. 7, 1726	2	246

	Vol.	Page
LOOMIS, LOOMYS, LOOMAS, LOMAS, LOOMYES, (cont.)		
Richard, s. Aaron & Deborah, b. Oct. 17, 1732	2	374
Right, s. Seth & Esther, b. Feb. 13, 1756	2	382
Rocksalany, d. Moses, Jr. & Elizabeth, b. Oct. 1, 1741	2	381
Rocksana, d. Ruben, Jr. & Laurana, b. Mar. 23, 1775	2	388
Roger, s. John & Abigail, b. Feb. 9, 1744/5	2	379
Roman W., m. Ann G. **BARBER**, Oct. 5, 1834, by Henry A. Rowland	2	489
Ruth, d. [Samuell], b. June 14, 1660	MG	
Ruth, d. Samuel, b. June 14, 1660	1	22
Ruth, d. [Thomas & Mary], b. Oct. 16, 1665	MG	
Ruth, d. Thomas, b. Oct. 16, 1665	Col.1	55
Ruth, d. Thomas, b. Oct. 16, 1665	1	22
Ruth, d. Tho[mas], bp. Apr. 8, [16]66	MG	
Ruth, d. John, b. Jan. 28, 1689	1	23
Ruth, m. Joseph **COLT**, Oct. 29, 1691	1	55
Ruth, d. Thomas, b. Dec. 27, 1698	1	24
Ruth, m. Peter **MILLS**, Jr., b. of Windsor, Feb. 1, 1726/7	2	177
Ruth, m. Robert **BARNARD**, b. of Windsor, Nov. 1, 1728	2	129
Ruth, d. Henry & Ruth, b. Aug. 24, 1729	2	373
Ruth, of Bolton, m. Daniel **GILLET**, of Windsor, Aug. 27, 1735	2	156
Ruth, m. Quartus **BEDORTHA**, b. of Windsor, Feb. 28, 1832, by Hiram Roberts, J. P.	2	150
Ruth R., of Windsor, m. Noah **GRISWOLD**, Jr., of Bloomfield, Apr. 27, 1836, by Rev. Charles Walker	2	481
Samuel, s. John, b. June 29, 1655	Col.2	161
Samuel, s. John, b. June 29, 1655	1	22
Samuell, s. [John & Elisbeth], b. June 29, 1655; d. [ ]	MG	
Samuell, adm. ch. Nov. 26, 1661	MG	
Samuell, 2nd, s. [John & Elisabeth], b. Aug. 12, 1666	MG	
Samuel, 2nd, s. John, b. Aug. 12, 1666	1	22
Samervel, bp. Aug. 19, [16]66	MG	
Samuell, had 5 children b. in Windsor. Dated Aug. 17, 1677	MG	
Samuel, of Windsor, m. Elizabeth **WHITE**, of Hatfield, July 2, 1688	1	58
Samuel, s. Samuel, b. Feb. 28, 1689	1	23
Samuel, s. Samuel, d. Mar. 14, 1689	1	47
Samuel, s. Samuel, b. July 17, 1692	1	23
Samuel, his w. [ ], adm. ch. [16]	MG	
Samuel, s. David & Elizabeth, b. May 21, 1731	2	374
Sam[ue]l, paid him 2-6-0 for cask of wine for sacrament	MG	
Samuel O., m. Charlotte **BLISS**, June 2, 1847, by T. A. Leete	2	175
Samuel O., m. Charlotte **BLISS**, June 2, 1847, by T. A. Leete	2	491
Sara, d. [Joseph & Sara], b. July 22, 1647; d. [ ], [16]54	MG	
Sarah, d. Joseph, b. July 22, 1647	1	22
Sara, 2nd d. [Joseph & Sara], b. Apr. 1, 1660	MG	
Sarah, d. Joseph, b. Apr. 1, 1660	1	22

	Vol.	Page

LOOMIS, LOOMYS, LOOMAS, LOMAS, LOOMYES, (cont.)

	Vol.	Page
A. Rowland	2	489
Stephen, s. [Joseph & Sara], b. Sept. 1, 1668	MG	
Stephen, m. Esther COLT, b. of Windsor, Jan. 1, 1690	1	58
Stephen, s. Stephen, b. July 21, 1693	1	24
Stephen, m. Mabell HOSKINS, Dec. 7, 1715	2	170
Stephen, s. Stephen, b. Aug. 21, 1716	2	58
Stephen, Jr., m. Grace LOOMIS, b. of Windsor, June 9, 1743	2	172
Stephen, s. Stephen, Jr. & Grace, b. Apr. 13, 1745	2	379
Submit, d, Moses, Jr. & Elizabeth, b. Oct. 20, 1736	2	381
Susannah, d. Stephen & Grace, b. Sept. 24, 1753	2	383
Susanna, d. Joseph & Keziah, b. Feb. 7, 1764	2	386
Sibell, d. Jedadiah & Sibell, b. Nov. 19, 1749	2	380
Sibel, d. Elijah & Rachel, b. May 12, 1759	2	385
Sibbel, m. Serajah LOOMIS, b. of Windsor, Oct. 21, 1767	2	488
Sibal, s. Daniel, Jr. & Elizabeth, b. Sept. 18, 1827*		
*(Probably "1727")	2	372
Sylvia, d. Jacob, Jr. & Jerusha, b. Feb. 14, 1807	2	390
Sylvia, of Windsor, m. William MUNSON, of Bethlem, Apr. 10, 1832, by John Bartlett	2	495
Tabitha, d. Benjamin & Joanna, b. Oct. 16, 1730	2	373
Temperance, d. Benajah & Temperance, b. Feb. 19, 1731/2	2	374
Thankful, d. Moses, b. Mar. 5, 1709/10	2	56
Theedeann, d. Eliplet & Thedosha, b. Sept. 13, 1754	2	382
Thomas, m. Hanna FOX, Nov. 1, 1653	MG	
Thomas, m. Hannah FFOXE, b. of Windsor, Nov. 1, 1653	Col.2	159
Thomas, m. Hannah FOX, Nov. 1, 1653	1	59
Thomas, s. [John & Elisabeth], b. Dec. 3, 1653	MG	
Thomas, s. John, b. Dec. 3, 1653	Col.2	161
Thomas, s. John, b. Dec. 3, 1653	1	22
Thomas, s. John, [bp.] Dec. 3, [16]53	MG	
Thomas, s. [Thomas & Hanna], b. Oct. 29, 1654; d. [ ]	MG	
Thomas, s. Thomas, b. Oct. 29, 1654	1	22
Thomas, s. Thomas, d. [ ], [16]54	MG	
Thomas, 2nd. s. [Thomas & Hanna], b. Mar. 17, 1655	MG	
Thomas, s. Thomas, b. Mar. 17, 1655. "The day of the month and the year annexed to this birth taken from an ancient book now in posssion of Theodore Sill, and entered here by William Howard, Register	1	22
Thomas, s. Tho[mas], b. Mar. 17, 1655/6	Col.2	157
Thomas, m. 2nd w. Mary JUDG, Jan. 1, 1662	MG	
Thomas, of Windsor, m. Mary JUDD, of Ffarmingtown, Jan. 1, [16]62, at Hartford, by Mr. Willes	Col.1	45
Thomas, m. Mary JUDD, Jan. 1, 1662, by Mr. Willis	1	58
Thomas, his w. [ ], d. [ ], [16]62	MG	
Thomas, adm. ch. Apr. 3, [16]66	MG	
Thomas, adm, ch. & communicant Apr. [ ], 1666	MG	
Thomas, his w. [ ], adm. ch. & communicant Apr.[ ], 16661	MG	

	Vol.	Page
LOOMIS, LOOMYS, LOOMAS, LOMAS, LOOMYES, (cont.)		
Thomas, taxed 4-0 on Feb. 10, [16]73	MG	
Thomas, had 10 children b. in Windsor. Dated Aug. 17, 1677	MG	
Thomas, m. Hannah **PORTER**, Dec. 17, 1682	1	58
Thomas, m. Hannah **PORTER**, Dec. 17, 1683	Col.D	54
Thomas, s. Thomas, Jr., b. Mar. 16, 1687/8	1	23
Thomas, Sr., d. Aug. 28, 1689	Col.D	57
Thomas, Sr., d. Aug. 28, 1689	1	47
Thomas, s. Thomas, bp. [ ], [16[ ]	MG	
Thomas, his w. [ ], adm. to Ch. Apr. [ ], 16[ ]	MG	
Thomas, d. Apr. 19, 1746	2	248
Thomas, m. Hanna **FOX**, b. of Windsor, Nov. 1, [ ]	Col.2	159
Thomas, contributed 0-2-6 to the poor in other colonies	MG	
Timothy, s. [John & Elisabeth], b. July 27, 1661	MG	
Timothy, s. John, b. July 27, 1661	1	22
Timothy, s. John, [bp.] July 28, [16]61	MG	
Timothy, m. Rebekah **PORTER**, Mar. 20, 1689/90	1	59
Timothy, s. Timothy, b. Feb. 22, 1691	1	24
Timothy, s. Timothy, b. Feb. 22, 1691	2	60
Timothy, d. May 19, 1710	2	245
Timothy, s. Timothy, of Windsor, m. Hannah **PHELPS**, d.		
Timothy, of Hartford, Apr. 5, 1722	2	171
Timothy, s. Timothy & Hannah, b. July 30, 1724	2	61
Timothy, d. Aug. 12, 1740	2	247
Timothy, m. Sarah **TALCOTT**, b. of Windsor, Jan. 31,		
1748/9	2	173
Timothy, s. Timothy & Sarah, b. June 3, 1750	2	381
Timothy, Ens., m. Jerusha **BISSELL**, b. of Windsor, Nov.		
3, 1763	2	173
Timothy, d. Dec. 9, 1786, in the 63rd y. of his age	2	250
Timothy, s. George & Anne, b. June 28, 1789	2	390
Triphena, d. Nathaniell, 3rd & Margaret, b. Oct. 9, 1753	2	382
Tryphena, d. Capt. Nathaniell & Margret, d. July 4, 1765	2	249
Tryphena, d. George & Anne, b. Feb. 21, 1783	2	389
Uriah, s. Timothy, b. May 8, 1703	1	25
Uriah, s. Timothy, b. May 8, 1703	2	60
Uriah, m. Hannah **WOLCUTT**, b. of Windsor, June 2, 1737	2	172
Uriah, s. Uriah & Hannah, b. Feb. 25, 1737/8	2	376
Uriah, Jr., of Windsor, m. Apphia **SHELDON**, of Suffield,		
July 5, 1764	2	488
Uriah, Jr. & Apphia, had child b. Feb. 12, 1767; d. in about		
12 hrs. after birth	2	387
Uriah, Jr., d. [ ], 1787	2	250
Uriah, d. Jan. [ ], 1788	2	250
Uriah, s. Oliver & Cloe, b. Mar. 17, 1793	2	390
Uriah & Hannah, had d. [ ], b. Dec. 3, [ ], ; d. next day	2	378
Ursalah, d. John & Abigail, b. July 19, 1740	2	379
Wait, d. Jonathan & Sarah, b. Aug. 14, 1732	2	375

	Vol.	Page
LOOMIS, LOOMYS, LOOMAS, LOMAS, LOOMYES, (cont.)		
Watson, s. Nathaniell, 3rd & Margret, b. Jan. 1, 1746/7	2	380
Welthy, d. Serajah & Sibbel, b. Feb. 11, 1777	2	388
Willard, m. Abigail **WARNER**, Feb. 17, 1830, by Henry A. Rowland	2	174
William, s. Samuel, b. Mar. 18, [16]72	1	22
William, s. Simeon & Keziah, b. Feb. 14, 1774	2	389
William S., of Granby, m. Elizabeth **GRISWOLD**, of Windsor, Apr. 11, 1838, by Eli Deniston	2	175
Worthy, d. Gidion & Joanna, b. Sept. 22, 1760; d. Oct. 17, 1760	2	384
Zachariah, s. John, b. Nov. [ ], 1681	1	23
Zeruiah, d. Joshua, b. Mar. 20, 1719/20	2	59
Zeruiah, d. Joshua & Deborah, d. Jan. 31, 1726/7	2	246
Zeruiah, d. Joshua & Deborah, b. Jan. 31, 1727/8	2	372
Zeruiah, d. Nathaniell, 4th & Deborah, b. Apr. 5, 1746	2	379
Surviah, d. Moses, Jr. & Elizabeth, b. Nov. 10, 1738; d. Dec. 10, 1740	2	381
-----, adm, communion, Oct. 11, 1640	MG	
-----, b. Mar. 17, [16]55; bp. Feb. 7, [16]57	MG	
LORD, Benjamin, m. Laury **ALLIS**, b. of Windsor, Oct. 18, 1848, by Rev. Samuel Law	2	491
LOTHROP, [see under **LATHROP**]		
LOVEL, [see under **LOVETT**]		
LOVETT, LOVET, [see also **LEVIT**], David, s. Noah & Deborah, b. Feb. [ ], 1746	2	384
Hannah, d. Noah & Deborah, b. Nov. 28, 1742	2	384
James*, s. Noah & Deborah, b. Aug. 12, 1754 *(Written "James **LOVEL**")	2	384
Jerusha, d. Noah & Deborah, b. July 21, 1744	2	384
John, s. Noah & Deborah, b. Nov. 13, 1749	2	384
Samuel, s. Noah & Deborah, b. Oct. 29, 1751	2	384
LUCK, W[illia]m, m. Julia **WILSON**, b. of Windsor, June 4, 1837, by Eli Deniston	2	490
LUDLO[W], -----, Mr., had 1 child b. in Windsor. Dated Aug. 17, 1677	MG	
LUNDON, John, had 2 children b. in Windsor. Dated Aug. 17, 1677	MG	
John, contributed 0-2-6 to the poor in other colonies his w. [ ] contributed 0-0-9 to the poor in other colonies	MG	
LYNDE, Nathanil, of Brookfield, Mass., m. Eunice **AUSTIN**, Mar. 26, 1822, by Rev. Henry A. Rowland	2	174
LYON, Aaron, s. Aaron & Rhode, b. Nov. 12, 1774	2	388
Esther, d. Aaron & Rhoda, b. Aug. 23, 1776	2	388
Rhode, d. Aaron & Rhode, b. June 18, 1769	2	387
LYTEL, [see also **LITTLE**], Mary, d. Thomas & Ann, b. Feb. 28, 1724/5	2	372

	Vol.	Page
LYTEL, (cont.)		
Thomas, s. Thomas & Ann, b. Jan. 28, 1726/7	2	372
McCARTER, James, s. James & Phebe, b. Feb. 10, 1760	2	406
John, s. James & Phebe, b. Nov. 26, 1755	2	406
Phebe, d. James & Phebe, b. Feb. 7, 1758	2	406
McCHESTER, Selina, of Windsor, m. Asa PEASE, of Enfield, Nov.* 12, 1848, by Rev. Samuel Lake *("Mar." crossed out)	2	194
McCRAY, David, s. William & Margret, b. Dec. 22, 1755	2	405
Elizabeth, d. William & Margret, b. Apr. 25, 1752	2	405
Ruben, s. William & Margret, b. Mar. 22, 1754	2	405
Sarah, d. William & Margret, b. Oct. 23, 1763	2	405
McCURDY, Elizabeth, m. Alford TYLER, b. of Windsor, Aug. 30, 1852, by Rev. Thomas H. Rouse	2	461
McDERMOT, Bridget, m. Thomas ENGLISH, Oct. 13, 1852, by Rev. James Smyth	2	460
MACK, Andrew, s. Andrew & Sarah, b. Nov. 19, 1780	2	575
Andrew, d. July 7, 1839	2	256
Andrew, of Windsor, m. Lydia S. MERRETT, of Whitingham, Vt., Aug. 6, 1843, by S. W. Scofield	2	517
Charlotte, of Windsor, m. William PERKINS, of East Hartford, Apr. 6, 1825, by Rev. Henry A. Rowland	2	192
Fanny, d. Andrew & Sarah, b. Sept. 14, 1799	2	575
George A., m. Eliza M. REYNOLDS, b. of Windsor, Nov. 30, 1837, by Eli Deniston	2	493
Hezekiah, s. Andrew & Sarah, b. Jan. 3, 1786	2	575
James, s. Andrew & Sarah, b. Aug. 19, 1788	2	575
Mary, d. Andrew & Sarah, b. Mar. 25, 1791	2	575
Sarah, d. Andrew & Sarah, b. Dec. 13, 1792	2	575
William, s. Andrew & Sarah, b. May 31, 1783	2	575
McKEE, [see also MACKEY], Salmon, of Glastenbury, m. Abigail COLLINS, of Hartford, July 7, 1822, by Rev. Augustus Bolles	2	494
MACKELL, Catharine, m. Patrick DUFFY, Sept. 3, 1852, by Rev. James Smyth	2	460
MACKENOREY, S. T., of Hartford, m. Maria Antoinette SOPER, of Windsor, Dec. 26, 1836, by Rev. Charles Walker	2	496
MACKEY, [see also McKEE], James, m. Ellen CARROLL, Oct. 14, 1852, by Rev. James Smyth	2	460
McKINSTRY, McKINTRY, MACKENSTRY, MEKINSTRE,		
Alexander, s. Paul & Sarah, b. Dec. 12, 1764	2	371
Salmon, s. Paul & Sarah, b. Oct. 19, 1766	2	405
William, s. John, b. Oct. 8, 1732	2	392
-----, had 2 children d. [ ], in "Elenton" prior to 1740	MG	
MACKMAN, Elizabeth, Mrs., m. John ELIOT, Oct. 31, 1699	1	56
James, m. Elizabeth STOUGHTON, Nov. 27, 1690	Col.D	55
James, m. Elizabeth STOUGHTON, Nov. 27, 1690	1	59
James, d. Dec. 18, 1698	1	48

	Vol.	Page
McLEAN, Betsey, m. Elizer **LATIMER**, Nov. 15, 1830, by John Bartlett	2	174
James, s. John & Sarah, b. May 6, 1779	2	575
McMORAN, MACMORAN, MACMORRAN, McMORRAN, MACKMORRAN, Elizabeth, d. John & Elizabeth, b. Aug. 18, 1735	2	395
Elizabeth*, wid. John, Jr., m. Daniel **HAYDON**, Jr., Apr. 13, 1748 *(In pencil)	2	163
Elizabeth, m. Ezekiel **THRALL**, b. of Windsor, July 26, 1763	2	205
John, s. John & Elizabeth, b. July 27, 1729	2	391
John, s. John & Elizabeth, d. July 17, 1730	2	253
John, 2nd, s. John & Elizabeth, b. May 17, 1731	2	393
John, m. Mindwell **THRALL**, b. of Windsor, Feb. 16, 1758	2	179
MACROBIES, Susan Maria, m. George W. **FOWLER**, b. of Windsor, Aug. 15, 1852, by Rev. Joseph D. Hull	2	461
MADER, [see under **MATHER**]		
MADISON, Francis W., of New York, m. Almira G. **COOK**, Nov. 19, 1840, by S. D. Jewett	2	515
MAGIRA, Edward S., of Hartford, m. Rosanna **SMITH**, of Windsor, Mar. 7, 1847, by Rev. George F. Kettell	2	493
MALLORY, Mary A., of Windsor, m. Philo **JOY**, of Amherst, Mass., Nov. 15, 1835, by Rev. Daniel Heminway	2	169
MANLEY, MANLY, Allyn, s. Ebenezer & Marcy, b. Feb. 8, 1765	2	405
Erastus, s. William & Lucy, b. July 12, 1801	2	576
Erastus, m. Abigail **BROWN**, Jan. 15, 1835, by Henry A. Rowland	2	182
Marcy, wid., m. Samuel **ENO**, Jr., b. of Windsor, May 7, 1777	2	147
Marcie, d. Russell & Rebeckah, b. Apr. 5, 1797	2	574
Margret, of Symsbury, m. Josiah **BUTLER**, of Windsor, Nov. 13, 1754	2	133
Poley, d. Ebenezer & Marcy, b. Nov. 15, 1763	2	405
Russell, s. Ebenezer & Marcy, b. Sept. 19, 1768	2	406
Russell Sherman, s. Russell & Rebeckah, b. Jan. 13, 1799	2	574
William, s. Ebenezer & Marcy, b. Sept. 9, 1771	2	406
MANSFIELD, MANSFEILD, John, m. Sarah **PHELPS**, Dec. 13, 1683	Col.D	54
John, s. John, b. Sept. 13, 1684	Col.D	51
John, s. John, b. Sept. 13, 1684	1	26
John, s. John, d. Feb. 10, 1690	1	48
John, d. Mar. 15, 1726/7	2	252
John, m. Sarah **PHELPS**, Dec. 13, [ ]	1	59
Mary, d. John, b. Aug. 16, 1689	1	26
Samuel, s. John, b. Sept. 16, 1687	1	26
Sarah, d. Jno, b. Jan. 5, 1685	Col.D	51
Sarah, d. John, b. Jan. 5, 1685	1	26
Sarah, m. Cornelius **PHELPS**, Nov. 2, 1704	2	186
Sarah, wid., d. Oct. 26, 1732	2	253

	Vol.	Page
MARBLE, William, of East Windsor, m. Maria HOLCOMB, Oct. 17, 1826, by Richard Niles, J. P.	2	182
MARSH, Ann, d. Rev. Jonathan & Margeret, b. Jan. 28, 1729/30	2	392
Darcos, d. Rev. Jonathan, b. Aug. 31, 1718	2	68
Hannah, d. Rev. Jonathan, b. May 28, 1723	2	68
Jonathan, of Windsor, m. Margaret WHITING, of Hartford, July 13, 1710	2	176
Jonathan, s. Jonathan, b. Jan. 1, 1713/14	2	66
Jonathan, Rev., d. Sept. 9, 1747	2	254
Joseph, s. Rev. Jonathan & Margeret, b. Nov*. 10, 1727 *("Jan." crossed out)	2	392
Lydia, m. David LOOMIS, Dec. 8, 1692	1	59
Margarett, d. Jonathan, b. June 10, 1711	2	65
Margret, wid. Rev. Jonathan, d. Dec. 9, 1747	2	254
Mary, d. Jonathan, b. July 19, 1716	2	66
Roswell, of New Hartford, m. Huldah M. TURNER, Mar. 18, 1829, by Henry A. Rowland	2	495
Sarah, Mrs. alias PINNEY, d. May 25, 1751	2	254
William, of Hartford, m. Huldah WILSON, of Windsor, May 9, 1822, by Rev. Henry A. Rowland	2	181
MARSHALL, MARSHAL, MARSHEL, MARSHELL, Aaron, s. Samuel & Abigaiel, b. May 11, 1735	2	393
Abigail, d. David, b. Jan. 9, 1687	1	26
Abigail, d. John, b. Dec. 10, 1693	1	27
Abigail, d. John, d. Feb. 18, 1693/4	1	48
Abigail, d. Edmond, b. Sept. 20, 1697	1	27
Abigail, w. John, d. Feb. 20, 1697/8	1	48
Abigail, m. Stephen WINCHEL, Mar. 10, 1697/8	1	63
Abigail, of Northampton, m. John BIRDGE, of Windsor, Nov. 10, 1702	1	54
Abigaell, m. Benjamin GIBBS, Sept. 16, 1708	2	154
Abigail, d. Samuel, b. Mar. 6, 1721	2	68
Abigail, wid., d. Feb. 13, 1774	2	255
Abner, s. Samuel & Abigail, b. Feb. 9, 1726/7	2	69
Abner, m. Hannah MARSHALL, b. of Windsor, Jan. 4, 1759	2	179
Alexander, s. Samuell, Jr. & Joanna, b. July 13, 1747	2	397
Alexander, s. Samuel, Jr. [ ] (Entry crossed out)	2	380
Almeda, d. Eliakim & Anna, b. Jan. 18, 1788	2	574
Amasa, s. Samuel & Abigail, b. Jan. 17, 1728/9	2	391
Anronetta Rebecca, d. Elihu & Mary Caroline, b. Nov. 27, 1836	2	576
Asenath, d. Samuel & Abigail, b. May 1, 1733	2	393
Asenath, d. Eliakim & Sarah, b. July 9, 1758	2	401
Asenath, had s. Job, b. Aug. 27, 1774	2	406
Benjamin, s. Thomas, b. Aug. 8, 1707	2	65
Benjamin, s. Thomas, d. July 4, 1708	2	251
Candace, m. Odiah L. SHELDON, Aug. 1, 1826, by Rev. Henry A. Rowland	2	203

	Vol.	Page
MARSHALL, MARSHAL, MARSHEL, MARSHELL, (cont.)		
Cathiern, d. Thomas, b. Apr. 11, 1699	2	62
Daniel, s. Thomas, b. [ ], 1705	2	65
Daniel, m. Hannah **DRAKE**, b. of Windsor, Nov. 10, 1742	2	178
Daniel, of Windsor, m. Martha **STEARNS**, of Tolland, June 23, 1747	2	179
Daniel, s. Eliakim & Sarah, b. Mar. 18, 1766	2	404
Dauid, s. [Samuell & Mary], b. July 24, 1661	MG	
David, s. Samuel, b. July 24, 1661	1	25
David, m. Abigail **PHELPS**, Dec. 9, 1686	1	59
David, s. David, b. Apr. 14, 1692	1	26
David, m. Sarah **PHELPS**, b. of Windsor, Dec. 15, 1721	2	176
David, s. David, b. June 1, 1722	2	68
David, s. David, d. Sept. [ ], 1725	2	252
David, s. David & Sarah, b. Oct. 21, 1728	2	391
David Elihu, s. Elihu & Mary Caroline, b. Aug. 11, 1843	2	576
Dinah, d. Eliakim, Jr. & Sarah, b. Apr. 1, 1749	2	397
Dorithy, d. Eliakim, b. Oct. 1, 1705	2	63
Dorithy, d. Oct. 25, 1736	2	253
Edward W., m. Julia A. **HAYDEN**, Nov. 10, 1836, by Rev. Charles Walker	2	489
Eliacem, s. [Samuell & Mary], b. July 10, 1669	MG	
Eliakim, of Windsor, m. Sarah **LEET**, of Gilford, Aug. 23, 1704	2	175
Eliakim, s. Samuel, b. Mar. 1, 1718/19	2	67
Eliakim, s. Eliakim, b. July 15, 1720	2	67
Eliakim, s. Eliakim, d. Aug. 8, 1720, ae 3 wks. 3 das.	2	252
Eliakim, m. Sarah **HODGE**, b. of Windsor, Nov. 10, 1743	2	178
Eliakim, s. Eliakim, Jr. & Sarah, b. Oct. 28, 1754	2	400
Elihu, s. David & Noamy, b. Mar. 21, 1765	2	404
Elihu, m. Mary C. **GRISWOLD**, June 10, 1829, by Henry A. Rowland	2	492
Elijah, s. Eliakim, Jr. & Sarah, b. Sept. 9, 1752	2	399
Elisha, s. Eliakim, Jr. & Sarah, b. Dec. 31, 1750	2	399
Elisha, s. David & Naomy, b. Apr. 16, 1763	2	404
Elizabeth, d. [Samuell & Mary], b. Sept. 27, 1674	MG	
Elizabeth, d. Samuel, b. Sept. 27, [16]74	1	26
Elizabeth, m. John **GAYLORD**, b. of Windsor, May 27, 1701	1	57
Elizabeth, m. Joseph **BAKER**, Jr., Nov. 11, 1829, by Henry A. Rowland	2	498
Ellen Elizabeth, d. Elihu & Mary Caroline, b. Aug. 8, 1846	2	576
Ellen Griswold, d. Elihu & Mary Caroline, b. Oct. 24, 1834	2	576
Emilla, d. Eliakim & Anna, b. July 18, 1794	2	574
Estelle Willehemine, d. Elihu & Mary Caroline, b. July 1, 1840	2	576
[E]unice, d. Thomas, b. May 3, 1709	2	65
Eunice, m. Samuel **ENO**, b. of Windsor, Dec. 24, 1735	2	147
Eunice, d. Eliakim, Jr. & Sarah, b. Jan. 14, 1745/6	2	396

	Vol.	Page
MARSHALL, MARSHAL, MARSHEL, MARSHELL, (cont.)		
Mary Caroline, d. Elihu & Mary Caroline, b. Mar. 13, 1833	2	576
Mercy, w. Edmund, d. Sept. 28, 1697	1	48
Nancy, d. Eliakim & Anna, b. Dec. 5, 1791	2	574
Nancy, m. Horace BECKWITH, Oct. 7, 1822, by Rev. Elisha Cushman, of Hartford	2	467
Naomy, d. David & Naomy, b. Sept. 30, 1757	2	404
Noah, s. Thomas, b. Apr. 24, 1703	2	63
Noah, s. Thomas, d. Dec. 22, 1712	2	251
Noah, s. Samuel, b. Apr. 29, 1723	2	68
Noah, m. Ruth* COOK, b. of Windsor, Jan. 19, 1748/9		
*("Joanna" crossed out)	2	179
Oliver, s. Samuel, Jr. & Sabra, b. Nov. 21, 1769	2	406
Oliver W., m. Julia A. BAINS, b. of Windsor, Jan. 1, 1838, by Eli Deniston	2	493
Rachell, d. Thomas, b. Apr. 12, 1696	2	62
Rachel, d. Samuel, b. Feb. 1, 1724/5	2	68
Rachel, d. Eliakim & Sarah, b. June 13, 1756	2	400
Rhode, d. Eliakim, Jr. & Sarah, b. July 26, 1747	2	397
Ruth, w. Noah, d. Nov. 13, 1749	2	227
Ruth, w. Noah, d. Nov. 13, 1749	2	254
Samuell, m. Mary WILTON, May 6, 1652	MG	
Samuell, m. Mary WILTON, b. of Windsor, May 6, 1652	Col.2	159
Samuel, m. Mary WILTON, May 6, 1652	1	59
Samuell, s. [Samuell & Mary], b. May 27, 1653	MG	
Samuel, s. Samuel, b. May 27, 1653	Col.2	154
Samuel, s. Samuel, b. May 27, 1653	1	25
Samuel, b. May 27, [16]53; bp. Feb. 7, [16]57	MG	
Samuel, adm. ch. May 3, 1663	MG	
Samuell, taxed 3-6 on Feb. 10, [16]73	MG	
Samuell, s. Samuell, m. Rebeca NEWBERY, June 22, 1675	Col.1	46
Samuel, d. Dec. 19, [16]75, in war	MG	
Samuel, Corp., d. Dec. 19, 1675	1	26
Samuel, Corp., d. Dec. 19, 1675	1	47
Samuell*, d. Dec. 19, 1675 *("In King Philip's War he was actively engaged appointed Oct. 14, 1675, Ensign in Maj. Treat's Army and was one of five Conn. Capts. who led the colony's forces to the attack on the Narragansett fort Dec. 19, 1675 where he fell at the head of his troops")	1	58
Samuell, had 9 children b. in Windsor. Dated Aug. 17, 1677	MG	
Samuell, s. Thomas, b. July 23, 1691	2	62
Samuel, m. Abigael PHELPS, b. of Windsor, July 12, 1716	2	176
Samuel, s. Samuel, b. Aug. 17, 1717	2	67
Samuel, Jr., m. Joanna COOK, b. of Windsor, Nov. 17, 1743	2	178
Samuell, s. Samuell, Jr. & Joanna, b. Mar. 27, 1744	2	396
Samuel, s. Samuel, Jr. & Joanna, d. July 26, 1744	2	254
Samuel, s. Samuel, Jr. & Joanna, b. July 27, 1745	2	396

	Vol.	Page
MARSHALL, MARSHAL, MARSHEL, MARSHELL, (cont.)		
Samuel, d. Oct. 24, 1749	2	254
Samuel, s. Samuel, Jr. & Sabra, b. Nov. 8, 1774	2	406
Sarah, d. Eliakim, b. June 27, 1709	2	64
Sarah, d. Eliakim, d. Jan. 20, 1709/10	2	251
Sarah, 2nd, d. Eliakim, b. Jan. 24, 1710/11	2	64
Sarah, d. David & Sarah, b. Apr. 4, 1727	2	391
Sarah, d. Eliakim, Jr. & Sarah, b. Oct. 17, 1744	2	396
Sarah, d. David & Naomy, b. Mar. 21, 1759; d. Feb. 6, 1761	2	404
Thomas, s. [Samuell & Mary], b. Apr. 23, 1659; d. [ ]	MG	
Thomas, s. Samuel, b. Apr. 23, 1659	1	25
Thomas, 2nd, s. [Samuell & Mary], b. Feb. 18, 1663	MG	
Thomas, s. Samuell, b. Feb. 18, [16]63	Col. 1	54
Thomas, s. Samuel, b. Feb. 18, [16]63	1	25
Tho[mas], m. Mary **DRAKE**, b. of Windsor, Mar. 3, 1685/6	Col.D	54
Thomas, m. Mary **DRAKE**, b. of Windsor, Mar. 3, 1685/6	1	59
Thomas, s. Thomas, b. Jan. 14, 1686	2	62
Thomas, m. Mary **DRAKE**, Mar. 2, 1686	2	175
Thomas, s. Thomas, d. Aug. 25, 1689	2	250
Tho[mas], s. Tho[mas], d. Aug. 26, 1689	Col.D	57
Thomas, s. Thomas, d. Aug. 26, 1689	1	48
Thomas, s. Thomas, b. Feb. 6, 1693	2	62
Thomas, Jr., m. Elizabeth **TUDOR**, b. of Windsor, Oct. 9, 1725	2	177
Thomas, s. Thomas, Jr. & Elizbeth, b. Oct. 13, 1726	2	69
Thomas, Dea., d. Nov. 8, 1735	2	253
Thomas, s. Thomas & Elizabeth, d. Dec. 15, 1736	2	253
Thomas, s. Thomas & Elizabeth, b. Aug. 24, 1738	2	395
Tryphena, d. Eliakim & Sarah, b. Mar. 31, 1762	2	403
Warren, s. Eliakim & Anna, b. Oct. 6, 1789	2	574
Warren, s. Eliakim & Ann, d. Aug. 27, 1837	2	256
MARSHFIELD, Prissila, d. Oct. 20, [1639]	MG	
MASKELL, MASKEL, Abigayl, d. [Thomas & Bethia], b. Nov. 27, 1663	MG	
Abigaill, d. Thomas, b. Nov. 27, 1663	Col. 1	54
Abigail, d. Thomas, b. Nov. 27, 1663	1	27
Bethia, d. [Thomas & Bethia], b. Mar. 6, 1660; d. [ ]	MG	
Bethial, d. Thomas, b. Mar. 6, 1660	1	25
Bethia, wid., m. John **WILLIAMS**, Aug. 8, 1672, by Capt. Newbery	MG	
Bethia, wid., m. John **WILLIAMES**, Aug. 8, [16]72	Col. 1	46
Elisabeth, d. [Thomas & Bethia], b. Oct. 19, 1669	MG	
John, s. Thomas, b. Nov. 9, 1667	1	27
John, s. [Thomas & Bethia], b. Nov. 19, 1667	MG	
Thomas, m. Bethia **PARSONS**, May 10, 1660	MG	
Thomas, m. Bathia **PARSONS**, b. of Windsor, May 10, 1660	1	59
Thomas, s. [Thomas & Bethia], b. Mar. 19, 1661; d. [ ]	MG	
Thomas, s. Thomas, b. Mar. 19, 1661	1	25

	Vol.	Page
MASKELL, MASKEL, (cont.)		
Thomas, 2nd, s. [Thomas & Bethia], b. Jan. 2, 1664	MG	
Thomas, s. Thomas, b. Jan. 2, 1665	Col.1	55
Thomas, s. Thomas, b. Jan. 2, 1665	1	27
Thomas, d. [Aug. 12*], [16]71 *(In pencil)	MG	
Thomas, bd. Aug. 12, [16]71	Col.1	58
Thomas, bd. Aug. 12, [16]71	1	47
Thomas, had 6 children b. in Windsor. Dated Aug. 17, 1677	MG	
MASON, MASSEN, Ann, d. Oct. 7, [1640]	MG	
David, s. Jonathan & Hannah, b. Feb. 23, 1742/3	2	396
Hannah, w. Jonathan, d. June 12, 1753	2	255
Hezakiah, s. Jonathan & Hannah, b. Apr. 2, 1748	2	402
Hezekiah, s. Jonathan & Hannah, d. Aug. 29, 1750	2	255
Isaac, s. Jonathan & Hannah, b. Oct. 24, 1743	2	402
Jzrell, m. John BISSELL, Jr., June 17, 1658	MG	
Isrell, of Saybrook, m. John BISSELL, of Windsor, June 17, 1658	1	54
Jonathan, m. Abigail DORCHESTER, b. of Windsor, Aug. 29, 1754	2	179
Lydia, d. Jonathan & Hannah, b. June 10, 1745	2	402
Zeruiah, d. Jonathan & Hannah, b. Sept. 29, 1751	2	403
Zeruiah, d. Jonathan & Hannah, d. May 1, 1759	2	255
-----, Capt., had 4 children b. in Windsor. Dated Aug. 17, 1677	MG	
MATHER, MADER, MATHERS, MARTHER, Abigail, d. Dr. Samuel, b. Sept. 1, 1714	2	67
Abigail, w. Dr. Samuel, d. Sept. 1, 1722	2	252
Allyn, s. Nathaniel & Elisabeth, b. Apr. 10, 1747	2	398
Atherton, m. Rebekah STOUGHTON, Sept. 20, 1694	1	59
Azariah, s. Samuell, b. Aug. 29, 1685	Col.D	51
Azariah, s. Samuel, b. Aug. 29, 1685	1	26
Benjamin, s. Samuel, b. Sept. 29, 1696	1	27
Charles, s. Capt. Samuel, b. Feb. 16, 1719/20	2	67
Charles, s. Nathaniel & Elizabeth, b. Sept. 26, 1742	2	396
Clarisa, m. William DIXON, b. of Windsor, Dec. 9, 1836, by Rev. Eli Deniston	2	145
Clorinah, d. Eliakim & Sarah, b. Oct. 10, 1758	2	402
Cynthia, m. Benjamin ALLYN, Oct. 16, 1823, by Rev. Henry A. Rowland	2	126
Doroth[y], m. Thomas NEWBERRY, b. of Windsor, Dec. 8, 1763	2	183
Ebenezer, s. Samuel, b. Sept. 3, 1687	1	26
Ebenezer, s. Samuel, d. Apr. 18, [ ]	1	48
Eleazer, m. Hester WAREHAM, Sept. 29, 1659	1	59
Eliakim, s. Samuell, Jr., b. Feb. 10, 1704/5	2	63
Eliakim, s. Dr. Samuell, d. Sept. 24, 1712	2	251
Eliakim, 2nd, s. Dr. Samuel & Hannah, b. Sept. 26, 1732	2	393
Eliakim, m. Sarah NEWBERRY, b. of Windsor, Dec. 4, 1755	2	179

MATHER, MADER, MATHERS, MARTHER, (cont.)

	Vol.	Page
Elijah, s. Nathaniel & Elizabeth, b. Dec. 1, 1743	2	396
Elizabeth, d. Samuel, b. Jan. 2, 1691	1	26
Elizabeth, d. Samuel, d. Jan. 17, 1696	1	48
Elizabeth, d. Joseph, b. Oct. 6, 1714	2	66
Elizabeth, d. Dr. Samuel & Hannah, b. Jan. 22, 1730/1	2	393
Elizabeth, m. Samuell WATSON, b. of Windsor, Feb. 25, 1741/2	2	209
Elisabeth, d. Nathaniel & Elisabeth, b. Oct. 1, 1745; d. Nov. 4, 1745	2	398
Elisabeth, m. John ALLYN, Jr., b. of Windsor, May 2, 1751	2	124
Elizabeth, d. Nathaniell & Elizabeth, b. May 13, 1754	2	401
Elizer, of Northampton, m. Hester WARHAM, of Windsor, Sept. 29, [16]59	Col.1	45
Hanah, d. Samuell, b. Sept. [ ], 1682	Col.D	51
Hanna, d. Samuel, b. Sept. [ ], 1682	1	26
Hannah, w. Rev. Samuell, d. Mar. 8, 1706/7	2	251
Hannah, d. Dr. Samuel & Hannah, b. Aug. 12, 1727	2	391
Hannah, d. Nathaniel, Jr. & Hannah, b. Nov. 12, 1765	2	404
Hannah, d. Samuell, d. [ ]	Col.D	56
Hannah, d. Samuel, d. [ ]	1	48
Increse, s. Nathaniel & Elizabeth, b. July 4, 1752	2	400
Jerusha, d. Atherton, b. July 18, 1700	1	27
Jerusha, m. Eli B. ALLYN, June 7, 1821, by Henry A. Rowland	2	125
John, s. Samuel, b. Sept. 22, 1699	1	27
John, s. Nathaniell & Elisabeth, b. Oct. 8, 1750	2	398
Joseph, s. Samuel, b. Mar. 6, 1688/9	1	26
Joseph, m. Elizabeth STOUGHTON, Nov. 12, 1713	2	176
Joseph, s. Samuel, d. Nov. 7, 1717	2	251
Joseph, s. Dr. Samuel, b. May 31, 1718	2	67
Joseph, s. Dr. Samuell, d. Dec. 27, 1732	2	253
Joseph, s. Dr. Samuel & Hannah, b. [ ]; d. [ ] (crossed out)	2	393
Joshua, s. Atherton, b. Nov. 26, 1706	2	65
Lucy, d. Dr. Samuel & Hannah, b. Feb. 18, 1728/9	2	391
Lucy, d. Nathaniel, Jr. & Hannah, b. Oct. 17, 1769	2	405
Marah, d. Joseph, b. Oct. 11, 1717	2	67
Mary, d. Atherton, b. Mar. 9, 1710/11	2	65
Naomi, m. Mannin BLANCHARD, Sept. 10, 1832, by Henry A. Rowland	2	469
Nathanael, s. Samuel, b. May 30, 1695	1	27
Nathanael, s. Dr. Samuel, b. Aug. 8, 1716	2	67
Nathanel, s. Nathanel & Elizabeth, b. Mar. 16, 1740/1	2	396
Nathaniel, Jr., m. Hannah FILLEY, 3rd, b. of Windsor, Nov. 11, 1762	2	180
Nathaniel, s. Nathaniel, Jr. & Hannah, b. May 14, 1763	2	404
Oliver, s. Nathaniell & Elizabeth, b. Mar. 21, 1749	2	396

	Vol.	Page
MATHER, MADER, MATHERS, MARTHER, (cont.)		
Oliver, s. Jemima **ELSWORTH**, b. of Windsor, Mar. 21, 1778	2	180
Oliver, s. Oliver & Jemima, b. Jan. 13, 1779	2	406
Richard, s. Atherton, b. Mar. 31, 1708	2	65
Robert T., s. Nathaniel & Sarah, d. Sept. 25, 1842 ae 17 y.	2	256
Samuel, Dr., m. Abigail **GRANT**, Apr. 13, 1704	1	59
Samuell, s. Dr. Samuell, b. Jan. 6, 1706/7	2	63
Samuel, Dr., m. Hannah **BUCKLAND**, b. of Windsor, May 15, 1723	2	177
Samuel, s. Eliakim & Sarah, b. Feb. 10, 1760	2	402
Samuel, m. Julia **SILL**, b. of Windsor, Nov. 22, 1843, by Rev. S. D. Jewett	2	508
Sarah, d. Eliakim & Sarah, b. Feb. 20, 1756; d. Mar. following	2	402
Sarah, d. Eliakim & Sarah, b. Sept. 4, 1757	2	402
Sarah N., of Windsor, m. Russell T. **CLARK**, of Hartford, Oct. 3, 1838, by Rev. Cephas Brainard	2	475
Talcott, m. Julia **PICKETT**, Jan. 11, 1821, by Rev. Henry A. Rowland	2	181
Timothy, s. Dr. Samuel, b. Apr. 23, 1710	2	64
Timothy, s. Nathaniell & Elizabeth, b. Nov. 15, 1755	2	401
William, s. Atherton, b. Mar. 2, 1697/8	1	27
MATSON, Keziah, of Hartford, m. William **COOK**, of Windsor, May 13, 1790	2	137
MAUDSLEY, MADESLY, MAWDSLEY, MADSLY, MAWDSLY, MAWDESLEY, Bathsheba, d. Benjamin, b. May 29, 1697	1	27
Beniamen, s. [John & Mary], b. Oct. 13, 1666	MG	
Beniamen, s. John, b. Oct. 13, 1666	Col.1	56
Benjamin, s. John, b. Oct. 13, 1666	1	26
Consider, s. [John & Mary], b. Nov. [ ]	MG	
Hannah, d. Capt. John, b. Apr. 3, 1690	Col.D	51
Hannah, d. Capt. John, b. Apr. 3, 1693* *("1690" written in pencil)	1	26
John, m. Mary **NEWBURY**, Dec. 14, 1664	MG	
John, m. Mary **NUBERY**, b. of Windsor, Dec. 14, 1664	Col.1	45
John, adm. ch. Oct. 7, 1666	MG	
John, adm. ch. & commnicant Oct. [ ], 1666	MG	
John, taxed 2-0 on Feb. 10, [16]73	MG	
John, taxed 4-0 on Feb. 10, [16]73	MG	
John, had 5 children b. in Windsor. Dated Aug. 17, 1677	MG	
John, Capt., d. Aug. 18, 1690	Col.D	57
John, Capt., d. Aug. 18, 1690	1	48
Joseph, s. [John & Mary], b. Dec. 21, 1670	MG	
Margret, d. [John & Mary], b. Feb. 4, 1668	MG	
Margret, d. John, bd. Oct. 31, 1673	Col.1	58
Margerit, d. John, bd. Oct. 31, [16]73	1	47

	Vol.	Page
MAUDSLEY, MADESLY, MAWDSLEY, MADSLY, MAWDSLY, MAWDESLEY, (cont.)		
Mary, d. [John & Mary], b. May 1, 1673	MG	
Mary, d. John, b. May 1, [16]73	1	26
Mary, of Windsor, m. Isack **PHELPS**, of Westfield, Dec. 17, 1690	Col.D	55
Mary, of Windsor, m. Isaac **PHELPS**, of Westfield, Dec. 17, 1690	1	60
Mary, contributed 0-7-6 to the poor in other colonies	MG	
MAY, Sarah, m. Isaac **DAY,** Apr. 17, 1823, b. of Windsor, by Richard Niles, J. P.	2	472
MAYBEE, Nicolas, d. [Mar. 1*], [16]65 *(In pencil)	MG	
Nicolas, d. Mar. 1, [16]66	Col.1	55
Nicholas, bd. Mar. 1, 1666/7	1	47
MEACHAM, MEACHUM, MEASHAM, [see also **MUCHMORE**], Barnabus, s. Barnabus & Margret, b. July 21, 1759	2	402
Paul, s. Barnabus & Margret, b. June 24, 1761	2	402
Phebe, d. Barnabus & Margret, b. Mar. 28, 1762	2	406
Titus, m. Anna **HOLCOMB,** June 22, 1820, by Richard Niles, J. P., Int. Pub.	2	181
Titus, m. [ ] **PLUM,** b. of Windsor, Apr. 2, 1827, by Richard Niles, J. P.	2	182
MEADCALF, Edward, of East Hartford, m. Anna Sophia **HUBBARD,** of Windsor, Mar. 25, 1824, by Rev. John Bartlett. Int. Pub.	2	494
MEARS, John, m. Lucy **ROCKWELL,** b. of Windsor, Jan. 14, 1761	2	179
Louisa, d. John & Lucy, b. Oct. 14, 1761	2	403
Lucy, d. John & Lucy, b. Sept. 3, 1763	2	403
[MEDCALF], [see under **MEADCALF**]		
MERRETT, Lydia S., of Whitingham, Vt., m. Andrew **MACK,** of Windsor, Aug. 6, 1843, by S. W. Scofield	2	517
MERRIMAN, Hannah, see Mrs. Hannah **NEWBERRY**	2	257
MESSENGER, MESENGER, MASSENGER, Deliveran[c]e, d. Edward, b. Apr. 7, [16]55	Col.2	181
Deliuerence, b. Apr. [ ], 16[ ]	MG	
Darkes*, d. [ ], b. Sept. 23, 1650 *("Dorcas")	MG	
Darkes*, d. Edward, b. Sept. 23, [16]50 *("Dorcas")	Col.2	181
Edward, had 3 children b. in Windsor. Dated Aug. 17, 1677	MG	
John, s. Nathan, b. Nov. 24, 1689	1	26
Joseph, s. Nathan, b. Sept. 20, 1687	1	27
Nathan, m. Rebeckah **KELSY,** Apr. 5, 1678	Col.D	54
Nathan, m. Rebekah **KELCIE,** Apr. 5, 1678	1	59
Nathan, s. Nathan, b. Apr. 7, [16]83	Col.D	51
Nathan, s. Nathan, b. Apr. 7, 1683	1	26
Nathan, s. Nathan, d. Dec. 30, 1684	Col.D	56
Nathan, s. Nathan, d. Dec. 30, 1684	1	48

	Vol.	Page
MESSENGER, MESENGER, MASSENGER, (cont.)		
Nathan, s. Nathan, b. Nov. 29, 1693	1	27
Nathaniell, s. Edward, b. June 18, [16]53	Col.2	181
Nathanael, s. Edward, b. June 18, [16]53	1	25
Nathaniell, b. June 18, 16[ ]	MG	
Rebekah, d. Nathan, b. Feb. 11, 1684	1	26
Rebeckah, d. Nathan, b. Feb. 11, 1685	Col.D	51
Return, s. Nathan, b. Aug. 4, 1691	1	27
-----, his d. [ ] 's. child d. May 24, [16]76	Col.1	58
-----, his d. [ ], d. [ ], [16]76	MG	
[METCALF], [see under **MEADCALF**]		
MILES, Lusindia C., of Windsor, m. E. Marshall **PEASE,** of		
Texas, Aug. 22, 1850, by Rev. N. B. Soule	2	502
Maria H., of Windsor, m. Rev. C. R. **MOORE.** of		
Brattleboro, May 14, 1851, by H. B. Soule	2	494
MILLER, Anna, d. Rev. William F. & Anna, b. July 23, 1796	2	575
Anna, of Windsor, m. William **HUDSON,** of Hartford, May		
15, 1832, by Rev. Ansel Nash	2	485
Edward, of Farmington, m. Lovinia **GOODWIN,** of		
Simsbury, Aug. 9, 1827, by Rev. John Bartlett	2	492
Elizabeth, d. Ruben & Elizabeth, b. Apr. 30, 1756	2	400
Elizabeth, w. Ruben, d. June 28, 1765	2	255
Emily M., m. William H. **ELLSWORTH,** b. of Windsor,		
Apr. 5, 1843, by Ezra J. Cook	2	148
Ephraim, s. Rev. William F. & Anna, b. Sept. 12, 1811	2	576
Esther, w. Ruben, d. Aug. 8, 1769	2	255
George, s. Rev. William F. & Anna, b. July 27, 1805	2	576
Hector, of Avon, m. Emily **FILLY,** of Windsor, Aug. 30,		
1830, by John Bartlett	2	492
Horatio, s. Rev. William F. & Anna, b. Feb. 16, 1799	2	575
Jemima, d. Ruben & Elizabeth, b. Apr. 11, 1762; d. June 17,		
1762	2	403
Julia, d. Rev. William F. & Anna, b. Apr. 27, 1803	2	575
Julia, of Windsor, m. Joseph W. **HUNTINGTON,** of		
Lancaster, Mass., Sept. 19, 1832, by Rev. Ansel Nash	2	484a
Lucy Hannah, d. Rev. William F. & Anna, b. July 14, 1801	2	575
Mary, d. Rev. William F. & Anna, b. Aug. 30, 1808	2	576
Mary, of Windsor, m. John C. **FURBER,** of Hartford, Apr. 8,		
1834, by Rev. Ansel Nash	2	153
Ruben, m. Elizabeth **THRALL,** b. of Windsor, July 17, 1755	2	179
Ruben, m. Esther **BISSELL,** b. of Windsor, Feb. 12, 1766	2	180
Roswell, m. Betsy **GAYLORD,** July 2, 1828, b. of Windsor,		
by Rev. Henry A. Rowland	2	495
Samuel, m. Abigael **HOLLIDAY,** Nov. 1, 1710	2	176
William F., Rev. of Windsor, m. Anna **STARR,** of Goshen,		
June 6, 1792	2	494
William Starr, s. Rev. William F. & Anna, b. Aug. 22, 1793	2	575
MILLIGAN, Ann, d. Samuel & Ann, b. June 28, 1734 (Crossed		

	Vol.	Page
MILLIGAN, (cont.)		
out)	2	321
MILLINGTON, MILLINTON, Abiah, d. Henry, b. May 16, 1711	2	66
Abia, m. William **FILLEY**, b. of Windsor, June 15, 1730	2	151
Abiah, m. William **FILLEY**, b. of Windsor, June 16, 1730	2	151
Ann, d. Samuel, b. June 28, 1734	2	393
Chloe, d. Samuel & Ann, b. Apr. 27, 1736	2	395
Jochebah, m. Joseph **COOK**, b. of Windsor, Nov. 26, 1744	2	136
John, m. Sara SMITH, Apr. 14, [16]68, by Mr. Mathew Allin	Col.1	45
John, m. Sarah **SMITH**, b. of Windsor, Apr. 14, 1668, by Mathew Allyn	1	59
John, Sr., d. Mar. 26, 1720 (Crossed out)	2	252
Mary, d. Henry, b. Aug. 20, 1716	2	67
Samuel, late of Coventry, now of Windsor, m. Ann **ELGAR**, of Windsor, Apr. 23, 1733	2	178
William, s. Henry, b. Sept. 18, 1713	2	66
MILLS, MILLES, Ammi, m. Rebecca **LOOMIS**, b. of Windsor, Nov. 16, 1825, by Rev. John Bartlett, of Wintonbury	2	492
Ann, d. Daniel & Jerusha, b. Mar. 24, 1735/6	2	395
Anne, d. Daniell & Jerusha, d. Mar. 25, 1737	2	253
Daniell, s. Peter, Jr., b. May 22, 1706	2	63
Daniel, of Windsor, m. Jerusha **STEEL**, of Hartford, Feb. 12, 1729/30	2	177
Daniel, s. Daniel & Jerusha, b. Nov. 19, 1730	2	394
Dorcas, w. Peter, d. May 18, 1688	1	48
Ebenezer, s. Peter, b. Feb. 8, 1687	1	26
Ebenezer, s. Peter, Sr., d. [ ]	1	48
Elijah, s. Pelitiah & Martha, b. May 30, 1726	2	68
Elizabeth, m. Thomas **HOSKINS**, Feb. 23, 1698/9	1	58
Esther, m. John **EGELSTON**, June 1, 1682	1	56
Gidian, s. Peter, Jr., b. Feb. 3, 1694	1	27
Hannah, m. Simon **DRAKE**, Dec. 15, 1687	1	55
Hester, m. John **EGLESTONE**, June 1, 1682	Col.D	54
Isaac, s. Daniel & Jerusha, b. Apr. [ ], 1738	2	395
Jedediah, s. Peter, Jr., b. Mar. 23, 1696/7	1	27
Jerusha, d. Daniel & Jerusha, b. Dec. 22, 1734	2	394
Joan, w. Simon, d. [ ]; bd. July 5, [16]59	1	47
Joanna, d. Pelletiah & Martha, b. Mar. 2, 1730/1	2	392
Joanna, m. Samuel Wolcott **ALLYN**, b. of Windsor, Feb. 20, 1755	2	124
John, s. Simon, b. June 23, 1668	MG	
John, s. Simon, b. June 23, 1668	1	26
John, s. Peter, b. Feb. 14, 1707/8	2	64
Julia Ann, m. Trumble **HUBBARD**, May 12, 1831, by Henry A. Rowland	2	485
Laura, m. Ebenezer **LATIMER**, Jr., Jan. 19, 1825, by Rev. Henry A. Rowland	2	489
Martha, m. Thomas **GILLIT**, b. of Windsor, Nov. 21, 1700	1	57

	Vol.	Page
MILLS, MILLES, (cont.)		
Martha, d. Pellatiah, b. Mar. 11, 1721/2	2	68
Mary, d. Simon, b. Dec. 8, 1662	MG	
Mary, d. Simon, b. Dec. 8, [16]62	Col.1	54
Mary, d. Simon, b. Dec. 8, 1662	1	26
Oliver William, m. Ann T. PHELPS, Feb. 23, 1825, by Rev.		
Henry A. Rowland	2	495
Pelatiah, s. Peter, b. Apr. 27, 1693	1	27
Pellatiah, of Windsor, m. Martha CHAPMAN, of Colchester,		
July 5, 1720	2	176
Pelatiah, s. Pellatiah, b. Jan. 19, 1723/4	2	68
Pelatia, Jr., m. Hannah OWEN, b. of Windsor, Mar. 29, 1743	2	178
Pelatiah, s. Pelatiah, Jr. & Hannah, b. Oct. 12, 1743	2	397
Peter, of Windsor, m. Jane WARRIN, of Hartford, Dec. 10,		
1691	1	59
Peter, Jr., m. Joanna PORTER, July 21, 1692	1	59
Peter, s. Peter, Jr., d. Apr. 28, 1700	1	48
Peter, s. Peter, Jr., b. Apr. 12, 1701	1	27
Peter, Sr., d. Apr. 17, 1710	2	251
Peter, Jr., m. Ruth LOOMIS, b. of Windsor, Feb. 1, 1726/7	2	177
Peter, contributed 0-1-3 to the poor in other colonies	MG	
Return, s. Peter, d. July 12, 1689	Col.D	56
Return, s. Peter, d. July 12, 1689	1	48
Samuell, s. [Simon & Mary], b. Apr. 23, 1661; d. [ ]	MG	
Samuel, s. Simon, b. Apr. 23, 1661	1	26
Samuel, d. May 19, 1661	1	47
Samuel, d. [ ], [16]61	MG	
Samuel, s. Pellatiah & Martha, b. Nov. 21, 1728	2	391
Samuell, s. Lieut. Peletiah, d. Nov. 20, 1734	2	253
Samuel, s. Lieut. Peletiah & Martha, d. Nov. 20, 1734	2	253
Samuel, s. Pelatiah, Jr. & Hannah, b. July 1, 1745	2	397
Samuel W., m. Candace ALLYN, May 8, 1823, by Rev.		
Henry A. Rowland	2	494
Sara, d. Simon, b. Sept. 16, 1670	MG	
Sarah, d. Simon, b. Sept. 16, 1670	1	26
Sarah, d. Capt. Peletiah & Martha, b. June 4, 1737	2	396
Simon, m. Jone* [ ], Oct. 18, 1639 *("Joan?")	1	59
Simon, m. Mary BUELL, Feb. 23, 1656	MG	
Simon, his w. [ ], d. [ ], [16]57	MG	
Simon, m. Mary BUEL, Feb. 23, 1659	1	59
Simon, s. [Simon & Mary], b. Jan. 21, 1661; d. [ ]	MG	
Simon, s. Simon, b. Jan. 21, 1661	1	26
Simon, his w. [ ], d. [ ], [16]62	MG	
Simon, s. Simon, b. May 1, 1667	MG	
Simon, s. Simon, b. May 1, 1667	1	26
Simon, had 6 children, b. in Windsor. Dated Aug. 17, 1677	MG	
Simon, s. [Simon & Mary], bp. May 11, 1679	MG	
Simon, contributed 0-2-6 to the poor in other colonies	MG	

	Vol.	Page
MILLS, MILLES, (cont.)		
Stone, s. Peter & Ruth, b. May 17, 1730	2	392
Susannah, d. Lieut. Peletiah & Martha, b. Mar. 2, 1733/4	2	393
Thomas, s. Daniel & Jerusha, b. Apr. 3, 1732	2	394
MINOR, MINER, MINERE, Grace, m. Samuel **GRANT,** Apr.		
11, 1688	2	154
Harry W., of Vernon, m. Mehitable **GRISWOLD,** of		
Windsor, Apr. 11, 1827, by Henry A. Rowland	2	182
Jesse, of Vernon, m. Hannah **POMEROY,** of Windsor, June		
10, 1825, by Rev. Augustus Bolles, of Wintonbury	2	181
Phillip, of Windsor, m. Elizabeth **CORNISH,** of Westfield,		
May 31, 1704	1	59
Philip, d. Dec. 7, 1711	2	251
MITCHELL, MITCHEL, Oliver, d. Mar. 10, 1840; bd. Mar. 13,		
1840	2	256
William, d. May 18, 1725	2	252
MITCHELSON, Abiguel, d. William, b. Sept. 22, 1714	2	66
Azispah, m. Azariah **SKINNER,** b. of Windsor, Aug. 10,		
1749	2	200
Margaret, d. William, b. May 4, 1717	2	66
William, m. Mary **HOWARD,** Apr. 26, 1713	2	176
MOFFET, MAFFET, MOFFAT, MOFFETT, Harriett, m.		
Edward **RAYMOND,** Jan. 11, 1835, by Rev. Nathaniel		
Kellogg	2	506
Huldah, m. James **CAMP,** Apr. 28, 1831, by H. A. Rowland	2	470
Mariette, m. John S. **GRIFFIN,** b. of Windsor, Dec. 23, 1851,		
by Rev. H. A. Weed	2	498
Mary, m. Gared **WELLS,** b. of Windsor, Dec. 13, 1832, by		
Henry A. Rowland	2	513
Robert L., of Hartford, m. Jane C. **CASE,** of Windsor,		
May 6, 1852, by Rev. H. N. Weed	2	494
Sophia, of Windsor, m. Charles **BROWN,** of New Haven,		
June 10, 1829, by Henry A. Rowland	2	150
MOLTON, [see under **MOULTON**]		
MOORE, MOOR, MORE, Abia, d. Thomas, b. July 9, 1706	2	63
Abiah, Mrs., d. Capt. Thomas **MOORE,** d. Aug. 30, 1747	2	254
Abiah, d. Thomas & Hannah, b. Nov. 4, 1747	2	397
Abiah, d. Joseph & Elizabeth, b. Feb. 13, 1749/50	2	398
Abigayl, m. Thomas **BISSELL,** Oct. 11, 1655	MG	
Abigall, m. Thomas **BISSELL,** b. of Windsor, Oct. 11, 1655	Col.2	159
Abigall, d. Andrew, b. Sept. 12, 1682	Col.D	51
Abigail, d. Andrew, b. Sept. 12, [16]82	1	26
Abigail, d. John, Jr., b. May 4, 1699	2	65
Abigael, m. William **STRATTON,** Jan. 17, 1705/6	2	197
Abigail, w. John, d. May 1, 1733	2	253
Abigail, d. Abijah & Abigail, b. June 5, 1773	2	407
Abigail, d. Abijah & Abigail, b. June 5, 1773	2	573
Abigail, of Windsor, m. Henry W. **DANIELS,** of Hartford,		

	Vol.	Page
MOORE, MOOR, MORE, (cont.)		
Nov. 26, 1834, by Rev. Henry A. Rowland	2	145
Abijah, m. Abigail **DRAKE,** b. of Windsor, Aug. 20, 1772	2	180
Abijah, s. Abijah & Abigail, b. Jan. 26, 1775	2	407
Abijah, s. Abijah & Abigail, b. Jan. 26, 1775	2	573
Allyn, s. Abijah & Abigail, b. Oct. 23, 1785	2	574
Almira, d. Abijah & Abigal, b. July 30, 1783	2	574
Alvin, s. Rachel, b. Sept. 25, 1776	2	406
Amos, s. Andrew, b. Oct. 19, 1698	1	27
Amos, m. Martha **OWIN,** b. of Windsor, May 21, 1720	2	176
Amos, s. Amos, b. Jan. 21, 1720/1	2	67
Andrew, m. Sara **PHELPES,** d. Samuell, b. Feb. 15, 1671, by		
Capt. Newbery	Col.1	46
Andrew, m. Sara **PHELPS,** Feb. [ ]	MG	
Andrew, s. [Andrew & Sara], b. Feb. 15, 1674	MG	
Andrew, had 2 children b. in Windsor. Dated Aug. 17, 1677	MG	
Andrew, d. Nov. 29, 1719	2	252
Ann, d. Samuel, d. July 4, 1714	2	251
Ann, d. Edward, b. Oct. 6, 1721	2	68
Ann, m. Reuben **LOOMIS,** b. of Windsor, Dec. 2, 1742	2	172
Ann, d. Samuell Goff & Elizabeth, b. Oct. 25, 1745	2	401
Ann, d. Joseph & Elizabeth, b. Apr. 27, 1752	2	400
Anna F., m. Oliver H. **BARNS,** b. of Simsbury, July 9, 1828,		
by Rev. John Bartlett	2	149
Anne, d. Samuell, b. Dec. 22, 1707	2	63
Anne, had d. Release, b. Jan. 26, 1770	2	405
Asa, s. Joseph & Elizabeth, b. May 12, 1744	2	396
Asa, s. Joseph & Elizabeth, d. Mar. 6, 1752	2	254
Asa, of Windsor, m. Huldah **KING,** of East Windsor, Nov. 1,		
1790	2	180
Bathsheba, d. John, Jr., b. July 30, 1707	2	65
Bathsheba, d. John, d. Jan. 11, 1723/4	2	252
Benjamin, s. Andrew, b. Dec. 5, 1693	1	27
Betey, d. Rachel, b. Feb. 14, 1780	2	407
C. N., of Bloomfield, m. Sarah C. **BAINES,** of Windsor,		
Dec. 25, 1850, by R. K. Reynolds	2	493
C. R., Rev., of Brattleboro, m. Maria H. **MILES,** of Windsor,		
May 14, 1851, by H. B. Soule	2	494
Catharine, m. Martin **BARBER,** Dec. 28, 1832, by Henry		
A. Rowland	2	498
Chester N., m. Esther M. **GOODWIN,** b. of Simsbury, Nov.		
27, 1828, by Rev. John Bartlett	2	495
Chloe, d. Elisha & Hannah, b. June 26, 1772	2	406
Chloe, m. Abel **GRISWOLD,** b. of Windsor, Oct. 14, 1779	2	159
Damiris, d. Samuel, b. Dec. 28, 1703	2	63
Debora, d. [Andrew & Sara], b. May 31, 1677	MG	
Deborah, d. Thomas, b. Aug. 6, 1699	1	27
Deborah, d. Thomas, b. Aug. 6, 1699	2	63

MOORE, MOOR, MORE, (cont.)

	Vol.	Page
Esther, w. Ebenezer, d. July 28, 1748	2	254
Esther, d. Elisha & Hannah, b. Nov. 6, 1762	2	403
Eunice, w. Benjamin, d. Feb. 23, 1732/3	2	253
Eunice, d. Thomas & Hannah, b. July 26, 1751	2	399
Fanny, m. Justin COOK, Jan. 18, 1835, by Henry A. Rowland	2	471
Goffe*, s. Samuel, b. Nov. 17, 1711 *("Gasse" written in pencil)	2	66
Goffe, s. Samuel, d. Dec. 4, 1711	2	251
Hanna, m. John DRAKE, Nov. [ ], [16]	MG	
Hannah, m. John DRAKE, Nov. 30, 1648	1	55
Hanna, taxed 2-0 on Feb. 10, [16]73	MG	
Hannah, Mrs., d. Apr. 4, 1697	1	48
Hannah, d. Thomas, b. Apr. 11, 1697	1	27
Hannah, d. Thomas, b. Apr. 11, 1697	2	63
Hannah, d. Samuel, b. Dec. 14, 1713	2	66
Hannah, d. Samuel, d. June 18, 1714	2	251
Hannah, m. Isaac SKINNER, Dec. 5, 1716	2	198
Hannah, d. Edward, b. Jan. 9, 1717/18	2	67
Hannah, m. Nathanael FILLEY, b. of Windsor, Nov. 24, 1737	2	151
Hannah, twin with Theophylus, d. Joseph & Elizabeth, b. Mar. 18, 1741/2	2	396
Hannah, d. Thomas & Hannah, b. Oct. 30, 1743	2	397
Hannah, d. Simeon & Hannah, b. May 28, 1754	2	400
Hannah, m. Elisha MOORE, b. of Windsor, Dec. 3, 1761	2	180
Harlow, m. Seliana CASE, May 4, 1825, by Rev. Henry A. Rowland	2	181
Harriot, d. Orson & Abigail, b. Mar. 11, 1799	2	575
Harriet, of Windsor, m. Henry HOLMAN, of East Windsor, Dec. 18, 1847	2	517
Hulda, w. Theophilus, d. May 21, 1790	2	255
James R., of Windsor, m. Harriet N. HUNT, of Northampton Dec. 1, 1850, by A. T. Leete	2	493
John, his w. [ ], adm. Ch. Apr. [ ], 16[ ]	MG	
John, ch. mem. 16[ ]	MG	
John, s. [Dea. John], b. Dec. 5, 1645	MG	
John, s. John, b. Sept. 5, 1645	1	25
John, m. Hanna GOFFE, Sept. 21, 1664, by Mr. Woolcot	Col.1	45
John, s. John, Jr., b. June 26, 1665	Col.1	54
John, s. John, Jr., b. June 26, 1665	1	25
John, ordained Dea. Jan. 11, 1651	MG	
John, m. Hanna GOFE*, Sept. 21, 1664 *("GOFF")	MG	
John, s. [John & Hanna], b. June 26, 1665	MG	
John, his w. [ ], adm. ch. & communicant Apr. [ ], 1666	MG	
John, had 5 children b. in Windsor. Dated Aug. 17, 1677	MG	
John, Dea., d. Sept. 18, [16]77; bd. Sept. 19, 1677	MG	

	Vol.	Page
MOORE, MOOR, MORE, (cont.)		
John, m. Abigail **STRONG**, Feb. 8, 1693/4	1	59
John, Jr., m. Abigael **STRONG**, Feb. 8, 1693/4	2	176
John, s. John, b. Mar. 21, 1694/5	1	27
John, s. John, Jr., b. Mar. 21, 1694/5	2	64
John, Sr., m. Mary **FARNSWORTH**, Dec. 17, 1701	2	175
John, d. June 21, 1718 (Crossed out)	2	252
John, Jr., m. Abigail **STOUGHTON**, d. Capt. Thomas, b. of Windsor, Dec. 2, 1724	2	176
John, Jr., m. Abigail **STOUGHTON**, d. Capt. Thomas, b. of Windsor, Dec. 2, 1724, by Samuel Humphris, J. P.	2	177
John, Jr., contributed 0-4-0 to the poor in other colonies	MG	
Jonathan, s. [Andrew & Sara], b. Feb. 6, [16]79	MG	
Joseph, twin with Josias, s. [John & Hanna], b. July 5, [16]79	MG	
Joseph, s. Aeseyh*, b. Aug. 11, 1712 (In pencil "Joseph")	2	66
Joseph, d. Aug. 15, 1713	2	251
Joseph, m. Elizabeth **ALLYN**, b. of Windsor, May 29, 1735	2	178
Joseph, s. Joseph & Elizabeth, b. May 2, 1736	2	395
Joseph, d. May 5, 1790	2	255
Joseph King, s. Asa & Huldah, b. July 11, 1791	2	574
Josiah, s. Joseph & Elizabeth, b. Sept. 17, 1737	2	395
Josiah, d. May 10, 1751	2	254
Josiah, m. Ann **GILLET**, b. of Windsor, Nov. 18, 1762	2	180
Josiah, s. Josiah & Ann, b. Sept. 28, 1765	2	404
Josias, twin with Joseph, s. [John & Hannah], b. July 5, [16]79	MG	
Julia, of Windsor, m. Ferdinand W. **CALKINS**, of Hamilton, N. Y., Oct. 20, 1836, by Charles Walker	2	471
Keziah, d. Thomas, b. Mar. 24, 1708/9	2	64
Kezia, d. Edward & Elizabeth, b. Mar. 28, 1737	2	395
Keziah, d. Thomas & Hannah, b. July 26, 1749	2	399
Kezia, m. Giles **ELLSWORTH**, Jr., b. of Windsor, Feb. [ ], 1756	2	158
Keziah, m. Simeon **LOOMIS**, b. of Windsor, Mar. 23, 1769	2	174
Lois, of Simsbury, m. Zebulon **HOSKINS**, of Windsor, Aug. 1, 1727	2	162
Lorania, m. Rodney **COOK**, b. of Windsor, Mar. 8, 1825, by Richard Niles, J. P.	2	139
Lorania, m. Rodney **COOK**, b. of Windsor, Mar. 8, 1825, by Richard Niles, J. P.	2	139
Lucretia, d. Abijah & Abigail, b. May 20, 1788	2	574
Lydia, d. Joseph, b. Aug. 8, 1710	2	64
Lydia C., m. Horace E. **ROBERTS**, Apr. 16, 1835, by Rev. Nathaniel Kellogg	2	506
Margerit, d. Edward, b. Aug. 5, 1724	2	68
Margaret O., m. James **ROBERTS**, Sept. 23, 1829, by Henry A. Rowland	2	505

	Vol.	Page
MOORE, MOOR, MORE, (cont.)		
Maria Ann, m. William E. **ST. JOHN**, Oct. 30, 1833, by		
Henry A. Rowland	2	508
Martha, d. John, Sr., b. Sept. 28, 1705	2	63
Martha, m. Job **DRAKE**, b. of Windsor, Nov. 16, 1730	2	141
Mary, d. John, Sr., b. Sept. 6, 1704	2	62
Mary, d. John, Sr., d. Sept. 27, 1704	2	250
Mary, d. Edward, b. May 13, 1707	2	64
Mary, m. Caleb **PHELPS**, b. of Windsor, Dec. 24, 1730	2	187
Mary, wid. Edward, d. July 15, 1751	2	254
Mindwell, d. [Dea. John], b. July 10, 1643	MG	
Mindwell, d. John, bp. [ ], 16, 1643	1	25
Mindwell, m. Nathanell **BISSELL**, Sept. 23, [16]	MG	
Mindwell, m. Nathanell **BISSELL**, b. of Windsor, Sept. 25,		
1662	Col. 1	45
Mindwell, m. Nathanael **BISSELL**, b. of Windsor, Sept. 25,		
1662	1	54
Mindwell see Mindwell **BISSELL**	Col.D	56
Nancy, d. Abijah & Abigail, b. Oct. 4, 1793	2	407
Nathanel, s. [John & Hannah], b. Sept. 20, 1672	MG	
Nathanael, s. John, b. Sept. 20, 1672	1	25
Oliver, s. John & Abigail, b. Jan. 27, 1734/5	2	394
Orren, s. Abijah & Abigail, b. Apr. 11, 1777	2	407
Orren, s. Abijah & Abigail, b. Apr. 11, 1777	2	574
Orson, s. Elisha & Hannah, b. Aug. 12, 1769	2	405
Orson, of Windsor, m. Abigail **GILLET**, of Torrington,		
Jan. 17, 1797	2	180
Orson, s. Elisha & Hannah, d. Aug. 1, 1799	2	255
Pelatiah, s. John, Jr., b. Feb. 26, 1700/1	2	65
Pelletiah, s. John, Sr., d. June 26, 1729	2	252
Pelatiah, s. Ebenezer & Easther, b. Aug. 24, 1736	2	396
Pelatiah, s. Ebenezer & Esther, d. Oct. 22, 1736	2	253
Perry, s. Abijah & Abigail, b. Apr. 23, 1791	2	407
Phebe, d. Joseph, b. Nov. 13, 1707	2	64
Phebe, m. John **SOPER**, b. of Windsor, Jan. 20, 1730/1	2	199
Phene, d. Abijah & Abigail, b. Feb. 13, 1781	2	574
Rachel, d. Andrew, b. Feb. 6, 1690	Col.D	51
Rachel, d. Andrew, b. Feb. 6, 1690/1	1	26
Rachel, m. Timothy **PHELPS**, smith, Dec. 10, 1707	2	185
Rachel, had s. Alvin, b. Sept. 25, 1776	2	406
Rachel, had d. Betey, b. Feb. 14, 1780	2	407
Release, d. Anne, b. Jan. 26, 1770	2	405
Return, s. Samuell, b. July 4, 1706	2	63
Reumah, [see under Rumah]		
Roger, s. Edward, b. Oct. 29, 1712	2	66
Roger, s. Edward, d. June 10, 1714	2	251
Roger, 2nd, s. Edward, b. Apr. 24, 1715	2	66
Rosel, s. John, Jr. & Abigail, b. May 17, 1728	2	391

	Vol.	Page
MOORE, MOOR, MORE, (cont.)		
Rumah, d. Samuel Goff & Elizabeth, b. Dec. 20, 1755	2	402
Reumah, of East Windsor, m. George **LOOMIS**, of Windsor, Dec. 29, 1791	2	174
Ruth W., m. William **CLARK**, Jan. 9, 1828, by Rev. Henry A. Rowland	2	469
Samuell, s. [John & Hannah], b. Dec. 24, 1669	MG	
Samuel, s. John, b. Dec. 24, 1669	1	25
Samuel, s. Thomas, b. Aug. 7, 1701	1	27
Samuell, s. Thomas, b. Aug. 7, 1701	2	63
Samuel, s. Thomas, d. Aug. 20, 1701	1	48
Samuell, s. Thomas, d. Aug. 20, 1701	2	251
Samuel Goffe*, s. Samuel, b. May 25, 1715 *(Written "Gasse")	2	66
Sara, d. [Andrew & Sara], b. Dec. [ ]	MG	
Sarah, d. Andrew, b. Dec. 6, 1672	1	26
Sarah, m. Thomas **WINCHEL**, Apr. 26, 1690	1	63
Sarah, d. Joseph, b. July 14, 1703	2	64
Sarah, d. John, Jr., b. Sept. 12, 1704	2	65
Sarah, m. Jedidiah **EGELSTON**, b. of Windsor, Apr. 6, 1726	2	146
Sarah, d. Joseph & Elizabeth, b. Apr. 25, 1755	2	400
Sarah, d. Abijah & Abigal, b. Feb. 7, 1779	2	407
Sarah, d. Abijah & Abigail, b. Feb. 7, 1779	2	574
Simeon, s. Benjamin & Eunice, b. Jan. 6, 1732/3	2	393
Simeon, m. Hannah **BARBER**, b. of Windsor, Nov. 22, 1753	2	179
Susanah, d. Josiah & Ann, b. June 1, 1763	2	403
Theophylus, twin with Hannah, s. Joseph & Elizabeth, b. Mar. 18, 1741/2	2	396
Theophilus, m. Hulda **GRISWOLD**, b. of Windsor, May [ ], 1779	2	180
Theophilus, m. Elizabeth **ROWEL**, b. of Windsor, Nov. 18, 1790	2	180
Thomas, d. [ ], [16]44	MG	
Thomas, s. [John & Hannah], b. July 25, 1667	MG	
Thomas, s. John, b. July 25, 1667	1	25
Thomas, m. Deborah **GRISWOLD**, b. of Windsor, Dec. 12, 1695	1	59
Thomas, m. Deborah **GRISWOLD**, b. of Windsor, Dec. 12, 1695	2	175
Thomas, s. Samuell, b. Mar. 20, 1704/5	2	63
Thomas, s. Capt. Thomas, b. Oct. 26, 1718	2	67
Thomas, s. Samuel & Damaris, d. Apr. 20, 1729, at New Haven	2	252
Thomas, Capt., d. Jan. 22, 1734/5	2	253
Thomas, s. Thomas & Hannah, b. Mar. 2, 1754	2	399
Thomas, d. May Nov [sic?] 21, 1755	2	254
Thomas, s. Thomas & Hannah, d. May 16, 1756	2	255
Thomas, s. Elisha & Hannah, b. Dec. 10, 1764	2	403

	Vol.	Page
MOORE, MOOR, MORE, (cont.)		
Thomas, of Plymouth, Penn., m. Maria Chloe **GOODRICH**,		
of Windsor, Nov. 21, 1830, by Rev. Augustus Bolles	2	493
Thomas Loomas, taxed 3-0 on Feb. 10, [16]73	MG	
Wareham, s. Samuell Goff & Elizabeth, b. Nov. 17, 1747	2	401
William, s. Elisha & Hannah, b. Dec. 24, 1780	2	406
William, s. Elisha & Hannah, b. Dec. 24, 1780	2	407
-----, Dea., had 3 children b. in Windsor. Dated Aug. 17,		
1677	MG	
-----, Dea., d. Sept. 18, 1677	MG	
-----, Dea., d. Sept. 18, 1677	Col.1	58
-----, Dea., his w. [ ], communicant from Dorchester;		
living in Windsor Dec. 22, 1677	MG	
-----, ch. mem. 16[ ], from Dorchester	MG	
-----, Dea., contributed 0-6-6 to the poor in other		
colonies	MG	
-----, Dea., his w. [ ], ch. mem. 16[ ], from Dorchester	MG	
MORAN, MORON, Addison, of Suffield, m. Laura **ALLYN**, of		
Windsor, July 31, 1820, by James Loomis, J. P.	2	181
Delia, of Suffield, m. John **ABBE**, of Warehouse Point,		
Apr. 11, 1847, by Ezra S. Cook	2	464
Harris H., m. Jane C. **LINDSEY**, Aug. 22, 1852, by Rev.		
H. N. Weed	2	494
John Mack, m. Elizabeth **GAYLORD**, b. of Windsor, Jan. 10,		
1727/8	2	177
MORGAN, Abigail T., of Windsor, m. James S. **SHERMAN**, of		
Suffield, Feb. 9, 1842, by Rev. S. D. Jewett	2	510
Griswold C., m. Amelia **ALLYN**, June 1, 1831, by Henry A.		
Rowland	2	493
Griswold C., m. Amelia **ALLYN**, June 1, 1831, by H. A.		
Rowland	2	495
Jasper, m. Abigail **CHAFFEE**, b. of Windsor, Mar. 10, 1823,		
by Rev. Henry A. Rowland	2	181
Jasper, m. Sarah M. **GILLET**, Sept. 12, 1832, by Henry A.		
Rowland	2	495
William G., m. Elizabeth **MOORE**, Nov. 27, 1828, by Rev.		
Henry A. Rowland	2	492
MORTON, Abigail, d. John & Jane, b. Aug. 9, 1724	2	394
Ann, twin with Jane, d. John & Jane, b. Mar. 1, 1717/18	2	394
Anne, m. Joseph **FILLEY**, b. of Windsor, May 8, 1740	2	151
Hannah, d. Thomas, decd., b. Mar. 14, 1706/7	2	39
Hannah, d. Thomas, decd., b. Mar. 14, 1706/7	2	65
Hannah, d. John & Jane, b. Dec. 21, 1726	2	394
Isaac, s. John & Jane, b. Feb. 19, 1713/14	2	393
Jane, twin with Ann, d. John & Jane, b. Mar. 1, 1717/18	2	394
John, m. Jane **WILLIAMS**, b. of Windsor, May 7, 1713	2	178
Lucie, d. John & Jane, b. Aug. 14, 1732	2	394
Mary, d. John & Jane, b. Dec. 27, 1722	2	394

	Vol.	Page
MORTON, (cont.)		
Mary, d. John & Jane, d. Aug. 21, 1727	2	253
Mary, d. John & Jane, b. Dec. 5, 1728	2	394
Sarah, m. Noah **LOOMIS,** b. of Windsor, May 7, 1713	2	170
Sarah, d. John & Jane, b. Mar. 26, 1721	2	394
Sebeal, d. John & Jane, b. Feb. 1, 1730/1	2	394
Thomas, d. July 19, 1708	2	251
Vashti, d. John & Jane, b. Apr. 26, 1736	2	395
William, s. John & Jane, b. Sept. 11, 1735	2	394
MOSES, MOOSES, Dary*, d. [John & Mary], b. Feb. 2, 1662		
*(Sarah)	MG	
John, m. Mary **BROWN,** May 18, 1653	MG	
John, m. Mary **BROWNE,** b. of Windsor, May 18, 1653	Col.2	159
John, s. John, b. June 1, 1654	1	25
John, s. [John & Mary], b. June 15, 1654	MG	
John, s. John, b. June 15, 1654	Col.2	158
John, had 9 children b. in Windsor. Dated Aug. 17, 1677	MG	
John, d. Oct. 14, 1683	Col.D	56
John, d. Oct. 14, 1683	1	48
John, contributed 0-5-6 to the poor in other colonies	MG	
Margret, d. [John & Mary], b. Dec. 2, 1666	MG	
Margerit, d. John, b. Dec. 2, 1666	1	26
Martha, b. Mar. 3, 1672	MG	
Martha, d. John, b. Mar. 8, 1672	1	26
Martha, d. John, b. Mar. 8, 1672	1	27
Martha, m. Samuel **CROW,** Jan. 30, 1689	Col.D	55
Martha, m. Samuel **CROW,** Jan. 30, 1689	1	55
Mary, d. [John & Mary], b. May 13, 1661	MG	
Mary, d. John, b. May 13, 1661	1	25
Mary, m. Samuel **FARNSWORTH,** Nov. [ ], 1685	1	56
Mary*, wid., d. Sept. 14, 1689 *(Note by LBB: "Mary		
(BROWN) MOSES")	Col.D	57
Mary, wid., d. Sept. 14, 1689	1	48
Mindwell, d. [John & Mary], b. Dec. 13, 1676	MG	
Mindwell, m. John **THRALL,** Jan. 6, 1697	1	62
Norman W., of Simsbury, m. Huldah **CADWELL,** of		
Windsor, Nov. 23, 1831, by Rev. Ansel Nash	2	495
Sarah*, b. Feb. 2, 1663 *("dau. of John?")	1	25
Thomas, s. [John & Mary], b. Jan. 14, 1658; d. July [ ]	MG	
Thomas, s. John, b. Jan. 14, 1658	1	25
Thomas, s. John, d. July 29, 1681; bd. July 30, 1681,		
ae 22 y.	1	47
Timothy, b. Feb. [ ], 1670	MG	
Timothy, s. John, b. Feb. [ ], 1670	1	26
William, s. [John & Mary], b. Sept. 1, 1656	MG	
William, s. John, b. Sept. 1, 1656	1	25
William, s. John, d. Nov. 27, 1681	1	47
MOSHIER, Henry, m. Mary **HOLCOMB,** b. of Windsor, Sept.		

	Vol.	Page
MUNSELL, MUNSEL, MUNCIL, MUNCELL, MUNSIE, MONSEL, (cont.)		
Eliakim, s. Gurden & Lucy, b. Nov. 27, 1762	2	404
Elisha, s. Jacob, b. Sept. 15, 1723	2	68
Elisha, m. Keziah TAYLOR, b. of Windsor, Dec. 27, 1750	2	179
Eunice, d. Jacob, Jr. & Sarah, b. Apr. 30, 1763	2	405
Gurdian, s. Jacob & Phebe, b. Apr. 26, 1730	2	392
Gurdon, m. Lucy STYLES, b. of Windsor, Nov. 7, 1751	2	179
Gurdon, s. Gurdon & Lucy, b. Oct. 31, 1752; d. Oct. 10, 1754	2	400
Gurden, s. Gurden & Lucy, b. Oct. 28, 1760	2	404
Hannah, d. Jonathan & Hannah, b. Apr. 15, 1747	2	399
Hezekiah, s. Elisha & Keziah, b. Dec. 7, 1751; d. 20th day of same month	2	398
Hezekiah, s. Elisha & Keziah, b. Jan. 7, 1753	2	399
Jacob, m. Phebe LOOMIS, b. of Windsor, Feb. 15, 1718	2	176
Jacob, s. Jacob & Phebe, b. Apr. 21, 1732	2	398
Jacob, Jr., m. Sarah BANCROFT, b. of Windsor, Jan. 2, 1750/1	2	179
Joel, s. Elisha & Keziah, b. July 3, 1755	2	400
John, s. Jacob & Phebe, b. Sept. 5, 1736	2	398
Jonathan, s. Jacob & Phebe, b. Oct. 7, 1725	2	392
Jonathan, s. Jonathan & Hannah, b. May 25, 1751	2	399
Joseph, s. Jacob & Phebe, b. Sept. 28, 1734	2	398
Keziah, d. Elisha & Keziah, b. Oct. 17, 1763	2	403
Lucy, d. Gurdon & Lucy, b. Nov. 31, 1755	2	400
Lucy, d. Gurdon & Lucy, b. Nov. 31, 1755	2	404
Lydia, d. Jonathan & Hannah, b. Feb. 9, 1749	2	399
Marcy, d. Jacob, b. Feb. 9, 1721	2	68
Marcy, d. Jacob & Phebe, b. Feb. 20, 1727/8	2	392
Marcy, d. Gurden & Lucy, b. Sept. 30, 1757	2	404
Mary, d. Calkin & Mary, b. Feb. 5, 1744	2	396
Meriam, d. Elisha & Keziah, b. Jan. 15, 1767	2	405
Naomy, d. Elisha & Keziah, b. Apr. 3, 1758	2	403
Phebe, d. Caulkins & Mary, b. Feb. 2, 1747/8	2	397
Rathel*, d. Jacob, Jr. & Sarah, b. Aug. 4, 1767 *(In pencil)	2	405
Sarah, d. Jacob, Jr. & Sarah, b. Apr. 23, 1754	2	400
Silas, s. Jacob & Sarah, b. June 2, 1751	2	398
Silas, s. Jacob & Sarah, b. Mar. 27, 1758	2	401
Solomon, s. Gurdon & Lucy, b. Apr. 3, 1754	2	400
Submit, d. Calkin & Mary, b. Apr. 16, 1757	2	401
Sibel, d. Caulkins & Mary, b. May 27, 1751	2	398
Thomas, s. Jacob, b. Apr. 9, 1720	2	67
Thomas, s. Jacob, d. Apr. 17, 1720	2	252
Thomas, s. Jacob, Jr. & Sarah, b. May 19, 1765	2	405
Tryphena, d. Gurden & Lucy, b. Nov. 25, 1764	2	404
Zaccheus, s. Calkin & Mary, b. Aug. 17, 1745	2	396
MUNSON, William, of Bethlem, m. Sylvia LOOMIS, of Windsor, Apr. 10, 1832, by John Bartlett	2	495

	Vol.	Page
MURPHY, George, m. Susan **DENSLOW**, Nov. 23, 1820, by Rev. Henry A. Rowland	2	181
John, m. Mrs. [ ] **CLARKHAN**, Oct. 15, 1852, by Rev. James Smyth	2	460
Mary, m. Patrick **WARD**, Oct. 12, 1852, by Rev. James Smyth	2	460
Prudence B., m. Sumner **CLARK**, Mar. 15, 1841, by Ezra S. Cook	2	475
MURRAY, John, m. Lydia **ROCK**, b. of Windsor, Oct. 15, 1832, by Rev. Ansel Nash	2	496
MUZY, Abigaell, m. William **PHELPS**, s. Timothy, Dec. 7, 1699	2	186
NAPES, Ephraim, his w. [ ], d. [ ], "in Elenton" prior to 1740	MG	
NASH, Elezer, s. Joel & Zuriviah, b. Nov. 28, 1759	2	71
Elizabeth, d. Joel & Zuriviah, b. Mar. 11, 1757	2	71
Joel, m. Zuriviah **LADD**, b. of Windsor, June 11, 1754	2	183
Joel, s. Joel & Zuriviah, b. May 5, 1755	2	71
Phinehas, of Windsor, m. Susannah **LADD**, of Tolland, Feb. 27, 1755	2	183
Phenihas, s. Phenihas & Susannah, b. Apr. 24, 1761	2	72
Susannah, d. Phenihas & Susannah, b. Sept. 8, 1758	2	72
NEAL, Chloe, of Farmington, m. Moses **WRIGHT**, of Windsor, Oct. 8, 1773	2	210
NEARING, Asahel H., m. Mary Ann **LATIMER**, b. of Windsor, Oct. 19, 1820, by Rev. John Bartlett. Int. Pub.	2	183
NETTLETON, Alfred, of East Windsor, m. Elizabeth **PECK**, Nov. 25, 1840, by S. D. Jewett	2	496
NEWBERRY, NEWBERY, NUBERY, NEWBURY, NEUBERY, Abigayl, d. [Beniamen & Mary], b. Mar. 14, 1659	MG	
Abigail, d. Benjamin, b. Mar. 14, 1659	1	27
Abigail, m. Ephraim **HAYWERD**, Jan. 8, 1684	Col.D	54
Abigail, m. Ephraim **HOWART**, Jan. 8, 1684	1	58
Abigael, d. Feb. 29, 1715/16	2	256
Abigail, d. Lieut. Roger & Elizabeth, b. Dec. 5, 1733	2	70
Albert, s. James & Sally, b. Sept. 25, 1817	2	409
Amasa, s. Benjamin & Jerusha, b. Oct. 27, 1752	2	71
Amelia, d. Thomas & Dorothy, d. Aug. 22, 1788	2	258
Anne, d. Joseph & Sibble, b. Oct. 17, 1750	2	71
Anne, d. Thomas & Dorothy, b. Oct. 28, 1771	2	408
Aurelia, d. Thomas & Dorothy, b. Sept. 3, 1764	2	408
Aurelia, d. James & Sally, b. July 25, 1815	2	409
Beniamen, m. Mary **ALLYN**, June 11, 1646	MG	
Benjamin, m. Mary **ALLYN**, June 11, 1646	1	59
Beniamen, s. [Beniamen & Mary], b. Apr. 20, 1669	MG	
Benjamin, s. Benjamin, b. Apr. 20, 1669	1	27
Benj[amin], s. Tho[mas], b. Feb. 18, 1686	Col.D	51
Benjamin, s. Thomas, b. Feb. 18, 1686	1	27
Benjamen, Maj., d. Sept. 11, 1689	Col.D	57

	Vol.	Page
NEWBERRY, NEWBERY, NUBERY, NEWBURY, NEUBERY, (cont.)		
Benjamin, Maj., d. Sept. 11, 1689	1	48
Benjamin, s. Benjamin, b. Jan. 31, 1692	1	28
Benjamin, of Windsor, m. Hannah DEWEY, of Westfield, Mar. 3, 1691/2	1	59
Benjamin, Jr., d. Sept. 24, 1709, at Camp Woodstock	2	256
Benjamin, Capt., d. Nov. 3, 1709	2	256
Benjamin, m. Ruth PORTER, b. of Windsor, Apr. 24, 1717	2	182
Benjamin, s. Benjamin, b. Aug. 22, 1718	2	69
Benjamin, s. Capt. Benjamin, decd., d. Sept. 11, 1718	2	256
Benjamin, s. Joseph, b. May 20, 1721	2	70
Benjamin, s. Roger & Elizabeth, b. Dec. 11, 1738	2	70
Benjamin, s. Benjamin & Ruth, d. May 2, 1739	2	257
Benjamin, m. Jerusha STOUGHTON, b. of Windsor, Feb. 13, 1745/6	2	182
Benjamin, s. Benjamin & Jerusha, b. Aug. 13, 1765	2	72
Chauncey, s. Benjamin & Jerush, b. July 22, 1750	2	71
Dolly, d. Thomas & Dorothy , b. Aug. 14, 1776	2	408
Dyer, s. Joseph & Sibbel, b. June 18, 1765	2	408
Elizabeth, d. Ens. Roger, b. June 28, 1728	2	70
Elizabeth, Jr., m. Daniel BISSELL, Jr., b. of Windsor, Feb. 16, 1746/7	2	132
Elizabeth, d. Benjamin & Jerusha, b. Sept. 13, 1754	2	71
Elizabeth, d. Roger & Eunice, b. Oct. 15, 1765; d. Sept. 27, 1766	2	407
Elizabeth W., d. James & Sally, b. June 11, 1825	2	409
Emma, d. James & Sally, b. June 23, 1821	2	409
Frederick, s. Thomas & Dorothy, b. Sept. 19, 1774	2	408
George, s. Joseph & Sibble, b. Nov. 5, 1753	2	72
Hanna, d. [Beniamen & Mary], b. Dec. 22, 1652; d.[ ]	MG	
Hannah, d. Beniamin, b. Dec. 22, 1652	Col.2	155
Hannah, d. Benjamin, b. Dec. 22, 1652	1	27
Hanna, d. Sept. 21, 1663	Col.1	55
Hanna, d. [ ], [16]63	MG	
Hanna, d. [Beniamen & Mary], b. July 1, 1673	MG	
Hannah, d. Benjamin, b. July 1, 1673	1	27
Hanna, d. [Thomas & Ann], b. Feb. 10, 1679	MG	
Hanna, d. Thomas, b. Feb. 10, 1679	Col.1	57
Hannah, m. John WOLCOTT, b. of Windsor, Dec. 14, 1703	1	63
Hannah, d. Capt. Benjamin, d. Oct*. 17, 1718 *("Sept." crossed out)	2	256
Hannah, d. Lieut. Roger & Elizabeth, b. Oct. 3, 1729	2	70
Hannah, Mrs. alias MERRIMAN, d. Aug. 30, 1749	2	257
Hannah, w. Roger, d. Feb. 23, 1760	2	257
Hannah, d. Thomas & Dorothy, b. Feb. 3, 1780	2	408
Harriet, d. James & Sally, b. Mar. 17, 1812	2	409
James, s. Thomas & Dorothy, b. Mar. 21, 1773	2	408

	Vol.	Page
NEWBERRY, NEWBERY, NUBERY, NEWBURY, NEUBERY, (cont.)		
Rebeca, d. [Beniamen & Mary], b. May 2, 1655; m. [ ]	MG	
Rebeca, d. Beniamin, b. May 2, 1655	Col.2	158
Rebekah, d. Benjamin, b. May 2, 1655	1	27
Rebeca, bp. May 6, [16]55	MG	
Rebeca, m. Samuell **MARSHALL**, s. Samuell, June 22, 1675	Col.1	46
Roger, s. Capt. Benjamin, b. June 4, 1706	2	69
Roger, m. Mrs. Elizabeth **WOLCUTT**, b. of Windsor, Aug. 24, 1727	2	182
Roger, s. Lieut. Roger & Elizbeth, b. June 19, 1735	2	70
Roger, Capt., d. about May 6, 1741, on his return from Carthegene to Jemeca	2	257
Roger, m. Hannah **ALLIN**, 3rd, b. of Windsor, Jan. 9, 1759	2	183
Roger, of Windsor, m. Eunice **ELY**, of Springfield, July 29, 1762	2	183
Roger, s. Roger & Eunice, b. Sept. 1, 1764; lived 6 wks. wanting 2 das.	2	407
Ruth, wid., m. Nathaniel **LOOMIS**, 2nd, b. of Windsor, Mar. 9, 1740/1	2	172
Sally, d. Thomas & Dorothy, b. May 3, 1767	2	408
Sally, d. Thomas & Dorothy, d. Aug. 3, 1786	2	258
Sally Maria, m. Anson A. **COLLINS**, b. of Windsor, Mar. 14, 1827, by Rev. Augustus Bolles	2	139
Sara, d. [Beniamen & Mary], b. Jun 14, 1650; m. [ ]	MG	
Sarah, d. Benjamin, b. June 14, 1650	1	27
Sara, d. Capt. Beniamen, of Windsor, m. Presance **CLAY***, s. of Capt. Roger, of Dorchester, June 4, 1668, by Mr. Talcott *(Note by LBB: "Preserve **CLAPP**")	Col.1	45
Sarah, d. Capt. Benjamin, of Windsor, m. Preserve **CLAP[P]**, s. Capt. Roger, of Dorchester, June 4, 1668, by Mr. Talcutt	1	55
Sara, m. Henery **WOLCOT**, Nov. 8, [16]	MG	
Sarah, d. Joseph, b. Aug. 14, 1716	2	69
Sarah, d. Lieut. Roger & Elizabeth, b. Dec. 31, 1736	2	70
Sarah, d. Joseph & Sibble, b. Mar. 7, 1751	2	72
Sarah, m. Eliakim **MATHER**, b. of Windsor, Dec. 4, 1755	2	179
Sarah, d. Joseph & Sibil, d. Aug. 17, 1759	Col.D	56
Sarah, see Sarah **WOOLCOT**	Col.D	56
Susan A., m. Henry **WILSON**, Jr., b. of Windsor, Nov. 17, 1842, by Rev. S. D. Jewett	2	516
Temmeson, d. Benjamin & Jerusha, b. Oct. 28, 1759	2	71
Thomas, s. [Beniamen & Mary], b. Sept. 1, 1657	MG	
Thomas, s. Benjamin, b. Sept. 1, 1657	Col.2	161
Thomas, s. Benjamin, b. Sept. 1, 1657	1	27
Thomas, m. Ann **FORD**, Mar. 12, [16]76	MG	
Thomas, m. Ann **FOORD**, Mar. 12, 1676	Col.1	46
Thomas, m. Ann **FORD**, Mar. 12, 1676	TR1	1

	Vol.	Page

NEWBERRY, NEWBERY, NUBERY, NEWBURY, NEUBERY,
(cont.)

	Vol.	Page
Thomas, m. Ann **FORD**, Mar. 12, 1676/7	1	59
Thomas, s. [Thomas & Ann, b. Jan. 20, 1677; d. Feb. 11, [16]80	MG	
Thomas, s. Thomas, bp. Jan. 27, [16]77	MG	
Thomas, s. Thomas, d. Feb. 10, 1680	Col.1	58
Tho[mas], s. Tho[mas], b. Mar. 28, 1681	Col.D	51
Thomas, s. Thomas, b. Mar. 22, [16]81	1	27
Thomas, d. Apr. 30, 1688	1	48
Thomas, d. Feb. 23, 1697/8	1	48
Thomas, s. Joseph, b. Nov. 7, 1714	2	69
Thomas, s. Sergt. Joseph & Sarah, d. May 24, 1735	2	256
Thomas, s. Roger & Elizabeth, b. Aug. 1, 1740	2	70
Thomas, m. Doroth[y] **MATHER**, b. of Windsor, Dec. 8, 1763	2	183
-----, Mrs., adm. ch. Apr. 1, 1655	MG	
-----, Mrs., adm. ch. & communicant Apr. [ ],1655	MG	
-----, Capt., adm. ch. Apr. 11, 1658	MG	
-----, Capt., adm. ch & communicant Apr. [ ], 1658	MG	
-----, Capt., taxed 4-0 on Feb. 10, [16]73	MG	
-----, Capt., had 9 children b. in Windsor. Dated Aug. 17, 1677	MG	
-----, Mrs., contributed 0-2-6 to the poor in other colonies	MG	
[**NEWELL**], **NEWEL**, [see also **NOWEL**], Abigail, d. Nathaniel		72
& Abigail, b. Oct. 4, 1762	2	72
Daniel, s. Nathaniel & Abigail, b. Dec. 14, 1755	2	72
Esther, d. Nathaniell & Abigail, b. Aug. 24, 1764	2	72
Jacob, s. Nathaniel & Abigail, b. Dec. 23, 1758	2	72
John, s. Nathaniel & Abigail, b. Aug. 16, 1757	2	
Nathaniel, of Windsor, m. Abigal **EBORN**, of Toland,		180
Nov. 13, 1754	2	72
Rebekah, d. Nathaniell & Abigail, b. Dec. 4, 1760	2	
Thomas, d.[ ], [16]48	MG	
NEWMAN, Rase, d. [ ], [16]44	MG	73
NEWTON, NUTON, Amos, s. Isaac & Sarah, b. Oct. 21, 1765	2	71
Asa, s. Stephen & Mary, b. Apr. 13, 1748	2	
Hanna, m. Joseph **PHELPS**, s. William, Sept. 20, 1660	MG	60
Hannah, m. Joseph **PHELPS**, Sept. 20, 1660	1	183
Isaac, m. Sarah **SEWETT**, b. of Windsor, Apr. 19, 1758	2	73
Isaac, s. Isaac & Sarah, b. June 23, 1759	2	
Jone, m. Benedictus **ALUARD**, Nov. 26, 1640	MG	53
Jane, m. Benedictus **ALFORD**, Nov. 26, 1640	1	71
Jonas, s. Stephen & Mary, b. Mar. 18, 1740	2	
Jonas, s. Stephen & Mary, d. Nov. 3, 1753, ae 13 y.		257
7 m. 16 d.	2	73
Martha, d. Isaac & Sarah, b. June 14, 1763	2	71

	Vol.	Page
NEWTON, NUTON, (cont.)		
Mary, d. Stephen & Mary, b. Nov. 8, 1737	2	71
Mary, m. Samuel **BELKNAP,** b. of Windsor, June 19, 1754	2	133
Oliver, s. Stephen & Mary, b. Apr. 2, 1742	2	71
Sary, d. Stephen & Mary, b. Nov. 29, 1745	2	71
Sarah, d. Isaac & Sarah, b. June 9, 1761	2	73
NICHOLOS, Hannah, Mrs. of Stanford, m. John **WOLCOTT,** of Windsor, June 22, 1692	1	63
Rebekah, d. William, of Lebanon, b. Dec. 5, 1714	2	70
NIGRIS, Dolly, m. Thomas **GOUDY,** Apr. 29, 1830, by John Bartlett	2	480
NILES, Augusta Floree, of Windsor, m. Eliphalet **LADD,** of New York, Oct. 6, 1846, by H. B. Soule	2	490
NOCK, Thomas G., m. Caroline M. **PROUTY,** b. of Windsor Locks, Nov. 12, 1851, by Rev. S. H. Allen	2	496
NORCOTT, Maria A., m. Anson B. **BURNHAM,** Apr. 30, 1837, by Gamaiel W. Griswold, J. P.	2	513
NORNER*, Ruth, m. David **BISSELL,** Feb. 24, 1703/4 *(Name in pencil)	2	127
NORTH, Charles, twin with John, s. Jonathan & Mary, b. May 14, 1736	2	70
Elizabeth, d. Jonathan & Mary, b. July 6, 1732	2	70
Elizabeth, d. Jonathan & Mary, b. July 6, 1732	2	117
John, twin with Charles, s. Jonathan & Mary, b. May 14, 1736	2	70
Jonathan, of Farmington, m. Mary **WOLCUTT,** of Windsor, Aug. 28, 1730	2	182
Mary, d. Jonathan & Mary, b. Apr. 1, 1734	2	70
Sarah, d. Jonathan & Mary, b. Apr. 27, 1738	2	70
NORTON, [see also **ORTON**], George, of Sowthfeild, m. Mercy **GILLET,** of Windsor, June 14, 1683	Col.D	54
George, of Suffield, m. Marcy **GILLIT,** of Windsor, June 14, 1683	1	59
Jane E., of Enfield, m. Allen N. **PRIOR,** of Somers, May 21, 1843, by Rev. S. D. Jewett	2	193
Mary, of Saybrook, m. Samuel **ROCKWELL,** of Windsor, Apr. 9, 1658	1	61
Mary, m. Samuell **ROCKWELL,** Apr. 7, 1660	MG	
Samuel I., of Hartford, m. Elizabeth **ALLYN,** of Windsor, Apr. 12, 1832, by Rev. Henry A. Rowland	2	183
NOWEL, [see also **NEWELL**], Elizabeth, m. Stephen **TAYLOR,** Oct. 25, 1649	1	62
NUBERY, [see under **NEWBERRY**]		
OAKLEY, Peter C., Rev., m. Mariah **LOOMIS,** Sept. 12, 1827, by Rev. Arnold Scholefield	2	185
O'CONNOR, Michael, m. Mrs. **CUNNINGHAM,** Oct. 14, 1852, by Rev. James Smyth	2	460
O'DONALL, Bridget, m. Phillip **KEONSAN,** [ ], [1852], by Rev.		

	Vol.	Page
O'DONALL, (cont.)		
James Smyth	2	460
OLCOTT, ALCOTT, OLCUT, Abigail, d. Benoni & Deborah, b.		
Jan. 1, 1759	2	79
Achsa, d. Benoni & Deborah, b. July 7, 1762	2	79
Asahel, s. Benoni & Deborah, b. Apr. 15, 1754	2	78
Asahel, s. Benoni & Deborah, b. Apr. 15, 1754	2	285
Deborah, d. Benoni & Deborah, b. Apr. 21, 1764	2	79
Eli, s. Benoni & Deborah, b. Apr. 1, 1756	2	79
Eunice, w. Benoni & d. of Charles **WOLCOTT,** & his w.		
Elizabeth, d. Aug. 4, 1750	2	523
Eunice, d. Benoni & Deborah, b. Sept. 2, 1752	2	78
Eunice, d. Benoni & Deborah, b. Sept. 2, 1752	2	285
Mary, w. Thomas, of Hartford, d. May 3, 1721	2	258
Ruben, s. Benoni & Deborah, b. Nov. 30, 1757	2	79
OLD, Allyn, d. Sept. 12, [16]75	1	40
Jonathan, s. Robert, b. Dec. 24, 1672	1	29
OLDAGE, OULDAG, Ann, m. John **OSBO[R]N,** May 19, 1645	MG	
Ann, m. John **OSBAND,** May 19, 1645	1	59
Richard, d. Jan. 27, 1660	1	48
Richard, d. [ ], [16]60	MG	
OLIVE, Mary, of Boston, m. William **ELSWORTH,** of Windsor,		
June 16, 1737	2	146
OLMSTED, OUMSTED, Maria C., of Windsor, m. Charles		
KING, of Hartford, June 17, 1850, by Rev. T. A. Leete	2	169
Nicolas, his child d. [ ], [16]46	MG	
OMES, Mary Ann, of Hartford, m. Jonathan Worthington **SMITH,**		
of Suffield, Jan. 31, 1832, by Rev. Augustus Bolles	2	508
ORTON, [see also **NORTON**], Elizabeth, d. Thomas, b. Oct. 1,		
1654	Col.2	158
Elizabeth, d. [Thomas & Margret], bp. Oct. 1, 1654	MG	
Elizabeth, d. Thomas, bp. Oct. 1, 1654	1	28
John, d. [ ], [16]46	MG	
John, s. [Thomas & Margret], b. Feb. 17, 1647	MG	
John, s. Thomas, b. Feb. 17, 1647	1	28
Mary, d. [Thomas & Margret], b. May 16, 1650	MG	
Mary, d. Thomas, b. May 16, 1650	1	28
Sara, d. [Thomas & Margret], bp. Aug. 22, 1652	MG	
Sarah, d. Thomas, bp. Aug. 22, 1652	1	28
Thomas, m. Margret **PALL,** June [ ], 1641	MG	
Thomas, m. Margaret **PALL,** June 1, 1641	1	59
Thomas, his two children d. [ ], [16]48	MG	
Thomas, had 4 children b. in Windsor. Dated Aug. 17, 1677	MG	
OSBORN, OSBAND, ORSBORN, OSBON, Abel, s. Joseph &		
Martha, b. Feb. 11, 1747/8	2	78
Abel, s. Joseph & Martha, d. Aug. 28, 1750	2	259
Abel, s. Joseph & Martha, b. Apr. 8, 1751	2	78
Abigal, d. [John, Jr. & Abigail], b. Mar. 2nd wk., [16]71	MG	

	Vol.	Page
OSBORN, OSBAND, ORSBORN, OSBON, (cont.)		
Abigal, d. John, Jr., b. Mar. 2, [16]71	Col.1	56
Abigail, m. Jacob **GIBBS**, May 16, 1689	1	57
Abigall, w. John, d. July 30, 1689 *(Note by LBB:		
"Abigail (**EGGLESTON**) OSBORN")	Col.D	56
Abigail, w. John, d. July 30, 1689	1	48
Abigail, w. John, d. Aug. 7, 1689	1	49
Abigaell, w. Samuell, Jr., d. Oct. 16, 1705	2	258
Abigail, d. Jacob, b. Mar. 24, 1724/5	2	74
Abigail, d. Samuel, 3rd & Mary, b. July 17, 1734	2	75
Abigail, d. Samuel & Mary, d. Apr. 16, 1737	2	259
Abigail, d. Samuel, 2nd & Mary, b. June 18, 1741	2	77
Abigail, d. Ezekiel & Abigail, b. July 24, 1745	2	78
Abigail, m. Zebedy **OSBAND**, b. of Windsor, Jan. 8, 1746	2	184
Abigail, w. Ezekiel, d. Sept. 28, 1749	2	259
Abigail, d. Israel & Damaras, b. Nov. 17, 1761	2	79
Abigail, m. Levi **BOOTH**, b. of Windsor, June 13, 1765	2	134
Alexander, s. Samuel, 2nd & Mary, b. Jan. 1, 1743/4	2	77
Ann, d. John, b. Jan. 15, 1647	Col.2	155
Ann, d. John, b. Jan. 15, 1647	1	28
Ann, d. [John & Ann], b. Jan. 18, 1647	MG	
Ann, m. Houmfery **PRIOR**, Nov. 12, 1663	MG	
Ann, m. Houmfery **PRIER**, Nov. 12, [16]63, by Mr. Allyn	Col.1	45
Ann, [d. John, Jr. & Abigail], b. Jan. "first week", [16]75	MG	
Ann, d. [John, Jr.], b. Jan. 1st wk., [16]75	Col.1	56
Ann, wid., d. Aug. 28, 1689	Col.D	57
Ann, wid., d. Aug. 28, 1689	1	49
Ann, d. John, d. Apr. 5, 1690	1	49
Ann, d. John & Sarah, b. Oct. 1, 1743	2	77
Ann, see Ann **PRYOR**	Col.D	56
Benjamin, s. John, b. Oct. 20, 1700	2	74
Benjamin, m. Persilla **HULSE**, b. of Windsor, June 11, 1720	2	184
Benjamin, s. Benjamin, b. June 2, 1721	2	74
Daniel, s. Samuel, Jr. & Mary, b. June 23, 1736	2	76
David, s. Joseph & Martha, b. Sept. 23, 1745	2	77
Dorcas, d. Joseph & Martha, b. Nov. 23, 1754	2	78
Ebenezer, s. Samuel, 3rd & Mary, b. Mar. 8, 1738/9	2	76
Elizabeth, d. John, b. Dec. 19, [16]84	Col.D	51
Elizabeth, d. John, b. Dec. 19, 1684	1	28
Elisabeth, m. Isaack **BISSELL**, May 2, 1706	2	127
Elizabeth, d. Benjamin & Prisilla, b. July 5, 1732	2	75
Elizabeth, m. Jonathan **BARBER**, Jr., b. of Windsor, Apr. 17,		
1760	2	133
Ester, d. [John & Ann], b. Aug. 9, 1662	MG	
Ester, d. [John], b. Aug. 9, 1662	Col.1	56
Ezekiel, s. John, b. May 18, 1710	2	74
Ezekiel, m. Abigail **WATSON**, b. of Windsor, Apr. 12, 1744	2	185
Hanna, d. [John & Ann], b. Dec. 18, 1657	MG	

	Vol.	Page
OSBORN, OSBAND, ORSBORN, OSBON, (cont.)		
Hannah, d. John, b. Dec. 18, 1657	1	28
Hanna, d. John, m. Elias **SHADOCK,** Nov. 26, 1675	Col.1	46
Hanna, d. John & wid. Shadock [ ], m. Beniamen		
EGELLSTON, Mar. 6, 1678, by Capt. Newbery	TR1	1
Hanah, d. John, b. June 14, 1680	Col.D	51
Hanna, d. John, b. June 14, 1680	1	28
Hannah, d. John, d. Dec. 25, 1689	1	49
Hannah, of Enfield, m. James **PASCO,** of Windsor, July [ ],		
1725	2	187
Hannah, d. Samuell & Hannah, b. July 22, 1747	2	78
Hannah, Jr., m. Lamson **WELLS,** Jr., b. of Windsor, Feb. 20,		
1757	2	210
Hannah, see Hannah **SHADRAKE**	1	56
Henry, s. Henry & Kesiah, b. Aug. 21, 1819	2	410
Isack, s. [John & Ann], b. Sept. 28, 1664	MG	
Isack, s. John, b. Sept. 28, 1664	Col.1	54
Isack, s. John, Sr., d. Nov. 24, [16]73	Col.1	58
Isaac, s. John, d. Nov. 24, [16]73	1	48
[Isaac*], s. John, Sr., bd. [Nov. 24*], [16]73 *(In pencil)	MG	
Isaac, s. John, b. June 6, 1694	1	29
Israel, s. Samuel, 2nd & Mary, b. Feb. 6, 1731/2	2	77
Israel, of Windsor, m. Damaras **BECRAFFT,** of Wethersfield,		
Apr. 18, 1751	2	185
Israel, illeg. s. Anna **STILES,** b. July 2, 1751; reputed f.		
Israel **OSBAND**	2	441
Israel,s. Israel & Damaras, b. Nov. 26, 1753	2	78
Jacob, s. John, Sr., b. Jan. 4, 1697/8	1	29
Jerusha, d. Ezekiel & Abigail, b. Jan. 3, 1747/8	2	78
John, s. [John & Ann], b. Jan. 10, 1645	MG	
John, s. John, b. Jan. 10, 1645	.Col.2	155
John, s. John, b. Jan. 10, 1645	1	28
John, m. Ann **OULDAG,** May 19, 1645	MG	
John, m. Ann **OLDAGE,** May 19, 1645	1	59
John, Jr., m. Abigail **EGELSTON,** Oct. 14, 1669	MG	
John, Jr., m. Abigall **EGELSTON,** Oct. 14, [16]69	Col.1	45
John, m. Abigail **EGELSTON,** Oct. 4, 1669	1	59
John, Sr., had 10 children b. in Windsor. Dated Aug. 17,		
1677	MG	
John, Sr., d. Oct. 27, 1686	Col.D	56
John, Sr., d. Oct. 27, 1686	1	48
John, had twin s. [ ], b. Feb. 3, 1692/3; d. same day	1	29
John, Jr., m. Elizabeth **GIBBS,** Dec. 7, 1696	1	64
John, s. John, b. Oct. 20, 1702	2	74
John, m. Sarah **STILES,** b. of Windsor, Apr. 15, 1730	2	184
John, s. John & Sarah, b. Jan. 20, 1731/2	2	75
John, s. John, Jr. & Sarah, b. Feb. 7, 1736/7	2	76
John, s. John & Sarah, d. Feb. 10, 1736/7	2	259

	Vol.	Page
OSBORN, OSBAND, ORSBORN, OSBON, (cont.)		
John, s. John & Sarah, b. Nov. 23, 1746	2	78
Joseph, s. [John], b. May 2, 1707	2	74
Joseph, m. Martha STYLES, b. of Windsor, Dec. 30, 1736	2	184
Joseph, s. Joseph & Martha, b. Feb. 13, 1739/40	2	76
Julia, d. Henry & Kesiah, b. Jan. 15, 1823	2	410
Julia R., m. Frederick P. HALSEY, Nov. 25, 1840, by S. D. Jewett	2	483
Keziah, w. Henry, d. May 4, 1825	2	260
Lucy, d. Jacob & Abigail, b. May 30, 1727	2	75
Margret, d. Joseph & Martha, b. Jan. 22, 1759	2	79
Martha, d. John, b. Apr. 10, 1687	1	28
Martha, d. Joseph & Martha, b. Jan. 13, 1737/8	2	76
Mary, d. [John & Ann], b. Apr. 16, 1655	MG	
Mary, d. John, b. Apr. 16, [16]55	Col.2	181
Mary, d. John, b. Apr. 16, 1655	1	28
Mary, m. Josias OWEN, Oct. 22, 1674	MG	
Mary, m. Josias OWEN, Oct. 22, 1674	Col.1	46
Mary, [d. John, Jr. & Abigail], b. Jan. "last week", [16]77	MG	
Mary, d. John, b. Jan. [ ], 1677	Col.D	51
Mary, d. John, b. Jan. [ ], 1677	1	28
Marey, d. [John, Jr.], b. Jan. last wk., [16]77	Col.1	56
Mary, d. John, d. Aug. 6, 1689	Col.D	57
Mary, d. John, d. Aug. 6, 1689	1	49
Mary, d. John, d. Aug. 13, 1689	1	49
Mary, w. Samuell, d. Aug. 30, 1690	Col.D	57
Mary, w. Samuel, d. Aug. 30, 1690	1	49
Mary, d. John, Sr., b. Feb. 10, 1695/6	1	29
Mary, m. John STILES, Jr., b. of Windsor, May 7, 1713	2	198
Mary, d. Samuel, 3rd & Mary, b. Nov. 23, 1727	2	75
Merriam, d. John & Sarah, b. Nov. 30, 1750	2	78
Mindwell, d. [John, Jr. & Abigail], b. Jan. 2nd wk., [16]73	MG	
Mindwell, d. John, Jr., b. Jan. 2nd wk. [16]73	Col.1	56
Mindwell, d. Joseph & Martha, b. Feb. 28, 1742/3	2	77
Nathanell, s. [John & Ann], b. Mar. 10, 1649	MG	
Nathanael, s. John, b. Mar. 10, 1649	Col.2	155
Nathanael, s. John, b. Mar. 10, 1649	1	28
Nathanael, s. John, d. Oct. 25, 1689	1	49
Nathanael, s. Samuel, 3rd & Mary, b. Jan. 24, 1729/30	2	75
Nathaniel, s. Israel & Damaras, b. Oct. 24, 1758	2	79
Nathanael Israel, s. Samauel & Mary, b. Feb. 6, 1731/2	2	75
Prisilla, d. Benjamin & Presilla, b. July 23, 1727	2	75
Rachel, d. John & Sarah, b. July 6, 1741	2	77
Rebekah, d. Samuel, b. Apr. 20, 1687	1	29
Rebekah, d. Samuel, b. July 9, 1691	1	29
Rebeckah, wid. Samuel, d. May 2, 1751	2	259
Ruth, d. Israel & Damaras, b. Apr. 1, 1756	2	79
Samuell, s. [John & Ann], b. July 25, 1652; d. [ ]	MG	

	Vol.	Page
OSBORN, OSBAND, ORSBORN, OSBON, (cont.)		
Samuel, s. John, b. July 25, 1652	Col.2	155
Samuel, s. John, b. July 25, 1652	1	28
Samuell, 2nd, s. [John & Ann], b. May 8, 1660	MG	
Samuel, s. John, b. May 8, 1660	1	28
Samuel, s. Samuel, b. Oct. 19, 1684	1	29
Samuel, s. James, m. Mary **BROOKS,** Nov. 14, 1688	1	63
Samuell, Jr., m. Abigaell **EGLSTONE,** May [ ] 1704	2	184
Samuell, s. Samuell, Jr., b. July 6, 1708	2	73
Samuel, Jr., of Windsor, m. Mary **PHELPS,** of Enfield, Apr. 14, 1725	2	184
Samuel, s. Samuel, 3rd, b. Nov. 23, 1725	2	74
Samuel, Sr., d. June 21, 1736	2	259
Samuel, Sergt., of Windsor, m. Hannah **PHELPS,** of Enfield, July 20, 1737	2	184
Samuel, s. Samuel & Mary, d. Mar. 6, 1746	2	259
Samuel, s. Samuel & Mary, b. Jan. 24, 1746/7	2	78
Samuel, d. June 17, 1756, ae 72	2	259
Samuel, m. Rebeckah **DENSLOW,** [ ]	Col.D	54
Samuel, m. Rebekah **DENSLOW,** Feb. 7, [ ]	1	63
Samuell, contributed 0-1-3 to the poor in other colonies	MG	
Sara, d. [John & Ann], b. Feb. 8, 1666	MG	
Sarah, d. John, b. Feb. 8, 1666	Col.1	45
Sarah, d. John, b. Feb. 8, 1666	Col.1	56
Sarah, d. John, b. Aug. 12, 1682	Col.D	51
Sarah, d. John, b. Aug. 12, 1682	1	28
Sarah, d. John, d. May 6, 1692	1	49
Sarah, d. John & Sarah, b. June 20, 1739	2	77
Sarah, m. Ashbel **BARBER,** b. of Windsor, Aug. 1, 1765	2	134
Thomas, s. Benjamin, b. Sept. 20, 1722	2	74
Thomas, s. Benjamin, d. Sept. 29, 1727	2	259
Thomas, s. Benjamin & Presilla, b. Aug. 7, 1729	2	75
Zebude, s. Benjamin, b. Jan. 25, 1724/5	2	74
Zebedy, m. Abigail **OSBAND,** b. of Windsor, Jan. 8, 1746	2	184
Zebedy, s. Zebedy & Abigail, b. Aug. 11, 1748	2	77
OULD, Jonathan, s. [Robard & Susanna], b. Jan. 4, 1672	MG	
Robard, m. Susanna H[A]NFORD, Dec. [ ]	MG	
Robard, m. Susan **HANFORD,** b. of Windsor, Dec. 31, 1669	Col.1	45
Robard, [s. Robard & Susanna], b. Oct. 9, 1670	MG	
Robard, had 2 children b. in Windsor. Dated Aug. 17, 1677	MG	
OWEN, OWIN, Aron, s. Nathaniel, Jr & Mary, b. July 21, 1756	2	80
Abia, d. Isaac & Mary, b. Dec. 30, 1739	2	76
Abijah, s. Asahel & Deborah, b. Apr. 9, 1754	2	80
Abner, s. Nathaniell, b. Mar. 17, 1706/7	2	73
Abner, s. Nathaniel, d. Mar. 10, 1708/9	2	258
Abner, s. Nathaniell & Mary, b. Jan. 4, 1735/6	2	76
Alice, d. Samuel, Jr. & Rachel, b. [ ]	2	409
Alvan, s. Nathaniell & Mary, b. Feb. 22, 1737/8	2	76

	Vol.	Page
OWEN, OWIN, (cont.)		
Ami, d. Nathaniel, b. July 31, 1709	2	74
Amos, s. Josiah, b. Mar. 4, 1704/5	2	73
Ann, d. Isaac, b. June 12, 1700	1	29
Anne, d. Nathaniell, b. July 17, 1705	2	73
Asahel, s. Josiah, b. Mar. 25, 1699	1	29
Asahel, m. Deborah **DRAKE,** b. of Windsor, June [ ], 1752	2	185
Asahel, s. Asahel & Deborah, b. Oct. 11, 1752	2	78
Azubah, d. Samuel, Jr. & Rachel, b. Jan. 6, 1765	2	80
Benajah, s. Isaac & Mary, b. June 1, 1743	2	77
Beniamen, s. [John & Rebeca], b. Sept. 20, 1664; d. [ ]	MG	
Beniamen, s. John, b. Sept. 20, 1664	Col.1	54
Benjamin, s. John, b. Sept. 20, 1664	1	28
Beniamen, d. May 26, 1665	Col.1	55
Caroline, of Windsor, m. Gilbert **ALLEN,** of Enfield, Nov. 20, 1823, by Rev. Francis L. Robbins, of Enfield	2	126
Christen, d. Obadiah, b. Jan. 10, 1702/3	2	73
Daniell, s. [John & Rebeca], b. Mar. 28, 1658	MG	
Daniel, s. John, b. Mar. 28, 1658	1	28
Daniel, m. Mary **BISSELL,** Jan. 24, 1681	Col.D	54
Daniel, s. Daniell, b. Nov. 25, 1682	Col.D	51
Daniel, d. Mar. 1, 1682/3	Col.D	56
Daniel, d. Mar. 1, 1682/3	1	49
Daniel, s. Jedadiah & Ruth, b. Dec. 7, 1738	2	76
Daniel, s. Elijah & Lydia, b. Dec. 15, 1768	2	79
Daniel, m. Mary **BISSELL,** Jan. 24, [ ]	1	63
Dazier, d. John & Hannah, b. Feb. 26, 1718/19	2	75
Elijah, s. Isaac, b. Oct. 7, 1706	2	73
Elijah, of Windsor, m. Lydia **CLARK,** of Symsbury, Mar. 8, 1762	2	185
Elijah, s. Elijah & Lydia, b. Apr. 17, 1763	2	79
Elizabeth, m. Samuel **THRALL,** b. of Windsor, Oct. 23, 1706	2	203
Erastus, s. Elijah & Lydia, b. Jan. 1, 1771	2	80
Easther, d. Nathaniell, Jr. & Mary, b. Nov. 12, 1761	2	80
[E]unice, d. Obediah, b. Aug. 8, 1696	1	29
Eunice, d. Samuel, Jr. & Rachel, b. Nov. 24, 1761	2	80
Hannah, d. Elijah & Hannah, b. July 17, 1740	2	76
Hannah, m. Pelatia **MILLS,** Jr., b. of Windsor, Mar. 29, 1743	2	178
Hannah, d. Elijah & Lydia, b. Feb. 11, 1775	2	80
Hezakiah, s. Nathaniell, Jr. & Mary, b. Sept. 1, 1766	2	80
Isack, s. John [& Rebeca], b. May 27, 1670	MG	
Isaac, s. John, b. May 27, 1670	1	28
Isack, s. [Josias & Mary], b. June 4, 1678	MG	
Isack, s. Josias, b. June 4, 1678	Col.1	56
Isaac, s. Josiah, b. June 4, 1678	1	28
Isaac, m. Sarah **HOLCOMB,** Dec. 20, 1694	1	64
Isaac, s. Isaac, b. Nov. 7, 1702	1	29
Isaac, s. Joseph, d. Dec. 3, 1709	2	258

	Vol.	Page
OWEN, OWIN, (cont.)		
Isaac, s. Isaac & Mary, b. Sept. 13, 1736	2	76
Jane, m. Oliver **HAYDEN**, b. of Windsor, Nov. 30, 1837,		
by Rev. Daniel Hemmenway	2	482
Jedidiah, s. Obadiah, b. May 22, 1712	2	74
Jedidiah, s. Obadiah, d. June 7, 1714	2	258
Jedidiah, 2nd, s. Obadiah, b. Apr. 21, 1715	2	74
Jedidiah, m. Ruth **PHELPS**, b. of Windsor, Oct. 4, 1735	2	184
Jemima, d. Obadiah, b. Nov. 18, 1700	2	73
Jerusha, d. Seth & Jemima, b. May 12, 1785	2	409
Joel, s. Elijah & Lydia, b. Sept. 6, 1785	2	410
John, s. [ ], b. Dec. 25, 1624 "so that in Dec. 25, 1664		
he was 40 y. old"	1	28
John, m. Rebeca **WADE**, Oct. 3, 1650	MG	
John, m. Rebekah **WADE**, Oct. 3, 1650	1	59
John, s. [John & Rebeca], b. Nov. 5, 1652; d. [ ]	MG	
John, s. John, b. Nov. 5, 1652	1	28
John, 2nd, s. [John & Rebeca], b. Apr. 23, 1654; d. [ ]	MG	
John, s. John, b. Apr. 23, 1654	Col.2	157
John, s. John, b. Apr. 23, 1654	Col.2	181
John, s. John, b. Apr. 23, 1654	1	28
John, his s. [ ], d. [ ], [16]65	MG	
[John*], s. John, b. [Jan. 13]*, [16]67 *(In pencil)	MG	
John, s. John, d. Jan. 13, [16]70	Col.1	55
John, s. John, d. Jan. 15, [16]70	1	48
John, had 11 children b. in Windsor. Dated Aug. 17, 1677	MG	
John, d. Feb. 18, 1697/8	1	49
John, s. John & Hannah, b. Mar. 18, 1711/12	2	75
John, contributed 0-1-0 to the poor in other colonies	MG	
Joseph, s. [John & Rebeca], b. Oct. 23, 1660	MG	
Joseph, s. John, b. Oct. 23, 1660	1	28
Joseph, s. Elijah & Lydia, b. June 26, 1779	2	81
Josiah, s. John, b. Sept. 8, 1651	Col.2	157
Josiah, s. John, b. Sept. 8, 1651	1	28
Josiah, s. Josiah, b. June 6, 1675	1	28
Josiah, Jr., m. Mary **HOSFORD**, Dec. 3, 1698	1	64
Josiah, d. Sept. 11, 1722	2	258
Josias, s. [John & Rebeca], b. Sept. 8, 1651	MG	
Josias, m. Mary **OSBORN**, Oct. 22, 1674	MG	
Josias, m. Mary **OSBON**, Oct. 22, 1674	Col.1	46
Josias, s. [Josias & Mary], b. June 6, 1675	MG	
Josias, had 1 child b. in Windsor. Dated Aug. 17, 1677	MG	
Keziah, d. Nathanael & Mary, b. Apr. 11, 1730	2	75
Keziah, d. Nathanael & Mary, b. Aug. 11, 1730	2	259
Keziah, d. Samuel, Jr. & Rachel, b. July 16, 1763	2	80
Kezia, d. Nathaniell, Jr. & Mary, b. June 15, 1764	2	80
Keziah, d. Samuel, [ ] (Crossed out)	2	392
Lydia, d. Elijah & Lydia, b. Apr. 9, 1773	2	80

	Vol.	Page
OWEN, OWIN, (cont.)		
Margeret, d. Samuel & Margeret, b. Aug. 14, 1731	2	341
Margret, d. Samuel & Margret, d. Apr. 28, 1741	2	259
Margret, d. Samuel & Margret, b. Apr. 28, 1742	2	77
Margret, w. Dea. Samuel, d. Feb. 7, 1783	2	259
Martha, d. Obediah, b. Aug. 31, 1698	1	29
Martha, m. Amos **MOORE**, b. of Windsor, May 21, 1720	2	176
Mary, d. [John & Rebecca], b. Dec. 5, 1662	MG	
Mary, d. John, b. Dec. 5, [16]62	Col.1	54
Mary, d. John, b. Dec. 5, 1662	1	28
Mary, d. [Josias & Mary], b. Feb. 15, 1679	MG	
Mary, m. Nath[an] **WILLIAMS**, Oct. 3, 1681	Col.D	54
Mary, w. Nathanael, d. Jan. 23, 1695/6	1	49
Mary, m. Enoch **PHELPS**, Apr. 13, 1704	1	60
Mary, d. Josiah, Jr., b. Apr. 13, 1707	2	74
Mary, d. Nathaniel & Mary, b. Sept. 12, 1731	2	75
Mary, d. Isaac & Mary, b. June 13, 1733	2	75
Mary, m. Nathanael **WILLIAMS**, Oct. 3, [ ]	1	63
Mary **BISSELL**, see Mary **BIRGE**	Col.D	57
Nathanel, s. [John & Rebeca], b. Aug. 9, 1656	MG	
Nathaniell, s. John, b. Aug. 29, 1656	Col.2	158
Nathanael, s. John, b. Aug. 29, 1656	1	28
Nathanael, m. Mary **GAYLORD**, June 14, 1694	1	63
Nathanael, m. Sarah **PALMER**, Feb. 2, 1697	1	64
Nathanael, s. Nathanael, b. Dec. 31, 1702	1	29
Nathanael, m. Mary **GRISWOLD**, b. of Windsor, July 2, 1729	2	184
Noah, s. Josiah, b. May 14, 1701	1	29
Obedia, s. John [& Rebeca], b. Dec. 12, 1662	MG	
Obediah, s. John, b. Dec. 12, 1667	1	28
Obediah, m. Christian **WINCHEL**, Sept. 21, 1693	1	59
Obedia, s. Obediah, b. July 8, 1694	1	29
Obediah, s. Obediah, d. July 18, 1694	1	49
Obadiah, s. Obadiah, b. Jan. 8, 1705	2	73
Obediah, Jr., d. Dec. 11, 1728	2	258
Obediah, s. Jedediah & Ruth, b. Jan. 14, 1736/7	2	76
Oliver, s. Elijah & Lydia, b. Apr. 24, 1777	2	81
Pegge, d. Samuel, Jr. & Rachel, b. Apr. 22, 1769	2	80
Pelatiah, s. Elijah & Lydia, b. Dec. 10, 1781	2	81
Rachel, m. Samuel **PHELPS**, s. Josiah, Aug. 28, 1712	2	186
Rachel, d. Samuel, Jr. & Rachel, b. June 29, 1760	2	80
Rebeca, d. John, b. Mar. 28, 1666	MG	
Rebeca, d. John, b. Mar. 28, 1666	Col.1	55
Rebekah, d. John, b. Mar. 28, 1666	1	28
Rebekah, m. Nathan **GILLIT**, b. of Windsor, Jan. 30, 1692	1	57
Rebekah, d. Isaac, b. Mar. 2, 1697/8	1	29
Rebecah, wid., d. Dec. 3, 1711	2	258
Rebekah, d. Elijah & Hannah, b. Nov. 28, 1736	2	76

	Vol.	Page
OWEN, OWIN, (cont.)		
Rebeckah, m. Benedict **ALFORD,** Jr., b. of Windsor, Dec. 28, 1761	2	125
Samuell, s. Obadiah, b. Aug. 3, 1707	2	73
Samuel, m. Margerit **GRISWOLD,** b. of Windsor, Nov. 19, 1730	2	184
Samuel, s. Samuel & Margaret, b. Feb. 24, 1736/7	2	76
Samuel, s. Samuel, Jr. & Rachel, b. June 11, 1775	2	410
Samuel, Dea., m. wid. Mary **TYLOR,** Feb. 26, 1783	2	185
Sarah, d. Isaac, b. Feb. 17, 1694/5	1	29
Sarah, d. Nathanael, b. May 3, 1700	1	29
Sarah, m. Ephraim **PHELPS,** b. of Windsor, Dec. 30, 1714	2	186
Sarah, w. Nathaniell, d. Apr. 25, 1731	2	259
Sarah, m. Noadiah **GILLET,** b. of Windsor, Sept. 29, 1737	2	156
Sarah, d. Isaac & Mary, b. Sept. 28, 1747	2	78
Sarah, d. Samuel, Jr. & Rachel, b. July 16, 1767	2	80
Seth, s. Samuel & Margaret, b. Jan. 1, 1744/5	2	77
Seth Calvin, s. Seth Owen & Jemima, b. May 2, 1783	2	409
Shem, s. Elijah & Lydia, b. Nov. 9, 1764	2	79
Silas, s. Josiah, Jr., b. Mar. 9, 1702/3	1	29
Silas, s. Elijah & Lydia, b. Oct. 11, 1766	2	79
Tabitha, d. Obidiah, b. Feb. 6, 1709/10	2	74
Tabitha, d. Obadiah, d. June 10, 1714	2	258
Tabitha, d. Jedediah & Ruth, b. Oct. 2, 1740	2	77
PAINE, PANE, Edward, s. David & Ann S., b. Jan. 24, 1829	2	578
Luther Henry, s. David & Ann, b. Mar. 7, 1824	2	577
Sarah, d. Phillip, b. July 21, 1693	1	31
Stephen, his child d.[ ], in "Elenton" prior to 1740	MG	
Theodore Sill, s. David & Ann, b. Aug. 28, 1825	2	577
PALL, Margret, m. Thomas **ORTON,** June [ ], 1641	MG	
Margaret, m. Thomas **ORTON,** June 1, 1641	1	59
PALMER, PALLMER, PALLMOR, Abigail, d. Hezekiah H. & Abigail, b. June 15, 1818	2	577
Amy, m. Daniel **GILLET,** b. of Windsor, Nov. 2, 1769	2	159
Ann, d. Nicholos, bp. Oct. 11, 1640	1	30
Anna, m. Tahan **GRANT,** b. of Windsor, Jan. 22, 1662	Col.1	45
Anna, m. Tahan **GRANT,** b. of Windsor, Jan. 22, 1662	1	57
Anne, d. Joel & Anne, b. May 16, 1762	2	421
Benjamen, s. Tim[othy], b. Feb. 24, 1681	Col.D	51
Benjamin, s. Timothy, b. Feb. 24, 1682	1	31
Benjamin, s. John, b. Dec. 23, 1703	1	32
Benjamin, s. John, d. Aug. 23, 1706	2	260
Benjamin, s. John, b. Oct. 11, 1707	2	82
Benjamin, s. John & Deborah, b. Apr. 10, 1742	2	412
Chloe, d. Benjamin & Mabel, b. Aug. [ ], 1763	2	423
Deborah, d. Ens. John & Deborah, b. June 21, 1746	2	414
Eli, s. John & Deborah, b. Oct. 13, 1733	2	91
Eli, m. Elizabeth **GILLET,** b. of Windsor, Apr. 1, 1756	2	189

	Vol.	Page
PALMER, PALLMER, PALLMOR, (cont.)		
Eli, d. Sept. 29, 1756	2	265
Elisabeth, d. [Nicolas], b. Aug. 7, 1644	MG	
Elizabeth, d. Nicholos, b. Aug. 7, 1644	1	30
Emeline, d. Hezekiah H. & Abigail, b. Apr. 5, 1815	2	577
Ezekiel, s. John & Deborah, b. Mar. 17, 1737/8	2	411
Ezekiel, s. Capt. John, d. Sept. 10, 1756	2	265
Ezekiel, s. Jonathan & Hannah, b. Feb. 7, 1770	2	430
Hanna, d. [Nicolas], b. Oct. [ ], 1640; bp. [Oct.] 11, 1640	MG	
Hanna, m. Tahan **GRANT**, Jan. 22, 1662	MG	
Hanna, d. [Timothy & Hanna], b. Oct. 3, 1666	MG	
Hannah, d. Timothy, b. Oct. 3, 1666	1	30
Hannah, m. Timothy **HOSFORD**, Dec. 5, 1689	Col.D	54
Hannah, m. Timothy **HOSFORD**, Dec. 5, 1689	1	58
Hannah, w. Timothy, d. Sept. 26, 1704	2	260
Hannah, d. Samuel & Ruth, b. Dec. 29, 1745	2	414
Hannah, w. Jonathan, d. May 1, 1796	2	266
Hervey, s. Joel & Anne, b. Nov. 20, 1770	2	425
Hezekiah H., m. Abigail **TAYLOR**, May 29, 1811	2	500
Hezakiah Haydon, s. Joel & Anna, b. Jan. 19, 1781	2	428
Horace, s. Joel & Anna, b. Mar. 5, 1783	2	428
Horace, m. Mary **HEATH**, Dec. [ ], 1823, by Rev. James F.		
Bridges, of Enfield	2	500
Israel I., m. Flora **WELLS**, Dec. 3, 1828, by John Bartlett	2	193
Jehiel, s. John & Deborah, b. Jan. 12, 1730/1	2	90
Jehiel, s. Capt. John, d. Oct. 10, 1756	2	265
Jehiel, s. John, 2nd & Jerusha, b. Mar. 18, 1757;		
d. June 9, 1757	2	417
Jehiel, s. Jonathan & Hannah, b. June 17, 1768	2	429
Jerusha, d. John, 3rd & Jerusha, b. Aug. 29, 1751;		
d. Oct. 2, 1751	2	416
Jerusha, d. John, 3rd & Jerusha, b. Nov. 11, 1752	2	416
Jerusha, w. John, Jr., d. Apr. 27, 1757	2	264
Joan, w. Nicho[las], d. Apr. 6, 1683	Col.D	56
Joane, w. Nicholas, d. Apr. 6, 1683	1	50
Joel, s. John & Deborah, b. May 4, 1736	2	410
Joel, m. Anne **HAYDON**, b. of Windsor, July 23, 1761	2	189
Joel, s. Joel & Anne, b. July 26, 1768	2	425
Joel, m. Emily **BARBER**, Feb. 19, 1834, by Henry A.		
Rowland	2	193
John, s. [Timothy & Hanna], b. Apr. 13, 1673	MG	
John, s. Timothy, b. Apr. 13, 1673	1	30
John, m. Sarah **MUDGG**, Jan. 14, 1695/6	1	60
John, s. John, b. June 11, 1698	1	32
John, Jr., m. Deborah **FILLEY**, b. of Windsor, Sept. 12, 1723	2	187
John, s. John, Jr., b. Feb. 7, 1724/5	2	89
John, s. John, 3rd & Jerusha, b. Apr. 21, 1730	2	415
John, 3rd, m. Jerusha **ALLYN**, b. of Windsor, Dec. 3, 1748/9	2	188

	Vol.	Page
PALMER, PALLMER, PALLMOR, (cont.)		
John, Dea., d. Sept. 10, 1756	2	264
John, Jr., m. wid. Jerusha **WADSWORTH**, b. of Windsor,		
Mar. 4, 1762	2	189
Jonathan, s. John & Deborah, b. May 31, 1740 (Crossed out)	2	296
Jonathan, s. John & Deborah, b. May 31, 1740	2	412
Jonathan, m. wid. Hannah **HUBBARD**, b. of Windsor, Jan.		
19, 1764	2	189
Jonathan, s. Jonathan & Hannah, b. July 14, 1766	2	424
Julia Ann, d. Hezekiah H. & Abigail, b. July 16, 1813	2	577
Lulima, see under Zulima		
Lydia, d. Samuel & Ruth, b. Aug. 25, 1743	2	412
Mabel, d. Benjamin & Mabel, b. Sept. 9, 1768	2	426
Martha, d, [Timothy & Hanna], b. Dec. 29, 1679	MG	
Martha, d. Tim[othy], d. Aug. 16, [16]83	Col.D	56
Martha, d. Nicholas*, d. Aug. 16, 1683 *(Written over		
"Timothy")	1	50
Martha, d. Nov. 21, 1732	2	263
Martin, s. Joel & Anna, b. Feb. 19, 1773	2	427
Martin, Jr., m. Sephrona **BARBER**, May 20, 1835, by Rev.		
Nathaniel Kellogg	2	500
Martin, d. Aug. 23, 1843	2	266
Mary, d. [Nicolas], b. May 3, 1637	MG	
Mary, d. Nicholos, b. May 3, 1637	1	30
Mary, d. [Timothy & Hanna], b. May 14, 1669	MG	
Mary, m. Samuel **HOSFORD**, Apr. 4, 1690	Col.D	55
Mary, m. Samuel **HOSFORD**, Apr. 4, 1690	1	58
Mary, d. John, b. Nov. 17, 1700	1	32
Mary, m. Phinehas **WILSON**, b. of Windsor, Nov. 21, 1750	2	209
Mary, m. John **HAYDEN**, b. of Windsor, Nov. 28, 1830, by		
Henry A. Rowland	2	485
Mary E., m. Charles H. **FITCH**, b. of Windsor, Sept. 15,		
1847, by F. A. Leete	2	478
Merriam, wid., d. May 31, 1727	2	262
Noami, d. Joel & Anne, b. Oct. 1, 1763	2	423
Nicolas, his w. [ ], d. [ ], [16]46	MG	
Nicolas, had 4 children b. in Windsor. Dated Aug. 17, 1677	MG	
Nicholas, d. Aug. 30, 1689	Col.D	57
Nicholas, d. Aug. 30, 1689	1	49
Ruba, d. Joel & Anna, b. July 5, 1775	2	427
Samuell, s. [Timothy & Hanna], b. Sept. 7, 1677	MG	
Samuell, s. Timothy, bp. Dec. 2, [16]77	MG	
Samuel, s. John, b. Apr. 5, 1712	2	85
Samuel, of Windsor, m. Ruth **PRATT**, of Hartford, Apr. 6,		
1738	2	188
Samuel, s. Samuel & Ruth, b. Mar. 16, 1755	2	417
Sara, d. [Timothy & Hanna], b. Feb. 25, 1671; d. [ ]	MG	
Sara, d. [Timothy & Hanna], b. Apr. 12, 1675	MG	

	Vol.	Page
PALMER, PALLMER, PALLMOR, (cont.)		
Sarah, m. Nathanael **OWIN**, Feb. 2, 1697	1	64
Sarah, d. Samuel & Ruth, b. Jan. 12, 1738/9	2	412
Sarah, d. Samuel & Ruth, d. Feb. 14, 1759	2	264
Stephen, s. Timo[thy], b. Jan. 20, 1686	Col.D	51
Stephen, s. Timothy, b. Jan. 20, 1686	1	31
Steven, m. Sarah **BARBOR**, b. of Windsor, Oct. 17, 1717	2	187
Stephen, s. Stephen, b. Jan. 18, 1718/19	2	87
Stephen, d. Nov. 17, 1720	2	262
Stephen, s. Samuel & Ruth, b. June 7, 1750	2	417
Sulima, see under Zulima		
Timothy, s. [Nicolas], bp. Mar. 20, 1641	MG	
Timothy, s. Nicholos, bp. Mar. 20, 1641	1	30
Timothy, m. Hanna **BUELL**, Sept. 17, 1663	MG	
Timothy, m. Hanna **BUELL**, Sept. 17, 1663	Col.1	45
Timothy, m. Hannah **BUELL**, Sept. 17, 1663	1	60
Timothy, s. [Timothy & Hanna], b. Aug. 25, 1664	MG	
Timothy, s. Timothy, b. Aug. 25, 1664	Col.1	54
Timothy, s. Timothy, b. Aug. 25, 1664	1	32
Timothy, had 6 children b. in Windsor. Dated Aug. 17, 1677	MG	
Timothy, d. Aug. 29, 1713	2	261
Timothy, s. Stephen, b. June 28, 1720	2	87
Timothy, s. Samuell & Ruth, b. Aug. 18, 1747	2	414
Timothy, contributed 0-2-6 to the poor in other colonies	MG	
William Lucius, s. Hezekiah H. & Abigail, b. Nov. 4, 1820	2	577
Zulima, d. Joel & Anne, b. Feb. 4, 1766 (Perhaps "Lilima")	2	425
-----, his child d. June 7, [16]39	MG	
-----, Mrs., contributed 0-2-10 to the poor in other colonies	MG	
PARKER, Experience, m. James **SLADE**, b. of Windsor, June 14, 1750	2	201
Miriam, of Southwick, m. Elijah **ALLYN**, of Windsor, Feb. 17, 1823, by Rev. Augustus Bolles, of Wintonbury	2	125
William, m. Johanna **REGAN**, Oct. 14, 1852, by Rev. James Smyth	2	460
PARKES, Hanna, m. William **PARSONS**, Oct. 26, 166[ ]	MG	
Hanna, m. William **PARSONS**, Oct. 26, 1666	Col.1	45
Hannah, m. William **PARSONS**, Oct. 26, 1666	1	60
PARKMAN, Samuel, s. Elias, b. Aug. 12, 1644	1	30
PARMELEE, PARMELE, Elizabeth, m. Richard S. **LAMBERSON**, b. of Suffield, Sept. 20, 1852, by Rev. S. H. Allen	2	492
Frances A., of Windsor, m. Henry L **GOWDY**, of Enfield, Dec. 12, 1849, by S. H. Allen	2	497
Nancy, of Windsor, m. Ezra **DAY**, of Ottawa, Ill., May 18, 1848, by Rev. Cephus Brainard	2	474
Silas, of Windsor, m. Phidelia M. **WELLS**, of Leyden, Mass., June 7, 1849, by Rev. S. H. Allen	2	502

	Vol.	Page
PARSONS, PARSON, PERSON, PERSONS,		
Abigayl, d. [Thomas & Liddia], b. Jan. 21, 1643; d. [ ]	MG	
Abigail, d. Thomas, b. Jan. 21, 1653	Col.2	155
Abigail, bd. Dec. 5, [16]59	1	49
Abigall, d. [ ], [16]62	MG	
Abigall, d. Ebenezer, b. Aug. 1, [16]75	MG	
Abigail, d. Ebenezer, b. Aug. [ ], 1675	1	31
Abigail, d. Samuel & Jerusha, b. May 27, 1744	2	413
Abigail, d. Hezekiah & Anna, b. Dec. 7, 1765	2	424
Anna, d. Hezakiah & Anna, b. May 7, 1764	2	424
Anne, d. Ephraim & Hannah, b. Nov. 19, 1756	2	418
Benjamin, s. Simon & Ruth, b. May 21, 1742	2	414
Benjamin, s. Ephraim & Hannah, b. May 28, 1763	2	423
Bethia, d. [Thomas & Liddia], b. May 21, 1642	MG	
Bethia, d. Thomas, b. May 21, 1642	Col.2	155
Bethia, m. Thomas MASKELL, May 10, 1660	MG	
Bathia, m. Thomas MASKEL, b. of Windsor, May 10, 1660	1	59
Ebenezer, s. [Thomas & Liddia], b. May 14, 1655	MG	
Ebenezer, s. Thomas, b. May 14, [16]55	Col.2	181
Ebenezer, s. Ebenezer, b. Apr. 16, [16]77	MG	
Ebenezer, had 1 child b. in Windsor. Dated Aug. 17, 1677	MG	
Electa, m. Linus GIDDINGS, b. of Windsor, Nov. 27, 1821,		
by Rev. John Bartlet. Int. Pub.	2	159
Emily, Mrs. of Windsor, m. William HALE, of Sandisfield,		
Mass., Jan. 4, 1846, by Rev. T. A. Leete	2	519
Ephraim, m. Hannah BARRET, b. of Windsor, Apr. 23, 1754	2	189
Ephraim, s. Ephraim, b. June 18, 1758	2	420
Eunice, d. John & Sarah, b. Aug. 6, 1731	2	427
Ezra, s. Simon & Ruth, b. Apr. 16, 1744	2	414
Hanna, d. [Thomas & Sara], b. Oct. 3, 1671; d. [ ]	MG	
Hanna, d. [William & Hanna], b. Nov. 3, [16]78	MG	
Hannah, w. Hezekiah, d. July 29, 1725	2	262
Hannah, d. Ephraim & Hannah, b. Apr. 1, 1755	2	418
Henrietta R., m. Niles M. GRISWOLD, b. of Windsor, Dec.		
2, 1841, by Rev. John Moore, of Hartford	2	482
Hezekiah, d. Hezekiah & Martha, b. May 28, 1736	2	410
Hezekiah, m. Ann [ ], b. of Windsor, July 15, 1756	2	189
Hezakiah, s. Hezekiah & Anna, b. June 13, 1757	2	422
Hezekiah, of Windsor, m. Ruth CASE, of Simsbury, May 14,		
1822, by Rev. John Bartlett. Int. Pub.	2	500
Hiram, of Sandisfield, Mass., m. Emely STEPHENS, of		
Windsor, Sept. 11, 1831, by Henry A. Rowland	2	193
Huldah, of Enfield, m. Zachariah ALLEN, of Windsor,		
Oct. 31, 1765	2	125
Jerusha, d. Samuel & Jerusha, b. Dec. 5, 1740	2	413
Jesse, s. Ephraim & Hannah, b. May 6, 1761	2	423
John, s. [Thomas & Liddia], b. Nov. 13, 1647	MG	
John, s. Thomas, b. Nov. 13, 1647	Col.2	156

	Vol.	Page
PARSONS, PARSON, PERSON, PERSONS, (cont.)		
John, s. Ebenezer, b. July 29, [16]78	MG	
John, s. Ebenezer, b. July 29, 1678	Col.1	56
John, s. Ebenezer, b. July 29, 1678	1	31
Jonathan J., m. Mary C. **GRISWOLD,** Dec.1, 1825, by Rev.		
John Bartlett	2	192
Joseph, s. [Thomas & Liddia], b. May 1, 1661	MG	
Louve, d. Samuel & Jerusha, b. Oct. 23, 1742	2	413
Lidea, wid., m. Eltwed **POMRY,** Nov. 30, 1664, by Mr.		
Wolcot	Col.1	45
Marcy, d. [Thomas & Liddia], b. July 23, 1652	MG	
Martha, d. Hezekiah & Martha, b. June 20, 1732	2	410
Martha, d. Hezakiah & Ann, b. Oct. 29, 1759	2	422
Mary, d. Thomas, b. July 23, 1652	Col.2	156
Mary, m. Nicolas **EUENES,** b. of Windsor, Nov. 17, 1670,		
by Capt. Newbery	Col.1	46
Meriam, of Summers, m. David **ALLIN,** of Windsor, Nov.		
14, 1755	2	124
Pelatiah, d. Hezakiah & Anna, b. Sept. 1, 1758	2	422
Pelatiah, s. Hezekiah & Ann, d. Jan. 29, 1759	2	265
Pelatiah, s. Hezekiah & Ann, b. Sept. 15, 1761	2	422
Ruth, m. Edward **MOORE,** Jr., b. of Windsor, Jan. 28, 1773	2	180
Salome, m. Russell **FOOT,** May 29, 1825, by Benjamin F.		
Lambord, Elder, of Warehouse Point	2	153
Samuell, s. [Thomas & Liddia], b. July 18, 1657	MG	
Samuell, s. Thomas, b. July 18, 1657	Col.2	161
Samuel, of Windsor, m. Jerusha **CIBBE,** of Enfield, Jan.		
17, 1739/40	2	188
Samuell, had 1 child d. [ ], in "Elenton" prior to		
1740	MG	
Samuel, s. Samuel & Jerusha, b. Dec. 23, 1745	2	414
Sara, d. [Thomas & Sara], b. Oct. 12, 1669	MG	
Sara, w. [Thomas], d. June 14, 1674	MG	
Sarah, m. Henry **STYLES,** Jr., b. of Windsor, Nov. 1, 1698	1	62
Sarah (**DARE**)*, w. Thomas, d. [June 14*, [16]74 *(In pencil)	MG	
Sarah (**DARE**)*, w. Thomas, d. June 14, [16]74 *(Name		
supplied by LBB)	Col.1	58
Simon, had 1 child d. [ ], in "Elenton" prior to 1740	MG	
Thomas, m. Liddia **BROWN,** June 28, 1641	MG	
Thomas, m. Lydia **BROWN,** June 28, 1641	1	60
Thomas, s. [Thomas & Liddia], b. Aug. 9, 1645; d. [ ]	MG	
Thomas, s. Thomas, b. Aug. 9, 1645	Col.2	155
Thomas, s. Thomas, b. Aug. 9, 1645	1	30
Thomas, d. Sept. 23, 1661	MG	
Thomas, d. Sept. 23, 1661	1	49
Thomas, d. [ ], [16]61	MG	
Thomas, m. Sara **DARE,** Dec. 24, 1668	MG	
Thomas, m. Sara **DARE,** Dec. 24, [16]6[8]?, by Mr. Wolcott	Col.1	45

	Vol.	Page
PARSONS, PARSON, PERSON, PERSONS, (cont.)		
Thomas, m. Sarah **DEARE**, Dec. 6, 1668, by Mr. Wolcott	1	60
Thomas, s. [Thomas & Sara], b. Jan. 2, 1673; d. [ ]	MG	
Thomas, s. Thomas, b. Jan. 2, 1673	1	30
Thomas, his w. [ ]*,d. June 14, [16]64 *(Note by		
LBB: "Sarah **DARE**")	Col.1	58
Thomas, his w. [ ], d. June 14, [16]74; bd. the 15th day	1	49
Thomas, Jr., had 3 children b. in Windsor. Dated Aug. 17,		
1677	MG	
Thomas, Sr., had 8 children b. in Windsor. Dated Aug. 17,		
1677	MG	
Thomas, d. Dec. 14, 1680	MG	
Thomas, d. Dec. 14, [16]80	Col.1	58
William, m. Hanna **PARKES**, Oct. 26, 166[ ]	MG	
William, m. Hanna **PARKES**, Oct. 26, 1666, by [ ]	Col.1	45
William, m. Hannah **PARKES**, Oct. 26, 1666	1	60
William, s. [William & Hanna], b. July 27, 1669	MG	
PARTMAN, [see under **PATRUM**]		
PASCO, PASKO, Elizabeth, d. James & Hannah, b. Jan. 29,		
1728/9	2	91
Hannah, d. James & Hannah, b. Aug. 16, 1726	2	91
James, of Windsor, m. Hannah **ORSBAND**, of Enfield, July		
[ ], 1725	2	187
James, s. James & Hannah, b. Mar. 28, 1731	2	91
Nelson, m. Charlotte **KING**, Feb. 1, 1827, by Rev. Henry		
A. Rowland	2	193
Rachel, of Stafford, m. Noah **PAULK**, of Windsor, Dec. 13,		
1764	2	190
PATRUM, PARTMAN, Elias, had 2 children b. in Windsor.		
Dated Aug. 17, 1677	MG	
George, d. [ ], [16]44	MG	
PAULK, POLK, Noah, of Windsor, m. Rachel **PASKO**, of		
Stafford, Dec. 13, 1764	2	190
Xerxes, s. Noah & Rachel, b. Jan. 14, 1766	2	424
PEARSON, [see also **PIERSON**], Ruth, d. Simon & Ruth, b. Oct.		
21, 1739	2	412
Simon, m. Ruth **TALER**, b. of Windsor, Dec. 25, 1738	2	188
PEASE, Abigail, of Windsor, m. Edward **HURLBURT**, of		
Hartford, Sept. 16, 1839, by Rev. Cephas Brainard	2	483
Asa, of Enfield, m. Selina **McCHESTER**, of Windsor, Nov.*		
12, 1848, by Rev. Samuel Lake *("Mar." crossed out)	2	194
Chauncey, of Springfield, m. Betsey or Elizabeth		
HOLCOMB, of Windsor, Nov. 7, 1821, by Richard		
Niles, J. P.	2	191
David, 2nd, m. Elizabeth **COOK**, Mar. 14, 1841, by Ezra S.		
Cook	2	501
E. Marshall, of Texas, m. Lusindia C. **MILES**, of Windsor,		
Aug. 22, 1850, by Rev. N. B. Soule	2	502

	Vol.	Page
PETERSON, Jane, m. Edward **WHITE**, b. of Windsor, Apr. 16, 1848, by Rev. Cephus Brainard	2	520
PETTIBONE, PETTEBON, PETTEBONE, PETYBON, Daniel, s. Daniel & Sarah, b. Oct. 22, 1770	2	427
John, m. Sara **EGELSTON**, Feb. 16, 1664	MG	
John, m. Sara **EGGLSTONE**, b. of Windsor, Feb. 16, 1664, by Mr. Wollcot	Col.1	45
John, m. Sarah **EGELSTON**, b. of Windsor, Feb. 16, 1664, by Mr. Wolcott	1	60
John, s. [John & Sara], b. Dec. 15, 1665	MG	
John, s. John, b. Dec. 15 1665	Col.1	55
John, s. John, b. Dec. 15, 1665	1	30
John, had 3 children b. in Windsor. Dated Aug. 17, 1677	MG	
John, s. Daniel & Sarah, b. July 10, 1774	2	427
John, his w. [ ], contributed 0-0-6 to the poor in other colonies	MG	
Levi, s. Daniel & Sarah, b. July 15, 1772	2	427
Lydia, of Simsbury, m. Ithamer **GAYLORD**, of Windsor, Dec. 4, 1800	2	479
Samuel, s. Daniel & Sarah, b. Apr. 18, 1780	2	427
Sara, d. [John & Sara], b. Sept. 24, 1667	MG	
Sarah, d. John, b. Sept. 24, 1667	1	30
Sarah, d. Daniel & Sarah, b. Jan. 24, 1776	2	427
Stephen, s. [John & Sara], b. Oct. 3, 166[ ]	MG	
Stephen, s. [John & Sara], b. Oct. 3, 1669	MG	
Stephen, s. John, b. Oct. 3, 1669	1	30
PETTIS, Thankful, of Bolton, m. Henry **DIXON**, of New Canan, N. Y., Oct. 24, 1830, by John Bartlett	2	473
PHELPS, PHELPES, PELPES, PHELPES, Aaron, s. Josiah & Abigail, b. Nov. 9, 1716	2	90
Aaron, of Windsor, m. Mercey **KENT**, of Suffield, Aug. 13, 1742	2	188
Aaron, s. Aaron & Marcey, b. Jan. 26, 1745/6	2	415
Aaron, s. Aaron, 3rd & Ruth, b. Mar. 3, 1772	2	426
Abell, s. Joseph, b. Feb.19, 1705/6	2	81
Abigayl, d.[ ], [16]48	MG	
Abigayl, d. [Nathanell & Elizabeth], b. Apr. 5, 1655	MG	
Abigaile, d. Nathaniell, b. Apr. 5, [16]55	Col.2	158
Abigayl, d. [Samuell & Sara], b. May 16, 1666	MG	
Abigail, d. Samuell, b. May 16, 1666	Col.1	55
Abigail, d. Samuel, b. May 16, 1666	1	29
Abigall, d. Timo[thy], b. June 5, 1682	Col.D	51
Abigail, m. David **MARSHEL**, Dec. 9, 1686	1	59
Abigail, d. Joseph, b. Oct. 15, 1693	1	31
Abigael, w. William (s. Timothy), d. Apr. 24, 1705	2	260
Abigaell, d. Samuell, b. Mar. 8, 1707/8	2	82
Abigail, d. Enoch, b. Feb. 9, 1708/9	2	84
Abigaell, d. Joseph (s. Joseph), b. Nov. 18, 1709	2	82

	Vol.	Page
PHELPS, PHELPES, FELPES, PHELPES, (cont.)		
Arah, s. Josiah, 3rd & Ann, b. Jan. 28, 1736/7	2	411
Asa, s. Ephraim, b. Oct. 1, 1720	2	87
Aurelia, d. John (s. Thomas) & Rachel, b. May 31, 1776	2	428
Austin, m. Deborah **MOORE**, b. of Windsor, Oct. 27, 1768	2	190
Belhuel, d. Lancelot & Jerusha, b. Feb. 16, 1787	2	429
Benajah, s. Aaron & Ruth, b. Apr. 8, 1773	2	426
Benj[amin], s. Abram, b. Oct. 1, 1683	Col.D	51
Benjamin, s. Abraham, b. Oct. 1, 1683	1	31
Benjamin, m. Hannah **BIRGE**, b. of Windsor, Apr. 12, 1705	2	185
Benjamin, s. Capt. Abraham, d. July 24, 1706	2	260
Benjamin, s. Josiah, Jr., b. May 12, 1711	2	84
Benjamin, s. Joseph, b. Nov. 11, 1717	2	86
Benjamin, s. Thomas, b. July 25, 1720	2	89
Benjamin, m. Rachel **BROWN**, b. of Windsor, June 24, 1731	2	187
Benjamin, s. Benjamin & Rachel, b. Nov. 12, 1732	2	410
Bennoni, s. Joseph, Sr., b. June 24, 1694	1	32
Benoni, s. Joseph, decd., d. Feb. [ ], 1709/10 (?), at		
Nathaniell Horsford	2	260
Bildad, s. Benjamin & Rachel, b. July 17, 1734	2	411
Bildad, s. Capt. Josiah & Ann, b. Aug. 22, 1739	2	427
Bildad, m. Mrs. Eunice **PHELPS**, b. of Windsor, Jan. 5, 1763	2	190
Caleb, s. William (s. Timothy), b. Jan. 11, 1708/9	2	83
Caleb, m. Mary **MOORE**, b. of Windsor, Dec. 24, 1730	2	187
Caleb, s. Caleb & Mary, b. June 24, 1738	2	411
Caleb, m. wid. Mary **HENDERSON**, b. of Windsor, June 22,		
1749	2	189
Candace, d. Bildad & Eunice, b. Jan. 28, 1773	2	426
Candis, of Windsor, m. Henry **THOMPSON**, of Enfield, June		
10, 1829, by Henry A. Rowland	2	206
Caroline, of Windsor, m. Warren **VIBERTS**, of Springfield,		
Mass., July 27, 1841, by Rev. John R. Adams	2	207
Catherine, of Windsor, m. Rev. Austin **CAREY**, of		
Sunderland, Mass., May 3, 1842, by Rev. S. D. Jewett	2	516
Charity, of Windsor, m. Paul **HARMON**, of Suffield, Apr.		
13, 1826, by Rev. Asahel Morse	2	166
Charles, s. William, Sr. (s. Samuell), b. Oct. 13, 1708	2	82
Charles, s. Charles & Hannah, b. July 21, 1752	2	420
Charles, Jr., m. Ann **COOK**, b. of Windsor, Apr. 13, 1776	2	190
Charles, m. Hannah **COOK**, b. of Windsor, [17]	2	137
Cicero, m. Catherine S. **GRISWOLD**, b. of Windsor, Jan.		
31, 1822, by Richard Niles, J. P.	2	500
Cicero I., m. Sarah **ALLIS**, b. of Windsor, June 28, 1840, by		
Rev. Ezra S. Cook	2	501
Cornelius, s. [Timothy & Mary], b. Apr. 26, 1671	MG	
Cornelious, s. Timothy, b. Apr. 26, 1671	1	31
Cornelius, m. Sarah **MANSFIELD**, Nov. 2, 1704	2	186
Cornelius, s. Cornelius, b. June 2, 1707	2	83

	Vol.	Page
PHELPS, PHELPES, FELPES, PHELPES, (cont.)		
Cornelius, m. Hannah **PHELPS**, b. of Windsor, Mar. 24,		
1742/3	2	188
Cornelius, s. Cornelius & Hannah, b. July 14, 1745	2	414
Cornish, s. Elisha & Elizabeth, b. July 18, 1772	2	426
Cyrus, s. Bildad & Eunice, b. Jan. 15, 1771	2	426
Damoros, d. Josiah, b. July 7, 1699	1	32
Damoras, had illeg. s. John, b. Nov. 2, 1724; reputed f. John		
THRALL, Jr.	2	108
Daniel, s. Joseph, b. Dec. 25, 1689	1	31
Daniel, s. Joseph, d. Jan. 4, 1690	Col.D	57
Daniel, s. Joseph, d. Jan. 4, 1690	1	50
Daniel, s. Joseph, b. Apr. 15, 1696	1	32
Daniel, s. William, Sr., b. Mar. 21, 1700/1	1	32
Daniel, s. Joseph, Jr., b. Mar. 28, 1707	2	82
Daniel, s. John, Jr., b. May 27, 1712	2	85
Daniel, m. Sarah **STRONG**, b. of Windsor, Mar. 23, 1726/7	2	187
Daniel, m. Mindwell **BUCKLAND**, b. of Windsor, Nov. 9,		
1728	2	187
Daniel, s. Daniel & Mindwell, b. Apr. 26, 1730	2	89
Daniel, s. John & Elizabeth, d. Jan. 6, 1732/3	2	263
Daniel, Jr., m. Damaris **LOOMIS**, b. of Windsor, Feb. 28,		
1744/5	2	188
Daniel, s. Timothy & Margret, b. Oct. 11, 1753	2	418
Daniel, Lieut., d. Sept. 17, 1777	2	265
Daniel, m. Delia **DRAKE**, b. of Windsor, Apr. 4, 1832, by		
Rev. Henry A. Rowland	2	193
Daniel B., m. Phebe L. **ELLSWORTH**, b. of Windsor, Mar.		
21, 1848, by Cephus Brainard	2	501
David, s. John, b. Jan. 17, 1689	1	32
David, twin with Jonathan, s. Ephraim, b. May 24, 1723	2	88
David, s. Thomas & Ann, b. Nov. 1, 1734	2	413
Deborah, d. Thomas & Ann, b. May 27, 1743	2	413
Deborah, d. Aaron & Marcy, b. Feb. 16, 1757	2	420
Ebenezer, s. William (s. Timothy), b. Apr. 2, 1705	2	82
Ebenezer, m. Mindwell **EGELSTON**, b. of Windsor, Dec. 7,		
1727	2	187
Ebenezer, s. Ebenezer & Mindwell, b. Mar. 18, 1734/5	2	91
Ebenezer, s. Ebenezer & Anna, b. July 27, 1764	2	422
Edward, of Simsbury, m. Lamitha **HUBBARD**, of Windsor,		
Nov. 28, 1822, by Rev. John Bartlett. Int. Pub.	2	191
Elinor, d. James & Esther, b. June 10, 1749	2	419
Eli, s. William & Martha, b. Aug. 16, 1746	2	414
Elihu, s. John, 3rd & Elizabeth, b. July 17, 1762	2	422
Elihu, m. Hulah P. **HOUSE**, b. of Windsor, Dec. 31, 1843, by		
Rev. S. W. Scofield	2	501
Elijah, s. Caleb & Mary, b. July 18, 1744	2	418
Elisha, s. John & Sarah, b. Mar. 27, 1737	2	414

	Vol.	Page

PHELPS, PHELPES, FELPES, PHELPES, (cont.)

Elisha, s. Elisha & Elizabeth, b. Aug. 9, 1770	2	426
Eliza A., of Windsor, m. Sheldon **KEENY**, Jr., of Winchester, Nov. 25, 1846/7, by Rev. Cephus Brainard	2	462
Eliza D., m. Frederick **DRAKE**, b. of Windsor, Mar. 6, 1843, by Rev. S. D. Jewett	2	473
Elizabeth, d. William, Sr., b. July 23, 1706	2	81
Elizabeth, d. John, Jr., b. Nov. 25, 1714	2	86
Elizabeth, d. John, Jr., b. Nov. 25, 1714 (Crossed out)	2	261
Elizabeth, d. Thomas & Ann, b. Sept. 28, 1740	2	413
Elizabeth, d. John & Sarah, b. May 21, 1744	2	416
Elizabeth, d. John, 3rd & Elizabeth, b. July 27, 1764	2	422
Elizabeth, d. John, 3rd & Elizabeth, d. Sept. 13, 1777	2	266
Elizabeth, d. Timothy & Ruth, b. Nov. 22, 1795	2	429
Ellsworth N., m. Lucy **MARSHALL**, b. of Windsor, Dec. 15, 1850, by T. A. Leete	2	502
Emily H., of Windsor, m. Edward H. **HOLLISTER**, of New York, Dec. 6, 1849, by J. H. Farnsworth	2	487
Enock, s. [John & Sarah], b. Jan. 21, 1675; bp. [Feb.] 3, [16]7[ ]	MG	
Enoch, m. Mary **OWIN**, Apr. 13, 1704	1	60
Enoch, d. Aug. 5, 1750	2	264
Enoch, s. Aaron & Marcy, b. Oct. [ ], 1751	2	420
Enoch, s. Aaron & Marcy, b. Nov. [ ], 1751	2	417
Ephraim, s. [Samuell & Sara], b. Nov. 1, 1663	MG	
Ephrem, s. Samuel, b. Nov. 1, [16]63	Col. 1	54
Ephraim, s. Samuel, b. Nov. 1, 1663	1	29
Ephraim, m. Mary **JAGGERS**, May 21, 1691	1	60
Ephraim, s. Ephraim, b. Sept. 28, 1692	1	31
Ephraim, d. Nov. 6, 1697	1	50
Ephraim, s. Sarah **OWEN**, b. of Windsor, Dec. 30, 1714	2	186
Ephraim, s. Ephraim, b. June 29, 1718	2	87
Easter, d. James & Esther, b. June 20, 1746	2	414
Esther, w. James, d. Apr. 3, 1767	2	265
Esther, d. Elijah & Esther, b. Sept. 27, 1772	2	426
Esther, m. Daniel **ENO**, b. of Windsor, Jan. 23, 1783	2	147
Eunice, Mrs., m. Bildad **PHELPS**, b. of Windsor, Jan. 5, 1763	2	190
Eunice, d. Bildad & Eunice, b. Aug. 18, 1769	2	426
Eunice, d. Timothy & Ruth, b. Nov. 17, 1788	2	429
Ezecia, child of Isack, bp. Sept. 9, [16]77	MG	
Fidelia, m. Isaac S. **CLARK**, [1835], by Richard G. Drake, J. P.	2	471
Flava, d. Timothy & Ruth, b. Mar. 28, 1794	2	429
Francis, d. John, b. Dec. [ ], 1683	1	31
Frances, m. Epheram **BANCRAFT**, b. of Windsor, Mar. 17, 1715	2	129
Georg[e], communicant 16[ ]	MG	

	Vol.	Page
PHELPS, PHELPES, FELPES, PHELPES, (cont.)		
George, his w. [ ], ch. mem. 16[ ], from Dorchester	MG	
George, m. 2nd w. Frances **DEWEY**, wid. Thomas, Nov.		
[ ], 164[ ]	MG	
George, his child d. [ ], [16]46	MG	
George, his child d. [ ], [16]47	MG	
George, his w. [ ], d. Apr. 29, 1648	MG	
George, m. Frances **DEWEY**, Nov. 30, 1648	1	60
George, his w. [ ], d. [ ], [16]48	MG	
George, had 6 children b. in Windsor. Dated Aug. 17, 1677	MG	
George, s. Lieut. Caleb & Mary, b. Jan. 9, 1755	2	419
George, m. [ ] **RANDAL**, d. Phillup, [ ]	MG	
George, contributed 0-4-6 to the poor in other colonies	MG	
Hannah, d. Timo[thy], b. Aug. 4, 1684	Col.D	51
Hannah, d. Sergt. Timothy, b. Aug. 4, 1684	1	31
Hanna, d. [Joseph & Hanna], b. Feb. 2, 1668	MG	
Hannah, d. William, b. Oct. 13, 1694	1	32
Hannah, d. Nathanael, b. Jan. 22, 1701/2	2	81
Hannah, wid., m. James **ENNO**, Jr., July 15, 1708	2	145
Hannah, d. Thomas, b. Sept. 28, 1709	2	85
Hannah, d. Timothy, of Hartford, m. Timothy **LOOMIS**, s.		
Timothy, of Windsor, Apr. 5, 1722	2	171
Hannah, of Windsor, m. Benjamin **SMITH**, of Springfield,		
Feb. 22, 1725/6	2	198
Hannah, d. Daniel & Sarah, b. Feb. 4, 1731/2	2	90
Hannah, d. Daniel & Sarah, b. Feb. 4, 1731/2	2	91
Hannah, of Enfield, m. Sergt. Samuel **ORSBORN**, of		
Windsor, July 20, 1737	2	184
Hannah, m. Cornelius **PHELPS**, b. of Windsor, Mar. 24,		
1742/3	2	188
Hannah, d. Cornelius & Hannah, b. Mar. 17, 1747/8	2	415
Hannah, d. Charles & Hannah, b. Sept. 2, 1748	2	420
Harriet, d. Capt. Austin & Deborah, b. Feb. 25, 1784	2	428
Henry Hatfield, s. Solomon & Deborah, b. Feb. 24, 1823	2	577
Hezekiah, s. Samuel & Abigail, b. Aug. 3, 1722	2	88
Hezekiah, Dr., of Windsor, m. Lydiah **GRISWOLD**, of		
Symsbury, Feb. 21, 1749/50	2	189
Hezekiah, Dr., d. July 12, 1752	2	264
Hezakiah, s. James & Esther, b. Oct. 6, 1754	2	419
Hezakiah, s. James & Esther, d. May 31, 1757	2	265
Hezakiah, s. Lieut. Caleb & Mary, b. Oct. 3, 1758;		
d. May 3, 1759	2	419
Hezakiah, s. Elijah & Esther, b. May 12, 1770	2	426
Hiram, s. Timothy & Ruth, b. Oct. 14, 1790	2	429
Horise, s. John, 3rd & Elizbeth, b. Dec. 19, 1766	2	427
Huldah, m. Timothy **WELLS**, b. of Windsor, July 20, 1828,		
by Rev. Henry A. Rowland	2	212
Icabod, s. Joseph, Sr., b. Apr. 3, 1708	2	82

	Vol.	Page
PHELPS, PHELPES, FELPES, PHELPES, (cont.)		
Isack, s. [George], b. Aug. 20, 1638	MG	
Isaac, s. George, b. Aug. 26, 1638	1	29
Isack, m. Ann **GAYLAR**, Mar. 11, 1662	MG	
Isack, m. Ann **GAYLER**, b. of Windsor, Mar. 11, 1662/3, by		
Mr. Allyn	Col.1	45
Isaac, m. Ann **GRISWOLD**, b. of Windsor, Mar. 11, 1662,		
by Mr. Allyn	1	60
Isaak, adm. ch. Jan. 27, 1666	MG	
Isack, s. [Isack & Ann], b. Sept. 10, 1666	MG	
Isack, s. Isack, b. Sept. 10, 1666	Col.1	56
Isaac, s. Isaac, b. Sept. 10, 1666	1	30
Isack, s. [Abraham & Mary], b. Aug. 5, 1673	MG	
Isaac, s. Abraham, b. Aug. 5, 1673	1	30
Isack, had 3 children b. in Windsor. Dated Aug. 17, 1677	MG	
Isack, of Westfield, m. Mary **MAWDSLY**, of Windsor, Dec.		
17, 1690	Col.D	55
Isaac, of Westfield, m. Mary **MAUDSLY**, of Windsor, Dec.		
17, 1690	1	60
Isaac, s. Capt. Abraham, d. Jan. 4, 1702/3	1	50
Isaac, s. Cornelius, b. July 22, 1722	2	89
Isaac, s. Joseph, b. Aug. 16, 1724	2	88
Israel, s. James & Esther, b. Sept. 26, 1757	2	424
Israel, s. James & Esther, b. Sept. 26, 1757; d. Mar. 25, 1763	2	424
Israel, s. James & Esther, b. June 27, 1758	2	419
Jacob, s. [George & Frances], b. Feb. 7, 1649	MG	
Jacob, s. William b. June 18, 1711	2	84
Jacob, m. Abigail **ALFORD**, b. of Windsor, Dec. 30, 1745	2	188
Jacob, s. Jacob & Abigail, b. June 16, 1747	2	415
James, s. Samuel, b. Aug. 12, 1713	2	85
James, s. Samuel, d. Apr. 3, 1718	2	261
James, s. Samuel, b. Jan. 23, 1719/20	2	87
James, s. James & Esther, b. Oct. 26, 1752	2	419
James, s. James & Esther, d. Oct. 27, 1757	2	265
James, s. James & Mary, b. Apr. 25, 1770	2	426
Jane E., of Windsor Locks, m. Herbert **CURTIS**, of Lee,		
Mass., June 20, 1849, by S. H. Allen	2	496
Jerijah, s. Joseph, b. Feb. 17, 1712/13	2	86
Jerijah, m. wid. Sarah **BISSELL**, b. of Windor, Feb. 10, 1763	2	190
Jerusha, d. Josiah, b. Nov. 8, 1705	2	82
Jerusha, d. Lieut. Samuel & Abigiel, b. Oct. [ ], 1729	2	89
Jerusha, d. Jacob & Abigail, b. Mar. 22, 1760	2	422
Jerusha, d. Lancelot & Jerusha, b. Nov. 1, 1782	2	429
Jerusha, d. Lancelot & Jerusha, d. Dec. 12, 1789	2	429
Jerusha, d. Lancelot & Jerusha, b. Jan. 27, 1791	2	429
Joab, s. Charles & Hannah, b. June 10, 1765	2	423
Joannah, d. Aaron & Mercy, b. July 31, 1743	2	412
Job, s. John, b. Apr. 27, 1692	1	32

	Vol.	Page
PHELPS, PHELPES, FELPES, PHELPES, (cont.)		
Job, s. John, d. Aug. 16, 1692	1	50
Job, s. John, b. Aug. 24, 1693	1	32
Job, s. Cornelius & Anna, b. Jan. 27, 1751	2	417
Job, s. Job & Lucy, b. Apr. 28, 1752	2	425
John, d. May 16, [16]39	MG	
John, s. [George & Frances], b. Feb. 15, 1651	MG	
John, s. George, bp. Feb. 15, 1652	Col.2	155
John, s. [Samuell & Sara], b. July 7, 1662; d. [ ]	MG	
John, s. Samuell, b. July 7, [16]62	Col.1	54
John, s. Samuel, b. July 7, 1662	1	29
John, s. [Isack & Ann], bp. June 29, 1672	MG	
John, had 1 child b. in Windsor. Dated Aug. 17, 1677	MG	
John, m. Sara **BUCKLAND**, [ ]	MG	
John, s. [John & Sara], b. Apr. 12, 1678	MG	
John, s. John, b. Apr. 12, 1678	Col.1	56
John, s. Samuell, d. Apr. 30, 1679	Col.1	58
John, adult, ch. men. 16[ ]	MG	
John, s. William, Sr., b. Mar. 21, 1702/3	1	32
John, m. Elizabeth **LUIS**, Jan. 15, 1707/8	2	186
John, s. John, Jr., b. Aug. 31, 1709	2	83
John, s. Cornelius, b. July 6, 1710	2	83
John, illeg. s. Damoras **PHELPS**, b. Nov. 2, 1724; reputed		
f. John **THRALL**, Jr.	2	108
John, Jr., m. Sarah **CORNISH**, b. of Windsor, Oct. 24, 1728	2	187
John, s. John & Sarah, b. May 14, 1733	2	410
John, s. John & Elizabeth, d. July 5, 1734	2	263
John, s. Thomas & Ann, b. Jan. 8, 1738/9	2	413
John, twin with Lanstoll, s. Timothy & Margret, b. May		
23, 1750	2	418
John, 3rd, of Windsor, m. Elizabeth **PINNEY**, of Symsbury,		
Mar. 10, 1762	2	189
John, 3rd, d. Sept. 19, 1776	2	265
John, Dea., d. Sept. 1, 1777	2	266
Jonathan, s. Joseph, Sr., b. Oct. 20, 1711	2	84
Jonathan, s. Joseph, b. Aug. 20, 1715	2	86
Jonathan, twin with David, s. Ephraim, b. May 24, 1723	2	88
Jonathan, s. Capt. Joseph, d. Feb. 23, 1758	2	264
Joseph, s. [George], b. June 24, 1647	MG	
Joseph, s. George, b. June 24, 1647	1	29
Joseph, bp. July 11, [16]47	MG	
Joseph, bp. July 11, [16]47	MG	
Joseph, s. William, m. Hanna **NUTIN**, Sept. 20, 1660	MG	
Joseph, m. Hannah **NUTON**, Sept. 20, 1660	1	60
Joseph, s. [Timothy & Mary], b. Sept. 27, 1666	MG	
Joseph, s. Timothy, b. Sept. 27, 1666	Col.1	55
Joseph, s. [Joseph & Hanna], b. Aug. 2, 1667	MG	
Joseph, s. Joseph, b. Aug. 2, 1667	1	30

	Vol.	Page
PHELPS, PHELPES, FELPES, PHELPES, (cont.)		
Joseph, m. Mary **PORTER,** June 26, 1673	MG	
Joseph, m. Mary **PORTER,** b. of Windsor, June 26, 1673, by		
Mr. Wolcott	Col.1	46
Joseph, [s.] W[ ], had 2 children b. in Windsor. Dated		
Aug. 17, 1677	MG	
Joseph, had 2 children, b. in Windsor. Dated Aug. 17, 1677	MG	
Joseph, s. [Joseph & Mary], b. Dec. 30, 1678; bp. May 4, [ ]	MG	
Joseph, s. Tim[othy], m. Sara **HOSFORD,** Nov. 18, 1686	Col.D	54
Joseph, s. Sergt. Timothy, m. Sarah **HOSFORD,** Nov. 18,		
1686	1	60
Joseph, s. Joseph, b. Mar. 16, 1692/3	1	31
Joseph, adult, ch. mem. 16[ ]	MG	
Joseph, m. Abigail **BISSELL,** b. of Windsor, Nov. 26, 1702	1	60
Joseph, s. Joseph, Jr., b. Sept. 20, 1703	1	32
Joseph, s. Joseph, Jr., d. Oct. 4, 1703	2	260
Joseph, s. Joseph, Jr., b. Mar. 20, 1704/5	2	82
Joseph, s. Capt. Timothy, m. Sarah **GILLET,** Feb. 22,		
1709/10	2	186
Joseph, s. Capt. Timothy, d. Aug. 30, 1716	2	261
Joseph, s. Capt. Joseph, d. Nov. 5, 1746	2	264
Joseph, Capt., d. Sept. 3, 1751	2	264
Joseph, s. Benjamin & Ruth, b. May 24, 1760	2	420
Joseph, s. Jerijah & Sarah, b. Mar. 18, 1766	2	424
Joseph, grandson of Capt. Timothy, m. Ann **ENNOE,** [17]	2	187
Joseph, contributed 0-5-0 to the poor in other colonies	MG	
Josias, s. [Samuell & Sara], b. Dec. 15, 1667	MG	
Josiah, s. Samuel, b. Dec. 16, 1667	1	29
Josia, s. [Joseph & Sara], b. Feb. 17, 1679	MG	
Josiah, m. Sarah **WINCHEL,** Apr. 26, 1690	1	60
Josiah, s. Josiah, b. Aug. 24, 1708	2	82
Josiah, s. John, m. Abigael **GRISWOLD,** d. Ens. Jos., June		
21, 1711	2	186
Josiah, s. Josiah & Abigail, b. Nov. 14, 1714	2	90
Josiah, m. Ann **GRISWOLD,** b. of Windsor, Sept. 14, 1733	2	187
Josiah, s. Josiah & Ann, b. July 28, 1734	2	91
Josiah, of Windsor, m. Hannah **SAXTON,** of Simsbury, Dec.		
18, 1734	2	188
Josiah, Jr., m. Emely **ALLYN,** Dec. 26, 1820, by Rev.		
Henry A. Rowland	2	190
Josiah, m. Susanna **HOLCOMB,** Nov. 6, 1822, by Horace		
Clark, J. P.	2	191
Josias, s. John, b. Feb. 17, 1679	Col.1	57
Lanstoll* , twin with John, s. Timothy & Margret, b.		
May 23, 1750 (Probably "Lancelot")	2	418
Lancelot, m. Jerusha **PINNEY,** b. of Windsor, July 6, 1779	2	190
Levi, s. John (s. Thomas) & Rachel, b. Oct. 20, 1767	2	428
Livia Drusilla, d. Bildad & Eunice, b. Sept. 8, 1766	2	425

	Vol.	Page
PHELPS, PHELPES, FELPES, PHELPES, (cont.)		
Lois, d. Josiah, b. July 14, 1696	1	32
Lott, s. Lancelot & Jerusha, b. Nov. 9, 1784	2	429
Lucy, d. Ebenezer & Mindwell, b. Sept. 13, 1747	2	414
Lucy, d. Charles & Hannah, b. June 18, 1750	2	420
Lucy, d. Caleb & Mary 2nd w., b. Jan. 3, 1752	2	419
Lucy, d. Job & Lucy, b. Apr. 4, 1754	2	425
Lucy Rosanna, twin with Lydia, d. Job & Lucy, b. Sept. 24, 1757	2	425
Lydia, d. Thomas, b. Jan. 12, 1725/6	2	89
Lydia, of Symsbury, m. Jacob **GILLET**, of Windsor, Dec. 13, 1744	2	157
Lydiah, d. Dr. Hezekiah & Lydia, b. Dec. 11, 1750	2	416
Lydia, twin with Lucy Rosanna, d. Job & Lucy, b. Sept. 24, 1757	2	425
Marsey, m. Thomas **BARBER**, Dec. 17, 1663, by Mr. Clark	Col.1	45
Marcy, d. Aaron & Marcy, b. May 8, 1749	2	416
Margerit, d. Thomas, b. Mar. 15, 1717/18	2	89
Margret, twin with Abraham, d. Thomas & Ann, b. July 20, 1730	2	413
Margret, d. Timothy & Margret, b. Mar. 2, 1752	2	418
Margret, d. Job & Lucy, b. July 13, 1759	2	425
Mark Tully Cecero, s. Bildad & Eunice, b. Mar. 10, 1768	2	425
Martha, d. Sergt. Timothy, b. Nov. 12, 1688	1	31
Martha, m. Samuel **HOLCOMB**, Oct. 13, 1709	2	161
Martha, d. John, Jr., b. Oct. 6, 1720	2	87
Martha, d. William & Martha, b. Apr. 8, 1742	2	412
Mary, d. [William], b. Mar. [ ], 1644	MG	
Mary, d. Will[ia]m, bp. Mar. 2, 1644	1	29
Mary, d. [Nathanell & Elizabeth], b. June 21, 1651	MG	
Mary, d. [Nathanael, b. June 21, 1651	1	30
Mary, d. [Samuell & Sara], b. Oct. [ ], 1658	MG	
Mary, [d. Samuel], b. Oct. [ ], 1658. "Not recorded until after her father's death"	1	29
Mary, d. [Timothy & Mary], b. Aug. 14, 1673	MG	
Mary, d. Timothy, b. Aug. 14, 1673	1	31
Mary, d. [Joseph & Mary], b. Jan. 13, 1674	MG	
Mary, Mrs., m. John **WOLCOTT**, Feb. 14, 1676	1	63
Mary*, [d. of Sarah (**GRISWOLD**) PHELPS, who later m. Nath[anie]l **PINNEY**, m. Dan[ie]ll **ADAMS**, Sept. 20, 1677 *("Mary **PINNE**" in Copy)	TR1	1
Mary*, w. Jose, d. Jan. 16, 1682 *(Note by LBB; "Mary (**PORTER**) PHELPS")	Col.D	56
Mary, w. Joseph, d. Jan. 16, 1682	1	50
Mary, d. Joseph, Jr., b. June 8, 1689	1	31
Mary, d. Lieut. Tim[othy], d. Mar. 23, 1690	Col.D	57
Mary, d. Lieut. Timothy, d. May 23, 1690	1	50
Mary, m. Thomas **BARBER**, Dec. [ ], [16]	MG	

	Vol.	Page
PHELPS, PHELPES, FELPES, PHELPES, (cont.)		
Mary, m. Nathanael **HOSFORD**, b. of Windsor, Apr. 19, 1700	1	58
Mary, d. Josiah, b. Aug. 18, 1702	1	32
Mary, d. Benjamin, decd., b. Sept. 4, 1706	2	81
Mary, d. Enoch, b. Sept. 11, 1706	2	84
Mary, m. Mathew **GRISWOLD**, June 6, 1709	2	154
Mary, d. Ephraim, b. Dec. 24, 1716	2	86
Mary, d. Ephraim, d. Feb. 13, 1716/17	2	261
Mary, d. Samuel, b. Feb. 20, 1718/19	2	87
Mary, d. Samuel*, d. Mar. 15, 1718/19 *("John" crossed out)	2	261
Mary, d. Joseph, b. Nov. 29, 1719	2	87
Mary, of Enfield, m. Samuel **OSBAND**, Jr., of Windsor, Apr. 14, 1725	2	184
Mary, w. Capt. Abraham, d. July 25, 1725	2	262
Mary, m. Samuel **STYLES**, b. of Windsor, Feb. 19, 1729/30	2	199
Mary, m. Samuel **BROWN**, b. of Windsor, June 15, 1730	2	130
Mary, d. Caleb & Mary, b. May 4, 1734	2	418
Mary, w. Caleb, d. Apr. 20, 1747	2	265
Mary, d. Cornelius & Anna, b. Apr. 2, 1755	2	417
Mary, d. Jacob & Abigail, b. Mar. 1, 1762	2	422
Mary, d. Elijah & Esther, b. Jan. 7, 1768	2	426
Mary, of Windsor, m. Jonathan **COLTON**, of East Windsor, Mar. 31, 1831, by Stephen Crosby	2	140
Mary G., m. Alonzo A. **MUNSEL**, b. of Windsor, Nov. 20, 1849, by Rev. Cephus Brainard	2	493
Mathew, s. Samuel, b. Jan. 25, 1714/15	2	86
Mercy, d. Will[ia]m, Sr., b. Feb. 11, 1644	1	30
Mindwell, m. Obediah **HOSFORD**, May 4, 1705	2	161
Mindwell, d. Ebenezer & Mindwell, b. Dec. 3, 1708 (Crossed out)	2	262
Mindwell, d. Thomas, b. Feb. 17, 1722	2	89
Mindwel, d. Ebenezer & Mindwel, b. Dec. 3, 1728	2	90
Mindwell, d. Daniel & Mindwell, b. Sept. 30, 1729	2	89
Mindwel, d. Ebenezer, d. Nov. 27, 1736	2	263
Mindwell, 2nd, d. Ebenezer & Mindwel, b. Mar. 21, 1736/7	2	411
Mindwell, had d. Phebe, b. May 23, 1739	2	412
Mindwell, m. Isaac **GRISWOLD**, b. of Windsor, May 19, 1748	2	479
Mindwell, w. Lieut. Daniel, d. Aug. 21, 1775	2	265
Miriam, m. Elihu **HOLCOMB**, b. of Windsor, Mar. 22, 1832, by Henry A. Rowland	2	485
Modia, s. Thomas, b. Jan. 7, 1715/16	2	86
Moses, s. Josiah & Abigail, b. Oct. [ ], 1718	2	90
Noami, of Symsbury, m. Joseph **EGELSTON**, of Windsor, Dec. 21, 1757	2	147
Naomi, d. James & Esther, b. Oct. 13, 1761	2	424
Nathanell, m. Elizabeth **COPLEY**, Sept. 17, 1650	MG	

	Vol.	Page
PHELPS, PHELPES, FELPES, PHELPES, (cont.)		
1849, by Thomas A. Leete	2	463
Sabra, d. Timothy & Margret, b. Oct. 7, 1755	2	418
Sabra, m. Isaac **PINNEY**, Jr., b. of Windsor, Feb. 22, 1781	2	190
Sally, m. Cyrus **HOW**, Feb. 7, 1830, by Rev. Asa Bushnell, Jr.	2	484
Samuell, m. Sara **GRISWOLD**, Nov. 10, 1650	MG	
Samuel, m. Sarah **GRISWOLD**, Nov. 10, 1650	1	60
Samuel, s. Samuel, b. Sept. 5, 1652	1	29
Samuell, s. [Samuell & Sara], bp. Sept. 6, 1652	MG	
Samuel, s. Samuel, bp. Sept. 5, 1652	Col.2	155
Samuell, d. May 15, 1669	MG	
Samuell, d. May 15, [16]69	Col.1	55
Samuell, d. [ ], [16]69	MG	
Samuel, d. [ ], [16]69	1	49
Samuell, s. [Timothy & Mary], b. Jan. 29, [16]75	MG	
Samuell, had 9 children b. in Windsor. Dated Aug. 17, 1677	MG	
Samuell, s. Samuell, m. Abiell **WILLIAMES**, d. John, June 21, 1678	Col.1	46
Samuel, s. Josiah, b. Jan. 21, 1690	1	32
Samuell, m. Abigaell **ENO**, b. of Windsor, Apr. 3, 1707	2	185
Samuel, s. Samuel, b. Apr. 5, 1710	2	83
Samuel, s. Josiah, m. Rachel **OWEN**, Aug. 28, 1712	2	186
Samuel, Lieut., d. Oct. 26, 1741	2	263
Samuel O., s. Henry, d. May 14, 1845, ae 22 y.	2	266
Sara, d. [Samuell & Sara], b. Mar. latter end, 1653	MG	
Sarah, [d. Samuel], b. Mar. latter end, 1653. "Not recorded until after her father's death"	1	29
Sarah, of Windsor, m. William **WADE**, of Middletown, June 9, 1658	1	63
Sara, d. [Isack & Ann], bp. July 4, 1670	MG	
Sara, wid. Samuel, m. Nathan **PINNE**, July 21, 1670	MG	
Sara, wid., m. Nathaniell **PINNE**, July 21, 1670	MG	
Sara, wid., m. Nathanell **PINNE**, b. of Windsor, July 21, 1670, by Capt. Newbery	Col.1	45
Sara, m. Andrew **MOORE**, Feb. [ ]	MG	
Sara, d. Samuell, m. Andrew **MOORE**, Feb. 15, 1671, by Capt. Newbery	Col.1	46
Sara, d. [Joseph & Mary], b. Apr. 4, 1677; bp. July 1, [16]7[ ]	MG	
Sara, d. Timothy, b. Dec. 27, 1679	MG	
Sarah, d. John, b. Mar. 2, 1681	Col.D	51
Sarah, d. John, b. Mar. 2, 1681	1	31
Sarah, m. John **MANSFEILD**, Dec. 13, 1683	Col.D	54
Sarah, d. Joseph, b. Aug. 14, 1687	1	31
Sarah, d. Timothy, b. Dec. 20, 1687	1	31
Sarah, w. Timothy, d. July 10, 1688	1	49
Sarah, w. Timothy, d. July 10, 1689	Col.D	57

	Vol.	Page
PHELPS, PHELPES, FELPES, PHELPES, (cont.)		
Sarah, d. Josiah, b. Aug. 18, 1693	1	32
Sarah, m. Samuel PINEY, Oct. 24, 1698	1	60
Sarah, d. Joseph, b. Mar. 17, 1703	2	81
Sarah, d. Cornelius, b. Dec. 19, 1705	2	83
Sarah, w. Joseph, Sr., d. Apr. 9, 1708	2	260
Sarah, d. Josiah & Abigail, b. June 14, 1712	2	90
Sarah, d. Thomas, b. Sept. 28, 1713	2	86
Sarah, m. David MARSHEL, b. of Windsor, Dec. 15, 1721	2	176
Sarah, d. Josiah & Abigail, b. Mar. [ ], 1723	2	90
Sarah, d. Josiah & Abigail, d. Aug. 9, 1725	2	262
Sarah, d. John & Sarah, b. Dec. 15, 1729	2	90
Sarah, d. Daniel & Sarah, b. June 17, 1730	2	90
Sarah, d. Daniel & Sarah, b. June 17, 1730	2	104
Sarah, w. Josiah, d. May 4, 1733	2	263
Sarah, d. Timothy & Abigail, d. June 18, 1736	2	263
Sarah, d. Ebenezer & Mindwell, b. July 3, 1744	2	413
Sarah, m. Thomas ALLYN, b. of Windsor, Dec. 13, 1750	2	124
Sarah, d. John, 3rd & Elizabeth, b. July 27, 1770	2	427
Sarah, d. John (s. Thomas) & Rachel, b. Sept. 8, 1771	2	428
Sarah, w. Dea. John, d. Sept. 5, 1777	2	266
Sarah, d. John, Sr., d. Feb. 27, 1709/10 (?)	2	260
Sarah, see Sarah WADE	1	52
Sarah, m. John MANSFIELD, Dec. 13, [ ]	1	59
Solomon, s. Timothy & Ruth, b. July 15, 1792	2	429
Solomon, m. Deborah BARBER, Apr. 16, 1822, by Henry A. Rowland	2	191
Sule, d. Austin & Deborah, b. July 22, 1776	2	428
Sulima, d. Austin & Deborah, b. May 29, 1774; d. June 5, 1775	2	428
Susannah A., of Windsor, m. Sturgis G. GREGORY, of New Milford, [, 18], by Rev. Ansel Nash	2	480
Silvester, s. Job & Lucy, b. Feb. 16, 1766	2	425
Tabitha, s. Samuel (s. Josiah), b. June 18, 1721	2	88
Tabitha, d. Job & Lucy, b. July 29, 1768	2	425
Talitha, d. Jacob & Abigail, b. June 25, 1754	2	416
Thankfull, d. Aaron & Marcy, b. Mar. 20, 1754	2	417
Thankfull, d. Aaron & Marcy, b. Mar. 20, 1754	2	420
Thomas, s. John, b. Aug. 21, 1687	1	32
Thomas, s. Thomas, b. July 27, 1711	2	85
Thomas, d. Jan. 6, 1750/1	2	264
Timothy, adult, ch. mem. 16[ ]	MG	
Timothy, s. [William], b. Aug. [ ], 1639	MG	
Timothy, s. William, b. Sept. 1, 1639	1	29
Timothy, s. [Samuell & Sara], b. Oct. [ ], 1656	MG	
Timothy, s. Samuel, bp. Oct. 26, 1656	1	29
Timothy, m. Mary GRISWOLD, Mar. 19, 1661	MG	
Timothy, m. Mary GRISWOLD, Mar. 19, 1661	1	60

	Vol.	Page

PHELPS, PHELPES, FELPES, PHELPES, (cont.)

	Vol.	Page
Timothy, s. [Timothy & Mary], b. Nov. 1, 1663	MG	
Timothy, m. Timothy, b. Nov. 1, [16]63	Col.1	54
Timothy, s. Timothy, bp. Nov. 8, [16]63	MG	
Timothy, bp. Nov. 8, [16]63	MG	
Timothy, had 6 children b. in Windsor. Dated Aug. 17, 1677	MG	
Tim[othy], s. Sergt. [ ], m. Martha **CROW**, Nov. 4, 1686	Col.D	54
Timo[thy], s. Sam[uel], m. Sara **GAYLER**, d. Walter, Nov. 18, 1686	Col.D	54
Timothy, s. Samuel, m. Sarah **GAYLORD**, d. Walter, Nov. 18, 1686	1	60
Timothy, s. Timothy, Jr., b. June 22, 1689	1	31
Timothy, s. Timothy, Jr., d. Sept. 28, 1689	1	49
Tim[othy], s. Tim[othy], Jr., d. Sept. 28, 1689	Col.D	57
Timothy, s. Samuel, of Windsor, m. Sarah **PRATT**, of Hartford, Nov. 13, 1690	Col.D	55
Timothy, s. Samuel, of Windsor, m. Sarah **PRATT**, of Hartford, Nov. 13, 1690	1	60
Timothy, smith, m. Rachel **MOORE**, Dec. 10, 1707	2	185
Timothy, s. Cornelius, b. Feb. 3, 1713/14	2	86
Timothy, m. Margaret **GILLET**, b. of Windsor, Apr. 24, 1746	2	188
Timothy, s. Timothy & Margret, b. July 14, 1748	2	415
Timothy, twin with Ruth, s. Timothy & Ruth, b. Feb. 24, 1787	2	429
Timothy, m. Elizabeth **LOOMIS**, b. of Windsor, Dec. 20, 1843, by Rev. S. D.Jewett	2	508
Timothy, contributed 0-3-6 to the poor in other colonies	MG	
William, adm., ch. & communicant Nov. [ ], 1639	MG	
[Wi]lliam, adm. communion Nov. 17, [16]39	MG	
William, m. 1st w. [ ], June 4, 1645	MG	
William, s. [William], m. Isabell **WILSON**, June 4, 1645; "now since 29 y. and has had no child July 15, [16]74"	MG	
William, m. Isable **WILSON**, June 4, 1645	1	60
William, has w. [ ], adm. ch. Mar. 11, [1654	MG	
William, s. [Nathanell & Elizabeth], b. June 22, 1657, at Northampton	MG	
William, s. [Samuell & Sara], b. Nov. 3, 1660	MG	
William, s. [Timothy & Mary], b. Feb. 4, 1668	MG	
William, s. Timothy, b. Feb. 4, 1668	1	29
William, s. Timothy, b. Feb. 4, 1668	1	31
William, d. [July 14*], [16]72 *(In pencil)	MG	
William, d. July 14, 1672	Col.1	58
William, d. July 14, 1672; bd. the 15th day	1	49
William, taxed 4-0 on Feb. 10, [16]73	MG	
William, has w. [ ], d. Nov. 27, [16]75	MG	
William, his w. [ ], d. Nov. 27, 1675	Col.1	58
William, his w. [ ], d. Nov. 27, [16]75	1	49

	Vol.	Page
PHELPS, PHELPES, FELPES, PHELPES, (cont.)		
William, m. 2nd w. Sara **PINNE,** Dec. 20, 1676	MG	
William, m. Sara **PINNE,** Dec. 20, 1676, by Capt. Newbery	Col.1	46
William, m. Sarah **PINNE,** Dec. 20, [16]76, by Capt. Newbery	TR1	1
Will[ia]m, m. Sarah **PINNEY,** Dec. 20, 1676, by Capt. Nubery	1	60
William, m. Sarah **PINNEY,** Dec. 20, 1676, by Capt. Nubery	1	64
Willliam, d. Feb. 17, 1681	Col.D	56
William, d. Feb. 17, 1681	1	49
W[illia]m, s. Joseph, d. Oct. 8, 1689	Col.D	57
William, s. Joseph, d. Oct. 8, 1689	1	49
William, m. Hannah **HAYDON,** Jan. 4, 1693	1	60
William, s. William, b. Jan. 13, 1698/9	1	32
William, s. Timothy, m. Abigaell **MUZY,** Dec. 7, 1699	2	186
William, communicant 16[ ]	MG	
William, s. William (s. of Timothy), b. Mar. 16, 1702	2	82
William, s. Timothy, m. Ruth **BARBER,** Apr. 18, 1706	2	186
William, Sr., d. Nov. 21, 1711	2	260
William, s. William & Martha, b. Sept. 22, 1740	2	412
William, s. Jacob & Abigail, b. May 2, 1752	2	416
William, contributed 0-9- 0 to the poor in other colonies	MG	
Worin, s. Lancelot & Jerusha, b. Jan. 10, 1794	2	429
Zacheas, s. Cornelius & Anna, b. Aug. 11, 1751	2	417
Zelolus, s. Elisha & Elizbeth, b. Apr. 13, 1774	2	426
-----, Mrs., taxed 2-0 on Feb. 10, [16]73	MG	
-----, old Mr., had 2 children b. in Windsor. Dated Aug. 17, 1677	MG	
-----, Mrs., comminicant from Dorchester; living in Windsor Dec. 22, 1677	MG	
-----, ch. mem. 16[ ], from Dorchester	MG	
-----, Mrs., ch. mem. 16[ ], from Dorchester	MG	
PHILLIPS, PHILLUPS, PHILLUP, PHILUPS, George, his w. [ ], d. [ ], [16]62	MG	
George, taxed 2-0 on Feb. 10, [16]73	MG	
George, communicant from Dorchester; living in Windsor Dec. 22, 1677	MG	
George, d. July 9, [16]78	MG	
George, d. July 9, 1678	Col.1	58
George, contributed 0-2-9 to the poor in other colonies	MG	
Harriet E., of Hartford, m. Anson B. **STONE,** of Springfield, May 5, 1839, by James Loomis, J. P.	2	510
Samuel, of Wilmantic, m. Juliette **GRISWOLD,** of Windsor, Nov. 26, 1851, by Rev. H. N. Weed	2	461
Sara, d. May 14, 1662	Col.1	55
-----, ch. mem. 16[ ], from Dorchester	MG	
PICKETT, Julia, m. Talcott **MATHER,** Jan. 11, 1821, by Rev. Henry A. Rowland	2	181

	Vol.	Page
PICKETT, (cont.)		
Phinehas, d. Aug. 11, 1841, ae 84	2	266
PIERCE, PEIRCE, PIRCE, Abigail, d. Nathanael & Mary, b.		
June 20, 1739	2	411
Benjamin, s. Nathaniel & Mary, b. Apr. 5, 1743	2	417
Ebenezer, s. Nathaniel & Mary, b. May 3, 1753	2	417
Ebenezer, s. Samuel & Lois, b. Jan. 4, 1754	2	416
Ephraim, s. Nathaniel & Mary, b. Feb. 26, 1745	2	417
Loice, d. Samuell & Loise, b. Nov. 28, 1748	2	415
Phebe A., m. Seth L. **STRONG**, b. of Windsor, Aug. 13,		
1848, by C. B. Everist	2	482
Samuel, s. Samuel & Lois, b. Apr. 3, 1750	2	416
PIERSON, See also **PEARSON**], Julia A., of Windsor, m. Samuel		
H. **ALLEN**, Rev., of Windsor Locks, Feb. 26, 1847, by		
T. A. Leete	2	462
Lydia, m. Charles H. **DEXTER**, Sept. 19, 1838, by William		
Thompson	2	473
PIKE, Mary R., of East Hartford, m. Thomas P. **LAIHAY**, of		
Manchester, Mar. ¦ ¦, 1848, by Samuel A. Seaman	2	491
PINE, David, m. Ann A. **SILL**, Sept. 12, 1822, by Rev. Henry A.		
Rowland	2	500
PINNEY, PINNE, PINEY, Abigayl, d. [Houmfery & Mary], b.		
Nov. 26, 1654	MG	
Abigaile, d. Humfery, b. Nov. 26, 1654; m. John **ADAMS**,		
Dec. 6, 1677* *(Marriage entered by LBB)	Col.2	158
Abigail, d. Humphrey, b. Nov. 26, 1654	1	30
Abigall, m. John **ADMES**, Dec. 6, 1677	Col.1	46
Abigal, m. John **ADAMS**, Dec. 6, 1677	TR1	1
Abigail, m. John **ADDAMS**, Dec. 6, 1677	1	53
Abigail, d. Humphrey, b. Oct. 2, 1720	2	87
Abigail, w. Daniel, d. June 15, 1766	2	190
Abigail, w. Daniel, d. June 15, 1766	2	265
Abraham, s. Nathaniel, b. Feb. [ ], 1709/10	2	84
Adeline H., of Windsor, m. Lunsford W. **HARTLEY**, of		
Oswegotche, N. Y., Jan. 4, 1842	2	515
Ami, d. Nathaniel, b. Oct. 6, 1704	2	84
Ann, d. Isaac, b. Jan. 24, 1712/13	2	85
Azariah, s. Nathaniel, b. June 10, 1700	2	84
Daniel, s. Noah & Elizabeth, b. June 5, 1766	2	423
Daniel, d. Dec. 19, 1768	2	265
Darius, s. Nathanael, Jr., b. June 5, 1724	2	88
David, s. Isaac & Mary, b. Apr. 30, 1744	2	413
David, m. Augusta F. **CLARK**, of Windsor, Apr. 31, 1848,		
by Rev. Cephas Brainard	2	501
Elizabeth, d. Isaac, b. Jan. 6, 1696	1	32
Elizabeth, d. Isaac, decd., d. Sept. 13, 1715	2	270
Elizabeh, d. Humphrey, b. Jan. 14, 1718	2	87
Elizabeth, of Symsbury, m. John **PHELPS**, 3rd, of Windsor,		

	Vol.	Page
PINNEY, PINNE, PINEY, (cont.)		
Mar. 10, 1762	2	189
Eveline, of Windsor, m. Joseph **WHIPPLE**, of East Windsor,		
Jan. [ ], 1841, by Rev. A. C. Washburn	2	515
Frances, m. Harvey **STOUGHTON**, Oct. 8, 1823, by Henry		
A. Rowland	2	202
Hannah, d. Samuel, Jr., b. May 19, 1713	2	85
Horatio, m. Eunice Mary Ann **ALLYN**, b. of Windsor, Mar.		
28, 1824, by Rev. Augustus Bolles, of Wintonbury	2	192
Huldah, of Symsbury, m. Abiel **GRISWOLD**, of Windsor,		
Oct. 25, 1775	2	159
Humphrey, d. Aug. 20, 1683	Col.D	56
Humphry, d. Aug. 20, 1683	1	50
Humphry, s. Isaac, b. Sept. 5, 1694	1	32
Humphrey, of Windsor, m. Abigail **DEMEN**, of Hartford,		
July 22, 1717	2	187
Humfrey, contributed 0-2-0 to the poor in other colonies	MG	
Houmfery, m. Mary **HULL**, in Dorchester, [ ]	MG	
Irane, d. Nathanael, Jr., b. Jan. 8, 1719/20	2	88
Isack, s. [Houmfery & Mary], b. Feb. 24, 1663	MG	
Isack, s. [H]umfery, b. Feb. 24, [16]63	Col.1	54
Isaac, s. Humphry, b. Feb. 24, 1663; bp. 28th day	1	30
Isaac, s. Isaac, b. Jan. 17, 1686	1	31
Isaac, Sergt., d. Oct. [ ], 1709, on board the vessel coming		
from Albany	2	260
Isaack*, m. Abigael **FILLY**, d. John, Jan. 26, 1709/10		
*("Josia" crossed out)	2	186
Isaac, s. Isaac, b. Jan. 15, 1716/17	2	87
Isaac, d. Aug. 12, 1717	2	261
Isaac, s. Isaac & Mary, b. July 4, 1741	2	412
Isaac, Jr., m. Sabra **PHELPS**, b. of Windsor, Feb. 22, 1781	2	190
Isibe, d.[ ], in "Elenton" prior to 1740	MG	
Jerusha, d. Humphrey & Abigail, b. Apr. [ ], 1731	2	91
Jerusha, wid., m. Benjamin **ENO**, Jan. [ ], 1741/2	2	146
Jerusha, d. John, of East Side of River, & Deboarh, b. Feb. 2,		
1764	2	423
Jerusha, m. Lancelot **PHELPS**, b. of Windsor, July 6, 1779	2	190
John, s. [Houmfery & Mary], b. Oct. [ ], [1651];		
bp. [Oct.] 19, 1651	MG	
John, s. Humphry, bp. Oct. 19, 1651	1	30
John, s. Nathaniel, b. Nov. 18, 1707	2	84
John, s. Sergt. Nathaniel, d. June 20, 1715	2	261
Jonathan, s. Isaac, b. Oct. 23, 1688	1	31
Jonathan, s. Humphrey & Abigail, b. Feb. 5, 1725/6	2	89
Jonathan, d. Sept. 21, 1737	2	227
Jonathan, d. Sept. [ ], 1737	2	263
Joseph, s. Nathaniel, b. Mar. 10, 1702	2	84
Joseph, s. Samuel, Jr., b. Feb. 13, 1710/11	2	83

	Vol.	Page
PINNEY, PINNE, PINEY, (cont.)		
Joseph, s. Joseph & Jerusha, b. July 15, 1734	2	91
Josia, s. Sam[ue]ll, b. Nov. 3, 1681	Col.D	51
Josiah, s. Samuel, b. Nov. 3, 1681	1	31
Josiah, d. Sept. 7, 1726	2	262
Josiah, s. Samuel & Lucresha, b. Aug. 19, 1764	2	423
Joyce*, w. Samuel, d. [ ] *(Note by LBB: "Joyce (BISSELL) PINNEY")	Col.D	57
Judah, s. Ens. Isaac & Mary, b. Sept. 18, 1757	2	423
Lucretia, d. Nathanael, Jr., b. Jan. 17, 1722/3	2	88
Lurana, d. Nathanael, Jr., b. July 20, 1721	2	88
Lydia, Mrs., of Hartford, m. Ambroes **ADAMS,** of Bloomfield, Feb. 4, 1851, by Rev. Ralph H. Bowls, of Tariffville	2	463
Mabel, d. Humphrey & Abigail, b. Sept. 31, 1723	2	89
Martha, d. Nathanael, b. Feb. 24, 1693	1	32
Martha, d. Sergt. Nathaniell, d. Apr. 25, 1715	2	261
Martha, d. Nathaniel, Jr., b. Feb. 22, 1716/17	2	86
Martin, s. Isaac & Mary, b. Aug. 19, 1747	2	415
Martin, s. Isaac & Mary, b. Aug. 21, 1747	2	423
Mary, d. [Houmfery & Mary], b. June [ ], [1644]; bp. [June] 16, 1644; m. [ ]	MG	
Mary, d. Humphry, bp. June 16, 1644	1	30
Mary, m. Abraham **PHELPS,** July 6, 1665	MG	
Mary, m. Abraham **PHELPS,** b. of Windsor, July 6, 1665, by Mr. Allyn	Col.1	45
Mary, m. Abraham **PHELPS,** b. of Windsor, July 6, 1665, by Mr. Allyn	1	60
Mary, d. [Samuell & Joyse], b. June 16, 1667	MG	
Mary, d. Samuell, m. Danell **ADAMS,** Sept. 20, 1677	TR1	1
Mary, d. Samuel, m. Daniel **ADDAMS,** Sept. 20, 1677	1	53
Mary, d. Samuel, m. Danell **ADAMES,** Dec.* 20, 1677 *(Note by LBB; "Sept.")	Col.1	46
Mary, Mrs., d. Aug. 18, 1684	Col.D	56
Mary, Mrs., d. Aug. 18, 1684	1	50
Mary, d. Isaac, b. Mar. 4, 1690	1	32
Mary, d. Samuel, Jr., b. Nov. 26, 1706	2	83
Mary, d. Humphrey & Abigail, d. Oct. 25, 1732	2	263
Mary, w. Noah, d. Feb. 22, 1744/5	2	263
Mary, d. Isaac & Mary, b. June 3, 1751; d. Sept. 21, 1753	2	423
Mary, d. Isaac & Mary, b. Nov. 28, 1754	2	423
Mary, d. Isaac, Jr. & Sabra, b. Nov. 3, 1781	2	428
Mary, m. Abiel B. **GRISWOLD,** b. of Windsor, Sept. 8, 1800	2	479
Nathan, m. Sara **PHELPS,** wid. Samuel, July 21, 1670	MG	
Nathanell, s. [Houmfery & Mary], b. Dec. [ ], 1641	MG	
Nathanael, s. Humphry, bp. Jan. 2, 1641	1	30
Nathanell, m. Sara **PHELPS,** wid., July 21, 1670	MG	
Nathanell, m. Sara **PHELPS,** wid., b. of Windsor, July		

	Vol.	Page
PINNEY, PINNE, PINEY, (cont.)		
21, 1670, by Capt. Newbery	Col. 1	45
Nathanell, s. [Nathanell & Sara], b. May 11, 1671	MG	
Nathanell, d. Aug. 7, [16]76	Col. 1	58
Nathanael, d. Aug. 7, [16]76	1	49
Nathanell, had 2 children b. in Windsor. Dated Aug. 17, 1677	MG	
Nathaniel, d. Aug. 7, [16]81	MG	
Nathanael, m. Martha THRALL, Sept. 21, 1693	1	60
Nathaniel, s. Nathaniel, b. Aug. 18, 1695	2	83
Nathanael, s. Sergt. Nathaneel, m. Elizabeth CARRIER, Jan. 12, 1716/17	2	187
Noah, s. Isaac, b. July 24, 1703	1	32
Noah, m. Mary ALLYN, b. of Windsor, Sept. 30, 1744	2	188
Noah, s. Noah & Elizabeth, b. Apr. 10, 1763	2	421
Oliver, s. Isaac, b. Mar. 23, 1714/15	2	86
Philander, s. Nathaniel, Jr. & Elizabeth, b. Mar. 3, 1725/6	2	89
Prudence, d. Isaac, b. Oct. 16, 1710	2	83
Ruhamah, d. Nathanael, Jr. & Elizabeth, b. [ ]	2	89
Salome, d. Ens. Isaac & Mary, b. May 5, 1760; d. May 30, 1762	2	423
Salome, d. John & Sarah, b. July 1, 1764	2	424
Samuell, m. Joyse BISSELL, Nov. 17, 1665	MG	
Samuell, m. Joyce BISSELL, b. of Windsor, Nov. 17, 1665, by Mr. Allyn	Col. 1	45
Samuel, m. Joyce BISSELL, b. of Windsor, Nov. 17, 1665, by Mr. Allyn	1	60
Samuell, s. [Samuell & Joyse], b. Nov. 20, 1668	MG	
Samuel, had 2 children b. in Windsor. Dated Aug. 17, 1677	MG	
Samuel, m. Sarah PHELPS, Oct. 24, 1698	1	60
Samuel, s. Samuel, Jr., b. Feb. 19, 1700/1	1	32
Samuell, his d. [ ], d. [ ], in "Elenton" prior to 1740	MG	
Samuell, s. [Houmfery & Mary], b. [ ], in Dorchester	MG	
Sara, d. [Houmfery & Mary], b. Nov. 19, 1648	MG	
Sarah, d. Humphry, b. Nov. 19, 1648	1	30
Sara, bp. Dec. 3, [16]48	MG	
Sara, d. [Nathanell & Sara], b. Oct. 11, 1673	MG	
Sarah, d. Nathan[ie]ll, b. Oct. 11, 1673	1	31
Sara, m. William PHELPS, Dec. 20, 1676	MG	
Sara, m. William PHELPES, Dec. 20, 1676, by Capt. Newbery	Col. 1	46
Sarah, m. William PHELPS, Dec. 20, [16]76, by Capt. Newbery	TR1	1
Sarah, m. William PHELPS, Dec. 20, 1676, by Capt. Nubery	1	60
Sarah, m. William PHELPS, Dec. 20, 1676, by Capt. Nubery	1	64
Sarah, d. Isaac, b. Mar. 7, 1692	1	32
Sarah, m. Thomas GRANT, Feb. 13, 1695/6	1	57

	Vol.	Page
PINNEY, PINNE, PINEY, (cont.)		
Sarah, d. Samuel, Jr., b. Nov. 21, 1703	2	83
Sarah, d. Nathaniel, b. Feb. 24, 1706/7	2	84
Sarah, w. Samuell, Sr., d. Nov. [ ], 1712	2	260
Sarah, wid., d. Nov. 16, 1715	2	261
Sarah, m. Ebenezer **STYLES**, b. of Windsor, Jan. 28, 1729/30	2	199
Sarah, d. Noah & Elizabeth, b. Sept. 30, 1760	2	421
Sarah, d. John & Sarah, b. Sept. 17, 1765	2	424
Sara, contributed 0-1-3 to the poor in other colonies	MG	
Sarah, see Mrs. Sarah **MARSH**	2	254
Susan Jane, m. L. F. **JOHNSON**, b. of Windsor, June 2,		
1852, by Rev. Ralp[h N. Bowles	2	462
-----, communicat 16[ ]	MG	
-----, Mrs., adm. ch. Feb. 9, 1639	MG	
-----, Mrs., adm. ch. & communicant Feb. [ ], 1639	MG	
-----, Mr., taxed 4-0 on Feb. 10, [16]73	MG	
-----, Mr., had 6 children b. in Windsor. Dated Aug.		
17, 1677	MG	
-----, Mr., communicant from Dorchester; living in		
Windsor Dec. 22, 1677	MG	
------, had seven children d. [ ], in "Elenton"		
prior to 1740	MG	
PITKIN, Martha, m. Simon **WOLCOT**, Oct. 17, 1661	MG	
Martha, late of England, m. Simon **WOLCOTT**, of		
Windsor, Oct. 17, 1661	1	63
Mary, of East Hartford, m. David **DEXTER**, of Windsor,		
Dec. 22, 1796	2	472
PLUM, -----, m. Titus **MEASHAM**, b. of Windsor, Apr. 2, 1827,		
by Richard Niles, J. P.	2	182
POLK, [see under **PAULK**]		
POMEROY, POMERY, PUMRY, POMRY, Caleb, s. [Eltewd],		
bp. Mar. 6, 1641	MG	
Caleb, s. Eltweed, bp. Mr. 6, 1641	1	30
Caleb, m. Hepsiba **BAKER**, Mar. 8, 1664	MG	
Caleb, m. Hepsiba **BAKER**, b. of Windsor, Mar. 8, 1664, by		
Mr. Allyn	Col.1	45
Caleb, had 1 child b. in Windsor. Dated Aug. 17, 1677	MG	
Eltwed, his w. [ ], d. [ ], [16]55	MG	
Eltwed, his w. [ ], d. July 5, 1655	Col.2	160
Eltwed, m. Lidea **PARSON**, wid., Nov. 30, 1664, by Mr.		
Wolcot	Col.1	45
Eltwed, had 5 children b. in Windsor. Dated Aug. 17, 1677	MG	
Eltwood, his w. [ ], d. July 5, [ ]	1	49
Hannah, of Northampton, m. Joseph **BAKER**, of Windsor,		
July 8, 1702, at Northampton	1	54
Hannah, of Windsor, m. Jesse **MINER**, of Vernon, June 10,		
1825, by Rev. Augustus Bolles, of Wintonbury	2	181
Hepsiba, d. [Caleb & Hepsiba], b. July 27, 1666	MG	

	Vol.	Page
POMEROY, POMERY, PUMRY, POMRY, (cont.)		
Hepsiba, d. Caleb, b. July 27, 1666	Col.1	56
Hephzibah, d. Caleb, b. July 27, 1666	1	30
John, d. [ ], [16]46	MG	
Joseph, s. [Eltewd], b. June [ ], [1652; bp. [June] 20, 1652	MG	
Joseph, s. Eltweed, bp. June 20, 1652	1	30
Josua, s. [Eltewd], b. Nov. [ ], [1646]; bp. Nov. 22, 1646	MG	
Joshua, s. Eltweed, bp. Nov. 22, 1646	1	30
Marcy, d. [Eltewd], b. Apr. [ ], [1644]; bp. [Apr.] 21, 1644; d. [ ]	MG	
Marcy, d. [ ], [16]57	MG	
Mary, d. Dec. 19, [16]40	MG	
Mary, d. Eltweed, bp. Apr. 21, 1644	1	30
Mary, d. Apr. 21, 1657	Col.2	160
Mary, d. Apr. 21, 1657	1	49
Meedad, s. [Eltewd], bp. Aug. 19, 1638	MG	
Medad, s. Eltweed, bp. Aug. 19, 1638	1	30
Nancy H., of New London, m. Charles A. CHASE, of Warehouse Point, Apr. 11, 1841, by Ezra S. Cook	2	475
Pheba, m. Thomas FOSTER, b. of Windsor, Jan. 12, 1762	2	152
POND, Hanna, d. [Isack & Hana], b. Feb. 10, 1646	MG	
Isack, s. [Samuell & Sara], b. Mar. 16, 1667; d. [ ]	MG	
Isaack, s. Samuel, b. Mar. 16, 1646	Col.2	155
Isaac, m. Hannah GRIFFIN, b. of Windsor, May 1, 1667, by Mr. Allyn	1	60
Isack, m. Hana GRIFFEN, May 10, 166[7?]	MG	
Isack, m. Hanna GRIFFEN, May 10, [16]67, by Capt. John Allin, at Hartford	Col.1	45
Isack, d. Nov. 15, [16]69	Col.1	55
Isaac, d. Nov. 15, 1669, ae 23 y.	1	49
Isack, d. [ ], [16]69	MG	
Nathanell, s. [Samuell & Sara], b. Dec. 21, 1650; d. [ ]	MG	
Nathanael, s. Samuel, b. Dec. 21, 1651	Col.2	155
Nathanael, s. Samuel, b. Dec. 21, 1650	1	30
Nathanel, d. Dec. 19, [16]75, in war	MG	
Nathaniel, d. Dec. 19, 1675	1	26
Nathanell, d. Dec. 19, 1675	Col.1	58
Nathanael, d. Dec. 19, 1675	1	47
Samuell, m. Sara [ ], Nov. 18, 1642	MG	
Samuell, his two children, d. [ ], [16]47	MG	
Samuell, s. [Samuell & Sara], b. Mar. 4, 1648	MG	
Samuel, s. Samuel, b. Mar. 4, 1648	Col.2	155
Samvell, d. Mar. 14, 1654	Col.2	160
Samuell, d. [ ], [16]54	MG	
Samuell, had 4 children b. in Windsor. Dated Aug. 17, 1677	MG	
Sara, d. [Samuell & Sara], b. Feb. 11, 1652	MG	
Sarah, d. Samuel, b. Feb. 11, 1652	Col.2	155
Sarah, wid. of Windsor, m. John LINSLEE, of Toket,		

	Vol.	Page
POND, (cont.)		
July 9, 1655	Col.2	159
POWDER, John*, m. Temprannc **BUCKLAND,** Jan. 26, 1668, at Hartford, by John Allyn *(Probably lived in Westfield,Mass., in 1666)	Col.1	45
John, m. Temperance **BUCKLAND,** June 26, 1668, at Hartford, by John Allyn	1	60
Martha, of Westfield, m. Samuel **BARBAR,** of Windsor, June 18, 1713	2	128
Martha, of Westfield, m. Samuel **BARBER,** of Windsor, June 18, 1713	2	129
Sarah, of Westfield, m. Josiah **COOK,** of Windsor, Jan. 14, 1702/3	1	55
POOLE, Bethesda, of Dorchester, m. John **FYLER,** of Windsor, Oct. 21, 1686	Col.D	54
Bethsda, of Dorchester, m. John **FYLER,** of Windsor, Oct. 21, 1686	1	56
POPE, John, d. Aug. 21, 1683	Col.D	56
John, d. Aug. 21, 1683	1	50
PORTER, Abiezer, s. Hezekiah & Sarah, b. Dec. 23, 1757	2	418
Abygall, d. Martha & reputed d. of Benjamin **ALLYN,** b. July 10, 1704	2	1
Abigael, d. Daniel, b. Aug. 26, 1710	2	83
Alexander, s. Daniel, b. Mar. 7, 1718/19	2	88
Amos, s. Nathaniel, b. May 25, 1713	2	85
Amos, of Windsor, m. Ami **GAINS,** of Glastenbury, Dec. 22, 1737	2	188
Ann, m. William **GAYLAR,** Jr., Feb. 24, 1641	MG	
Ann, d. [John, Jr. & Joanna], b. Aug. 26, 1679	MG	
Ann, d. John, Jr., b. Aug. 26, 1679	Col.1	56
Ann, d. John, Jr., b. Aug. 26, 1679	1	31
Ann, d. John, b. Oct. 13, 1714	2	87
Ann, d. John, d. June 1, 1716	2	261
Anna, m. William **GAYLORD,** Feb. 24, 1641	1	56
Anne, d. John, b. Apr. 2, 1706	2	81
Anne, d. David, b. Sept. 25, 1710	2	83
Anne, m. William **WALLIS,** b. of Windsor, Sept. 9, 1738	2	209
Betty, d. Jonathan & Elisabeth, b. Dec. 16, 1739	2	415
Cathrien, d. John, b. Sept. 14, 1707	2	87
Daniel, s. John, Jr., b. Nov. 13, 1683	1	31
Dan[ie]ll, s. John, Jr., b. Nov. 13, 1683* *(Note by LBB: "1681")	Col.D	51
Daniel, of Windsor, m. Mindwell **ALEXAND,** of Northampton, Feb. 19, 1706/7	2	186
Daniel, s. Daniel, b. Oct. 11, 1712	2	88
Daniel, d. Apr. 17, 1724	2	262
Daniel, d. Nov. 30, 1733	2	263
Daniel, s. William & Mary, b. July 18, 1814	2	577

	Vol.	Page
PORTER, (cont.)		
Isaac, s. James, b. July 13, 1683	1	31
Isack, s. James, d. May 1, 1684	Col.D	56
Isaac, s. James, d. May 1, 1684	1	50
Isaac, s. John, Jr., b. Sept. 23, 1687	1	31
Isaac, s. John, Jr., d. Oct. 10, 1687	1	49
Israel, s. Hezakiah & Sarah, b. Sept. 27, 1759	2	420
J., his w. [ ], adm. ch. & communicant May [ ], 1663	MG	
James, s. [John], b. Dec. 22, 1657	MG	
James, s. John, b. Dec. 22, 1657	Col.2	161
James, ae 6 y., s. John, bp. May 10, [16]63	MG	
James, s. John, Sr., m. Sara **TUDER,** Jan. 15, 1679, by Mr. Wolcot	MG	
James, s. John, Sr., m. Sara **TUDOR,** d. Owen, Jan. 15, 1679, by Mr. Wolcott	Col.1	46
James, s. John, Sr., m. Sarah **TUDER,** d. Owen, Jan. 15, [16]79, by Mr. Wolcot	TR1	1
James, s. John, Sr., m. Sarah **TUDOR,** d. Owin, Jan. 15, 1679, by Mr. Wolcott	1	60
James, s. James, d. Jan. 14, 1680	Col.1	58
James, s. James [& Sara], b. Oct. 13, 1680; d. Jan. 14,[16]80/[1]	MG	
James, his d. [ ], d. Aug. 13, 1689	Col.D	57
James, s. John, Sr., m. Sarah **TUDOR,** d. Owen, Jan. 15, 1697, by Mr. Wolcott	1	64
James, s. Hezekiah, b. May 11, 1706	2	82
James, Sergt., d. Sept. 29, 1727	2	262
James, contributed 0-2-6 to the poor in other colonies	MG	
Jerusha, d. David, b. Sept. 15, 1712	2	85
Jerusha Ann, of Windsor, m. William J. **SKINNER,** of Hartford, Sept. 21, 1852, by Rev. H. N. Weed	2	482
Joanna, d. [John, Jr. & Joanna], b. Feb. 7, 1670	MG	
Johana, of Farmington, m. Stephen **TAYLAR,** Jr., Nov. 8, [16]76	Col.1	46
Johana, of Farmington, m. Stephen **TAYLAR,** Jr., Nov. 8, [16]76	TR1	1
Joanna, of Farmington, m. Stephen **TAYLOR,** Jr., Nov. 8, 1676	1	62
Joanna, m. Peter **MILLS,** Jr., July 21, 1692	1	59
Joanna, d. Joseph & Joanna, b. Oct. 13, 1734	2	91
John, Sr., came from England and settled in Windsor, 1639	MG	
John, Sr., his w. [ ], d. [ ], [16]47	MG	
John, Sr., d. Apr. 21, 1648	MG	
John, d. [ ]; bd. Apr. 22, 1648	Col.2	160
John, d. [ ]; bd. Apr. 22, 1648	1	49
John, Sr., d. [ ], [16]48	MG	
John, [s. John], b. June 3, 1651; m. [ ]	MG	
John, s. John, Jr., b. June 3, 1651	Col.2	155

	Vol.	Page
PORTER, (cont.)		
John, s. John, Jr., b. June 3, 1651	1	30
John, his w. [ ], adm, ch. May 3, [16]63	MG	
John, ae 12 y., s. John, bp. May 10, [16]63	MG	
John, Jr., m. Joanna **GAYLAR,** Dec. 16, 1669	MG	
John, Jr., m. Joanna **GAYLAR,** Dec. 16, 1669, by Capt. Newbery	Col.1	45
John, Jr., m. Joanne **GAYLORD,** d. Walter, Sept. 16, 1669, by Capt. Nubery	1	60
John, bp. Feb. 7, 1670	MG	
John, s. [John, Jr. & Joanna], b. Jan. 17, 1674	MG	
John, Sr., had 2 children b. in Windsor. Dated Aug. 17, 1677	MG	
John, now Sr., had 12 children b. in Windsor. Dated Aug. 17, 1677	MG	
John, Jr., had 4 children b. in Windsor. Dated Aug. 17, 1677	MG	
John, Sr., d. Aug. 2, 1688	1	49
John, m. Mary **DRAKE,** Sept. 23, 1697	1	60
John, Sergt., d. Jan. 4, 1698/9	1	50
John, s. John, b. Mar. 7, 1699	2	81
John, his w. [ ], adm. ch. May 3, [16][ ]	MG	
John, s. [John, Sr.] ch. mem. 16[ ]	MG	
John, Sr., adult, ch. mem. 16[ ]	MG	
John, s. John, d. July 2, 1712	2	261
John, s. David, b. Apr. 18, 1714	2	85
John, m. Sarah **HILL,** b. of Windsor, June 27, 1723	2	187
John, d. Apr. 28, 1724	2	262
John, s. Jonathan & Elisabeth, b. June 29, 1738	2	415
John, Jr., contributed 0-3-0 to the poor in other colonies	MG	
John, Sr., contributed 0-10-0 to the poor in other colonies	MG	
John Frederick, s. William & Mary, b. Aug. 18, 1822	2	578
Jonathan, s. Jonathan & Elisabeth, b. Nov. 20, 1748	2	415
Joseph, s. [John], b. Feb. 7, [16]75; bp. [Feb.] 13, [1675]	MG	
Joseph, of Windsor, m. Hannah **BUEL,** of Killinsworth, Dec. 5, 1699	1	60
Joseph, s. Joseph, b. Sept. 14, 1700	1	32
Joseph, s. Joseph, d. Feb. 2, 1700/1	1	50
Joseph, s. Joseph, b. Jan. 20, 1701/2	1	32
Joseph, s. Joseph & Joanna, b. Oct. 27, 1732	2	91
Joseph, s. Joseph & Joanna, d. Feb. 24, 1736/7	2	263
Joseph, s. Joseph & Joanna, b. July 11, 1742	2	412
Kathrien, m. Jacob **DRAKE,** b. of Windsor, Jan. 10, 1727/8	2	142
Lois, d. Hezekiah, b. Mar. 19, 1707/8	2	82
Lois, of Windsor, m. James **ROCKWELL,** of Norrige, June 28, 1734	2	194
Luther, m. Sarah Ann **ELLIS,** b. of Windsor, Feb. 12, 1850, by Rev. Cephas Brainard	2	194

	Vol.	Page

PORTER, (cont.)

Lydia, twin with Esther, d. John, b. Nov. 28, 1689	1	31
Lydia, d. John, b. May 4, 1711	2	87
Lydia, d. Jonathan & Elisabeth, b. June 16, 1744	2	415
Lydia, m. Simon **BURROUGHS**, Oct. 30, 1745	2	131
Martha, d. Jno, b. Sept. 16, [16]83	Col.D	51
Martha, d. John, b. Sept. 16, 1683	1	31
Martha, had illeg. d. Abygall, b. July 10, 1704; reputed		
f. Benjamin **ALLYN**	2	1
Mary, d. [John], b. July 17, 1653; m. [ ]	MG	
Mary, d. John, b. July 17, 1653	Col.2	155
Mary, d. John, b. July 17, 1653	1	30
Mary, m. Samuel **GRANT**, May 27, 1658	MG	
Mary, ae 10 y., d. John, bp. May 10, 16]63	MG	
Mary, d. [John, Jr. & Joanna], b. Nov. 20, 1672	MG	
Mary, d. John, Jr., b. Nov. 20, 1672; bp. 24th day	1	30
Mary, m. Joseph **PHELPS**, June 26, 1673	MG	
Mary, m. Joseph **PHELPS**, b. of Windsor, June 26, 1673, by		
Mr. Wolcott	Col.1	46
Mary, d. James, b. June 4, 1682	Col.D	51
Mary, d. James, b. June 4, 1682	1	31
Mary, d. James, d. June 9, 1684	Col.D	56
Mary, d. James, d. June 9, 1684	1	50
Mary, d. James, b. Sept. 23, [16]84	Col.D	51
Mary, d. James, b. Sept. 23, 1684	1	31
Mary, wid., d. Sept. 13, 1688	1	49
Mary*, m. Hezekiah **LOOMIS**, Apr. 30, 1690 *(First		
written "Mary **LOOMIS**")	2	169
Mary, d. John, b. July 10, 1703	2	81
Mary, d. Joseph, b. May 27, 1713	2	85
Mary, w. John, d. Sept. 12, 1717	2	261
Mary, d. Sergt. Joseph, d. Mar. 16, 1718/19	2	261
Mary, d. Joseph & Joanna, b. Dec. 11, 1739/40	2	415
Mary, see Mary **PHELPS**	Col.D	56
Mary Jones, d. William & Mary, b. Dec. 16, 1805	2	577
Mehitabell, d. Joseph, b. June 27, 1707	2	81
Mehitable, d. Joseph & Jemima, b. May 27, 1737	2	410
Mindwell, d. Daniell, b. Mar. 26, 1708	2	83
Nathanell, s. [John, Sr.], b. July 19, 1640; bp. 1640	MG	
Nathanael, s. John, bp. July 19, 1640	Col.2	155
Nathanael, s. John, bp. July 19, 1640	1	30
Nathanell, s. [John], b. Apr. 20, 1660	MG	
Nathanael, s. John, b. Apr. 20, 1660	1	30
Nathanell, ae 3 y., s. John, bp. May 10, [16]63	MG	
Nathaniel, s. Joseph, b. Jan. 14, 1710/11	2	84
Nathaniel, of Windsor, m. Elizabeth **GILLET**, of Colchester,		
June 4, 1712	2	186
Nathanael, of Windsor, m. Elizabeth **DOD[D]**, of Hartford		

	Vol.	Page
PORTER, (cont.)		
Oct. 3, 1838 [1738?]	2	188
Nathanel, contributed 0-1-0 to the poor in other colonies	MG	
Philo, of Ellington, m. Clarissa B. SKINNER, of Windsor,		
Mar. 29, 1838, by Eli Deniston	2	193
Rebeca, d. [John], b. Mar. 8, 1666	MG	
Rebeca, d. John, b. Mar. 8, 1666/7	Col.1	55
Rebecca, bp. Mar. 10, [16]66	MG	
Rebekah, m. Timothy LOOMIS, Mar. 20, 1689/90	1	59
Reuben, s. Jonathan & Elisabeth, b. Jan. 12, 1741/2	2	415
Rocksalany, d. Hezekiah & Sarah, b. Jan. [ ], 1762;		
d. Dec. 9, 1762	2	422
Rose, d.[ ], [16]48	MG	
Rose, d.[ ]; bd. May 12, 1648	Col.2	160
Rose, bd. May 12, 1648	1	49
Ruth, d. [John], b. Aug. 7, 1671	MG	
Ruth, bp. Aug. 20, [16]71	MG	
Ruth, m. Nath[an] LOOMY[S], s. John, Nov. 28, 1689	Col.D	55
Ruth, m. Nathanael LOOMIS, s. John, Nov. 28, 1689	1	58
Ruth, m. Benjamin NEWBERY, b. of Windsor, Apr. 24,		
1717	2	182
Sally, d. William & Mary, b. Apr. 17, 1817	2	577
Samuell, s. [John], b. Mar. 5, 1664	MG	
Samuell, s. John, b. Mar. 5, [16]64/5	Col.1	55
Samuell, s. John, b. Mar. 5, 1664	Col.1	54
Samuell, bp. Mar. 12, [16]64	MG	
Samuel, d. Nov. 16, 1694	1	50
Samuel, s. Hezekiah, b. Mar. 23, 1709/10	2	84
Samuel, s. Joseph & Joanna, b. June 3, 1750	2	415
Sara, d. [John], b. Sept. 5, 1655; m. [ ]	MG	
Sarah, d. John, b. Sept. 5, 1655	Col.2	181
Sara, m. Nathanell WINCHELL, Apr.[ ], [16]	MG	
Sara, ae 8 y., d. John, bp. May 10, [16]63	MG	
Sara, of Farmingtowne, m. Nathanell WINCHELL, of		
Windsor, Apr. 8, 1664, by Anthony Howkins	Col.1	45
Sarah, of Farmington, m. Nathanael WINCHEL, of Windsor,		
Apr. 8, 1664, by Anthony Hawkins	1	63
Sara, d. [John, Jr. & Joanna], b. June 1, [16]77	MG	
Sara, d. John, Jr., bp. June 3, [16]77	MG	
Sara, ae 25 on June 5, 1680, m. Enoch DRAK[E], who was		
ae 25 on [Dec.] 8, [1680], Nov. 11, 1680	MG	
Sara, d. John, Sr., m. Enock DRAK[E], s. John, Nov. 11,		
1680	Col.1	47
Sarah, d. James, b. May 31, 1686	Col.D	51
Sarah, d. James, b. May 31, 1686	1	31
Sarah, d. Daniel, b. Dec. 11, 1714	2	88
Sarah, w. Sergt. James, d. Aug. 16, 1725	2	262
Sarah, m. Isaac HIGLEY, b. of Windsor, Feb. 13, 1734/5	2	162

	Vol.	Page
PORTER, (cont.)		
Timothy, s. Hezekiah & Sarah, b. Feb. 5, 1764	2	422
Wareham, s. Hezakiah & Sarah, b. Oct. 1, 1766	2	424
William, m. Mary **BIRT,** Jan. 24, 1805	2	500
William, s. William & Mary, b. Feb. 21, 1807	2	577
POTTER, Milton, 1st s. Marcus & Sally, b. Jan. 15, 1809	2	430
POWELL, POWEL, PUELL, Ann, d. [Thomas & Alse], b. Apr. 19, 1678	MG	
Ann, d. Thomas, b. Apr. 19, 1678	Col.1	56
Ann, d. Thomas, b. Apr. 19, 1678	1	31
Haneball, s. Tho[mas], b. Oct. 3, 1682	Col.D	51
Hanable, s. Thomas, b. Oct. 3, 1682	1	31
Hanibel, s. Tho[mas], d. Jan. 15, 1684	Col.D	56
Hannaball, s. Thomas, d. Jan. 15, 1684	1	50
John, d. Jan. 17, 1685	Col.D	56
John, d. Jan. 17, 1685	1	50
Thomas, m. Alse **TRAHARN,** Aug. 25, 1676	MG	
Thomas, m. Alse **TREHARNE,** Aug. 25, 1675, by Capt. Newbery	Col.1	46
Thomas, m. Allse **TRAHARNE,** Aug. 25, [16]76	Col.1	46
Thomas, m. Alse **TREHAREN,** Aug. 25, 1675*, by Capt. Nubery *(In pencil "1676")	TR1	1
Thomas, m. Allse **TRAHAVEN,** Aug. 25, 1676	1	60
Thomas, m. Allse **TRAHAVEN,** Aug. 25, 1676	1	64
Thomas, m. Allse **TREAHAREN,** Aug. 25, 1676 *("Dec." crossed out)	TR1	1
Thomas, s. [Thomas & Alse], b. July 11, 1680	MG	
Thomas, s. Thomas, b. July 11, 1680	Col.1	57
Thomas, contributed 0-4-0 to the poor in other colonies	MG	
POWERS, John N., of Charleston, S. C., m. Sarah N. **HAYDEN,** of Windsor, Aug. 25, 1847, by T. A. Leete	2	501
Jonathan, s. Walter & Sarah, b. Feb. 12, 1734/5	2	91
PRATT, PRAT, Luther, of Granby, m. Eliza **LATIMER,** of Windsor, Aug. 30, 182[ ], by Rev. John Bartlett. Int. Pub.	2	190
Ruth, of Hartford, m. Samuel **PALMER,** of Windsor, Apr. 6, 1738	2	188
Sarah, of Hartford, m. Timothy **PHELPS,** s. Samuel, of Windsor, Nov. 13, 1690	Col.D	55
Sarah, of Hartford, m. Timothy **PHELPS,** s. Samuel, of Windsor, Nov. 13, 1690	1	60
PRESCOTT, Eliza, m. Andrew **ATKINSON,** b. of Boston, Mass., Dec. 22, 1846, by Rev. George F. Kettel	2	465
Eliza, m. Andrew **ATKINSON,** b. of Boston, Mass., Dec. 22, 1846, by Rev. George F. Rettell	2	466
PRIOR, PRIER, PRYER, Abigail, d. John & Sarah, b. Feb. 9, 1729	2	90
Abner, s. John & Sarah, b. June 2, 1732	2	411

	Vol.	Page
PRIOR, PRIER, PRYER, (cont.)		
Abner, s. Abner & Abigail, b. June 10, 1758	2	419
Allen N., of Somers, m. Jane E. **NORTON**, of Enfield, May		
21, 1843, by Rev. S. D. Jewett	2	193
Ann, w. Humphry, d. Sept. 29, 1682	1	50
An[n]*, w. Humphrey, d. Sept. 29, 1682 *(Note by LBB:		
"Ann **(OSBORN) PRYOR**")	Col.D	56
Ann, d. John, b. Mar. 31, 1690	1	32
Ann, d. Daniel, b. May 10, 1696	1	32
Ann, d. John, Jr. & Ann, b. Nov. 8, 1748	2	416
Asa, of East Windsor, m. Amanda **COOK**, of Windsor, Dec.		
22, 1839, by Rev. W. C. Hoyt	2	501
Azariah, s. John & Sarah, b. Apr. 6, 1734	2	411
Bette, d. John, Jr. & Ann, b. July 10, 1762	2	424
Daniell, s. [Houmfery & Ann], b. Dec. 19, 1667	MG	
Daniel, m. Sarah **EGELSTON**, Feb. 8, 1692	1	60
Daniel, of Windsor, m. Sarah **EGELSTON**, of Middletown,		
Feb. 9, 1692/3	1	60
Elanor, d. John, Jr. & Ann, b. Feb. 26, 1755	2	418
Gideon, s. John & Sarah, b. Feb. 17, 1736/7	2	411
Houmfery, m. Ann **OSBO[R]N**, Nov. 12, 1663	MG	
Houmfery, m. Ann **OSBON**, Nov. 12, [16]63, by Mr. Allyn	Col.1	45
Humphery, m. Mary **WHITCOMBE**, [ ]	Col.D	54
Humfrey, contributed 0-2-6 to the poor in other colonies	MG	
Jerusha, d. John, Jr. & Ann, b. Jan. 12, 1753	2	418
Joel, s. John & Sarah, b. Jan. 16, 1739/40	2	412
John, s. [Houmfery & Ann], b. Feb. 14, 1664	MG	
John, s. John, b. May 16, 1695	1	32
John, s. John, Jr. & Ann, b. Aug. 8, 1764	2	424
Mary, d. John, b. Mar. 6, 1692	1	32
Mary, wid., d. July 10, 1723	2	262
Mahittable, d. John, Jr. & Ann, b. Aug. 15, 1751	2	416
Roswell, s. John, Jr. & Ann, b. Jan. 30, 1749/50	2	416
Roswell, s. John, Jr. & Ann, d. Feb. 20, 1756	2	264
Roswell, s. John, Jr. & Ann, b. May 30, 1758	2	419
Roxa, d. John, Jr. & Ann, b. Oct. 14, 1756	2	419
Sarah, d. Daniel, b. Mar. 4, 1693/4	1	32
Sarah, m. Samuel **WATSON**, b. of Windsor, Feb. 25, 1741/2	2	209
Sarah, d. John, Jr. & Ann, b. July 12, 1760	2	424
PROUTY, Caroline M., m. Thomas G. **NOCK**, b. of Windsor		
Locks, Nov. 12, 1851, by Rev. S. H. Allen	2	496
RAHM, Samuel, of Harrisburg, Pa., m. Dorcas S. **ALLEN**, of		
Suffield, Dec. 19, [probably 1830], by Henry A.		
Rowland	2	505
RALSTON, Archibald, of Berthier, S. C., m. Francis M.		
WOLCOTT, [, 18--], by Rev. S. D. Jewett	2	506
RANDALL, RANDEL, RANDLE, RANDELL, Abraham, m.		
Mary [ ], Dec. 8, 1640; had no child"	MG	

	Vol.	Page
RANDALL, RANDEL, RANDLE, RANDELL, (cont.)		
Abraham, m. Mary [ ], Dec. 1, 1640	1	61
Abraham, his w. [ ], adm. ch. Aug. 17, [16]45	MG	
Abraham, taxed 4-0 on Feb. 10, [16]73	MG	
Abraham, his w. [ ], d. July 8, [16]77	MG	
Abraham, his w. [ ], d. July 8, 1677	Col.1	58
Abraham, of Windsor, m. Elizabeth **KERBRE**, of		
Middletown, Oct. 27, 1681	1	61
Abraham, d. Aug. 21, 1690	Col.D	57
Abraham, d. Aug. 21, 1690	1	50
Abram, communicant from Dorchester; living in Windsor,		
Dec. 22, 1677	MG	
Abram, contributed 0-2-6 to the poor in other colonies	MG	
Mary, w. Abraham, d. July 8, [1677]	MG	
Phillup, d. [ ], [16]48	MG	
Phillip, d. [ ]; bd. Sept. 26, 1648	1	50
Phillup, d. [ ], [16]62	MG	
Phillup, d. May 6, 1662	Col.1	55
------, wid., d. [ ], [16]65, ae 87	MG	
------, wid., d. Aug. 24, 1665	Col.1	55
------, d. Phillup, m. George **PHELPS**, [ ]	MG	
RANDOLPH, Abraham, of Windsor, m. Elizabeth **KIRBY**, of		
Middletown, Oct. 27, 1681	Col.D	54
RAYMOND, Anna, d. Samuel & Lois, b. Nov. 10, 1744	2	438
Anna, m. Elisha **COOK**, b. of Windsor, Jan. 16, 1767	2	137
Edward, m. Harriett **MOFFAT**, Jan. 11, 1835, by Rev.		
Nathaniel Kellogg	2	506
READ, REED, REEDE, Benjamin, s. Hezkeiah & Hannah, b.		
Sept. 3, 1748	2	432
Chloe, d. Ebenezer & Mary, b. June 1, 1764	2	438
Ebenezer, m. Mary **FITCH**, b. of Windsor, Dec. 6, 1759	2	195
Elijah Fitch, s. Ebenezer & Mary, b. May 11, 1767	2	438
Elizabeth, alias Rite, had d. Kathrain, b. June 12, 1721	2	94
Elizabeth, d. David & Hannah, b. May 26, 1751	2	434
Fradrick, s. Isaac & Dinah, b. Nov. 22, 1754	2	435
Helen S., m. James **HOOKER**, Jan. 24, 1816	2	522
Helen S., m. James **HOOKER**, Jr., Jan. 24, 1841	2	165
Hezekiah, m. Hannah **HADLOCK**, b. of Windsor, Feb. 16,		
1746/7	2	195
Justus, s. Ebenezer & Mary, b. Oct. 17, 1760	2	436
Kathrain, d. Elizbeth **REED** alias Rite, b. June 12, 1721	2	94
Lewis, m. Elizabeth **FISH**, b. of Windsor, Sept. 28, 1830, by		
Henry Sill, J. P.	2	505
William B., of Granby, m. Louisa **DRAKE**, Sept. 20, [1830?],		
by Henry A. Rowland	2	505
RECKARD, Hosea, of Palmer, Mass., m. Mary **PEASE**, of Ludlo,		
Mass., Sept. 14, 1848, by Rev. S. H. Allen	2	507
REGAN, Johanna, m. William **PARKER**, Oct. 14, 1852, by Rev.		

	Vol.	Page
REGAN, (cont.)		
James Smyth	2	460
REMINGTON, RIMINGTON, Daniel G., of Hartford, m.		
Elizabeth **ALFORD,** Jan. 25, 1843, by Rev. S. W.		
Scofield	2	507
George N., of Suffield, m. Charlott S. **HALSEY,** of Windsor,		
Sept. 24, 1838, by Rev. Cephas Brainard	2	474
Joseph, s. Thomas, b. Sept. 1, [16]75; bp. Nov. 7, [1675	1	33
Thomas, had 1 child b. in Windsor. Dated Aug. 17, 1677	MG	
RENNARD, John, contributed 0-2-6 to the poor in other colonies	MG	
REYNOLDS, Eliza M., m. George A. **MACK,** b. of Windsor,		
Nov. 30, 1837, by Eli Deniston	2	493
Lorin M., m. Amanda M. **WARE,** Nov. 21, 1830, by Smith		
Dayton, Elder	2	505
Nancy, of Windsor, m. Richmond **HALL,** of Suffield, Nov.		
26, 1834, by Richard G. Drake, J. P.	2	243
Roxey L, m. Silas H. **BROWN,** Oct. 7, 1829, by Rev. Asa		
Bushnell, Jr.	2	498
RICHARDS, Mary, of New London, m. Dr. Alexander		
WOLCOTT, of Windsor, Apr. 3, 1745	2	209
RICHARDSON, Sarah E., m. Algenion Sidney **ALLIN,** Sept. 4,		
1835, by Henry A. Rowland	2	127
RILEY, Chloe, m. Henry **CLARK,** Jan. 1, 1821, by Rev. Henry A.		
Rowland	2	138
Chloe, m. Elisha **BARBER,** Dec. 30, 1828, by Rev. Henry A.		
Rowland	2	150
RIPNER, Elisabeth, d. John & Elisabeth, b. Aug. 15, 1745	2	431
John, s. John & Elisabeth, b. Nov. 12, 1745	2	431
RISING, Hanna, contribute 0-1-3 to the poor in other colonies	MG	
James, his w. [ ], d. [ ], [16]69	MG	
James, his w.[ ], d. Aug. 11, [16]69	Col.1	55
James, m. Martha **BARTLET,** wid., Aug. 13, 1673	Col.1	46
James, his w. [ ], d. [Apr. 20*], [16]74 *(In pencil)	MG	
James, his w. [ ], d. Apr. 2, 1674	1	50
James, his w. [ ]*, d. Apr. 20, 1674 *(Note by LBB:		
"wid. Martha **BARTLETT**")	Col.1	58
James, contributed 0-5-0 to the poor in other colonies	MG	
John, contributed 0-1-6 to the poor in other colonies	MG	
RISLEY, Eri, of East Hartford, m. Chloe **DUNLAP,** of Windsor,		
Sept. 20, 1826, by Rev. Joseph Hough	2	197
Hervey, of East Windsor, m. Minerva **LOOMIS,** June 23,		
1825, by Rev. Henry A. Rowland	2	196
RITTER, Joseph, of Hartford, m. Elizabeth **PEASE,** of Windsor,		
Nov. 30, 1845, by Rev. Rev. Horace Winslow	2	508
ROARK, Farl, m. Margaret **GREENAN,** June 13, 1852, by Rev.		
James Smyth	2	460
ROBERTS, Allyn, s. John, Jr. & Mary, b. Nov. 9, 1769	2	578
Ann, d. John & Mary, b. [ ]	2	432

	Vol.	Page
ROBERTS, (cont.)		
Cathrine, of Hartford, m. Samuel **HOLMAN**, of Windsor, Jan. 17, 1715/16	2	161
Cicero, m. Julia **STOUGHTON**, b. of Windsor, Apr. 11, 1849, by Rev. Samuel Law	2	502
Clark, s. John, Jr. & Mary, b. Sept. 16, 1761	2	436
Elihu, of Windsor, m. Ann R. **LATHROP**, of Middletown, Dec. 6, 1826, by Rev. Henry A. Rowland	2	196
Elisha, s. James & Jerusha, b. June 24, 1779	2	579
Elizabeth T., of Windsor, m. Erastus S. **ROBERTS**, of Tallahassa, Fla., Oct. 1, 1832, by Rev. Ansel Nash	2	505
Erastus S., of Tallahassa, Fla., m. Elizabeth T. **ROBERTS**, of Windsor, Oct. 1, 1832, by Rev. Ansel Nash	2	505
Habbe Humphry, d. John, Jr. & Mary, b. Dec. 24, 1766	2	438
Henry, s. John & Mary, b. Nov. 20, 1759	2	436
Horace E., m. Lydia C. **MOORE**, Apr. 16, 1835, by Rev. Nathaniel Kellogg	2	506
Isaac, of West Springfield, m. Cornelia **CLARK**, of Windsor, Apr. 3, 1834, by Henry A. Rowland	2	506
James, s. John & Mary, b. May 2, 1739	2	430
James, m. Jerusha **TALCOTT**, b. of Windsor, Oct. 5, 1766	2	196
James, s. James & Jerusha, b. June 15, 1771	2	578
James, m. Margaret O. **MOORE**, Sept. 23, 1829, by Henry A. Rowland	2	505
James, s. Elihu & Deborah, d. Oct. 13, 1837, ae 34	2	258
Jerusha, d. James & Jerusha, b. Sept. [ ], 1767; d. Oct. 8, following	2	438
Jerusha, d. James & Jerusha, b. Aug. 17, 1769	2	578
John, m. Mary **ALYN**, b. of Windsor, Oct. 22, 1734 (This entry crossed out)	2	95
John, m. Mary **ALLYN**, b. of Windsor, Oct. 22, 1734	2	195
John, s. John & Mary, b. May 9, 1737	2	430
John, d. Dec. 11, 1771	2	268
John, s. John & Mary, b. Mar. 28, 1780	2	579
Laura R., m. Levi L. **DEMMING**, Oct. 12, 1840, by Rev. Ezra S. Cook	2	473
Lucina, d. William & Violet, b. Mar. 10, 1751/2	2	434
Lucy, d. John & Mary, b. Aug. 15, 1745	2	431
Mary, of Hartford, m. John **THRALL**, Jr., of Windsor, May 4, 1727	2	204
Mary, d. John & Mary, b. May 22, 1743	2	431
Mary, Jr., m. Elijah **ANDRUS**, b. of Windsor, Dec. 1, 1763	2	125
Mary, d. John & Mary, b. July 22, 1772	2	579
Paul, s. John & Mary, b. May 19, 1741	2	431
Pelatiah, s. John & Mary, b. Aug. 30, 1756	2	435
Peter, d. May 26, 1752	2	268
Peter, s. John, Jr. & Mary, b. June 26, 1764	2	437
Ruhamah, d. John & Mary, b. June 15, 1752	2	434

	Vol.	Page
ROBERTS, (cont.)		
Salla, d. James & Jerusha, b. Oct. 25, 1776	2	579
Sarah, d. John & Mary, b. Oct. 18, 1747	2	432
Susa, d. John & Mary, b. Dec. 12, 1775	2	579
Susa, d. John, d. Feb. 17, 1776	2	268
Susa, d. John & Mary, b. Mar. 4, 1777	2	579
Triphena L., m. Elihu **LATIMER,** Jr., b. of Wintonbury, Oct. 17, 1834, by John Bartlett	2	489
ROBINSON, Charles, s. John & Eunice, b. July 5, 1808	2	582
Elizabeth W., m. Sardis **PECK,** b. of Windsor, Mar. 8, 1821, by James Loomis, J. P.	2	191
John, s. John & Eunice, b. Dec. 19, 1805	2	582
Silvester, s. John & Eunice, b. Aug. 17, 1801	2	582
ROCHE, Mary, m. Martin **HENRY,** Oct. 18, 1852, by Rev. James Smyth	2	460
ROCK, Lydia, m. John **MURRAY,** b. of Windsor, Oct. 15, 1832, by Rev. Ansel Nash	2	496
ROCKWELL, ROCKWEL, Abigayle, d. [Samuell & Mary], b. Aug. 23, 1664; d. [ ]	MG	
Abigal, d. Samuell, b. Aug. 23, 1664	Col. 1	54
Abigaile, d. May 3, 1665	Col. 1	55
Abigall, d. [Samuell & Mary], b. Apr. 11, [16]76	MG	
Abigael, m. John **SMITH,** Nov. 9, 1704	2	197
Abigael, d. John, b. Aug. 9, 1713	2	93
Abigail, d. James & Abigail, b. Dec. 19, 1733	2	95
Abigail, d. James & Abigail, d. Feb. 13, 1733/4	2	267
Abner, s. Daniel & Margret, b. Mar. 6, 1737/8	2	430
Abner, s. Daniel & Margaret, d. Aug. 7, 1741	2	268
Abner, s. Daniell & Margret, b. Oct. 10, 1744	2	432
Alpheus, m. Selene **BOWER,** b. of Windsor, Dec. 19, 1821, by Rev. Oliver Wilson, of North Haven	2	196
Ann, d. Joel & Sarah, b. Oct. 23, 1755	2	436
Anna, d. [ ], [16]43	MG	
Anne, d. John, b. Jan. 18, 1704	2	92
Azubah, d. Ebenezer, Jr. & Lucy, b. Apr. 3, 1755	2	435
Benjamin, s. Joseph, b. Oct. 26, 1700	1	33
Benjamin, s. Job & Merriam, b. Jan. 25, 1742/3	2	431
Bulah, d. Daniel & Margret, b. May 20, 1735	2	430
Bulah, d. Daniel & Margaret, d. July 20, 1741	2	268
Bulah, d. Daniel & Margret, b. Jan. 20, 1742/3	2	432
Beulah, d. Daniel & Margaret, b. July 3, 1748	2	433
Charles, s. Job & Merriam, b. Dec. 22, 1737	2	95
Charles, m. Abigail **WOLCOTT,** b. of Windsor, Apr. 9, 1764	2	195
Charles, s. Charles & Abigail, b. July 2, 1765	2	438
Daniell, s. John, b. May 30, 1707	2	92
Daniel, of Windsor, m. Margrit **LOOMIS,** of Lebanon, Feb. 20, 1732/3	2	195
Daniel, s. Daniell & Margaret, b. Sept. 4, 1746	2	432

	Vol.	Page
ROCKWELL, ROCKWEL, (cont.)		
David, s. John, b. Aug. 15, 1709	2	92
David, of Windsor, m. Margrit **VANHORN,** of Springfield,		
Feb. 22, 1735/6	2	195
Deliurance, wid. of John, of Windsor, m. Robard		
WARRENNAK, of Middletown, Feb. 2, 1674, by Mr.		
Wolcott	Col.1	46
Ebenezer, s. John, b. Jan. 5, 1717/18	2	93
Ebenezer, s. James & Abigaiel, b. Sept. 27, 1728	2	95
Ebenezer, Jr., m. Lucy **BARBER,** b. of Windsor, Aug. 16,		
1749	2	195
Ebenezer, s. Ebenezer & Lucy, b. July 5, 1752	2	435
Elijah, of East Windsor, m. Nancy **GREEN,** of Windsor, Oct.		
3, 1832, by Henry A. Rowland	2	505
Elisabeth, d. [John & Deliuerance], b. Feb. 5, 1670	MG	
Elizabeth, d. Joseph, b. Dec. 12, 1698	1	33
Elizabeth, d. Joseph, d. Nov. [ ], 1699	1	50
Elizabeth, d. Joseph, b. July 24, 1713	2	93
Elizabeth, m. Thomas **GRANT,** Jr., b. of Windsor, July 9,		
1722	2	155
Elizabeth, wid. Dea. Samuell, d. Dec. 12, 1727	2	267
Elizabeth, d. James & Abigail, b. Apr. 9, 1742	2	431
Elizabeth, d. Dr. Mathew & Jemima, b. Mar. 26, 1756	2	436
Elizabeth, m. Thomas D. **ELLIOT,** b. of Windsor, Nov.		
30, 1843, by Rev. S. D. Jewett	2	508
Ephraim, s. Joel & Sarah, b. Sept. 16, 1750	2	435
Eunice, d. Josiah & Rebeckah, b. June 3, 1727	2	94
Eunice, d. Daniell & Eunice, b. Sept. 7, 1742	2	431
Ezra, s. Josiah, b. Apr. 15, 1721	2	94
Frances, s. Isaac & Desire, b. June 2, 1765	2	438
Hanna, d. [John & Deliuerance], b. May 30, 1665	MG	
Hanna, d. John, b. May 30, 1665	Col.1	55
Hannah, d. Joseph, b. Dec. 25, 1717	2	93
Isaac, s. John, b. Mar. 14, 1715/16	2	93
Isaac, s. John & Ann, d. June 23, 1732. Was drowned in the		
Great River	2	267
Isaac, s. Daniel & Margret, b. Jan. 26, 1733/4	2	430
Isaac, s. Daniel & Margret, d. Feb. 5, 1733/4	2	267
Isaac, s. Joel & Sarah, b. Sept. 9, 1742	2	431
Isaac, m. Desire **MUNSELL,** b. of Windsor, July 22, 1764	2	195
James, s. Joseph, b. June 3, 1704	2	92
James, s. James & Abigail, b. Sept. 27, 1728	2	94
James, m. Abigail **LOOMIS,** b. of Windsor, Nov. 7, 1728	2	194
James, of Norrige, m. Lois **PORTER,** of Windsor, June		
28, 1734	2	194
Jane (?), see under Jone		
Jemima, d. Mathew & Jemima, b. Oct. 8, 1744	2	431
Jemima, d. Mathew & Jemima, d. Nov. 19, 1744	2	267

	Vol.	Page
ROCKWELL, ROCKWEL, (cont.)		
Jemima, d. James & Abigail, d. July 31, 1746	2	268
Jerusha, twin with [ ], d. Joseph, b. June 15, 1720	2	93
Job, s. Joseph, b. Apr. 13, 1709	2	92
Job, m. Meriam HAYDON, b. of Windsor, Jan. 20, 1736/7	2	194
Job, d. Aug. 23, 1750	2	268
Joel, s. John, b. about Sept. 25, 1718	2	94
Joel, s. John, b. Sept. 8, 1719	2	94
Joel, m. Sarah DRAKE, b. of Windsor, Dec. 3, 1741	2	195
Joel, of Granville, Mass., m. Monimia CLARK, of Windsor, July 7, 1823, by Rev. Augustus Bolles, of Wintonbury	2	196
John, m. Sara ENSIGNE, May 6, 1651	MG	
John, m. Sarah GORSIGNE, May 6, 1651	1	61
John, adm. ch. July 31, [16]53	MG	
John, d. May 10, 1662	Col.1	55
John, m. 2nd w. Deliuerance HAYES, Aug. 18, 1662	MG	
John, of Windsor, m. Deliverance HAYNES, of Dorchester, Mass., Aug. 18, [16]62, at Dorchester, Mass.	1	61
John, Sr., d. [ ], [16]62	MG	
John, s. [John & Deliuerance], b. Sept. 5, 1663; d. [ ]	MG	
John, his s. [ ], d. [ ], [16]63	MG	
John, s. Samuel, b. Mar. 31, 1673	1	33
John, s. [Samuell & Mary], b. May 31, 1673	MG	
John, d. Sept. 3, 1673, ae 46	MG	
John, d. Sept. 3, 1673, ae 46	Col.1	58
John, d. Sept. 3, [16]73; bd. [ ], ae 46 y.	1	50
John, had 7 children b. in Windsor. Dated Aug. 17, 1677	MG	
John, s. John, b. Dec. 18, 1701	1	33
John, his twins b. May 12, 1706; d. 3 das. after	2	92
John, s. John, d. Feb. 3, 1725/6	2	267
John, s. John, b. Dec. 5, 1728	2	94
John, s. Daniel & Margarett, b. Aug. 5, 1757	2	434
John, m. Ann SKIN[N]ER, [ ]	1	60
Jonathan, s. Joseph, Jr., b. May 2, 1723	2	94
Jone, m. Jefery BAKER, Nov. 15, 1642 *("Joan" or Jane?")	MG	
Joseph, s. [John & Deliuerance], b. July 8, 1668	MG	
Joseph, s. [Samuell & Mary], b. May 22, 1670	MG	
Joseph, m. Elizabth DRAKE, Jan. 23, 1694	1	61
Joseph, s. Joseph, b. Nov. 23, 1695	1	33
Joseph, Jr., m. Hannah HUNTINGTON, Nov. 11 or 15, 1714	2	194
Joseph, s. Joseph, Jr., b. Mar. 15, 1715/16	2	93
Josia, s. [Samuell & Mary], b. Mar. 10, [16]78; bp. [Mar.] 23, [1678]	MG	
Josiah, s. Samuel, b. Mar. 10, 1678/9	1	33
Josiah, of Windsor, m. Rebeckah LOOMIS, of Lebanon*, Dec. 10, 1713 *("Hebron" crossed out)	2	194
Josiah, s. Josiah, b. Mar. 7, 1718/19	2	93
Josias, s. Samuell, b. Mar. 10, 1678/9	Col.1	56

	Vol.	Page
ROCKWELL, ROCKWEL, (cont.)		
Lucretia, d. Dr. Mathew & Jemima, b. Nov. 5, 1751	2	434
Lucresha, d. Joel & Sarah, b. June 18, 1757	2	436
Lucey, d. Ebenezer, Jr. & Lucey, b. July 30, 1749	2	433
Lucy, w. Ebenezer, Jr., d. Apr. 3, 1755	2	268
Lucy, m. John **MEARS**, b. of Windsor, Jan. 14, 1761	2	179
Lidia, d. John, b. Nov. 23, 1656	Col.2	161
Liddia, d. [John & Sara], b. Nov. 28, 1656	MG	
Lydia, d. Daniel & Margret, b. Oct. 4, 1740	2	431
Mabel, d. Mathew & Jemima, b. Apr. 22, 1749	2	432
Margret, d. Daniel & Margret, b. Feb. 20, 1734/5		
(Crossed out)	2	430
Marietta, of Windham, m. Harry **SIMMONS**, of Durham,		
Dec. 25, 1833, by Henry A. Rowland	2	508
Martha, d. John, b. Aug. 28, 1720	2	94
Mary, m. Robard **WATSON**, Dec. 10, 1646	MG	
Mary, m. Robard **WATSON**, Dec. 10, 1646	1	62
Mary, d. [Samuell & Mary], b. Jan. 18, 1661	MG	
Mary, [d.] Sam[uel], [bp.] Jan. 26, [16]61	MG	
Mary, m. Josiah **LOOMYS**, Oct. 23, 1683	Col.D	54
Mary, m. Josiah **LOOMIS**, Oct. 23, 1683	1	58
Mary, d. John, b. July 10, 1711	2	93
Mary, d. Daniel & Margret, b. Aug. 18, 1736	2	430
Mary, d. Job & Miriam. b. Sept. 10, 1750	2	435
Mary, d. Job & Meriam, d. Nov. 9, 1751	2	268
Mary, m. Oliver **SKINNER**, b. of Windsor, Jan. 26, 1763	2	201
Mathew, s. Samuel, Jr., b. Jan. 30, 1707/8	2	92
Mathew, m. Jemima **COOK**, b. of Windsor, Jan. 19, 1743/4	2	195
Merriam, d. Job & Merriam, b. Jan. 23, 1739/40	2	430
Nathaniel, s. James & Abigail, b. Nov. 3, 1746	2	432
Noah, s. Daniel & Margret, b. Mar. 31, 1753	2	435
Orator P., of Bloomfield, m. Rosalia E. **GRISWOLD**, Aug.		
15, 1852, by Rev. T. H. Rouse	2	502
Owen, of Terris Vill, m. Ann **FRANCES**, of Windsor, Apr.		
25, 1827, by Rev. Henry A. Rowland	2	197
Rachel, d. John & Ann, b. June 20, 1726	2	94
Rachel, m. Hezekiah **CRANE**, Apr. 2, 1747	2	136
Rebeckah, d. Josiah, b. Mar. 24, 1714/15	2	93
Ruth, d. [John & Sara], b. Mar. 5, 1654	MG	
Ruth, d. John, b. Mar. 5, 1654	Col.2	158
Ruth, bp. Mar. 11, [16]54	MG	
Ruth, d. Josiah, b. Jan. 6, 1716/17	2	93
Ruth, wid., d. June 11, 1831	2	269
Samuell, communicant 16[ ]	MG	
Samuell, b. Mar. 28, 1631; m. Mary **NORTON**, Apr. 7, 1660	MG	
Samuell, adm. ch. Apr. 6, 1652	MG	
Samuel, of Windsor, m. Mary **NORTON**, of Saybrook, Apr.		
9, 1658	1	61

	Vol.	Page
ROCKWELL, ROCKWEL, (cont.)		
Samuel, adm. ch. & communicant Apr. [ ], 1662	MG	
Samuel, his d. [ ], d. [ ], [16]65	MG	
Samuell, s. [Samuell & Mary], b. Oct. 19, 1667	MG	
Samuel, s. Samuel, b. Oct. 19, 1667	1	33
Samuel, taxed 2-0 on Feb. 10, [16]73	MG	
Samuell, had 6 children b. in Windsor. Dated Aug. 17, 1677	MG	
Samuel, m. Elizabeth GAYLORD, Jan. 10, 1694	1	61
Samuel, s. Samuel, Jr., b. Jan. 11, 1702/3	1	33
Samuel, Jr., d. Apr. 21, 1725	2	267
Samuel, Dea., d. May 13, 1725	2	267
Samuel, s. Joseph, Jr. & Hannah, b. Mar. 9, 1725/6	2	94
Samuel, s. Joseph, Jr. & Hannah, d. Sept. 10, 1727	2	266
Samuel, s. Joseph, Jr. & Hannah, b. Jan. 19, 1728	2	94
Samuell, s. Mathew & Jemima, b. Sept. 6, 1747; d. Oct. 28, 1747, ae 7 wks. 3 das.	2	432
Samuell, contributed 0-2-0 to the poor in other colonies	MG	
Sara, b. May 12, [16]53	MG	
Sara, d. [John & Sara], b. May 12, 1653	MG	
Sarah, d. John, b. May 12, 1653	Col.2	156
Sarah, m. Walter GAYLAR, Mar. 22, 1658	MG	
Sara, w. John, d. June 23, 1659	MG	
Sarah, w. John, bd. June 23, 1659, at Hartford	1	50
Sarah, m. Walter GAYLORD, b. of Windsor, Mar. 22, 1659/60	1	56
Sarah, d. David & Margrit, b. Sept. 12, 1737	2	95
Sarah, d. Joel & Sarah, b. Apr. 2, 1744	2	435
Sarah, see Sarah GAYLOR	Col.D	56
Silence, m. John ELLIS, b. of Windsor, Oct. 13, 1826, by Rev. David Miller	2	196
Simon, d. [ ], [16]65	MG	
Simon, d. June 22, 1665	Col.1	55
Susannah, m. Mathew GRANT, May 29, 1645	1	56
Susannah, d. Joel & Sarah, b. June 28, 1753	2	436
Silvanus, s. John, b. Jan. 7, 1723/4	2	94
Salvanus, s. Joel & Sarah, b. Feb. 1, 1747	2	435
Waitstil, d. Josiah, b. Sept. 6, 1723	2	94
Waitstill, m. Thomas SADD, Jr., b. of Windsor, May 31, 1744	2	199
William, d.[ ], [16]40	MG	
William, d.[ ]; bd. May 15, 1640	1	50
William, had 1 child b. in Windsor. Dated Aug. 17, 1677	MG	
William, s. Samuel, Jr., b. Nov. 11, 1704	2	92
William, d. Apr. 22, 1725	2	267
William, s. James & Abigail, b. Sept. 19, 1731	2	95
Wilmoth, w. [John], d. May 12, 1662	Col.1	55
-----, twin with Jerusha, s. Joseph, b. June 15, 1720; d. same day	2	93
ROGER, Peter, bd. June 13, 1651	1	50

	Vol.	Page
ROOD, Abigail, m. Josiah **BLOCHET**, b. of Windsor, Jan. 15, 1746(7) sic?	2	132
ROOT, Anna, m. Noah **ALLIN**, b. of Windsor, Mar. 25, 1756	2	124
ROPER, Charles A., of Bristol, m. Maria **ARNOLD**, of Windsor, May 15, 1833, by Henry A. Rowland	2	506
ROSS, James, s. John & Patience, b. Oct. 31, 1767	2	578
John, m. Patience **DENSLOW**, b. of Windsor, Mar. [ ], 1763	2	196
Lucinda, m. Henry **WILLIAMS**, Oct. 13, 1834, by Henry A. Rowland	2	513
Roxana, d. John & Patience, b. Mar. 6, 1764	2	578
Sabra, d. John & Patience, b. Feb. 5, 1771	2	578
[ROSSITER], **ROSETER**, Abigayl, d. [ ], [16]48	MG	
Elizabeth, d.[ ], [16]51	MG	
Ester, d.[ ], [16]49	MG	
Peter, d. [ ], [16]51	MG	
Samuel, d. June 10, 1640	MG	
Timothy, d. [ ], [16]46	MG	
-----, Mr., had 6 children b. in Windsor. Dated Aug. 17, 1677	MG	
ROUNSAVELL, John, of Baltimore, m. S. **STONE**, of Litchfield, Dec. 12, 1841, by William Thompson	2	506
ROWE, Martha Ann, of Westfield, Mass., m. George **ANNIS**, of Manchester, Sept. 16, 1839, by Rev. S. D. Jewett	2	464
ROWELL, **ROWEL**, **ROUELL**, Abigail, d. Thomas, b. Feb. 10, 1686	1	33
Abigaell, had s. Daniell, b. Jan. 3, 1709/10	2	92
Amy, d. Job & Ruth, b. May 30, 1791	2	579
Ann, d. Thomas, Jr., b. Sept. 24, 1703	2	92
Ann, d. Daniel & Eunice, b. Mar. 17, 1745/6	2	432
Bette, d. Silas & Christian, b. Aug. 15, 1792	2	580
Bildad, s. Job & Ruth, b. Aug. 17, 1795	2	580
Birum, s. Philander & Joanna, b. Sept. 28, 1797	2	581
Cate, d. Samuel & Elizabeth, b. Dec. 9, 1766	2	579
Charlotte, d. Philander & Joana, b. Mar. 20, 1785	2	580
Crisse, d. Silas & Christian, b. Oct. 4, 1787; d. Sept. 16, 1788	2	580
Crisse, d. Silas & Christian, b. Sept. 11, 1789	2	580
Daniell, s. Abigaell, b. Jan. 3, 1709/10	2	92
Daniel, s. Thomas, b. Oct. 11, 1717	2	93
Daniel, m. Eunice **BROWN**, b. of Windsor, June 23, 1736	2	194
Daniel, s. Daniel & Eunice, b. Apr. 25, 1737	2	95
Daniel, s. Daniel & Eunice, d. Oct. 20, 1741	2	267
David, s. Daniel & [E]unice, b. Apr. 6, 1739	2	430
David, s. Daniel & Eunice, d. Oct. 28, 1741	2	267
Elizabeth, m. Theophilus **MOORE**, b. of Windsor, Nov. 18, 1790	2	180
Fanna, d. Philander & Joanna, b. July 10, 1801	2	581
Gurdon, s. Philander & Joanna, b. Aug. 13, 1792	2	581

	Vol.	Page
ROWELL, ROWEL, ROUELL, (cont.)		
Hannah, d. Thomas, Jr., b. July 5, 1700	2	92
Hannah, d. Thomas, d. Jan. 5, 1719/20	2	266
Hannah, d. Thomas, b. Feb. 11, 1720/1	2	93
Hannah, d. Daniel & Eunice, b. Apr. 9, 1758	2	436
Hiram, s. Silas & Christian, b. Oct. 19, 1795; d. Apr. 25, 1799	2	580
James, s. Samuel, Jr. & Catharine, b. Apr. 9, 1774	2	579
Jesse, s. Philander & Joana, b. Oct. 4, 1777	2	579-80
Job, s. Samuel & Elisabeth, b. Apr. 15, 1752	2	434
Job, s. Job & Ruth, b. Aug. 11, 1787	2	579
John, his w. [ ], d. [ ], [16]62	MG	
John, s. Thomas, b. Apr. 4, 1714	2	93
John, m. Mary FILLEY, b. of Windsor, Jan. 4, 1743/4	2	195
John, s. John & Mary, b. Feb. 20, 1744/5	2	431
Levy, s. Philander & Joana, b. Mar. 24, 1780	2	580
Lindia, d. Samuel, Jr. & Catharine, b. Nov. 11, 1775	2	579
Loomis, s. Job & Ruth, b. Apr. 13, 1797	2	580
Lusina, had d. Orma, b. June 15, 1784	2	557
Lusina, had d. Orma, b. June 15, 1784	2	580
Martin, s. John & Mary, b. Aug. 18, 1748	2	432
Mary, wid., d. June 14, 1739	2	267
Nabey King, d. Silas & Christian, b. May 2, 1798	2	580
Odadorman, s. Philander & Joanna, b. Aug. 29, 1790	2	580
Orma, d. Lusina ROWEL, b. June 15, 1784	2	557
Orma, d. Lusina, b. June 15, 1784	2	580
Philander, s. John & Mary, b. Dec. 20, 1755	2	435
Philander, of Windsor, m. Joana HAZE, of Symsbury, Jan. 5, 1775	2	196
Philander, s. Philander & Joana, b. Oct. 19, 1775	2	579
Ruben, s. John & Mary, b. Oct. 11, 1746	2	431
Ruben, s. John & Mary, d. July 11, 1764, in the 18th y. of his age	2	268
Ruben, s. John & Mary, b. July 11, 1764	2	438
Ruth, d. Job & Ruth, b. June 4, 1789	2	579
Samuel, s. Thomas, d. Aug. 11, 1697	1	50
Samuel, s. Thomas, b. Mar. 11, 1710/11	2	92
Samuel, s. Samuel & Elisabeth, b. May 29, 1746	2	432
Samuel, s. Samuel, Jr. & Catharine, b. May 22, 1772	2	578
Sarah, d. Thomas, b. Sept. 17, 1708	2	92
Silas, s. Samuel & Elizabeth, b. Dec. 2, 1759	2	436
Silas, s. Silas & Christian, b. Nov. 19, 1785	2	580
Solomon, s. Philander & Joanna, b. May 5, 1796	2	581
Stephen, s. Samuell & Elizabeth, b. Mar. 21, 1755	2	435
Stephen, d. Apr. 30, 1778	2	269
Susanna, d. Philander & Joana, b. Feb. 20, 1782	2	580
Susine, d. Samuel & Elizabeth, b. Mar. 10, 1762	2	436
Thomas, m. Mary DENSLOW, May 5, 1669, by Mr. Wolcott	2	61

	Vol.	Page
SADD, SADDS, (cont.)		
Matthew, s. Thomas, b. Feb. 8, 1717/18	2	100
Mathew, s. Thomas & Hannah, d. May 10, 1728	2	271
Mathew, s. Thomas & Hannah, b. July 11, 1729	2	103
Thomas, s. Thomas, b. Aug. 3, 1723	2	101
Thomas, Jr., m. Waitstill **ROCKWELL**, b. of Windsor, May		
31, 1744	2	199
Thomas, s. Thomas & Waitstill, b. Mar. 29, 1748	2	440
SAFFORD, Jonathan, of Windsor, m. Susanna **BUTT**, of		
Canterbury, Nov. 1, 1759	2	200
Jonathan, s. Jonathan & Susannah, b. Aug. 2, 1760	2	444
ST. JOHN, William E., m. Maria Ann **MOORE,** Oct. 30, 1833, by		
Henry A. Rowland	2	508
SAMWAYES, SAMMAIS, SAMWAYS, Richard, his child d.		
[ ], [16]48	MG	
Richard, bd, Oct. 23, 1648* *(Line drawn through date)	1	50
Richard, d. [ ], [16]50	MG	
Richard, had 3 children b. in Windsor. Dated Aug. 17, 1677	MG	
SANDERS, Christopher, had 1 child b. in Windsor. Dated Aug.		
17, 1677	MG	
Danell, s. [Christopher], b. Oct. 27, 1678	MG	
Danell, s. Cristopher, b. Oct. 27, 1678	Col.1	56
Daniel, s. Christopher, b. Oct. 27, 1678	1	34
Elizabeth, d. [Christopher], b. Aug. 30, 1681	MG	
Elizabeth, see Henery **WOLCOT**	Col.2	160
George, his child d. May 31, [16]76	MG	
George, m. Abigail **BISSELL,** Dec. 17, 1691	1	61
George, Ens., d. Dec. 5, 1697	1	51
George, contributed 0-1-3 to the poor	MG	
Hana, d. George, b. May 23, 1690	Col.D	51
Hannah, d. George, b. May 23, 1691	1	34
Susana, d. Christopher, b. Nov. 20, 1676	MG	
-----, adult, ch. mem. 16[ ]	MG	
SANDS, Chloe, m. Harmon **WAY,** Nov. 11, 1830, by Henry A.		
Rowland	2	513
George, his child bd. May 31, [16]76	Col.1	58
SAWN, Daniel, m. Jane M. **HUMASON,** b. of Windsor, [ ] 31,		
[18], by Rev. Francis L. Robins, of Enfield	2	509
SAXTON, SAXSTON, SAXTONE, Frances, s. [Richard & Sara],		
b. Jan. 17, 1661; d. May 6, [16]66	MG	
Francis, s. Richard, b. Jan. 1, 1661	1	34
Frances, d. [ ], [16]62	MG	
Ffrances, d. May 6, 1662	Col.1	55
Hannah, of Simsbury, m. Josiah **PHELPS,** of Windsor,		
Dec. 18, 1734	2	188
John, adult, ch. mem. 16[ ]	MG	
John, s. [Richard & Sara], b. Mar. 4, 1649	MG	
John, s. Richard, b. Mar. 4, 1649	Col.2	156

	Vol.	Page
SAXTON, SAXSTON, SAXTONE, (cont.)		
John, s. Richard, b. Mar. 4, 1649	1	34
John, s. George, b. May 26, 1673	1	33
John, m. Mary **HILL**, July 30, 1677	MG	
John, m. Mary **HILL**, July 30, 1677	Col.1	46
John, m. Mary **HILL**, July 30, [16]77	TR1	1
John, m. Mary **HILL**, July 30, 1677	1	61
John, contributed 0-1-3 to the poor in other colonies	MG	
Mary, bp. & adm. ch. June [ ], [16]	MG	
Mary, d. [Richard & Sara], b. Feb. 27, 1651	MG	
Mary, d. Richard, b. Feb. 27, 1651	Col.2	156
Mary, d. Richard, b. Feb. 27, 1651	1	34
Mary, adm. ch. & communicant Apr. [ ], 1671	MG	
Mary, d. John, b. May 4, 1678	Col.1	56
Mary, d. John, b. May 4, 1678	1	34
Patience, d. [Richard & Sara], b. Jan. 28, 1658	MG	
Patience, d. Richard, b. June 28, 1658	1	34
Richard, m. Sara **COOK**, Apr. 16, 164[ ]	MG	
Richard, m. Sarah **COOK**, Apr. 16, 1647	1	61
Richard, s. [Richard & Sara], b. Mar. 1, 1654; d. [ ]	MG	
Richard, s. Richard, b. May 1, 1654/5	1	34
Richard, d. [ ], [16]62	MG	
Richard, d. May 3, 1662	MG	
Richar[d], d. May 3, 1662	Col.1	55
Richard, d. Dec. 19, [16]57, in war	MG	
Richard, d. Dec. 19, 1675	1	26
Richard, d. Dec. 19, 1675	Col.1	58
Richard, d. Dec. 19, 1675	1	47
Richard, had 6 children b. in Windsor. Dated Aug. 17, 1677	MG	
Sara, d. [Richard & Sara], b. Mar. 23, 1647	MG	
Sarah, d. Richard, b. Mar. 23, 1647	Col.2	156
Sarah, d. Richard, b. Mar. 23, 1647	1	34
Sara, w. Richard, d. June 13, 1674	MG	
-----, wid., [d. June 13*], [16]74 *(In pencil	MG	
-----, wid., d. June 13, 1674	Col.1	58
-----, wid., d. [ ]; bd. June 13, 1674	1	50
SCHULZE, Henry, m. Elizabeth **THRALL**, b. of Hartford, Nov.		
25, 1846, by Rev. George Burgess, of Hartford	2	511
SCOTT, SCOT, Elisabeth, m. John **LOOMYS**, Feb. 3, 1648	MG	
Elizabeth, John **LOOMIS**, Feb. 3, 1648, at Hartford	1	58
Rachel, of Hartford, m. Peter **BROWN**, of Windsor, Aug. 14,		
1722	2	129
Rachel, w. Robert, d. Jan. 3, 1737/8	2	271
Reuben, of Poultney, Vt., m. Esther M. **COOK**, of Windsor,		
June 11, 1835, by John Bartlett	2	509
Timothy, s. Timothy & Thankfull, b. Mar. 30, 1738/9	2	106
Timothy, had 1 child d. [ ], in "Elenton" prior to		
1740	MG	

Vol.   Page

SCOVILL, Charlotte, m. William W. HILLS, b. of Windsor, Mar.
    24, 1852, by Theodore A. Leet   2   487
SEARLS, Elisha, s. John & Margret, b. Jan. 22, 1751; d. Mar. 9,
    1751   2   447
    Eunice, d. John & Margret, b. Sept. 29, 1761   2   447
    Gedion, s. John & Margret, b. Nov. 13, 1742   2   446
    Gideon, of Windsor, m. Cynthia SWETLAND, of Hartford,
        Sept. 9, 1761   2   200
    Gedion, s. Gedion & Cynthia, b. Mar. 11, 1762   2   445
    John, s. John & Margret, b. Jan. 24, 1745   2   446
    Lemuel, s. John & Margret, b. Mar. 27, 1754   2   447
    Margret, d. John & Margret, b. Jan. 25, 1752   2   447
    Reuben, s. John & Margret, b. Jan. 17, 1747   2   447
    Ruth, of Northampton, m. Jonathan GILLET, of Windsor,
        Nov. 18, 1707   2   154
    Ruth, d. John & Margret, b. Oct. 9, 1756   2   447
    Sarah, d. John & Margret, b. Feb. 11, 1759   2   447
SEARS, Hezekiah H., of Hartford, m. Julia O. HALSEY, of
        Windsor, June 23, 1847, by T. A. Leete   2   514
    W[illia]m H., of Glastenbury, m. Catherin ANDERSON, of
        Wethersfield, June 27, 1842, by Rev. S. D. Jewett   2   206
SEDGWICK, Chester, of Hartford, m. Cyrene DRAKE, of
        Windsor, Nov. 27, 1822, by Rev. John Bartlett. Int.   2   202
    Pub.
SELDEN, SELDON, Edward, d. Dec. 17, 1828, ae 69   2   274
    Nancy, m. Joel THAYER, of Palmyra, N. Y., Sept. 30, 1823,
        by Rev. Henry A. Rowland   2   205
SENTION, SENSION, SENCHON, SENSHON, Isabell, w.
        Nicho[las], d. Oct. 2, 1689   Col.D   57
    Isabell, w. Nicholas, d. Oct. 2, 1689   1   51
    N., his w. [   ], adm, ch. & communicant Jan. [   ], 1649   MG
    Nicholos, m. Isable [   ], June 12, 1645   1   61
    Nicolas, his w. [   ], adm. ch. Jan. 22, [16]49   MG
    Nicolas, taxed 2-0 on Feb. 10, [16]73   MG
    Nicholas, d. Sept. 18, 1689   Col.D   57
    Nicholas, d. Sept. 18, 1689   1   51
    Nicolas, adult, ch. mem. 16[   ]   MG
SEWARD, [see also SEWETT], Frederick R., s. Frederick A.
        & Mary A., b. Aug. 31, 1846   2   558
SEWETT, [see also JEWETT & SEWARD], Sarah, m. Isaac
        NEWTON, b. of Windsor, Apr. 19, 1758   2   183
SEXTON, Allyn, s. Thomas & Sibbel, b. Mar. 4, 1760; d. Oct. 6,
    1760   2   445
    Lovicia, d. Thomas & Sibbel, b. Nov. 21, 1761   2   445
    Thomas, m. Sibbel FOSTER, b. of Windsor, Nov. 26, 1759   2   200
SHADOCK, SHADRAKE, Elias, m. Hanna OSBOND, d. John,
        Nov. 26, 1675   Col.1   46

	Vol.	Page
SHADOCK, SHADRAKE, (cont.)		
Elias, d. May 26, [16]76	MG	
Elias, bd. May 26, 1676	Col. 1	58
Elias, d. [ ]; bd. May 26, [16]76	1	51
Hanna, wid., m. Beniamen **EGELSTON**, Mar. 6, 1678, by Capt. Newbery	MG	
Hanna, wid. & d. John **OSBON**, m. Beniamen **EGELSTON**, Mar. 6, 1678, by Capt. Newbery	Col. 1	46
Hannah, wid. & d. of John **OSBAND**, m. Benjamin **EGELSTON**, Mar. 6, 1678, by Capt. Nubery	1	56
Hanna, contributed 0-1-3 to the poor in other colonies	MG	
SHARE, SHEARS, John, m. Sara **GIBBS**, Dec. 5, 1661	MG	
John, m. Sarah **GIBBS**, b. of Windsor, Dec. 5, 1661	1	61
John, s. [John & Sara], b. Dec. 11, 1662	MG	
John, s. John, b. Dec. 11, 1662	1	33
John, d. [ ], [16]69	MG	
John, bd. Sept. 29, [16]69	Col. 1	55
John, d. [ ]; bd. Sept. 29, 1669	1	51
John, had 1 child b. in Windsor. Dated Aug. 17, 1677	MG	
John, d. Dec. 7, 1688	1	51
SHARWOOD, Ruth, m. Josua **HOLCOM[B]**, June 4, 1663	MG	
Ruth, m. Josua **HOLCOM**, June 4, 1663, by Mr. Wolcot	Col. 1	45
SHEARS, [see under **SHARES**]		
SHEFFINGTON, Henry, m. Catharine **DAWSON**, Nov. 21, 1852, by Rev. James Smyth	2	460
SHELDON, SHELDING, SHELDEN, Allyn, s. Epaphras & Eunice, b. July 30, 1755	2	443
Apphia, of Suffield, m. Uriah **LOOMIS**, Jr., of Windsor, July 5, 1764	2	488
Eli, s. Remembrance, Jr. & Sarah, b. Sept. 4, 1761	2	445
Elisha, s. Rememberance, b. Feb. 29, 1719/20	2	100
Epephras, s. Remembrance & Hannah, b. Sept. 4, 1726	2	102
Epaphras, m. Eunice **ALLYN**, b. of Windsor, Apr. 30, 1752	2	200
Epaphras, s. Epaphras & Eunice, b. Aug. 2, 1753	2	442
Gad, m. Lusinda A. **CHANDLER**, Apr. 5, 1831, by Henry A. Rowland	2	508
Hannah, w. Remembrance, d. Mar. 31, 1758	2	273
Jerusha, d. Remembrance, b. Nov. 27, 1722	2	101
Odiah L., m. Candace **MARSHALL**, Aug. 1, 1826, by Rev. Henry A. Rowland	2	203
Rachel, of Suffield, m. Isaac **DAVICE**, Jr., of Windsor, May 15, 1745	2	142
Remembrance, of Hartford, m. Hannah **DRAKE**, of Windsor, Feb. 19, 1718/19	2	198
Remembrance, s. Sergt. Remembrance & Hannah, b. Oct. 23, 1728	2	103
Remembrance, Jr., m. Sarah **EGELSTONE**, b. of Windsor, Jan. 31, 1751	2	200

	Vol.	Page
SHELDON, SHELDING, SHELDEN, (cont.)		
Remembrance, m. Marcy **KEENY,** b. of Windsor, Mar. 17, 1762	2	201
Remembrance, s. Remembrance & Marcy, b. Jan. 20, 1763	2	446
Sarah, d. Remembrance, Jr. & Sarah, b. May 19, 1753	2	442
Sarah, w. Remembrance, Jr., d. Nov. 7, 1761	2	273
SHEPARD, SHEPPARD, SHEPPERD, Elisha, Jr., of Hartford, m. Aurelia **ELMER,** of Windsor, May 20, 1824, by Rev. Augustus Bolles	2	202
Hannah, d. William & Hannah, b. Apr. 8, 1756	2	443
Mary L., m. Russel W. **CADWELL,** b. of Windsor, Nov. 28, 1832, by Rev. Ansel North	2	470
William, m. Hannah **GILLET,** b. of Windsor, Mar. 28, 1754	2	200
William, s. William & Hannah, b. Oct. 3, 1758	2	444
William, of Farmington, m. Sally **HIGLEY,** of Windsor, Nov. 29, 1821, by John Bartlett. Int. Pub.	2	201
SHERMAN, James S., of Suffield, m. Abigail T. **MORGAN,** of Windsor, Feb. 9, 1842, by Rev. S. D. Jewett	2	510
[SHERWOOD], [see under **SHARWOOD**]		
SIGLUR, Austin, of Fowler, O., m. Malissa L. **LAMBERTON,** of Windsor, May 13, 1849, by Rev. Cephus Brainard	2	514
SILL, Alfred H., m. Mary R. **HOPKINS,** b. of Cugahoga Falls, O., [ ], 1852, by Theo. A. Leete	2	503
Ann A., m. David **PINE,** Sept. 12, 1822, by Rev. Henry A. Rowland	2	500
Ann Allyn, d. Elisha N. & Chloe, b. Feb. 17, 1799	2	449
Charles Schott, s. Elisha N. & Chloe, b. Nov. 21, 1809	2	449
Edward Josiah, s. Elisha N. & Chloe, b. Aug. 21, 1811	2	449
Elisha N., d. May 14, [ ], ae 85	2	274
Elisha Noyes, m. Chloe **ALLYN,** d. Lieut. Josiah, Feb. 11, 1796	2	507
Elisha Noyes, s. Elisha N. & Chloe, b. Jan. 6, 1801	2	449
Elizabeth, d. May 8, 1819, ae 89 y.	2	274
Emily, m. Elisha S. **ALFORD,** b. of Windsor, Sept. 30, 1850, by Rev. James Rankin	2	463
George Denison, s. Elisha N. & Chloe, b. Oct. 25, 1819; d. Mar. 20, 1820	2	449
Henry Allyn, s. Elisha N. & Chloe, b. Sept. 19, 1805	2	449
Horace Hooker, s. Elisha Noyes & Chloe, b. Mar. 2, 1797	2	449
Horace Hooker, m. Charlotte **STRONG,** May 17, 1820	2	507
James Kingsbury, s. Elisha N. & Chloe, b. Apr. 15, 1813	2	449
Joseph F., s. John, d. Aug. 13, 1839, ae 58	2	533
Julia, m. Samuel **MATHER,** b. of Windsor, Nov. 22, 1843, by Rev. S. D. Jewett	2	508
Mary M., m. Oliver R. **HOLCOMB,** of East Granby, Mar. 3, 1851, by Rev. James Rankin	2	476
Theodore, m. Elisha N. & Chloe, b. Jan. 12, 1808	2	449
Theodore, m. Elizabeth N. **ROWLAND,** June 20, 1833, by		

	Vol.	Page
SILL, (cont.)		
Henry A. Rowland	2	508
William Frederick Augustus, s. Elisha N. & Chloe, b.		
June 16, 1817	2	449
SIMMONS, Abel, s. Abel & Rhoda, d. Nov. 15, 1833, at Athens,		
Ga., ae 24	2	274
Eunice N., of Windsor, m. Anson **LOOMIS**, of Bethlem,		
Conn., Oct. 25, 1836, by Rev. Charles Walker	2	489
Harry, of Durham, m. Marietta **ROCKWELL**, of Windham,		
Dec. 25, 1833, by Henry A. Rowland	2	508
Mary Ann, m. Robert **BEST**, Apr. 1, 1849, by Cornelius B.		
Everest	2	503
SIZER, Ephraim, of Westfield, m. Candice M. **GRISWOLD**, of		
Poquonock, Feb. 26, 1852, by Rev. T. H. Rouse	2	503
SKINNER, SKINER, Abigail, d. Daniel & Abigail, b. Sept. 22,		
1729	2	103
Abigail, m. Benjamin **COOK**, b. of Windsor, Nov. 30, 1758	2	137
Abigail, m. Giles **ALEXANDER**, Nov. 11, 1823, by Rev.		
Henry A. Rowland	2	125
Abijah, s. Joseph, Jr., b. Apr. 9, 1709	2	97
Ann, d. Joseph, Jr., b. Oct. 31, 1701	1	35
Ann, d. Azariah & Persilla, b. Nov. 25, 1761	2	445
Ann, of Windsor, m. Sylvester **HYNE**, of Ticonderoga, N.		
Y., Oct. 19, 1848	2	487
Ann, m. John **ROCKWELL**, [ ]	1	60
Anna, d. Thomas, b. Aug. 12, 1712	2	98
Anna, m. Jonah **LOOMIS**, b. of Windsor, June 19, 1734	2	172
Ashbell, s. Thomas, b. May 6, 1716	2	99
Aulia, m. William **LAMBERTON**, b. of Windsor, Aug. 5,		
1822, by Joseph H. Russell, J. P.	2	488
Azariah, s. Dea. Joseph, b. Dec. 10, 1719	2	100
Azariah, m. Azispah **MITCHELSON**, b. of Windsor, Aug.		
10, 1749	2	200
Azariah, s. Azariah & Rispah, b. July 27, 1750	2	441
Azariah, m. Persilla **STEVASON**, b. of Windsor, Mar. 16,		
1758	2	200
Benjamin, s. Richard, b. July 20, 1716	2	100
Benjamin, of Windsor, m. Prudence **EASTON**, of Hartford,		
Nov. 9, 1747	2	200
Benjamin, s. Benjamin & Prudance, b. Apr. 20, 1762	2	445
Clarissa B., of Windsor, m. Philo **PORTER**, of Ellington,		
Mar. 29, 1838, by Eli Deniston	2	193
Daniel, s. Joseph, Jr., b. Apr. 1, 1703	2	97
Daniel, m. Abigail **SMITH**, b. of Windsor, Mar. 6, 1727/8	2	198
Daniel, s. Daniel & Abigail, b. Mar. 6, 1733/4	2	104
Daniel, m. Esther **WHITE**, b. of Windsor, May 15, 1765	2	201
David, s. Richard, b. May 21, 1707	2	97
David, m. Elizabeth **ELSWORTH**, b. of Windsor, Nov. 20,		

	Vol.	Page
SKINNER, SKINER, (cont.)		
1728	2	200
David, s. David & Elizabeth, b. Sept. 13, 1741	2	438
David, s. David & Elizabeth, d. May 26, 1751	2	272
Deborah, d. Isaac & Hannah, b. Sept. 15, 1733	2	104
Dorcas, d. Isaac & Dorcas, b. Dec. 10, 1755	2	443
Dosha, d. Benjamin & Prudance, b. Jan. 1, 1760	2	444
Dosha, d. Benjamin & Prudance, d. Nov. 23, 1762	2	273
Dosha, d. Benjamin & Prudance, b. [ ]; d. [ ]	2	443
Edatha, d. David & Elizabeth, b. Oct. 4, 1737	2	105
Edatha, m. Aaron **BOOTH**, b. of Windsor, Apr. 13, 1756	2	133
Eli, twin with Levi, s. Azriah & Persilla, b. Mar.13, 1763	2	446
Elizabeth, d. [Joseph & Marey], b. Jan. 23, 1669	MG	
Elizabeth, m. John **GRANT**, June 1, 1690	Col.D	55
Elizabeth, m. John **GRANT**, June 5, 1690	1	57
Elizabeth, d. Joseph, Jr., b. Oct. 21, 1706	2	97
Elisabeth, d. David & Elisabeth, b. Aug. 27, 1730	2	440
Esther, w. Dea. Joseph, d. Dec. 28, 1755	2	273
Esther, d. John & Sarah, b. Sept. 15, 1763; d. Jan. 9, 1764	2	446
Esther, d. Azariah & Persilla, b. Jan. 11, 1767	2	448
Eunice, m. Thomas **DRAKE**, b. of Windsor, Jan. 25, 1750	2	143
Ezekiel, s. Thomas, b. June 26, 1710	2	96
Ezekiel, s. Thomas, d. Dec. 4, 1726	2	270
Fidelia, m. Henry H. **HOSKINS**, Sept. 28, 1832, by Henry A. Rowland	2	486
Gid[e]on, had 1 child d. [ ], in "Elenton" prior to 1740	MG	
Hannah, d. Joseph, Jr., b. Apr. 2, 1700	1	35
Hannah, d. Isaac, b. Sept. 21, 1720	2	101
Hannah, m. Noah **DRAKE**, b. of Windsor, Oct. 1, 1741	2	142
Hezakiah, s. Isaac & Dorcas, b. Apr. 10, 1758	2	444
Hezakiah, s. Isaac & Dorcas, d. May 7, 1761	2	273
Hezakiah, s. Isaac & Dorcas, b. Feb. 2, 1764	2	446
Isaac, s. Joseph, b. Aug. 16, 1691	1	34
Isaac, m. Hannah **MOORE**, Dec. 5, 1716	2	198
Isaac, s. Isaac, b. Oct. 7, 1717	2	100
Isaac, s. Isaac, Jr. & Dorcas, b. Mar. 11, 1746/7	2	440
Jemima, d. David & Elizabeth, b. Feb. 18, 1733/4	2	105
Jemima, m. William **BISSELL**, b. of Windsor, June 4, 1754	2	133
Jerusha, twin with Martha, d. Richard, b. May 19, 1714	2	100
John, s. Dea. Joseph, b. Apr. 19, 1725	2	102
John, of Windsor, m. Sarah **CANADA**, of Hartford, Nov. 21, 1762	2	201
John, s. John & Sarah, b. Mar. 5, 1765	2	447
Jonathan, s. Richard, b. June 30, 1709	2	97
Joseph, adult, ch. mem. 16[ ]	MG	
Joseph, m. Marey **FILLEY**, Apr. 5, 1666	MG	
Joseph, m. Mary **FFILLY**, b. of Windsor, Apr. 5, 1666	Col.1	45
Joseph, m. Mary **FILLEY**, b. of Windsor, Apr. 5, 1666	1	61

	Vol.	Page
SKINNER, SKINER, (cont.)		
Joseph, bp. Feb. 17, [16]78	MG	
Joseph, m. Mary **GRANT,** b. of Windsor, Mar. 13, 1694	1	62
Joseph, s. Joseph, Jr., b. Apr. 30, 1698	1	35
Joseph, Dr., m. Ester **DRAKE,** b. of Windsor, Aug. 21, 1718	2	198
Joseph, Dea., d. May 31, 1724	2	270
Joseph, Dea., d. Jan. 19, 1756	2	273
Joseph, contributed 0-2-6 to the poor in other colonies	MG	
Keziah, d. Isaac & Hannah, b. June 14, 1728	2	103
Levi, twin with Eli, s. Azariah & Persilla, b. Mar. 13, 1763	2	446
Luci, d. Dea. Joseph, b. Mar. 6, 1721/2	2	101
Lucia, d. Dea. Joseph, b. Oct. 12, 1723	2	101
Lucie, d. Dea. Joseph, d. Sept.* 3, 1724		
*("Apr." crossed out)	2	270
Lucie, d. Dea. Joseph, d. Oct. 28, 1736	2	271
Lucy, d. Isaac, Jr. & Dorcas, b. Feb. 16, 1745/6	2	439
Lucy, d. Azariah & Persilla, b. Sept. 22, 1759	2	444
Lucy, had s. William, b. Dec. 2, 1763	2	446
Martha, twin with Jerusha, d. Richard, b. May 19, 1714	2	100
Mary, wid., m. Owen **TUDOR,** Nov. 13, 16[ ]	MG	
Mary, wid., m. Owen **TUDOR,** b. of Windsor, Nov. 13, 1651	Col.2	159
Mary, m. Owin **TUDOR,** Nov. 13, 1651	1	62
Mary, d. [Joseph & Marey], b. Sept. 22, [16]67	MG	
Mary, d. Joseph, b. Sept. 22, 1667	1	33
Mary, d. Joseph, Jr., b. Dec. 26, 1695	1	35
Mary, w. Joseph, Jr., d. Apr. 15, 1711	2	270
Mary, d. Richard & Mary, b. July 12, 1728	2	103
Mary, d. Isaac & Hannah, b. Apr. 7, 1730	2	103
Mary, wid. Dea. Joseph (Elder), d. Aug. 26, 1734	2	271
Mary, d. Daniel & Abigail, b. May 18, 1738	2	106
Mary, d. Daniel & Abigail, d. Oct. 1, 1741	2	272
Mary, d. Oliver & Mary, b. Feb. 4, 1764	2	446
Maryanah, d. David & Elizabeth, b. Jan. 13, 1747/8	2	440
Masoanh*, d. David & Elizabeth, d. Oct. 22, 1749		
*(Probably "Maryann")	2	272
Noah, s. Thomas, b. Feb. 27, 1707/8	2	96
Oliver, s. Daniel & Abigail, b. May 29, 1736	2	105
Oliver, m. Mary **ROCKWELL,** b. of Windsor, Jan. 26, 1763	2	201
Prudence, d. Benjamin & Prudence, b. Dec. 31, 1750	2	441
Prudance, d. Benjamin & Prudance, b. Mar. 20, 1755	2	444
Rachel, d. Richard, b. Nov. 20, 1718	2	101
Richard, m. Sarah **GAINES,** Dec. 25, 1702	2	197
Richard, s. Richard, b. Jan. 3, 1703/4	2	97
Richard, m. Mary **GILLET,** b. of Windsor, Sept. 5, 1727	2	198
Rispah, d. Azariah & Rispah, b. Nov. 9, 1752	2	442
Rispah, w. Azariah, d. May 14, 1756	2	273
Roswell, s. Azariah & Rispah, b. Feb. 20, 1754	2	443
Samuell, s. Richard, b. Dec. 4, 1705	2	97

	Vol.	Page
SKINNER, SKINER, (cont.)		
Samuel, m. Sarah **WARD**, b. of Windsor, Mar. 24, 1741	2	200
Samuell, s. Samuell & Sarah, b. Oct. 18, 1747	2	440
Sarah, d. Richard, b. Apr. 9, 1711	2	100
Sarah, d. Samuel & Sarah, b. Aug. 27, 1743	2	440
Silas, s. Azariah & Persilla, b. Nov. 27, 1764	2	447
Thomas, s. Joseph, bp. Dec. 23, [16]77	MG	
Thomas, m. Sarah **GRANT**, July 19, 1705	2	197
Thomas, s. Thomas, b. May 1, 1706	2	96
Timothy, s. Daniel & Abigail, b. Apr. 18, 1732	2	104
Timothy, s. Daniel & Abigail, d. Mar. 7, 1737/8	2	271
Timothy, s. Daniell & Abigail, b. Apr. 4, 1741	2	439
William, s. Lucy, b. Dec. 2, 1763	2	446
William J., of Hartford, m. Jerusha Ann **PORTER**, of Windsor, Sept. 21, 1852, by Rev. H. N. Weed	2	482
SLADE, Aaron, s. James & Experience, b. July 4, 1751	2	448
Abner, s. James & Experience, b. May 5, 1756	2	448
Daniel, s. James & Experience, b. Jan. 14, 1759	2	448
Experience, d. James & Experience, b. Dec. 26, 1754	2	448
Hannah, d. James & Expereance, b. Apr. 12, 1765	2	448
Jacob, s. James & Experience, b. Mary 18, 1763	2	448
James, m. Experience **PARKER**, b. of Windsor, June 14,1750	2	201
James, s. James & Experience, b. Nov. 3, 1752	2	448
John, m. wid. Martha **GLESON**, b. of Windsor, Sept. 12, 1751	2	200
John, s. John & Martha, b. June 10, 1752	2	444
Martha, d. John & Martha, b. July 22, 1754	2	444
Mary, m. John **DORCHESSTER**, Dec. 13, 1744	2	142
Mary, d. James & Experience, b. Apr. 21, 1761	2	448
Samuell, s. William, Jr. & Esther, b. Sept. 3, 1747	2	440
Thankfull, d. Will[iam], Jr. & Esther, b. July 13, 1749	2	440
SLATER, SLAUGHTER, John, m. Abia **BARTLET**, formerly w. Esaia, July 15, 1669	Col.1	45
John, m. Abiah **BARTLETT**, formerly w. Elisha, July 15, 1669	1	61
SLAUGHTER, [see under **SLATER**]		
SLOPER, Elizabeth, had d. Mary, b. May 24, 1762	2	448
Mary, d. Elizabeth, b. May 24, 1762	2	448
SMITH, Abigail, d. John, b. June 22, 1707	2	101
Abigail, m. Daniel **SKINNER**, b. of Windsor, May 6, 1727/8	2	198
Alonzo, m. Almira **DRAKE**, Nov. 26, 1835, by H. A. Rowland	2	509
Benjamin, of Springfield, m. Hannah **PHELPS**, of Windsor, Feb. 22, 1725/6	2	198
Chauncey, m. Emily H. **SMITH**, b. of Suffield, Oct. 30, 1839, by Rev. S. D. Jewett	2	510
Eleanor, of Granby, m. Levi **ANDRUS**, of Suffield, Sept. 3, 1839, by Rev. Cephas Brainard	2	127

	Vol.	Page

SMITH, (cont.)

Emily H., m. Chauncey **SMITH**, b. of Suffield, Oct.
30, 1839, by Rev. S. D. Jewett — 2 — 510

Hannah, d. Samuell & Hannah, b. Oct. 10, 1749 — 2 — 441

Hannah, of Windsor, m. Samuel **AUSTIN**, of Hartford, Nov.
28, 1847, by Cephus Brainard — 2 — 463

Horatio N., of Oxford, N. H., m. Jane C. **VELEY**, of
Windsor, [ ], 30, [18], by Rev. Edmund Tenney, of
Hartford — 2 — 510

James, of Morrisvill, N. Y., m. Sally **HUBBARD**, of
Windsor, June 15, 1824, by Luther Fitch, J. P., Int. Pub. — 2 — 202

Joel, s. Samuell & Hannah, b. May 28, 1751 — 2 — 441

John, m. Abigael **ROCKWELL**, Nov. 9, 1704 — 2 — 197

John, m. John, b. Sept. 6, 1714 — 2 — 99

John, m. Sally **COOLIDGE**, June 11, 1826, by Rev. David
Miller — 2 — 507

John C., of Wallingford, m. Mary **BROWN**, of Windsor, Oct.
25, 1824, by Rev. John Bartlett. Int. Pub. — 2 — 203

Jonathan Worthington, of Suffield, m. Mary Ann **OMES**, of
Hartford, Jan. 31, 1832, by Rev. Augustus Bolles — 2 — 508

Martin, s. Samuel & Hannah, b. Aug. 3, 1759 — 2 — 445

Mary, Mrs., of Middletown, m. Samuel **TUDOR**, of Windsor,
Dec. 10, 1729 — 2 — 204

Prudence, d. Samuel & Hannah, b. Oct. 13, 1746 — 2 — 440

Rosanna, of Windsor, m. Edward S. **MAGIRA**, of Hartford,
Mar. 7, 1847, by Rev. George F. Kettell — 2 — 493

Ross, d. July 16, [16]61; bd. the 17th day (Drowned at
Massaco) — 1 — 51

Samuell, s. John, b. Aug. 10, 1717 — 2 — 100

Samuel L., of North Haven, m. Maria D. S. **GRISWOLD**, of
Windsor, Oct. 18, 1849, by E. B. Everest — 2 — 515

Sara, d. [ ], [16]61 — MG

Sara, m. John **MILLINGTON**, Apr. 14, [16]68, by Mr.
Mathew Allin — Col.1 — 45

Sarah, m. John **MILLINGTON**, b. of Windsor, Apr. 14,
1668, by Mathew Allyn — 1 — 59

Sarah, of Granby, m. Benjamin E. **BROWN**, of Suffield,
Nov. 25, 1838, by Rev. Jared R. Avery — 2 — 465

Theoder, s. Samuel & Hannah, b. May 12, 1753 — 2 — 442

Theoder, s. Samuel & Hannah, b. Mar. 28, 1757 — 2 — 445

Uriah, m. Fanny **COOK**, b. of Windsor, July 13, 1823, by
James Loomis, J. P. — 2 — 202

-----, m. Anne **BROWN**, b. of Windsor, Oct. 12, 1824, by
Rev. John Bartlett, of Wintonbury, In. Pub. — 2 — 203

SOOKES, Henery, d. [ ], [16]40 — MG

SOPER, SOOPER, Abigail, d. John & Phebe, b. May 6, 1741 — 2 — 442

David, s. John & Phebe, b. Dec. 15, 1738 — 2 — 442

Elizabeth, d. John & Phebe, b. Oct. 31, 1736 — 2 — 105

	Vol.	Page
SOPER, SOOPER, (cont.)		
Elizabeth, d. John & Phebe, b. Oct. 31, 1736	2	442
Frances C., of Windsor, m. Birge **CHAPMAN**, of Hartford, Nov. 27, 1851, by Cornelius B. Everest	2	497
Hellen M., of Windsor, m. Timothy **WICKHAM**, of Glastenbury, May 30, 1848, by C. B. Everest	2	520
Joel, s. John & Phebe, b. Feb. 1, 1734/5	2	442
John, m. Phebe **MOORE**, b. of Windsor, Jan. 20, 1730/1	2	199
John, s. John & Phebe, b. May 15, 1733	2	104
Maria Antionette, of Windsor, m. S. T. **MACKENOREY**, of Hartford, Dec. 26, 1836, by Rev. Charles Walker	2	496
Phebe, d. John & Phebe, b. Sept. 19, 1731	2	104
Samuel, of Sandersfield, Mass., m. Rhoda **DRAKE**, Nov. 30, 1828, by Rev. Henry A. Rowland	2	507
Sarah E., m. Edwin B. **HOLCOMB**, b. of Windsor, Apr. 4, 1852, by Cornelius B. Everest	2	520
Timothy, s. John & Phebe, b. Aug. 12, 1742	2	442
Virgil, of New Harmony, Ind., m. Martha **THRALL**, of Windsor, Sept. 16, 1833, by Rev. Daniel Heminway	2	508
SOUTHARD, Amanda, of Ware, Mass., m. Henry W. **DAYTON**, of Glastenbury, Apr. 5, 1847, by Rev. T. A. Leete	2	473
SPARKS, Noah, m. Margeret **STRONG**, b. of Windsor, July 29, 1736	2	199
SPEIR, David, s. David, now of Windsor, formerly of the Town of Coldrea, in the Cty. of Londondery, Ireland, b. Aug. 15, 1725	2	102
SPENCER, SPENSER, Asahel, m. Sarah **COOK**, b. of Windsor, Dec. 25, 1736	2	199
James H., of Windham, m. Pamela G. **GILLETT**, of Windsor, Jan. 19, 1823, by Rev. Augustus Bolles	2	202
Jeremiah M., of Hartford, m. Ann **CROSS**, of Windsor, Dec. 3, 1826, by Rev. Joseph Hough	2	507
John, of Suffield, m. Experience **GIBBS**, of Windsor, Oct. 30, 1706	2	197
Lamaria, d. George Otis & Theresa, b. Sept. 25, 1838	2	391
SPERRY, Philemon P., of Avon, m. Jane M. **GRISWOLD**, of Windsor, Sept. 23, 1832, by Rev. Ansel Nash	2	508
Theodore, m. Ann **GODDARD**, b. of East Windsor, Mar. 5, 1847, by T. A. Leete	2	482
SQUIRES, Eunice, m. Simeon **BLANCHARD**, Oct. 29, 1823, by Rev. Henry A. Rowland	2	149
Henry S., m. Delia **VELA**, b. of Windsor, May 5, 1841, by Rev. Daniel Hemenway	2	514
STAFFORD, Caroline L., m. Charles G. **BALDWIN**, May [2], 1847, by Rev. S. H. Allen	2	503
STAMFORD, [see under **STANFORD**]		
STANFORD, STAMFORD, STANNIFORD, Mary, m. Nicolas **WILTON**, Nov. 20, 1656	MG	

	Vol.	Page
STANFORD, STAMFORD, STANNIFORD, (cont.)		
Mary, m. Nicholas **WILTON**, Nov. 20, 1656	Col.2	159
Mary, m. Nicholas **WILTON**, b. of Windsor, Nov. 20, 1656	1	63
Mary, see Mary **WILTON**	Col.D	56
STANLEY, STANDLY, Sarah, m. Joseph **GAYLAR**, s. Walter,		
July 11, 1670	MG	
Sara, of Farmingtown, m. Joseph **GAYLAR**, s. Walter, of		
Windsor, July 14, 1670	Col.1	45
Timothy, of Farmington, m. Mary **STRONG**, d. John, of		
Windsor, Nov. 22, 1676	Col.1	46
Timothy, of Farmington, m. Mary **STRONG**, d. John, of		
Windsor, Nov. 22, 1676	TR1	1
Timothy, of Farmington, m. Mary **STRONG**, d. John, of		
Windsor, Nov. 22, 1676	1	61
STANNARD, STANARD, John, s. John & Eunice, b. Feb. 24,		
1729/30	2	103
John, of Hartford, m. Sally **GRAHAM**, of Windsor, Apr.		
3, 1834, by Rev. Henry Stanwood	2	509
Joseph, s. John & Eunice, b. Mar. 20, 1739	2	438
Josiah, of Haddam, m. Mrs. Betsey **CLARK**, of Windsor,		
Apr. 21, 1839, by Rev. Daniel Heminway	2	206
Mary, d. John & Eunice, b. Sept. 24, 1733	2	438
STANWOOD, John, of Newberryport, Mass., m. Candace		
GRAHAM, of Windsor, Nov. 30, 1820, by Rev.		
Augustus Bolles	2	201
STARKS, Cynthia, of Windsor, m. Lorenzo D. **ALLEN**, of		
Springfield, Jan. 1, 1827, by Rev. Henry A. Rowland	2	126
STARR, Anna, of Goshen, m. William F. **MILLER**, of Windsor,		
June 6, 1792	2	494
STEARNS, Martha, of Tolland, m. Daniel **MARSHEL**, of		
Windsor, June 23, 1747	2	179
STEBBINS, STEBENS, Lucy, m. Edward B. **MUNSEL,** Oct. 19,		
1834, by H. A. Rowland	2	496
Mary, m. Walter **GAYLAR**, Apr. [ ], 1648	MG	
STEDMAN, STEADMAN, Abigail, d. Joseph, Jr. & Abigail, b.		
May 24, 1753	2	443
Alexander, s. Joseph, Jr. & Abigail, b. May 26, 1748	2	441
Ebenezer, s. Joseph, b. Aug. 31, 1721	2	102
Joseph, m. Sarah **TAYLOR**, b. of Windsor, June 7, 1709	2	198
Joseph, s. Joseph, Jr. & Abigail, b. Aug. 10, 1748	2	441
Levi, s. Joseph, Jr. & Abigail, b. Nov. 26, 1740	2	439
Martha, d. Stephen & Martha, b. Mar. 14, 1743	2	441
Martha, m. Ebenezer **DRAKE,** Jr., b. of Windsor, Feb. 18,		
1762	2	143
Nathan, s. Joseph, Jr. & Abigail, b. Jan. 6, 1750	2	443
Phinias, s. Joseph, b. Nov. 26, 1723	2	102
Sarah, d. Joseph, b. May 22, 1710	2	98
Sarah, d. Joseph, d. July 3, 1710	2	269

	Vol.	Page

STEDMAN, STEADMAN, (cont.)

Sarah, 2nd, d. Joseph, b. Oct. 31, 1711	2	98
Stephen, s. Joseph, b. July 30, 1718	2	101
Stephen, s. Stephen & Martha, b. Aug. 28, 1749	2	441
Timothy, s. Joseph, Jr. & Abigail, b. Nov. 3, 1743	2	439
Violet, of Hartford, m. Thomas ROWEL, Jr., of Windsor, Mar. 16, 1699/1700	2	194

STEEL, Jerusha, of Hartford, m. Daniel MILLS, of Windsor,

Feb. 12, 1729/30	2	177

STEPHENSON, STEVANSON, Betty, d. Sarar, negro, b. Aug. 12,

17[ ]	2	449
Persilla, m. Azariah SKINNER, b. of Windsor, Mar. 16, 1758	2	200

STEVENS, STEPHENS, Abigail, d. John, b. Mar. 30, 1718

	2	101
Emely, of Windsor, m. Hiram PARSONS, of Sandisfield, Mass., Sept. 11, 1831, by Henry A. Rowland	2	193
Hannah, of Symsbury, m. Isaac GILLET, of Windsor, Dec. 28, 1742	2	157
Silvanus, s. John & Abigail, b. Apr. 2, 1726	2	102
William, of Southwick, Mass., m. Caroline A. ARNOLD, of Granby, Dec. 27, 1850, by Rev. S. H. Allen	2	502

STILES, STYLES, STILLES, STILLS, Abel, s. John, Sr., b. Mar.

5, 1708/9	2	98
Amelia, m. William WELCH, b. of Windsor, Aug. 14, 1821, by Joseph H. Russell, J. P.	2	210
Amos, s. Henry, Jr., b. Feb. 14, 1702/3	1	35
Ann, w. Ebenezer, d. July 7, 1726	2	271
Anna, had illeg. s. Israel OSBAND, b. July 2, 1751; reputed f. Israel OSBAND	2	441
Delia, m. Ruel VANHORN, Dec. 21, 1820, by Rev. Henry A. Rowland	2	207
Ebanezer, m. Ann DRAKE, b. of Windsor, Nov. 2, 1725	2	198
Ebenezer, m. Sarah PINNEY, b. of Windsor, Jan. 28, 1729/30	2	199
Elisabeth, d. [Henery & Elizabeth], b. Nov. 30, 1664	MG	
Elissabeth, d. Henery, b. Nov. 30, 1664	Col.1	54
Elizabeth, d. Henry, b. Nov. 30, 1664	1	33
Elizabeth, d. Samuel, b. Oct. 14, 1708	2	99
Elizabeth, m. John DENSLOW, b. of Windsor, Mar. [ ], 1720/1	2	141
Elizabeth, d. John, Jr. & Mary, b. Feb. 20, 1731/2	2	104
Ephraim, s. Frances, b. Aug. 3, 1645	1	34
Frances, had 4 children, b. in Windsor. Dated Aug. 17, 1677	MG	
Hanna, d. John, b. Mar. 23, [16]64/5	Col.1	55
Hannah, d. John, b. Mar. 23, 1664/5	1	33
Hannah, d. John, b. Mar. 23, 1664/5	1	35
Hannah, d. John, Jr., b. Oct. 9, 1711	2	98
Hannah, m. Isaac HAYDON, Nov. 19, 1736	2	162
Henery, d. [ ], [16]51	MG	
Henery, d. [ ], bd. Nov. 3, 1651	Col.2	160

	Vol.	Page
STILES, STYLES, STILLES, STILLS, (cont.)		
Henery, m. Elizabeth **WILLCOCKSON**, Apr. 16, 1663	MG	
Henry, m. Elizabeth **WILCOKSON**, Apr. 16, 1663	Col. 1	45
Henry, m. Elizabeth **WILCOXSON**, Apr. 16, 1663	1	61
Henery, had 5 children, b. in Windsor. Dated Aug. 17, 1677	MG	
Henry, s. Henry, Jr., b. Feb. 19, 1693	1	35
Henry, Jr., m. Sarah **PARSONS**, b. of Windsor, Nov. 1, 1698	1	62
Isaac, s. John, b. July 30, 1697	1	34
John, d. [ ], [16]62	MG	
John, d. June 4, 1662	Col. 1	55
John, d. June 4, 1662	1	51
John, s. John, b. Dec. 10, [16]63	Col. 1	54
John, s. John, b. Dec. 10, 1665	1	35
John, his w. [ ], d. Sept. 3, [16]74	Col. 1	58
John, his w. [ ], d. Sept. 3, [16]74	1	50
John, had 2 children b. in Windsor. Dated Aug. 17, 1677	MG	
John, his w. [ ], d. [Sept. 3*], [16]76 *(In Pencil)	MG	
John, d. Dec. 8, 1683	Col. D	56
John, d. Dec. 8, 1683	1	51
John, s. John, b. Dec. 17, 1692	1	34
John, Jr., m. Mary **OSBORN**, b. of Windsor, May 7, 1713	2	198
John, s. John, Jr., b. May 12, 1714	2	99
John, Sergt., m. Elizabeth **TAYLOR**, b. of Windsor, May 19, 1724	2	199
John, Sergt., d. Nov. 12, 1728	2	271
John, s. Sergt. John & Elizabeth, b. May 6, 1729	2	103
Jonah, s. Henry, Jr., b. June 24, 1700	1	35
Jonathan, m. Sarah **EGLSTONE**, Jan. 12, 1708/9	2	197
Jonathan, s. Jonathan, b. Apr. 28, 1722	2	101
Jonathan, s. Jonathan & Sarah, b. Mar. 18, 1725/6	2	102
Jonathan, Jr., d. Sept. 8, 1775	2	273
Jonathan, d. Dec. 30, 1775	2	274
Julia, of Windsor, m. Frederick H. **HALE**, of Glastenbury, Apr. 7, 1825, by Rev. Henry A. Rowland	2	166
Lucy, m. Gurdon **MUNSEL**, b. of Windsor, Nov. 7, 1751	2	179
Margret, d. [Henery & Elizbeth], b. Feb. 6, 1666	MG	
Margret, d. Henery, b. Feb. 6, 1666	Col. 1	45
Margret, d. Henery, b. Feb. 6, 1666	Col. 1	56
Margerit, d. Henry, b. Feb. 6, 1666	1	33
Margerit, d. John, b. Feb. 23, 1694/5	1	34
Margaret, m. Joseph **PECK**, Feb. 23, 1714/15	2	186
Martha, d. Samuel, b. Apr. 1, 1702	1	35
Martha, d. Samuel, b. Apr. 1, 1702	2	99
Martha, d. Samuel & Mary, b. Apr. 9, 1731	2	104
Martha, m. Joseph **OSBORN**, b. of Windsor, Dec. 30, 1736	2	184
Mary, d. [Henery & Elizabeth], b. Sept. 28, 1669	MG	
Mary, m. Isaac **EGELSTON**, Mar. 21, 1694/5	1	56
Mary, m. Isaak **EGESTONE**, b. of Windsor, Mar. 21, 1694/55	2	145

	Vol.	Page
STILES, STYLES, STILLES, STILLS, (cont.)		
Mary, wid. Job, d. Mar. 15, 1839, ae 77	2	526
Mary, wid. Job & d. of Job **DRAKE**, d. Mar. 15, 1839, ae 77	2	533
Mindwell, d. [Henery & Elizabeth], b. Dec. 19, 1671	MG	
Mindwell, d. Henry, d. Nov. 6, 1685	Col.D	56
Mindwell, d. Henry, d. Nov. 6, 1685	1	51
Noah, s. John, b. Jan. 31, 1703	1	35
Noah, s. Noah, b. Mar. 8, 1735/6	2	105
Rachel, d. Henry, Jr., b. June 21, 1696	1	35
Rachell, wid., d. [ ]	Col.D	57
Ruth, d. John, b. Feb. 5, 1690	Col.D	51
Ruth, d. John, b. Feb. 5, 1690/1	1	34
Ruth, m. Nathaniel **TAYLOR**, b. of Windsor, May 31, 1711	2	204
Samuell, s. [Henery & Elizabeth], b. May 16, 1674	MG	
Samuel, m. Martha **ELSWORTH**, b. of Windsor, Dec. [ ], 1701	1	62
Samuel, s. Samuel, b. Jan. 10, 1705	2	99
Samuel, d. Dec. 18, 1712	2	270
Samuel, m. Mary **PHELPS**, b. of Windsor, Feb. 19, 1729/30	2	199
Sara, d. John, m. Ep[h]ra[i]m **BANCROFT**, May 1, 1681	MG	
Sarah, m. Ephraim **BANCROFT**, May 5, 1681	Col.D	54
Sarah, m. Ephraim **BANCRAFT**, May 5, 1681	1	54
Sarah, d. Jonathan, b. July 26, 1711	2	98
Sarah, m. John **OSBORN**, b. of Windsor, Apr. 15, 1730	2	184
Sarah, d. Ebenezer & Ann, b. Apr. 25, 1731	2	104
Sarah, d. Feb. 19, 1784	2	274
Thomas, s. Henry, Jr., b. Aug. 12, 1690	1	35
STOCKBRIDGE, Lyman, of Hartford, m. Abigail A. **BARBER**, of Windsor, Dec. 11, 1829, by Henry A. Rowland	2	507
STONE, Anson B., of Springfield, m. Harriet E. **PHILLIPS**, of Hartford, May 5, 1839, by James Loomis, J. P.	2	510
S., of Litchfield, m. John **ROUNSAVELL**, of Baltimore, Dec. 12, 1841, by William Thompson	2	506
STOUGHTON, STOTON, STOWTON, Abiah, d. Samuel & Abiah, b. Mar. 6, 1734/5	2	439
Abiah, m. Solomon **ALLYN**, b. of Windsor, Dec. 8, 1756	2	125
Abigael, d. Capt. Thomas, b. Dec. 21, 1704	2	96
Abigail, d. Capt. Thomas, of Windsor, m. John **MOORE**, Jr., of Windsor, Dec. 2, 1724	2	176
Abigail, d. Capt. Thomas, m. John **MOORE**, Jr., b. of Windsor, Dec. 2, 1724, by Samuel Humphris, J. P.	2	177
Abigail, d. Sergt. Israel & Mary, b. May 30, 1731	2	104
Abigail, d. William & Abigail, b. Dec. 27, 1761	2	446
Alexander, s. Benjamin & Elizabeth, b. Sept. 8, 1749	2	447
Alce, d. Nathanael & Martha, b. May 1, 1736	2	105
Allice, d. Nath[anie]ll & Martha, b. Oct. 10, 1743	2	440
Ami, twin with Ann, d. John, b. Oct. 24, 1719	2	100
Amy, of Windsor, m. Nehemiah **DICKINSON**, of		

	Vol.	Page

STOUGHTON, STOTON, STOWTON, (cont.)

Hannah, d. John, b. Aug. 7, 1705	2	95
Hannah, d. Israel, b. June 3, 1719	2	100
Hannah, m. Giles ELSWORTH, b. of Windsor, Feb. 6, 1728/9	2	146
Harvey, m. Frances PINNEY, Oct. 8, 1823, by Henry A. Rowland	2	202
Harvey, s. Israel, d. Jan. 27, 1846, ae 59	2	533
Isaac, s. Capt. Thomas, b. Nov. 2, 1714	2	99
Isrell, s. [Thomas & Mary], b. Aug. 21, 1667	MG	
Israel, s. Thomas, b. Aug. 21, 1667	1	33
Israel, s. Samuel, decd., d. Dec. 14, 1712	2	270
Israel, s. Samuell, decd., d. Dec. 14, 1712 (Crossed out)	2	277
Israel, Sergt., m. Mary BIRGE, b. of Windsor, May 7, 1713	2	198
Israel, s. Israel, b. July 21, 1714	2	99
Israel, Sergt., d. Sept. 17, 1736	2	271
Jemima, d. Sergt. Israel & Mary, b. July 16, 1729	2	103
Jerusha, d. William & Elizabeth, b. Apr. 12, 1725	2	103
Jerusha, m. Benjamin NEWBERRY, b. of Windsor, Feb. 13, 1745/6	2	182
John, s. [Thomas & Mary], b. June 20, 1657	MG	
John, s. Thomas, b. June 20, 1657	Col.2	161
John, s. Thomas, b. June 20, 1657	1	33
John, m. Elizabeth BISSELL, Aug. 24, 1682	Col.D	54
John, s. John, b. Oct. 16, 1683	Col.D	51
John, s. John, b. Oct. 16, 1683	1	34
John, m. Sary FITCH, Jan. 23, 1689	Col.D	55
John, m. Sarah FITCH, Jan. 23, 1689	1	61
John, Jr., m. [E]unice BISSELL, b. of Windsor, May 28, 1706	2	197
John, s. John, Jr., b. Dec. 11, 1710	2	97
John, Sr., d. May 24, 1712	2	270
John, s. John, d. June 14, 1714	2	270
John, s. William & Elizabeth, b. Apr. 6, 1723	2	103
John, s. Nathanel & Martha, b. Nov. 22, 1733	2	105
John, d. Apr. 22, 1746	2	272
John, s. William, Jr. & Abigail, b. Jan. 18, 1746/7	2	440
John, m. Elizabeth BISSELL, Aug. 11, [ ]	1	61
Jonathan, s. Capt. Thomas, b. Oct. 21, 1710	2	97
Jonathan, d. Aug. 10, 1733	2	271
Jonathan, s. Benjamin & Elizabeth, b. Aug. 1, 1754	2	448
Joseph, s. John, Sr., d. June 11, 1709	2	269
Joseph, s. Nathaniel & Martha, b. July 31, 1738	2	439
Julia, m. Cicero ROBERTS, b. of Windsor, Apr. 11, 1849, by Rev. Samuel Law	2	502
Justavus, s. Daniel & Joanna, b. July 25, 1733	2	104
Lemmuel, s. Nathanel & Martha, b. Aug. 9, 1731	2	104
Lucie, d. Israel & Mary, b. June 8, 1727	2	102

	Vol.	Page

STOUGHTON, STOTON, STOWTON, (cont.)

Mabell, d. Capt. Thomas, b. Aug. 19, 1708	2	96
Mable, m. Samuel **BELCHER,** b. of Windsor, Aug. 17, 1732	2	130
Martha, d. John, Jr., b. Jan. 16, 1711/12	2	98
Martha, m. Samuel **STRONG,** b. of Windsor, Dec. 12, 1734	2	199
Martha, d. Nathaniell & Martha, b. Aug. 3, 1748	2	441
Mary, d. [Thomas & Mary], b. Jan. 1, 1658	MG	
Mary, d. Thomas, b. Jan. 1, 1658	1	33
Mary, d. Thomas, of Windsor, m. Samuell **FFARNWORTH,** of Dorchester, June 3, [16]77	MG	
Mary, d. Thomas, of Windsor, m. Samuel **FARMESWORTH,** of Dorchester, Mass., June 3, 1677, by Capt. Newbery	Col.1	46
Mary, d. Thomas, of Windsor, m. Samuell **FFARNWORTH,** of Dorchester, Mass., June 3, 1677, by Capt. Nubery	TR1	1
Mary, d. Thomas, of Windsor, m. Samuel **FARNSWORTH,** of Dorchester, Mass., June 3, 1677, by Capt. Newbery	1	56
Mary, d. Capt. Thomas, b. Jan. 4, 1692/3	1	35
Mary, d. John, Sr., b. Nov. 25, 1708	2	96
Mary, m. Pelitiah **ALLYN,** b. of Windsor, Aug. 26, 1711	2	123
Mary, Mrs., d. Feb. 8, 1711/12	2	270
Mary, d. Sergt. Israel, b. Feb. 28, 1715/16	2	99
Mary, wid. Israel, d. Aug. 23, 1755	2	273
Mary, see Mary **FARNSWORTH**	Col.D	56
Mahetabel, d. Lieut. Thomas & Mahetabel, b. Apr. 18, 1725	2	105
Mihitabel, w. Lieut. Thomas, d. Jan.19, 1731/2	2	271
Mehitabel, d. Lieut. Thomas & Mehitabel, d. Feb. 5, 1744/5	2	272
Noami, d. William, b. Nov. 13, 1713	2	99
Naomi, d. William, Jr. & Abigail, b. Mar. 8, 1744/5	2	439
Nathanael, s. John, b. June 23, 1702	1	35
Nathanael, m. Martha **ELSWORTH,** b. of Windsor, Sept. 11, 1729	2	198
Nathaniel, s. Nathaniel & Martha, b. Mar. 6, 1746	2	440
Oliver, s. William & Elizabeth, b. May 19, 1727	2	103
Rachel, d. John, Sr., b. Aug. 25, 1711	2	98
Rachel, m. Nathaniel **STRONG,** b. of Windsor, June 2, 1747	2	200
Rebeca, d. [Thomas & Mary], b. June 19, 1673	MG	
Rebekah, d. Thomas, b. June 19, 1673	1	33
Rebekah, m. Atherton **MATHER,** Sept. 20, 1694	1	59
Rebekah, d. Israel, b. Mar. 10, 1720/1	2	101
Roxolania, d. Daniel & Joanna, b. Oct. 13, 1734	2	104
Russell, s. William & Abigail, b. Apr. 3, 1752	2	443
Samuell, s. [Thomas & Mary], b. Sept. 8, 1665	MG	
Samuel, s. Thomas, b. Sept. 8, 1665	1	33
Samuel, s. Samuel, b. Dec. 10, 1702	1	35
Samuell, d. Dec. 1, 1711	2	269
Samuel, s. Samuell & Abiah, b. May 27, 1737	2	439
Samuel W., m. Emely **GRISWOLD,** b. of Windsor, Nov. 22,		

	Vol.	Page
STOUGHTON, STOTON, STOWTON, (cont.)		
1824, by Rev. Augustus Bolles, of Wintonbury	2	203
Sara, d. [ ], [16]52	MG	
Sarah, d. [ ]; bd. May 31, 1652	Col.2	160
Sarah, d. John, b. June 26, 1723	2	101
Sarah, d. Sergt. Israel, b. Sept. 26, 1724	2	102
Sarah, d. Israel, d. Oct. 7, 1755	2	273
Sarah, m. John A. **HEMPSTED,** Sept. 7, 1830, by John Bartlett	2	484
Sibil, d. William & Elizabeth, b. June 9, 1730	2	103
Sibble, m. Joseph **NEWBERRY,** Jr., b. of Windsor, July 6, 1749	2	182
Thomas, of Windsor, m. Mary **WADSWORTH,** of Hartford, Nov. 30, 1655	Col.2	159
Thomas, Sr., d. [ ], [16]61	MG	
Thomas, Sr., d. Mar. 25, 1661; bd. the 27th day	1	51
Thomas, s. [Thomas & Mary], b. Nov. 21, 1662	MG	
Thomas, s. Thomas, b. Nov. 21, [16]62	Col.1	54
Thomas, s. Thomas, b. Nov. 21, 1662	1	33
Thomas, had 7 children b. in Windsor. Dated Aug. 17, 1677	MG	
Tho[mas], d. Sept. 15, 1684	Col.D	56
Thomas, d. Sept. 15, 1684	1	51
Thomas, Ens., of Windsor, m. Dorithi **TALCUTT,** of Hartford, Dec. 31, 1691	1	61
Thomas, Capt., of Windsor, m. Abigail **LOTHROP,** of Hartford, May 19, 1697	1	62
Thomas, s. Capt. Thomas, b. Apr. 9, 1698	1	35
Thomas, Jr., of Windsor, m. Mehitable **LOTHRUP,** of Norwich, Oct. 3, 1722	2	198
Thomas, s. Thomas, Jr., b. Sept. 29, 1723	2	102
Thomas, Capt., d. Jan. 14, 1748/9	2	272
Thomas, m. Mary **WADSWORTH,** [ ]	MG	
Thomas, contributed 0-2-6 to the poor in other colonies	MG	
Timothy, s. Capt. Thomas, b. June 27, 1703	2	96
W[illia]m, s. John, b. Mar. 10, 1685/6	Col.D	51
William, s. John, b. Mar. 10, 1685/6	1	34
William, m. Elizabeth **STRICKLAND,** July 6, 1710	2	197
William, s. William, b. Aug. 2, 1715	2	99
William, Sergt., m. Martha **WOLCUTT,** b. of Windsor, July 17, 1735	2	199
William, Jr., m. Abigail **WOLCUTT,** b. of Windsor, Feb. 8, 1743/4	2	199
William, s. William & Abigail, b. June 6, 1750	2	443
Zerviah, d. Lieut. Thomas & Mahetabel, b. Mar. 26, 1729	2	105
STOWELL, Bishop, of Brookline, m. Lovina **PEASE,** of Suffield, Feb. 27, 1837, by Rev. Henry Robinson	2	509
STRATTON, Nancy, m. Isaac P. **DAVIS,** of Northampton, Nov. 19, 1840, by S. D. Lewett	2	145

	Vol.	Page
STRONG, STRONGE, (cont.)		
David, s. Samuel, d. Apr. 18, 1708	2	269
David, s. Samuel & Martha, b. June 4, 1736	2	105
Elijah, s. John Wareham & Azubah, b. Dec. 22, 1735	2	106
Elijah, s. John Wareham, d. Nov. 22, 1737	2	271
Elijah, 2nd, s. John Wareham & Azubah, b. Feb. 20, 1738/9	2	106
Elijah, s. Abel & Elizabeth (WAKEMAN), b. Nov. 28, 1780	2	448
Elisha, s. John Wareham & Azubah, b. Dec. 31, 174[ ]	2	442
Elisha Bebee, m. Dolly G. HOOKER, June 24, 1813	2	201
Elisha Bebee, m. Dolly G. HOOKER, June 24, 1813	2	522
Elisabeth, d. John, Sr., b. Feb. 24, 1674	MG	
Elizabeth, d. John, b. Feb. 24, 1647	1	34
Elisabeth, d. [Return & Sara], b. Feb. 20, 1670	MG	
Eliz[abeth], w. John, d. June 7, 1684	Col.D	56
Elizabeth, w. John, d. June 7, 1684	1	51
Elizabeth, d. John, b. Sept. 21, 1689	1	34
Elizabeth, d. Return, Jr., b. Nov. 19, 1701	1	34
Elizabeth, d. Return, Jr., d. Dec. 30, 1701	1	51
Elisabeth, of Windsor, m. Nathan[ie]ll **BOREMAN**, of Wethersfield, Apr. 30, 1707	2	128
Elizabeth, d. Reuben, Jr., b. Aug. 13, 1708	2	96
Elizabeth, m. Thomas **BURNHAM**, Jr., Nov. 9, 1711	2	128
Elizabeth, d. Return, Jr., decd., d. July 9, 1714	2	270
Elizabeth, d. John Wareham & Abigail, b. Aug. 9, 1728	2	103
Elizabeth, m. David **DRAKE**, b. of Windsor, Mar. 12, 1747	2	142
Elizabeth, d. Abel & Elizabeth (WAKEMAN), b. Feb. 6, 1776	2	448
Elizabeth, d. Asel & Elizabeth (WAKEMAN), d. July 11, 1791	2	274
Ellen, d. Return & Sarah, b. Apr. 1, 1756; d. May 15, 1756, ae 6 wks.	2	443
Ellin, d. John, Jr. & Sarah, b. Jan. 22, 1759	2	445
Elnathan, s. John & Hephzibah, b. July 30, 1740	2	438
Elnathan, s. John & Hephzibah, d. Sept. 25, 1751	2	272
Est[h]e[r], d. John, of Northampton, m. Thomas **BISSELL**, s. Thomas, Sr., Oct. 15, 1678	MG	
Esther, d. John, b. Apr. 12, 1699	2	98
[E]unice, d. Jacob, b. Aug. 17, 1710	2	97
Eunice, d. Samuel, Jr. & Martha, b. Dec. 21, 1737	2	105
Eunice, d. Abel & Elizabeth (WAKEMAN), b. Feb. 21, 1790	2	449
Experenc[e], d. [John, Sr.], b. & bp. Aug. 4, 1650	MG	
Experience, d. John, bp. Aug. 4, 1650	1	34
Experence, m. Zarobabel **FYLAR**, May 27, 1669	MG	
Experenc, m. Sur Roball* **FYLAR**, b. of Windsor, May 27, 1669, by Mr. Newbery *(Note by LBB: "Zerubbabel")	Col.1	45
Experience, m. Zerubbable **FYLER**, b. of Windsor, May 27, 1669, by Mr. Nubery, Com.	1	56
Hanna, d. [John, Sr.], b. May 30, 1659	MG	

	Vol.	Page
STRONG, STRONGE, (cont.)		
Hannah, d. John, b. May 30, 1659	1	34
Hanna, d. [John, Jr. & Mary], b. Aug. 11, 1660	MG	
Hannah, d. John, b. Aug. 11, 1660	1	33
Hanna, [bp.] Sept. 2, [16]60	MG	
Hannah, d. John, Jr., b. May 8, 1692	1	34
Hannah, m. Nicholas **BUCKLAND**, June 16, 1698	1	54
Hannah, m. Samuel **CHAPMAN**, b. of Windsor, Aug. 8,		
1717	2	135
Hannah, had illeg. d. Rachel, b. Mar. 28, 1723/4; reputed		
f. Joseph **ROOSE**, of Boston	2	102
Hannah, d. Abel & Elizabeth (**WAKEMAN**), b. Dec. 18,		
1785	2	449
Hannah, d. Lieut. Return, b. [ ]	1	34
Harve, s. Nathaniel & Elizabeth, b. Mar. 22, 1763	2	446
Hephzibah, d. John & Hephzibah, b. Apr. 11, 1742	2	439
Hester, d. [John, Sr.], b. June 7, 1661	MG	
Hester, d. John, b. June 7, 1661	1	34
Hester, d. John, elder, m. Thomas **BISSELL**, Jr., s. Thomas,		
Sr., Oct. 15, 1678, at Northampton	Col.1	46
Hester, d. John, Elder, m. Thomas **BISSELL**, s. Thomas, Sr.,		
Oct. 15, 1678, at Northampton	TR1	1
Hester, d. John, Elder, m. Thomas **BISSELL**, s. Thomas,		
Sr., Oct. 15, 1678, at Northampton	1	54
J., his w. [ ], adm. ch. & communicant Aug. [ ], 1666	MG	
Jacob, s. [John, Jr. & Elizabeth], b. Apr. 8, 1673	MG	
Jacob, s. John, b. Apr. 8, 1673	1	33
Jacob, m. Abigail **BISSELL**, Nov. 10, 1698	1	61
Joannah, d. Josiah, b. Oct. 12, 1699	1	34
John, Jr., m. Mary **CLARK**, Nov. 26, 1656	MG	
John, m. Mary **CLARKE**, Nov. 26, 1656	Col.2	159
John, m. Mary **CLARK**, b. of Windsor, Nov. 26, 1656	1	61
John, his w. [ ], d. [ ], [16]63	MG	
John, his w. [ ], d. Apr. 28, 1663	Col.1	55
John, Jr., m. 2nd w. Elizabeth **WARRENOR**, [ ]	MG	
John, s. John, Jr. & Elizabeth, b. Dec. 25, 1665	MG	
John, s. John, b. Dec. 25, 1665	Col.1	55
John, s. John, b. Dec. 25, 1665	1	33
John, taxed 2-0 on Feb. 10, [16]73	MG	
John, Jr., had 4 children b. in Windsor. Dated Aug. 17, 1677	MG	
John, Sr., had 6 children b. in Windsor. Dated Aug. 17, 1677	MG	
John, of Windsor, m. Hana **TRUMBLE**, of Suffield, Nov.		
26, 1686	Col.D	54
John, of Windsor, m. Hannah **TRUMBLE**, of Suffield,		
Nov. 26, 1685* *("1689?")	1	61
John, d. Feb. 20, 1697/8	1	51
John, his w., bp. & adm. ch. Aug. [ ], [16]	MG	
John, adult, ch. mem. 16[ ]	MG	

	Vol.	Page
STRONG, STRONGE, (cont.)		
John, contributed 0-11-0 to the poor in other colonies	MG	
John, s. Josiah, b. June 17, 1701	1	34
John, s. John, b. July 14, 1707	2	98
John, s. John Wareham & Abigail, b. June 24, 1733	2	106
John, m. Hepzibah **WOLCUTT**, b. of Windsor, Nov. 10, 1737	2	199
John, d. May 29, 1749	2	272
John, s. John & Hepzibah, b. Aug. 12, 1754	2	444
John, s. John & Sarah, b. May 28, 1760	2	445
John Stoughton, s. Samuel & Martha, b. Mar. 8, 1746/7	2	440
John Rearam*, s. Reuben, Jr., b. Sept. 30, 1706 ("Rearam" in pencil. Probably meant for "Wareham")	2	95
John Wareham, m. Abigael **THRALL**, b. of Windsor, Nov. 30, 1727	2	198
John Wareham, m. Azubah **GRISWOLD**, b. of Windsor, Mar. 27, 1734/5	2	199
John Wareham, d. Apr. 25, 1752, in the 46th y. of his age	2	273
Jonathan, s. John, b. Apr. 22, 1694	1	34
Joseph, twin with Samuell, s. [John, Sr.], b. & bp. Aug. 5, 1652	MG	
Joseph, twin with Samuel, s. John, b. Aug. 5, 1652	Col.2	156
Joseph, twin with Samuel, s. John, b. [ ]; bp. Aug. 5, 1652	1	34
Joseph, s. Return, b. Feb. 7, 1694	1	34
Joseph, s. Lieut. Return, d. Dec. [ ], 1696	1	51
Josia, s. [John, Jr. & Elizabeth], b. Jan. 11, [1678]; bp. Jan. 12, 1678	MG	
Josia, s. John, b. Jan. 11, 1678	Col.1	56
Josiah, m. Joannah **GILLIT**, Jan. 5, 1698/9	1	61
Josiah, s. John, b. Jan. 11, [ ]; bp. 12th day	1	34
Loranah, d. John & Hepzibah, b. Feb. 8, 1739	2	106
Lucie, d. Samuel, Jr. & Martha, b. Apr. 4, 1735	2	105
Margerit, d. Lieut. Return, b. Apr. 28, 1700	1	34
Margeret, m. Noah **SPARKS**, b. of Windsor, July 29, 1736	2	199
Martha, d. Samuel, b. June 3, 1704	2	95
Martha, d. Samuell, d. June 26, 1704	2	269
Martha, d. Samuell, b. Nov. 25, 1709	2	96
Martha, d. Samuel, Jr. & Martha, b. May 6, 1739	2	106
Martha, wid. Samuel, d. Dec. 5, 1770	2	273
Mary, d. [John, Sr.], b. Oct. 26, 1654	MG	
Mary, d. John, b. Oct. 26, 1654	Col.2	158
Mary, d. John, b. Oct. 26, 1654	1	34
Mary, d. [John, Jr. & Mary], b. Apr. 22, 1658	MG	
Mary, d. John, b. Apr. 22, 1658	1	33
Mary, [bp.] Apr. 25, [16]58	MG	
Mary, w. John, Jr., d. Apr. 28, 1663	MG	
Mary, d. John, of Windsor, m. Timothy **STANDLY**, of		

	Vol.	Page
STRONG, STRONGE, (cont.)		
Farmington, Nov. 22, 1676	Col.1	46
Mary, d. John, of Windsor, m. Timothy **STANDLY,** of		
Farmington, Nov. 22, 1676	TR1	1
Mary, d. John, of Windsor, m. Timothy **STANLY,** of		
Farmington, Nov. 22, 1676	1	61
Mary, d. John, b. May 24, 1688	1	34
Mary, d. Return, Sr., d. Oct. 28, 1708	2	269
Mary, d. Sergt. John, d. Dec. 12, 1718	2	270
Mary, d. Samuel, b. Feb. 20, 1719/20	2	101
Mary, w. John, d. July 4, 1747	2	272
Mary, d. John & Hephzibah, b. Sept. 14, 1749	2	441
Mary, d. John & Hephzibah, d. Sept. 18, 1751	2	272
Mindwell, d. Jacob, b. July 19, 1701	2	97
Nathan, s. Abel & Elizabeth (**WAKEMAN**), b. Oct. 30, 1783	2	449
Nathaniel, s. Jacob, b. Sept. 11, 1712	2	100
Nathaniel, m. Rachel **STOUGHTON,** b. of Windsor, June 2,		
1747	2	200
Nathaniel, m. Elizabeth **GRANT,** b. of Windsor, Apr. 20,		
1755	2	200
Nathaniel, s. Nathaniel & Elizabeth, b. Feb. 13, 1756	2	443
Rachel, illeg. d. Hannah **STRONG,** b. Mar. 28, 1723/4;		
reputed f. Joseph **ROOSE,** of Boston	2	102
Rachel, d. Nathaniel & Rachel, b. June 2, 1750	2	441
Rachel, w. Nathaniell, d. June 16, 1750	2	272
Rachel, d. Nathaniell & Rachel, d. Oct. 26, 1751	2	272
Return, bp. Mar. 12, [16]64	MG	
Return, m. Sara **WARHAM,** May 11, 1664	MG	
Returne, m. Sara **WARHA,** May 11, 1664, by Mr. Clark	Col.1	45
Return, his w. [ ], adm. ch & communicant Jan. [ ],		
1665	MG	
Returne, s. [Return & Sara], b. Feb. 10, 1668	MG	
Return, s. Return, b. Feb. 10, 1668	1	33
Return, had 7 children b. in Windsor. Dated Aug. 17, 1677	MG	
Returne, his w. [ ]*, d. Dec. 26, 1678, ae 36 *(Note by		
LBB; "Sarah (**WARHAM**) STRONG")	Col.1	58
Return, Cornet, m. Margaret **NEWBERY,** May 23, 1689	Col.D	54
Return, Cornet, m. Margret **NUBERY,** May 23, 1689	1	61
Return, adult, ch. mem. 16[ ]	MG	
Return, his w. [ ], adm. to Ch. [16]	MG	
Return, of Windsor, m. Elizabeth **BURREL,** of Stratford,		
June 19, 1700	1	62
Return, s. Return, Jr., b. Dec. 30, 1702	1	35
Return, s. Return, Jr., d. Jan. 24, 1702/3	1	51
Return, Jr., 3rd child [Lieut. Return], b. Jan. 8, 1703/4;		
d. 10th day of same month	1	35
Return, Jr., d. Aug. 6, 1708	2	269
Return, Lieut., d. Apr. 9, 1726	2	270

	Vol.	Page
STRONG, STRONGE, (cont.)		
Return, contributed 0-5-0 to the poor in other colonies	MG	
Reuben, s. Samuel, b. Feb. 26, 1712/13	2	99
Ruth, d. Samuel & Martha, b. Dec. 2, 1744	2	439
Samuell, twin with Joseph, s. [John, Sr.], b. & bp.		
Aug. 5, 1652	MG	
Samuel, twin with Joseph, s. John, b. Aug. 5, 1652	Col.2	156
Samuel, twin with Joseph, s. John, b.[ ]; bp. Aug. 5, 1652	1	34
Samuell, s. [Return & Sara], b. May 20, 1673; d. at the age		
of 10 wks.	MG	
[Samuel*], s. Return, d. [July 28*], [16]73 *(In pencil)	MG	
Samuel, s. Return, d. July 28, 1673	Col.1	58
Samuel, s. Return, d. [ ]; bd. July 28, [16]73, ae 10 wks.	1	51
Samuel, s. Return, b. Dec. 26, 1675	1	34
Samuell, s. [Return & Sara], b. Dec. 27, [16]75; bp. Jan. 2,		
[16]75	MG	
Samuel, m. Martha **BUCKLAND**, b. of Windsor, Nov. 9,		
1699	1	61
Samuell, s. Samuell, b. July 16, 1705	2	96
Samuel, m. Martha **STOUGHTON**, b. of Windsor, Dec. 12,		
1734	2	199
Samuel, d. Jan. 15, 1741/2	2	271
Samuel, s. Samuel & Martha, b. July 8, 1743	2	439
Sara, d. [Return & Sara], b. Mar. 14, 1664	MG	
Sarah, d. Returne, b. Mar. 14, 1664	Col.1	54
Sara, w. Return, d. Dec. 26, [16]78, ae 36 y. last Aug.	MG	
Sara, w. Return, d. Dec. 26, 1678	MG	
Sarah, m. Joseph **BISSELL**, July 7, 1687	1	54
Sarah, d. Samuel, b. Jan. 1, 1700/1	1	34
Sarah, m. Daniel **PHELPS**, b. of Windsor, Mar. 23, 1726/7	2	187
Sarah, d. John Wareham & Abigail, b. May 13, 1731	2	106
Seth L., m. Phebe A. **PIERCE**, b. of Windsor, Aug. 13, 1848,		
by C. B. Everist	2	482
Thomas, m. Mary **HEWIT**, b. of Windsor, Dec. 5, 1660	Col.1	45
Thomas, m. Mary **HUIT**, b. of Windsor, Dec. 5, 1660	1	61
Zerviah, d. John, Jr. & Hephzibah, b. Dec. 13, 1745	2	440
Zeruiah, d. John & Hephzibah, d. Sept. 17, 1751	2	272
Zeruiah, d. John & Hephzibah, b. July 25, 1752	2	442
STYLES, [see under **STILES**]		
SULLIVAN, Timothy, m. Mrs. [ ] **BROOKS**, Sept. 19, 1852, by		
Rev. James Smyth	2	460
SWEET, Ellen, m. Sylvester **VANHORN**, b. of Hartford, Nov. 27,		
1838, by Rev. Jared R. Avery	2	511
SWEETSER, Henry P., of Hartford, m. Mary E. **ALLEN**, of		
Windsor, May 21, 1842, by Rev. S. D. Jewett	2	516
SWETLAND, Cynthia, of Hartford, m. Gideon **SEARLS**, of		
Windsor, Sept. 9, 1761	2	200
Isaac, s. Benjamin & Sarah, b. June 21, 1762	2	446

	Vol.	Page
TAYLOR, TAYLER, TALER, TAYLAR, (cont.)		
Hannebal, of Fowler, O., m. Belinda **LAMBERT**, of		
Windsor, June 2, 1850, by Rev. T. A. Leet	2	206
Jerusha, d. Nathaniel, b. Mar. 15, 1713/14	2	107
Joanna, m. Ephraim **BISSELL**, b. of Windsor, Dec. 24, 1702	1	54
Joanna, m. Samuell **TUDOR**, Feb. 7, 1708/9	2	203
John, s. [Stephen & Sara], b. Mar. 22, 1652	MG	
John, bp. Mar. 28, [16]52	MG	
John, had 3 children b. in Windsor. Dated Aug. 17, 1677	MG	
Keziah, d. Nathanael & Ruth, b. Oct. 23, 1726	2	108
Keziah, m. Elisha **MUNCIL**, b. of Windsor, Dec. 27, 1750	2	179
Margerit, d. Nathanael & Ruth, b. July 12, 1724	2	108
Mary, d. [Stephen & Sara], b. June 18, 1661	MG	
Mary, d. Stephen, b. June 18, 1661	1	35
Mary, [bp.] June 23, [16]61	MG	
Mindwell, d. [Stephen & Sara], b. Nov. 6, 1663	MG	
Mindwell, [bp.] Nov. 8, [16]63	MG	
Nath[an], s. Stev[en], d. July 3, [16]82	Col.D	56
Nathanell, s. [Stephen & Sara], b. May 24, 1668	MG	
Nathanael, s. Stephen, b. May 24, [ ], bp. the 31st	1	35
Nathanael, s. Stephen, d. July 3, [ ]	1	51
Nathaniel, m. Ruth **STILES**, b. of Windsor, May 31, 1711	2	204
Nathanael, d. May 6, 1736	2	275
Nathaniell, had 3 children d. [ ], in "Elenton"		
prior to 1740	MG	
Nathaniel, d. [ ], in "Elenton" prior to 1740	MG	
Ruth, d. Nathaniel, b. Apr. 3, 1712	2	107
Ruth, m. Simon **PEARSON**, b. of Windsor, Dec. 25, 1738	2	188
Samuell, s. [Stephen & Sara], b. Oct. 8, 1647	MG	
Samuell, m. Mary **BANKES**, Oct. 27, 1670, by Mr. Wolcot	Col.1	46
Samuell, s. John, b. Apr. 11, 1691	Col.D	51
Samuel, s. John, b. Apr. 11, 1691	1	36
Sarah, m. Joseph **STEDMAN**, b. of Windsor, June 7, 1709	2	198
Stephen, m. Sara **HOSFORD**, Nov. 1, 1642	MG	
Stephen, m. Ann **HOSFORD**, Nov. 1, 1642	1	62
Stephen, s. [Stephen & Sara], b. Mar. 11, 1644	MG	
Stephen, bp. Mar. 16, [16]44	MG	
Stephen, adm. ch. & communicant Mar. [ ], 1644	MG	
Stephen, m. Elizbeth **NOWEL**, Oct. 25, 1649	1	62
Ste[phe]n, his w. [ ], adm. ch. & communicant Aug.		
[ ], 1666	MG	
Stephen, taxed 4-0 on Feb. 10, [16]73	MG	
Stephen, Jr., m. Johana **PORTER**, of Farmington, Nov. 8,		
[16]76	Col.1	46
Stephen, Jr., m. Johana **PORTER**, of Farmington, Nov. 8,		
[16]76	TR1	1
Stephen, Jr., m. Johana **PORTER**, of Farmington, Nov. 8,		
[16]76	1	62

	Vol.	Page
TAYLOR, TAYLER, TALER, TAYLAR, (cont.)		
Stephen, had 8 children b. in Windsor. Dated Aug. 17, 1677	MG	
Stephen, s. Stephen, b. May 8, 1685	1	36
Stephen, s. Stephen, b. May 9, 1685	Col.D	51
Stephen, s. Stephen, b. May 9, 1685	1	36
Stephen, Sr., d. Sept. 1, 1688	1	51
Stephen, communicant 16[ ]	MG	
Stephen, his w. [ ], adm. ch. Aug. [ ], 16[ ]	MG	
Stephen, Sr., d. Aug. 8, 1707	2	274
Stephen, d. Oct. [ ], 1709	2	274
Stephen, Jr., contributed 0-4-0 to the poor in other colonies	MG	
Stephen, Sr., contributed 0-5-0 to the poor in other colonies	MG	
Thomas, s. [Stephen & Sara], b. Oct. 5, 1655	MG	
Thomas, s. Stephen, b. Oct. 5, 1655	Col.2	181
Thomas, [bp.] Oct. 12, [16]55	MG	
William, s. Stephen, b. Mar. 14, 1689/90	1	36
-----, wid., d. Aug. 5, 1689	Col.D	57
-----, wid., d. Aug. 5, 1689	1	51
TERRY, TERY, Abigayl, d. [Stephen], b. Sept. 21, 1646	MG	
Abigail, d. Stephen, bp. Sept. 27, 1646	1	35
Elisabeth, d. [Stephen], b. Jan. 4, 1641	MG	
Elizabeth, d. Stephen, bp. Jan. 9, 1641	1	35
Elisabeth, d. [John & Elisabeth], b. Dec. 16, 1663	MG	
Elizabeth, d. John, b. Dec. 16, 1663	Col.1	54
Elizabeth, d. John, b. Dec. 16, 1663	1	36
John, s. [Stephen], b. Mar. 6, 1637	MG	
John, m. Elisabeth **WADESWORTH,** Nov. 27, 1662	MG	
John, of Windsor, m. Elisabeth **WADSWORTH,** of Hartford, Nov. 27, [16]62	Col.1	45
John, of Windsor, m. Elizabeth **WADSWORTH,** of Hartford, Nov. 27, 1662, at Hartford	1	62
John, s. John, b. Mar. 22, [16]69	1	36
John, s. [John & Elisabeth], b. Mar. 22, 1670; d. [ ]	MG	
John, s. John, d. Dec. 30, [16]70	Col.1	55
John, has d. [ ], d. [ ], [16]70	MG	
John, had 8 children, b. in Windsor. Dated Aug. 17, 1677	MG	
Josias, d. Aug. 25, [1640]	MG	
Mary, d. [Stephen], b. Dec. 31, 1633, in Dorchester	MG	
Mary, d. [ ], [16]44	MG	
Mary, of Windsor, m. Richard **GOODMAN,** of Hartford, Dec. 8, 1659	Col.1	45
Mary, of Windsor, m. Richard **GOODMAN,** of Hartford, Dec. 8, 1659	1	56
Mary, d. [John & Elisabth], b. July 19, 1673; d. [ ]	MG	
Mary, d. John, b. July 19, 1673	1	36
Rebeca, d. [John & Elisabeth], b. Jan. 7, 1671; d. [ ]	MG	
Rebekah, d. John, b. Jan. 7, 1671	1	36

	Vol.	Page
TERRY, TERY, (cont.)		
[Rebecca*], d. John, bd. [Dec. 10*], [16]73 *(In pencil)	MG	
Rebeck[a], d. John, d. Dec. 10, 1673	Col.1	58
Rebekah, d. John, d. Dec. 10, 1673	1	51
Rebeca, d. [John & Elisabeth], b. Feb. 27, [16]76	MG	
Rebekah, d. John, b. Feb. 27, [16]76	1	36
Sara, d. [John & Elisabeth], b. Nov. 16, 1668	MG	
Sarah, d. John, b. Nov. 16, 1668	1	36
Sollomon, s. [John & Elisabeth], b. Mar. 29, [16]75	MG	
Solloman, s. John, b. Mar. 29, [16]75	1	36
Falomon*, s. John, d. Oct. 27, [16]77 *("Solomon")	MG	
Sallomon, s. John, d. Oct. 27, [16]77	Col.1	58
Stephen, d. Dec. 17, [1640]	MG	
Stephen, his w. [ ], d. [ ]; bd. June 5, 1647	1	51
Stephen, his w. [ ], d. [ ], [16]47	MG	
Stephen, s. [John & Elisabeth], b. Oct. 6, 1666	MG	
Stephen, s. John, b. Oct. 6, 1666	Col.1	55
Stephen, s. John, b. Oct. 6, 1666	1	36
Stephen, had 4 children b. in Windsor. Dated Aug. 17, 1677	MG	
Stephen, m. [ ], [ ], in Dorchester	MG	
William, m. Nancy **HARRIS**, Dec. 24, 1821, by Rev. Henry A. Rowland	2	205
THAYER, THAYRE, Joel, of Palmyra, N. Y., m. Nancy **SELDEN**, Sept. 30, 1823, by Rev. Henry A. Rowland	2	205
Lucius W., of Westfield, Mass., m. Sarah G. **ELLSWORTH**, of Windsor, Sept. 5, 1848, by C. B. Everest	2	511
THOMAS, Faney E., m. Joel A. **LOOMIS**, b. of Windsor, Mar. 24, 1850, by Rev. Samuel W. Law	2	175
THOMPSON, THOMSON, TOMSON, Ame, d. John, Jr. & Ame, b. Mar. 22, 1759	2	451
Bennoni, s. Hugh & Elizabeth, b. Sept. 25, 1737	2	109
Elizabeth, d. John, b. Jan. 2, 1645	1	36
Eunice, d. Job & Rhoda, b. Sept. 21, 1753	2	451
Henry, of Enfield, m. Candis **PHELPS**, of Windsor, June 10, 1829, by Henry A. Rowland	2	206
Hugh, m. Elisabeth **ELLSWORTH**, b. of Windsor, Jan. 11, 1727/8	2	204
Hugh, s. Hugh & Elizabeth, b. Aug. 26, 1736	2	109
Job, s. Hugh & Elizabeth, b. Nov. 24, 1728	2	108
Job, m. Rhoda **CRANE**, b. of Windsor, July 12, 1750	2	205
John, his child d. [ ], [16]44	MG	
John, had 2 children, b. in Windsor. Dated Aug. 17, 1677	MG	
John, s. Hugh & Elizabeth, b. Nov. 1, 1730	2	108
John, m. Ame **ELSWORTH**, May 24, 1753	2	204
Martha, m. Eliezer **GAYLER**, Aug. 18 (?), 1686	Col.D	54
Martha, m. Eleazer **GAYLORD**, Aug. 18, 1686	1	57
Rhoda, d. Job & Rhoda, b. Apr. 9, 1752	2	451
William, s. Hugh & Elizabeth, b. Jan. 11, 1732/3	2	108

	Vol.	Page
THORNTON, Ann, d. [ ], [16]46	MG	
Prissila, d. [ ], [16]46	MG	
Samuel, s. Thomas, b. July 13, 1645	1	36
Thomas, d. [ ], [16]46	MG	
Thomas, had 5 children b. in Windsor. Dated Aug. 17, 1677	MG	
THRALL, TRALL, Aaron, s. John, b. Sept. 27, 1704	2	106
Aaron, d. July 9, 1731	2	275
Aaron, s. John & Mary, b. Aug. 31, 1732	2	108
Aaron, s. John & Mary, d. July 29, 1740	2	275
Abel, s. Charles & Hannah, b. July 20, 1751	2	451
Abigall, twin with Samuel, d. Tim[othy], b. Feb. 22, 1681	Col.D	51
Abigail, twin with Samuel, d. Timothy, b. Feb. 22, 1681	1	36
Abigael, d. Capt. Timothy, b. May 13, 1708	2	106
Abigael, m. John Wareham **STRONG**, b. of Windsor, Nov. 30, 1727	2	198
Ami, d. John, b. Jan. 10, 1706/7	2	106
Benjamin, s. John & Mary, b. Feb. 18, 1744/5	2	452
Charity, m. Jonathan **ALFORD**, b. of Windsor, Dec. 17, 1744	2	123
Charles, s. Sergt. John, b. July 30, 1718	2	107
Charles, of Windsor, m. Hannah **CLARK**, of Symsbury, Mar. 24, 1744	2	205
Chloe, d. Ezekiel & Elizabeth, b. July 27, 1771	2	452
Daniel, s. John, b. Dec. 13, 1712	2	107
David, s. David & Jane, b. Sept. 23, 1749	2	453
Debroa, d. [Timothy & Debro], b. Aug. 19, 1660	MG	
Deborah, d. Timothy, b. Aug. 19, 1660	1	35
Deborah, w. Timothy, d. Jan. 17, 1694	1	51
Drusilla M., of Windsor, m. Spencer **CLAPP**, Jr., of Easthampton, Mass., Jan. 26, 1848, by T. A. Leete	2	496
Elinor, d. Charles & Hannah, b. Aug. 4, 1766	2	452
Eli, s. Charles & Hannah, b. June 30, 1764	2	452
Elisabeth, d. [Timothy & Debro], b. May 1, 1667	MG	
Elizabeth, d. Timothy, b. May 1, 1667	1	35
Elizabeth, of Windsor, m. James **CORNISH**, of Westfield, Nov. 10, 1693	1	55
Elizabeth, d. Samuel, b. Mar. 23, 1706/7	2	107
Elizabeth, d. Moses & Elizabeth, b. Nov. 29, 1731	2	108
Elizabeth, d. David & Jane, b. May 12, 1751	2	453
Elizabeth, m. Ruben **MILLER**, b. of Windsor, July 17, 1755	2	179
Elizabeth, d. Ezekiel & Elizabeth, b. Apr. 24, 1764	2	452
Elizabeth, d. David & Jane, d. Aug. 13, 1769; drowned in Ferry River	2	276
Elizabeth, m. Henry **SCHULZE**, b. of Hartford, Nov. 25, 1846, by Rev. George Burgess, of Hartford	2	511
Ezekiel, s. John & Mary, b. Sept. 30, 1742	2	109
Ezekiel, s. John & Mary, b. Sept. 30, 1742	2	452
Ezekiel, m. Elizabeth **McMORRAN**, b. of Windsor, July 26, 1763	2	205

	Vol.	Page
THRALL, TRALL, (cont.)		
Mary, d. Thomas, b. Sept. 2, 1707	2	107
Mary, d. John, Jr. & Mary, b. May 21, 1730	2	108
Mary, d. David & Jane, b. Feb. 28, 1747	2	453
Mary, d. David & Jane, d. Aug. 13, 1769; drowned in		
Ferry River	2	276
Mary G., m. Amos **HATHEWAY,** b. of Windsor, Jan. 5,		
1831, by Stephen Crosby	2	485
Mehettabell, d. [Timothy & Debro], b. Mar. [ ], 1664	MG	
Mehitteble, d. Timothy, b. Mar. [ ], 1664	1	35
Mindwell, d. John & Mary, b. Feb. 9, 1739/40	2	109
Mindwell, wid., d. Sept. 2, 1750	2	275
Mindwell, m. John **McMORAN,** b. of Windsor, Feb. 16,		
1758	2	179
Mindwell, twin with William, d. Charles & Hannah, b.		
Jan. 29, 1761	2	451
Mindwell, d. Ezekiel & Elizabeth, b. Apr. 12, 1767	2	452
Mooses, s. John, b. Apr. 29, 1702	1	36
Moses, m. Elizabeth **FYLER,** b. of Windsor, Feb. 4, 1730/1	2	204
Old Goode, d. July 30, 1676	1	51
Oliver, s. John & Rebeckah, b. Mar. 25, 1751	2	451
Oliver, s. John, d. Dec. 27, 1758	2	276
Oliver, s. John & Elizabeth, b. Nov. 13, 1762	2	452
Phillup, m. John **HOSFORD,** Nov. 5, 1657	MG	
Phillip, m. John **HOSFORD,** Nov. 5, 1657	Col.2	159
Phillip, m. John **HOSFORD,** b. of Windsor, Nov. 5, 1657	1	57
Rebeckah, w. John, d. Dec. 10, 1758	2	275
Rebecah, d. John & Elizabeth, b. Jan. 24, 1766	2	452
Ruphas, s. Charles & Hannah, b. Nov. 28, 1757	2	451
Samuel, twin with Abigall, s. Tim[othy], b. Feb. 22, 1681	Col.D	51
Samuel, twin with Abigail, s. Timothy, b. Feb. 22, 1681	1	36
Samuel, m. Elizabeth **OWEN,** b. of Windsor, Oct. 23, 1706	2	203
Samuell, s. Samuell, b. Feb. 25, 1708/9	2	107
Samuel, d. Oct. [ ], 1709	2	274
Samuel, d. May 20, 1730	2	275
Samuel, s. John & Mary, b. July 11, 1737	2	109
Sarah, d. Timothy, b. Oct. 19, 1704	2	106
Sarah, d. David & Jane, b. Feb. 3, 1742	2	452
Thomas, s. [Timothy & Debro], b. May 5, [16]75; d. [ ]	MG	
Thomas, s. Timothy, b. May 5, [16]75	1	36
Thomas, s. Timothy, d. Aug. 12, [16]75	Col.1	58
Thomas, s. Timothy, d. Aug. 12, 1675, ae 14 wks.	1	51
Thomas, 2nd, s. [Timothy & Debro], b. July 10, 1676	MG	
Thomas, s. Timothy, b. July 10, [16]76	1	35
Thomas, m. Elizabeth **HOSKINS,** Nov. 2, 1699	1	62
Thomas, s. Thomas, b. Apr. 13, 1700	1	36
Thomas, Jr., d. Jan. 29, 1724/5 *("John T." crossed out)	2	275
Timothy, b. July 25, 1641; bp. [1641], m. Debro **GUNN,**		

	Vol.	Page
THRALL, TRALL, (cont.)		
Nov. 10, 1659	MG	
Timothy, m. Deborah **GUNN**, b. of Windsor, Nov. 10, 1659	1	62
Timothy, s. [Timothy & Debro], b. Dec. 7, 1662	MG	
Timothy, s. Timothy, b. Dec. 7, [16]62	Col.1	54
Timothy, s. Timothy, b. Dec. 7, 1662	1	35
Timothy, had 10 children b. in Windsor. Dated Aug. 17, 1677	MG	
Timothy, his s. [ ], d. [ ], [16]81	MG	
Timothy, m. Sarah **ALLYN**, Dec. 21, 1699	1	62
Timothy, s. Timothy, b. Dec. 19, 1713	2	107
Timothy, Capt., d. Jan. 31, 1723/4	2	274
Timothy, d. Feb. 6, 1756	2	275
Timothy, contributed 0-2-6 to the poor in other colonies	MG	
William, his w. [ ], d. [ ], [16]76	MG	
William, had 2 children b. in Windsor. Dated Aug. 17, 1677	MG	
William, d. Aug. 3, 1679, ae 73	MG	
William, d. Aug. 3, [16]79	Col.1	58
William, s. Timothy, b. Oct. 2, 1700	1	36
William, Ens., m. Hannah **THRALL**, b. of Windsor, Oct. 11, 1728	2	204
William, Lieut., d. Oct. 25, 1738	2	275
William, twin with Mindwell, s. Charles & Hannah, b. Jan. 29, 1761	2	451
William, contributed 0-2-6 to the poor in other colonies	MG	
TILTON, Elizabeth, d. Peter, bp. June 19, 1642	1	35
Elisabeth, d. [Peter & Elisabeth], b. June [ ], [16[ ]; bp. [June] 19, [16[ ]	MG	
Elisabeth, d. Peter, d. July 17, 1655	Col.2	160
Elizabeth, d. Peter, d. July 17, [ ]	1	51
Mary, d. [Peter & Elisabeth], bp. Feb. 18, 1643	MG	
Mary, d. Peter, bp. Feb. 18, 1643	1	35
Peter, m. Elisabeth [ ], May 10, 16[ ]	MG	
Peter, m. Elizabeth [ ], May 10, 1641	1	62
Peter, s. [Peter & Elisabeth], b. Dec. 5, 1647	MG	
Peter, his d. [ ], d. [ ], [16]53	MG	
Peter, had 3 children b. in Windsor. Dated Aug. 17, 1677	MG	
TOD[D], Margaret, m. John **WHURY**(?), b. of Windsor, May 30, 1852, by Rev. H. N. Weed	2	520
TOURTELOT, Newton, of Thompson, m. Francis C. **BARRETT**, of Windsor, June 10, 1850, by Cornelius B. Everest	2	512
TOWNSEND, Mary, m. David **BOSTON**, colored, Jan. 8, 1833, by Henry A. Rowland	2	498
TRACY, Chester, of Vernon, m. Harriet E. **HOLCOMB**, of Windsor, May 23, 1849, by Cornelius B. Everest	2	511
TRALL, [see under **THRALL**]		
TREHAREN, TRAHARNE, TREAHAREN, TRAHAVEN, TRAHARNE, Alse, m. Thomas **POWELL**, Aug. 25, 1676	MG	
Alse, m. Thomas **POWELL**, Aug. 25, 1675, by Capt.		

	Vol.	Page

TREHAREN, TRAHARNE, TREAHAREN, TRAHAVEN, TRAHARNE, (cont.)

Newbery	Col.1	46
Alse, m. Thomas POWELL, Aug. 25, 1675*, by Capt. Nubery *(In pencil "1676")	TR1	1
Allse, m. Thomas POWELL, Aug. 25, [16]76	Col.1	46
Allse, m. Thomas POWELL, Dec.* 25, 1676 *("Aug." also written)	TR1	1
Allse, m. Thomas POWEL, Aug. 25, 1676	1	60
Allse, m. Thomas POWEL, Aug. 25, 1676	1	64
TROY, Patrick, m. Mrs. [ ] DUFFY, May [ ], 1852, by Rev. James Smyth	2	460

TRUMBLE, TROUMBLE, TRUMBEL, Ammi, m. Ann

BURNHAM, May 9, 1711	2	204
Ammi, s. Ammi, b. June 17, 1712	2	107
Ammi, m. Sabra GAYLORD, b. of Windsor, Nov. 9, 1738	2	204
Ann, d. Ammi, b. Sept. 24, 1714	2	107
Ann, m. Ebenezer WATSON, b. of Windsor, Dec. 31, 1741	2	209
Ann, w. Ammy, d. Aug. 10, 1753	2	275
Benoni, m. Sarah DRAKE, Aug. 31, 1709	2	203
David, s. Ammi, Jr. & Sabra, b. Nov. 10, 1744	2	109
Elizabeth, d. Capt. Ammi & Sebra, b. Apr. 13, 1761	2	452
Hannah, of Suffield, m. John STRONG, of Windsor, Nov. 26, 1685* *("1689"?)	1	61
Hana, of Suffield, m. John STRONG, of Windsor, Nov. 26, 1686	Col.D	54
Hannah, d. Oct. 5, 1689	Col.D	57
Hannah, d. Oct. 5, 1689	1	51
Hanna, contributed [ ]-1-3 to the poor in other colonies	MG	
Joseph, s. Ammi, Jr. & Sebra, d. Aug. 7, 1753	2	375
Jude, contributed 0-1-3 to the poor in other colonies	MG	
Mary, m. Job ELSWORTH, Dec. 19, 1695	1	56
Mary, d. Ami, b. July 9, 1717	2	107
Mary, m. Ebenezer HAYDON, Jr., b. of Windsor, June 16, 1737	2	163
Mary, d. Ammi, Jr. & Sabra, b. Sept. 6, 1739	2	109
Mary, m. Job ELSWORTH, b. of Windsor, May 4, 1762	2	147
Sabra, d. Ammi, Jr. & Sabra, b. Nov. 5, 1742	2	109
Sebra, w. Capt. Ammi, Jr., d. July 12, 1764	2	276
Sarah, of East Windsor, m. George HOWARD, of Windsor, May 28, 1810	2	482
Zeraviah, d. Capt. Ammy, Jr. & Sebra, b. May 28, 1756	2	451

TRYES, Michell, his w. [ ], d. [ ], [16]46 — MG

Michael, his w. [ ], d. May 19, 1646	1	51

TUCKER, TUKER, Mary, b. Oct. 4, 1653, in England; m.

Thomas DEBELL, Jr., Oct. 10, 1676	MG	
Mary, of England, m. Thomas DEBLE, Jr., Oct. 10, [16]72	Col.1	46
Mary, m. Thomas DEBLE, Jr., Oct. 10, 1676* *(In pencil		

	Vol.	Page
TUCKER, TUKER, (cont.)		
"1672"?)	TR1	1
Mary, m. Thomas **DIBLE,** Jr., Oct. 10, 1676	1	55
TUDOR, TUTOR, TUDER, Abigail, d. Samuel, b. Oct. 12, 1686	1	36
Abigaell, w. Samuell, d. Jan. 8, 1707/8	2	274
Anne, d. Owen, b. Oct. 16, 1657	Col.2	161
Elihu, s. Samuel & Mary, b. Feb. 3, 1732/3	2	109
Elizabeth, d. Samuel, b. July 8, 1700	1	36
Elizabeth, m. Thomas **MARSHEL,** Jr., b. of Windsor, Oct. 9, 1725	2	177
Jane, d. [Owen & Mary], b. Oct. 16, 1657	MG	
Jane, d. Owin, b. Oct. 16, 1657	1	35
Jane, [d. Ouen], bp. May 12, [16]61	MG	
Margret, d. Samuel, b. Nov. 17, [16]97	1	36
Mary, d. [Owen & Mary], b. Mar. 6, 1660	MG	
Mary, [d. Ouen], bp. May 12, [1661]	MG	
Mary, w. Owen, d. Aug. 19, 1680; bd. Aug. 20, 1680	MG	
Mary, d. Samuel, b. Aug. 31, 1689	1	36
Mary, d. Samuell, b. Aug. 31, 1690	Col.D	51
O., his w. [ ], adm. ch. & communicant Apr. [ ], 1661	MG	
Owen, m. Mary **SKIN[N]ER,** wid., Nov. 13, 16[ ]	MG	
Owen, adult, ch. mem. 16[ ]	MG	
Owen, s. [Owen & Mary], b. Mar. 12, 1654	MG	
Ouen, his w. [ ], adm. ch. Apr. 28, [16]61	MG	
Owen, [s. Ouen], bp. May 12, [16]61	MG	
Owen, m. Mary **SKINNER,** wid., b. of Windsor, Nov. 13, 1651	Col.2	159
Owin, m. Mary **SKINNER,** Nov. 13, 1651	1	62
Owen, s. Owen, b. Mar. 12, 1654	Col.2	158
[O]wen, had 5 children b. in Windsor. Dated Aug. 17, 1677	MG	
Owen, his w. [ ], d. Aug. 19, 1680	Col.1	58
Owen, d. Oct. 30, 1690	Col.D	57
Owen, Sr., d. Oct. 30, 1690	1	51
Ouen, contributed 0-6-7 to the poor in other colonies	MG	
Rode, d. Samuel & Mary, b. Feb. 25, 1734/5	2	109
Samuel, twin with Sara, s. [Owen & Mary], b. Nov. 26, 16[ ]	MG	
Samuel, twin with Sarah, s. Owen, b. Dec. 5, 1652	Col.2	156
Samuell, [s. Ouen], bp. May 12, [16]61	MG	
Samuel, m. Abigail **BISSELL,** Oct. 20, 1685	1	62
Samuel, s. Samuell, b. Mar. 8, 1704/5	2	106
Samuell, m. Joanna **TAYLOR,** Feb. 7, 1708/9	2	203
Samuel, d. July 6, 1727	2	275
Samuel, of Windsor, m. Mrs. Mary **SMITH,** of Middletown, Dec. 10, 1729	2	204
Samuel, s. Samuell & Mary, b. June 22, 1737	2	109
Samuell, contributed 0-4-0 to the poor in other colonies	MG	
Sara, twin with Samuel, d. [Owen & Mary], b. Nov. 26, 16[ ]	MG	
Sarah, twin with Samuel, d. Owen, b. Dec. 5, 1652	Col.2	156

	Vol.	Page
TUDOR, TUTOR, TUDER, (cont.)		
Sara, [d. Owen], bp. May 12, [16]61	MG	
Sara, m. James **PORTER,** s. John, Sr., Jan. 15, 1679, by		
Mr. Wolcot	MG	
Sara, d. Owen, m. James **PORTER,** s. John, Sr., Jan. 15,		
1679, by Mr. Wolcott	Col.1	46
Sarah, d. Owen, m. James **PORTER,** s. John, Sr., Jan. 15,		
[16]79, by Mr. Wolcot	TR1	1
Sarah, d. Owin, m. James **PORTER,** s. John, Sr., Jan. 15,		
1679, by Mr. Wolcott	1	60
Sarah, d. Samuel, b. Sept. 19, 1692	1	36
Sarah, d. Samuel, b. May 25, 1695	1	36
Sarah, d. Owen, m. James **PORTER,** s. John, Sr., Jan. 15,		
1697, by Mr. Wolcott	1	64
Sarah, d. Samuel, d. June [ ], 1697	1	51
Theophilous, s. Samuel & Mary, b. Sept. 20, 1730	2	109
TULLER, William, of Symsbury, m. Damiris **CORNISH,** of		
Windsor, Apr. 12, 1711	2	204
TURNBULL, Catherine, of Windsor, m. Joseph Adams **CLARK,**		
of Simsbury, June 18, 1843, by Rev. S. D. Jewett	2	517
TURNER, Huldah M., m. Roswell **MARSH,** of New Hartford,		
Mar. 18, 1829, by Henry A. Rowland	2	495
TUTTLE, Curtis, of Otis, Mass., m. Prudence **LOOMIS,** Sept. 17,		
1833, by Henry A. Rowland	2	206
George, of Hartford, m. Mary **LOOMIS,** of Windsor, Jan. 8,		
1832, by Rev. Gurdon Robins, of East Windsor	2	206
TYLER, TYLOR, Alford, m. Elizabeth **McCURDY,** b. of		
Windsor, Aug. 30, 1852, by Rev. Thomas H. Rouse	2	461
Mary, wid., m. Dea. Samuel **OWEN,** Feb. 26, 1783	2	185
Sarah, of Tolland, m. David **BURROUGHS,** of Windsor,		
May 24, 1744	2	131
ULRICH, Elizabeth, of Suffield, m. Robert **BOOME,** of New		
York, Apr. 21, 1850, by Rev. Samuel Warren Law	2	504
VADITIN, Henry, of East Granby, m. Ruth Marinda **BARNES,** of		
Barkhemsted, Feb. 14, 1836, by Walter Thrall, J. P.	2	511
[VALENTINE], VOLLENTINE, Samuel, of Eastbury, m. Delia		
COOK, of Windsor, Sept. 18, 1828,by Henry A.Rowland	2	498
VANHORN, Margrit, of Springfield, m. David **ROCKWEL,** of		
Windsor, Feb. 22, 1735/6	2	195
Ruel, m. Delia **STILES,** Dec. 21, 1820, by Rev. Henry A.		
Rowland	2	207
Sylvester, m. Ellen **SWEET,** b. of Hartford, Nov. 27, 1838,		
by Rev. Jared R. Avery	2	511
VELA, Delia, m. Henry S. **SQUIRES,** b. of Windsor, May 5,		
1841, by Daniel Hemenway	2	514
VELEY, Jane C., of Windsor, m. Horatio N. **SMITH,** of Oxford,		
N. H., [ ] 30, [18], by Rev. Edmund Tenney, of		
Hartford	2	510

	Vol.	Page
VIBBERT, VIBERTS, Nancey, of Hartford, m. Nathaniel		
HOWARD, Jr., of Windsor, Nov. 30, 1800	2	482
Warren, of Springfield, Mass., m. Caroline **PHELPS**, of		
Windsor, July 27, 1841, by Rev. John R. Adams	2	207
VIETTS, Cathrien, of Simsbury, m. John **HOSKINS**, of Windsor,		
Aug. 17, 1738	2	162
VINING, VINEING, Abijah, s. Samuel & Mary, b. Apr. 11, 1743	2	110
Alexander, s. Samuell & Elizabeth, b. Sept. 21, 1751	2	110
Edwin C., of Simsbury, m. Harriet **HUBBARD**, of Windsor,		
Dec. 11, 1831, by Rev. Ansel Nash	2	511
Elias, s. Samuell & Elizabeth, b. Oct. 23, 1743	2	110
Elizabeth, d. John & Rosannah, b. Feb. 28, 1764	2	110
Hannah, d. Samuel & Mary, b. Jan. 23, 1740/1	2	110
John, s. John & Rosannah, b. Apr. 13, 1762	2	110
Jonah, s. Samuel & Mary, b. Feb. 18, 1735/6	2	110
Jonah, s. John & Rosannah, b. Sept. 22, 1765	2	111
Josiah, s. Samuel & Mary, b. Oct. 22, 1733	2	110
Lucey, d. Samuell & Elizabeth, b. Apr. 22, 1750	2	110
Mary, d. John & Rosannah, b. Oct. 4, 1767	2	110
Sarah, d. Samuel & Mary, b. Sept. 16, 1738	2	111
VOAR, VORE, Abigall, m. Timothy **BUCKLAND**, Mar. 27,		
[16]62	MG	
Abigail, m. Timothy **BUCKLAND**, b. of Windsor, Mar. 27,		
[16]62	1	54
An[n], d. Dec. 7, 1683	Col.D	56
Lidia, m. Nathanell **COOK**, June 29, 1649	MG	
Lydia, m. Nathanael **COOK**, June 29, 1649	1	55
Mary, m. Allixander **ALUARD**, Oct. 29, 1646	MG	
Mary, m. Alexander **ALFORD**, Oct. 29, 1646	1	53
Richard, taxed 4-0 on Feb. 10, [16]73	MG	
Richard, had 1 child b. in Windsor. Dated Aug. 17, 1677	MG	
Richard, his w. [ ] communicant from Dorchester;		
living in Windsor Dec. 22, 1677	MG	
Richard, communicant from Dorchester; living in Windsor		
Dec. 22, 1677	MG	
Richard, d. Aug. 22, 1683	Col.D	56
Richard, contrubuted 0-1-3 to the poor in other colonies	MG	
Richard, his w.[ ], ch. mem. 16[ ], from Dorchester	MG	
W-----, Robart, his s. [ ], adm, ch. Jan. 22, [1649	MG	
W[ ]ER, Richard, his w. [ ], d. [ ], [16]53	MG	
WADE, Rebeca, m. John **OWEN**, Oct. 3, 1650	MG	
Rebekah, m. John **OWIN**, Oct. 3, 1650	1	59
Sarah, w. William & d. of Mr. **PHELPS**, d. July 10, [16]59;		
bd. [ ]	1	52
William, of Middletown, m. Sarah **PHELPS**, of Windsor,		
June 9, 1658	1	63
WADSWORTH, WADESWORTH, Elisabeth, m. John **TERY**,		
Nov. 27, 1662	MG	

	Vol.	Page
WADSWORTH, WADESWORTH, (cont.)		
Elisabeth, of Hartford, m. John TERY, of Windsor, Nov. 27, [16]62	Col.1	45
Elizabeth, of Hartford, m. John TERRY, of Windsor, Nov. 27, 1662, at Hartford	1	62
Jerusha, wid., m. John PALMER, Jr., b. of Windsor, Mar. 4, 1762	2	189
Mary, m. Thomas STOTON, [ ]	MG	
William, his w. [ ], d. [ ], [16]62	MG	
WAKEFIELD, WACKFELD, WACKFEELD, WAKEFELD,		
Aden, s. Patteshell & Margret, b. Nov. 25, 1773	2	456
Bethuel, s. Patteshell & Margret, b. Apr. 28, 1772	2	455
Harve, s. Patteshell & Margret, b. Jan. 6, 1777	2	456
Hezakiah, s. Patteshell & Sarah, b. Feb. 25, 1783	2	457
Margret, w. Patteshell, d. Oct. 4, 1779	2	280
Martha, m. [ ] BUCKLAND, Oct. 21, [16]68	MG	
Martha, of New Hauen, m. Nicolas BUCKLAND, of Windsor, Apr. 14, [16]68, by Mr. Mathew Allyn	Col.1	45
Martha, of New Haven, m. Nicholas BUCKLAND, of Windsor, Oct. 21, 1668, at New Haven, by Mr. Johnes	1	54
Martha, see Martha BUCKLAND	Col.D	56
Mary, m. Ebenezer DEBLE, Oct. 27, [16]63	MG	
Mary, of New Hauen, m. Ebenezer DEBLE, of Windsor, Oct. 27, 1663, by Mr. Jones, at New Hauen	Col.1	45
WALBRIDGE, Horace, of Stafford, m. D. Emeline ANIHUS*, July 4, 1821, by Henry A. Rowland *(In pencil)	2	210
WALDO, Alvin, of Bennington, N. Y., m. Nancy E. BUTLER, of Windsor, Oct. 16, 1825, by Rev. Augustus Bolles, of Wintonbury	2	211
Alvin, of Bennington, N. Y., m. Nancy E. BUTLER, of Windsor, Oct. 16, 1825, by Rev. Augustus Bolles, of Wintonbury	2	512
WALLIS, William, m. Anne PORTER, b. of Windsor, Sept. 9, 1738	2	209
WALTERS, Hepzibah, m. Job DRAKE, 3rd, b. of Windsor, Feb. 7, 1774	2	143
WAPLES, [see under WHAPLES]		
WARD, John, m. Clarissa HOLCOMB, Dec. 25, 1833, by Richard Niles, J. P.	2	213
Lucy I., m. William LATHROP, May 15, 1849, by Rev. S. H. Allen	2	491
Patrick, m. Mary MURPHY, Oct. 12, 1852, by James Smyth	2	460
Sarah, m. Samuel SKINNER, b. of Windsor, Mar. 24, 1741	2	200
WARDWELL, Elizabeth, d. Isaac & Hannah, b. May 8, 1780	2	457
Isaac, s. Isaac & Hannah, b. May 6, 1778	2	457
Sarah, of Windsor, m. Benjamin BOWE, of Springfield, Aug. 22, 1847, by Cornelius B. Everest	2	503
Sarah M., of Springfield, m. Lemuel ABBE, of Enfield,		

	Vol.	Page
WARDWELL, (cont.)		
Nov. 13, 1838, by Rev. R. Avery	2	464
WARE, Amanda M., m. Lorin M. **REYNOLDS**, Nov. 21, 1830,		
by Smith Dayton, Elder	2	505
WAREHAM, WARHAM, WARAM, WARHA, WARRAM,		
Abigayl, d. John & Jane, b. [ ]; bp. May 27, 1638	MG	
Abigail, d. John, bp. May 27, 1638	Col.2	156
Abigayl, m. Thomas **ALLYN**, Oct. [ ], 16[ ]	MG	
Abigail, m. Thomas **ALLYN**, b. of Windsor, Oct. 21, 1658	1	53
Abigal, Mrs., d. May 18, 1684	Col.D	56
Abigail, Mrs., d. May 18, 1684	1	52
Hepsiba, d. [John & Jane], bp. Aug. 9, 1640; d. [ ]	MG	
Hepsiba, d. [ ], [16]47	MG	
Hester, d. [John & Jane], bp. Dec. 8, 16[ ]	MG	
Hester, d. John, bp. Dec. 8, 1644	Col.2	156
Hester, of Windsor, m. Elizer **MATHER**, of Northampton,		
Sept. 29, [16]59	Col.1	45
Hester, m. Eleazer **MADER**, Sept. 29, 1659	1	59
Jane, w. John, d. Apr. [ ]3, 16[ ]5, at Norwake	MG	
John, m. 2nd w. Mrs. Abigayl **BRAUKER**, Oct. 9, [16]	MG	
John, m. wid. Abigail **BRANKER**, b. of Windsor, Oct. 9,		
1662	Col.1	45
John, m. Abigail **BRANKER**, b. of Windsor, Oct. 9, 1662	1	63
John, d. Apr. 1, 1670	MG	
John, d. Apr. 1, 1670	Col.1	55
John, d. Apr. 1, 1670; bd. Apr. 4, [1670]	1	52
John, had 4 children b. in Windsor. Dated Aug. 17, 1677	MG	
Samuell, d. [ ], [16]47	MG	
Sara, d. [John & Jane], b. Aug. 28, 1642	MG	
Sarah, d. John, bp. Aug. 28, 1642	Col.2	156
Sara, m. Return **STRONG**, May 11, 1664	MG	
Sara, m. Returne **STRONG**, May 11, 1664, by Mr. Clark	Col.1	45
Sarah, see Returne **STRONG**	Col.1	58
-----, began the practise of publicly catechizing		
candidates for church membership Jan. 31, 1657 until		
Mar. 19, 1664	MG	
-----, Mr., d. [ ], [16]70	MG	
WARFIELD, Curtis, of Hartford, m. Laura **KING**, of Windsor,		
Dec. 9, 1824, by Rev. Phinehas Cook	2	211
WARHAM, [see under **WAREHAM**]		
WARINER, Ebenezer, see Samuel **WARNER**	2	135
Elizabeth, m. as 2nd w. John **STRONG**, Jr., [ ]	MG	
WARNER, Abigail, m. Willard **LOOMIS**, Feb. 17, 1830, by		
Henry A. Rowland	2	174
Ann, w. Ebenzer, d. Mar. 8, 1749/50	2	279
Bethia, m. Nathanael **GRANT**, Oct. 12, 1699	1	57
Cleony, d. John & Margret, b. July 5, 1772	2	456
Ebenezer, d. Oct. 26, 1754	2	279

	Vol.	Page
WATSON, (cont.)		
Abigail, w. Ebenezer, d. June 16, 1752	2	279
Abigail, d. Samuel & Sarah, b. July 21, 1759	2	455
Ann, m. Benjamin **ALLYN**, b. of Windsor, Dec. 18, 1707	2	123
Ann, d. Ebenezer & Ann, b. Oct. 22, 1749	2	120
Anna, of East Windsor, m. Nathaniel **HOWARD**, of Windsor, Apr. 26, 1776. Mar. 25, 1773* *(Written along side of date, "Mar. 25, 1773")	2	164
Betty, d. Samuel & Sarah, b. Aug. 28, 1757	2	454
David, s. Samuel & Sarah, b. May 31, 1753	2	453
Ebenezer, s. [Robard & Mary], b. Apr. 25, 1661	MG	
Ebenezer, s. Robert, b. Apr. 25, 1661	1	37
Ebenez[e]r, [bp.] Apr. 28, [16]61	MG	
Ebenezer, m. Abigail **KELSIE**, b. of Windsor, Apr. 1, 1703	1	63
Ebenezer, s. Ebenezer, b. Mar. 20, 1703/4	1	39
Ebenezer, s. Ebenezer, b. Mar. 20, 1703/4	2	111
Ebenezer, 2nd, s. Ebenezer, b. Nov. 23, 1705	2	111
Ebenezer, s. Ebenezer, d. Nov. 28, 1705	2	276
Ebenezer, m. Ann **TRUMBLE**, b. of Windsor, Dec. 31, 1741	2	209
Ebenezer, s. Ebenezer & Ann, b. Oct. 16, 1742	2	119
Ebenezer, s. Robert, d. Oct. 3, 1747	2	279
Elizabeth, w. Samuel, d. Apr. 1, 1744	2	278
Hanna, d. [Robard & Mary], b. Aug. 8, 1658	MG	
Hanna, [d. Robart], bp. Aug. 15, [16]58	MG	
Hanna, m. John **BIRG**, Mar. 28, 1678	MG	
Hanna m. John **BIRG**, Mar. 18, 1678	Col.1	46
Hanna, m. John **BIRG[E]**, Mar. 28, 1678	TR1	1
Hannah, m. John **BIRDGE**, Mar. 28, 1678	1	54
Hannah, d. Ebenezer, b. Apr. 4, 1713	2	114
Hannah, m. John **BISSEL**, b. of Windsor, Dec. 2, 1733	2	130
Hannah, see Hanah **BIRGE**	Col.D	57
Jededia, s. [Robard & Mary], b. Sept. 30, 1666	MG	
Jededia, s. Robart, b. Sept. 30, 1666	Col.1	55
Jededia, [bp.] Oct. 7, [16]66	MG	
Jedediah, s. Robert, b. Sept. 30, 1668	1	37
Jedadiah, his w. [ ], d. Dec. 13, 1741	2	279
John, s. [Robard & Mary], b. Mar. 7, 1653	MG	
John, [s. Robart], bp. Jan. 25, [16]56	MG	
John, d. Sept. 8, 1730	2	278
John, s. Ebenezer & Ann, b. Jan. 8, 1743/4	2	119
John, m. Anna **BLISS**, b. of Windsor, July 1, 1767	2	210
Jona A., of Charleston, S. C., m. Bede **CAMP**, of Windsor, Jan. 1, 1836, by Eli Deniston	2	513
Lucretia, d. Samuel & Sarah, b. Sept. 4, 1761	2	455
Mary, d. [Robard & Mary], b. Jan. 11, 1651	MG	
Mary, [d. Robart], bp. Jan. 25, [16]56	MG	
Mary, m. John **DRAKE**, s. John, b. of Windsor, Mar. 20, [16]71, by Capt. Newbery	Col.1	46

	Vol.	Page
WATSON, (cont.)		
Mary, w. Rob, d. Aug. 21, 1684	Col.D	56
Mary, w. Robert, d. Aug. 21, 1684	1	52
Mary, d. Ebenezer, b. Mar. 2, 1707/8	2	112
Mary, m. William **WEBSTER**, June 3, 1731	2	209
Mary, w. Jedediah, d. Apr. 14, 1738	2	278
Mary, w. Jedediah, d. Apr. 14, 1738	2	278
Mary, see Mary **DRAKE**	Col.D	57
Maryann, d. Samuel & Sarah, b. July 24, 1763	2	455
Nath[an], m. Dorethy **BISSELL**, b. of Windsor, Jan. 21, 1685	Col.D	54
Nath[an], d. Aug. 19, 1690	Col.D	57
Nathanel, s. [Robard & Mary], b. Jan. 28, 1663	MG	
Nathanell, s. Robart, b. Jan. 28, [16]63	Col.1	54
Nathanael, s. Robert, b. Jan. 28, 1663	1	37
Nath[ie]l, [bp.] Jan. 30, [16]63	MG	
Nathanael, m. Dorithy **BISSELL**, b. of Windsor, Jan. 21, 1685	1	63
Nathanael, d. Aug. 19, 1690	1	52
Nathanael, d. Sept. 10, 1733	2	278
Nathaniel, s. Ebenezer & Ann, b. June 18, 1745	2	119
Robard, m. Mary **ROCKWELL**, Dec. 10, 1646	MG	
Robert, m. Mary **ROCKWELL**, Dec. 10, 1646	1	62
Robard, adm, ch. & communicant Jan. [ ], 1649	MG	
Robart, adm, ch. [16]49; dismis. from ch. May 11, [16]51, until Jan. 18, [16]56. Had 3 children between 1651 & 1656	MG	
Robard, taxed 6-0 on Feb. 10, [16]73	MG	
Robard, had 7 children b. in Windsor. Dated Aug. 17, 1677	MG	
Rober, d. July 19, 1689	Col.D	56
Robert, d. July 19, 1689	1	52
Robert, s. Ebenezer, Jr. & Ann, b. Sept. 4, 1747	2	120
Robard, contributed 0-8-0 to the poor in other colonies	MG	
Samuell, s. [Robard & Mary], b. Jan. 14, 1655	MG	
Samuell, [s. Robart], bp. Jan. 25, [16]56	MG	
Samuel, s. Ebenezer, b. Nov. 13, 1710	2	113
Samuel, d. Oct. 29, 1711	2	276
Samuell, m. Elizabeth **MATHER**, b. of Windsor, Feb. 25, 1741/2	2	209
Samuel, m. Sarah **PRYOR**, b. of Windsor, Feb. 25, 1741/2	2	209
Samuel, s. Samuel & Sarah, b. Oct. 16, 1749	2	120
Timothy, s. Ebenezer & Ann, b. Feb. 18, 1751/2	2	120
William, of Torrington, m. Molissa **CADWELL**, Jan. 30, 1828, by Rev. John Bartlett	2	212
WAY, Harmom, m. Chloe **SANDS**, Nov. 11, 1830, by Henry A. Rowland	2	513
WEATHERBY, C. S., m. F. A. **HOLLISTER**, b. of Glastenbury, Nov. 18, 1846, by Rev. T. A. Leete	2	519
WEBB, Clorany, d. Nathan & Margret, b. May 11, 1756	2	454

	Vol.	Page

WEBB, (cont.)

Judeth, m. Jonathan **BURROUGHS,** b. of Windsor, Mar. 5,
1752 — 2 — 132

Judeth, d. Zebulon, Jr. & Mahitable, b. Mar. 9, 1754 — 2 — 454

Lidia, d. Zebulon & Judah, b. Jan. 23, 1750/1 — 2 — 120

Mahittabel, d. Zebulon, Jr. & Mahittabel, b. Apr. 23, 175[ ] — 2 — 121

Myron Safford, of Bennington, Vt., m. Mary Caroline
DENSLOW, of Windsor, Oct. 12, 1800, by Dwight
Ives, of Suffield — 2 — 510

Nathan, m. Margret **KELLOGG,** b. of Windsor, Mar. 20,
1755 — 2 — 209

Sibbel, d. Zebulon & Mahittabel, b. Feb. 20, 1749/50 — 2 — 120

Zebulon, Jr., of Windsor, m. Mahetable **HUNTINGTON,** of
Windham, Nov. 24, 1748 — 2 — 209

WEBSTER, Azubah, w. Jacob, d. Jan. 9, 1758 — 2 — 279

Daniel, m. Rhoda **FYLOR,** b. of Windsor, Oct. 14, 1821, by
Angustus Bolles — 2 — 210

Hezekiah, s. Jacob & Azubah, b. Oct. 23, 1749 — 2 — 130

Hezekiah, s. Jacob & Azubah, d. Dec. 16, 1749 — 2 — 279

Jacob, m. Azubah **BARBER,** b. of Windsor, Jan. 19, 1748/9 — 2 — 209

James, s. William & Mary, b. Nov. 11, 1740 — 2 — 454

Mary, m. Fflurance **DRISCOLL,** b. of Windsor, Apr. 24,
1674, by Capt. Newbery — Col.1 — 46

Mary, d. William & Mary, b. Mar. 5, 1746 — 2 — 454

Mary, w. William, d. May 6, 1754 — 2 — 279

Nancy, of Windsor, m. Edwin **GRISWOLD,** of Simsbury,
Apr. 20, 1825, by Rev. John Bartlett. Int. Pub. — 2 — 479

Rhoda, m. Chauncey R. **JOHNSON,** b. of Avon, Jan. 9,
[   ], by John Bartlett — 2 — 486

Sarah, d. William & Mary, b. Jan. 8, 1735/6 — 2 — 453

Susanna, d. William & Mary, b. June 29, 1743 — 2 — 454

William, m. Mary **WATSON,** June 3, 1731 — 2 — 209

William, s. William & Mary, b. July 29, 1738 — 2 — 453

-----, wid., d. [   ], [16]44 — MG

WEEKS, Joseph, of Hartford, m. Delia **BIRGE,** of Windsor, Dec.
14, 1836, by William H. Shailer — 2 — 513

WELCH, Isaac, s. Isaac & Climenia, b. Oct. 22, 1770 — 2 — 455

Julia, m. Stanton **BABCOCK,** b. of Windsor, Jan. 6, 1840, by
Rev. S. D. Jewett — 2 — 466

Julia Elizabeth, d. Lemuel, Jr. & Anna, b. Apr. 23, 1822 — 2 — 460

Lemuel A., m. Harriet S. **COOK,** Jan. 12, 1848, by Rev.
Samuel A. Stedman — 2 — 519

Lemuel Augustus, s. Lemuel, Jr. & Anna, b. Feb. 4, 1812 — 2 — 459

Nancy, d. Lemuel, Jr. & Anna, b. Jan. 23, 1814 — 2 — 460

Nancy Ann, m. Horace **BOWER,** Nov. 18, 1835, by H. A.
Rowland — 2 — 499

William, m. Amelia **STILES,** b. of Windsor, Aug. 14, 1821,
by Joseph H. Russell, J. P. — 2 — 210

	Vol.	Page
WELLER, Eliasor, s. [Richard & Ann], b. Nov. 20, 1650	MG	
Eleazar, s. Richard, bp. Nov. 20, 1650	Col.2	157
Eleazer, s. Richard, b. Nov. 20, 1650	1	37
Eliaser, s. Richard, b. Nov. 20, 1650	1	37
John, s. Richard, b. Aug. 9, 1645	1	38
John, s. [Richard & Ann], bp. Aug. 10, 1645	MG	
John, s. Richard, bp. Aug. 10, 1645	Col.2	157
Nathanell, s. [Richard & Ann], b. July 15, 1648	MG	
Nathanael, s. Richard, bp. (sic), b. July 15, 1648	Col.2	157
Nathanael, s. Richard, b. July 15, 1648	1	37
Rebeca, d. [Richard & Ann], b. May 10, 1641	MG	
Rebekcha, d. Richard, bp. May 16, 1641	Col.2	157
Rebekah, d. Richard, bp. May 16, 1641	1	37
Richard, m. Ann **WILSON**, Sept. 17, 16[ ]	MG	
Richard, m. Ann **WILSON**, Sept. 17, 1640	1	62
Richard, his w. [ ], d. July 10, 1655	Col.2	160
Richard, had 6 children b. in Windsor. Dated Aug. 17, 1677	MG	
Sara, d. [Richard & Ann], b. Apr. 10, 1643	MG	
Sarah, d. Richard, bp. Apr. 16, 1643	Col.2	157
Sarah, d. Richard, bp. Apr. 16, 1643	1	37
Thomas, s. [Richard & Ann], b. Apr. 10, 1653	MG	
Thomas, s. Richard, b. Apr. 10, 1653	Col.2	157
Thomas, s. Richard, b. Apr. 10, 1653	1	37
WELLES, WELLS, WILLES, WILLS, [see also **WILLIS**],		
Elizabeth, d. Joshua, Jr., b. Apr. 19, 1698	1	38
Elizabeth, w. Joshua, Jr., d. Oct. 9, 1707	2	276
Elizabeth, d. Lamson & Mabel, b. June 5, 1740	2	119
Flora, m. Israel I. **PALMER**, Dec. 3, 1828, by John Bartlett	2	193
Hana, d. Joshua, b. Aug. 24, 1682	Col.D	51
Hannah, d. Joshua, b. Aug. 24, [16]82	1	38
Hannah, w. Joshua, d. Nov. [ ], 1694	1	52
Harlow, of Farmington, m. Almira **KELSEY**, of Windsor, Oct. 22, 1823, by Rev. Augustus Bolles, of Wintonbury	2	211
Henry, s. Joshua, b. Oct. 14, 1690	1	38
Hezekiah, s. Lamson & Mabel, b. June 25, 1736	2	118
Hiram, of Hartford, m. Maria **MARSHALL**, of Windsor, July 22, 1824, by Rev. John Bartlett, of Wintonbury, Int. Pub.	2	211
Ira, s. Lamson & Mabel, b. Mar. 23, 1744/5	2	119
Jacob, s. Joshua, b. Oct. 21, 1693	1	38
Jacob, of Windsor, m. Dinah **PECK**, of Norwich, May 17, 1720	2	208
James H., m. Susan Ann **HAYDON**, Feb. 26, 1840, by S. D. Jewett	2	514
Gared*, m. Mary **MOFFETT**, Dec. 13, 1832, b. of Windsor, by Henry A. Rowland *("Jared")	2	513
John, s. Joshua, b. June 14, 1687	1	38
John, s. Jacob, b. May 26, 1721	2	115

	Vol.	Page
WELLES, WELLS, WILLES, WILLS, (cont.)		
John, of Dearfield, m. Sarah **ALLYN**, of Windsor, Jan.		
2, 1728/9	2	208
Jonathan, s. [Josua & Asubath], b. Dec. 24, [16]70	MG	
Jonathan, s. Joshua, Jr., b. Dec. 31, 1703	1	39
Josua, m. Asubath **LAMSON**, May 5, 1670, by Capt.Newbery	MG	
Josua, m. Asubath **LAMSON**, May 5, 1670, by Capt.		
Newbery	Col.1	46
Joshua, s. Joshua, b. Apr. 10, [16]72	1	38
Josua, his w. [ ], d. Sept. 12, 1676 *(Note by LBB;		
"Azubah (**LAMSON**) **WELLS**")	Col.1	58
Joshua, his w. [ ]*, d. Sept. 12, 1676	1	52
Josua, m. Hanna **BUCKLAND**, d. Thomas, Sr., Aug. 11,		
1681, by Capt. Hewbery	MG	
Josua, m. Hanna **BUCKLAND**, [ ] 11, 1681, by Capt.		
Newbery	TR1	1
Joshua, m. Hannah **BUCKLAND**, Aug. 11, 1681, by Capt.		
Nubery	1	63
Josua, his w. [ ], d. Sept. 12, [16]81	MG	
Joshua, m. Elizabeth **GRANT**, May 12, 1697	1	63
Joshua, s. Joshua, Jr., b. May 11, 1700/1	1	39
Joshua, s. Lamson & Mabel, b. Feb. 22, 1741/2	2	119
Lamson, s. Lamson & Mabel, b. Nov. 27, 1737	2	118
Lamson, Jr., m. Hannah **ORSBAND**, Jr., b. of Windsor, Feb.		
20, 1757	2	210
Lucy, m. Gilbert **FILLEY**, b. of Windsor, Dec. 29, 1821, by		
Rev. Augustus Bolles, of Wintonbury	2	476
Mary, d. Joshua, Jr., b. Apr. 1, 1700	1	39
Mary, d. Joshua, Jr., b. Apr. 1, 1700	1	52
Mary, m. Jehu P. **ELLSWORTH**, b. of Windsor, Nov. 28,		
1843, by Rev. S. W. Scofield	2	501
Orson, of Simsbury, m. Malissa **HUMPHREY**, of		
Farmington, Aug. 21, 1822, by John Bartlett. Int. Pub.	2	512
Phidelia M., of Leyden, Mass., m. Silas **PARMELE**, of		
Windsor, June 7, 1849, by Rev. S. H. Allen	2	502
Ralph, of Farmington, m. Eunice E. **ALLYN**, of Windsor,		
Oct. 28, 1829, by John Bartlett	2	212
Sarah, of Farmington, m. [ ] **JOHNSON**, of Harwinton,		
Aug. 22, 1827, by Rev. John Bartlett	2	486
Thomas, s. Thomas & Dorothy, b. Jan. 7, 1770	2	457
Timothy, m. Huldah **PHELPS**, b. of Windsor, July 20, 1828,		
by Rev. Henry A. Rowland	2	212
Ursula, m. Josiah **CORNING**, Oct. 15, 1834, by Henry A.		
Rowland	2	471
Zerviah, d. Joshua, Jr., b. Jan. 9, 1711/12	2	114
WEST, Asa, s. Samuel, b. Nov. 19, 1721	2	115
Benjamin, s. Samuel & Dorithy, b. Aug. 1, 1733	2	118
Dority, d. Samuel, b. Aug. 19, 1723	2	116

	Vol.	Page
WEST, (cont.)		
Elizabeth, d. Samuel & Dorithy, b. June 7, 1730	2	117
Gilbert, of Rockville, m. Mrs. Mary Ann **HEMMINGWAY**		
of Windsor, Sept. 21, 1857, by Levi Smith	2	520
Hannah, d. Samuel & Dorithy, b. Aug. 13, 1727	2	117
Joseph, s. Samuel, b. Mar. 2, 1711/12	2	113
Judah, w. Zebulon, d. Feb. 5, 1750/1	2	279
Rhoda, d. Samuell, b. Dec. 8, 1709	2	112
Samuell, m. Dorithee **EGLSTONE**, Feb. 24, 1708/9	2	207
Samuel, s. Samuel, b. Oct. 28, 1714	2	114
Stephen, s. Zebulon & Judah, d. Sept. 6, 1751	2	279
Thomas, s. Samuel, b. July 21, 1719	2	115
William, s. Samuel, b. Mar. 26, 1717	2	115
WESTLAND, Amos, s. Robert & Thankfull, b. July 30, 1723	2	116
Amos, s. Amos & Marey, b. Aug. 19, [1749]	2	121
Amos, Jr., m. Mary **BROWN**, [ ]	2	210
Austin, s. Amos, Jr. & Mary, b. May 20, 1787	2	458
Candis, d. Joseph & Lusina, b. Feb. 13, 1798	2	458
Caroline Amanda, of Windsor, m. W[illia]m Warner		
BILLINGS, of East Windsor, July 18, 1847, by Samuel		
A. Seaman	2	503
Cata, d. Joseph & Lusina, b. Feb. 8, 1790	2	458
Deborah, d. Robert, Jr. & Thankfull, b. Feb. 24, 1725/6	2	117
Elizabeth, d. Amos, Jr. & Mary, b. Sept. 4, 1779	2	457
Grove, s. Joseph & [Lusina], b. June 2, 1793	2	458
Hannah, d. Amos, Jr. & Mary, b. June 26, 1784	2	457
Julia Ann, of Windsor, m. John D. **ALDERMAN**, of		
Hamilton, N. Y., Nov. 26, 1841, by [ ]	2	464
Lydia, d. Robert & Thankfull, b. Dec. 12, 1729	2	117
Lydia, had s. Phenihas, b. Jan. 1, 1752	2	455
Lydia, m. Noah **COOK**, b. of Windsor, Feb. 21, 1758	2	137
Marcy, d. Robert & Thankfull, b. June 15, 1734	2	117
Mary, m. Ephraim **BROWN**, Jr., b. of Windsor, Apr. 13,		
1757	2	133
Mary, d. Amos, Jr. & Mary, b. Apr. 15, 1782	2	457
Olive, m. William **ADDAMS**, b. of Windsor, June 16, 1823,		
by James Loomis, J. P.	2	125
Phenihas, s. Lydia, b. Jan. 1, 1752	2	455
Robert, of Windsor, m. Thankfull **ADDAMS**, of Simsbury,		
May 17, 1721	2	208
Robert, d. Apr. 15, 1728	2	278
Robert, s. Robert & Thankfull, b. Sept. 15, 1731	2	117
Sally, d. Joseph & Lusina, b. Nov. 25, 1787	2	458
Thankfull, wid., d. Feb. 13, 1733/4	2	278
William, s. Joseph & Lusina, b. Aug. 22, 1795	2	458
William, of O., m. Nancy **GILLET**, 2nd, of Windsor, June		
13, 1822, by Rev. John Bartlett. Int. Pub.	2	512
William D., m. Mary Ann **ALDERMAN**, Nov. 9, 1834, by		

	Vol.	Page
WESTLAND, (cont.)		
Henry A. Rowland	2	513
WESTON, Almira, m. Harvey **LATIMER**, Apr. 11, [18], by		
Rev. Asa Bushnell, Jr.	2	175
Luke, s. Samuel & Sarah, b. Dec. 6, 1756	2	454
Sarah, d. Samuel & Sarah, b. June 27, 1751	2	120
WESTOUER, Jonas, m. Hanna **GRISWOLD**, Nov. 19, 1663	Col.1	45
Jonas, s. Jonas, b. Sept. 20, 1664	Col.1	54
[WHAPLES], WAPLES, Nathan, of Hartford, m. Grace		
EGLSTONE, d. Thomas, of Windsor, Aug. 3, 1714	2	208
WHEELER, Hannah M., of Windsor, m. William **CALVERT**, of		
Manchester, Nov. 9, 1842, by Moses Stoddard	2	516
William C., m. Dorothy S. **GRISWOLD**, of Windsor,		
May 4, 1842, by Rev. David S. Marks	2	516
WHIPPLE, Joseph, of East Windsor, m. Eveline **PINNEY**, of		
Windsor, Jan. [ ], 1841, by Rev. A. C. Washburn	2	515
WHITCOMB, WHITTCOMB, Abigail, m. William **KELCIE**, b.		
of Windsor, Mar. 23, 1694/5	1	58
Jemimah, m. Ebenezer **LOOMIS**, Apr. 15, 1697	1	59
Mary, m. Humphery **PRIOR**, [ ]	Col.D	54
Mehetebel, d. Joseph & Mary, b. July 1, 1749	2	455
WHITE, Anne, w. Daniell, d. Apr. 21, 1709	2	276
Betty, Mrs., of Bolton, m. Rev. John **BLISS**, of Windsor,		
Jan. 15, 1766	2	134
Daniel, of Hartford, m. Anne **BISSELL**, of Windsor, July 6,		
1704	2	207
Daniel, of Windsor, m. Elisabeth **BLISS**, of Norwich,		
Apr. 25, 1710	2	207
Daniel, Capt., d. June 22, 1726	2	277
Edward, m. Jane **PETERSON**, b. of Windsor, Apr. 16, 1848,		
by Rev. Cephus Brainard	2	520
Elifelet, s. Robert & Elisabeth, b. June 12, 1745	2	120
Elisha, s. Daniell, b. Nov. 11, 1706	2	111
Elizabeth, of Hatfield, m. Samuel **LOOMIS**, of Windsor,		
July 2, 1688	1	58
Elizabeth, d. Capt. Daniel, b. May 18, 1717	2	116
Elisabeth, d. Robert & Elisabeth, b. Oct. 19, 1742	2	119
Esther, of Hatfield, m. John **ELSWORTH**, of Windsor,		
Dec. 9, 1696	1	56
Esther, m. Daniel **SKINNER**, b. of Windsor, May 15, 1765	2	201
Friend, s. Robert & Elizabeth, b. Nov. 1, 1748	2	121
Henry, of East Windsor, m. Jerusha **BARBER**, June 9, 1825,		
by Rev. Henry A. Rowland	2	211
Joell, s. Daniel, b. Apr. 6, 1705	2	111
Luce, d. Daniel, b. June 16, 1715	2	114
Mary, d. Robert & Elizabeth, b. Mar. 13, 1751/2	2	121
Mehitabel, of Hatfield, m. Jerimiah **BISSELL**, of Windsor,		
Dec. 18, 1705	2	128

	Vol.	Page
WHITE, (cont.)		
Oliver, s. Capt. Daniel, b. Mar. 26, 1720	2	116
Sarah, m. Daniell **GRISWOLD**, Jr., b. of Windsor, Sept.*		
5, 1716 *("Dec." crossed out)	2	155
Seth, s. Daniel, b. Mar. 6, 1712/13	2	114
Simeon, s. Daniell, b. Mar. 11, 1707/8	2	111
WHITEMARSH, Samuel, s. Nicolas & Elizabeth, b. Dec. 4, 1741	2	119
WHITING, Almira, of Hartford, m. Joab **HUBBARD**, 2nd, of Windsor, May 9, 1822, by Rev. Augustus Bolles, of Wintonbury	2	165
Margaret, of Hartford, m. Jonathan **MARSH**, of Windsor, July 13, 1710	2	176
Nathaniel, of West Hartford, m. Mahala **CADWELL**, Mar. 31, 1831, by John Bartlett	2	213
WHITMAN, Stillman F., m. Cynthia L. **LATHROP**, b. of Windsor, Mar. 28, 1852, by Rev. S. H. Allen	2	520
WHITON, Simeon, of Ashford, m. Cordelia **BIDWELL**, of Windsor, Apr. 18, 1832, by Ansel Nash	2	513
WHURY (?), John, m. Margaret **TOD[D]**, b. of Windsor, May 30, 1852, by Rev. H. N. Weed	2	520
WIARD, Lois, of Farmington, m. Martin **DESSLOW**, of Windsor, Apr. 11, 1770	2	143
WICKHAM, Timothy, of Glastenbury, m. Hellen M. **SOPER**, of Windsor, May 30, 1848, by C. B. Everest	2	520
WICKWARE, Albert G., of Bristol, m. Rebecca G. **GRISWOLD**, of Windsor, Jan. 20, 1834, by Rev. Stephen Martindale	2	213
WIGHT, Samuel, of Windsor, m. Elizabeth **JUPSON**, of West Springfield, Nov. 4, 1849, by Rev. Cephas Brainard	2	516
WILCOX, [see also **WILCOXSON**], Martha, d. Ebenezer, b. June 3, 1710	2	112
WILCOXSON, WILCOKSON, WILLCOCKSON, WILCOKEN, [see also **WILCOX**], Ebenezer, m. Martha **GAYLORD**, Jan. 15, 1707/8	2	207
Elizabeth, m. Henery **STILLES**, Apr. 16, 1663	MG	
Elizabeth, m. Henry **STILLES**, Apr. 16, 1663	Col.1	45
Elizabeth, m. Henry **STYLES**, Apr. 16, 1663	1	61
Hanna, m. Daniell **HAYDON**, Mar. 17, 1664	MG	
Hanna, m. Daniel **HAYDON**, Mar. 17, [16]64, by Mr. Allyn	Col.1	45
Hannah, m. Daniel **HAYDON**, Mar. 17, 1664, by Mr. Allyn	1	57
Samuell, s. Samuell, b. Apr. 15, 1666	Col.1	56
Samuel, s. Samuel, b. Apr. 15, 1666	1	37
WILES, Ruth Aurelia, of Cabotville, Mass., m. Nathan G. **FILLEY**, of Bloomfield,, Jan. 8, 1847, by George F. Kettell	2	478
WILLIAMS, WILLIAM, WILLIAMES, A. R., m. Mary C. **EARL**, b. of Buffalo, N. Y., May 17, 1847, by T. A. Leete	2	519
Abiell, d. [John & Mary], b. Sept. 2, 1655	MG	

	Vol.	Page
WILLIAMS, WILLIAM, WILLIAMES, (cont.)		
Abiell, d. John, m. Samuell **PHELPS**, s. Samuell, June 21,		
1678	Col.1	46
Abigall, d. John, b. Sept. 2, 1655	Col.2	181
Abigayle, d. [John & Mary], b. May 31, 1658	MG	
Abigail, m. Edward **GRISWOLD**, Nov. 3, 1681	Col.D	54
Abigail, m. Edward **GRISWOLD**, Nov. 3, [ ]	1	57
Arther, m. Cathrine **CARTER**, Nov. 30, 1647	1	62
Arter, had 1 child b. in Windsor. Dated Aug. 17, 1677	MG	
Asahel, m. Emeline **CIESAR***, Oct. 1, 1839, by Henry A.		
Rowland *(In pencil)	2	212
Dauid, d. Sept. 7, 1684	Col. D	56
David, d. Sept. 7, 1684	1	52
Ebenezer, twin with John, s. [John & Bethia], b. Jan. 7, 1675	MG	
Ebenezer, twin with John, s. John, b. Jan. 7, [16]75	1	38
Elisabeth, twin with Mary, d. [John & Mary], b. Jan. 5, 1652	MG	
Elizabeth, twin with Mary, d. John, b. Jan. 5, 1652	1	37
Elizabeth, d. John, d. Feb. 22, 1652	1	52
Esther, wid., (It is reported she was first female child		
b. in Hartford. Formerly wid. of James **EGLESTON**),		
d. July 10, 1720	2	277
Frances, s. John, [& Bethia], b. May 25, 1673	MG	
Hanna, d. [John & Mary], b. Apr. 13, 1651; d. [ ]	MG	
Hannah, d. John, b. Apr. 13, 1651	1	37
Hannah, d. John, b. Apr. 13, 1651	1	37
Hanna, d. John, m. Nathanell **BANCROFT**, Dec. 26, 1677,		
by Capt. [ ] Newbery	MG	
Hanna, d. John, m. Nathanell **BANCROFT**, Dec. 26, [16]77,		
by Capt. Newbery	Col.1	46
Hanna, m. Nathanell **BANCROFT**, Dec. 26, 1677, by Capt.		
Newbery	TR1	1
Hannah, m. Nathanael **BANCROFT**, Dec. 26, 1677, by Capt.		
Nubery	1	54
Henry, m. Lucinda **ROSS**, Oct. 13, 1834, by Henry A.		
Rowland	2	513
Jane, m. John **MORTON**, b. of Windsor, May 7, 1713	2	178
John, m. Mary **BURLLY**, June 29, 1644	MG	
John, s. [John & Mary], b. Mar. 26, 1646; d. [ ]	MG	
John, s. John, b. Mar. 26, 1646	1	37
John, his d. [ ], d. [ ], [16]52	MG	
John, d. Aug. 8, 1665	Col.1	55
John, Jr., d. [ ], [16]65	MG	
John, m. Bethia **MASKELL**, wid., Aug. 8, 1672, by Capt.		
Newbery	MG	
John, m. wid. Bethia **MASKELL**, Aug. 8, [16]72	Col.1	46
John, twin with Ebenezer, s. [John & Bethia], b. Jan.		
7, 1675	MG	
John, twin with Ebenezer, s. John, b. Jan. 7, [16]75	1	38

	Vol.	Page
WILSON, WILLSON, (cont.)		
Cortney, s. Calvin & Submit, d. Jan. 11, 1798	2	280
Ebenezer, s. Ebenezer, b. Dec. 26, 1708	2	112
Ebenezer, s. Samuel & Jemima, b. Mar. 28, 1734/5	2	118
Eli, s. Phenihas & Mary, b. Aug. 23, 1757	2	454
Eli, his wid. [ ], d. Nov. 3, 1845, ae 84	2	281
Eli, s. Phinehas, d. Mar. 9, [ ], ae 84	2	280
Eliza, d. Calvin & Submit, b. Nov. 4, 1800	2	459
Eliza, d. Calvin & Submit, d. Sept. 12, 1803	2	280
Eliza, m. Hector **HUBBARD**, b. of Windsor, Mar. 4, 1822, by Rev. John Bartlett. Int. Pub.	2	165
Eliza, m. Horace **THRALL**, b. of Windsor, Mar. 18, 1823, by James Loomis, J. P.	2	205
Emma, d. Calvin & Submit, b. Jan. 9, 1795	2	458
Grigs, s. Calvin & Submit, b. Feb. 10, 1793	2	458
Griggs, s. Calvin & Submit, d. July 31, 1800	2	280
Hannah, d. John & Mary, b. Oct. 19, 1713	2	116
Hannah, m. Josiah **DRAKE**, b. of Windsor, May 7, 1735	2	142
Hannah, d. Abiel & Hannah, b. May 2, 1786	2	459
Hannah, m. George **LOOMIS**, b. of Windsor, Feb. 10, 1807	2	488
Henry, Jr., m. Susan A. **NEWBERRY**, b. of Windsor, Nov. 17, 1842, by Rev. S. D. Jewett	2	516
Huldah, of Windsor, m. William **MARSH**, of Hartford, May 9, 1822, by Rev. Henry A. Rowland	2	181
Isabell, m. William **PHELPS**, s. [William], June 4, 1646; "now since 29 y. and has had no child July 15, [16]74"	MG	
Isable, m. William **PHELPS**, June 4, 1645	1	60
Isable, d. Samuel, b. Feb. 24, [16]72	1	37
Jezabell, d. Samuell & Mary, b. Feb. 24, [16]73	MG	
Jemima, d. Samuel, b. Feb. 15, 1723/4	2	116
Joab, s. Joel & Abigail, b. Dec. 22, 1761	2	455
Job, s. Abigail, b. Jan. 18, 1703/4	1	39
Joel, s. John & Mary, b. Apr. 17, 1718	2	116
Joel, s. Joel & Abigail, b. May 1, 1746	2	120
John, s. Sam[ue]l, b. May 24, 1686	Col.D	51
John, s. Samuel, b. May 24, 1686	1	38
John, m. Mary **MARSHALL**, June 16, 1709	2	207
John, s. John & Mary, b. Nov. 7, 1711	2	116
John, s. Joel & Abigail, b. Oct. 3, 1757	2	455
Julia, m. W[illia]m **LUCK**, b. of Windsor, June 4, 1837, by Eli Deniston	2	490
Keziah, d. Samuel & Jemima, b. Sept. 21, 1725	2	116
Laura, d. Calvin & Submit, b. Jan. 19, 1790	2	458
Lurannah, d. James & Margret, b. Nov. 15, 1778	2	457
Lyda, d. James & Luranna, b. Mar. 10, 1777	2	456
Mary, d. [Samuell & Mary], b. Aug. 5, 1675	MG	
Mary, d. Samuel, b. Aug. 5, [16]75; bp. the 8th day	1	38
Mary, m. John **FILLY**, b. of Windsor, Oct. 9, 1707	2	151

	Vol.	Page
WILSON, WILLSON, (cont.)		
Mary, d. John, b. July 16, 1710	2	112
Mary, m. Jonathan **FILLEY**, b. of Windsor, Jan. 2, 1728/9	2	151
Mary, d. Samuel & Jemima, b. Feb. 18, 1729/30	2	117
Mary, d. Phinehas & Mary, b. Apr. 4, 1752	2	121
Mary, w. Dea. John, d. Feb. 11, 1772, in the 83rd y. of her age	2	280
Mary, d. Eli & Lydia, b. July 14, 1822	2	459
Millissent, d. Eli & Lydia, b. Nov. 23, 1819	2	459
Millissent, d. Eli, d. Sept. 5, 1845, ae 26	2	281
Moses, s. Joel & Abigael, b. Sept. 11, 1748	2	120
Moses, m. Wealthy Ann **BARNES**, b. of Windsor, Feb. 5, 1824, by Joseph H. Russell, J. P.	2	211
Moses, d. May 20, 1837	2	280
Noah, s. John & Mary, b. Feb. 12, 1715/16	2	116
Oliver, s. Calvin & Submit, b. Oct. 14, 1785	2	458
Oliver, s. Calvin & Submit, d. Jan. 22, 1787	2	280
Oliver, s. Calvin & Submit, b. Jan. 10, 1788	2	458
Olivia C., m. Lucius B. **CHAPMAN**, b. of Windsor Locks, Dec. 4, 1849, by Rev. S. H. Allin	2	140
Orson*, m. Rhoda **LOOMIS**, b. of Windsor, Apr. 11, 1849, by Rev. Samuel Law *("Orson Wilson **AUSTIN**" crossed out in the original)	2	520
Phenihas, s. John & Mary, b. Mar. 16, 1728	2	118
Phinehas, m. Mary **PALMER**, b. of Windsor, Nov. 21, 1750	2	209
Phinehas, s. Phinahas & Mary, b. Aug. 26, 1753	2	121
Polly, d. James & Margret, b. Nov. 30, 1780	2	457
Rachel, d. John & Mary, b. June 6, 1720	2	116
Richard Griswold, s. Calvin & Submit, b. Nov. 8, 1802	2	459
Richard Griswold, s. Calvin & Submit, d. Oct. 6, 1803	2	280
Ruth, d. Phinihas & Mary, b. Mar. 10, 1755	2	454
Samuell, s. Samuell & Mary, b. May 1, 1672	MG	
Samuell, m. Mary **GRIFFEN**, b. of Windsor, May 1, 1672	Col.1	46
Samuel, b. May 1, 1672	1	37
Samuel, m. Mary **GRIFFIN**, b. of Windsor, May 1, 1672	1	63
Samuell, had 2 children b. in Windsor. Dated Aug. 17, 1677	MG	
Samuell, s. [Samuell & Mary], b. Nov. 21, 1678	MG	
Samuell, s. Samuel, b. Nov. 21, 1678	Col.1	56
Samuel, s. Samuel, b. Nov. 21, [16]78	1	38
Sam[ue]ll, s. Sam[ue]ll, d. July 31, 1689	Col.D	56
Samuel, s. Samuel, d. July 31, 1689	1	52
Samuel, d. Aug. 3, 1697	1	52
Samuel, adult, ch. mem. 16[ ]	MG	
Samuel, of Windsor, m. Jemima **LEWIS**, of East Haddam, May 9, 1723	2	208
Samuel, s. Samuel & Jemima, b. Dec. 14, 1727	2	117
Samuell, s. Joel & Abigail, b. Feb. 17, 1754	2	453
Samuel, m. Delia **CHAPMAN**, Nov. 29, 1827, by Rev.		

	Vol.	Page
WILSON, WILLSON, (cont.)		
Henry A. Rowland	2	212
Samuell, contributed 0-1-3 to the poor in other colonies	MG	
Sarah, d. Samuel & Jemima, b. Apr. 9, 1732	2	118
Thomas, s. Samuell & Mary, b. July 18, [1676]; bp. [July] 23, 1676	MG	
------, m. Mary **GRIFFEN**, [ ]	MG	
WILTON, Dauid, s. [Nicolas & Mary], b. Jan. 13, 1660	MG	
David, s. Nicholos, b. Jan. 13, 1660	1	37
John, s. [Nicolas & Mary], b. Aug. 8, 1664	MG	
John, s. Nicholos, b. Aug. 8, 1664	1	37
Mary, m. Samuell **MARSHALL**, May 6, 1652	MG	
Mary, m. Samuell **MARSHALL**, b. of Windsor, May 6, 1652	Col.2	159
Mary, m. Samuel **MARSHEL**, May 6, 1652	1	59
Mary*, w. Nich[olas], d. Aug. 4, 1683 *(Note by LBB: "Mary (STANFORD) WILTON")	Col.D	56
Mary, w. Nicholas, d. Aug. 4, 1683	1	52
Mary, see Mary **MARSHALL**	Col.D	56
Nicolas, m. Mary **STANNIFORD**, Nov. 20, 1656	MG	
Nicholas, m. Mary **STANFORD**, Nov. 20, 1656	Col.2	159
Nicolas, m. Mary **STANFORD**, b. of Windsor, Nov. 20, 1656	1	63
Nicolas, had 2 children b. in Windsor. Dated Aug. 17, 1677	MG	
Nicho[las], d. Aug. 4, 1683	Col.D	56
Nicholas, d. Aug. 4, 1683	1	52
Nicolas, contributed 0-1-8 to the poor in other colonies	MG	
Robard, d. Feb. 11, [16]40	MG	
------, wid. Daued, m. Osmer **GOODMAN**, of Hartford, May 6, [16]79, at Hartford	MG	
WINCHELL, WINCHEL, Beniamen, s. [Robard], bp. July 11, 16[5?]2	MG	
Beniamin, s. Robert, bp. July 11, 1652	Col.2	157
Benjamin, s. Robert, bp. July 11, 1652	1	37
Beniamen, d. [ ], [16]56	MG	
Benjamin, d. June 24, 1656	Col.2	160
Benjamin, s. Robert, bd. June 24, 1656	1	52
Caleb, s. Stephen, b. Dec. 6, 1701	2	113
Christian, d. [Dauid & Elisabeth], b. Mar. 9, 1672	MG	
Christian, m. Obediah **OWIN**, Sept. 21, 1693	1	59
Daniel, s. John, b. Apr. 22, 1718	2	115
Daniel, s. John, d. Apr. 19, 1733	2	278
Dauid, s. [Robard], bp. Oct. 22, 1643	MG	
David, s. Robert, bp. Oct. 22, 1643	Col.2	156
Dauid, m. Elisabeth **FFILLY**, Nov. 17, 1669	MG	
Daued, m. Elizabeth **FFILLYE**, Nov. 17, 1669	Col.1	45
David, m. Elizabeth **FILLEY**, Nov. 17, 1669	1	63
Dauid, bp. Sept. 18, [16]70	MG	
Daued, had 3 children, b. in Windsor. Dated Aug. 17, 1677	MG	

	Vol.	Page
WINCHELL, WINCHEL, (cont.)		
Dauid, contributed 0-2-6 to the poor in other colonies	MG	
Dorithy, d. Stephen, b. Oct. 2, 1703	2	113
Ebenezer, s. John, b. Sept. 15, 1719	2	115
Ebenezer, s. John, d. Apr. 8, 1721	2	277
Ebenezer, s. John, b. Mar. 31, 1722	2	116
Elisabeth, d. [Dauid & Elisabeth], b. Dec. 9, 1675	MG	
Eunice C., m. Jehiel HOUSE, b. of Windsor, Jan. 13, 1839,		
by Rev. Cephas Brainard	2	483
Hannah, d. Thomas, b. May 18, 1693	1	38
Hannah, d. Nathanael, b. Nov. 5, 1695	1	38
Hannah, m. Ebenezer HURLBURT, May 11, 1710	2	161
Hannah, d. John, b. Feb. 13, 1715/16	2	114
Hezekiah, s. Nathanael, b. June 20, 1697	1	38
John, m. Martha ENNO, Jan. 3, 1705/6	2	207
John, s. John, b. Apr. 5, 1707	2	112
John, d. Dec. 1, 1773	2	280
Jonathan, m. Abigayl BRUNSON, May 16, [16]	MG	
Jonathan, m. Abigall BRUNSON, May [ ], 1666, at Farming		
Town, by Mr. H[a]wkins	Col.1	45
Jonathan, m. Abigail BRUSAN, May [ ], 1666, in		
Farmington, by Mr. Hukins	1	63
Jonathan, s. [Jonathan & Abigayl], b. Feb. [ ], 16[ ]	MG	
Jonathan, bp. Feb. [ ], [16]67	MG	
Jonathan, had 1 child b. in Windsor. Dated Aug. 17, 1677	MG	
Joseph, s. [Robard], bp. Apr. 5, 1646	MG	
Joseph, s. Robert, bp. Apr. 5, 1646	Col.2	156
Joseph, s. [Dauid & Elisabeth], b. Sept. 13, 1670	MG	
Joseph, of Suffield, m. wid. Anne DENSLOW, of Windsor,		
Apr. 11, 1751	2	209
Lydia, d. Robert & Lydia, b. July 8, 1734	2	118
Martha, d. [Robard], bp. June 18, 1648	MG	
Martha, d. Robert, bp. June 18, 1648	Col.2	157
Martha, d. [ ], [16]53	MG	
Martha, d. July 12, 1655	Col.2	160
Martha, d. July 12, [16]55, ae 7 y.	1	52
Martha, of Suffield, m. Benajah HOLCOMB, of Windsor,		
May 17, 1705	2	161
Martha, d. John, b. Aug. 24, 1713	2	114
Martha, d. John & Martha, b. Dec. 5, 1726	2	117
Martha, d. John & Martha, d. Jan. 27, 1728/9	2	278
Martin, s. Stephen, b. Dec. 23, 1708	2	113
Mary, d. [Robard], bp. Sept. 5, 1641	MG	
Mary, d. Robert, bp. Sept. 5, 1641	Col.2	156
Mary, m. Samuel GIBBS, b. of Windsor, Mar. 4, 17[0]2/3	1	57
Mary, m. Joseph HOLCOMB, Nov. 15, 1714	2	161
Mercy, d. Nathanael, b. Feb. 29, 1699/1700	1	38
Nathanell, m. Sara PORTER, Apr. [ ], [16]	MG	

	Vol.	Page
WINCHELL, WINCHEL, (cont.)		
Nathan[ie]l, his w. [ ], adm, ch. Aug. [ ], [16]	MG	
Nathanell, of Windsor, m. Sarah **PORTER**, of Farmingtowne, Apr. 8, 1664, by Anthony Howkins	Col.1	45
Nathanael, of Windsor, m. Sarah **PORTER**, of Farmington, Apr. 8, 1664, by Anthony Hawkins	1	63
Nathanell, s. [Nathanell & Sara], b. Aug. 5, 1665	MG	
Nathanell, s. Nathanell, b. Aug. 7, [16]65	Col.1	56
Nathanael, s. Nathanael, b. Aug. 7, [16]65	1	37
Nat[hananiel]*, his w. [ ], adm, ch. & communicant Aug. [ ], 1671 (Written "Nat[hananiel] **WINCLS**(?)")	MG	
Nathanell, had 4 children b. in Windsor. Dated Aug. 17, 1677	MG	
Nathanael, of Windsor, m. Mary **GRAVES**, of Hartford, Mar. 15, 1693/4	1	63
Nathanael, s. Nathanael, Jr., b. Dec. 24, 1694	1	38
Nathanael, Sr., d. Mar. 8, 1699/1700	1	52
Phebe, d. Robard, bp. Mar. 29, 163[7?]	MG	
Phebe, d. Robert, bp. Mar. 29, 1639	Col.2	156
Pheby, d. [ ], [16]62	MG	
Phebe, d. May 23, 1662	Col.1	55
Rob, d. [Jan. 21*], [16]67 *(In pencil)	MG	
Robard, his w. [ ], d. [ ], [16]55	MG	
Robert, his w. [ ], d. July 10, 1655	Col.2	160
Robert, his w. [ ], d. July 10, [16]55	1	52
Robard, d. Jan. 21, 1667	MG	
Robard, d. Jan. 21, [16]67	Col.1	55
Robert, d. Jan. 21, [16]67	1	52
Robard. had 6 children b. in Windsor. Dated Aug. 17, 1677	MG	
Robert, s. Stephen, b. May 28, 1705	2	113
Robert, of Simsbury, m. Lydia **HOLLEBIRT**, of Woodberry, Sept. 6, 1733	2	208
Samuel, s. Thomas, b. Jan. 5, 1690	1	38
Samuel, s. John, b. Mar. 15, 1710/11	2	113
Sara, d. [Nathanell & Sara], b. Dec. 26, 1674	MG	
Sarah, m. Josiah **PHELPS**, Apr. 26, 1690	1	60
Sarah, wid., d. Oct. 7, 1725	2	277
Silence, d. John, b. Jan. 6, 1708/9	2	112
Silence, m. Simon **CHAPMAN**, b. of Windsor, Dec. 25, 1730	2	136
Stephen, s. [Nathanell & Sara], b. Aug. 13, 1677	MG	
Stephen, s. Nat[han], bp. [16]	MG	
Stephen, m. Abigail **MARSHELL**, Mar. 10, 1697/8	1	63
Stephen, s. Stephen, b. Nov. 20, 1698	1	38
Stephen, s. Stephen, b. Nov. 20, 1698	2	113
Thomas, s. [Nathanell & Sara], b. May 25, 166[ ]	MG	
Thomas, s. Nathanae, b. May 25, [16]69	1	37
Thomas, m. Sarah **MOORE**, Apr. 26, 1690	1	63
Thomas, d. Aug. [ ], 1697	1	52

	Vol.	Page
WOLCOTT, WOLCOT, WOLCUTT, WOOLCOT,		
WOOLCOTT, (cont.)		
Charles, s. John, b. Sept. 3, 1681	Col.D	51
Charles, s. John, b. Sept. 3, 1681	1	38
Charles, m. Elizabeth **HAWLY,** Dec. 19, 1706	2	207
Charles, s. Charles, b. June 17, 1716	2	114
Charles, s. Charles, d. June 27, 1716	2	277
Charles, Lieut., d. July 20, 1754	2	279
Christopher, d. [ ], [16]62	MG	
Christopher, d. Sept. 7, 1662	Col.1	55
Christopher, s. Simon, b. July 4, 1672	1	38
Daniell, s. [Simon & Martha], b. Aug. [ ], 1676	MG	
Elisabeth, d. [Simon & Martha], b. Aug. 12, 1662	MG	
Elizabeth, d. Simon, b. Aug. 19, 1662	Col.1	54
Elizabeth, d. Simon, b. Aug. 19, [16]62	1	53
Elisabeth, d. [Henery, Jr. & Abia], b. Aug. 27, 1665	MG	
Elizabeth, d. Henry, Jr., b. Aug. 27, 1665	1	37
Eliz[abeth], m. Mathew **ALLYN,** b. of Windsor, Jan. 5, 1686	Col.D	57
Elizabeth, m. Mathew **ALLYN,** b. of Windsor, Jan. 5, 1686	1	53
Eliz[abeth], d. George, m. Gabriel **CORNISH,** of Westfeild, Dec. 15, 1686	Col.D	54
Elizabeth, d. George, m. Gabriell **CORNISH,** of Westfield, Dec. 15, 1686	1	55
Elisabeth, d. Roger, b. Apr. 10, 1706	2	111
Elizabeth, d. Roger, b. Apr. 20, 1707/8 (This entry crossed out)	2	112
Elizabeth, d. Charles, b. June 15, 1712	2	113
Elizabeth, Mrs., m. Roger **NEWBERY,** b. of Windsor, Aug. 24, 1727	2	182
Elizabeth, d. Lieut. Charles & Elizabeth, d. Mar. 5, 1727/8	2	277
Elizabeth, see Elizabeth **ALLYN**	2	522
[Elizabeth (**SANDERS**)*], w. Henery, d. July 5, 1655 *(Supplied by LBB)	Col.2	160
Epaphras, twin with Erastus, s. Roger, b. Feb. 8, 1720/1	2	115
Ephraim, s. William, b. Mar. 13, 1714/15	2	114
Ephraim, s. Ephraim & Mary, b. Feb. 25, 1762	2	455
Erastus, twin with Epaphras, s. Roger, b. Feb. 8, 1720/1	2	115
Esther, d. Dr. Alexander & Mary, b. Sept. 17, 1746	2	121
Esther, d. Dr. Alexander & Mary, d. Oct. 9, 1746	2	279
Esther, d. Dr. Alexander & Mary, b. July 17, 1749	2	121
[E]unice, d. Simon, b. Sept. 24, 1697	1	38
Eunice, d. Lieut. Charles, b. June 14, 1725	2	116
Eunice, d. Will[iam], Jr. & Abigail, b. Dec. 11, 1747	2	120
Eunice, see Eunice **OLCOTT**	2	523
Francis M., m. Archibald **RALSTON,** of Berthier, S. C., [18], by Rev. S. D. Jewett	2	506
George, s. John, b. Oct. 20, 1683	Col.D	51
George, s. John, b. Oct. 20, 1683	1	38

	Vol.	Page
WOLCOTT, WOLCOT, WOLCUTT, WOOLCOT,		
WOOLCOTT, (cont.)		
George, s. Charles, b. Mar. 3, 1713/4	2	114
George, s. Lieut. Charles & Elizabeth, d. Mar. 16, 1727/8	2	278
George, s. Dr. Alexander & Mary, b. May 23, 1751	2	121
George, s. Dr. Alexander & Mary, d. Oct. 17, 1751	2	279
George, s. Dr. Alexander & Mary, b. Oct. 17, 1753	2	453
H., his w. [ ], adm, ch. & comminicant Apr. [ ], 1666	MG	
H., Jr., contributed 0-5-0 to the poor in other colonies	MG	
Hanna, d. [Henery & Sara], b. Mar. 7, 1653	MG	
Hannah, d. Henry, b. Mar. 7, 1653	Col.2	157
Hannah, d. Henry, b. Mar. 7, 1653	Col.2	181
Hannah, d. John, Jr., b. Oct. 21, 1706	2	111
Hannah, m. Uriah LOOMIS, b. of Windsor, June 2, 1737	2	172
Henery, m. Sara NEWBERY, Nov. 8, [16]	MG	
Henery, his w. [ ], adm. ch. Apr. [ ], 16[ ]	MG	
Henery, s. [Henery & Sara], b. [ ]; bp. Jan. 8, 1642	MG	
Henery, s. Henery, [Jr.], bp. Jan. 8, 1642	Col.2	156
Henry, s. Henry, bp. Jan. 8, 1642	1	37
Henery, his child d. [ ], [16]48	MG	
Henery, d. May 30, 1655	Col.2	160
Henry, Sr., his w. [ ], d. [ ], [16]55	MG	
Henery, w. [ ]*, d. July 5, 1655 *(Note by LBB:		
"Elizabeth (SANDERS) WOLCOT")	Col.2	160
Henery, Sr., d. [ ], [16]55	MG	
Henery, Jr., m. Abia GOFFE, Oct. 12, 1664	MG	
Henery, m. Abia GOFF, Oct. 12, 1664, by Mr. Wolcot	Col.1	45
Henery, s. Henery, Jr., b. Apr. 13, 1667	Col.1	45
Henery, s. [Henery, Jr. & Abia], b. Apr. 13, 1667;		
d. [ ]	MG	
Henery, s. Henery, b. Apr. 13, 1667	Col.1	56
Henry, s. Henry, b. Apr. 13, 1667	1	38
[Henry*], s. Henery, d. [May 14*], [16]67 *(In pencil)	MG	
Henery, s. Henery, Jr., d. May 14, 1667	Col.1	55
Henery, s. Simon, b. May 20, 1670	1	38
Henery, s. [Henery, Jr. & Abia], b. Mar. 30, 1673	MG	
Henry, s. Henry, b. Mar. 30, 1673	1	37
Henery, Jr., had 6 children b. in Windsor. Dated Aug. 17,		
1677	MG	
Henery, had 7 children, b. in Windsor. Dated Aug. 17, 1677	MG	
Henry, s. John, b. Aug. 7, 1679	Col.D	51
Henery, s. John, b. Aug. 7, 1679	1	38
[Henery], [Sr.], d. July 12, [1680]; bd. July 13, 1680	MG	
Henry, s. Henry, d. Apr. 29, 1680* *(This entry crossed		
out)	1	52
Henry, s. John, d. Apr. 29, 1680	Col.D	56
Henry, s. John, d. Apr. 29, 1680	1	52
Henery, d. July 12, 1680	Col.D	58

	Vol.	Page
WOLCOTT, WOLCOT, WOLCUTT, WOOLCOT,		
WOOLCOTT, (cont.)		
Henry, Jr., m. Jane **ALLYN**, b. of Windsor, Apr. 1, 1696	1	63
Henry, s. Henry, Jr., b. Feb. 28, 1697	1	39
Henry, d. Aug. 5, 1697	1	52
Henry, d. Feb. 18, 1709/10	2	276
Henry, Jr., of Windsor, m. Abigael **COOLEY**, of Springfield,		
Dec. 28, 1716	2	208
Henry, Lieut., m. Mrs. Hannah **PORTER**, b. of Windsor,		
Apr. 11, 1727	2	208
Hepzibah, d. Roger, b. June 23, 1717	2	115
Hepzibah, m. John **STRONG**, b. of Windsor, Nov. 10, 1737	2	199
Hope, d. John, Jr. & Mary, b. Dec. 29, 1742	2	119
Jane, w. Henry, Jr., d. Apr. 11, 1702	1	52
Jane, d. Henry, b. Oct. 20, 1710	2	113
Jane, d. Henry*, d. Mar. 16, 1710/11 *("Willia[m]"		
crossed out)	2	276
Jane Catharine, m. Elles **RUSSELL**, b. of Windsor, Nov. 14,		
1751	2	195
Jerusha, d. John, b. Jan. 18, 1718/19	2	115
Joanna, d. [Simon & Martha], b. June 30, 1668	MG	
Joanna, d. Simon b. June 30, 1668	1	38
John, s. [Henery & Sara], b. [Feb.]; bp. [ ], 1644	MG	
John, s. Henery, bp. Mar. 2, 1644	Col.2	156
John, s. Henry, bp. Mar. 2, 1644	1	37
John, m. Mrs. Mary **CHESTER**, Feb. 14, 1676	Col.D	54
John, m. Mrs. Mary **PHELPS**, Feb. 14, 1676	1	63
John, s. John, b. Nov. 20, 1677	Col. D	51
John, s. John, b. Nov. 20, 1677	1	38
John, of Windsor, m. Mrs. Hannah **NICHOLOS**, of Stanford,		
June 22, 1692	1	63
John, m. Hannah **NUBERY**, b. of Windsor, Dec. 14, 1703	1	63
John, s. John, Jr., b. Apr. 24, 1709	2	112
John, Sr., d. Jan. 23, 1711/12	2	276
John, 3rd, of Windsor, m. Mary **HAWLEY**, of Middletown,		
Jan. 9, 1734/5	2	208
John, d. Aug. 20, 1750	2	279
Josia, bp. July 25, [16]58	MG	
Josiah, s. Roger, b. Feb. 6, 1718/19	2	115
Josias, s. [Henry & Sarah], b. July 21, 1658	MG	
Justus, s. George & Mary, b. Feb. 1, 1735/6	2	118
Lorana, d. John & Mary, b. June 5, 1739	2	117
Luci, d. William, b. May 7, 1710	2	112
Marah, d. Roger & Marah, b. Oct. 15, 1730	2	117
Mara, d. Roger, Jr. & Mara, b. Apr. 4, 1742	2	455
Mara, m. Jesie **GOODELL**, b. of Windsor, Apr. 22, 1764	2	158
Martha, d. [Simon & Martha], b. May 17, 1664	MG	
Martha, d. Simon, b. May 17, 1664	Col.1	54

	Vol.	Page
WOLCOTT, WOLCOT, WOLCUTT, WOOLCOT,		
WOOLCOTT, (cont.)		
Sara, d. [Henery & Sara], b. July [ ], 1649	MG	
Sarah, d. Henery, bp. July 5, 1649	Col.2	156
Sarah, d. Henry, b. July 5, 1649	1	37
Sara, bp. July 8, [16]49	MG	
Sara, d. [Henery, Jr. & Abia], b. Mar. 27, 1671; d. [ ]	MG	
Sarah, d. Henry, b. Mar. 27, [16]71	1	37
[Sarah*], d. Henery, d. [July 20*], [16]71 *(In pencil)	MG	
Sara, d. Henery, Jr., bd. July 20, 1671	Col.1	58
Sarah, d. Henry, bd. July 20, [16]71	1	52
Sara, 2nd, d. [Henery, Jr. & Abia], b. Apr. 16, [16]76	MG	
Sarah, d. Henry, b. Apr. 16, [16]76; bp. May 14, [16]76	1	37
Sarah*, Mrs., d. June 16, 1684 *(Note by LBB: "Sarah (NEWBERRY) WOOLCOT")	Col.D	56
Sarah, Mrs., d. July 16, 1684	1	52
Sarah, of Windsor, m. Charles CHANCY, of Fairfield, Mar. 16, 1698/9	1	55
Sarah, d. Charles, b. Sept. 29, 1707	2	111
Sarah, d. Roger, b. Jan. 31, 1714/15	2	114
Sarah, d. Roger, b. Jan. 31, 1714/15	2	115
Sarah, d. Lieut. Charles & Elizabeth, d. Mar. 24, 1727/8	2	278
Sarah, d. Ephraim & Mary, b. Feb. 25, 1760	2	455
Simon, m. Joanna COOKE, Mar. 19, 1656	Col.2	159
Simon, m. Joanna COOK, b. of Windsor, Mar. 19, 1656/7	1	63
Simon, his w. [ ]*, d. Apr. 27, 1657 *(Note by LBB: "Joanna (COOK) WOOLCOT")	Col.2	160
Simon, his w. [ ], d. Apr. 27, 1657	1	52
Simon, m. Martha PITKIN, Oct. 17, 1661	MG	
Simon, of Windsor, m. Martha PITKIN, late of England, Oct. 17, 1661	1	63
Simon, s. [Simon & Martha], b. June 24, 1666	MG	
Simon, s. Simon, b. June 24, 1666	Col.1	55
Simon, s. Simon, b. June 24, 1666	1	38
Simon, had 7 children b. in Windsor. Dated Aug. 17, 1677	MG	
Simon, d. Sept. 11, 1687	1	52
Simon, of Windsor, m. Sara CHESTER, of Wethersfield, Dec. 5, 1689	Col.D	54
Simon, of Windsor, m. Sarah CHESTER, of Weathersfield, Dec. 5, 1689	1	63
Simon, s. Dr. Alexander & Mary, b. Aug. 8, 1747	2	120
Simon, s. Dr. Alexander & Mary, b. Aug. 9, 1747	2	121
Thomas, s. Henry, Jr., b. Apr. 1, 1702	1	39
Trypheny, m. Theophilus ALLYN, b. of Windsor, Oct.[ ], 1751	2	124
William, m. Simon, b. Nov. [ ], 1676	1	38
William, m. Abiah HAWLY, b. of Windsor, Nov. 5, 1707	2	207
William, s. William, b. July 29, 1711	2	113

	Vol.	Page
WOLCOTT, WOLCOT, WOLCUTT, WOOLCOT,		
WOOLCOTT, (cont.)		
William, Jr., m. Mrs. Abigail **ABBOTT**, Feb. 26, 1746/7	2	209
----, Mrs., adm. ch. & communicant Apr. [ ], 1640	MG	
----, Mrs., adm. ch. Apr. 26, 1640	MG	
----, Mr., taxed 4-0 on Feb. 10, [16]73	MG	
----, Sr., Mr., communicant from Dorchester, living in		
Windsor, Dec. 22, 1677	MG	
----, Mr., contributed 0-10-0 to the poor in other colonies	MG	
WOOD, WOODS, Abigail, m. Elijah **BARBER**, b. of Windsor,		
Dec. 29, 1768	2	134
Cloe, of East Windsor, m. Oliver **LOOMIS**, of Windsor,		
Feb. 9, 1792	2	488
Harriett Elisabeth, d. Asa B. & Elisabeth, b. Aug. 13, 1832	2	459
WOODARD, [see under **WOODWARD**]		
WOODBRIDGE, WOODBREDG, Beniamen, had 2 children b.		
in Windsor. Dated Aug. 17, 1677	MG	
Beniamen, d. Sept. [ ], 1680	Col.1	58
Benjamin, 2nd, s. Benjamin, b. Oct. 12, 1680	1	37
Benjamin Ruggles, s. Rev. Jno & Tryphena, b. Oct. 16, 1733	2	118
Dudley, s. Benjamin, b. Sept. 7, 1677	1	37
Elizabeth, d. Benjamin, b. Apr. 31, 1673	1	37
John, s. Rev. John & Tryphena, b. July 24, 1732	2	118
Mary, Mrs., of Groton, m. Rev. Hezekiah **BISSEL**, of		
Windsor, Nov. 20, 1740	2	131
Tryphena, d. Rev. John & Tryphena, b. July 21, 1731	2	117
WOODFORD, Mary Cordelia, d. Benjamin B. & Laura, b. Sept. 1,		
1831	2	459
WOODWARD, WOODARD, Charles, m. Eliza **HILLS**, Dec. 23,		
1823, by Rev. Henry A. Rowland	2	210
Electa, of Suffield, m. Thaddeus **GRISWOLD**, of Windsor,		
Mar. 5, 1833, by Rev. Daniel Hemienway	2	480
WOODWORTH, Timothy, m. Mary **COOLEY**, Sept. 28, 1829,		
by Asa Bushnell, Jr.	2	212
WOOLWORTH, Hannah, of Suffield, m. Thomas **DIBBEL**, of		
Windsor, Dec. 22, 1743	2	142
WRIGHT, RIGHT, RITE, Abel, s. Abel & Jerusha, b. Mar. 4,		
1773	2	457
Abiah, d. Jonathan & Abial, b. Sept. 7, 1737	2	118
Asenath, d. Abel & Jerusha, b. Apr. 20, 1770	2	455
David, s. Jonathan & Abiah, b. Feb. 24, 1742/3	2	119
Edmund, s. Henry & Deborah, b. Oct. 28, 1813	2	459
Elam, s. Abel & Jerusha, b. Dec. 1, 1774	2	457
Elizabeth, see Elizabeth **REED**	2	94
Eunice, d. Jonathan & Abiah, b. Apr. 22, 1741	2	119
Eunice, d. Jonathan & Abiah, d. May 28, 1741	2	278
Gedion, s. Mahitabal, b. Apr. 29, 1761	2	446
Henry, s. Moses & Chloe, b. Nov. 8, 1774	2	456

	Vol.	Page
WRIGHT, RIGHT, RITE, (cont.)		
Henry, m. Chloe **COOK,** b. of Windsor, Aug. 12, 1840, by		
Rev. Ezras Cook	2	515
Jerusha, d. Abel & Jerusha, b. Aug. 16, 1768	2	455
Jerusha, d. Abel & Jerusha, b. Aug. 16, 1768	2	578
Joel, s. Abel & Jerusha, b. Oct. 1, 1777	2	457
John, s. Jonathan & Abiah, b. Apr. 24, 1745	2	119
John, s. Henry & Lois, b. Oct. 14, 1748	2	435
John, s. Henry & Lois, b. Oct. 14, 1748	2	454
Jonathan, s. Jonathan & Abiah, b. July 2, 1739	2	119
Mahitabal, had s. Gedion, b. Apr. 29, 1761	2	446
Moses, s. Henry & Lois, b. Oct. 1, 1750	2	454
Moses, of Windsor, m. Chloe **NEAL,** of Farmington, Oct. 8,		
1773	2	210
Sarah, d. Abel & Jerusha, b. Sept. 23, 1781	2	457
Silas, s. Henry & Deborah, b. Feb. 19, 1810	2	459
Sybel, d. Henry & Lois, b. Sept. 11, 1752	2	454
YATES, Andrew, Rev., m. Hannah A. **HOOKER,** June 11, 1810	2	213
Andrew, m. Hannah A. **HOOKER,** June 11, 1810	2	522
YOUNG, YOUNGS, Anna, d. Seth & Hannah, b. Oct. 17, 1750	2	122
Calven, s. Seth & Hannah, b. June 18, 1757	2	122
Ebenezer, s. Sarah **ALLYN,** b. Oct. 19, 1777	2	122
Ebenezer, illeg. s. Sarah **ALLYN,** b. Oct. 19, 1777;		
reputed f. Ebenezer **YOUNGS**	2	535
Frederick s. Seth & Hannah, b. Apr. 25, 1759	2	122
Hannah, d. Seth & Hannah, b. July 31, 1744	2	121
James, m. Martha **HUNT,** b. of Windsor, Apr. 27, 1834, by		
Rev. David Miller	2	213
James I., m. Elizabeth **HUNT,** b. of Windsor, Jan. 10, 1843,		
by Rev. S. W. Scofield	2	517
James Indicot, s. Ebenezer & Mary, b. Aug. 1, 1807	2	122
John, s. Seth & Hannah, b. Dec. 12, 1748	2	122
John, s. Seth & Hannah, b. Oct. 4, 1752	2	122
Joseph, d. Apr. 21, 1765	2	281
Mary, d. Seth & Hannah, b. Nov. 4, 1754	2	122
Mary F., m. Silas **PERKINS,** of East Hartford, May 4, 1825,		
by Rev. Henry A. Rowland	2	192
Mary Fisher, d. Ebenezer & Mary, b. Sept. 18, 1805	2	122
Seth, s. Seth & Hannah, b. Feb. 10, 1746/7	2	122
[ ]ELS, Mary, m. Danell **LOOMYS,** [ ], 23, 1680	TR1	1
[ ]FELD, ------, ch. mem. 16[ ], from Dorchester	MG	
[ ]RD, Thomas, his w.[ ], d. [ ], [16]42	MG	
[ ]SELL, m. Nathanell **GAYL**[ ], [Oct.], 17, 1678	TR1	1
[ ]YLAR, -----, adm. communion Mar. 31, [16]44	MG	
NO SURMANE, Abigaile, [ ], Feb. 14, 1639	MG	
Abigayl, ae 10y., bp. Jan. 4, [16]65	MG	
Ann, m. Hezekiah **PERSONS,** b. of Windsor, July 15, 1756	2	189
Cirious, negro, d. Apr. 29, 1699	1	48

	Vol.	Page
NO SURNAME, (cont.)		
Debora, ae 3 y., bp. Jan. 4, [16]65	MG	
Elezer, s. Eliakim & Elizabeth, b. May 14, 1753	2	350
Elizabeth, m. Peter TILTON, May 10, 1641	1	62
Elizabeth, bp. Feb. 18, [16]65	MG	
Elisabeth, m. Peter TILTON, May 10, 16[ ]	MG	
Hanna, ae 4 yrs. bp. Jan. 4, [16]65	MG	
Hannah, m. Abel FOSTER, b. of Windsor, Dec. 18, 1755	2	335
Hannah, m. Abel FOSTER, b. of Windsor, Dec. 18, 1757	2	152
Immanuel, s. Elmor & Ann, b. Dec. 23, 1728	2	31
Isabell, m. Nicolas FENCHON, June 12, 1645; "in 1680 they had been m. 35 yrs and had no child"	MG	
Isable, m. Nicholos SENTION, June 12, 1645	1	61
Jane, m. Thomas BARBER, Oct. 7, 1640	MG	
Jone*, m. Simon MILLS, Oct. 18, 1639 *("Joan?")	1	59
Jone, m. Thomas BARBOR, Oct. 7, 1640 *(In pencil "Joan?")	1	53
John, communicant 16[ ]	MG	
John, mem. Jury 16[ ]	MG	
Joseph, s.[ ], ch. mem. 16[ ]	MG	
Jos[i]as, contributed 0-2-6 to the poor in other colonies	MG	
Lydia, d. [ ]	1	7
Marcy, d. Aaron & Marcy, b. Sept. 13, 1726	2	289
Margret, m. William FILLY, Sept. 2, 164[ ]	MG	
Mary, m. Abraham RANDELL, Dec. 8, 1640; had no child	MG	
Mary, m. Abraham RANDEL, Dec. 1, 1640	1	61
Mary, d. John, Jr. & Deborah, b. Sept. 10, 1728	2	89
Mary, m. John ENO, [ ]	TR1	1
Nath[aniel], communicant 16[ ]	MG	
Oliver, s. John & Mary, b. July 25, 1754	2	434
Rich[ard], communicant 16[ ]	MG	
Ruth, ae 12 y., bp. Jan. 4, [16]65	MG	
Samuell, ae 6 y., bp. Jan. 4, [16]65	MG	
Sara, m. Samuell POND, Nov. 18, 1642	MG	
Susan, m. George ALLIXANDER, Mar. 18, 1[6]	MG	
Thom[as], communicant 16[ ]	MG	
Th[o]m[as], mem. Jury 16[ ]	MG	
Thomas, his s. [ ], b. July 8, [1639]; d. [July] 9, [1639]	MG	
Wi[ ], Lieut. "removed from Windsor Church to go to No[rth] [ ], to help further a church there in the beginning [ ], Mar. 25.; bd. Feb. 6, 1677, in Windsor & d. the day before"	MG	
-----ott, ch. mem 16[ ], from Dorchester	MG